Hand Drawing for **Designers**

fb

Hand Drawing for **Designers**

COMMUNICATING IDEAS THROUGH ARCHITECTURAL GRAPHICS

DOUGLAS R. SEIDLER
Leed® AP, NCIDQ, Associate AIA, IDEC
Marymount University

AMY KORTÉ
Leed® AP, NCIDQ
Boston Architectural College
Arrowstreet

Fairchild Books
New York

Executive Editor: Olga T. Kontzias

Senior Associate Acquisitions Editor: Jaclyn Bergeron

Assistant Acquisitions Editor: Amanda Breccia

Editorial Development Director: Jennifer N. Crane

Associate Development Editor: Lisa Vecchione

Associate Art Director: Erin Fitzsimmons

Production Director: Ginger Hillman

Senior Production Editor: Elizabeth Marotta

Copyeditor: Susan Hobbs

Cover Art: Jie Zhao, Arrowstreet

Interior Drawings: Douglas R. Seidler

Cover Design: Erin Fitzsimmons

Text Design and Layout: Shu Shu Design

Library of Congress Catalog Card Number: 2009925894

ISBN: 978-1-56367-780-9

GST R 133004424

TP15

EXTENDED

Chapter 12: Rendering Techniques 239

WHY DO YOU NEED TO KNOW HOW TO DRAW?

Walk through any foundation design studio and you will likely hear at least one student ask, "Why do I need to learn how to draw?" This seems a fair question when you stop to consider that many design students arrive in college or graduate school preprogrammed with knowledge of multiple digital drawing technologies, such as AutoCAD, Google SketchUp, Revit, 3D Studio Max, and Photoshop.

Even if a student does not know how to draw with the computer, the question is reinforced by the digital drawings that hang on the walls of upper-level studios and fill the pages of design magazines. After reviewing these drawings and hearing praise from peers and critics, the student may ask, "If professional designers and upper-level students don't draw by hand, why should I take the time to learn?" The question is still flawed. In posing this question (or resisting learning a seemingly antiquated drawing technique), the beginning designer assumes that hand drawings were not a part of the creative problem solving process leading up to these digital presentations. The student may assume that once you know how to create computer drawings and digital renderings, hand drawing is removed from the design process. This is not the case.

To successfully develop a unique and responsive design solution, that is, to fully understand the design problem, a designer must challenge existing assumptions and form new conclusions while evaluating the strengths and weaknesses of multiple responses through an iterative process. Each of these responses may be an alternative to an original assumption or may represent a unique approach to the design problem. Although the quantity of design responses will vary for each designer and with each project, the ability to quickly generate and visually evaluate responses (individually and simultaneously) is essential in the investigation of a critically unique design response. We believe this process can only be accomplished through hand drawing.

Drawing versus Drafting

It seems at this point we should pause to define and compare the terms drawing and drafting, as they relate to this textbook and the design profession. Hand drawing and hand drafting are unique design and communication tools used to investigate or visually describe a design response.

The term hand drawing describes the process of intuitively sketching organizational diagrams, loose (but proportional) orthogonal drawings, and perspectives. Hand drawings are created with a pen, pencil, or marker on paper-based media. They may also be created with acrylic paint, watercolor, or charcoal. Hand drawings evolve during the act of drawing. Although you may have an idea of what you want to describe in a hand drawing, the fluid nature of the drawing process allows you to modify and refine your ideas as you see them emerge on the sheet of paper.

The term hand drafting almost always describes the process of creating a measured two-dimensional or three-dimensional drawing in perspective, isometric, plan, elevation, or section. Because of the precise nature of these drawings, they tend to be less intuitive than hand drawings. The process of hand drafting requires more understanding of what you are drafting before you begin the drawing.

The term computer drafting is used to describe the process of creating a measured drawing with computer-aided design (CAD) software. CAD software allows you to simultaneously generate perspective, plans, sections, and elevations from a single drawing or model. If you move a door in plan, it is automatically moved in elevation, section, and perspective. This strength of CAD software is also its weakness as a design tool. The amount of information needed to understand a project before beginning a new computer drawing can be paralyzing, especially if formal ideas have not been initially investigated and resolved through hand drawing or hand drafting. This is one example illustrating the importance of knowing how to draw and sketch.

We should be clear: as authors and educators we are not advocating the elimination of computer drafting in design education or in the profession. In fact, we rely heavily on computer drafting software in teaching studios, in our professional careers, and even in designing this textbook. Although the content of this textbook focuses mostly on hand drawing as a design tool and hand drafting as a communication technique, it is important to understand how each concept, drawing principle, and technique applies directly to computer drafting. Behind every polished computer drawing is a designer with a strong understanding of architectural graphic standards and a solid foundation of drawing principles. We believe you cannot achieve one without understanding the other.

Hand Drawing in the Profession

Design educators and professionals see hand drawing as an important skill needed to lead a design team in an interior design or architecture firm. When the spatial complexities of a project or detail are unclear, firms rely on a designer's capacity to quickly create a hand drawing. This hand drawing visually communicates the idea in an instant to other designers, contractors, or clients. Designers must also be able to hand draw plans, elevations, sections, and details to guide a draftsperson or intern in creating or modifying a computer drawing. Hand drawing is a powerful tool used by firms in conceptual design presentations. Hand drawings help emphasize a project's objectives and ideas by omitting nonessential details about material or methods of assembly.

Content Overview

Each chapter introduces you to a unique drawing convention or a new way of thinking about drawing as a tool for design and communication. Beginning with an overview of the drawing convention, chapters illustrate how each drawing technique is used in both school and in practice through examples from professional design firms and student projects.

Chapters 1 through 3 introduce you to hand drawing, the textbook's learning objectives, and foundation drawing principles. In these chapters, you will build an understanding of appropriate drawing techniques. You will also learn how to use hand drawing as a tool to communicate architectural ideas and spatial relationships.

Chapters 4 through 7 introduce plans, sections, elevations, and reflected ceiling plans. In these chapters, emphasis is placed on the relationship between each orthographic view. For example, you will understand how to construct a section or interior elevation by projection from a plan drawing and how to work back and forth between these different views. These chapters also describe how different orthographic views can be optimized to communicate your core design ideas. These techniques include choosing an appropriate location of the "building slice" in a section drawing, selecting appropriate line weight to emphasize various relationships within a space, and understanding the relationship that a drawing has to the sheet of paper as well as the relationship that a drawing has to other drawings in a presentation.

Chapters 8 and 9 introduce three-dimensional drawing conventions, including isometric, axonometric, and perspective. Each chapter contains examples of professional and student work followed by a comparison between different three-dimensional drawing techniques. They also include a comprehensive step-by-step guide for each drawing convention.

Chapter 10 is devoted solely to creating two-dimensional drawings of projects with complex geometry or elements that are not orthogonal to the cutting plane. The drawing techniques and examples introduced in this chapter provide students with the tools they need to design with curved or oblique geometries. Chapter 10 includes a step-by-step guide for using a printed SketchUp model as a tool to generate hand-drawn perspectives.

Chapters 11 and 12 introduce diagrams, analytical drawings, presentation drawing techniques, and methods of integrating hand drawing with digital technologies. Chapter 11 builds on the drawing conventions introduced in earlier chapters by introducing diagrams and analytical drawing tools for developing and presenting your ideas during the design process. Chapter 12 introduces various rendering techniques, with an emphasis on how each can be used to communicate design ideas. We also demonstrate how to digitally render hand drawings, sketches, and diagrams in Adobe Photoshop.

Companion Download

Hand Drawing for Designers: Communicating Ideas through Architectural Graphics has a companion download that aims to strengthen your understanding of visual representation through sample digital drawings that combine hand and digital drawing techniques. This companion download contains sample Photoshop, SketchUp, and AutoCAD drawings that expand on the exercises featured in the text. You can access these files at the following Web site: *http://fairchildbooks.com/book.cms?bookid=273*. If you have trouble accessing the files, please go to *http://HDFDbook.com*.

Summary

The strategies, lessons, and pedagogical approach in *Hand Drawing for Designers: Communicating Ideas through Architectural Graphics* come from a combination of our experiences teaching foundation design studio to interior design and architecture students, our educational research, and our professional experience using the act of drawing as a communication tool in design firms.

This textbook aims to strengthen your understanding of visual representation and technical drawing by visually teaching for understanding. Through this understanding of hand drawing, you will be able to critically evaluate your digital drawings and images as tools for visual communication.

When you understand how to use hand drawing as a tool for design, we believe you will become a more responsive designer.

—Douglas R. Seidler and Amy Korté

ACKNOWLEDGMENTS

We started talking about this project in March 2007, while attending the International Conference on the Beginning Design Student in Savannah, Georgia. The challenge, as we saw it, was to develop a resource by which we could reintroduce hand drawing into our increasingly computer-driven studios. We realized that to create a significant text, we would have to engage our colleagues and the students in our classrooms in education and in practice.

We would like to thank the following educators whose discussions, critical feedback, and enthusiasm helped shape and test the pedagogical approach of the material in the book:

Anne Brockleman
David Brothers
Richard Griswold
Karen Nelson
Lee Peters
Ariane Purdy

We are also grateful for the time that Heather Gray gave to this book. Heather's enthusiasm and energy in doing everything we asked of her was critical to our progress in its completion. We are grateful for Suffolk University's Faculty Research Assistance Program, which compensated Heather for her time assisting us on this project. We also want to thank our colleagues at the New England School of Art & Design, Suffolk University and at the Boston Architectural College for the conversations on "drawing in design" that helped shape this book.

Many individuals have graciously contributed their drawings and images to these pages. This diverse group of talented designers all embraces drawing as a tool for design. A special thank you is owed to:

Tharon Anderson
Christopher Angelakis
Kevin Asmus
Donald Barany
Billie Jo Baril
Robert Beson
Kibwe Daisy
Lian Davis
Sarah Eigen
Theadora Elliott
Tim Ervin
Jonathan C. Garland
Heather Gray
Richard Griswold
William Harper
David Haugen
Chienlan Hsu
Soo Im
Brian Kerr
Meghan Krieger
Ciara Langley
Patrick S. Lausell
Kirsten Lawson
Rania Makkas
Kate McGoldrick
Lee Morrissette
Ryan Nevidomsky
Elena Raya
Katrina Reyes Rollan
Tamison Rose
John Rufo
Alison Smith
Ryota Uchida
Matthew Varley
Lori Anderson Wier
Jie Zhao
Arrowstreet
ARC, Architectural Resources Cambridge
Bernard Tschumi Architects
Diller Scofidio + Renfro
Toyo Ito & Associates, Architects

We also greatly appreciate the enthusiasm, guidance, patience, and collaboration of the editorial and production teams at Fairchild Books. The efforts and talents of Olga Kontzias, Jennifer Crane, Liz Marotta, Lisa Vecchione, and Erin Fitzsimmons are more than we could have asked for in an editorial team.

Finally, we would like to thank our families. Amy Korté would like to thank her husband, Jeff Thompson, for his love and encouragement; her mom, Sarah Korté, for teaching her how to draw; and her dad, Robert Korté, for helping her realize that she can accomplish anything.

Douglas Seidler is thankful for the love and support from his family. Thank you, Tricia, for your encouragement and friendship; Laura and Jeff, for your feedback, laughter, and support; and Mom and Dad, for teaching me to learn through investigation in an environment ripe for exploration.

Hand Drawing for **Designers**

WHY DO I NEED TO DRAW?

Many beginning design students ask this question during the first few years of their education. Looking ahead to the digital drawing programs (such as AutoCAD, SketchUp, and Revit) that dominate the office and upper-level studio coursework, it is difficult for students to understand why hand drawing is a valuable skill in both the academic and practice environments.

Hand Drawing for Designers answers this question by situating the lessons and learning goals of hand drawing within both environments. Throughout the book, examples from professional design firms are coupled with student projects in order to illustrate how hand drawing techniques are used in both school and practice.

The following pages provide an overview of the learning objectives for this book:

- **Drawing and Ideation** – How is hand drawing used in both school and practice to explore and develop ideas?
- **Visual Communication** – How is hand drawing used in both school and practice to communicate design ideas?
- **Learning to Draw** – What are the fundamentals of orthographic projection and architectural representation?
- **Drawing and Meaning** – How do different drawing conventions and techniques affect what we design and how we communicate our ideas?
- **Hand and Digital Drawing** – How can hand and digital drawing techniques be used together during the design process to maximize the potential of both mediums?

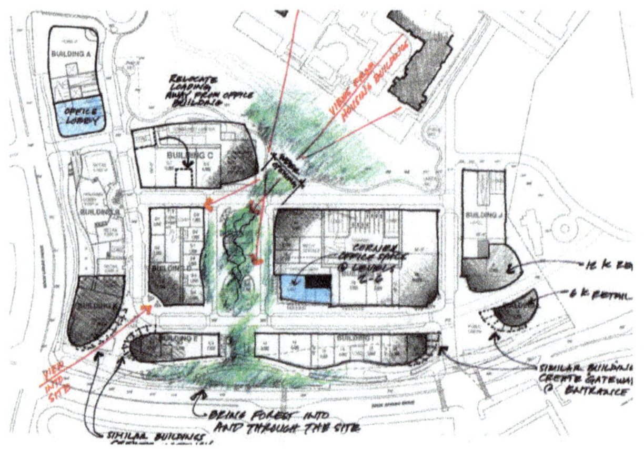

Site Plan Scheme

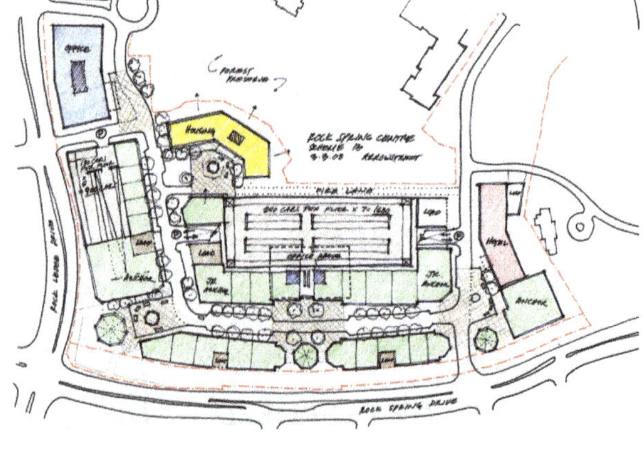
SitePlan Scheme

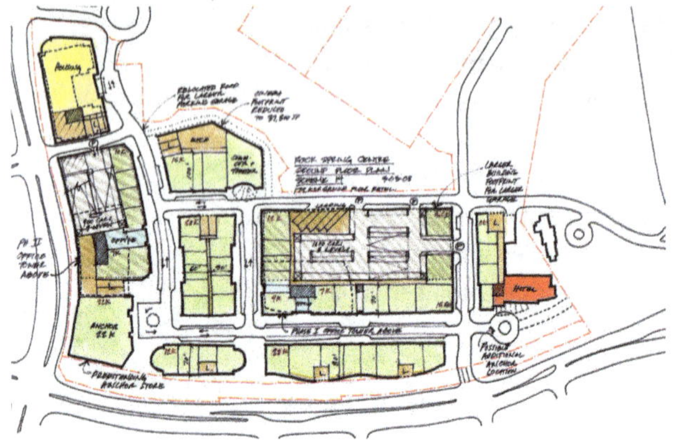
Site Plan Scheme

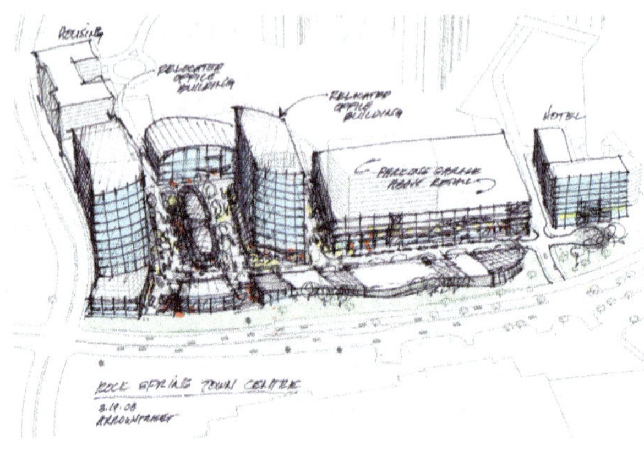

Axonometric Scheme

ARROWSTREET
Mixed-use project

Architects and interior designers use hand drawing intensively during the ideation process to generate, evaluate, and distill their design ideas.

Ideation is the process of generating and developing ideas and design concepts. Also known as conceptual design, ideation is characterized by the use of multiple iterations of sketches, drawings, and models to explore and critically evaluate solutions to a design problem. Sketches are typically notated with text to capture and develop ideas simultaneously through writing. Although the process of ideation varies greatly among designers, most rely on hand drawing and an abundance of trace paper during this process.

The production of multiple design sketches does not guarantee a strong design. As a good designer, you must use the process of ideation to critique, analyze, and refine the project. You should challenge your assumptions and form new conclusions as you evaluate the strength and weakness of each sketch, drawing, or model. At the end of the ideation process, you should have a strong understanding of both the design problem and the criteria for evaluating appropriate design solutions.

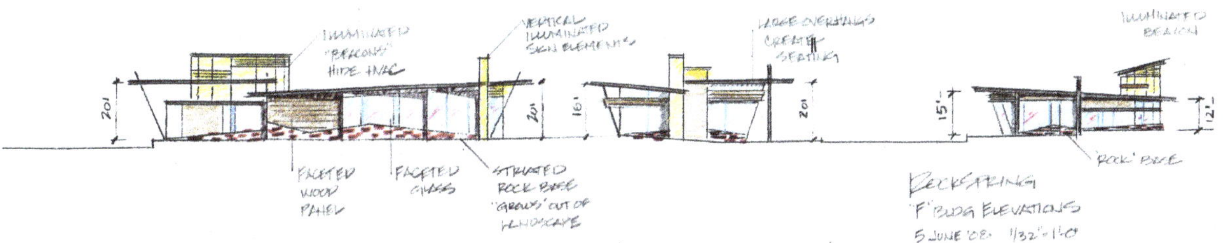

Pavilion Elevations Option A

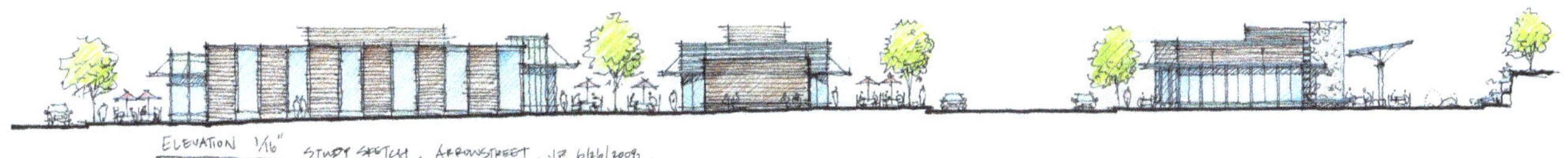

Pavilion Elevations Option B

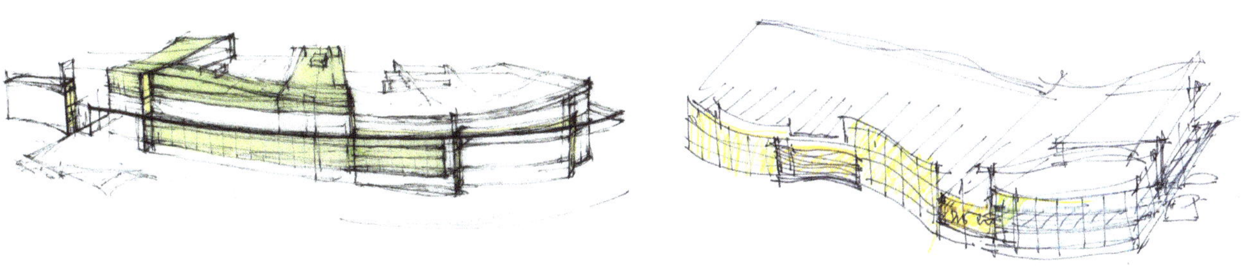

Building Design Sketches

In both the academic and practice environment, drawing makes a designer's thoughts and ideation process visible, helping communicate his or her ideas to other people.

In the academic studio the process of ideation is usually accomplished through independent investigation. Through drawing, students graphically develop and represent their ideas individually and present them to their peers, studio instructor, and guest critics for feedback. The opportunities for project feedback in studio are usually limited to a weekly or biweekly basis, making it vital for students to learn how to use ideation to critically self-assess their own work. In the professional design firm, the process of ideation is typically much more collaborative and occurs on a daily basis.

Project teams can be composed of more than one designer, with multiple people sketching over each other's drawings to discuss and explore ideas.

These sketches illustrate a small portion of a professional design firm's ideation process. Multiple drawing conventions, such as plan, elevation, and axonometric, were used throughout the ideation process in order to study and develop the design three dimensionally. Over the course of the project, the size of the design team ranged from a couple of designers to a dozen.

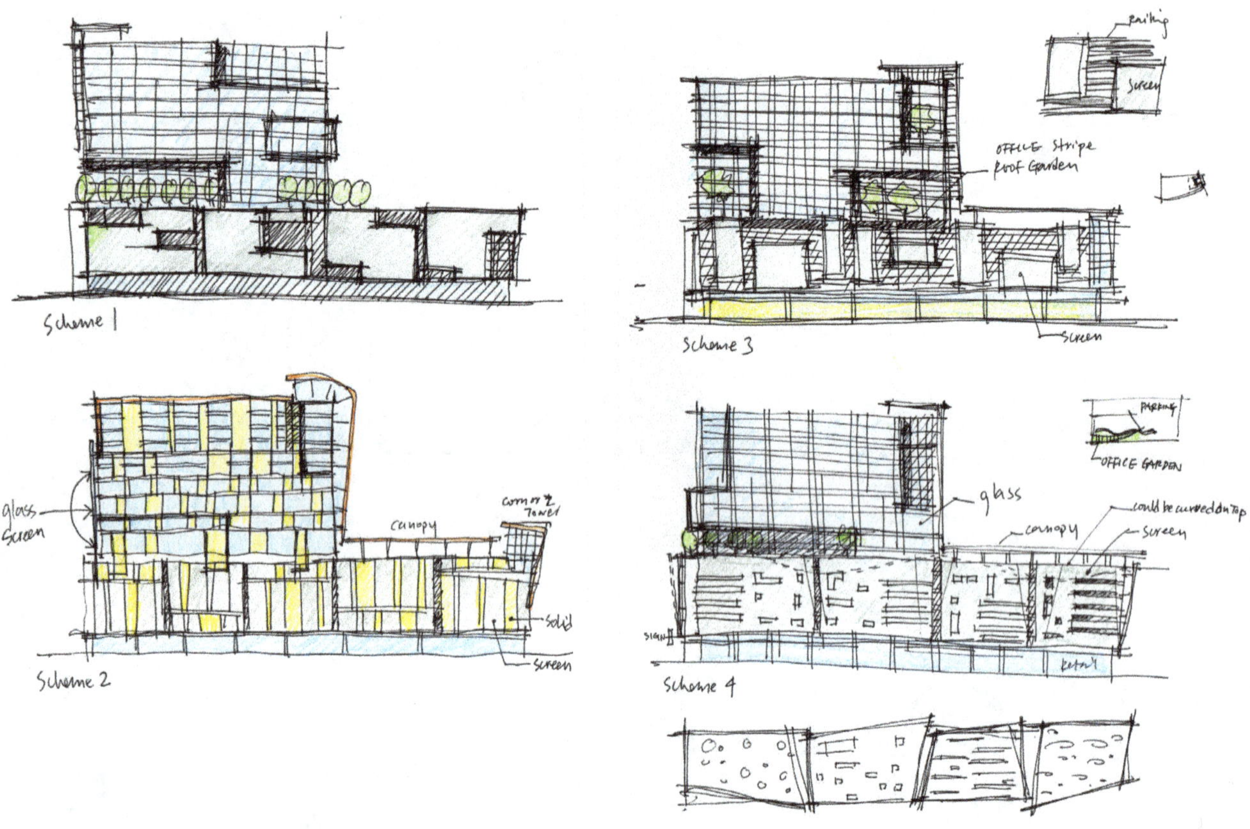

JIE ZHAO
Elevation studies
Arrowstreet

Loose hand sketches often communicate ideas more clearly and quickly than digital drawings.

Sketching ideas on the spot, both in front of clients and internally within the firm, is a crucial tool for visually communicating design ideas. Despite the increased reliance on digital media, hand drawing remains a powerful tool in the early design phases, primarily because it minimizes specifics while emphasizing the larger idea.

The sketches above are an example of how hand drawing can be used to visually communicate a designer's ideas. The drawings depict four different building elevation options, with a liberal use of textual notations and colors to describe materials. These elevation schemes were drawn by the project designer in her sketchbook, scanned in, and sent to the client for discussion.

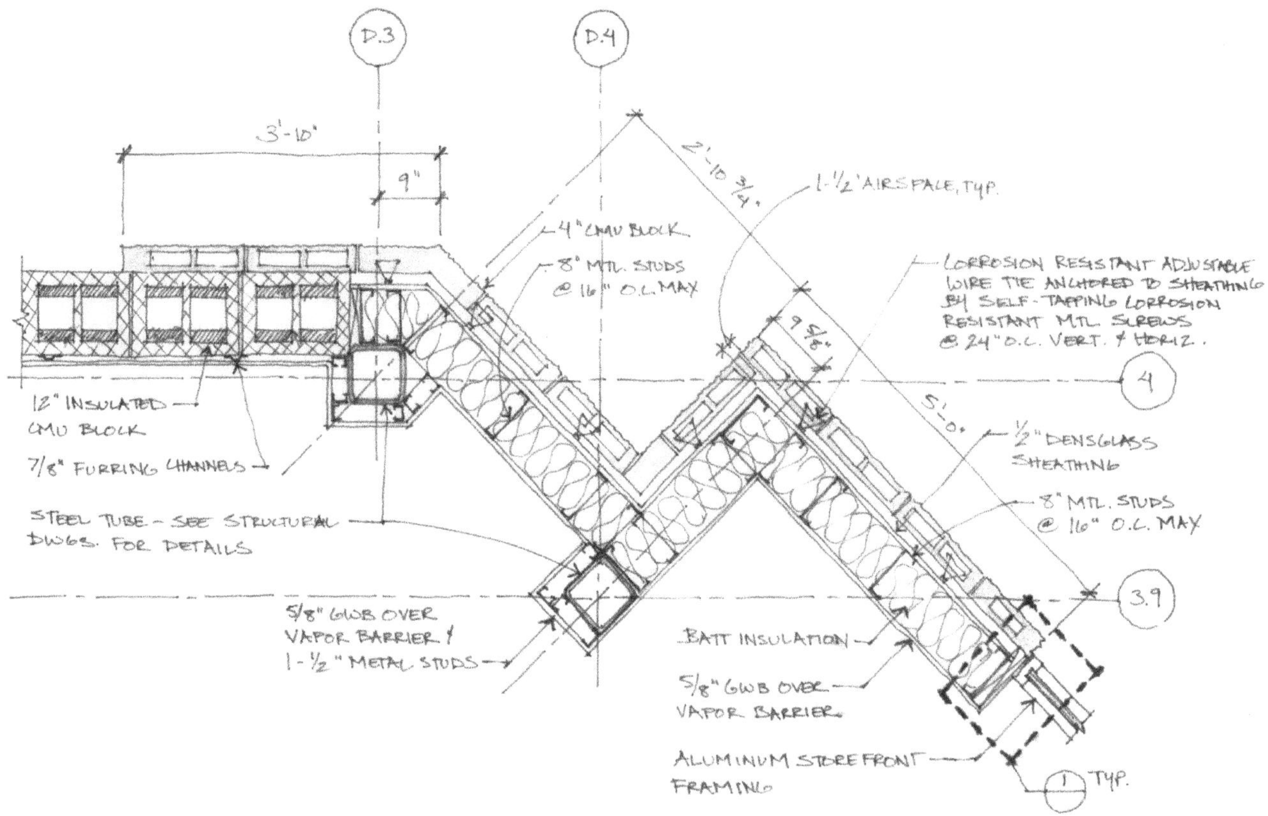

CARTER-BURGESS
Ink on trace paper
Alamance Crossing, Burlington, North Carolina

Hand drawing is an important skill that one needs to have to position one's self as an interior designer or architect within a firm.

To advance beyond the intern level, a designer needs to be able to hand draw details or sketch out portions of the project and pass them to a draftsperson to draw digitally. These types of hand drawings communicate the design intent to someone who typically is not familiar with how buildings are constructed, and are also used by architects and interior designers in the field when talking to contractors.

The sketch above is an example of a hand-drawn construction detail that was translated into a digital drawing to become part of the construction document set. Drawn by the project architect during the construction document phase, it describes the plan relationship between different wall materials and structure.

Drawing allows designers to visually represent three-dimensional spaces on two-dimensional surfaces.

At a fundamental level, *Hand Drawing for Designers* will teach you how to visually communicate and represent spaces through the conventions of architectural drawing. After reading this book and completing the exercises associated with each chapter, you will understand how to hand draw and hand draft plan, section, elevation, paraline, and perspective drawings. Drawing techniques, such as line weight and hatching, are introduced with each drawing convention; the techniques of rendering and diagramming are reviewed in later chapters.

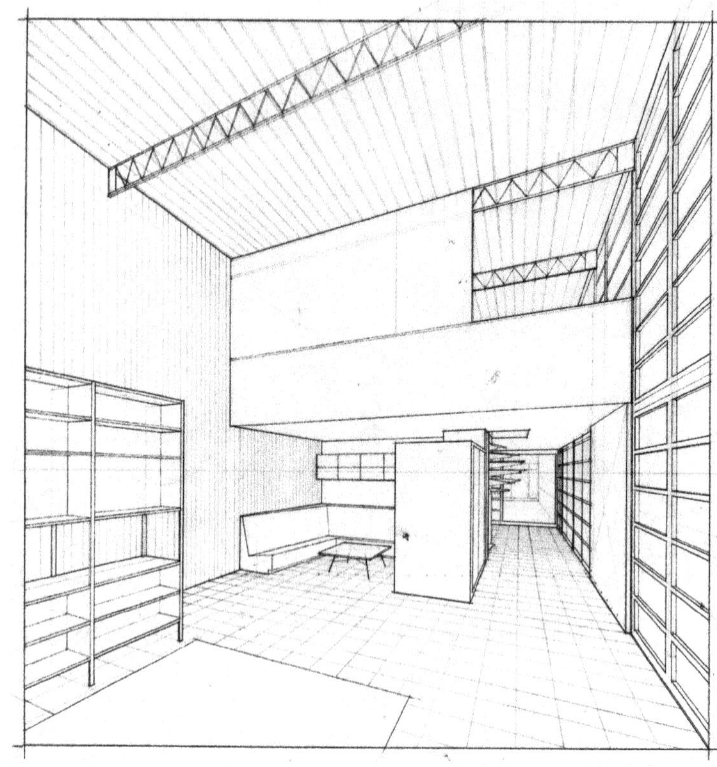

Perspective drawing

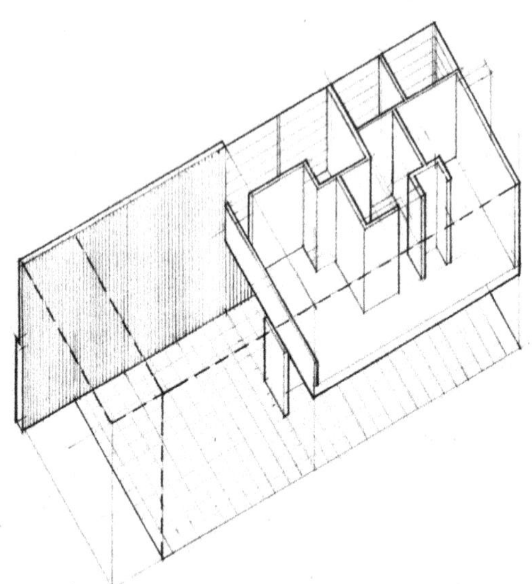

Paraline projection

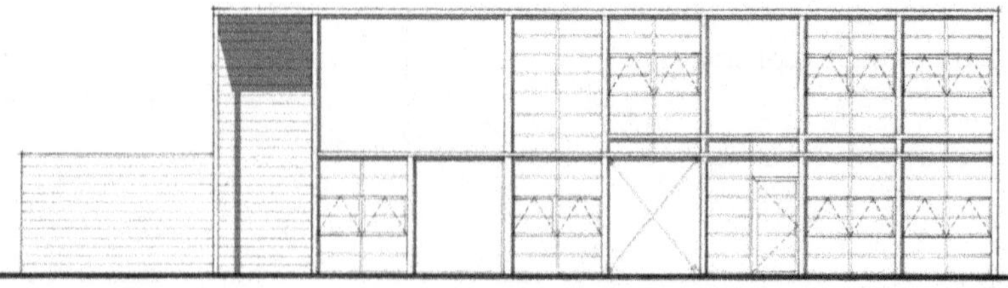

Elevation drawing

CHARLES (1907–78) AND RAY (1912–88) EAMES
Multiple drawing views of the Eames House (1949)
Drawings by Douglas Seidler

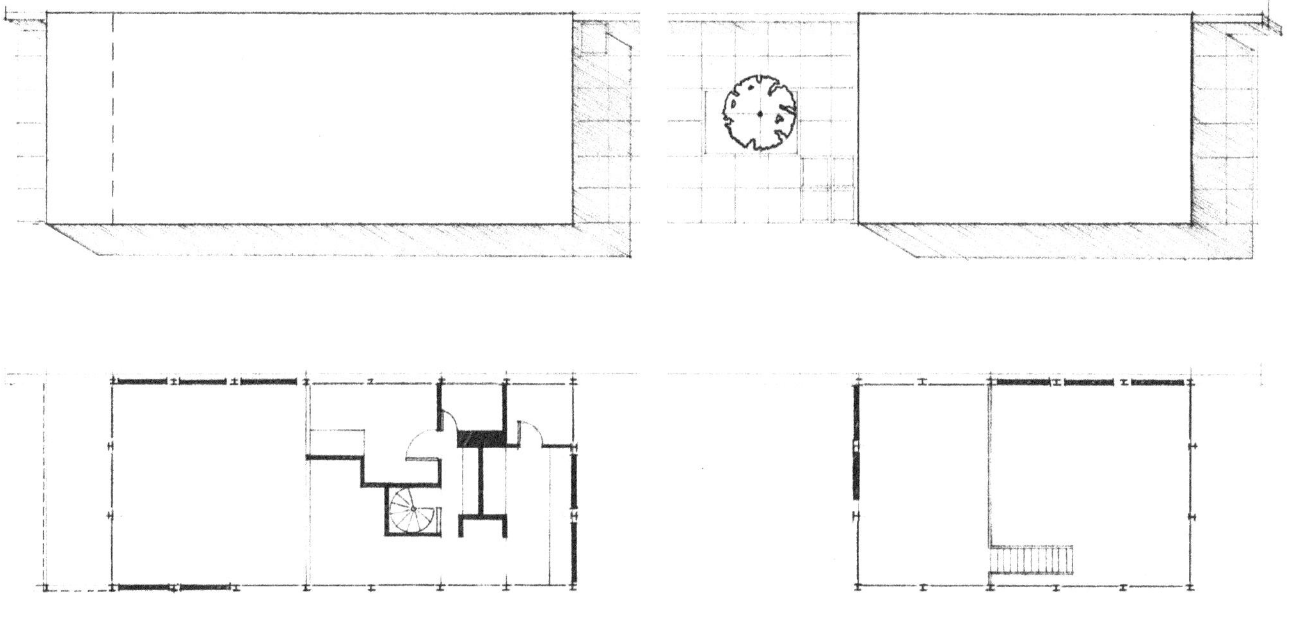

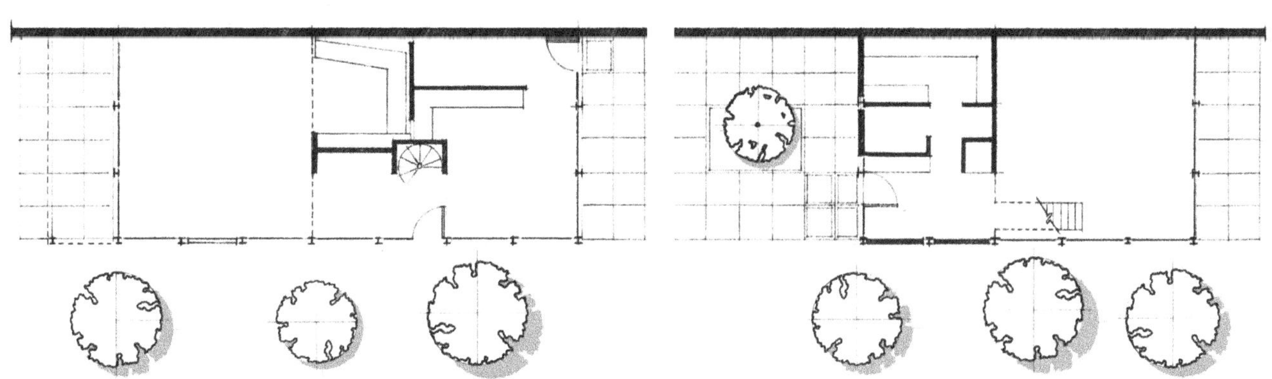

Plan drawings

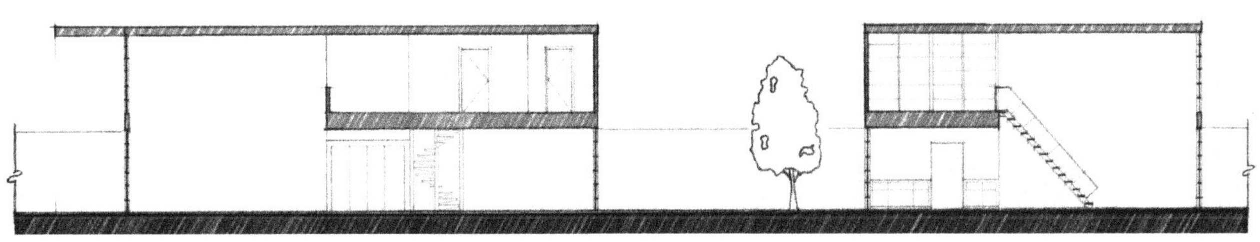

Section drawing

Each drawing convention uniquely represents the spatial conditions in a design project.
Plan, section, elevation, paraline, and perspective drawings allow designers to explore their ideas in different ways. The types of drawings in which you choose to design will influence your ideation process in terms of how design concepts are generated and communicated. For example, when perspective drawings are used to design a project, experiential qualities, such as a person's path of movement through a space and visual relationships along this path, are typically emphasized as the design ideas. By understanding how drawings influence your design solution, you can more appropriately use each drawing type to develop your design ideas.

The principles of graphic design also affect how drawings are understood and interpreted. Drawing composition and ordering principles such as hierarchy, scale, and balance are introduced and referenced throughout this book in terms of how they help visually communicate design ideas.

The perspectives on the right were generated as part of a student's design project and were used to explore how a person moves through and experiences the spaces. The student was studying how different wall and ceiling planes could frame a person's view, and how these planes could help guide people through the spaces of her building.

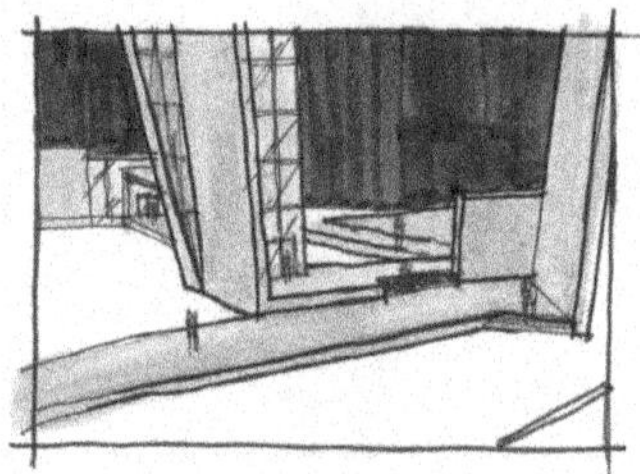

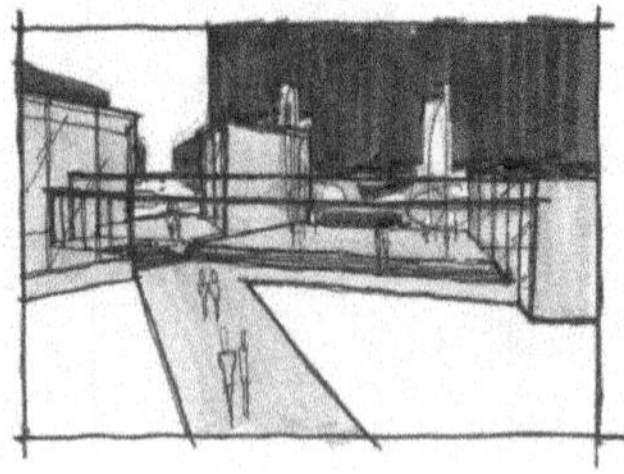

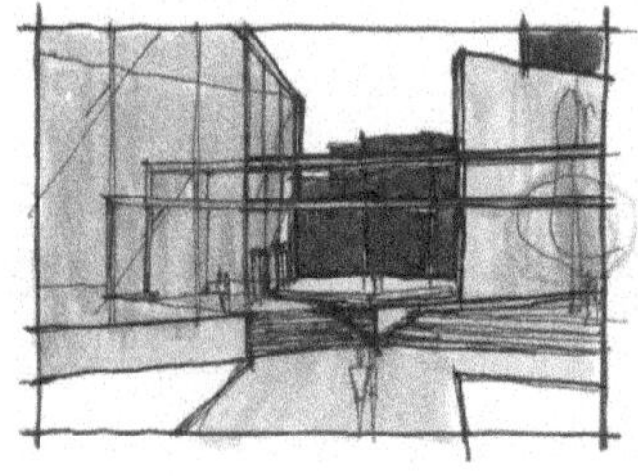

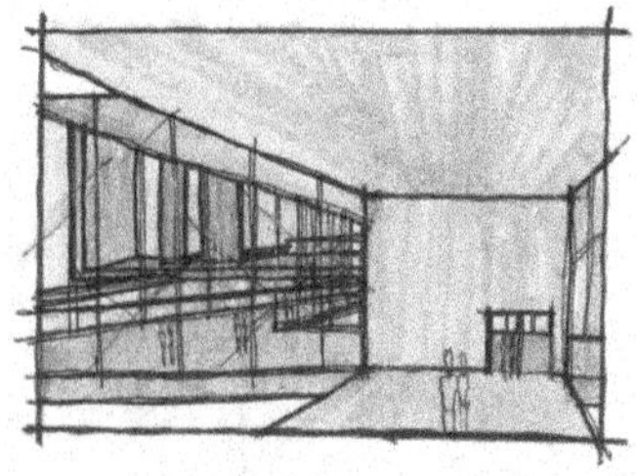

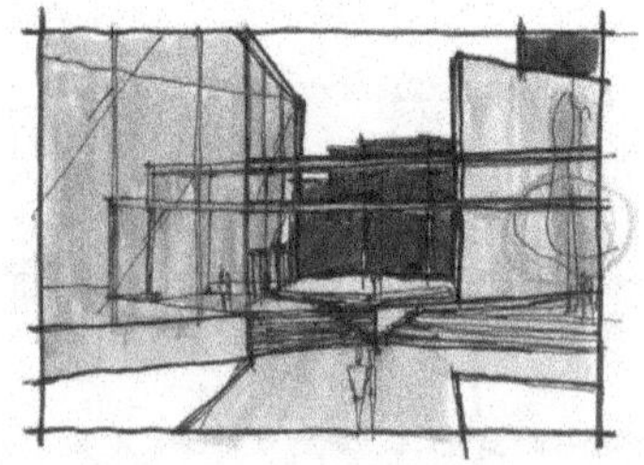

KATRINA REYES ROLLAN
Perspective Drawings
Degree Project Studio,
Boston Architectural College

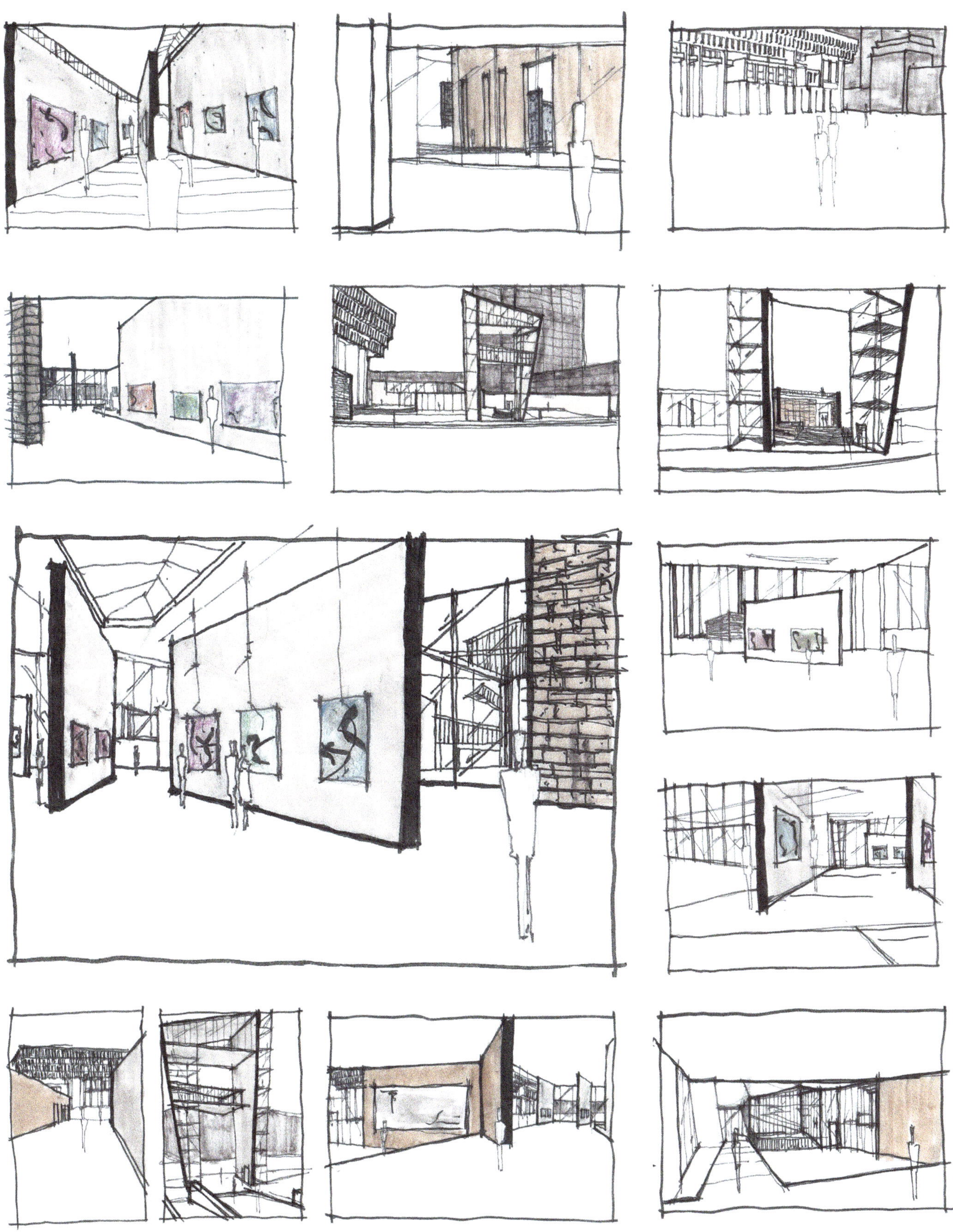

Hand and digital drawing techniques can be used together to exploit the potential of both mediums.

By understanding the limitations and potential of both hand and digital drawings, designers can draw from a wider range of tools to develop and generate ideas. *Hand Drawing for Designers* introduces basic techniques for integrating hand drawing with digital technologies and methods for designing simultaneously through various hand drawing conventions and digital programs. Many design firms rely on these hybrid techniques, which continue to evolve with the introduction of new digital technologies in the academic and practice environments.

The following drawings rely on a combination of hand drawing and SketchUp, a three-dimensional digital drawing program, to engage the ideation process. This process takes advantage of the digital technology to construct perspective drawings more quickly and allows the designer to use these digital underlays to develop the project in more detail. A step-by-step overview of this method is introduced in Chapter 9.

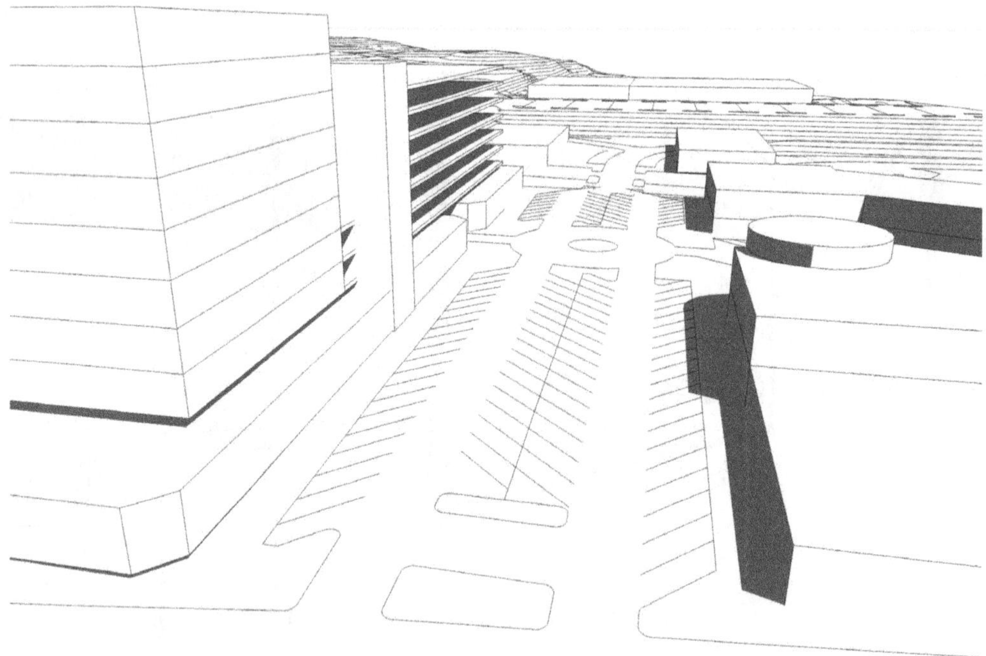

Step 1

For this project, a simple digital model was built of the overall building volumes, with the sidewalks and roads imported as a two-dimensional file from AutoCAD. A wireframe perspective view of the digital model was exported as a JPEG image, to create a digital underlay.

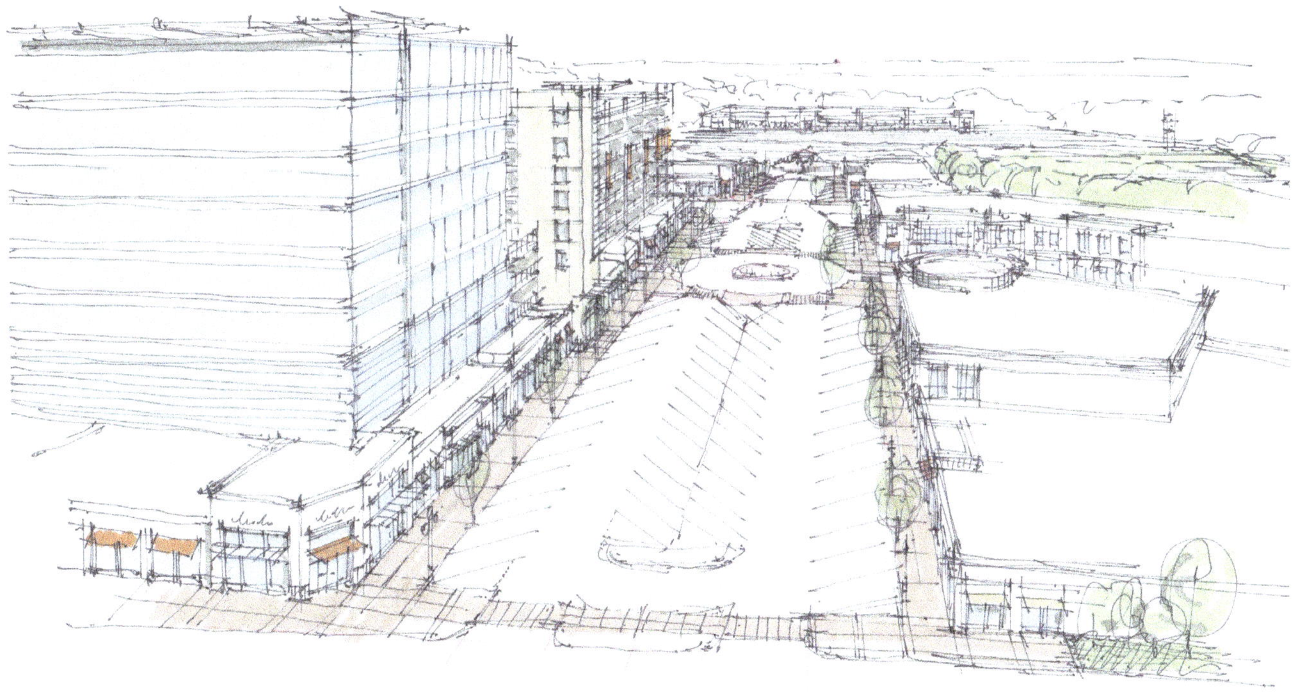

Step 2
Using trace paper, the design was adjusted and more details such as windows were added by sketching over the printed perspective view. The perspective view was widened, using drawing, to capture more of the streetscape. This sketch was one of a series of perspectives generated during the ideation phase for the project. As the design process continued, additional perspective underlays were created to help develop the building designs in greater detail.

John Rufo and Lee Morrissette
Aerial perspective of mixed-use project
Arrowstreet

DRAWING TOOLS

In this chapter, you are introduced to the different tools you will use to sketch, draw, and draft by hand. The chapter explores tools and media used for both lead and ink drawings.

The premise of this textbook is that your abilities as a designer are directly linked to your capacity to think critically and explore your ideas through hand drawing. That said, we do not expect you to invest in specific drafting tools that you will not use in a contemporary design firm. When it is appropriate, we will offer advice on which tools are required for the few semesters you are required to draft by hand and which tools you will use for your career as a designer.

Consider the following questions as you read this chapter:

- How do different drawing tools affect what we design and how we communicate our ideas?
- What are the different ways to achieve multiple line weights, using both pencils and pens?

A good drafting surface is a critical investment that will affect the quality of your drawings. You may consider purchasing a preassembled drafting board or constructing your own drafting surface, using a hollow core door; a Borco or Vyco board cover; and a T square, Mayline, or Paral-Liner straightedge.

- Borco is a self-healing drawing surface that, if kept clean, will recover from hard pencil marks and compass points.
- Your drafting table should be a minimum of 38" wide and 26" deep. If you construct your drafting surface from a hollow core door, you may also use it as a computer drafting table. It will have enough space for your computer and to lay out your printed drawings.

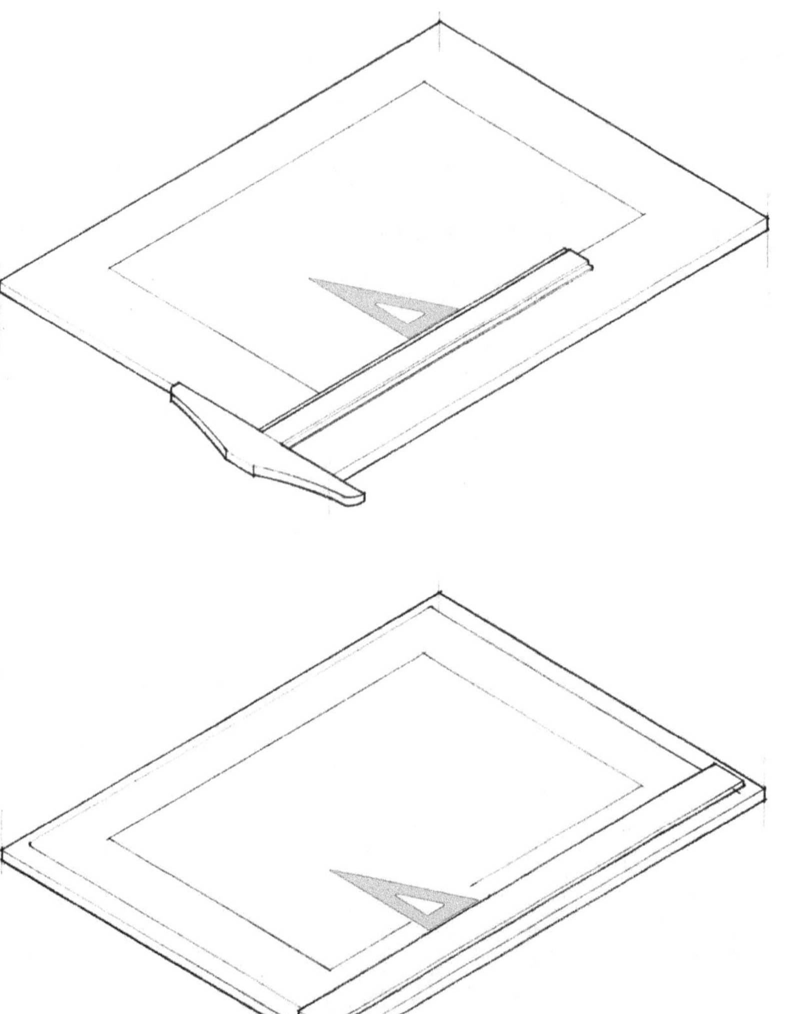

T Square

- Align the edge of the T square with the side of your drafting board. Slide the T square up the edge of the drafting board to draw parallel horizontal lines.
- Combine a drafting triangle with your T square to draw parallel vertical lines.
- Because T squares are not physically attached to the drafting surface, this configuration provides the most flexibility if you chose to use your drafting surface as a computer drafting table.

Mayline / Paral-Liner

- The Mayline Parallel Rule and Paral-Liner Mobile Straightedge are both physically attached to the drafting table.
- Slide the straightedge up and down your drafting table to draw parallel horizontal lines. Use a drafting triangle to draw parallel vertical lines.
- Although these drawing edges are more accurate than T squares, they typically cost more to install and provide less flexibility when you transition from hand drafting to digital drawing.

Architectural and engineering scales are used to accurately draw plan, section, and elevation drawings at a reduced size. Architects and interior designers use specific industry standard scales for each drawing convention.

- This type of triangular scale has four architectural scales per side.
- There are a total of twelve architectural scales on a triangular scale.

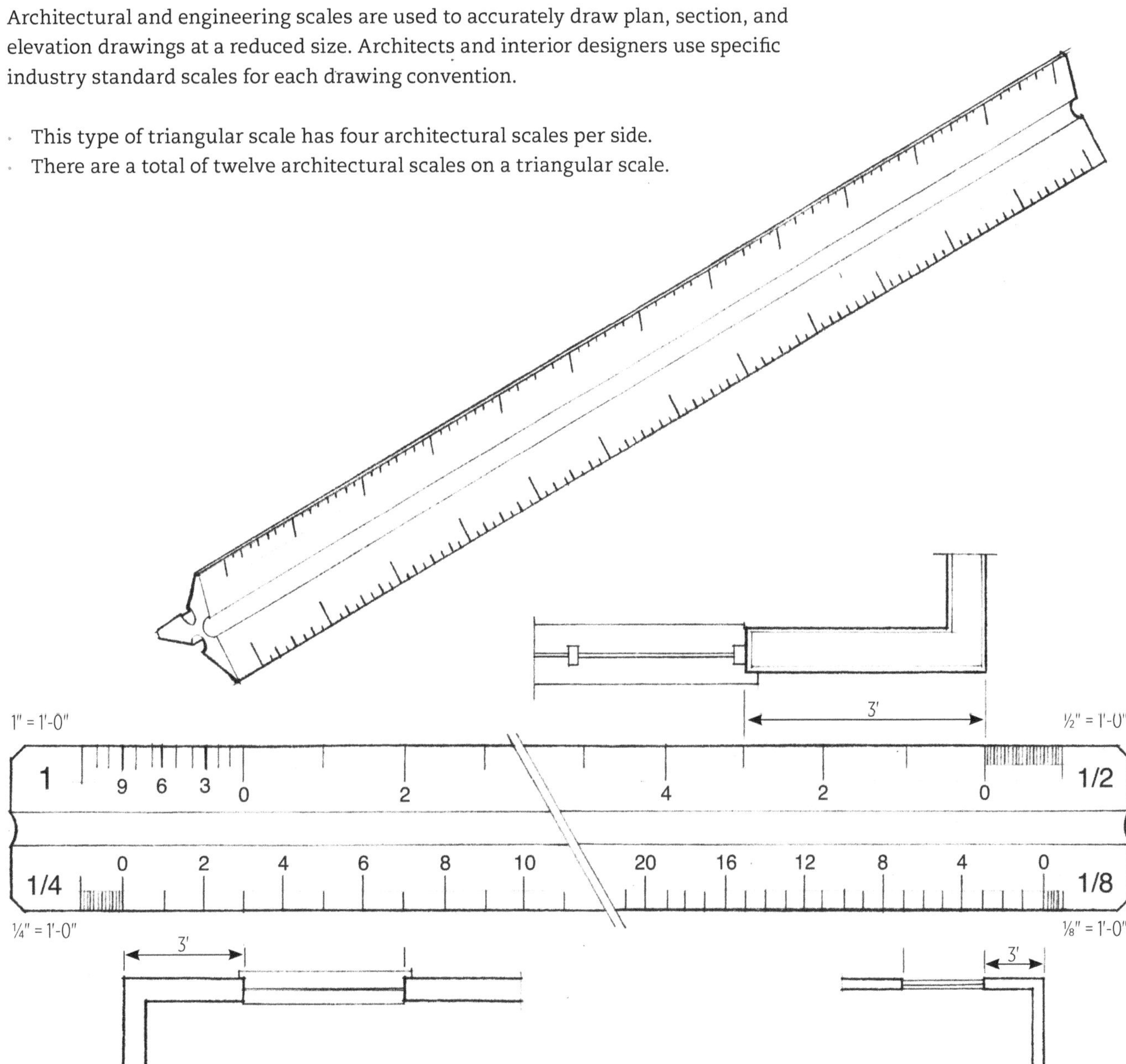

When you look at a single side of an architectural scale, you will find four unique scales or ratios starting at each corner.

- In this example the four scales are 1" = 1'-0", ½" = 1'-0", ¼" = 1'-0", and ⅛" = 1'-0".
- Note the relative size of each floor plan drawn adjacent to the architectural scale.
- Starting at the zero mark and moving toward the middle of the scale, each tick represents one foot.
- The ticks to the outside of the zero mark represent inches at the indicated architectural scale.
- Rotate the scale to find the appropriate side for your selected drawing scale.

Drawing with Ink-Based Media

Designers communicate the three-dimensional space represented in each drawing through clear and legible line weight.

- When drafting with ink, adjust the thickness of your lines by using a variety of pens.

For drafted ink presentation drawings, you may use Pigma Micron pens, Itoya Finepoint System pens, or Koh-I-Noor Rapidograph pens. All are available in multiple nib sizes for drawing different line widths.

- **Extra light lines:** Use a Pigma Micron 005 (.20 mm nib) or similar size pen.
- **Light lines:** Use a Pigma Micron 01 (.25 mm nib) or similar size pen.
- **Medium lines:** Use a Pigma Micron 03 (.35 mm nib) or similar size pen.
- **Dark lines:** Use a Pigma Micron 08 (.50 mm nib) or similar size pen.

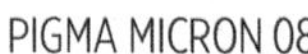

When you sketch or draw, you may also use the following selection of fiber-tipped pens. These pens are available in most office supply stores. Because the ink color may vary, these pens are not appropriate for presentation drawings.

- **Light lines:** Use a Pilot Razor Point or a Pilot Razor Point II.
- **Medium lines:** Use a Pentel Sign Pen.
- **Dark lines:** Use a Sharpie Fine Point permanent marker.

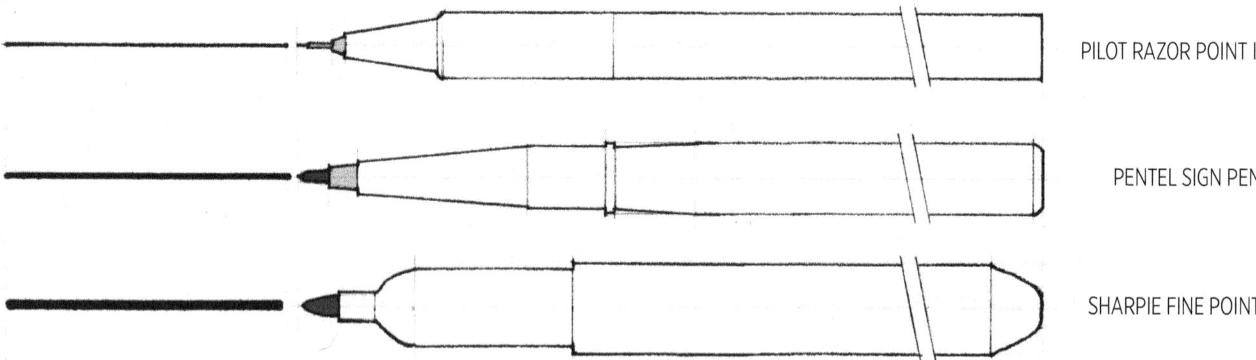

Drawing with Lead-Based Media

When drafting with lead, adjust the thickness of your lines by using different lead weights.

- For hand-drafted presentation drawings, you may use a lead holder and different lead weights.

A **lead holder** is designed to hold drafting lead. You can purchase multiple lead weights and interchange them in your lead holder to adjust the line weight in your drawings.

The **lead pointer** is a special sharpener used with lead holders. Lead pointers and holders are available at most art supply stores.

- To sharpen the lead, extend it to the depth indicated by one of the two gauges on the top of the lead pointer.
- Holding the lead pointer with one hand and the lead holder with the other, put the tip of the lead holder in the opening on the top of the lead pointer.
- Rotate the lead holder in a clockwise direction to sharpen the lead. You will feel the lead grinding against the pointer.
- Continue to rotate the lead holder until the lead is sharpened to a fine point.
- Use a tissue to gently wipe the lead dust off the freshly sharpened lead.

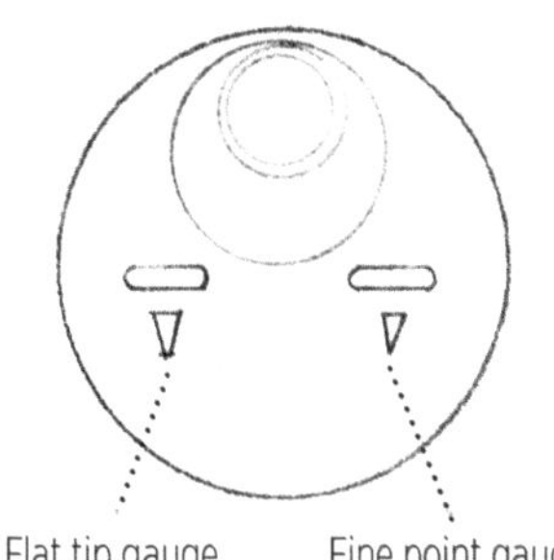

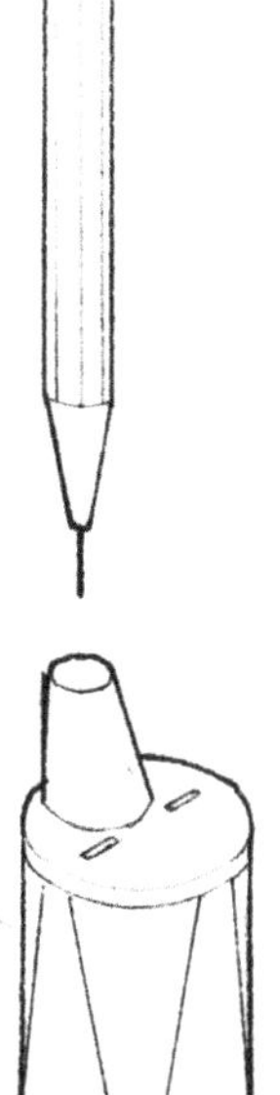

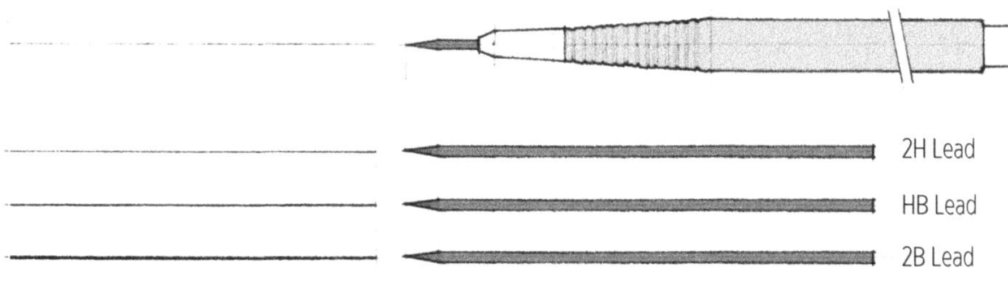

Line Weight

- Extra-light lines: Use a 4H lead.
- Light lines: Use a 2H lead.
- Medium lines: Use an HB lead.
- Dark lines: Use a 2B lead.

For pencil sketches and freehand drawings, you can also use wooden drafting pencils that are sharpened with a standard pencil sharpener. These pencils are available in a variety of lead weights.

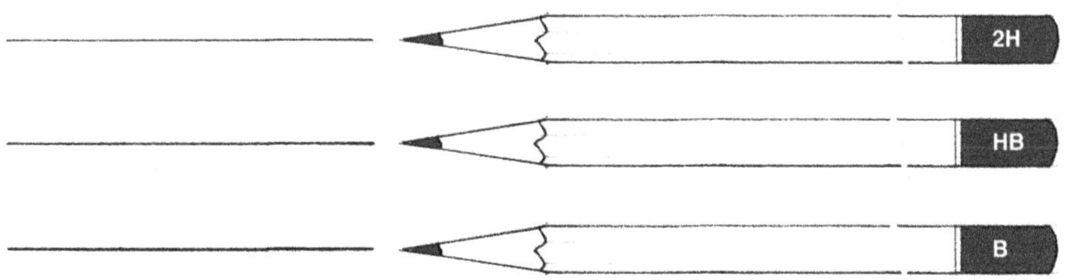

Triangles

Drafting triangles are used in combination with a horizontal drafting straightedge to draft vertical and angled lines.

- The edges of a drafting triangle are raised slightly above the drawing surface to prevent drafting ink from seeping between the triangle and the sheet of paper.
- In addition to drawing angled lines in plan, elevation, and section, a 45/45/90-degree triangle is used to draw 45-degree isometric drawings.
- A 30/60/90-degree triangle is used to draw axonometric drawings and 30-degree isometric drawings.
- An adjustable triangle can be set to draft lines at any angle. If you want to purchase only one drafting triangle, an adjustable triangle can be used as both a 30/60/90-degree triangle and a 45/45/90-degree triangle.

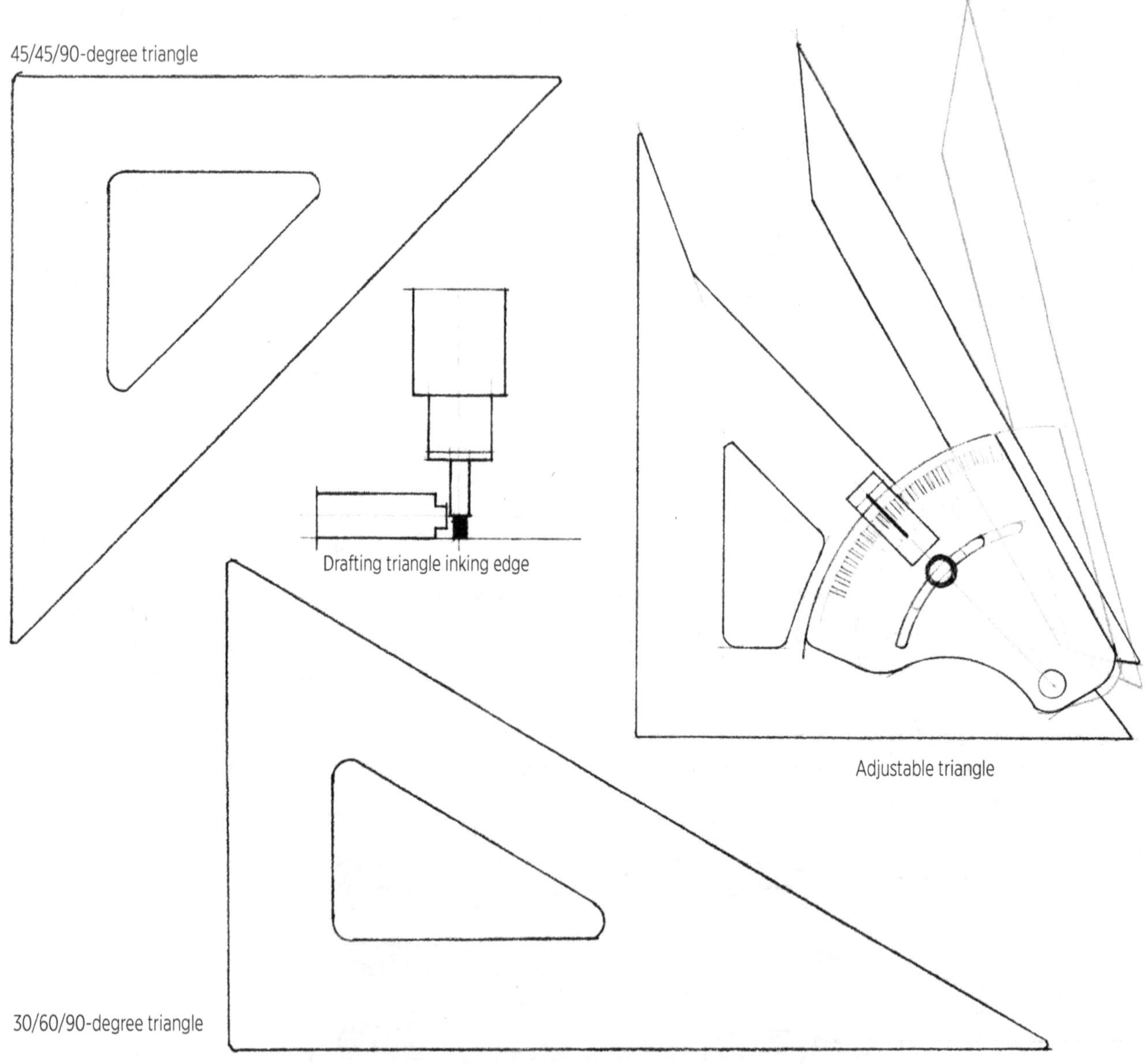

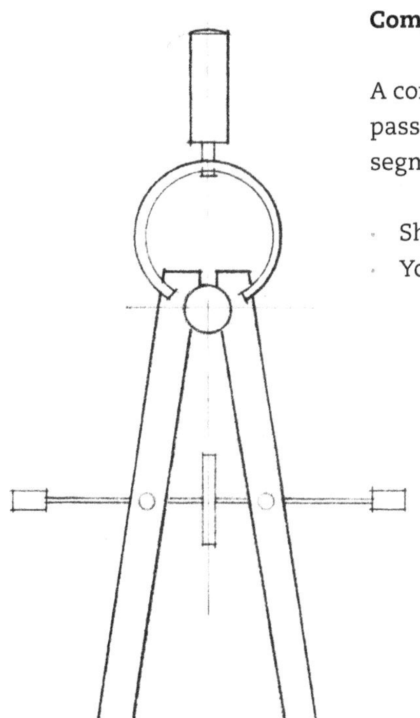

Compass

A compass is used to draw large circles in plan, section, or elevation. The compass is also used to construct geometric shapes and to subdivide lines into equal segments.

- Sharpen the drafting compass's lead with a lead holder and a lead pointer.
- You may also purchase drafting templates to draw ellipses and circles.

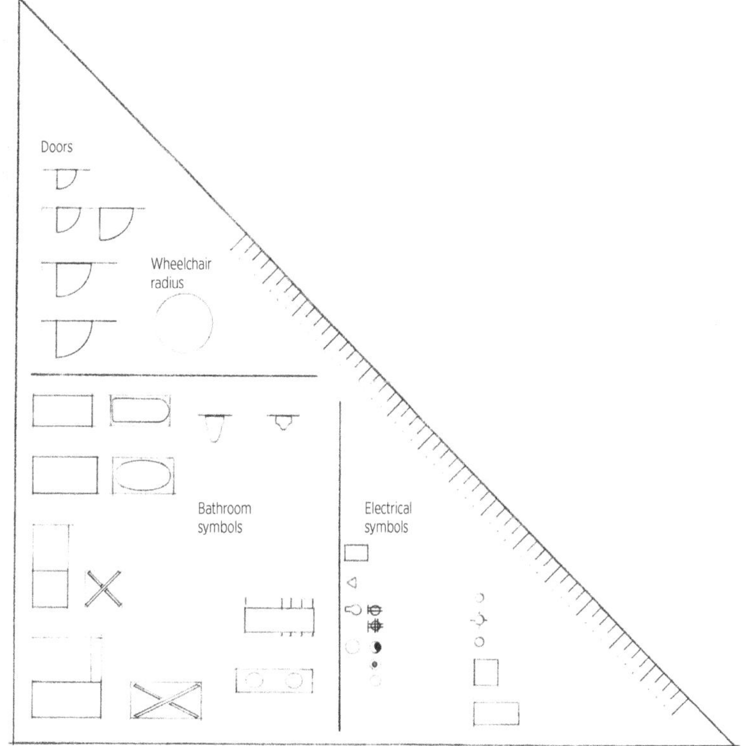

Interior Drafting Templates

Interior drafting templates contain typical furniture symbols at standard architectural scales. These templates help you quickly add interior detail, such as doors, toilets, and furniture to any hand-drafted presentation drawing. They also provide a quick method for locating and sizing typical room dimensions in space planning exercises.

- Consider purchasing a good template that includes door swings, plumbing fixtures, and electrical symbols.
- Typical template scales are ¼" = 1'-0" and ⅛" = 1'-0".

Circle template

Eraser Shield

An eraser shield is used with an eraser to precisely erase portions of your drawing. Use the shield to cover the portion of your drawing that you do not want to erase. The different openings inside the shield are used to precisely erase segments of lines and arcs.

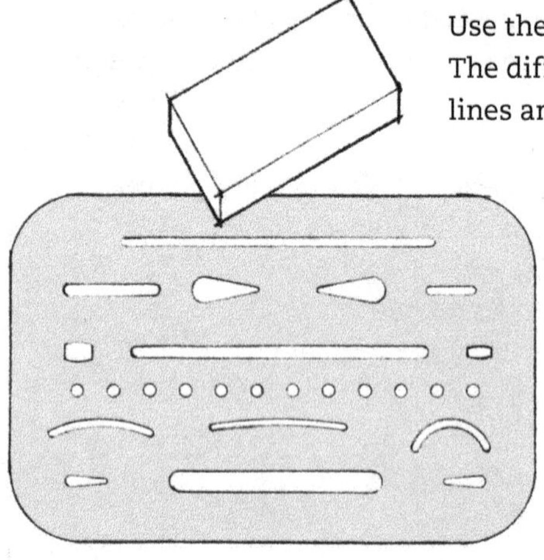

Eraser shield

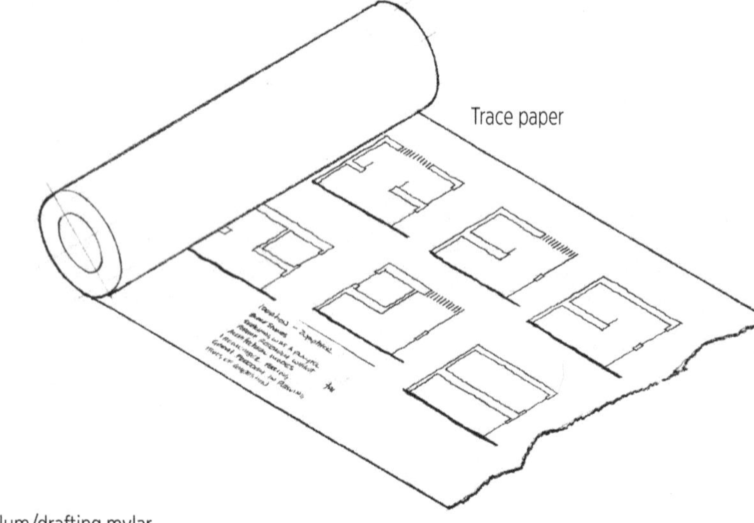

Trace paper

Trace Paper

Lightweight tracing paper is appropriate for preliminary design drawings in both pencil and pen.

- Because the paper is translucent, you can overlay multiple sheets to test different design schemes.
- By layering trace paper over an existing presentation drawing, you can explore alternate design options during or after a design review.
- Depending on the scale of your project, you can purchase a roll of trace paper 12", 18", or 24" wide. The paper is available in white and canary yellow.

Vellum/drafting mylar

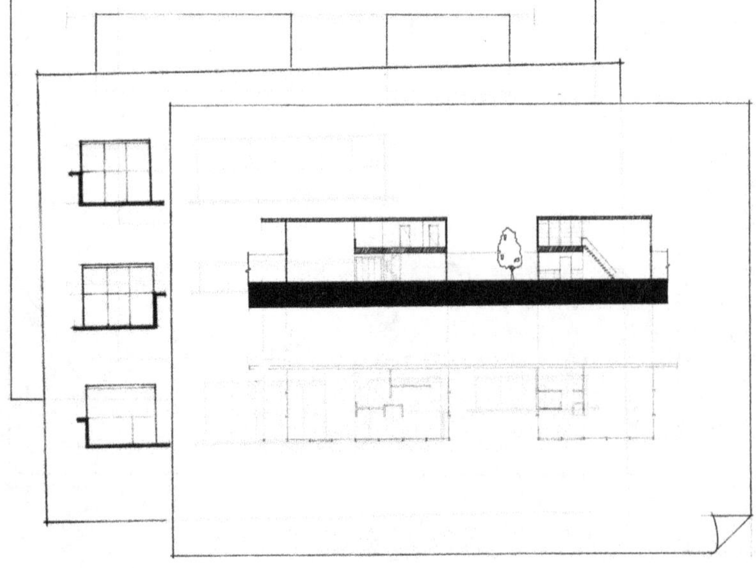

Vellum/Drafting Mylar

Presentation drawings are often drafted on drafting Mylar or vellum.

- Drafting vellum is available in different levels of translucency.
- Vellum is durable enough to withstand the stress of erasing lines as you modify your design or correct errors in your drawing.
- Drafting Mylar is available with a matte finish on either one or both sides. Draft on the side of the paper with the matte finish.
- Mylar is the preferred surface for drafting with ink pens. Using an ink eraser, you can erase the ink completely from the Mylar surface without damaging the paper.

DESIGN PRINCIPLES

In this chapter, you are introduced to foundation design principles, including ordering, figure-ground, spatial relationships, and proportion. The chapter presents design principles in two dimensions and three dimensions to communicate how each principle is used to compose spatial relationships and to develop strong design ideas in plan, section, and elevation.

Consider the following questions as you read this chapter:

- How is hand drawing used in both school and in practice to explore and develop ideas?
- How is hand drawing used in both school and in practice to communicate design ideas?
- How do different drawing conventions and techniques affect what we design and how we communicate our ideas?

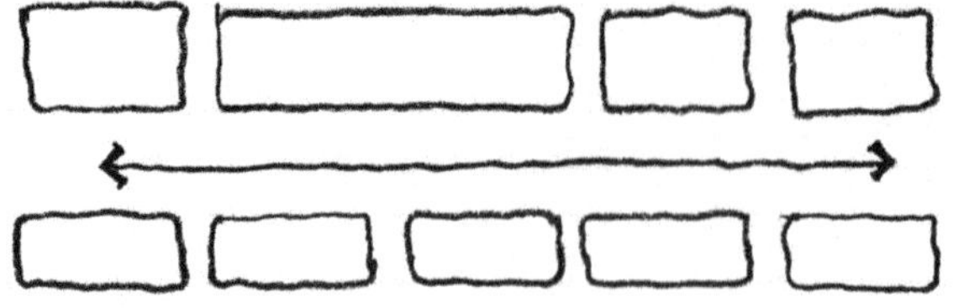

Single Axis
In the axial organized plan, objects are arranged symmetrically or in balance about the axis of one real or imaginary line.

- Examples of single-axis organization in architecture and interior design are a dual-loaded corridor and an urban city street.

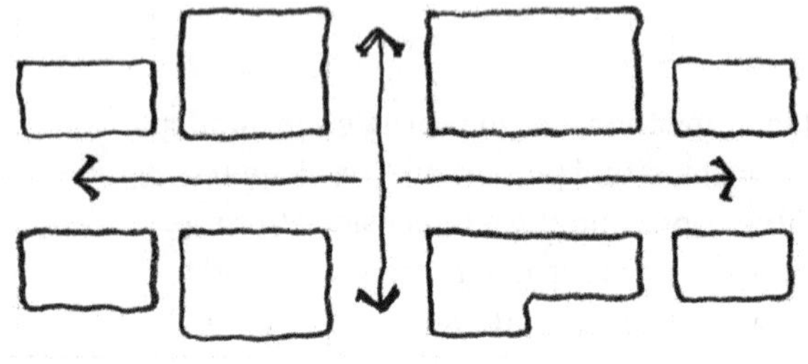

Dual Axis
In the dual-axial organized plan, objects are arranged in a balanced and organized manner around two real or imaginary intersecting lines.

- Examples of dual-axis organization in architecture and interior design are intersecting corridors and the intersection of two urban city streets.

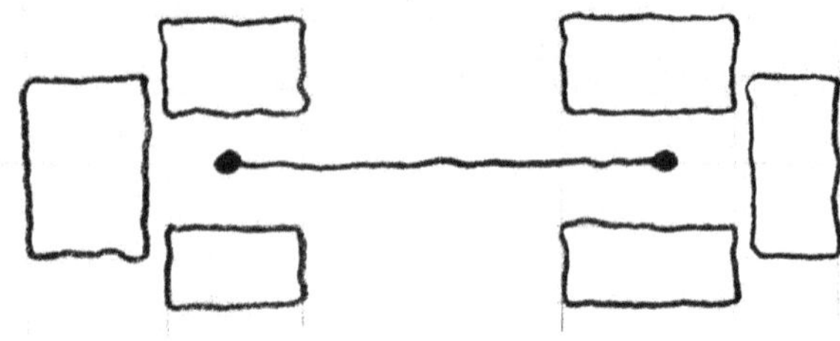

Binodal
In the binodal organized plan, objects are clustered around two nodes. A straight, uninterrupted line connects the two nodes.

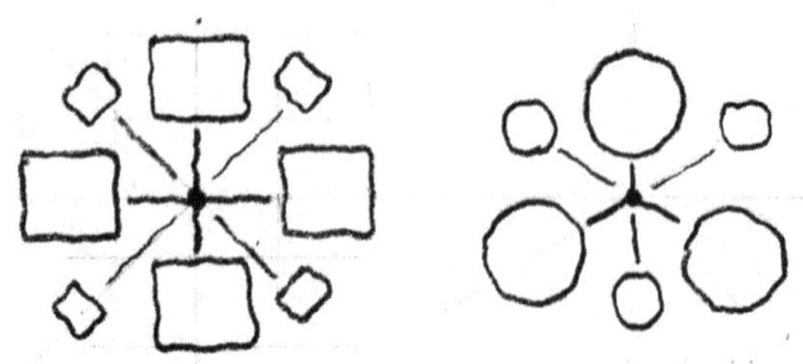

Radial
In the radial organized plan, objects stem from a series of lines that radiate from a central node.

Grid
Grid organization is achieved through a series of real or imaginary intersecting lines about which a series of objects, masses, or spaces are composed. The spacing of the grid may vary according to context and the individual needs within each grid.

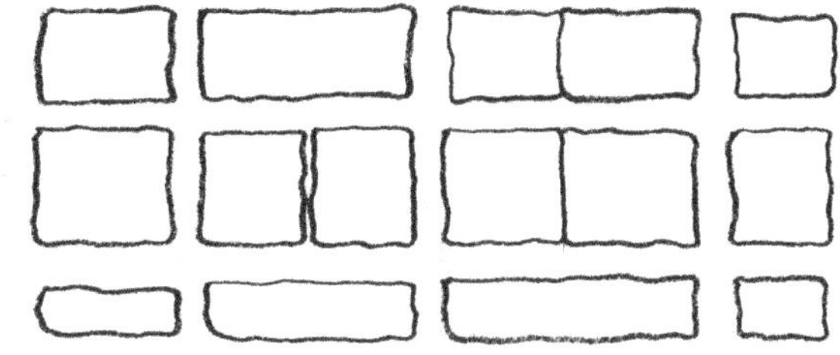

- Grids are used to organize cities, building structure, floor plans, and surfaces on the interior and exterior of a building.

Regular Grid
In the regular grid, spacing between the intersecting lines is consistent. Objects placed in a regular grid conform to this standard module. Regular grids may occur in both two and three dimensions.

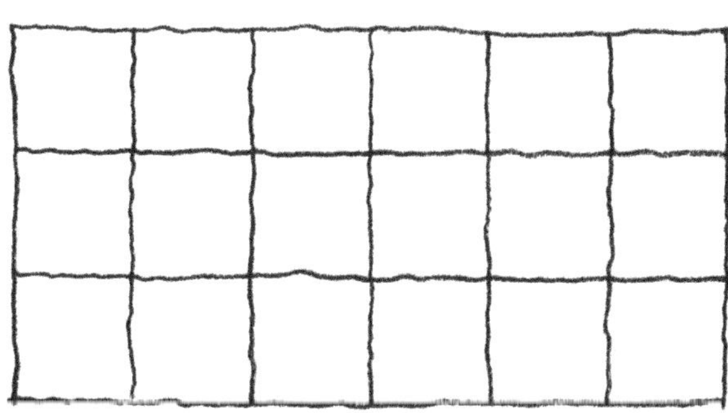

Irregular Grid/Matrix
The spacing in an irregular grid/matrix is modified by internal program requirements or the external context surrounding the grid.

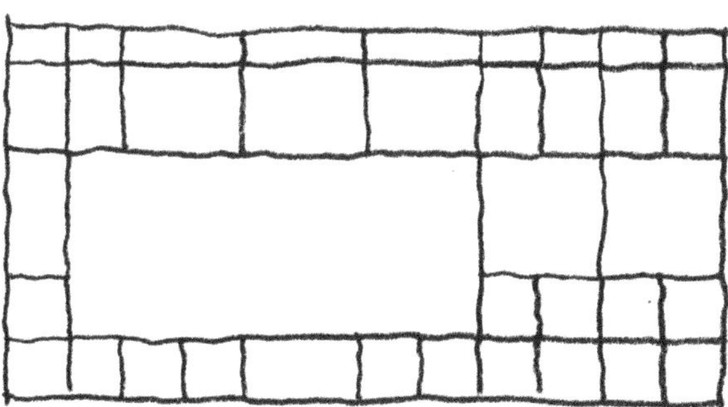

Rotated Grid
Two grids may be rotated and overlapped to react to a contextual condition or to programmatic requirements. The space created by overlapping grids creates a unique threshold opportunity within a design project.

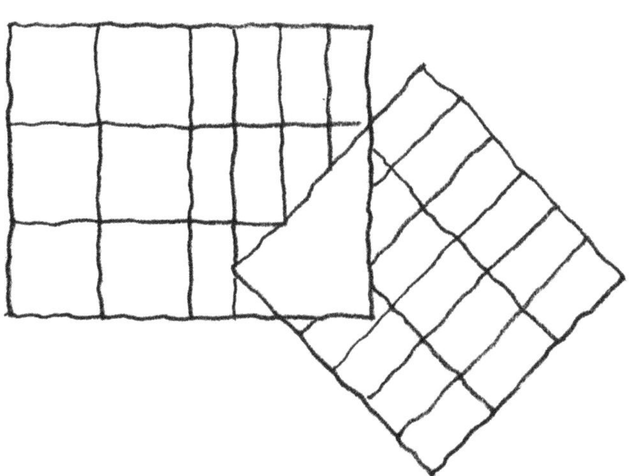

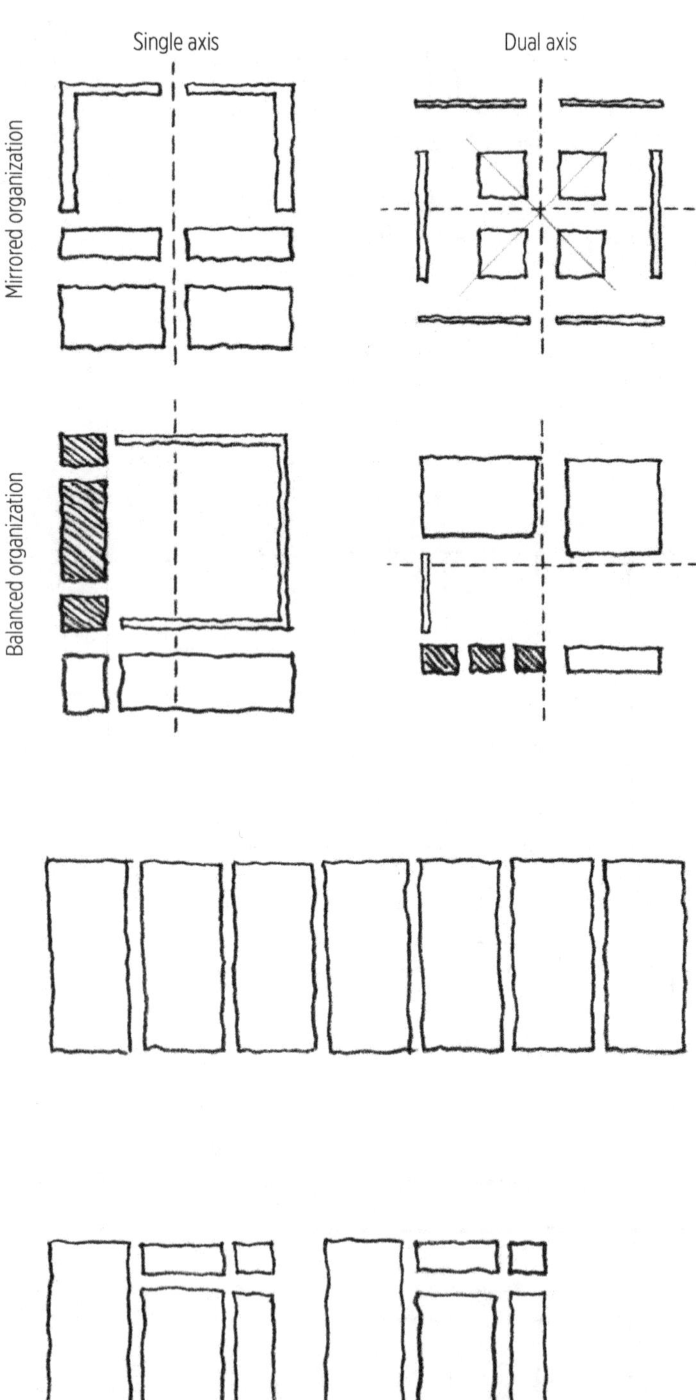

Symmetry
Symmetrical organization is the mirrored, or balanced, organization around an axis.

- Mirrored organization is an exact duplication of spatial elements on both sides of an axis. The strict organizational constraints of a mirrored floor plan often prevent an appropriate response to a site or program.
- Balanced organization is the measured arrangement of dissimilar spatial elements on either side of an axis.

Repetition
Repetition is the systematic duplication of a spatial element or a series of elements. Repetition occurs in both two and three dimensions.

Rhythm
Rhythm is a recurring sequence of spatial elements. Variation within a pattern ranges from subtle modification between elements to a more distinct change.

Hierarchy

Hierarchy is the clear ranking among similar elements in a category or design. Within a design there may be a hierarchy of spaces, mass, and spatial elements.

- Positional hierarchy occurs when one element is clearly removed from a predetermined organizational pattern.
- Object hierarchy occurs when one element clearly differs in value or geometry.
- Hierarchy in scale occurs when one element's scale is clearly larger or smaller than that of a similar element's scale.

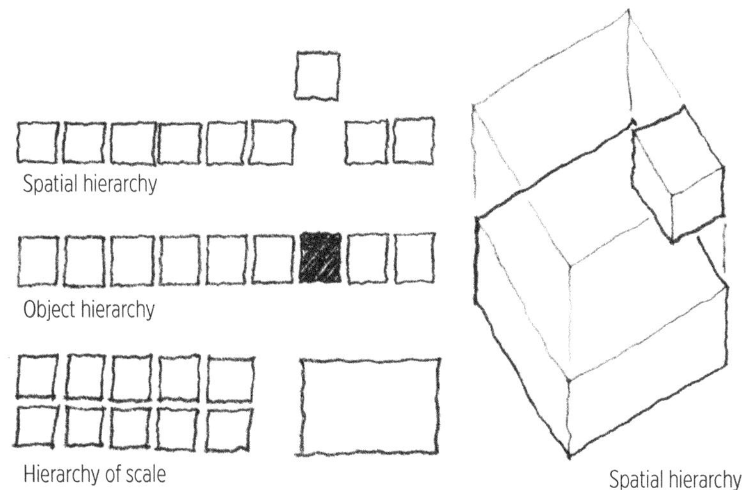

Displacement

Displacement is the implied movement, or shift of volume or mass, to a new position within a spatial composition.

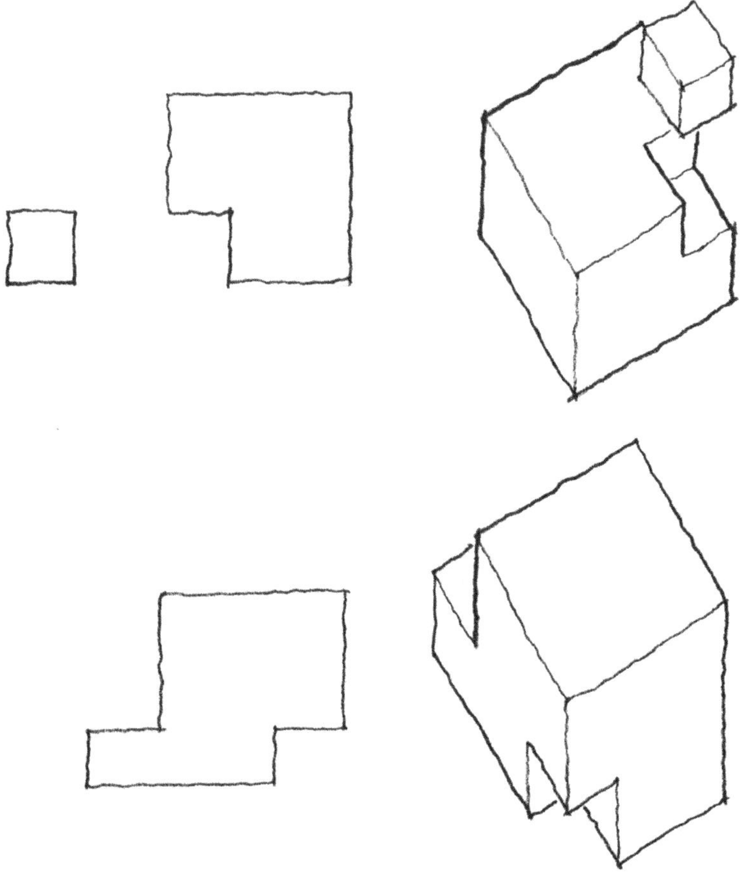

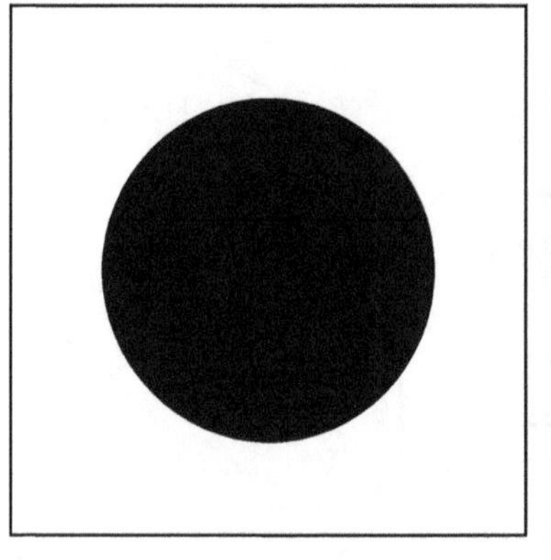
A

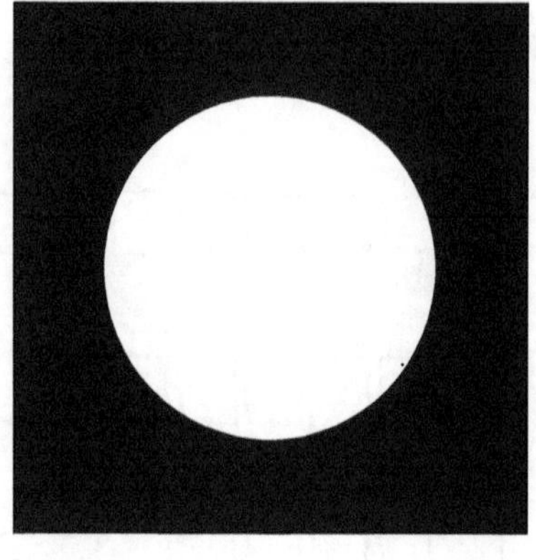
B

Figure-ground compositions clearly distinguish the figural element from the background.

- A black circle is located on a white background (Figure A).
- The inverse composition, with a white circle located on a black background (Figure B).

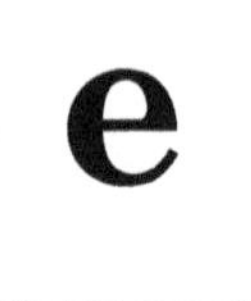

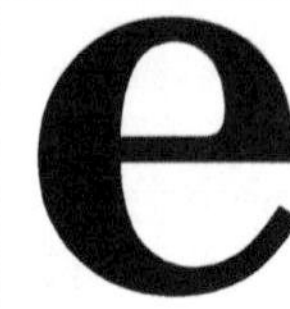

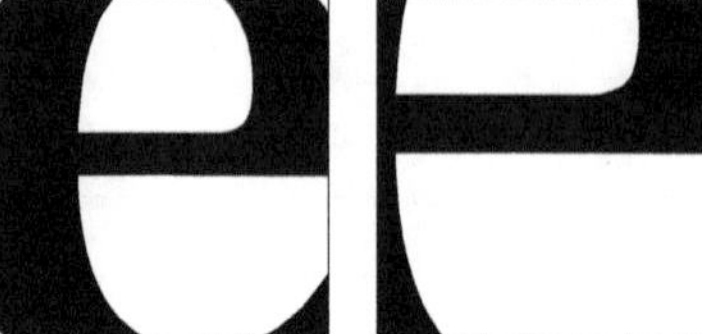
C

- The letter "e" in Figure C is increasingly expanded on a white background until it becomes indistinguishable as a letter.

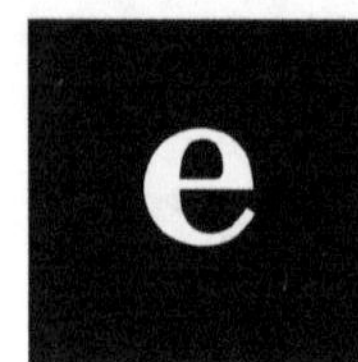

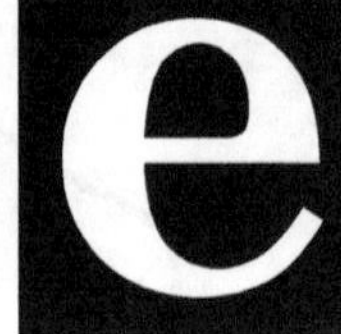

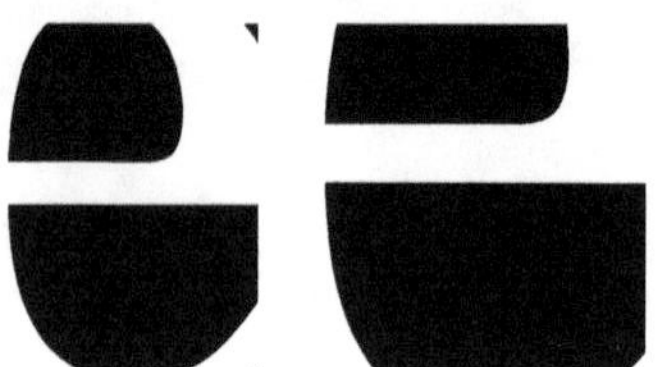
D

- Figure D illustrates the inverse figure-ground comp-ositions, allowing one to see how both foreground and background are critical in the visual reading of the letter "e."

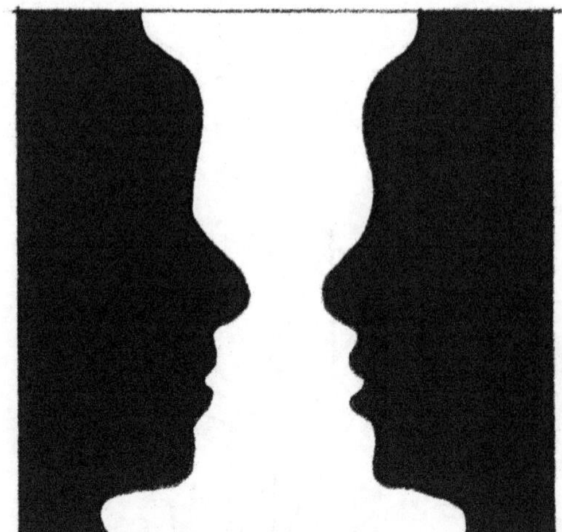

Figure-Ground Reversal
The figure-ground reversal composition creates an ambiguous relationship between the figure or figures and the background.

- This example can be seen as a white vase (figure) on a black background.
- Conversely, this example can also be seen as two black faces on a white background.

Two-dimensional compositional exercises like these examples challenge students to create visual ambiguity, or oscillation, between the foreground and background elements in a composition. The compositions are made from white and black paper on brown chipboard.

In a successful composition, ambiguity between foreground and background is achieved when the brown chipboard becomes a figural element and the white and black paper become the background.

In the essay "Transparency: Literal and Phenomenal" (1963), Colin Rowe and Robert Slutzky use examples from architecture and cubist paintings to define this visual oscillation as phenomenal transparency, an inherent quality of spatial organization in which an element can simultaneously appear in two different locations. In this student work, the two locations are foreground and background.

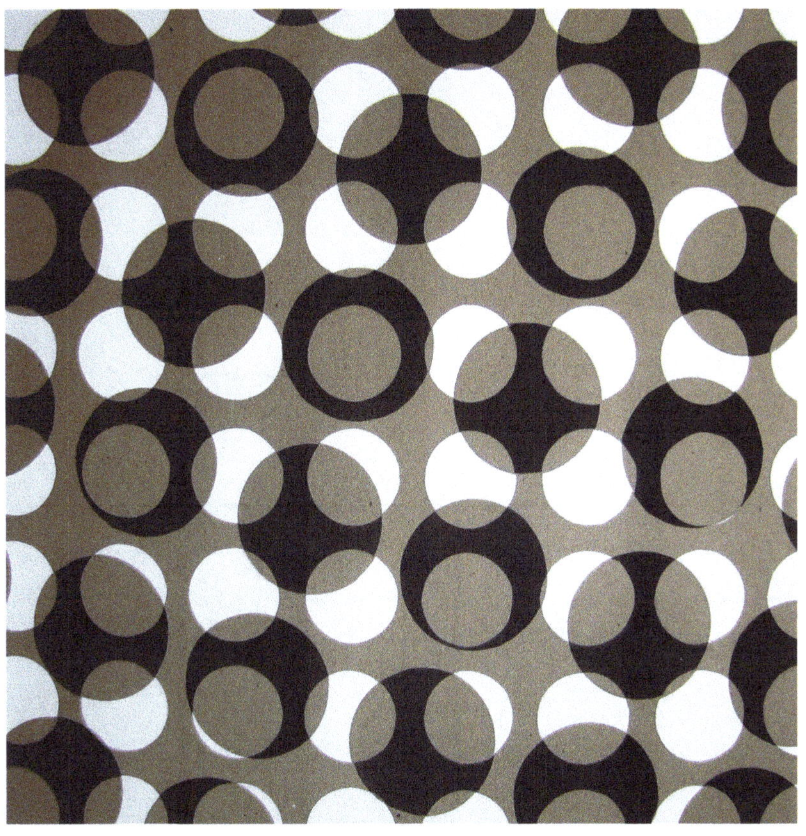

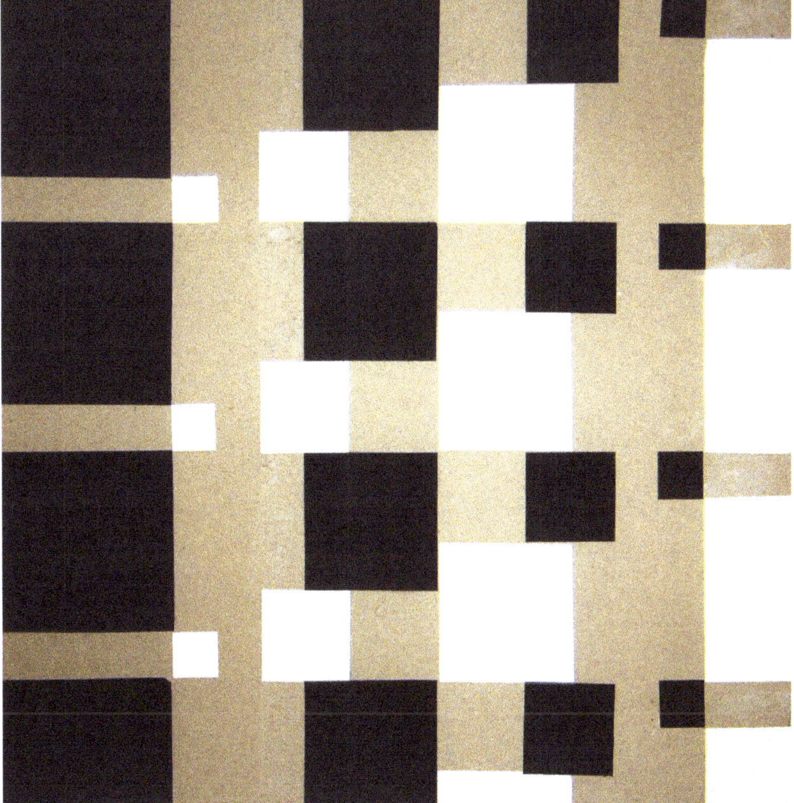

WILLIAM HARPER
Points composition
Masters A Foundation Design Studio, Boston Architectural College

DAVID HAUGEN
Points composition
Masters A Foundation Design Studio, Boston Architectural College

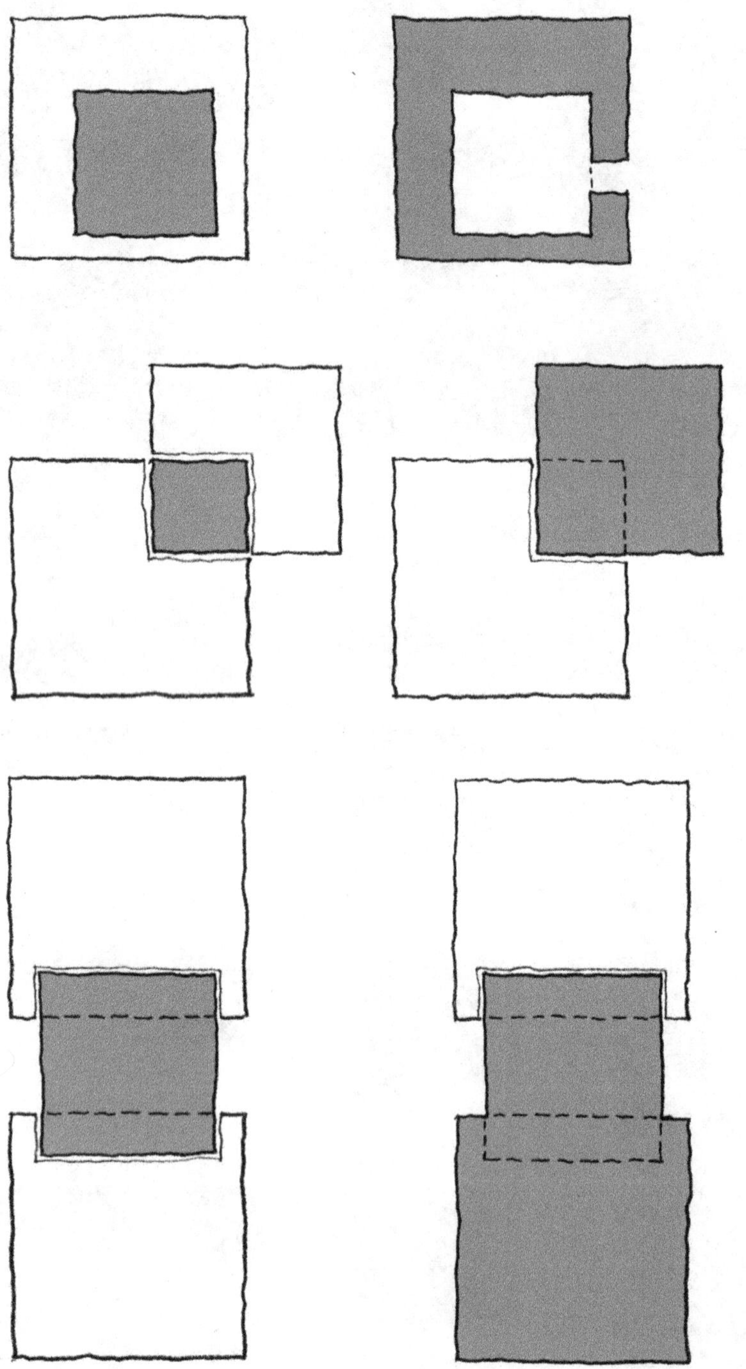

Two unique spaces can assume three distinct spatial relationships in plan or section.

Enclosed Spaces

Enclosed spaces occur when one space is completely surrounded by a second space. Depending on the relationship, the primary space can be either the surrounding space or the enclosed space.

Partially Overlapping Spaces

- Partially overlapping spaces can create a unique separate space shared by both spaces.
- In a different relationship the overlapping space may belong in large part to one space, with an implied relationship to the second space.

Linked Spaces

- Linked spaces are physically isolated spaces that are connected by a third, unique space.
- Similar to this example, the linking space may take on the physical or spatial qualities of one of the two spaces.
- The linking space does not have to be physically enclosed and can be the implied space created by the placement of two separate objects.

Circulation
The floor plan is an organization of objects, masses, and spaces that are experienced through the system of circulation.

In addition to an understanding of ordering principles and proportion, strong plans result from a clear understanding of circulation and human occupation.

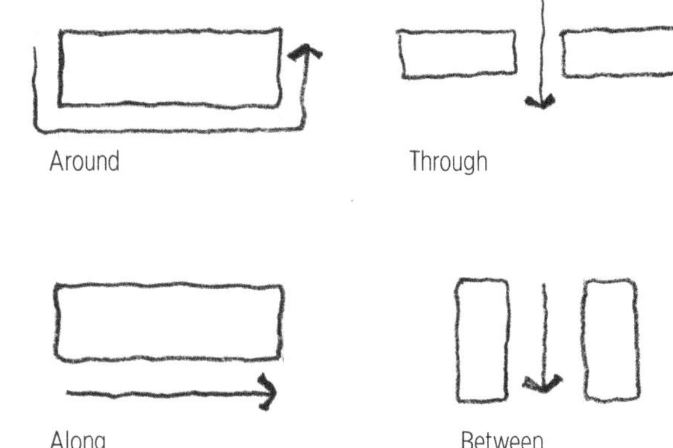

Ideation and Transformation
Critical analysis in design relies on your ability to explore and examine multiple solutions to a design problem.

The transformative process is a tool for refining and clarifying your design intent through both deliberate modifications and modifications that occur by chance. This process can be used to examine the influence of multiple variables on a design idea. The result of this investigation should relate in part or in whole to your original conceptual ideas.

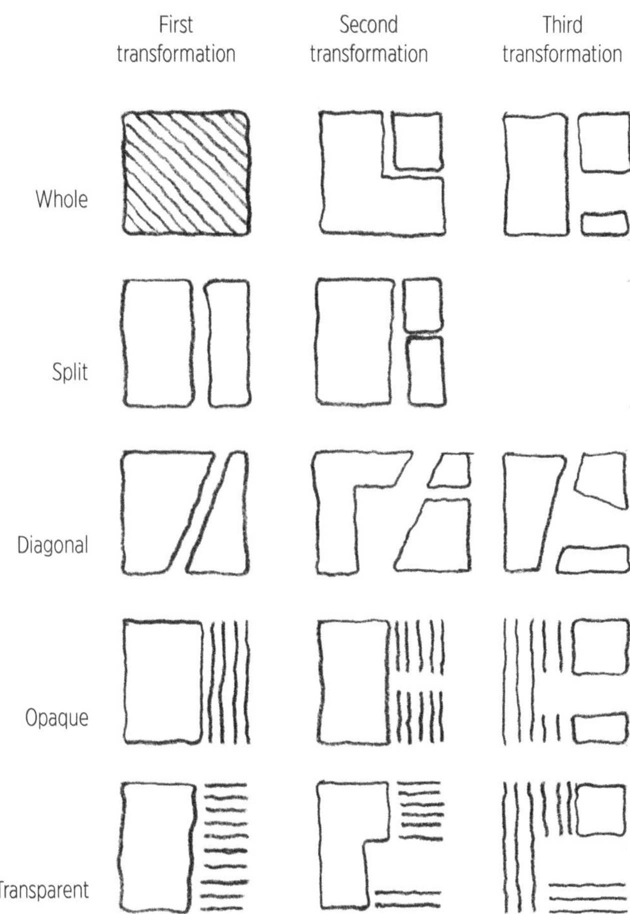

Learning Exercise
Using the following concepts, transform a square and a rectangle:

- part, whole
- grid, binodal
- opaque, transparent
- split, connect

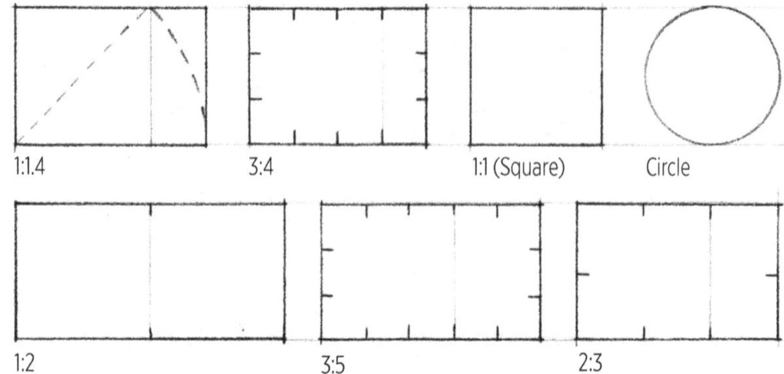

Palladian Proportions

In his *Four Books on Architecture* (1570), Andrea Palladio (1508–1580) identifies the seven "most beautiful and proportional manner of rooms." Palladio used these proportions to shape rooms in many of his villas.

Villa Foscari

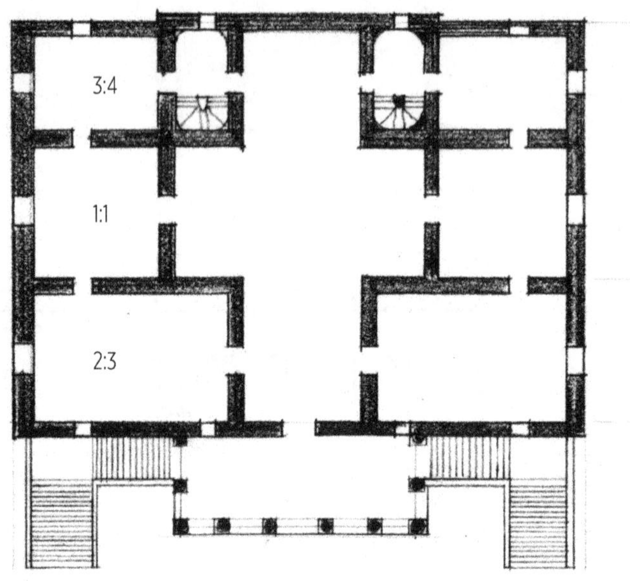

Villa Foscari (1558–1560) was commissioned by Nicolo and Alvise Foscari and built outside of Venice, Italy. This villa is a good example of Palladio's use of symmetrical organization and how ideal proportions shape and organize the floor plan. The room proportions are indicated in the floor plan to the left.

The symmetrical organization of this and other Palladian villas was based in large part on Palladio's understanding of structure, specifically masonry construction. By utilizing mirrored organization with rooms the same size on each side of the villa, the walls can equally bear the weight of the roof and the upper floors.

Proportional Diagram

2 1 2 1 2

1.5 2 2 1.5

3:4

1:1

2:3

Colin Rowe's essay "The Mathematics of the Ideal Villa" (1947) compares Palladio's Villa Foscari with Le Corbusier's Villa Garches.

This diagram illustrates Rowe's analysis of the spatial proportions and the position of solid walls in Villa Foscari.

- The floor plan is 8 units in length by 5½ units in breadth.
- The spaces alternate between double and single intervals from left to right.
- Including the portico, the front to back spaces are sequenced 1½ : 2 : 2 : 1½, from front to back.

Golden Section/Regulating Lines
Le Corbusier (1887–1965) followed Palladio in his use of regulating lines to refine his designs in plan, section, and elevation. In *Towards a New Architecture* (1923; translated 1927), he writes, "A regulating line is an assurance against capriciousness." Le Corbusier argues that the regulating lines are not the generator of plan, but a tool to bring in "this tangible form of mathematics which gives the reassuring perception of order."

The relationship between design and mathematics expressed by Le Corbusier is similar to the relationship between hand drawing and computer drawing: the computer should not be used as the generator for design, but as a tool to refine and clarify your design intent.

In Villa Garches (1927), Le Corbusier locates the primary structure, using proportions similar to those of Villa Foscari.

- The golden section is used by Le Corbusier at Villa Garches to order a sequence of square spaces.
- The free plan allows Le Corbusier to separate the load-bearing columns in this house from the walls to divide interior spaces.
- Unlike Palladio's Villa Foscari, the size of the interior spaces and relationships between them are independent of the building's structure.

This diagram illustrates Rowe's analysis of the spatial proportions at Villa Garches.

- Like Villa Foscari, this floor plan is 8 units in length by 5½ units in breadth.
- Left to right, the spaces also follow the order of those of Villa Foscari, alternating between double and single intervals.
- The front to back spaces do not follow the sequence in Villa Foscari. They are sequenced 1½ : ½ : 1½ : 1½ : 1½ : ½.

Golden Section

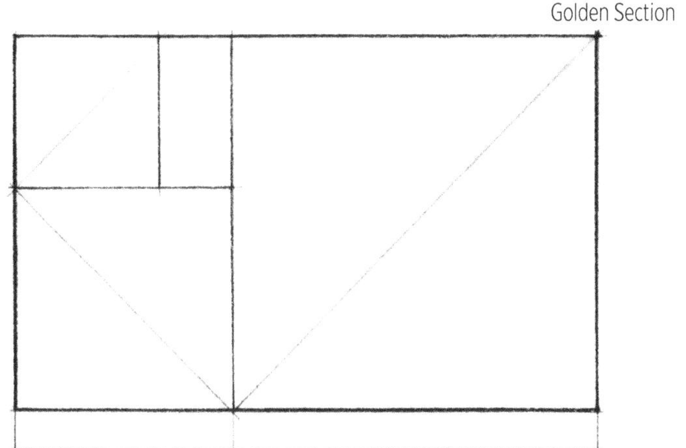

Villa Garches

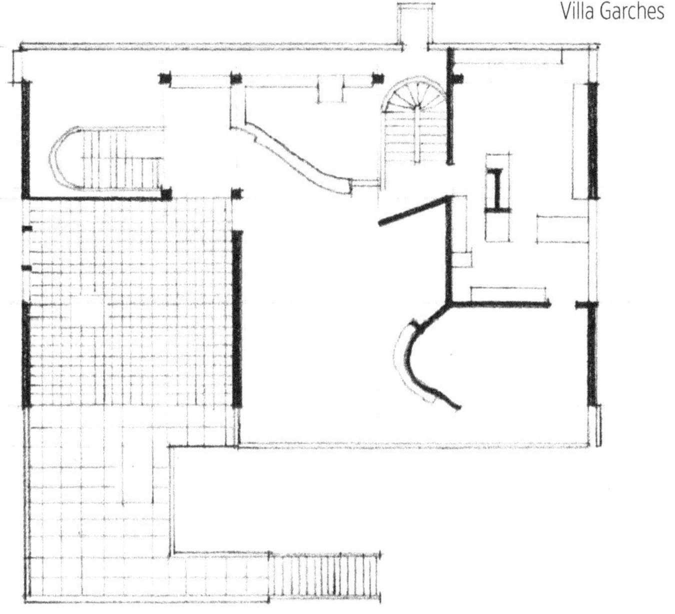

Proportion Diagram

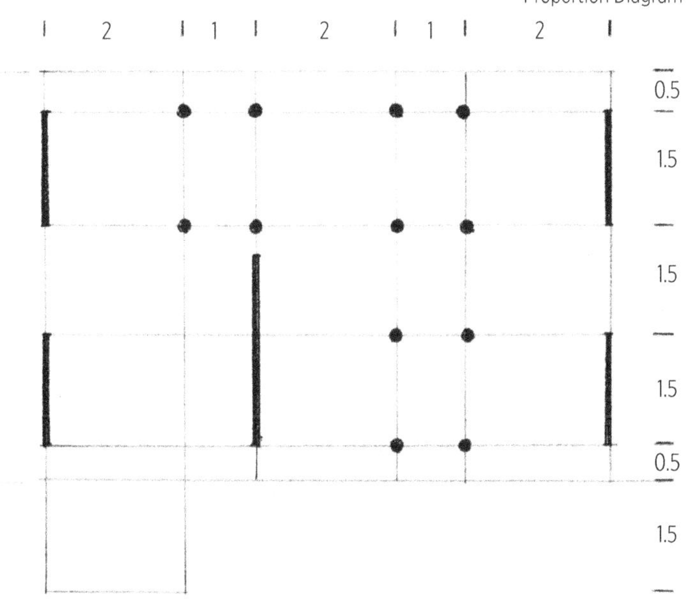

FLOOR PLANS

This chapter introduces the floor plan as a tool for the generation of ideas and discusses architectural drawing conventions to help you draw legible floor plans. The instruction in this chapter directly addresses what students and instructors are trying to accomplish in the design studio: to translate physical models and three-dimensional ideas into two-dimensional drawings.

Depending on the educational approach of your college or university, you may use the plan as a primary tool for design, or the plan may reveal itself at the end of a project to communicate the organization and ideas of your built models. Regardless of when you introduce it in your design process, the plan is an important tool for refining and clarifying your design ideas and intent.

> Without a good plan nothing exists, all is frail and cannot endure, all is poor even under the clutter of the richest decoration.
>
> —LE CORBUSIER, *Towards a New Architecture*

Consider the following questions as you read this chapter:

- How is hand drawing used in both school and in practice to explore, develop, and communicate ideas?
- What are the fundamental drawing conventions used to construct floor plans?
- How do floor plans support the design process?

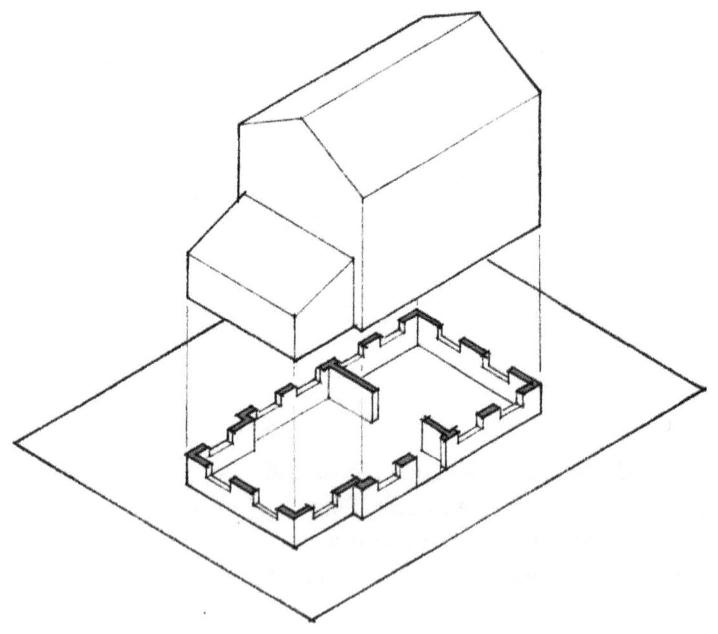

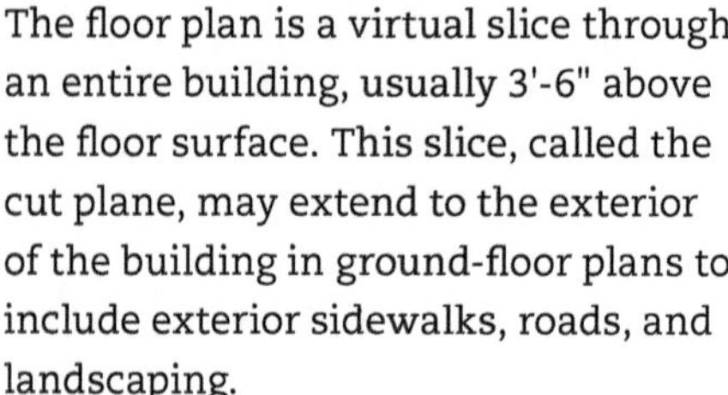

The floor plan is a virtual slice through an entire building, usually 3'-6" above the floor surface. This slice, called the cut plane, may extend to the exterior of the building in ground-floor plans to include exterior sidewalks, roads, and landscaping.

Floor plans are two-dimensional drawings that visually communicate the spatial conditions in a building or project including the relationship between adjacent spaces.

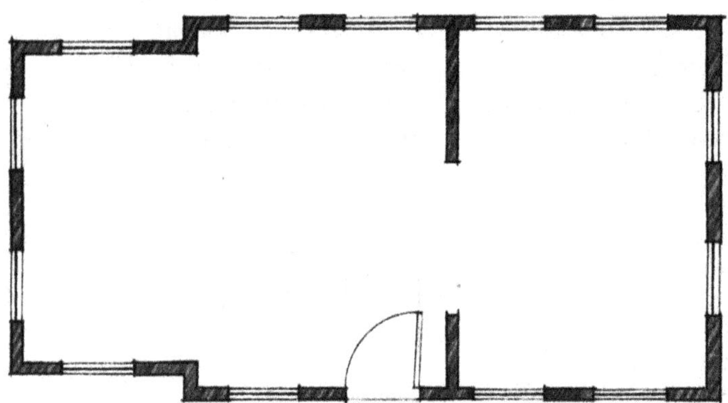

Objects that are "sliced" in the floor plan, such as doors and walls, are drawn with a very dark line. These objects are also rendered with solid tone, also called poché, in presentation drawings to communicate the relationship between mass and void. Interior furniture is drawn with a medium line. Floor surface patters are drawn with light lines.

The scale of floor plans varies, depending on the size of the project. Typical presentation plans are drawn at $\frac{1}{16}$" = 1'-0", $\frac{1}{8}$" = 1'-0", or $\frac{1}{4}$" = 1'-0".

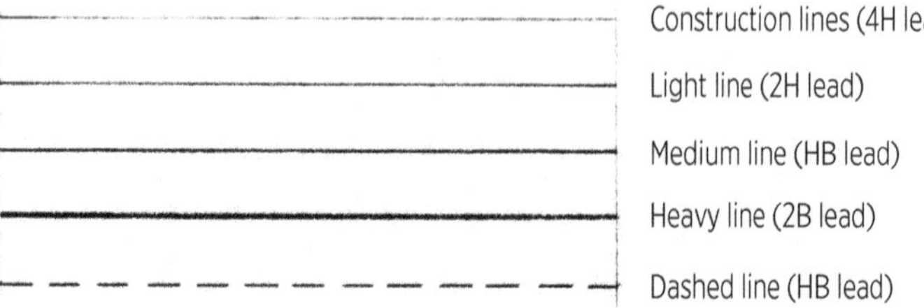

Line Weight

Designers communicate the three-dimensional space represented in a floor plan through clear and legible line weight.

- When drafting by hand, adjust line thickness by adjusting the type of lead in your pencil, the thickness of your pen, and the pressure applied to the paper.

Ideation through Hand-Drawn Plans
Ideation, also referred to as conceptual design, is the process of exploring multiple design iterations and critically evaluating each as an appropriate solution to a design problem. The ideation process most often occurs at the beginning of a project, during or after research and programming. Ideation involves the translation of a written design problem to a spatial design solution.

- In plan, ideation is most evident through the rapid execution of multiple design solutions or options, often at a reduced scale.
- Working at a reduced scale allows you, the designer, to focus on larger programmatic issues, including adjacencies, scale, and proportion.
- Designers use quick sketches in plan to study the organization and circulation of a project. These drawings vary in media, which can include charcoal, marker, pencil, and watercolor.

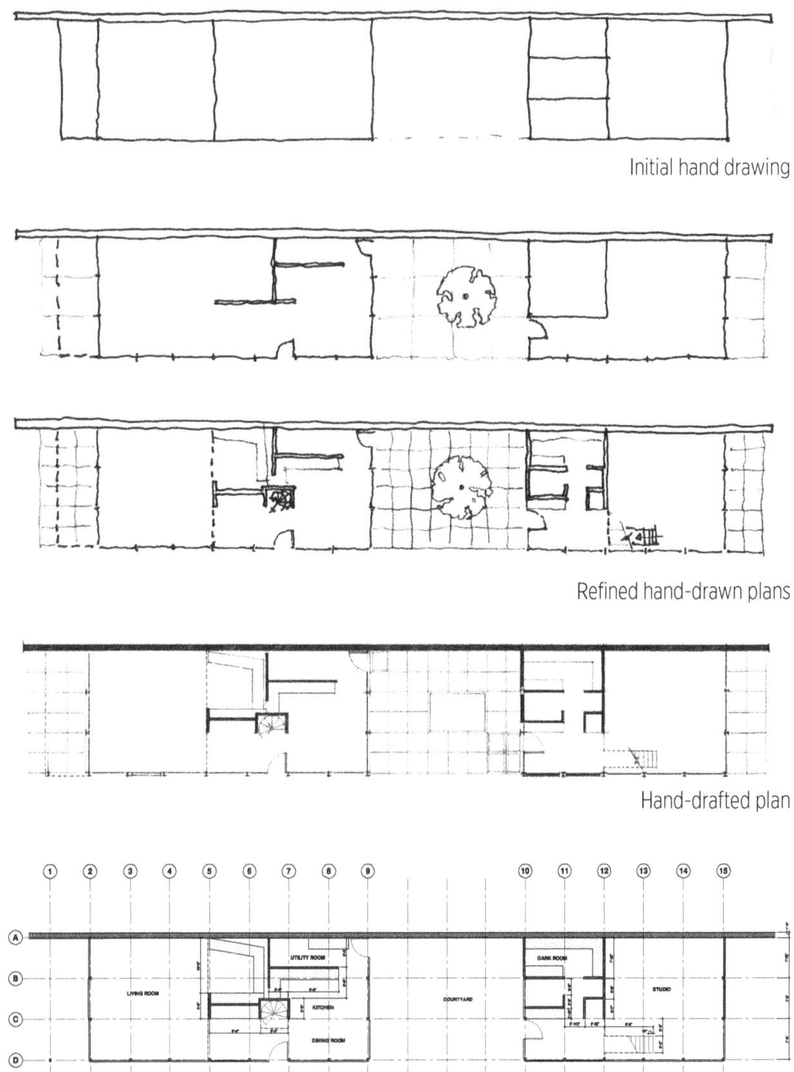

Initial hand drawing

Refined hand-drawn plans

Hand-drafted plan

Digitally drafted plan

CHARLES (1907–78) AND RAY (1912–88) EAMES
Eames House (1949)
Drawings by Douglas Seidler

Hand and Digital Drafting
At some point in the design process, you will need to create a more precise drawing for a presentation, client meeting, or set of construction drawings. Using the accuracy of a drafting table or computer drafting software, you can quickly translate the ideas in your hand drawings to drafted floor plans that contain appropriate line weight and conform to drawing conventions. These more precise drawings often contain additional information, such as floor patterns, notes, and dimensions.

It is important to note that a strong floor plan is measured both in its technical accuracy and in the strength of the design solution. Loose hand drawings are the most effective method to explore, refine, and strengthen a design. Hand-drafted or digitally drafted drawings are the most effective methods to create technically accurate and consistent floor plans for presentations or construction documents.

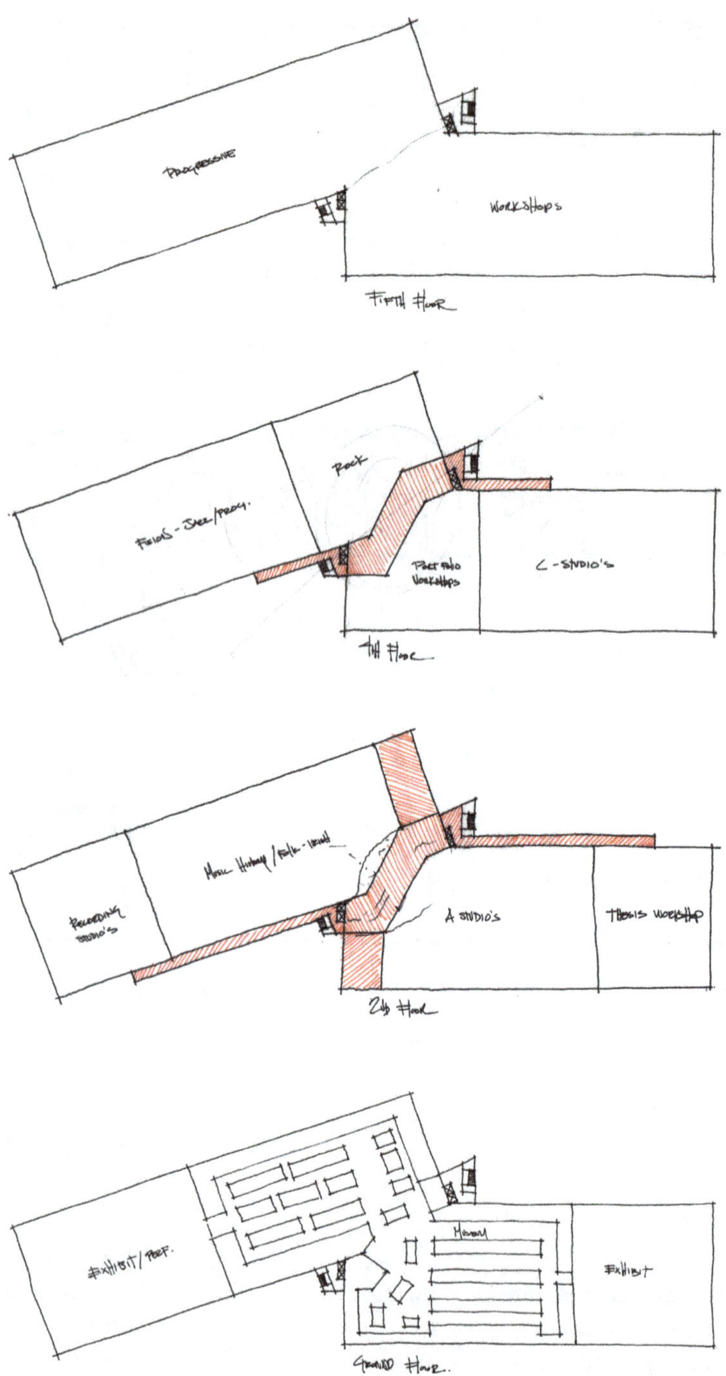

I created these presentation drawings to describe my project's interior organization, and I wanted to represent volumes rather than designed spaces. By shading the edges of the spaces and controlling the tone so the shading fades to the center of the space, I was able to give the drawing a sense of depth. Altering where the shading starts to fade can also suggest shadow and heights of spaces.

Everyone wants to use programs like SketchUp and Revit as design tools. Although they are definitely useful for spatial and materiality exploration, I believe students too often use these programs as design tools right from the start. Being able to express your ideas and communicate form, volume, and space by hand is an invaluable tool because you can quickly realize a design idea with just a few simple sketches.

Because this is a skill that requires practice, I try to draw by hand whenever possible.

—KEVIN ASMUS

KEVIN ASMUS
Schematic design plans
Degree Project Studio,
Boston Architectural College

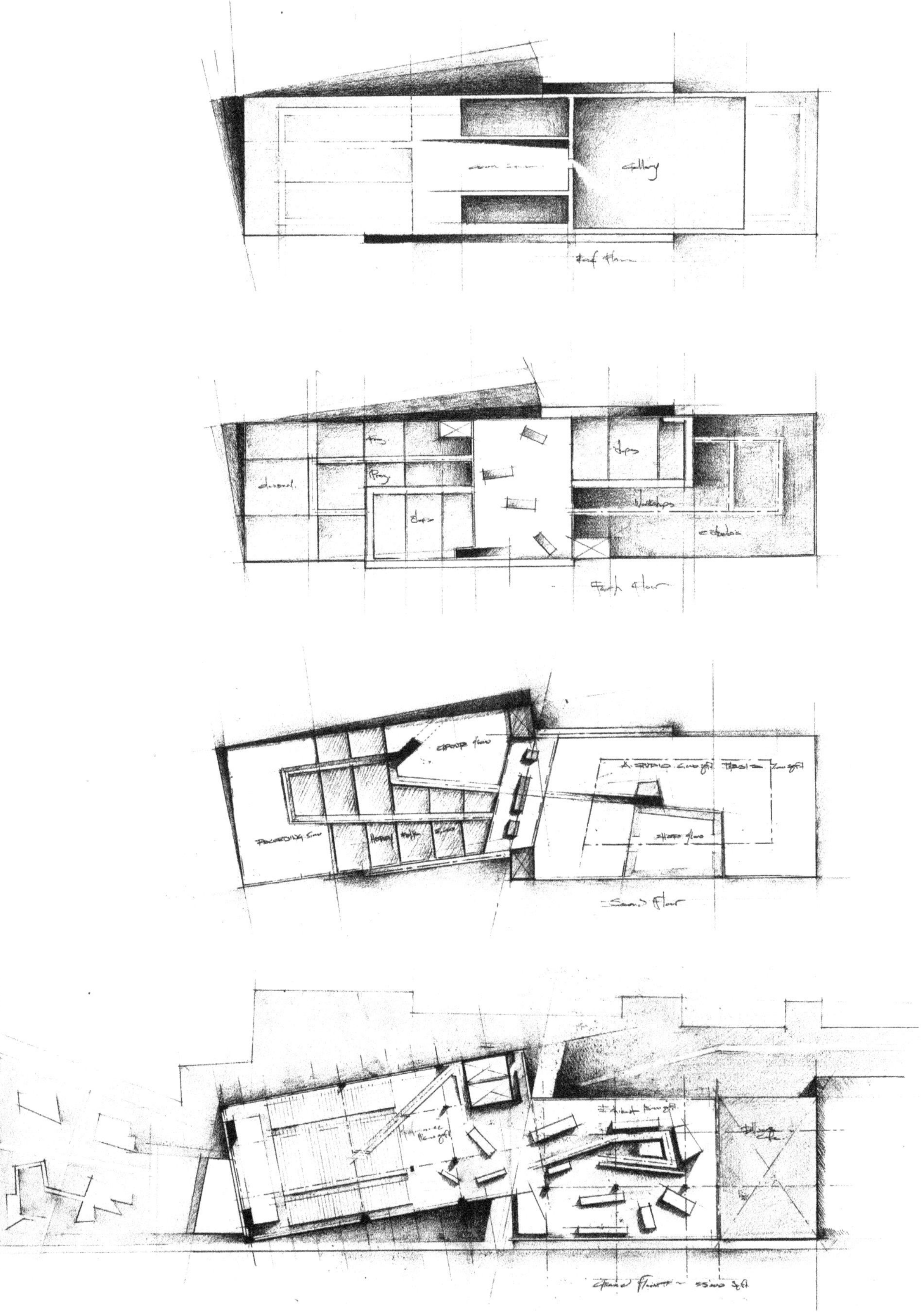

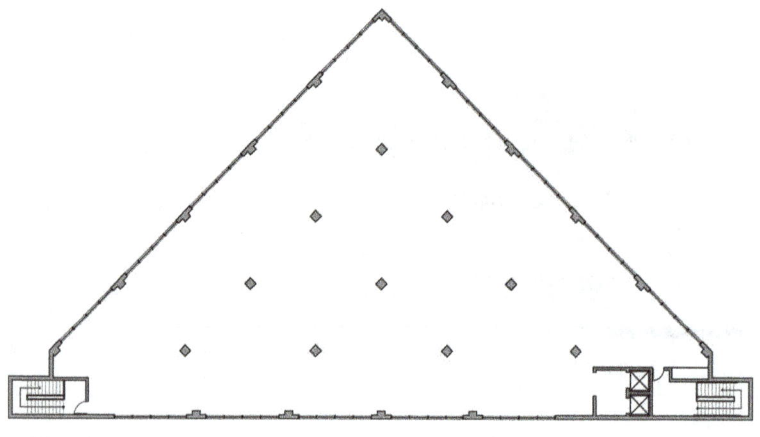

Building shell

Space Planning

For both architects and interior designers, the schematic design phase includes determining the appropriate sizes of and relationships between interior spaces in a given project. Space planning, the process of evaluating these relationships, most often occurs in floor plan drawings because of the clear relationship between circulation, square footage requirements, and program adjacencies.

Strong designs are most often the result of the multiple investigations and refinements that occur through a rigorous design process.

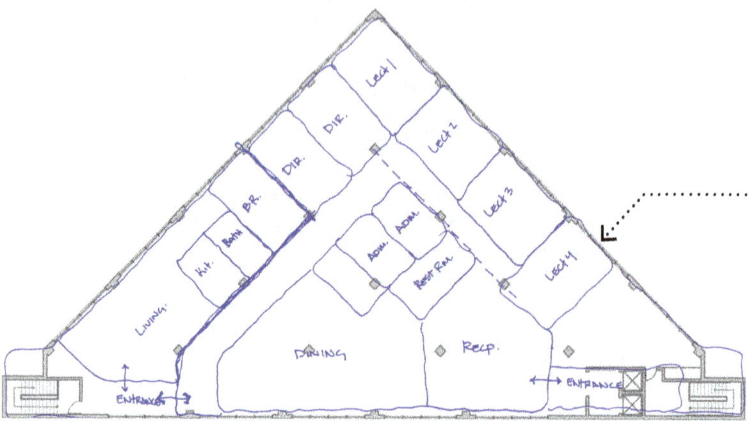

Block diagram

Block Diagrams

Starting with a building shell and a program, interior designers draw multiple iterations using a technique called block diagramming.

- The shapes of the blocks in this drawing represent the approximate size of each space in the program.
- This drawing technique provides an opportunity for a designer to investigate several design alternatives in a short period of time.
- Good block diagrams test program adjacencies, entrances, egress, relative scale, and circulation patterns.

Preliminary Floor Plan

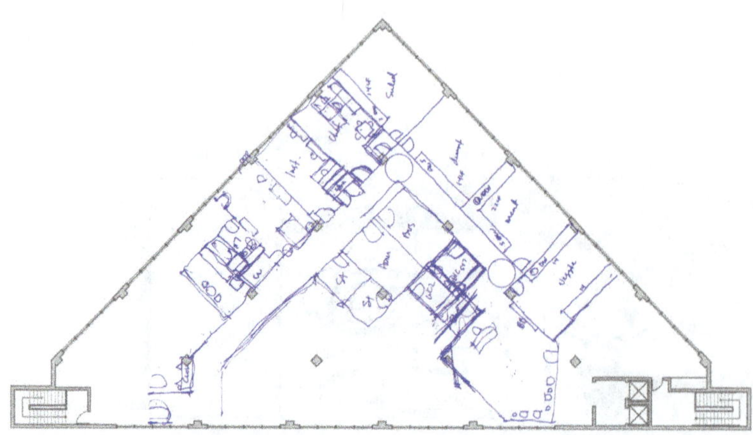

Preliminary Floor Plan

- Using the resulting analysis from the block diagrams, a designer may refine the design in plan through sketches that locate walls, doors, and windows.
- The preliminary plan provides additional opportunities to investigate and refine the design.
- This drawing is also an opportunity to evaluate life safety criteria, including room egress, building egress, common path of travel distances, and maximum travel distances to egress.

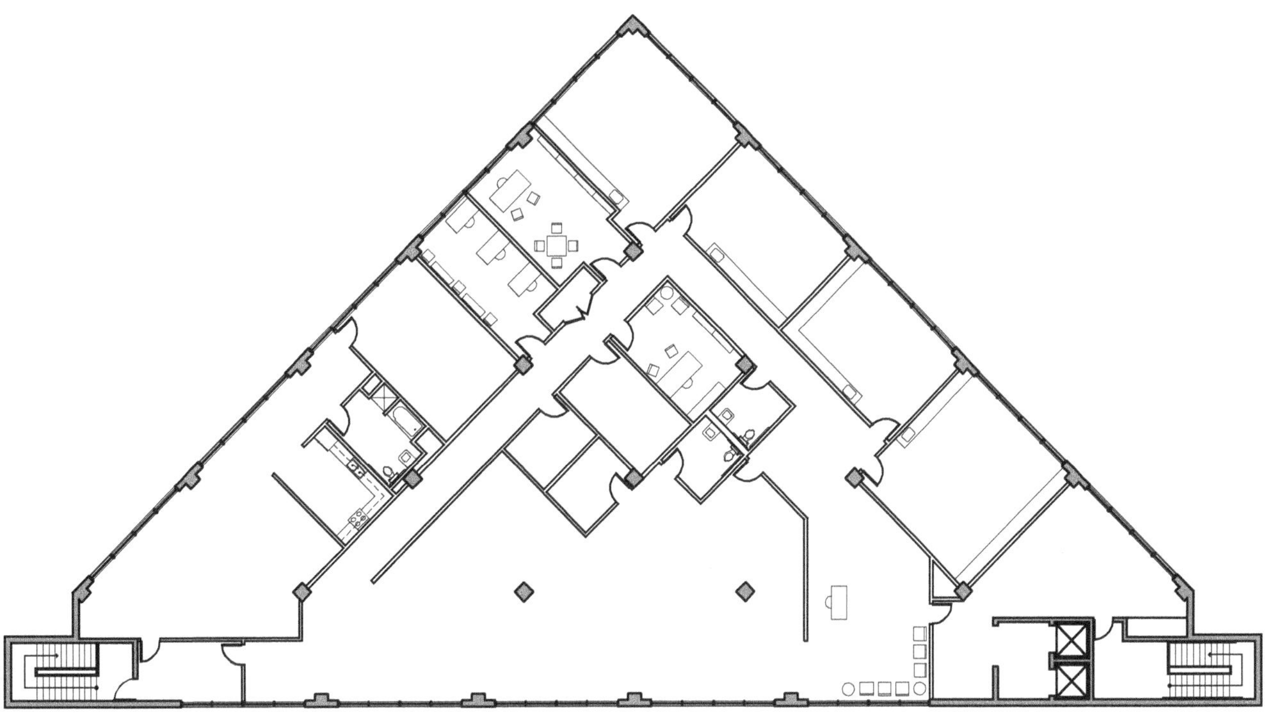

Presentation floor plan

Presentation Floor Plan

The presentation plan is often prepared to communicate design ideas and building organization to a client or for a design presentation. This is perhaps the first drawing that attempts to resolve the quantitative programmatic issues and the qualitative design methodology for a project.

- These drawings often include furniture layouts to communicate the intended uses of individual spaces.
- Notes or legends are incorporated in good presentation floor plans to identify the programmed use for each space.
- Despite the availability of digital drawing software in design offices, design firms may choose to hand draw presentation plans. Hand-drawn floor plans better communicate the flexibility of the current design solution to a client, who may misunderstand computer drawings as a completed design solution.

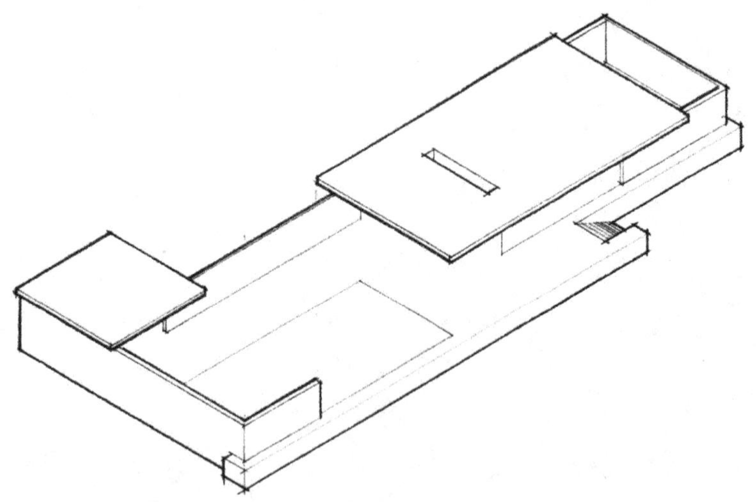

Analytical Drawing
Analysis drawings are a useful tool for investigating a project's context, precedents, and human occupation and to evaluate the strength of a current design. Good analysis drawings clearly identify the portion of the project that is under critique by editing or removing unnecessary information from the drawing. They also visually communicate the conclusions learned through the focused research or analysis.

These drawings are usually drawn at a reduced scale and can include color or other graphic elements to visually communicate the main ideas or objectives for each drawing.

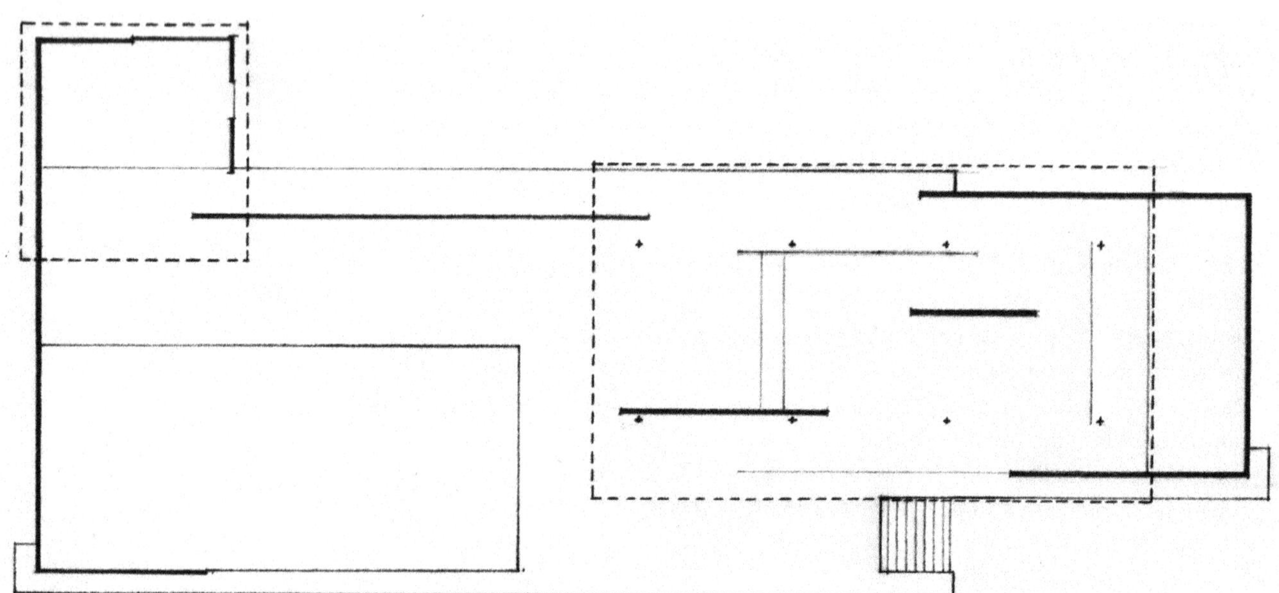

LUDWIG MIES VAN DER ROHE
(1886–1969)
The German Pavilion for the Barcelona Universal Exposition, 1929 (Rebuilt 1988)

Circulation Analysis

- The circulation within the pavilion is primarily defined by implicit edges made from glass and water.
- Travertine walls define the remaining circulation edge conditions.
- The yellow in this drawing identifies the primary spaces for movement.

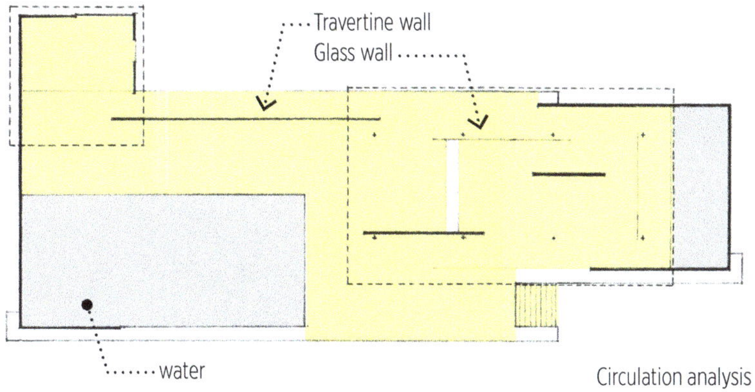

Circulation analysis

Vertical Enclosure

- The roof planes of the pavilion explicitly define the vertical boundaries of interior and exterior spaces.
- The yellow in this drawing identifies the primary spaces that are contained by overhead planes.

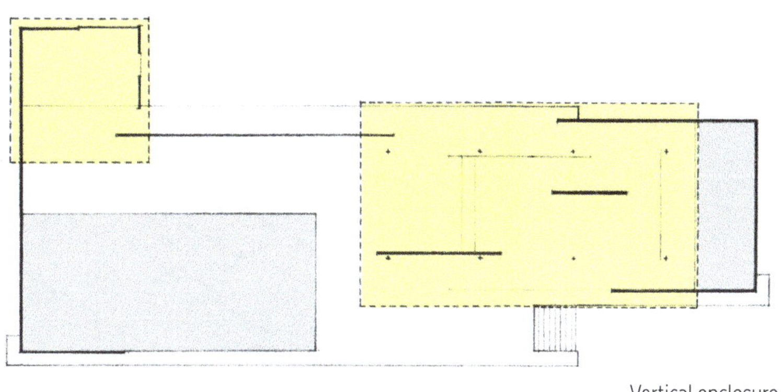
Vertical enclosure

Horizontal Enclosure

- Travertine walls in the pavilion explicitly define the horizontal boundaries of interior and exterior spaces.
- The yellow in this drawing identifies the primary spaces that are contained by solid walls.

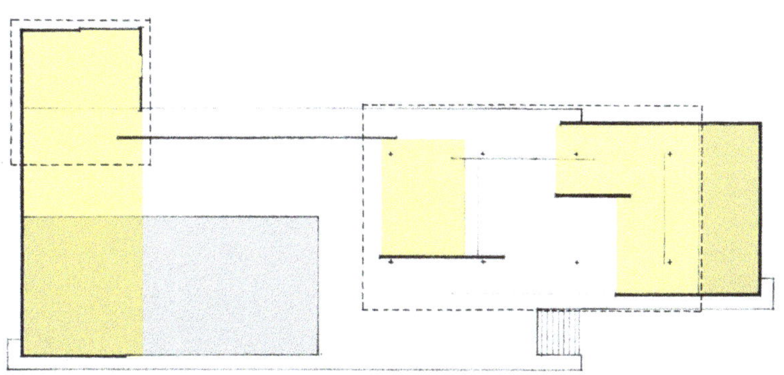
Horizontal enclosure

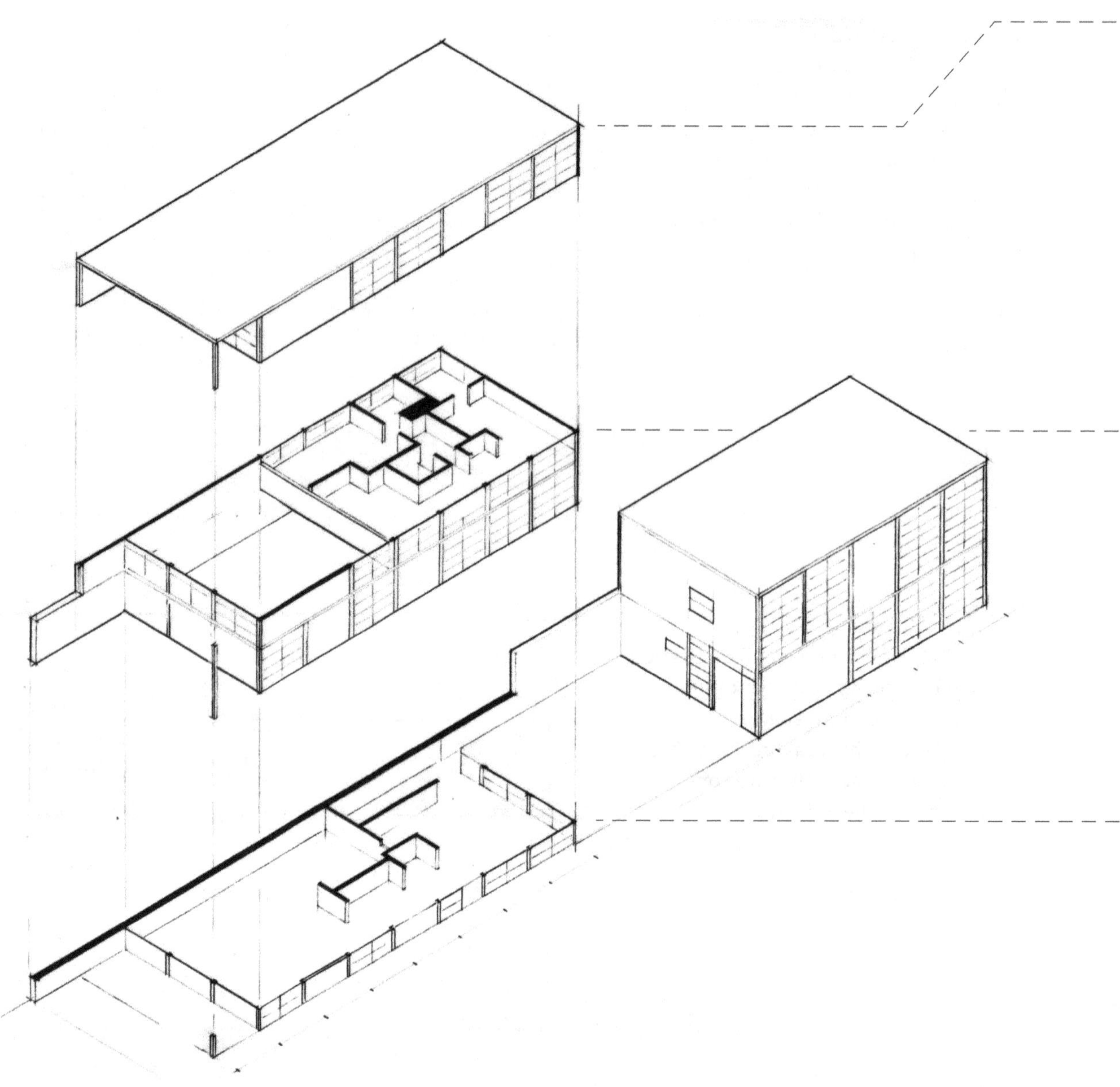

CHARLES (1907–78) AND RAY (1912–88) EAMES
The Eames House (1949) represents one of 25 "case study" homes. The Case Study Home Project, commissioned by *Art & Architecture* magazine, challenged architects to design homes that could be built and furnished with building technologies used during World War II.
Drawings by Douglas Seidler

A strong understanding of architectural graphic standards is critical for clearly communicating and developing design ideas through plan. The remaining portion of this chapter introduces drawing techniques, terminology, and graphic standards to increase your understanding and your ability to draw legible floor plans.

Roof plan

Roof Plan

The roof plan is an aerial view of the building and includes everything that is visible from above the roof. This plan may also include the landscape or cityscape that is adjacent to the building.

- Medium lines are used to delineate a change in plane or a corner in elevation.
- Light lines are used to delineate objects on the ground or on the roof.
- Construction lines are very light lines that help define the overall scope of the drawing or drawings on a sheet of paper.
- Dashed lines are used to identify major architectural elements below the roof.

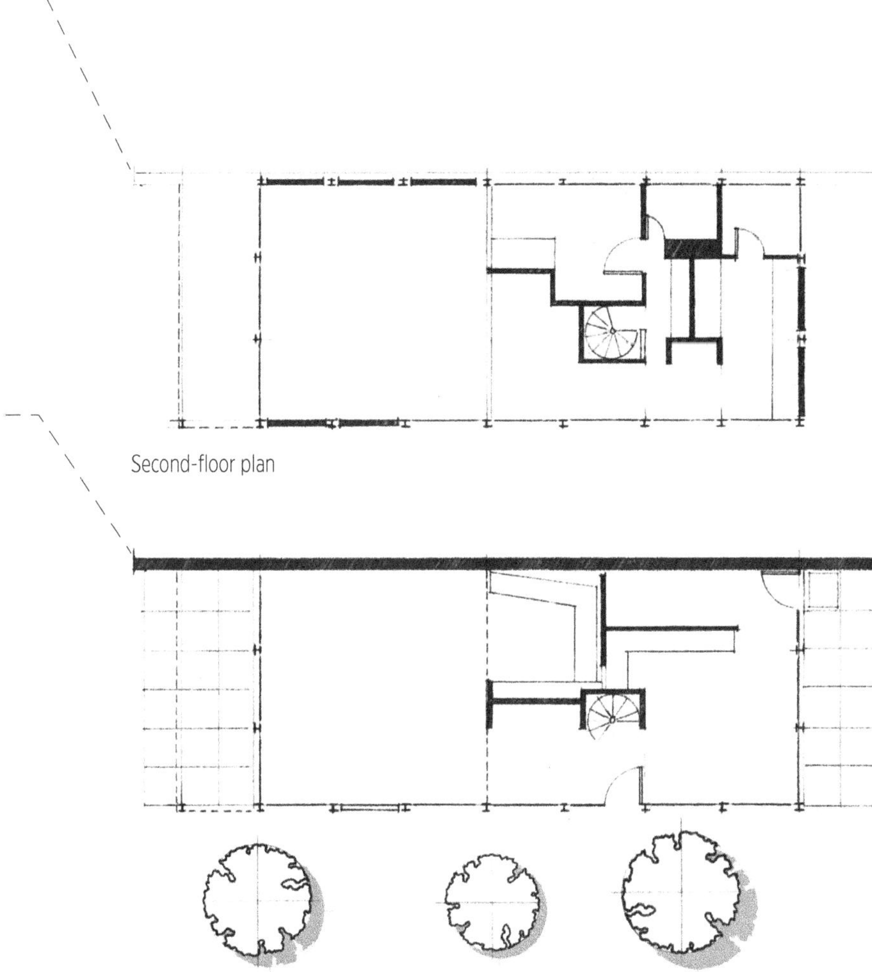

Second-floor plan

First-floor plan

Second-Floor Plan

- Plans are usually sliced 3'-6" above the floor but may vary according to the project. This imaginary slice is referred to as the cut plane.
- The cut plane slices through walls, doors, windows, and columns. Below the slice, we see furniture, flooring material, countertops, and so on.

First-Floor Plan

- Heavy lines delineate elements in plan that are sliced by the cut plane.
- Medium lines are used for furniture, casework, or handrails.
- Light lines are used for floor patterns and transitions between floor materials.
- Construction lines are very light lines that help define the overall scope of the drawing or drawings on a sheet of paper.
- Dashed lines are used to identify major architectural elements above the cut plan.
- The first-floor plan often includes landscape or cityscape that is adjacent to the building.

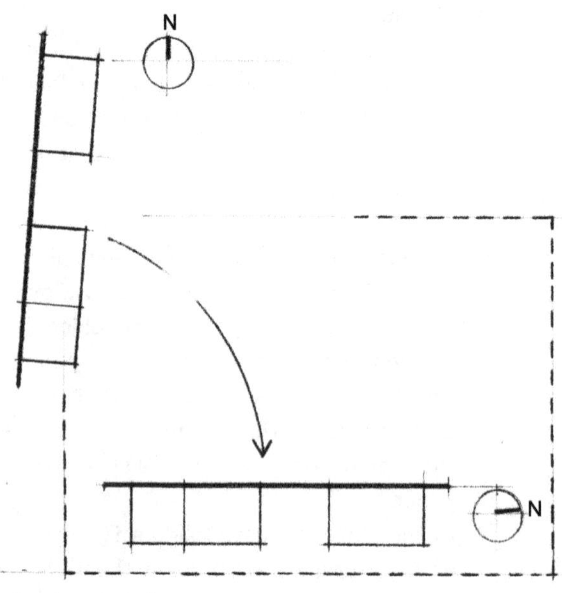

Drawing orientation

Drawing Orientation

Before you begin a drawing, identify the most appropriate orientation for the floor plan.

- When possible, orient your plan so that north is toward the top of the paper.
- In this example the plan was rotated clockwise 90 degrees to accommodate the orientation of the paper. North is identified on the plan with a north arrow.

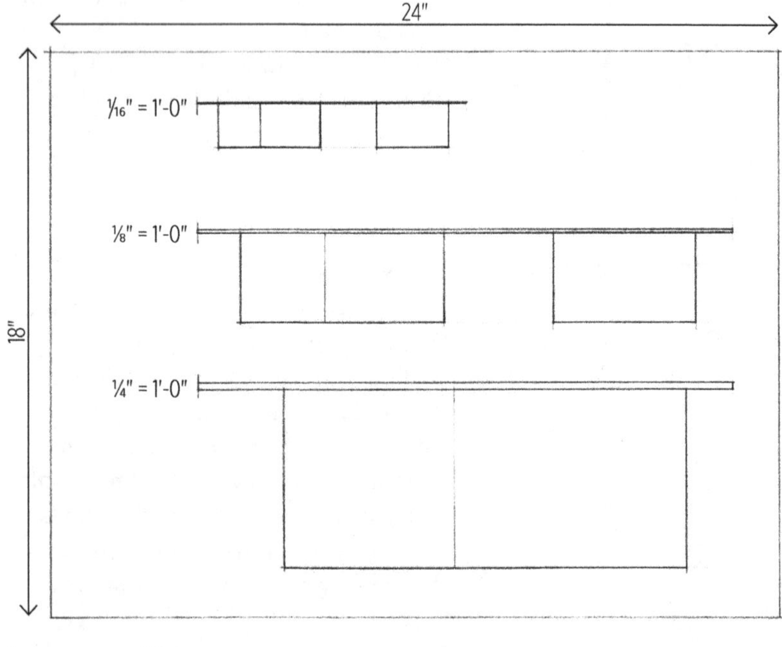

Drawing composition

Drawing Composition

Drawing composition involves the thoughtful arrangement of the drawing on a sheet of paper. Before you begin drawing, identify the boundaries of the floor plan or plans, using construction lines.

- Calculate the drawn size of your floor plan to determine what size sheet of paper you will need to complete your drawing. Plans drawn at a larger scale occupy a larger portion of the paper.
- In this example, the 1/8"=1'-0" drawing is the most appropriate size for the selected 18" × 24" sheet of paper.
- Leave a ¾" to 1" margin on all sides of your paper and between different drawings on the same sheet of paper.
- Center your drawings on the sheet of paper.

There are different methods available to designers for drawing and projecting plans on a sheet of paper. The overlay method relies on multiple overlays of trace paper, Mylar, or translucent vellum to trace over previously constructed drawings. When you want to present and develop your drawings on a single page, the construction line method allows you to project light lines up from the first plan in order to draw the geometry of all subsequent plans.

Overlay Method

- Use translucent vellum to overlay and construct new drawings from an existing floor plan.
- Insert a white sheet of paper between the two sheets of translucent vellum to review your progress and hide the existing floor plan.
- In this example the second-floor plan is constructed from the first-floor plan.

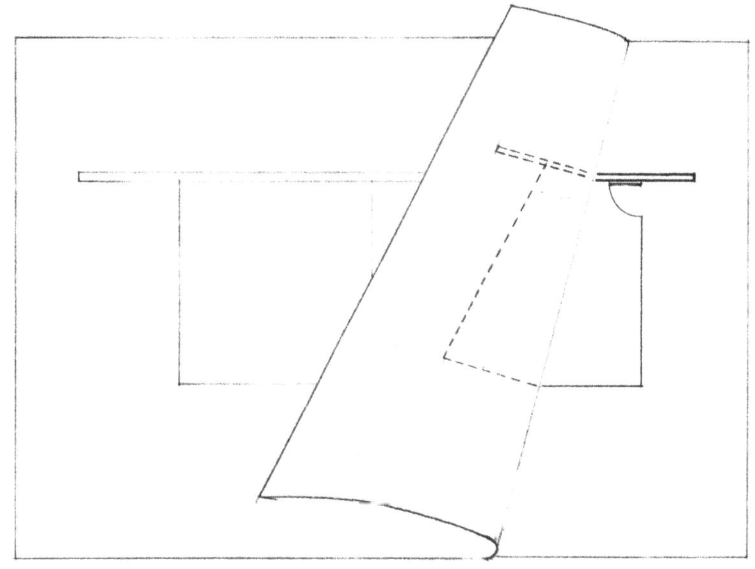

Overlay method

Construction Line Method

- Organize plans that are drawn on a single sheet of paper, with the lower floors drawn below the upper floors and roof plan.
- Use very light lines to construct the geometry for upper floors from the first-floor plan.

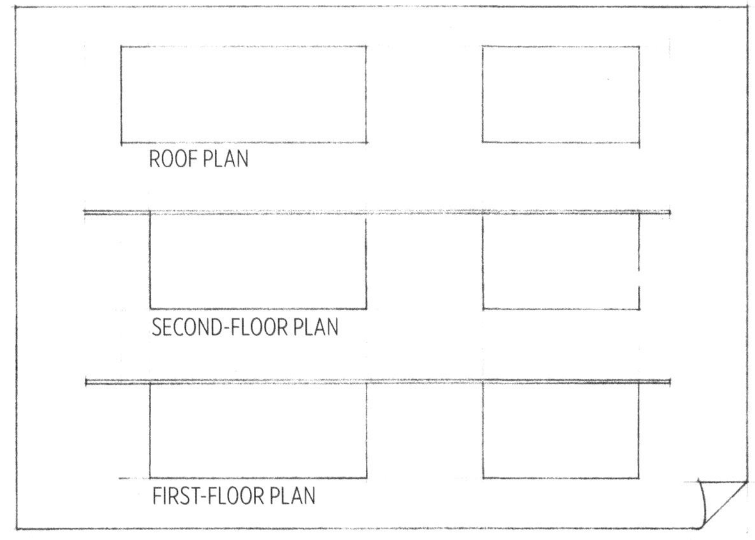

Construction line method

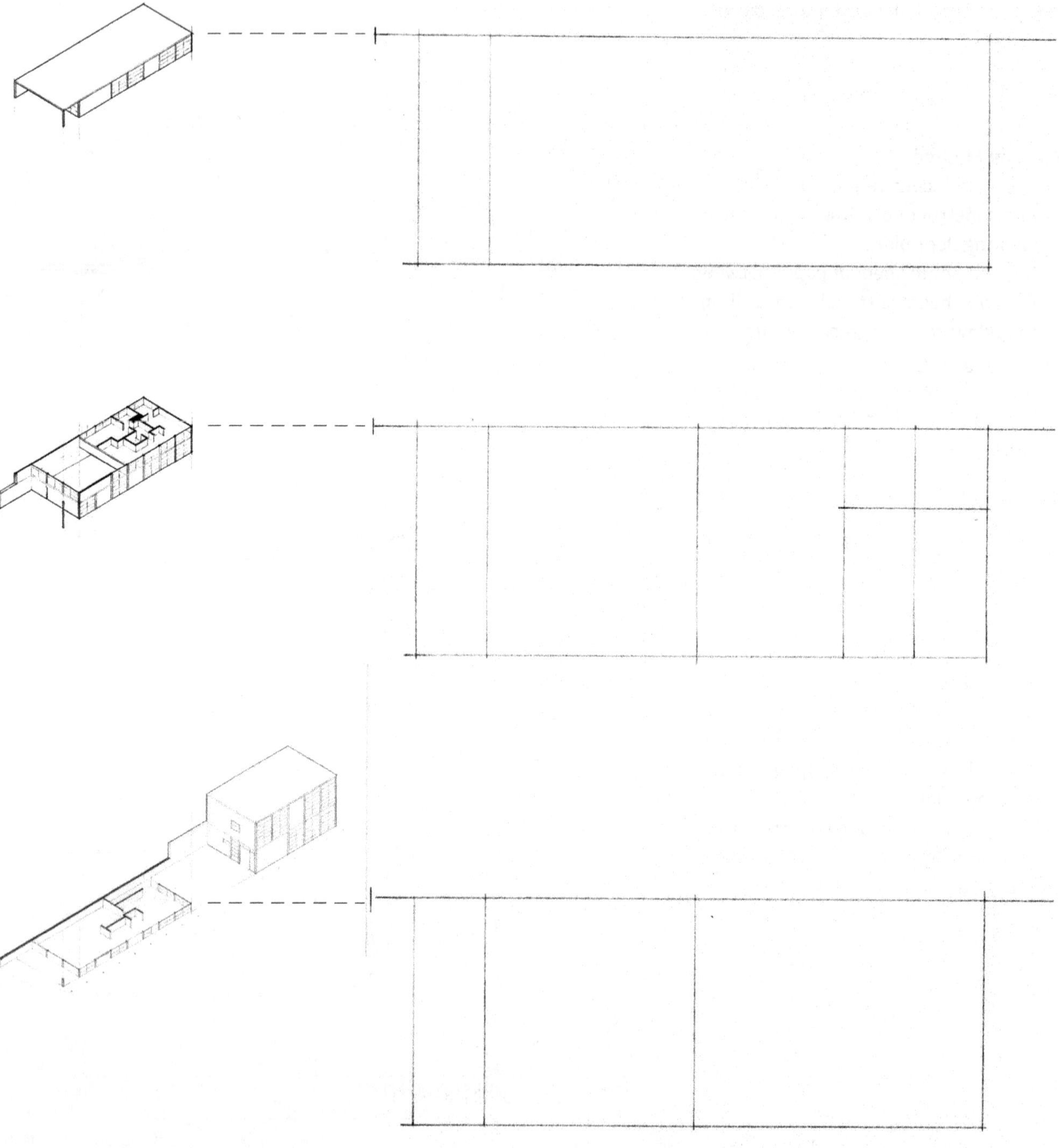

Plan Boundaries and Geometry

When starting a new drawing, it is important to identify the boundaries of the floor plan with construction lines.

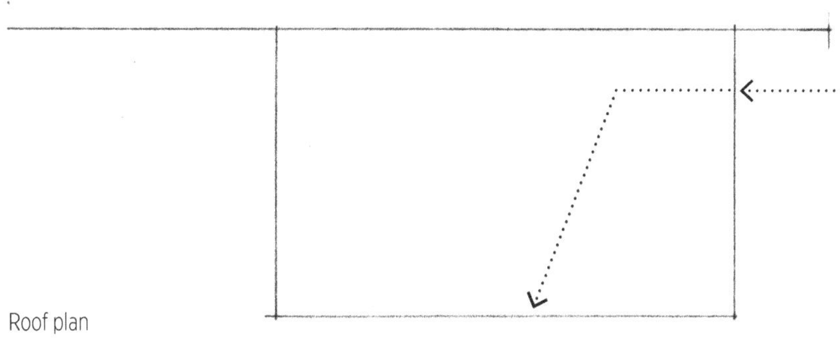

Roof plan

Roof Plan

- Use construction lines to identify major geometry on the roof plan.
- **Construction lines** are very light lines that help define the overall scope of the drawing or drawings on a sheet of paper. These lines are projected from adjacent floor plans or measured with an architectural scale.

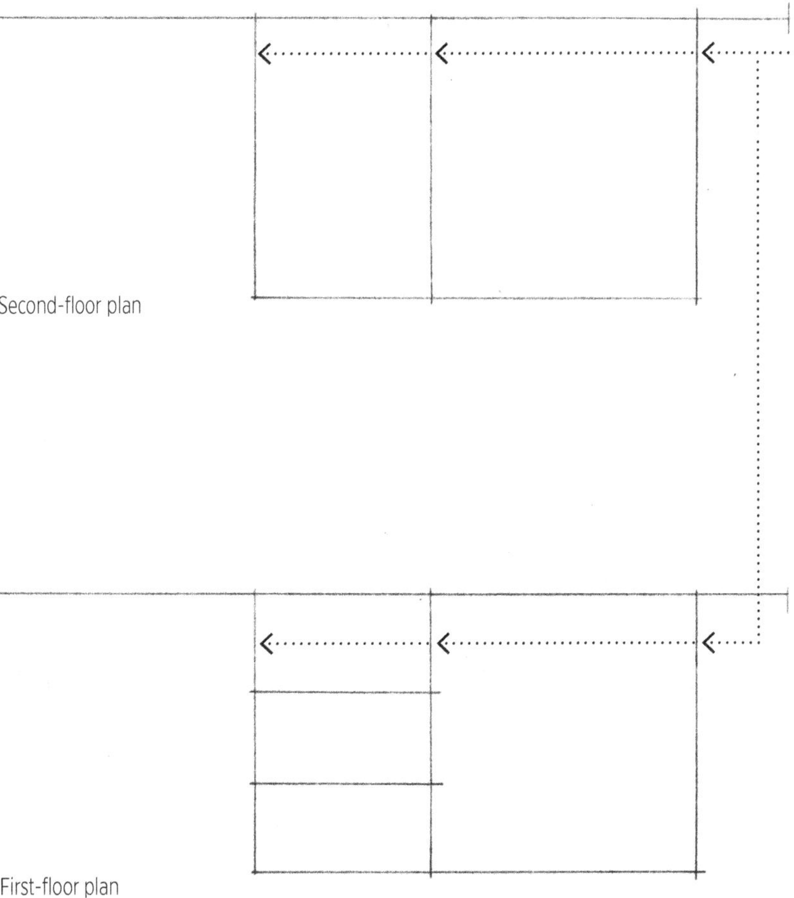

Second-floor plan

First-floor plan

Second-Floor Plan

- You can construct floor plans from geometry that is shared between different levels. For example, all the vertical lines in the roof plan and the second-floor plan are constructed from the first-floor plan.

First-Floor Plan

- The structural bays in the Eames House are 7'-6" wide x 20'-0" deep. This module is used to locate major walls within the floor plan.

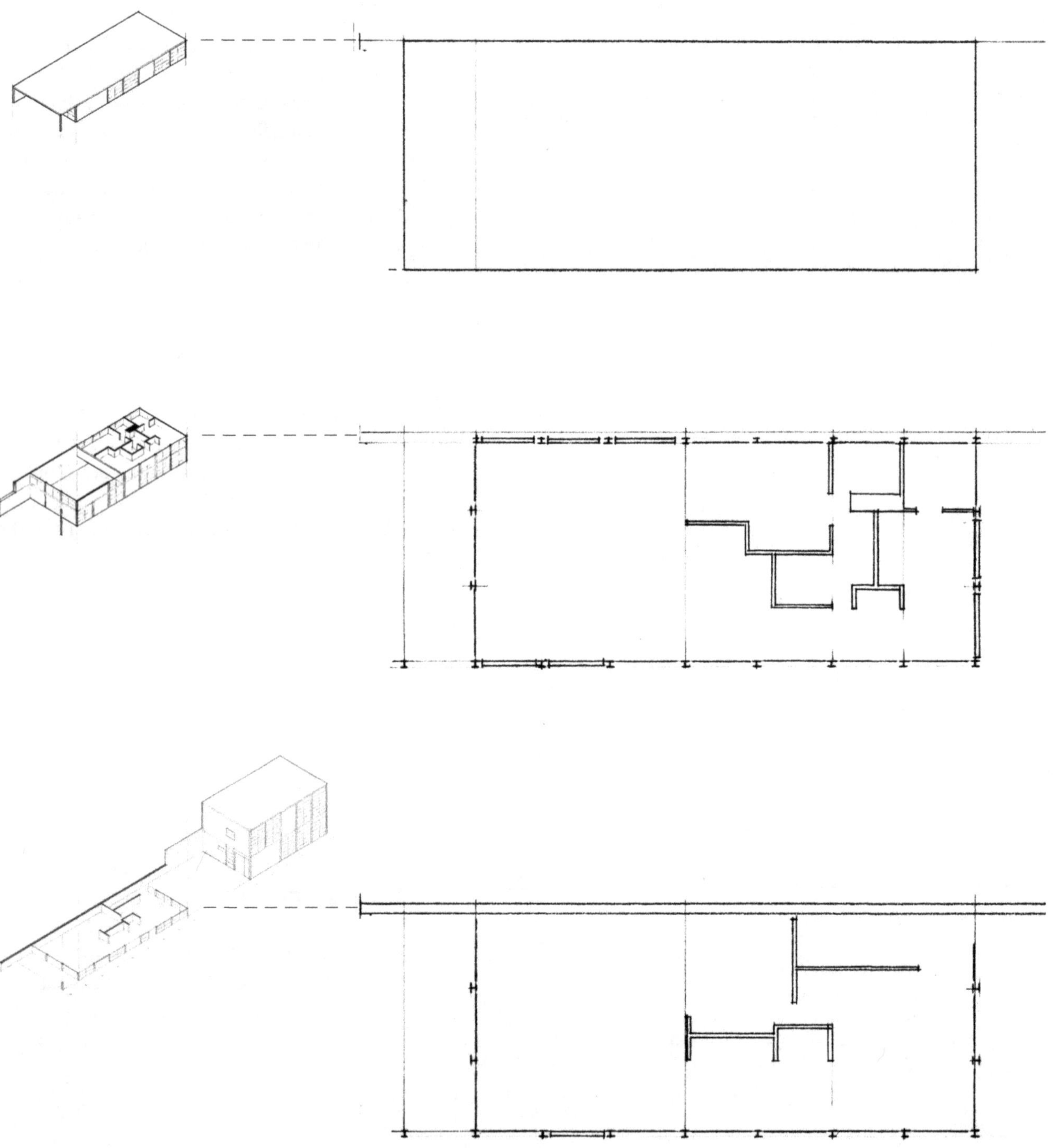

Sliced Objects

The second step in drawing floor plans involves locating walls and any wall openings for windows and door.

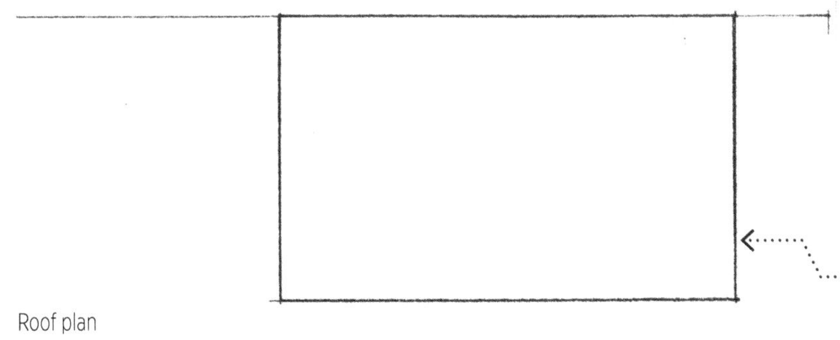

Roof plan

Roof Plan

For roof plans, which often do not slice through objects, the second step involves drawing the perimeter around the roof plane.

- Use medium lines to identify the perimeter around the roof.
- Use dashed lines to identify major architectural elements that are hidden below the roof.

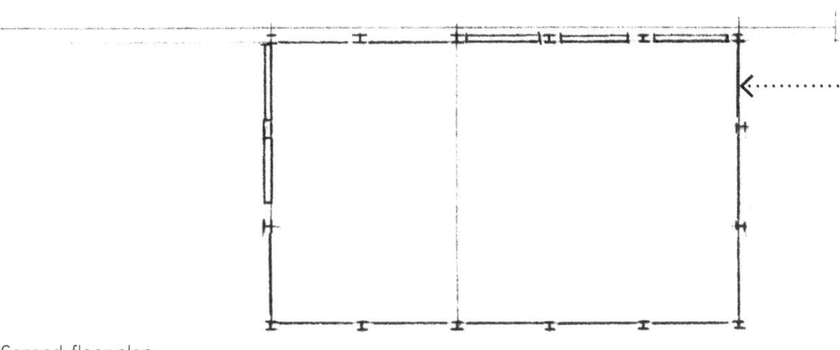

Second-floor plan

Second-Floor Plan

- Use dark lines to draw all objects that are sliced by the cut plane, including walls, windows, and columns.

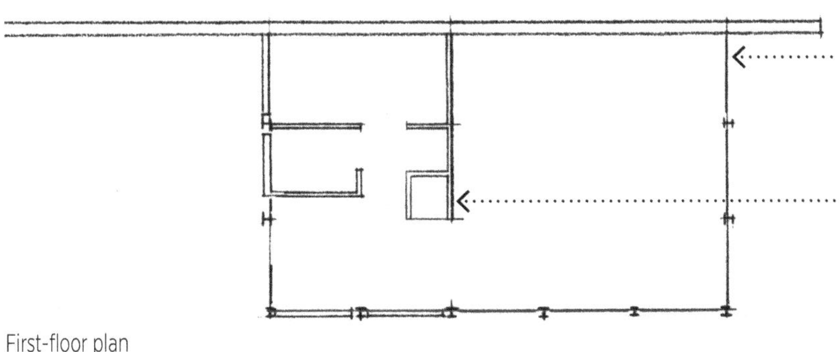

First-floor plan

First-Floor Plan

- At the scale of this and most presentation drawings, windows are represented with a single line identifying the location of the glazing.
- Rather than draw the actual thickness of the wall (which can change through project design and development), walls are most often represented with a double line identifying the nominal thickness of the wall (usually 6" or 8" thick).

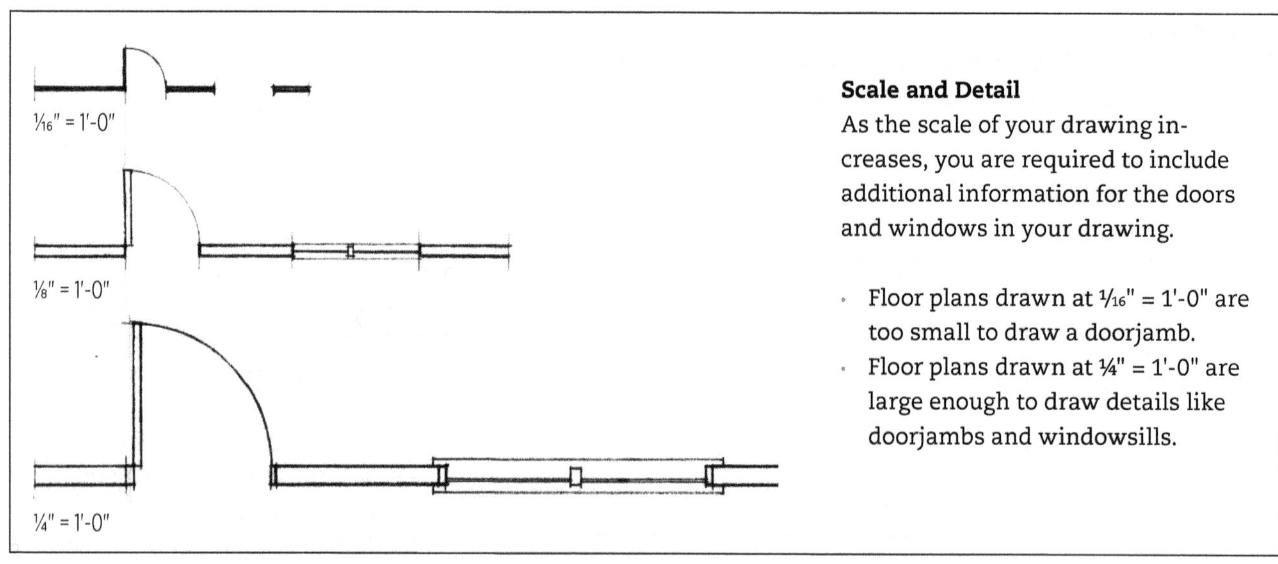

Scale and Detail

As the scale of your drawing increases, you are required to include additional information for the doors and windows in your drawing.

- Floor plans drawn at 1/16" = 1'-0" are too small to draw a doorjamb.
- Floor plans drawn at ¼" = 1'-0" are large enough to draw details like doorjambs and windowsills.

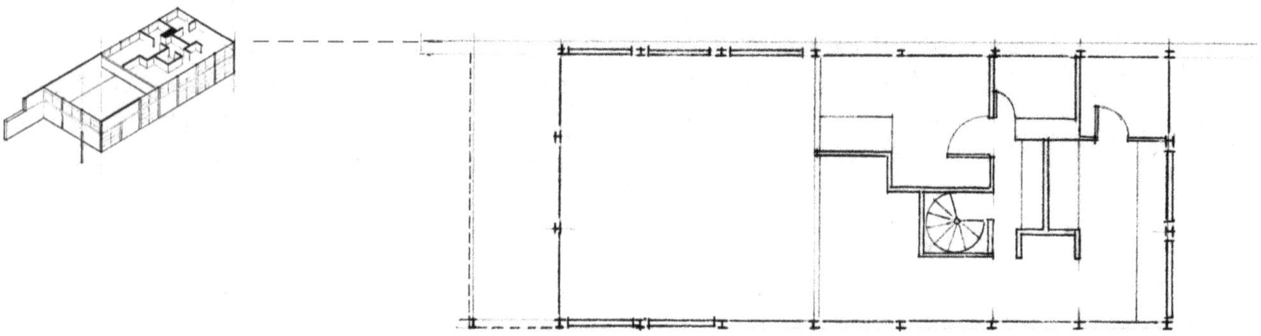

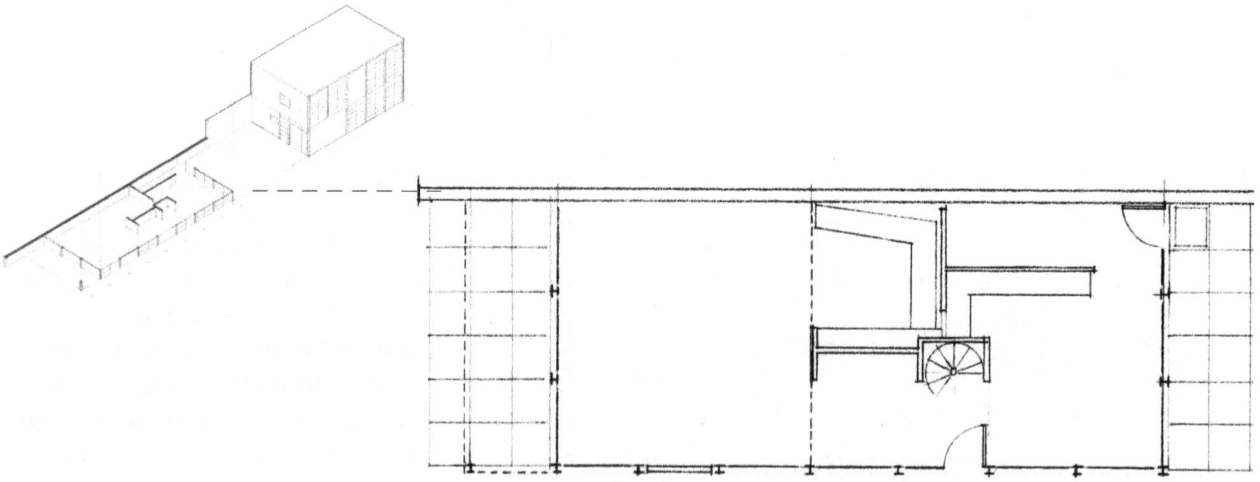

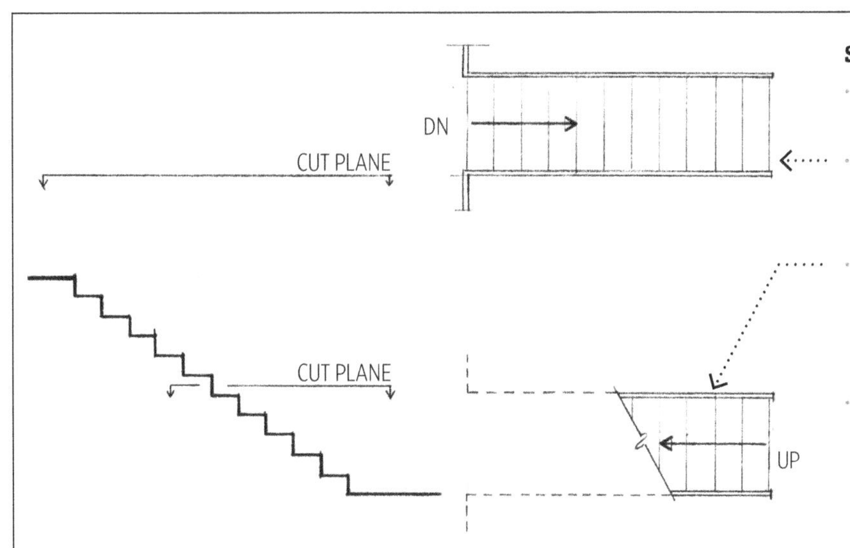

Stairs in Plan

- Use light lines for stairs in floor plans.
- Stairs that go down to the first floor are visible unless they pass under the floor opening.
- Stairs that go up to the second floor are sliced at the cut plane. Above the cut plane, stairs are identified with dashed lines.
- Add an arrow and label indicating the direction of travel from the current plan.

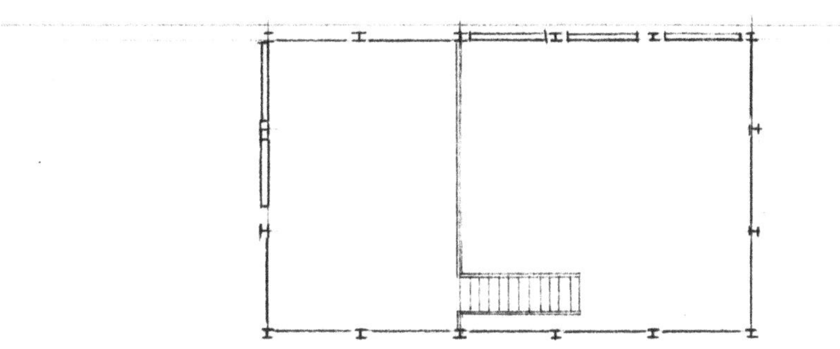

Second-Floor Plan

Using the graphic standards described for the first-floor plan, draw all appropriate content that is visible in the second-floor plan.

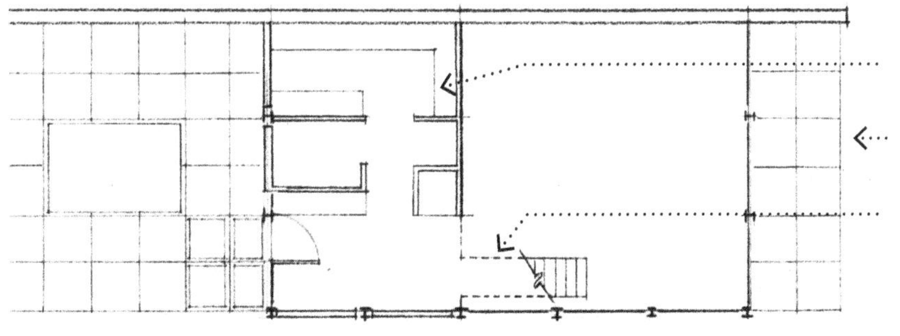

First-Floor Plan

- Use medium lines to draw furniture, handrails, and built-in casework.
- Use light lines to draw doors and floor patterns.
- Use dashed lines to draw major architectural elements that are above the cut plane.

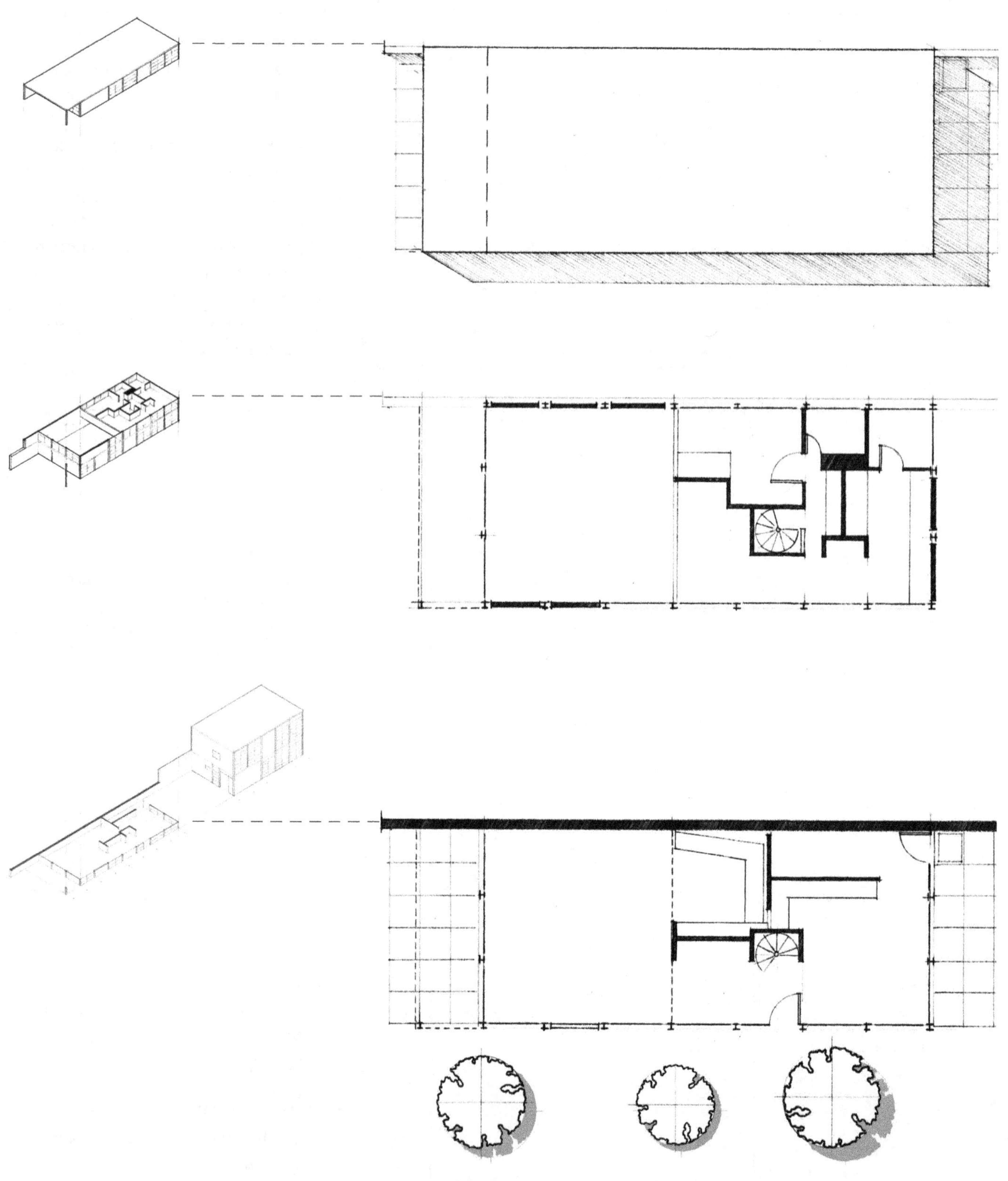

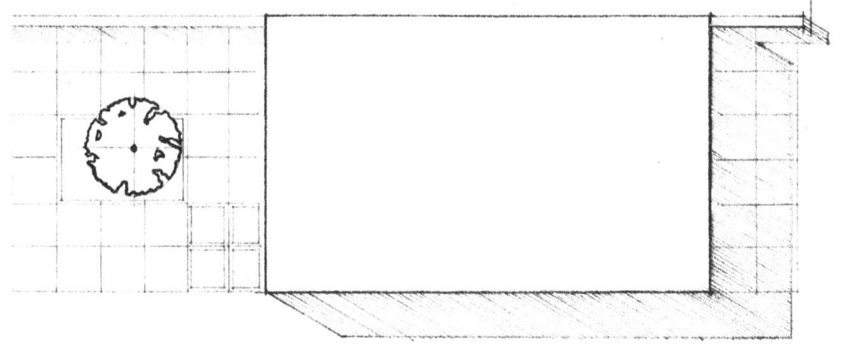

Projecting Shadows

- Shadows are most often projected from the south toward the north side of a building because of the path the sun follows through the sky.
- In this drawing, shadows are projected at a 30-degree angle, from the southwest toward the northeast.

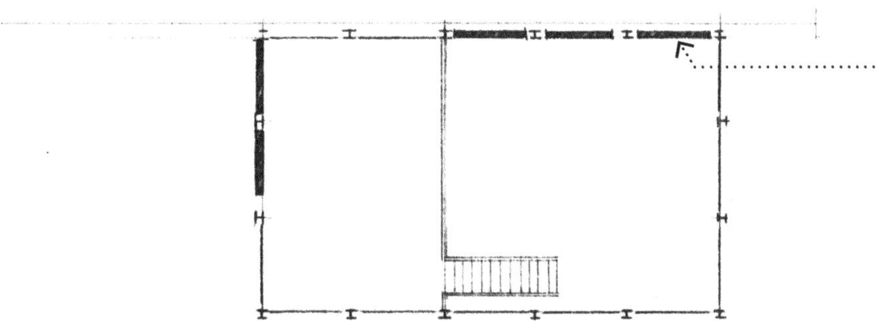

Poché

Add solid tone to wall thickness in a drawing to communicate space by creating contrast between the mass and the void.

- The solid dark tone is added with a soft lead pencil to the front or back of the sheet of paper.
- Grayscale tone is added with multiple angled lines. Depending on the density of the lines, this technique creates different grayscale values for the poché.
- This technique is particularly valuable for presentation drawings that need to be legible at a distance of several feet.

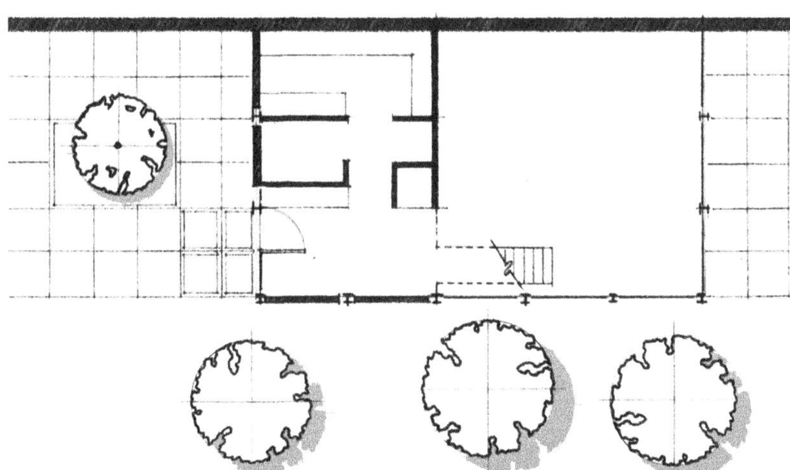

GERRIT RIETVELD (1888–1964) IN COLLABORATION WITH MRS. TRUUS SCHRÖDER-SCHRÄDER

Bureau (1931)
Erasmuslaan 9, the model home for Reitveld's housing block in Utrecht, was a showroom for him to display his furniture designs, including the Bureau. Both projects represent a shift in Rietveld's design from the De Stijl movement to Dutch functionalist architecture.
Drawings by Douglas Seidler

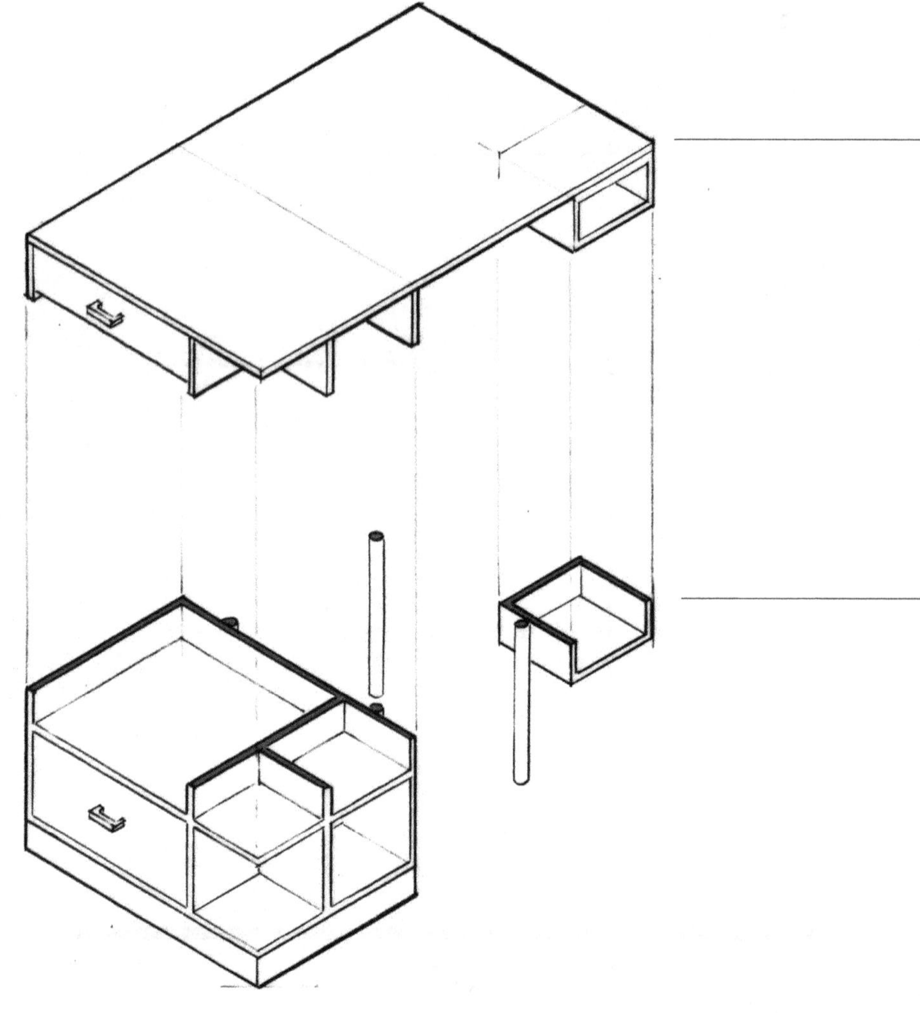

Top View

Furniture design drawings use a unique naming convention. The top view drawing is an aerial view of a piece of furniture or object and shares many technical qualities with the roof plan.

- Medium lines are used to delineate the perimeter around the object or a change in plane.
- Light lines are used to delineate a change in material on the top surface.
- Construction lines are very light lines that help define the overall scope of the drawing or drawings on a sheet of paper.
- Dashed lines are used to identify major objects hidden below the piece of furniture, such as cabinets or drawers.

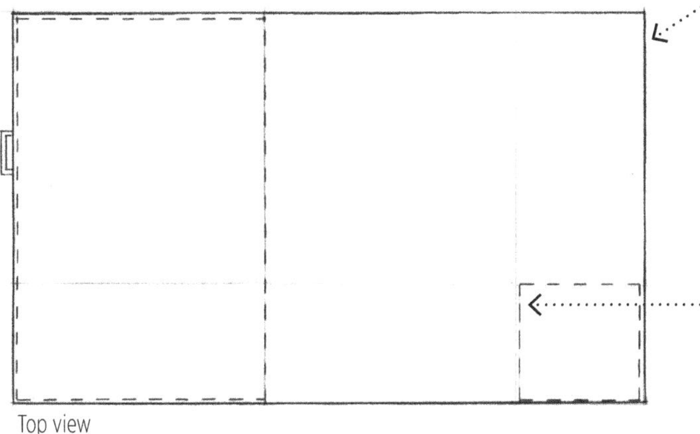

Top view

Plan-Section

The plan-section drawing is a horizontal section taken through a piece of furniture or an object. This imaginary slice is referred to as the cut plane.

- The cut plane slices through wood, glass, and other building materials.
- Furniture may require multiple plan-sections at different heights.
- Heavy lines are used to delineate objects sliced by the cut plane.
- Medium lines are used to delineate the perimeter around the object or a change in plane.
- Light lines are used to delineate a change in material on visible surfaces.
- Construction lines are very light lines that help define the overall scope of the drawing or drawings on a sheet of paper.
- Dashed lines are used to identify major objects above the cut plane or hidden below the object.

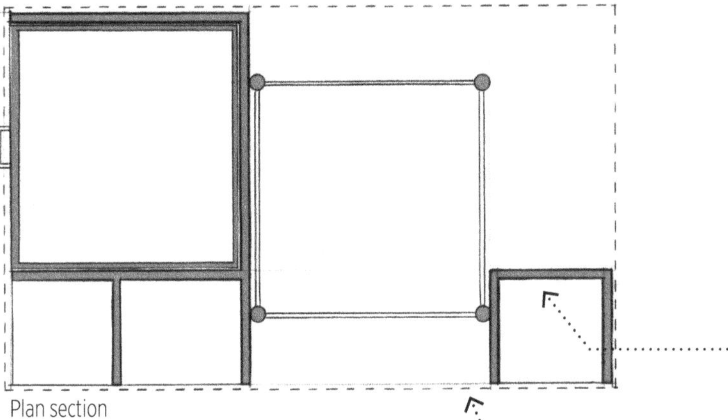

Plan section

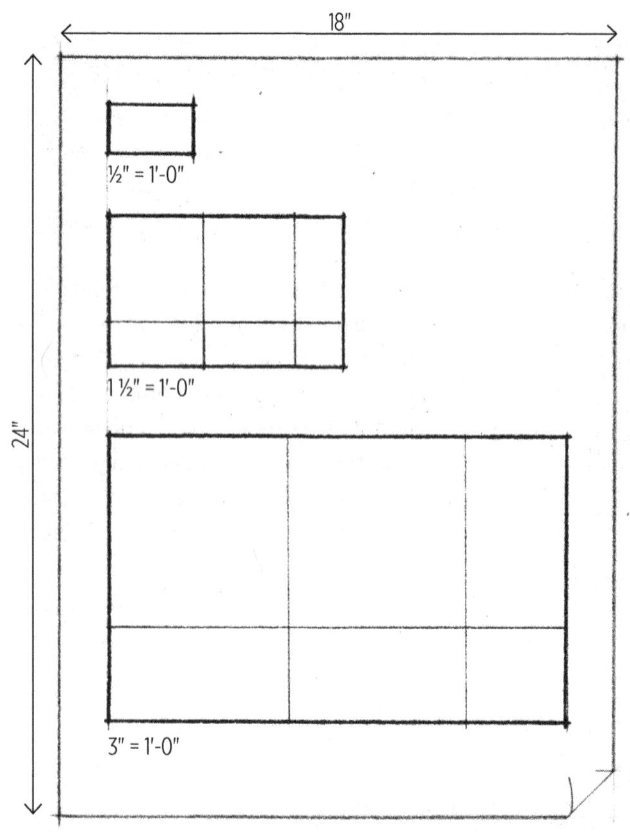

Typical Drawing Scales

To effectively communicate an appropriate level of detail to a contractor or fabricator, furniture design drawings are typically drawn at the following scales:

- 1½" = 1'-0"
- 3" = 1'-0"
- The ½" = 1'-0" scale drawing illustrates how the largest scale a piece of furniture would appear in a presentation floor plan.

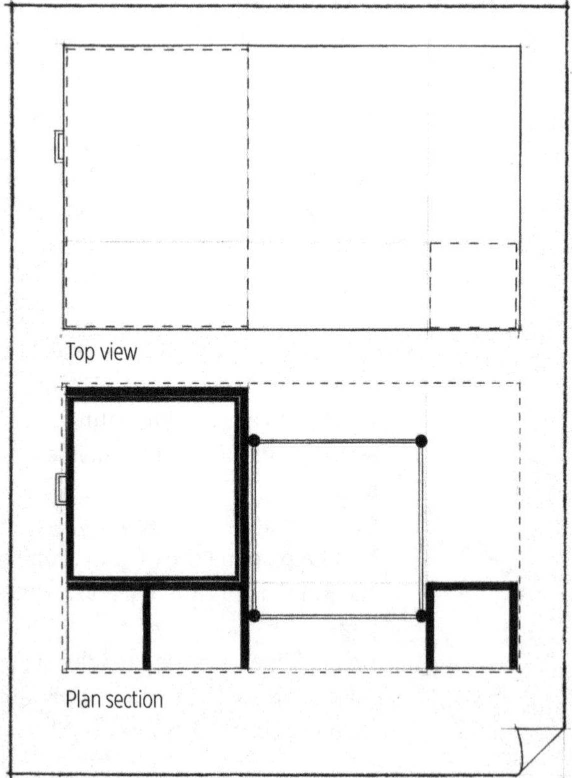

Drawing Composition

Before you begin drawing, you should identify the boundaries of what you are drawing with construction lines on your sheet of paper.

- Calculate the drawn size of your furniture plan to determine what size sheet of paper you will need to complete your drawing.
- Leave a ¾" to 1" margin on all sides of your paper.
- Consider leaving room for drawing labels below each drawing.
- Center or appropriately arrange your drawings on the sheet of paper.

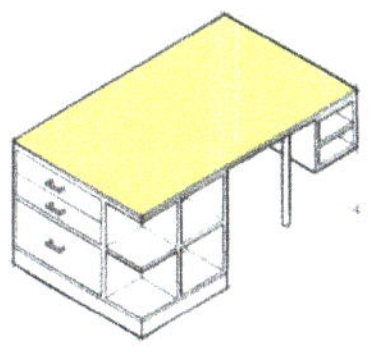

Top View
The top view in furniture design drawings is an aerial view of a piece of furniture or an object. Top view drawings share many of the technical qualities of the roof plan. These drawings indicate overall dimensions and identify specific materials in the furniture design.

Step 1
- Select an appropriate architectural scale for your drawing.
- Identify the boundaries and geometry of what you are drawing with construction lines on your sheet of paper.

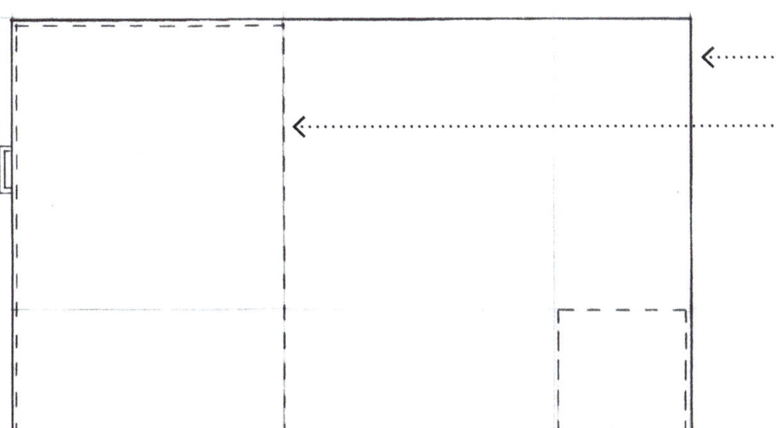

Step 2
- Use medium lines to identify the perimeter around the furniture or object.
- Use dashed lines to identify major elements that are hidden below the top surface of the piece of furniture.

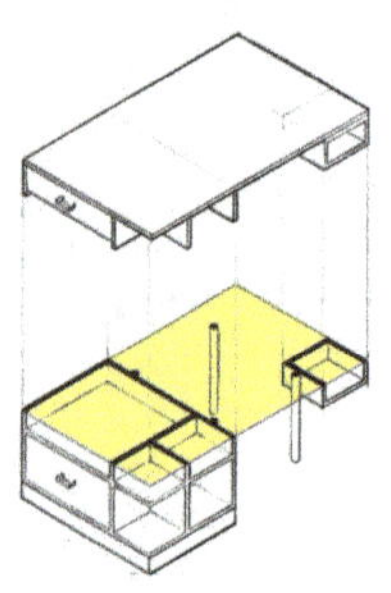

Plan-Section
The plan-section is a horizontal section taken through a piece of furniture or an object. This imaginary slice, referred to as the cut plane, should be located to maximize the amount of construction information communicated with the drawing.

Step 1
- Select an appropriate architectural scale for your drawing.
- Identify the boundaries and geometry of what you are drawing with construction lines on your sheet of paper.

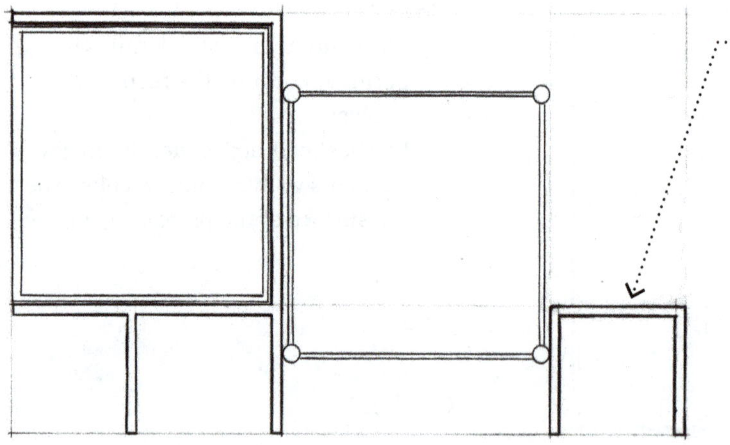

Step 2
- Use dark lines to draw all objects that are sliced by the cut plane, including wood, glass, and metal.

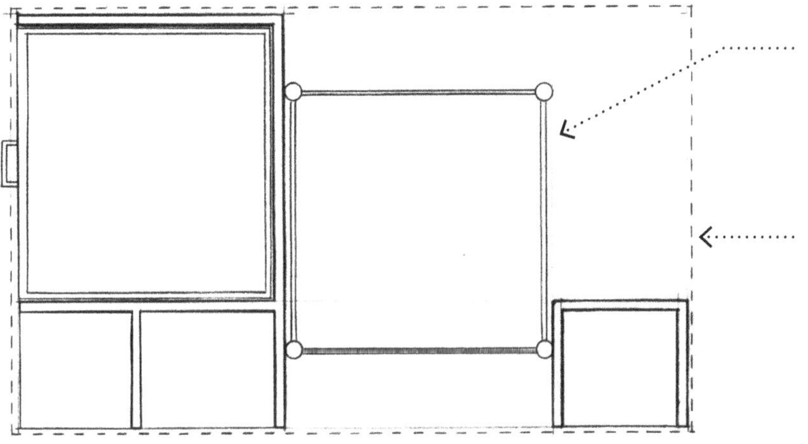

Step 3

- Use medium lines to delineate the perimeter around the object or a change in plane.
- Use light lines to delineate a change in material on visible surfaces.
- Use dashed lines to identify major objects above the cut plane or hidden below the object.

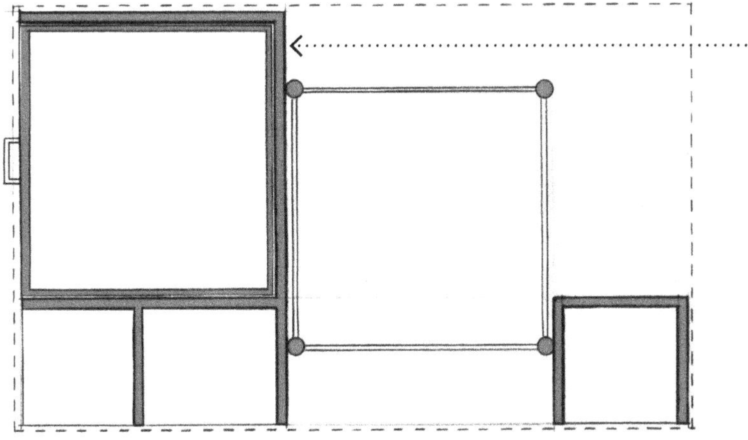

Step 4

- Use poché to darken the sliced objects in your plan-section.
- In furniture design plans, poché helps clarify the difference between solid mass and void.

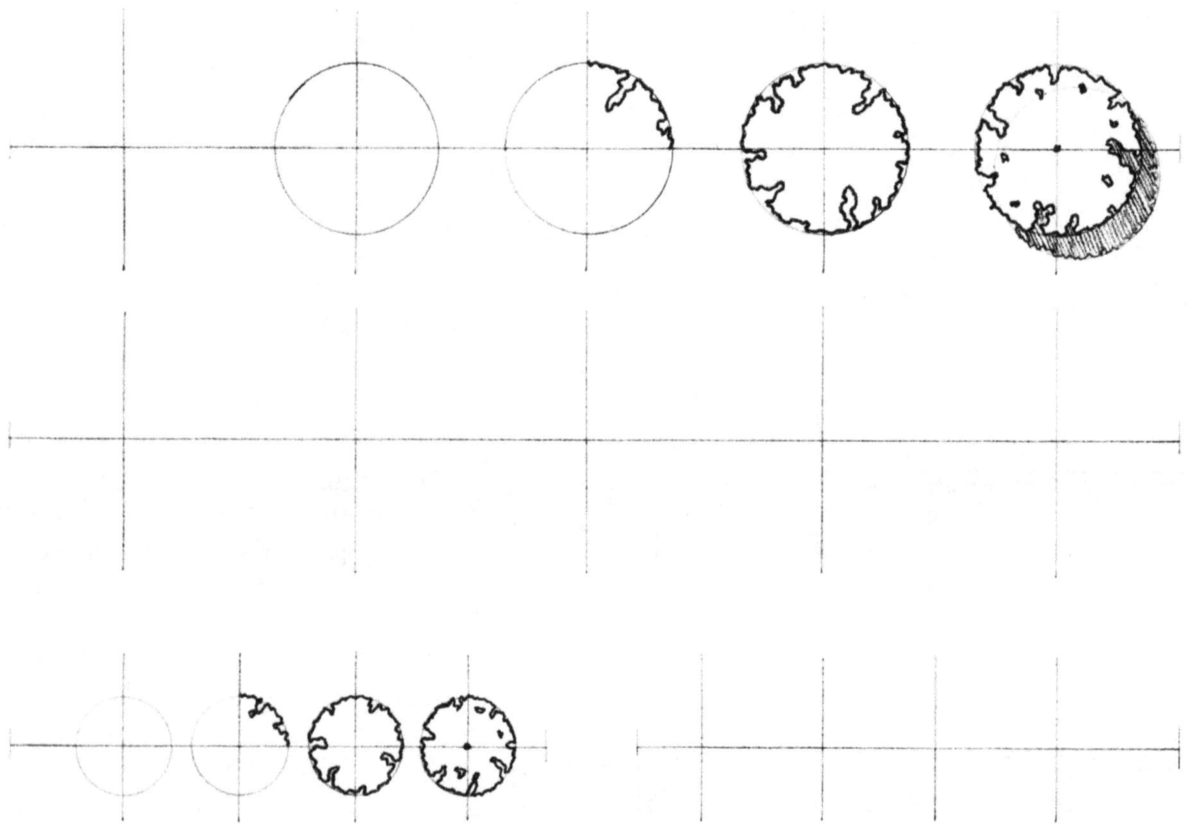

Learning Exercise: Drawing Trees

Trees are easily drawn by hand in plan following these steps:

- Using a circle template, draw the circle that is appropriately sized for the diameter of your tree.
- Starting at one part of the circle, slowly trace over the circle with a medium line that represents the edges of the tree.
- Add a shadow to the tree by offsetting a second circle in the direction of projected shadows.
- Using the construction lines above, draw five large and four small trees directly on this page.
- Draw these trees using both a pencil and a pen.

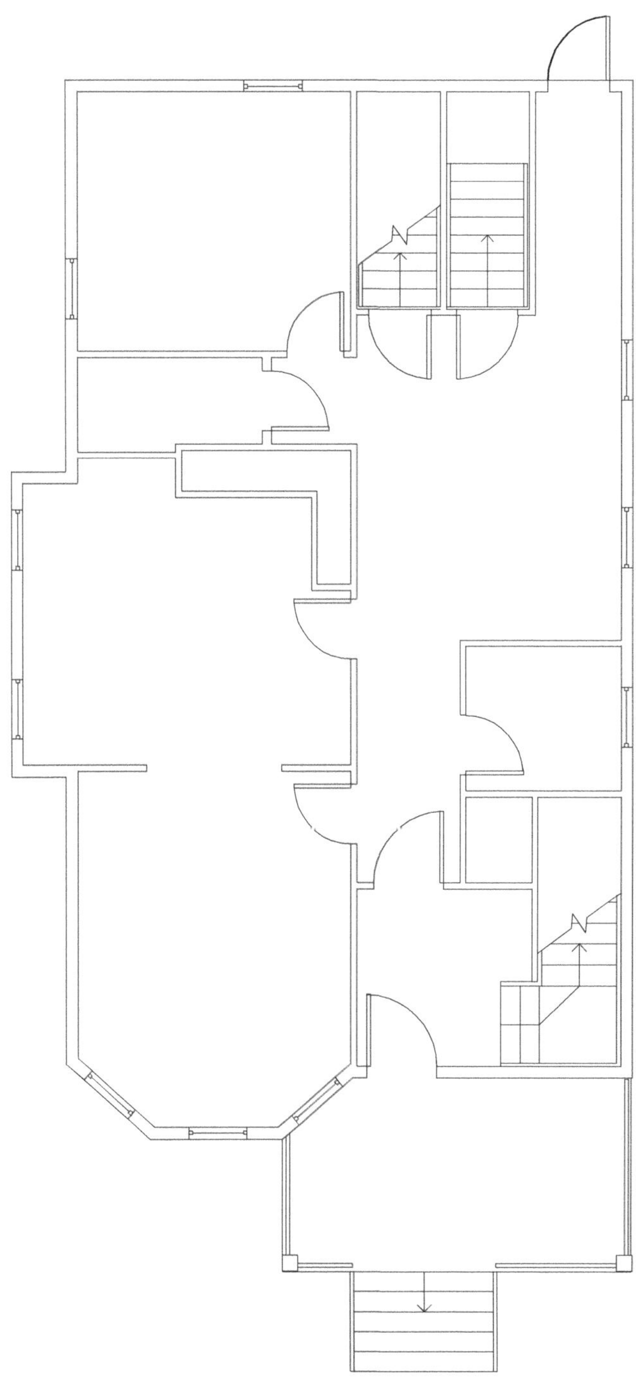

Floor plan
Scale: ⅛" = 1'-0"

Learning Exercise: Line Weight
This exercise is intended to help you improve your understanding of line weight in communicating the spatial properties of a floor plan.

- Using a dark line, carefully trace over all the walls in this drawing.
- Using a medium line, carefully trace over the windows in this drawing.
- Using a medium line, carefully trace over the doors in this drawing.
- Using a light line, draw the floor material in each of the rooms in this drawing.
- Use poché to fill the walls in this drawing.

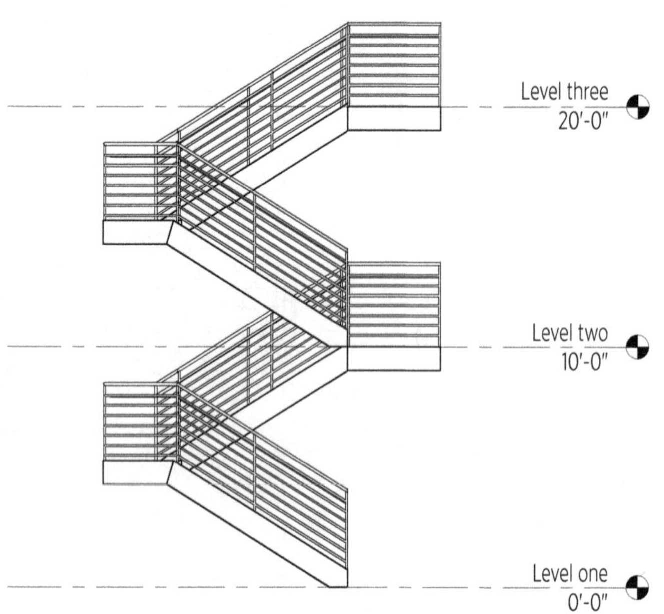

Stair elevation
Scale: ⅛" = 1'-0"

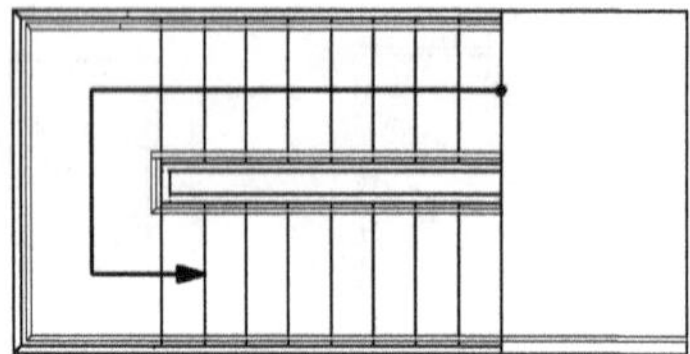

Stair plan: level three
Scale: ⅛" = 1'-0"

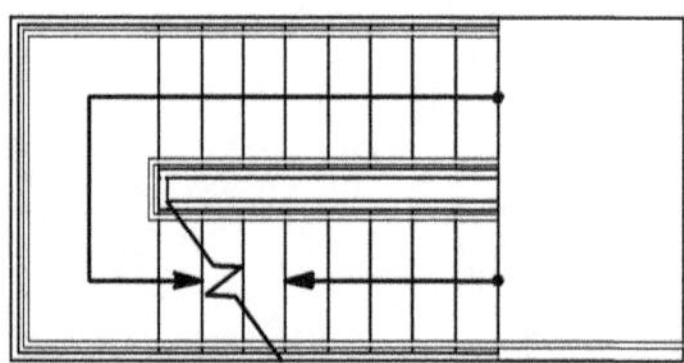

Stair plan: level two
Scale: ⅛" = 1'-0"

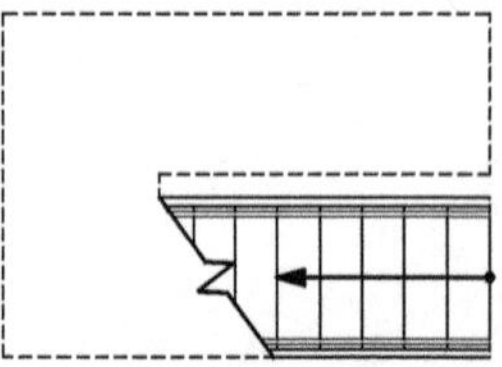

Stair plan: level one
Scale: ⅛" = 1'-0"

Learning Exercise: Stairs
This exercise is intended to help you improve your understanding of stair notation in floor plans.

- For each of the stair plan drawings, identify if the stair is moving up or down from the current level by writing the letters "UP" or "DN".

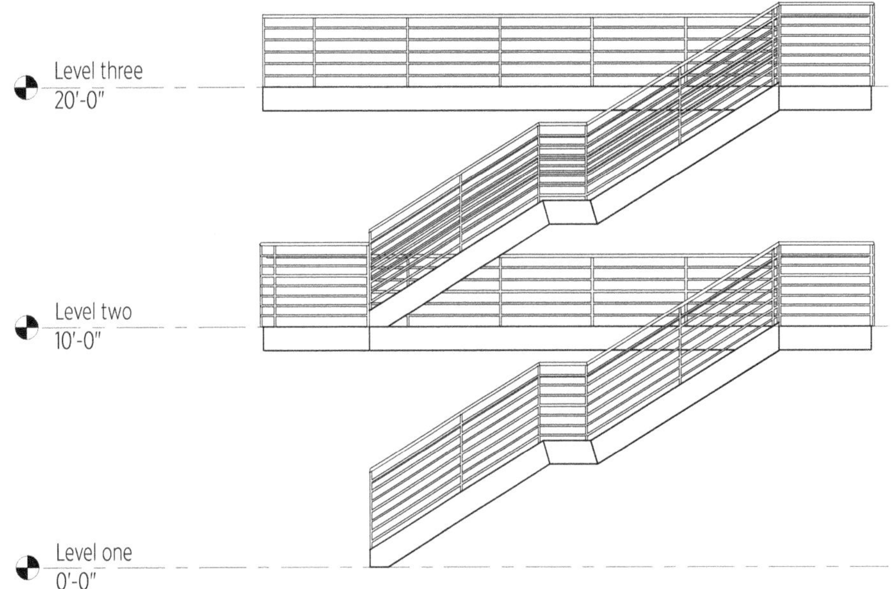

Stair elevation
Scale: ⅛" = 1'-0"

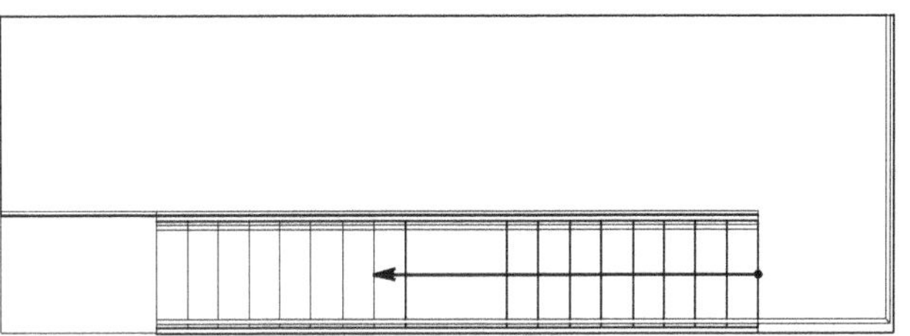

Stair plan level three
Scale: ⅛" = 1'-0"

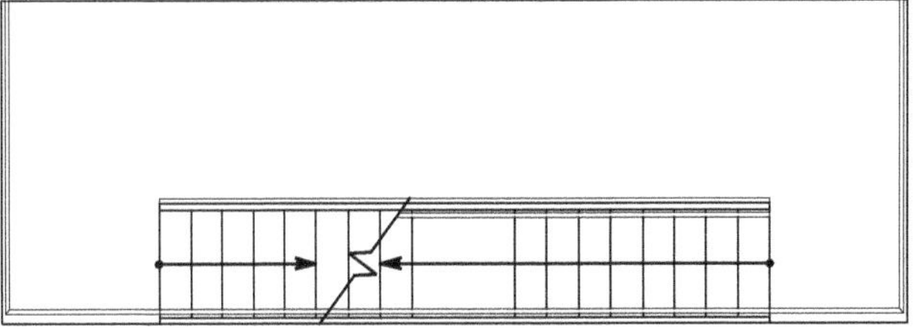

Stair plan: level two
Scale: ⅛" = 1'-0"

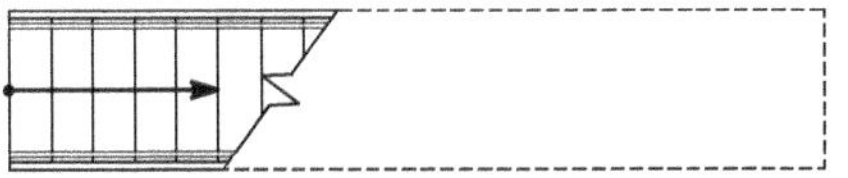

Stair plan: level one
Scale: ⅛" = 1'-0"

CHAPTER 5

REFLECTED CEILING PLANS

This chapter introduces the reflected ceiling plan (RCP) as a tool for generating ideas while discussing the technical aspects of drawing and designing the ceiling plane. The instruction in this chapter directly addresses what interior design students and instructors are trying to accomplish in the design studio. This will help design students transition from the academic studio to the professional studio.

This chapter provides appropriate reference material for students to access outside the classroom through both step-by-step guides and finished examples of RCPs.

Consider the following questions as you read this chapter:

- How are line weight, poché, and color used to clearly communicate space in floor plans?
- How is manual drawing used for ideation in ceiling plans?
- How do analytical drawings help you critically evaluate your design ideas and intentions?
- How are digital drawing and manual drawing used together in the design process? Is one more appropriate than the other at different stages in design?

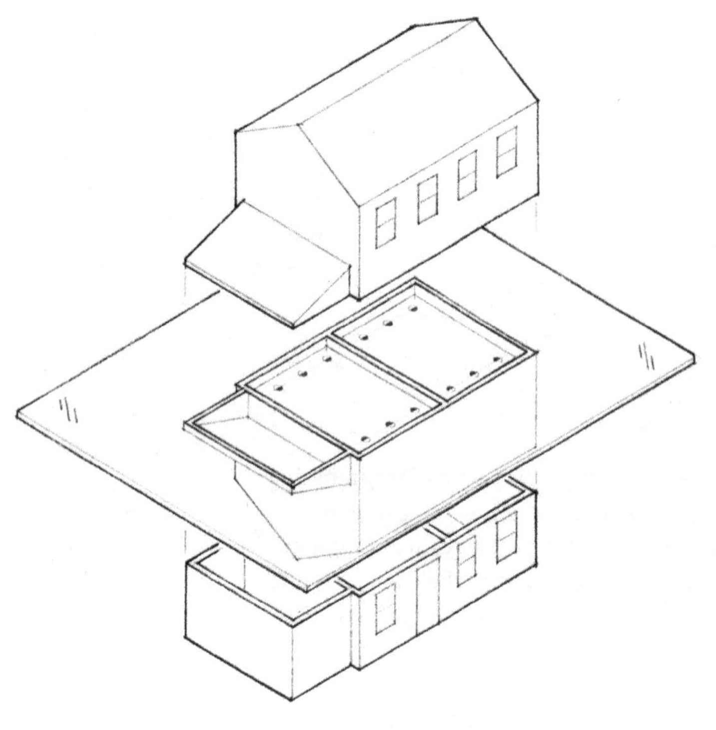

The RCP is a virtual slice through an entire building usually 12" below the ceiling surface. The drawing is similar to what you would see if you could place a mirror under the cut plane to see the reflected surface of the ceiling.

RCPs are two-dimensional drawings that communicate the ceiling conditions in a building or project, including the location of lights, ceiling materials, and ceiling height.

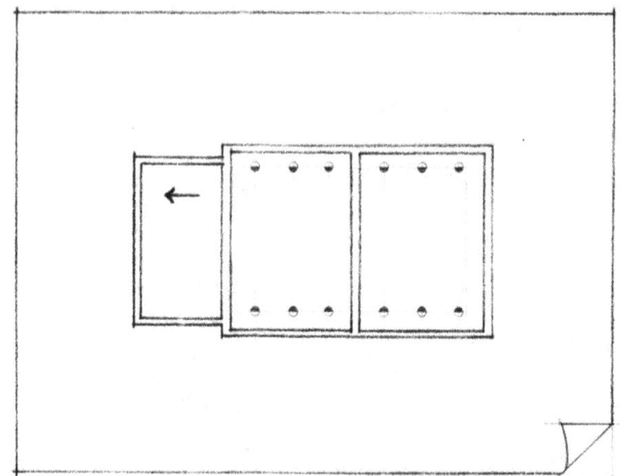

Objects that are "sliced" in the RCP, such as walls, are drawn with a very dark line. Door and window headers are also drawn with dark lines. Light fixtures, heating, ventilation, and air conditioning grills are drawn with medium lines. Ceiling material patterns, including acoustic ceiling tile grids, are drawn with light lines.

The scale of RCP varies, depending on the size of the project. It is usually drawn at the same scale as the floor plan.

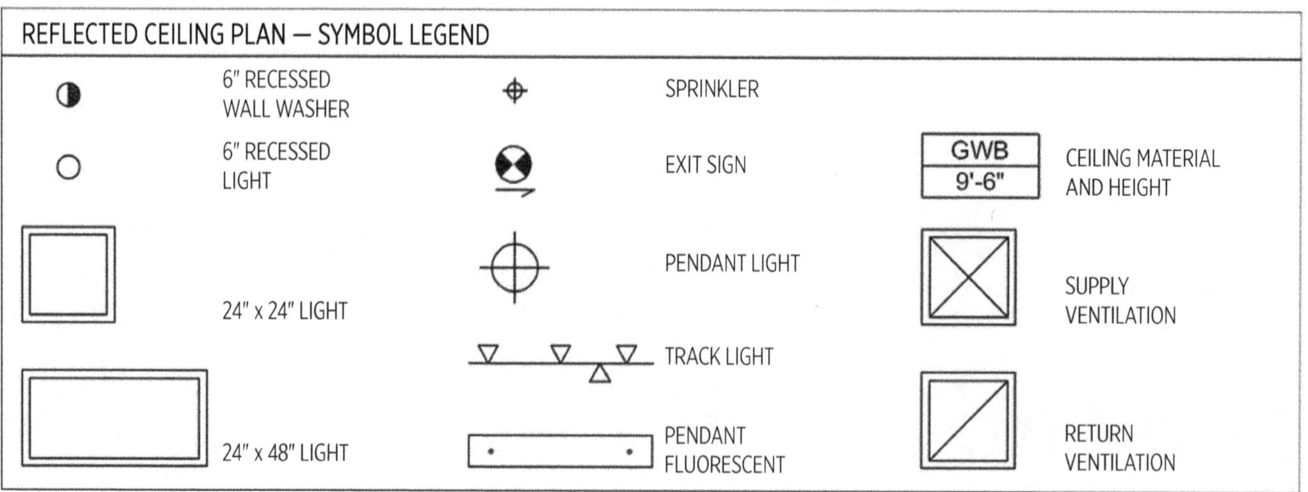

Ideation through Hand-Drawn Reflected Ceiling Plans

Ideation, also referred to as conceptual design, is the process of exploring multiple design iterations and critically evaluating each as an appropriate solution to a design problem. The ceiling ideation process often occurs in the middle of project design, after the following have been addressed in the floor plan: room locations, room sizes, and special program requirements.

- In RCP, ideation often involves the exploration of multiple ceiling design solutions or options, which are frequently traced over the floor plan.
- Working with trace paper over a current floor plan allows you, the designer, to focus on material and lighting issues that are relevant to room sizes and the location of built-ins or furniture.
- These drawings vary in media, which may include pen, pencil, marker, and colored pencil.

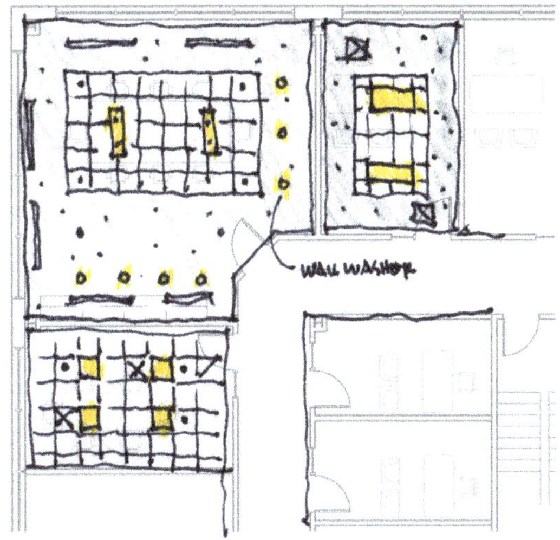

Initial hand-drawn RCP

Hand and Digital Drafting

At some point in the design process you will need to create a more precise drawing for a presentation, client meeting, or set of construction drawings. You can quickly translate the ideas in your hand drawings to a drafted RCP that contains appropriate line weight and conforms to drawing conventions, using the accuracy of a drafting table or computer drafting software. These more precise drawings often contain additional information, such as ceiling height, notes, and dimensions.

It is important to note that a strong RCP is measured by its success in shaping and organizing the many services that are located on the ceiling. Loose hand drawings are the most effective method to explore, refine, and strengthen this design. Hand-drafted or digitally drafted drawings are the most effective methods for creating technically accurate and consistent RCPs for presentations or construction documents.

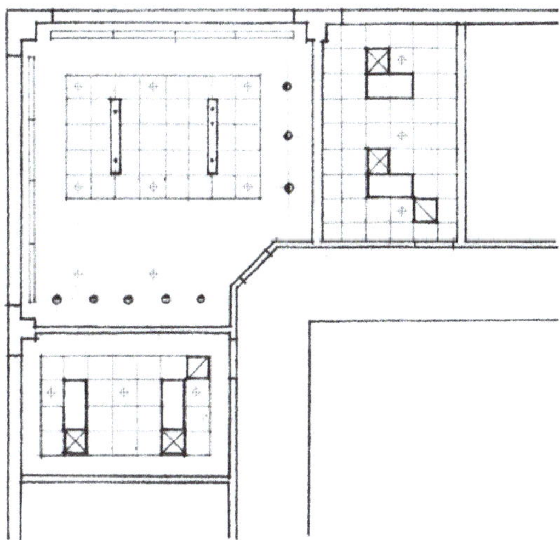

Hand-drafted RCP

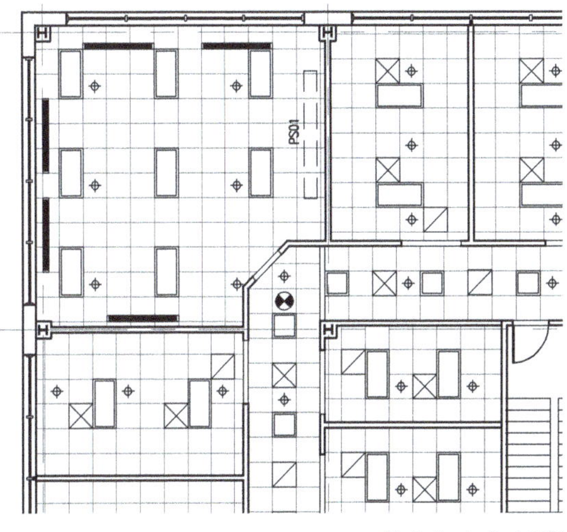

Digitally drafted RCP

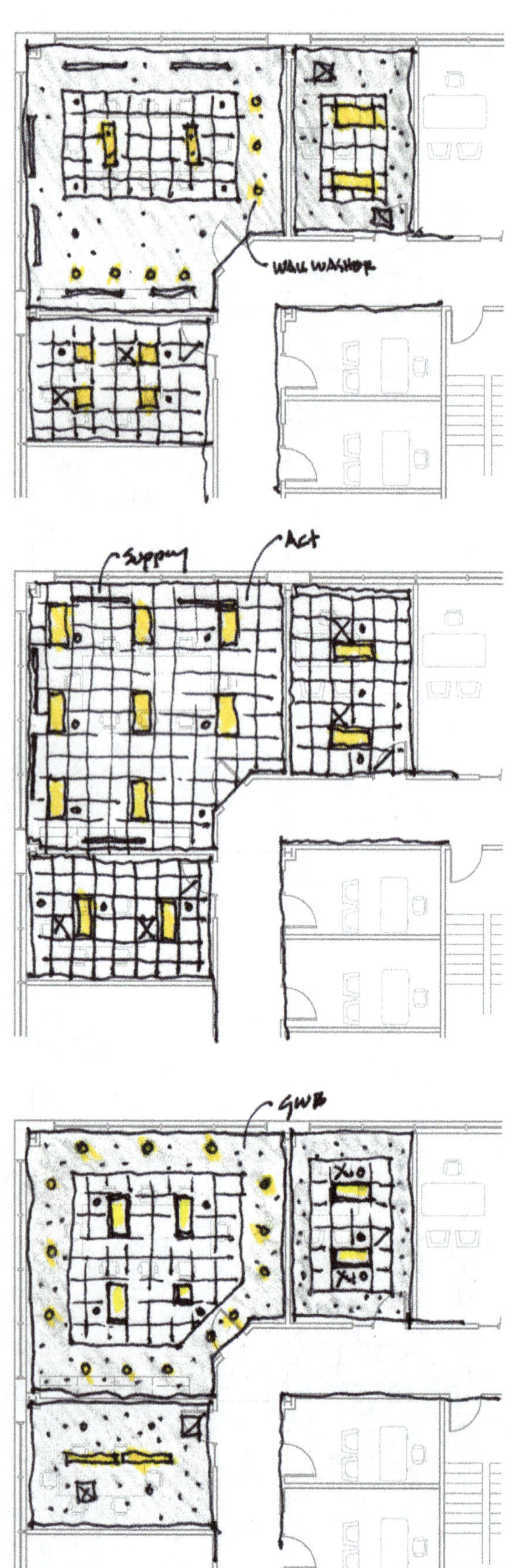

Multiple Design Schemes

These three early ceiling design RCPs explore different lighting configurations and ceiling systems for a conference room and two adjacent offices in a corporate office building.

- Each drawing was traced from an existing floor plan using trace paper and a pen.
- The drawings use yellow pencil to render the location of lighting in each scheme.
- Each scheme explores different ceiling systems, including acoustic ceiling tile and painted gypsum wallboard.

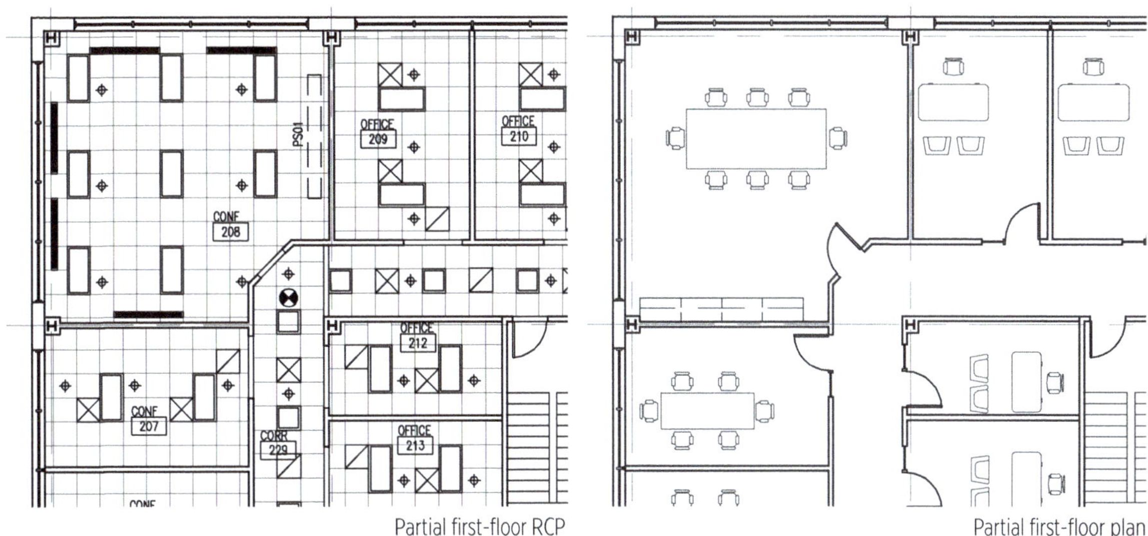

Partial first-floor RCP

Partial first-floor plan

In design firms, RCPs are usually drafted digitally, using computer software. This is because they are most often developed after a project has transitioned from hand drawings to more precise digital computer drawings.

- Both computer-drafted and hand-drafted RCPs are constructed from existing floor plans.
- Both computer-drafted and hand-drafted RCPs are drawn by a similar strategy, which is to start with walls and then add ceiling grids, light fixtures, and HVAC equipment.
- Both computer-drafted and hand-drafted RCPs are drawn using the same line weights and similar drawing symbols.
- Because of the repetitive nature of RCPs, using the computer is often quicker to initially draw and is more efficient to maintain as the project is modified and developed.

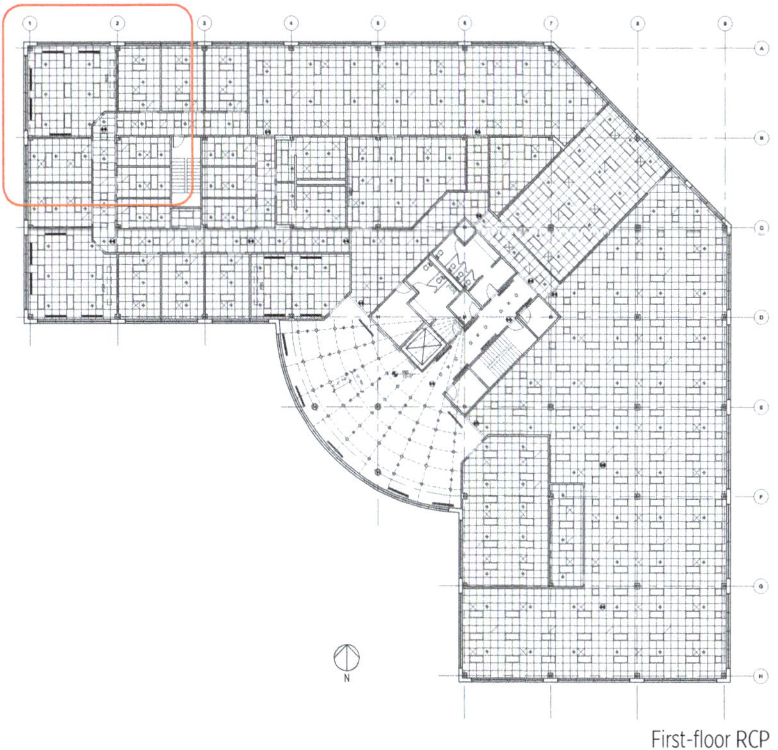

First-floor RCP

Heather Gray
Corporate reflected ceiling plan
Construction Documents Studio,
The New England School of Art & Design at Suffolk University

Drawing Reflected Ceiling Plans

A strong understanding of architectural graphic standards is critical for clearly communicating and developing design ideas in an RCP. The remaining portion of this chapter introduces drawing techniques, terminology, and graphic standards to increase your understanding and your ability to draw legible RCPs.

There are two primary methods used to draw RCPs. One is the overlay method, which uses multiple layers of trace paper, Mylar, or translucent vellum to trace over previously constructed floor plans. The second is the construction line method, which is used when you want to present and develop your floor plan and RCP on a single page. The construction line method allows you to project light lines up from the floor plan in order to draw the geometry of the corresponding ceiling plan.

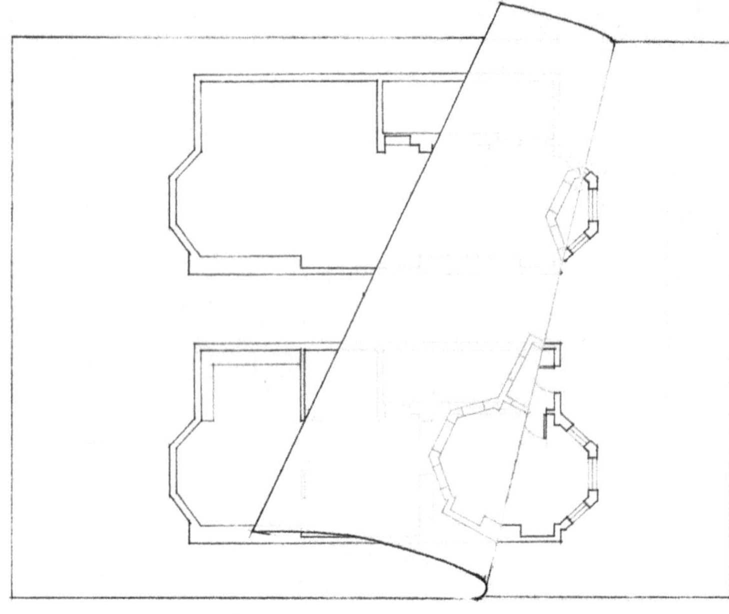

Overlay Method

- Use translucent drafting vellum to overlay and construct the new RCP from an existing floor plan.
- Insert a white sheet of paper between the two sheets of translucent vellum to review your progress and hide the existing floor plan.

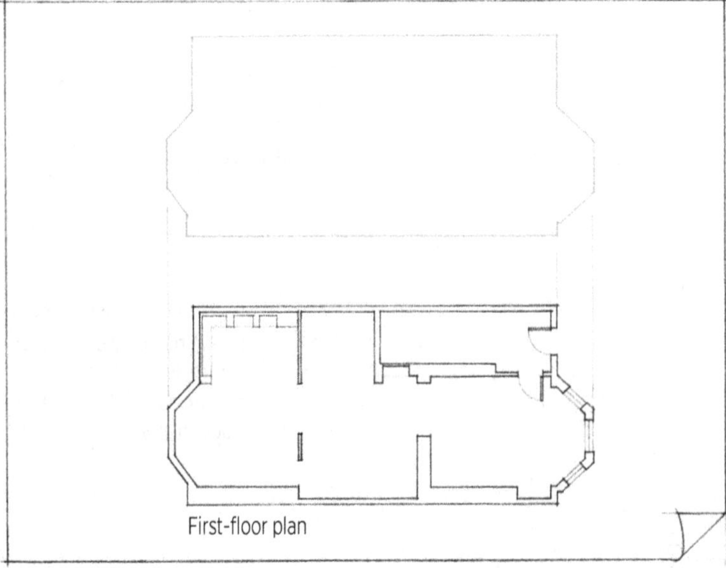

Construction Line Method

- Organize plans that are drawn on a single sheet of paper, with the floor plans drawn below the reflected ceiling plan.
- Use very light lines to construct the geometry for RCP from the floor plan.

FRANK LLOYD WRIGHT (1867–1959)
George Furbeck House (1897)
Drawings by Douglas Seidler

Drawing Composition
Strong drawing composition involves the thoughtful arrangement of multiple drawings on a sheet of paper. Before you begin drawing, identify the boundaries of the floor plans, using construction lines.

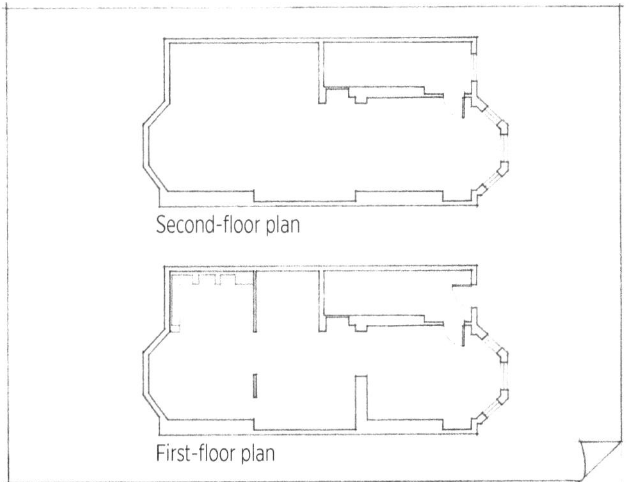

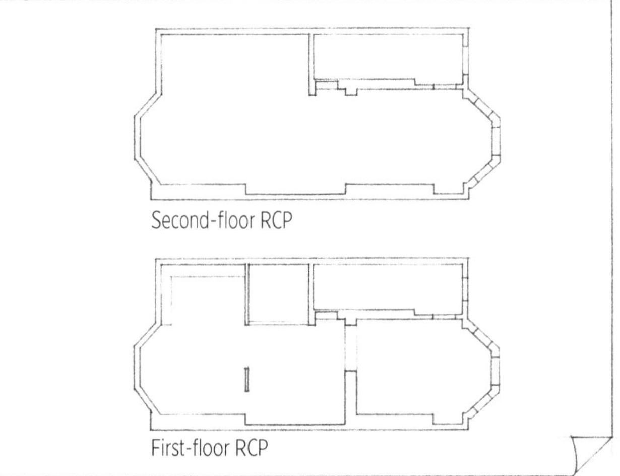

- If you have arranged multiple floor plans on a single sheet of paper, use the overlay method to construct the RCPs on a second sheet of paper. In a design presentation, hang the two sheets next to each other.

- If you arrange a single floor plan on each sheet of paper, you can use the construction line method to draw the corresponding RCP above the floor plan.
- Leave a ¾" to 1" margin on all sides of your paper and between the two drawings.
- Center your drawings on the sheet of paper.

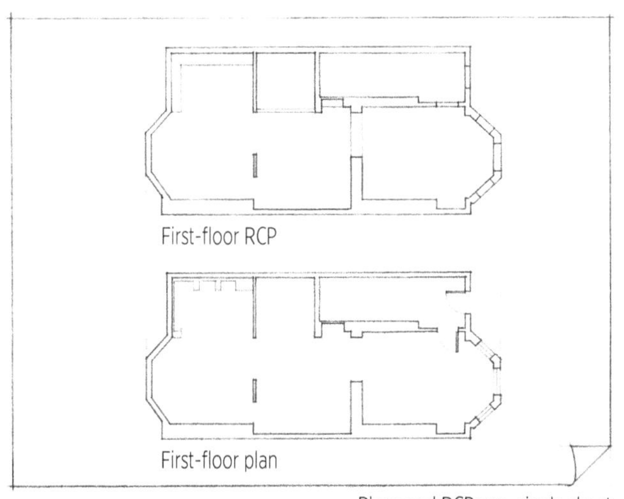

Plans and RCPs on single sheet

Drawing Reflected Ceiling Plans

Following steps 1 and 2 of the residential RCPs, this example illustrates the final steps for drawing a typical residential RCP.

- Small residential projects may combine the RCP information on a single drawing with the floor plan.
- Large residential projects and projects with complex ceiling designs will separate the RCP and the floor plan on two separate drawings.

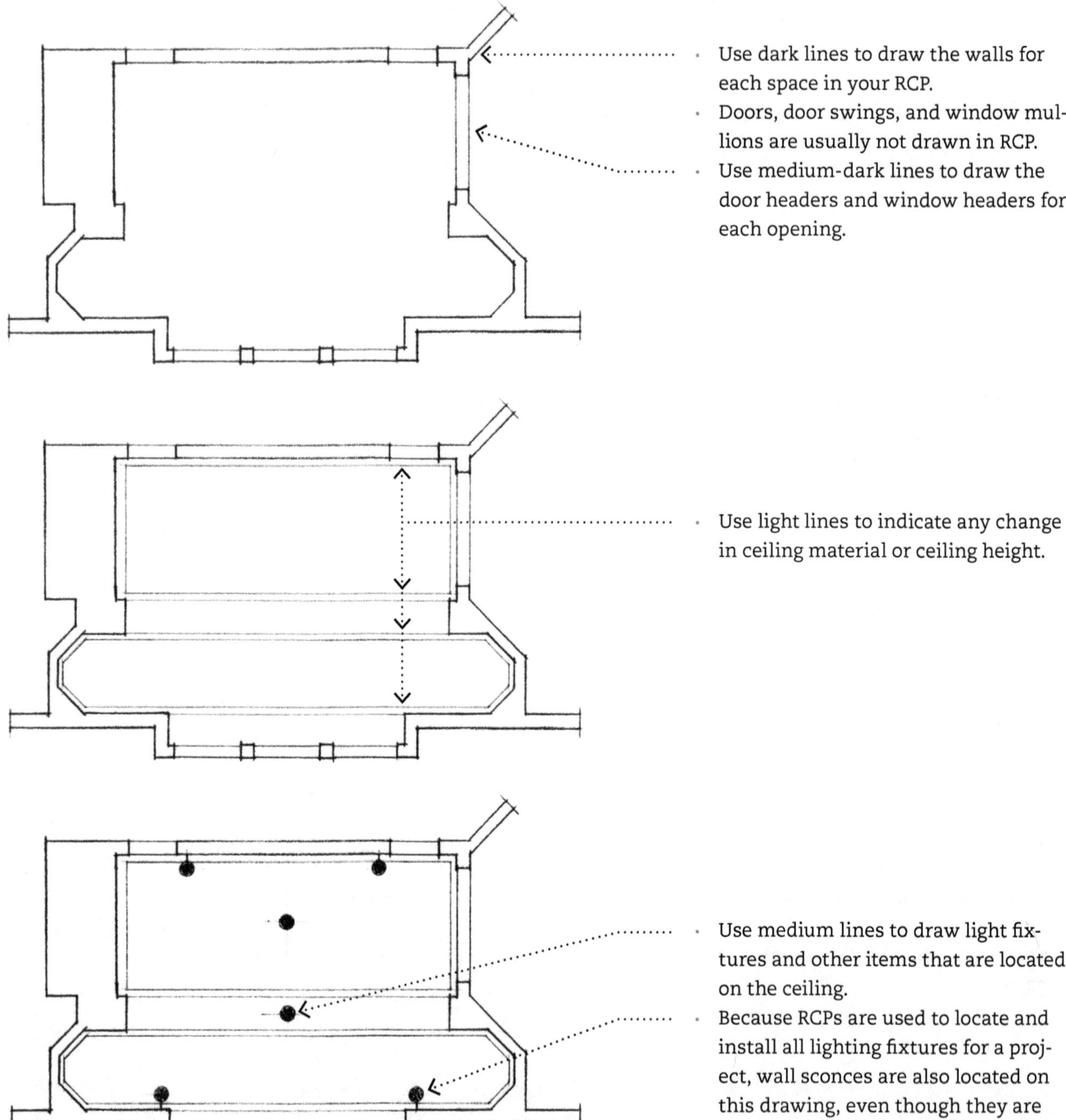

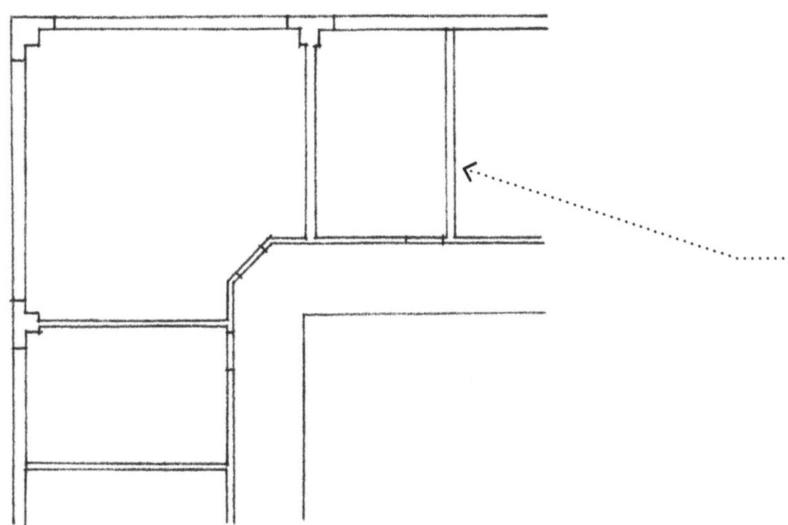

Drawing Reflected Ceiling Plans
This example illustrates the steps for drawing a typical corporate RCP. When starting a new RCP, it is important to have a resolved floor plan in order to identify the location of walls for each space.

- Use dark lines to draw the walls, door headers, and window headers for each space in your RCP.
- Doors, door swings, and window mullions are usually not drawn in RCP.

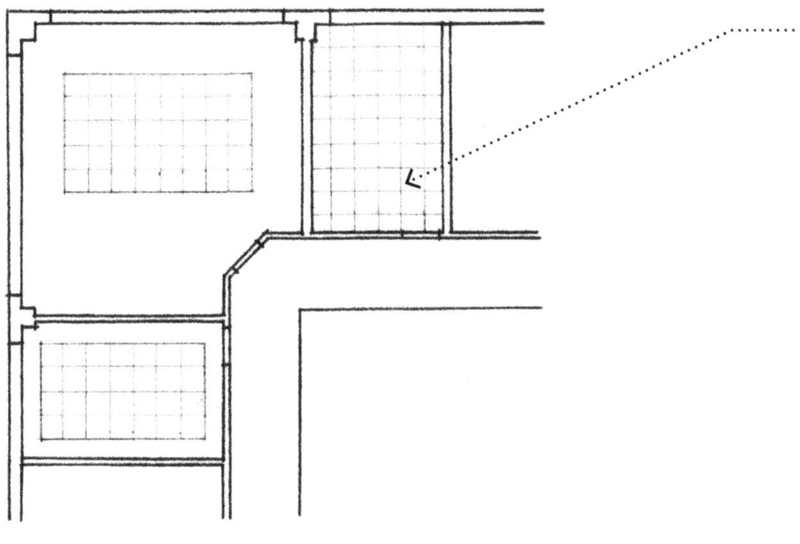

- Use light lines to show the location of any change in ceiling material and to identify the size and location for acoustic ceiling tile grids.

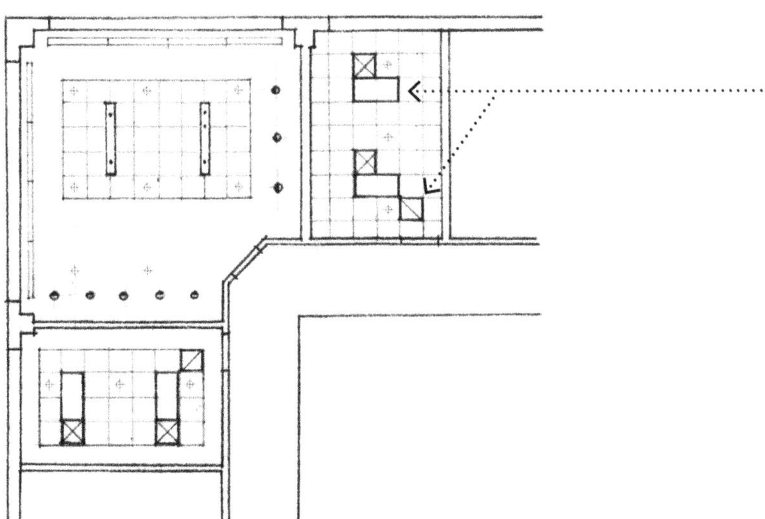

- Use medium lines to draw light fixtures, HVAC supply and return registers, and other items that are located on the ceiling.
- The term HVAC is used to identify most mechanical equipment used to heat, ventilate, or cool the building. HVAC stands for heating, ventilation, and air conditioning.

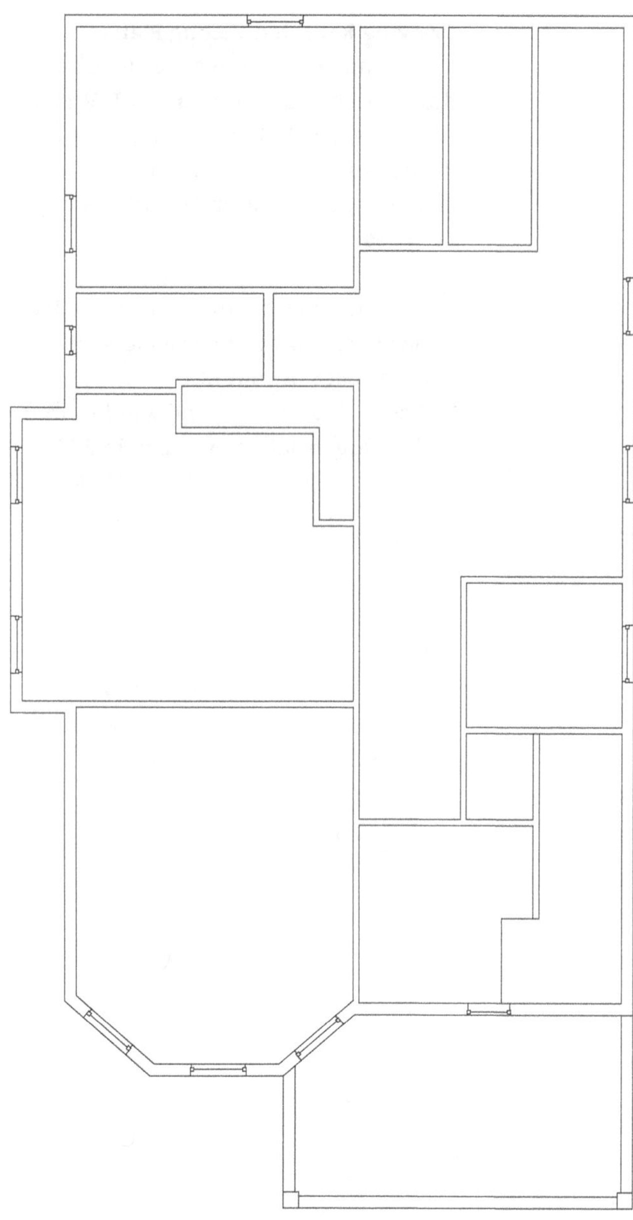

RCP
Scale: ⅛" = 1'-0"

Learning Exercise: Line Weight
This exercise is intended to help you improve your understanding of line weight in communicating the spatial properties of an RCP.

- Using a dark line, carefully trace over all the walls in this drawing.
- Use trace paper to develop a lighting scheme for this residence.
- Your lighting design should include both direct and indirect light sources.
- Using a medium line, carefully locate the ceiling-mounted light fixtures in your lighting scheme.

Learning Exercise: Drawing Reflected Ceiling Plans

This exercise is intended to help you improve your understanding of constructing RCPs from plans and sections or elevations.

- Construct the RCP from the room elevations.
- Using a dark line, carefully trace over all the walls in this drawing.
- Use trace paper to develop a lighting scheme that includes both direct and indirect light sources.
- Using a medium line, carefully locate the ceiling-mounted light fixtures in your lighting scheme.

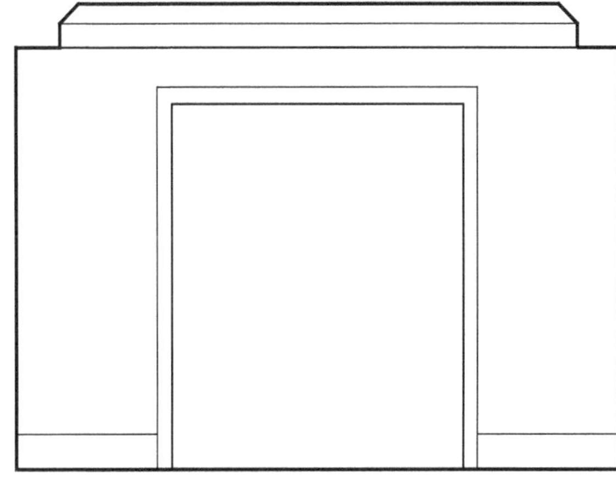

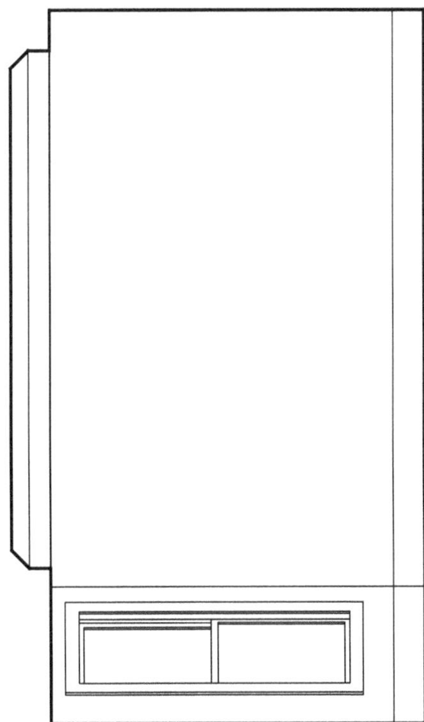

RCP
Scale: ¼" = 1'-0"

SECTIONS

This chapter introduces students to the most revealing two-dimensional drawing: the section. The instruction in this chapter directly addresses what students and instructors are trying to accomplish in the design studio: communicating their three-dimensional ideas in two-dimensional drawings.

This chapter provides appropriate reference material for students to access outside the classroom through both step-by-step guides and finished examples of section design drawings.

Depending on the educational approach of your college or university, you may use the section as a primary tool for design. Conversely, the section may reveal itself at the end of a project, communicating the spatial organization and ideas of your built models. Regardless of when you introduce the section in your design process, it is an important tool for refining and clarifying your design ideas and intent.

Consider the following questions as you read this chapter:

- How is hand drawing used in both school and in practice to explore, develop, and communicate ideas?
- What are the fundamental conventions used to construct section drawings?
- How do section drawings support the design process?

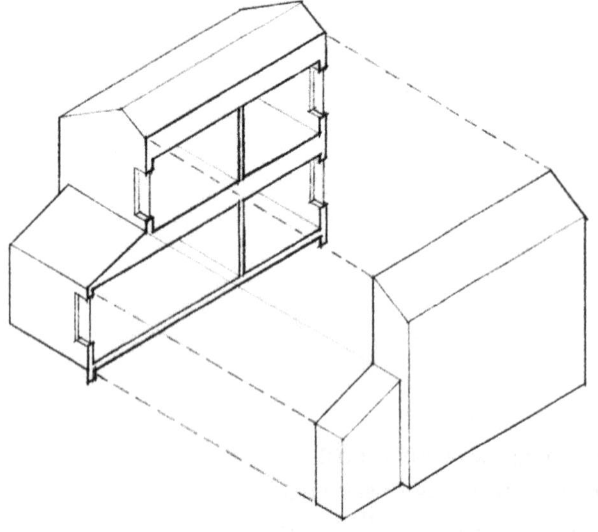

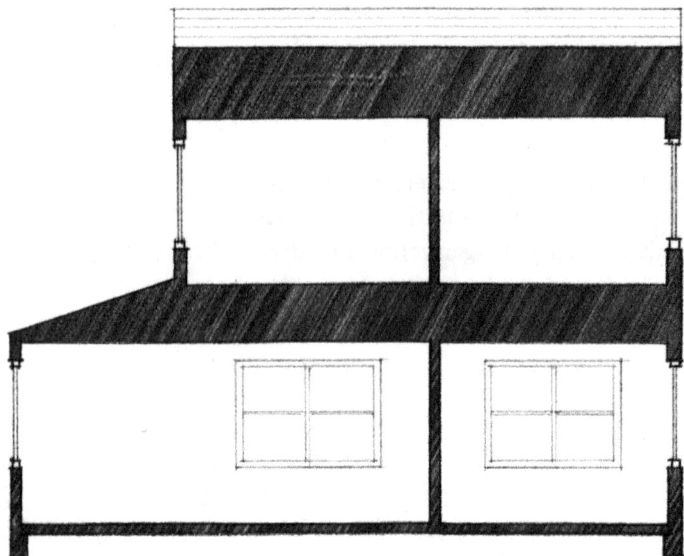

The section drawing is a virtual slice through an entire building or a series of adjacent rooms in a building. This slice, called the cut plane, often extends to the exterior of the building to include exterior sidewalks, roads, and landscaping.

Section drawings are two-dimensional drawings that visually communicate the spatial conditions in a building or project, including the relationship between adjacent spaces. The location of the cut plane in a section should slice through the most important programmatic spaces. It should also face the direction that best communicates the architectural character of these spaces.

Objects that are "sliced" in the section drawing, such as floors and walls, are drawn with a dark line. These objects are also rendered with solid poché to communicate the relationship between mass and void. The ground plan is drawn with a very dark line. Interior and exterior surfaces visible in the section cut are drawn with the same line weight principles as interior and exterior elevations.

Section drawings are often drawn at ⅛" = 1'-0" or ¼" = 1'-0".

Construction lines (4H lead)

Surface patterns and joints / light line (2H lead)

Object profiles and edges / medium line (HB lead)

Section cut line / heavy line (2B lead)

Hidden objects / dashed line (HB lead)

Line Weight

Designers communicate the three-dimensional space represented in a section through clear and legible line weight.

- When drafting by hand, adjust line thickness by adjusting the type of lead in your pencil, the thickness of your pen, and the pressure applied to the paper.

Ideation through Hand-Drawn Sections
When section drawings are integrated in the design process, they often develop from large ideas about scale and proportion. The drawings become increasingly refined, describing surface material and overhead ceiling conditions and locating wall openings, including windows and doors.

Initial section drawings are loosely drawn by hand. They clarify ideas of scale and proportion, as they relate to site conditions and the floor plan. Through the design process, these hand drawings are refined to address the programmatic requirements for each space represented in the drawing or project.

This ideation process is developed through the rapid and thoughtful execution of multiple hand drawings. These hand drawings should be proportionally accurate and drawn to an approximate architectural scale, and they should use line weight that is appropriate for a section drawing.

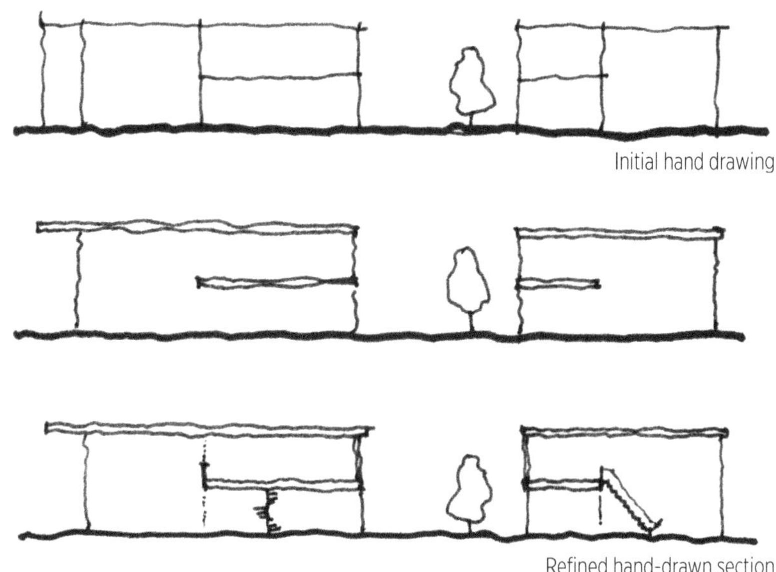

Initial hand drawing

Refined hand-drawn section

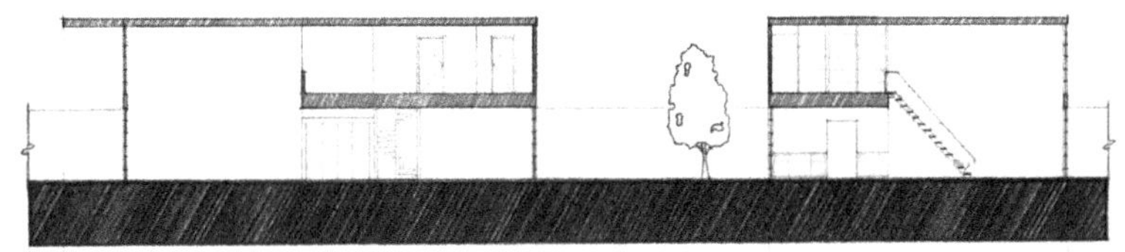

Hand-drafted section

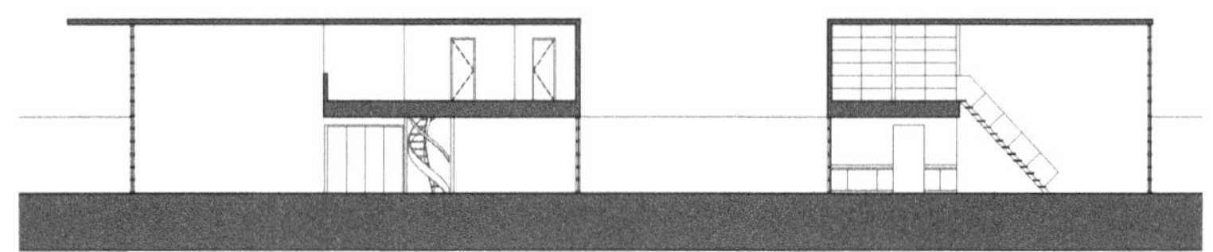

Digitally drafted section

CHARLES (1907–78) AND RAY (1912–88) EAMES
Eames House (1949)
Drawings by Douglas Seidler

Hand and Digital Drafting
At some point in the design process, you will need to create a more precise drawing for a presentation, client meeting, or set of construction drawings. Using the accuracy of a drafting table or computer drafting software, you can quickly transform the ideas in your hand drawings into drafted sections that contain appropriate line weight and conform to drawing conventions. These more precise drawings often contain additional information, such as material patterns, scale figures, notes, and dimensions.

It is important to note that a strong section is measured both in its technical accuracy and in the strength of the design solution. Loose hand drawings are the most effective method to explore, refine, and strengthen a design. Hand-drafted or digitally drafted drawings are the most effective methods for creating technically accurate and consistent section drawings for presentations or construction documents.

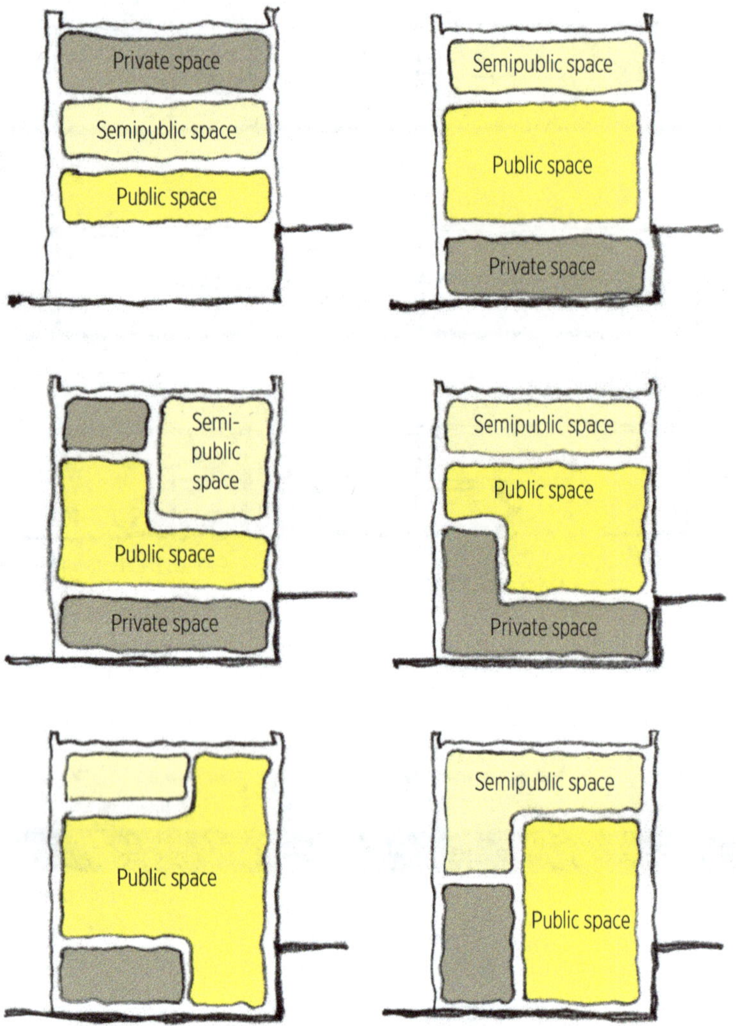

Vertical Space Planning

Ideation, also referred to as conceptual design, is the process of exploring multiple design iterations and critically evaluating each as an appropriate solution to a design problem.

- In section, ideation is most evident through the rapid execution of multiple design solutions, often at a reduced scale.
- Each design solution should investigate unique spatial relationships between major programmatic elements.
- For a single building, designers use quick sketches in section to study the organization and circulation of a project. These drawings vary in media, which can include charcoal, marker, pencil, and watercolor.
- The example drawings seen here explore six possible relationships between public, semipublic, and private spaces in a four-story building.
- Some design iterations separate private and public spaces vertically throughout the building. In these schemes, public spaces are closer to the sidewalk and the public entrance of the building.
- Other iterations make a clear distinction between the public front entrance of the building and the private back entrance.
- The site section below was used as an underlay to sketch these design iterations. This site section drawing is helpful in communicating the public and private edges of a particular site. It would ultimately be modified to reflect the strongest design solution.

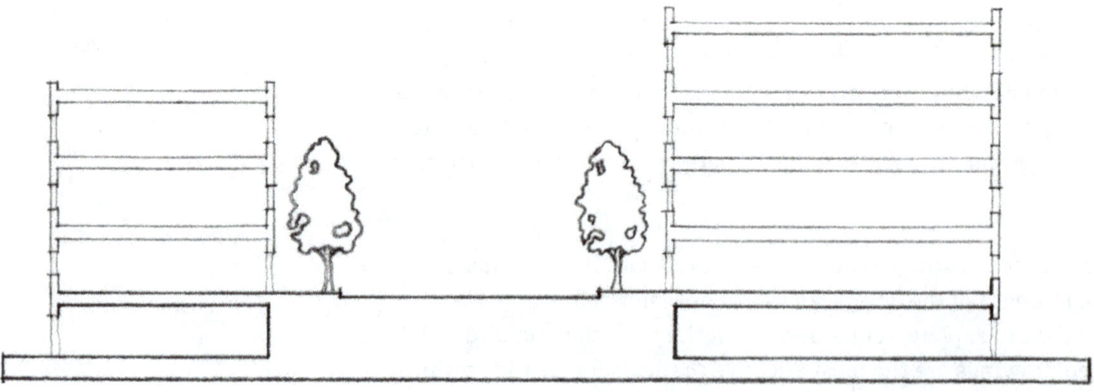

Urban Planning in Section
Traditional buildings are designed for a single type of occupancy or use. Many cities in the United States contain multiple blocks that were planned for single-commercial use, such as a business district. Because activities in business districts are limited to normal business hours, this type of urban planning may leave large portions of a city empty during off-peak hours.

- In this example the public theater and restaurant are next to a commercial office tower, which is likely empty during evenings and on weekends.

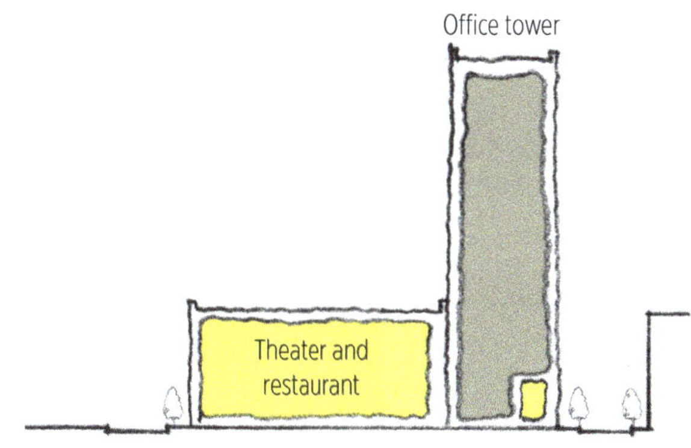

Mixed-Use Urban Planning
Mixed-use buildings attempt to activate the immediate urban landscape by combining multiple occupancy types within a single building.

- In this example the public theater, restaurant, and stores are located in close vertical proximity to the sidewalk.
- Private spaces, such as residential and office spaces, are located above the public spaces.

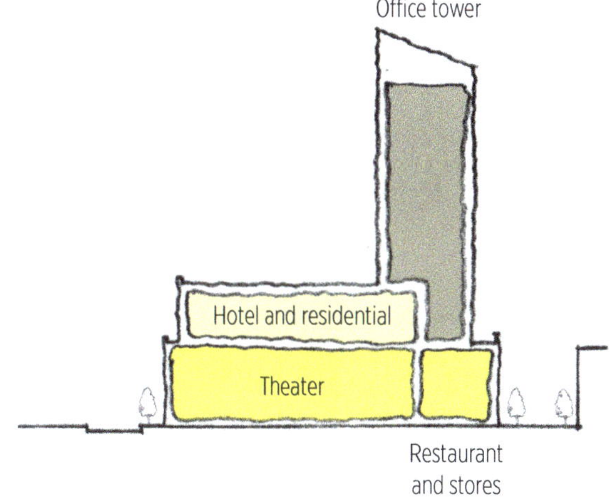

Horizontal Urban Planning
Many urban and suburban landscapes zone commercial building occupancies along a single street, with private residential buildings on parallel streets.

- This section drawing of the Back Bay neighborhood in Boston, Massachusetts, illustrates the spectrum of changes, from private residential buildings to public commercial buildings.

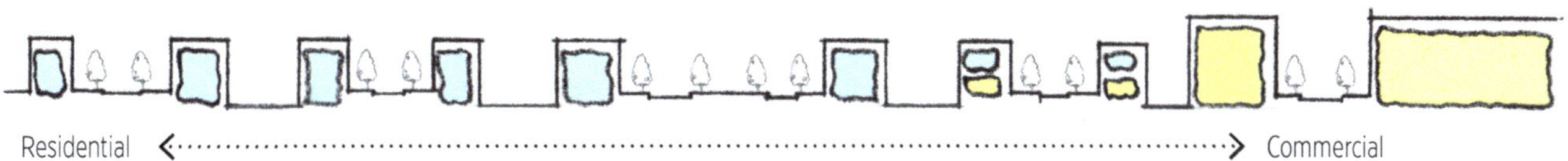

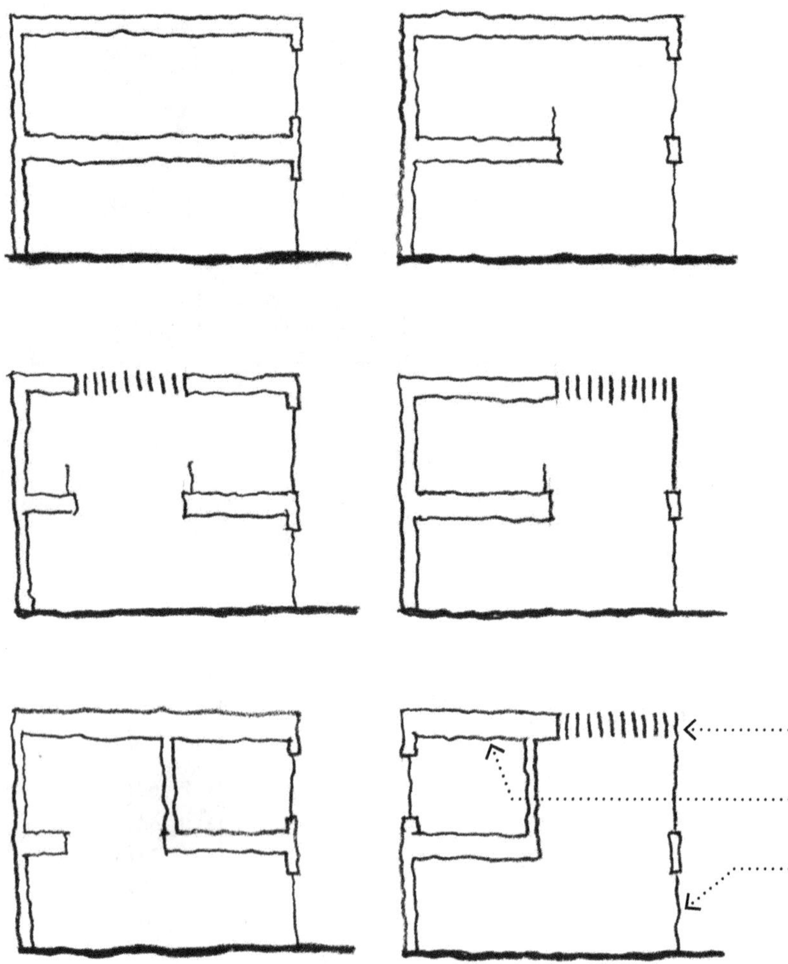

Shaping Interior Space
The section allows you to investigate the relationship between vertical spaces in a project. Each section diagram on the left investigates a unique relationship between the first and second floor of a retail store.

The location and size of floor openings may dramatically change the spatial experience of the interior environment. Designers may imply larger vertical interior spaces by placing floor openings under existing skylights or by locating new skylights over interior floor openings.

These diagrams also explore material use and surface opacity within the space.

- Translucent skylights are drawn with multiple vertical lines.
- Solid walls and ceilings are drawn with a double line.
- Glass walls are drawn with a single line.

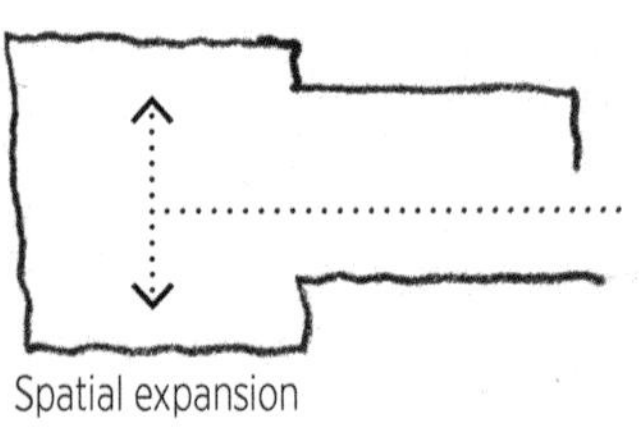

Spatial expansion

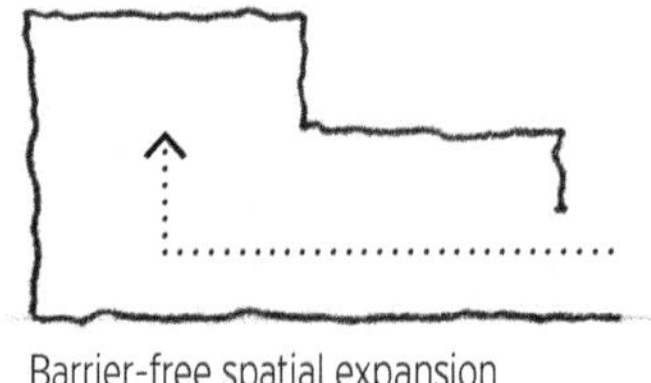

Barrier-free spatial expansion

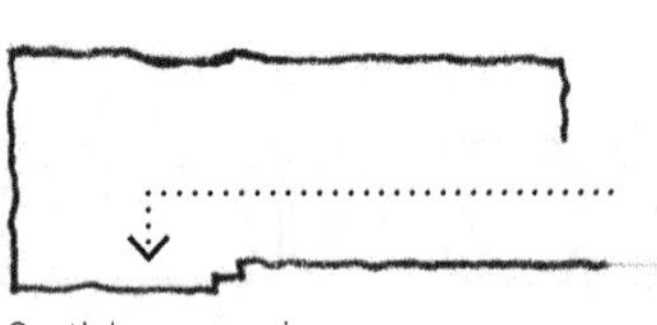

Spatial compression

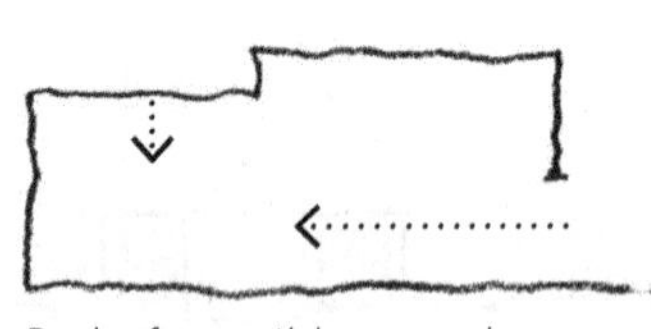

Barrier-free spatial compression

Barrier-Free Design
New construction in the United States must meet strict accessibility codes, which include barrier-free design for individuals in wheelchairs.

Prior to the adoption of these building codes, designers manipulated the interior ground plane to create unique interior spatial conditions. By manipulating the overhead condition and ceiling plane, designers created similar spatial conditions accessible to all.

These diagrams explore interior spatial conditions with either a manipulated interior ground plane or a manipulated overhead ceiling condition.

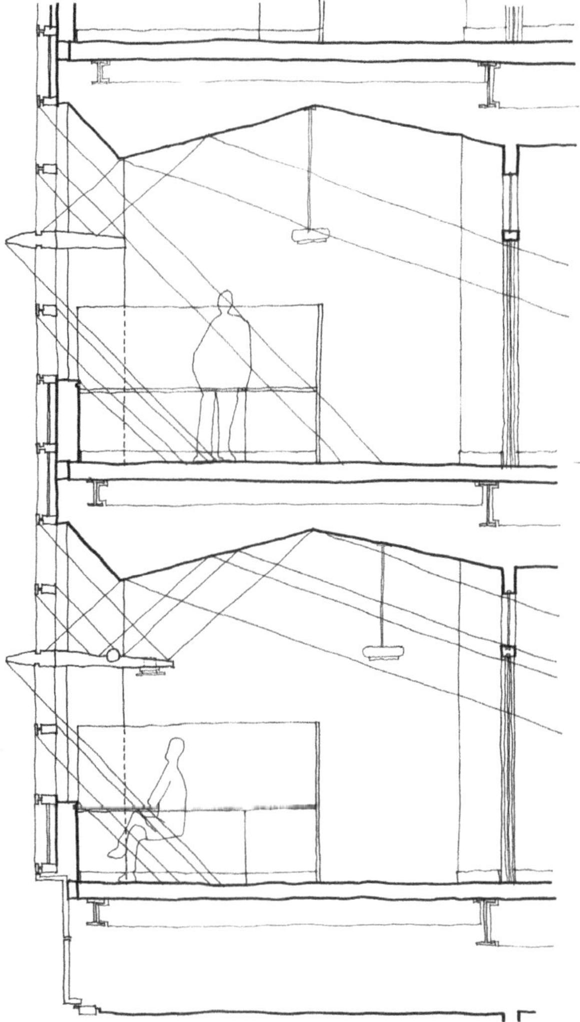

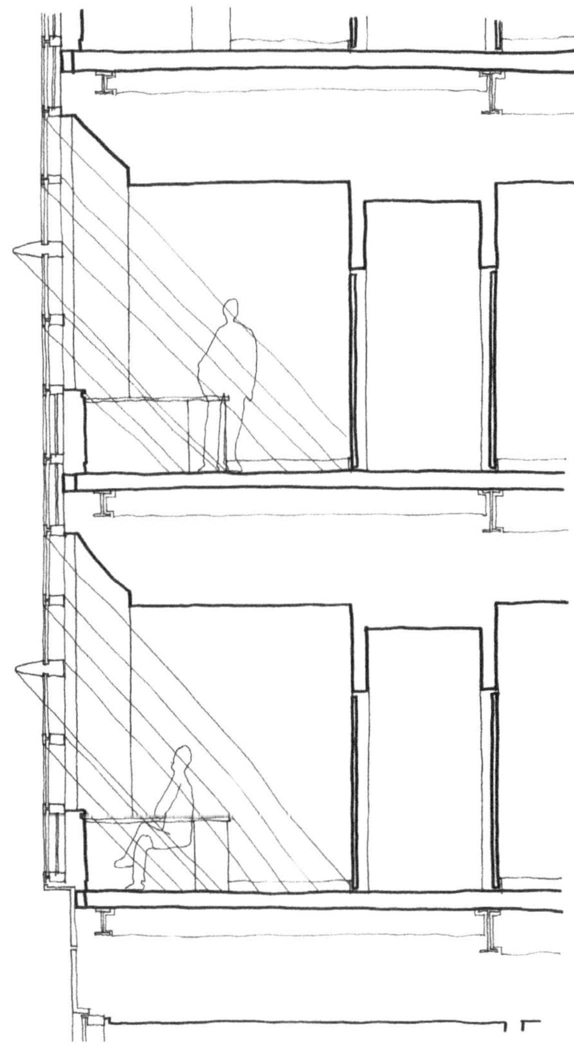

CHRISTOPHER ANGELAKIS
Daylight analysis drawings
ARC/Architectural Resources Cambridge

These section drawings were all studies of methods to bounce daylight deep into the building plan. The left drawing is an open office/write-up area where we wanted light to bounce into the adjacent interior spaces. The right section drawings are an office block that did not need light deep in the floor plan.

These concept section drawings were presented to the client early in the design process. Our goal was to create clear diagrams to help our client understand how we would bounce light deep into the plan and also provide shade in the workspace at the same time.

– CHRISTOPHER ANGELAKIS

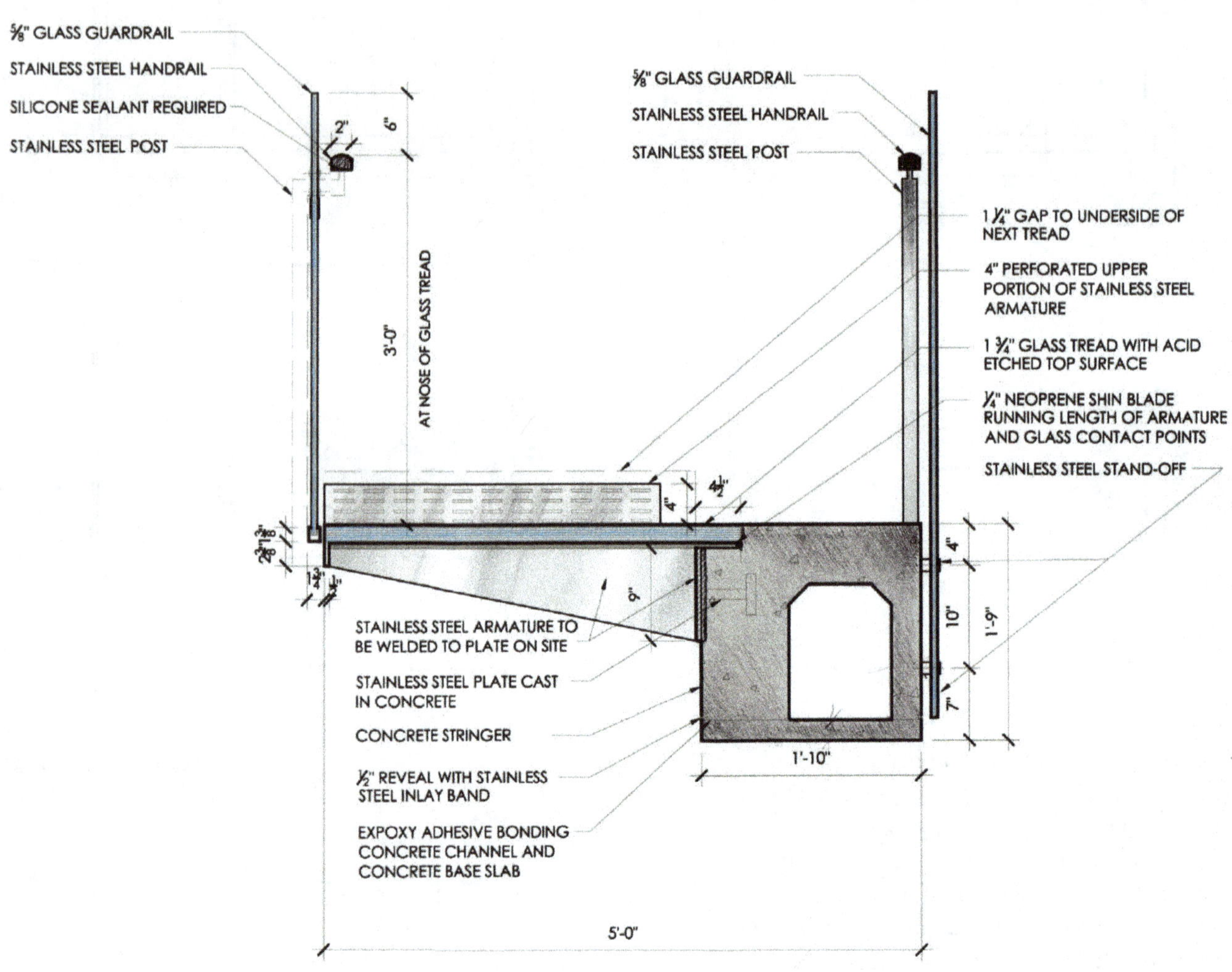

CIARA LANGLEY

Stair Section Drawing

Advanced Materials and Methods Studio, The New England School of Art & Design at Suffolk University

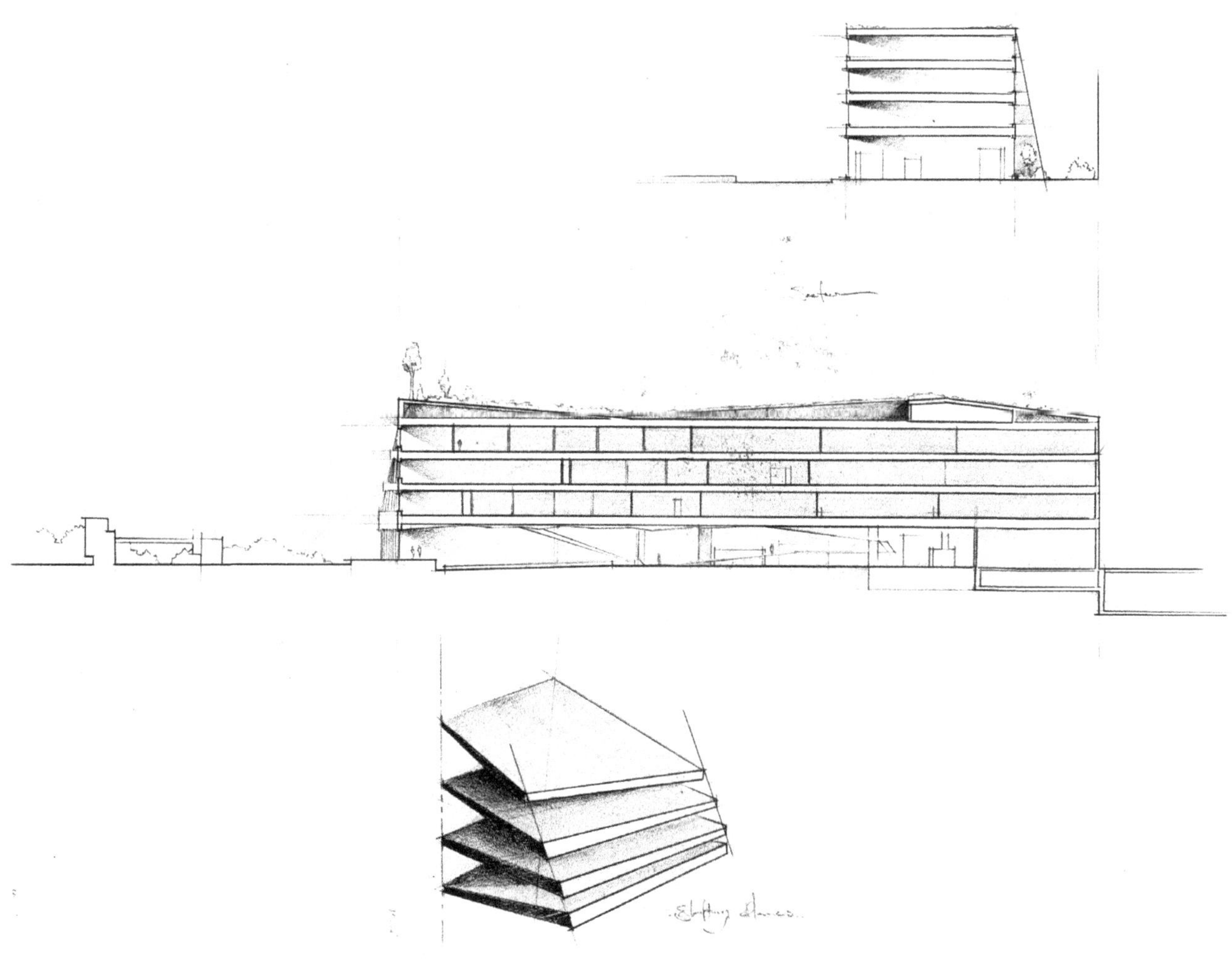

Kevin Asmus
Schematic design sections
Degree Project Studio,
Boston Architectural College

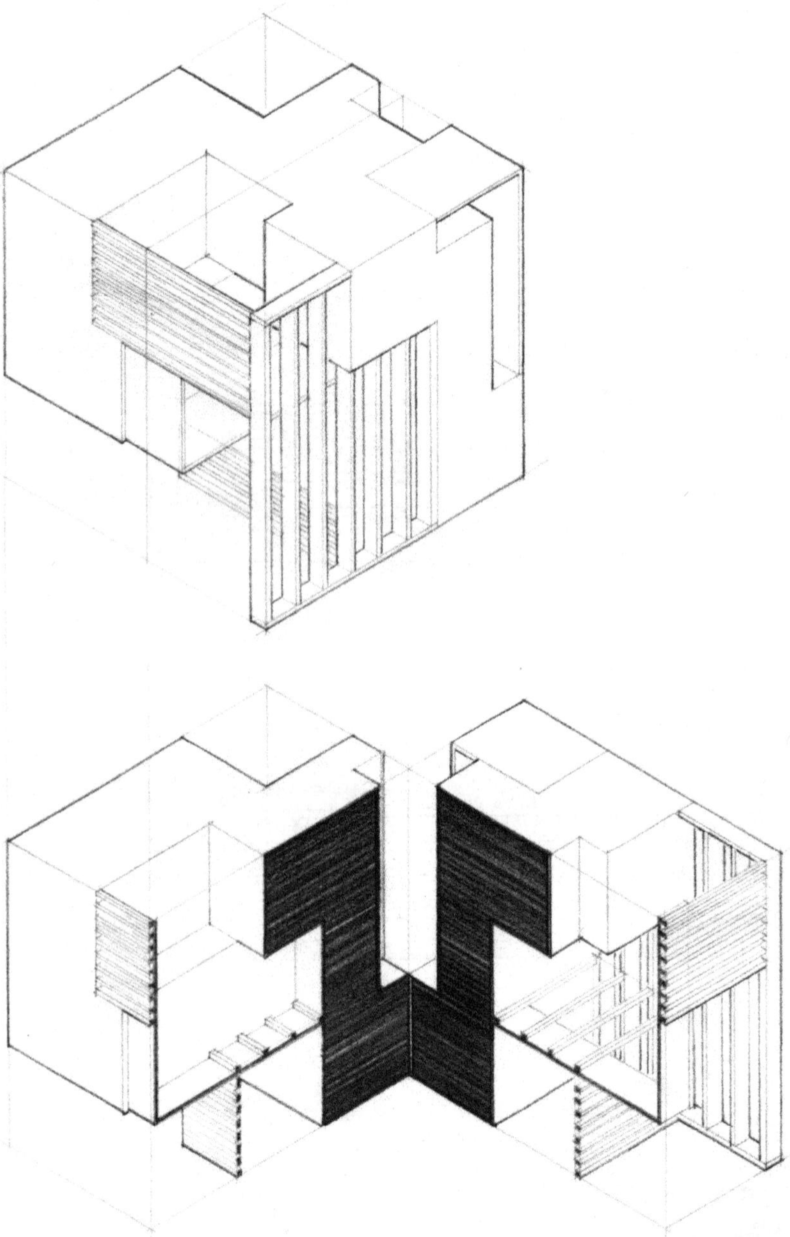

Design Sections
Early conceptual foundation projects, like the 9" cube, begin through built model. They are further developed through section drawings. The section drawings you complete are virtual slices through your project, usually parallel to one of the cube's surfaces.

The section drawing is an opportunity to visually communicate interior spatial relationships in a project.

- In the isometric drawing it is difficult to understand completely the interior spatial conditions of the cube.
- The section drawing more accurately communicates the interior space of the cube model.
- Compare the spatial condition revealed in the hinged section drawing below with the space in the isometric drawing to the left.

The section drawing reveals new information and presents an opportunity to refine and clarify your project.

- As you draw sections, evaluate the spatial conditions in the drawing. Compare this evaluation with your original design intentions, which can be gleaned in built model or in written conceptual statements.
- Most early design studios use the section drawing as an iteration in the project's development. That said, these drawings do not need to precisely match the built model and often contain design changes that improve the overall project.

Drawing Sections

A strong understanding of architectural graphic standards is critical for clearly communicating and developing design ideas through section. The remaining portion of this chapter introduces drawing techniques, terminology, and graphic standards to increase your understanding and enhance your ability to draw legible sections.

Constructing Sections from a Design Model

In foundation design studio, it is common for sections to be drawn at the same scale as the physical model.

- Use an architectural scale or ruler to measure your model and construct your section drawing with a 1:1 scale. Objects that are 3" wide in the model will be 3" wide in the drawing.
- In this example the cube model measures 9" wide, and the section is drawn 9" wide.
- Drawings are thoughtfully arranged on the sheet of paper, with an appropriate margin on all four sides of each drawing.

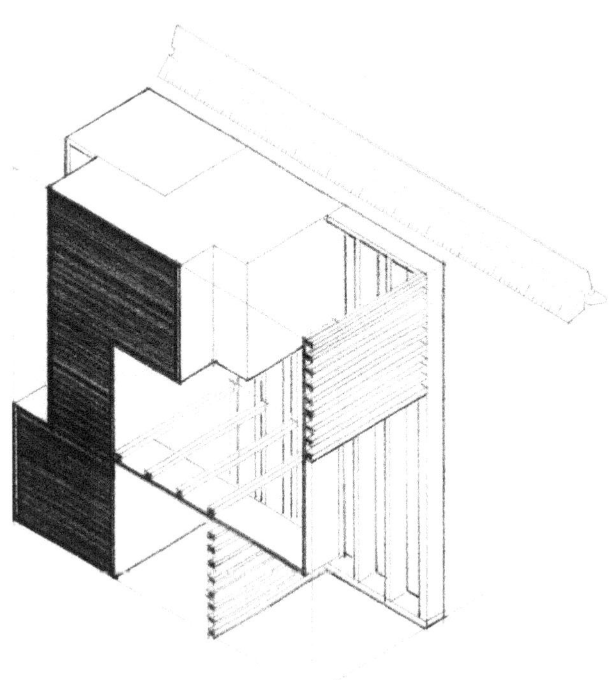

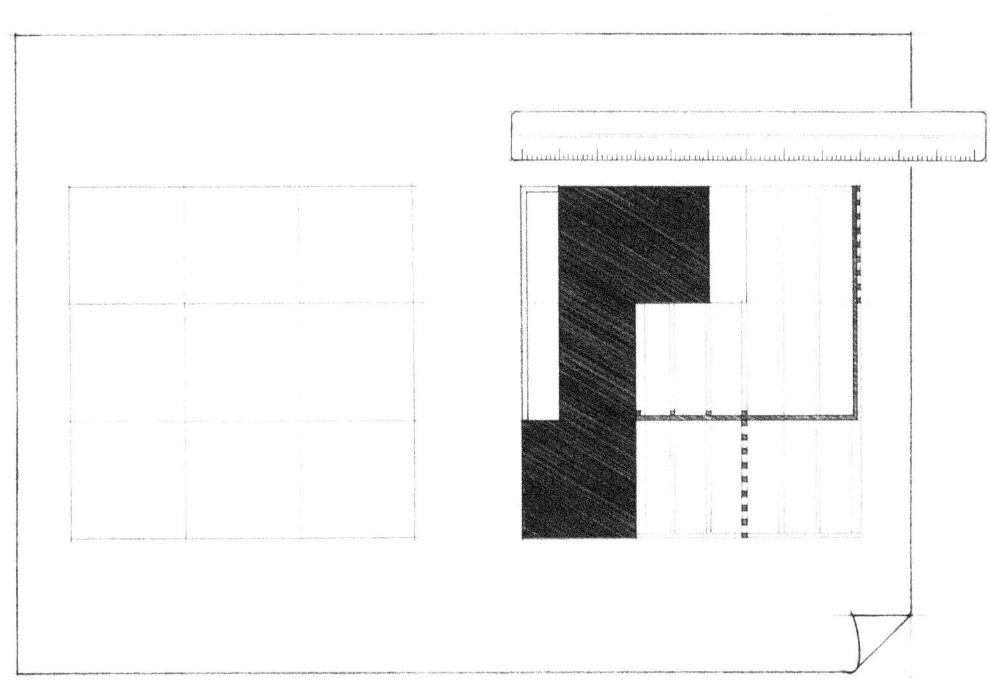

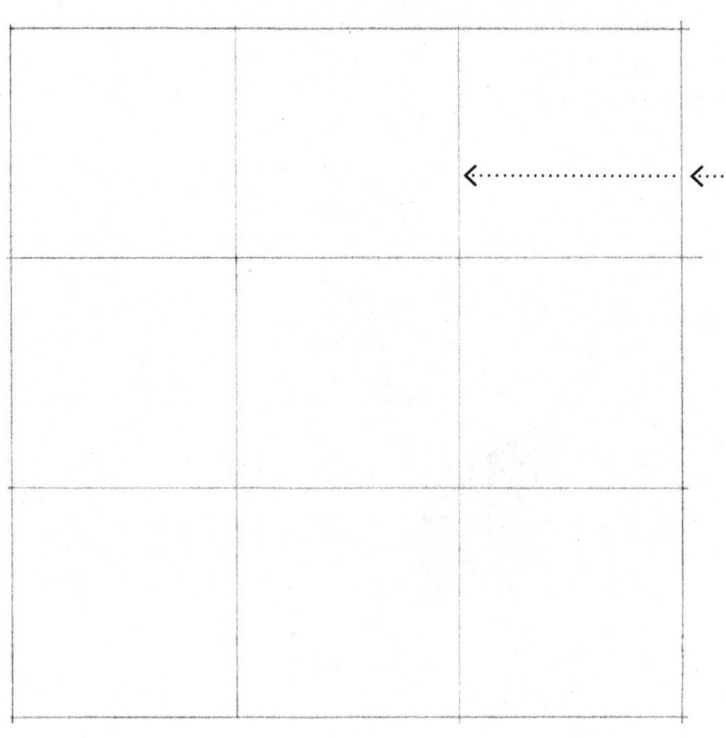

Boundaries and Geometry
When starting a new section, it is important to identify the boundaries of the drawing with construction lines.

- Use construction lines to identify the major geometry of your model.
- In this example the 9"× 9" square is divided into nine 3" modules.

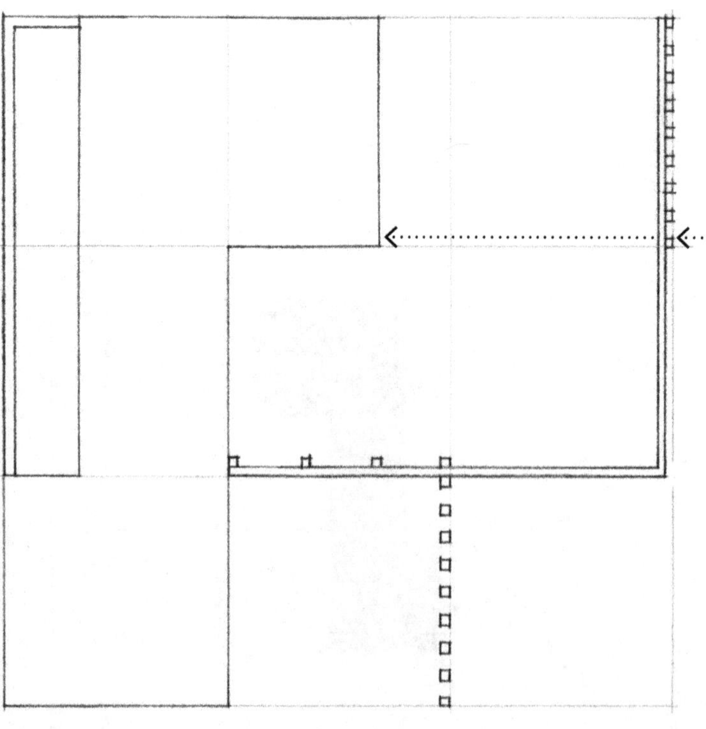

Sliced Objects
The third step in drawing sections involves drawing the perimeter around any object that is sliced by the section cut plane.

- Use dark lines to draw all objects that are sliced by the cut plane.
- In a model, masses are often constructed as hollow boxes of chipboard, corrugated cardboard, or foam board. In a section drawing, disregard the hollow nature of these masses, and draw them as solid objects.

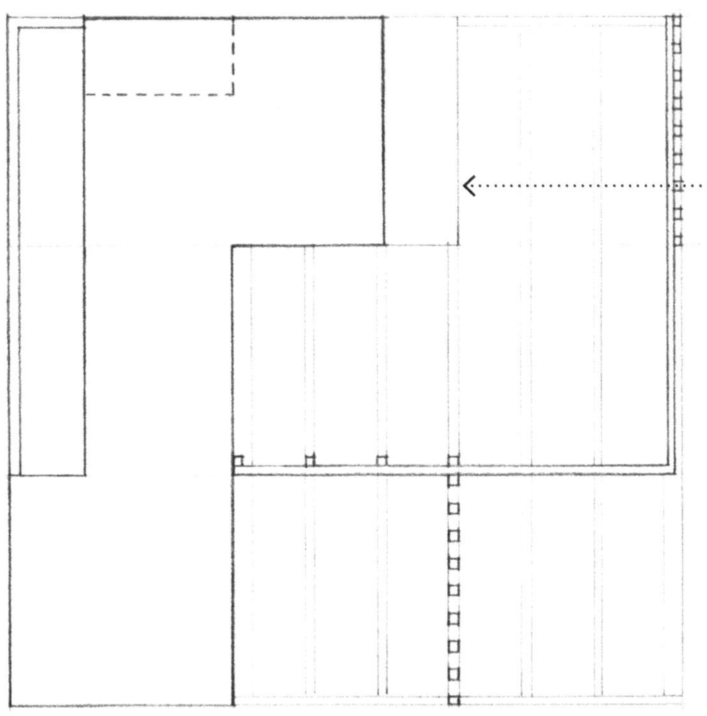

Objects in Elevation

The fourth step in drawing sections involves drawing any object visible in elevation.

- Use medium lines to draw the perimeter around all objects visible in elevation.
- Use light lines to draw surface patterns and joints between materials visible in elevation.

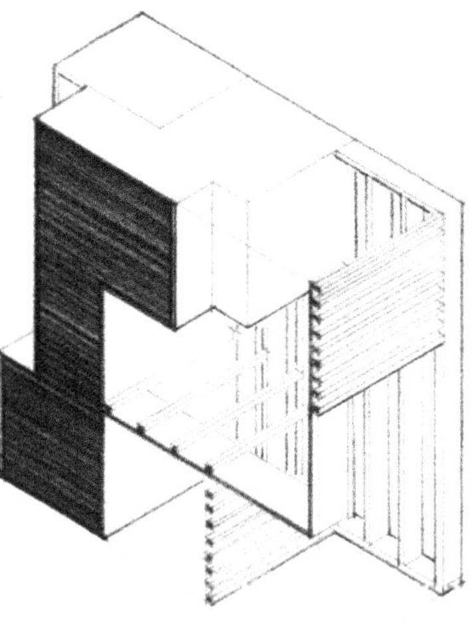

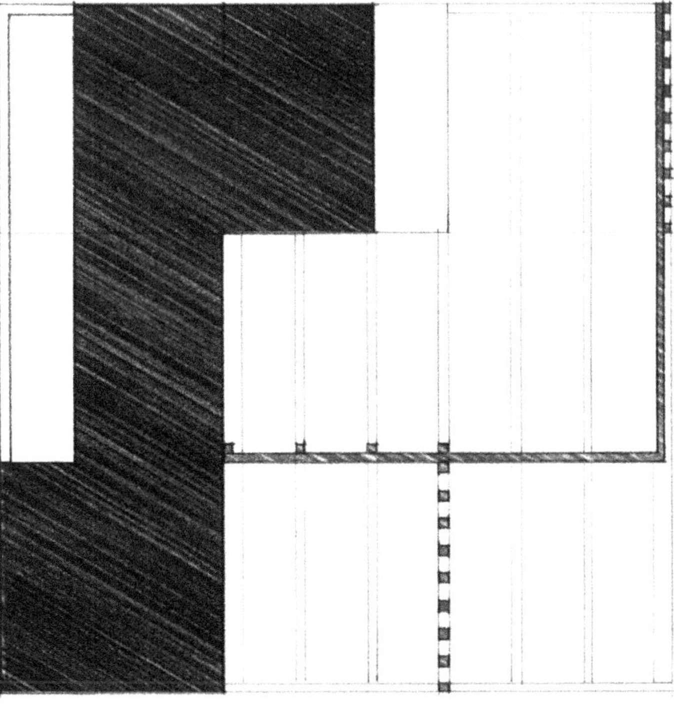

Poché

The final step in drawing sections involves adding tone to the sliced objects in the drawing. Tone communicates space by creating contrast between the mass and the void in a project.

- The solid dark tone is added with a soft lead pencil to the front or back of the sheet of paper.
- Grayscale tone is added with multiple angled lines. Depending on the density of the angled lines, this technique creates different grayscale values for the poché.

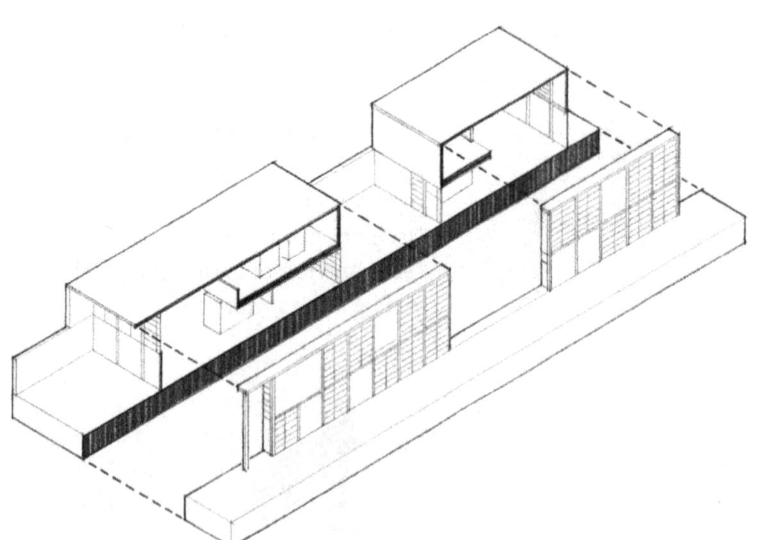

Building Sections
The building section is an opportunity to reveal and to visually communicate the interior spatial relationships in a design project. Depending on the individual project and your design process, these presentation drawings may be completed at the beginning, middle, or end of your project.

- Building sections should slice through major architectural elements, such as windows, doors, and openings in interior walls.
- Building sections should never slice through interior or exterior columns.
- Section drawings are usually drawn parallel to a perimeter wall.

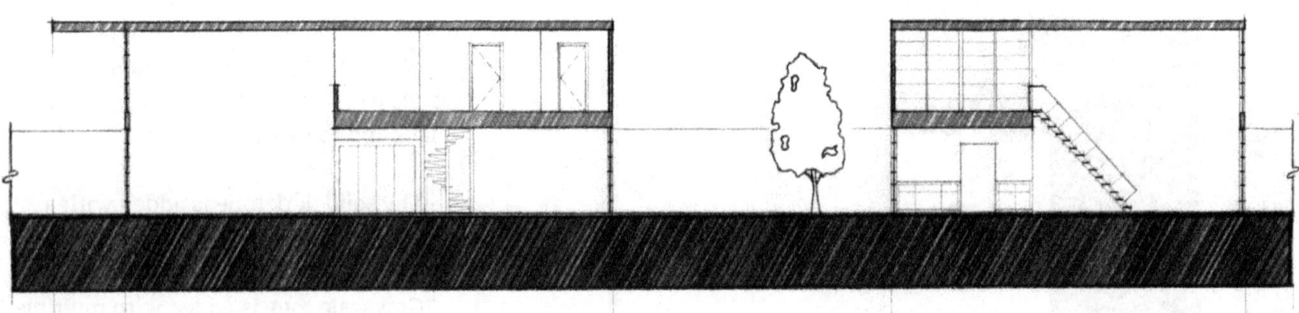

CHARLES (1907–78) AND RAY (1912–88) EAMES
Eames House (1949)
Drawings by Douglas Seidler

Drawing Scale
Calculate the size of your building section drawing to determine what size sheet of paper you will need to complete your drawing. Sections drawn at a larger scale occupy a larger portion of the paper.

- In this example the ⅛" = 1'-0" drawing is the most appropriate size for the selected 18" × 24" sheet of paper.

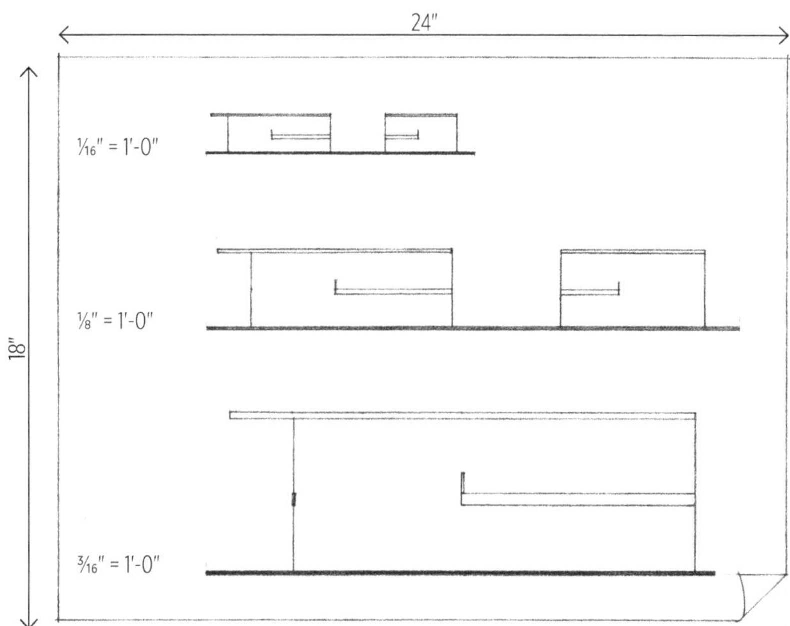

Drawing Composition
Drawing composition involves the thoughtful arrangement of the drawings on a sheet of paper. Before you begin a new drawing, identify the boundaries of the section or sections, using construction lines.

- The ground plane should be consistent across a row of sections. If the ground plane shifts up or down, the base of the sections should also shift up or down.
- Leave a ¾" to 1" margin on all sides of your paper.
- Leave a ¾" to 1" margin between different drawings on the same sheet of paper.
- Compare these sections with the section locations in the key plan.

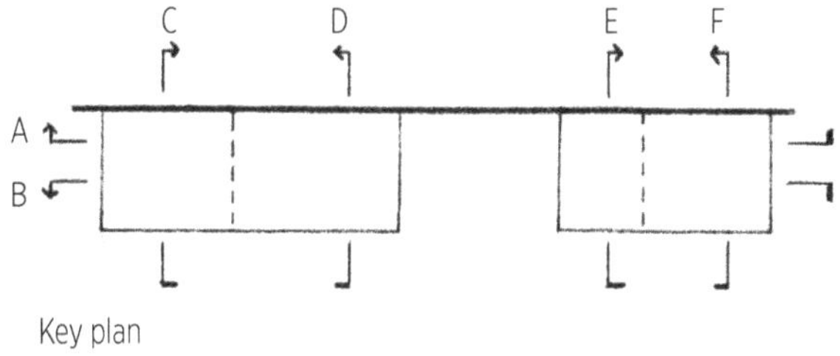

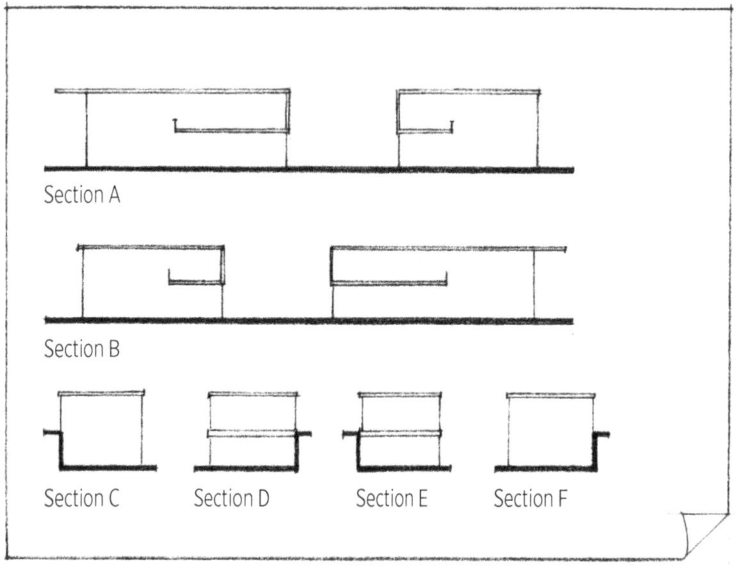

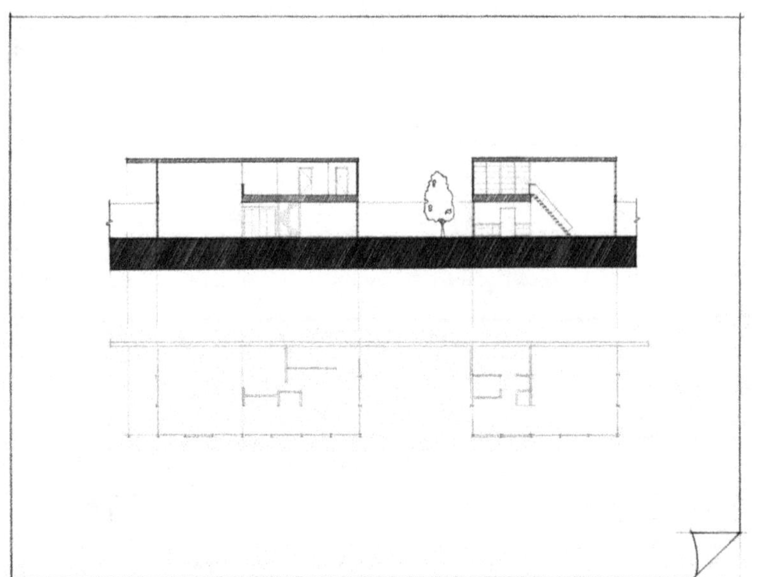

Construction Line Method

- Most sections are constructed from a floor plan drawn on the same sheet of paper.
- Use very light lines to construct the horizontal geometry in the section from the floor plan.
- Use an architectural scale to measure the vertical distances in the building section.

Boundaries and Geometry

When starting a new section, it is important to identify the boundaries of the drawing with construction lines.

- Use construction lines to identify the major geometry of your project.
- In this example the geometry is constructed from a floor plan of the same project.

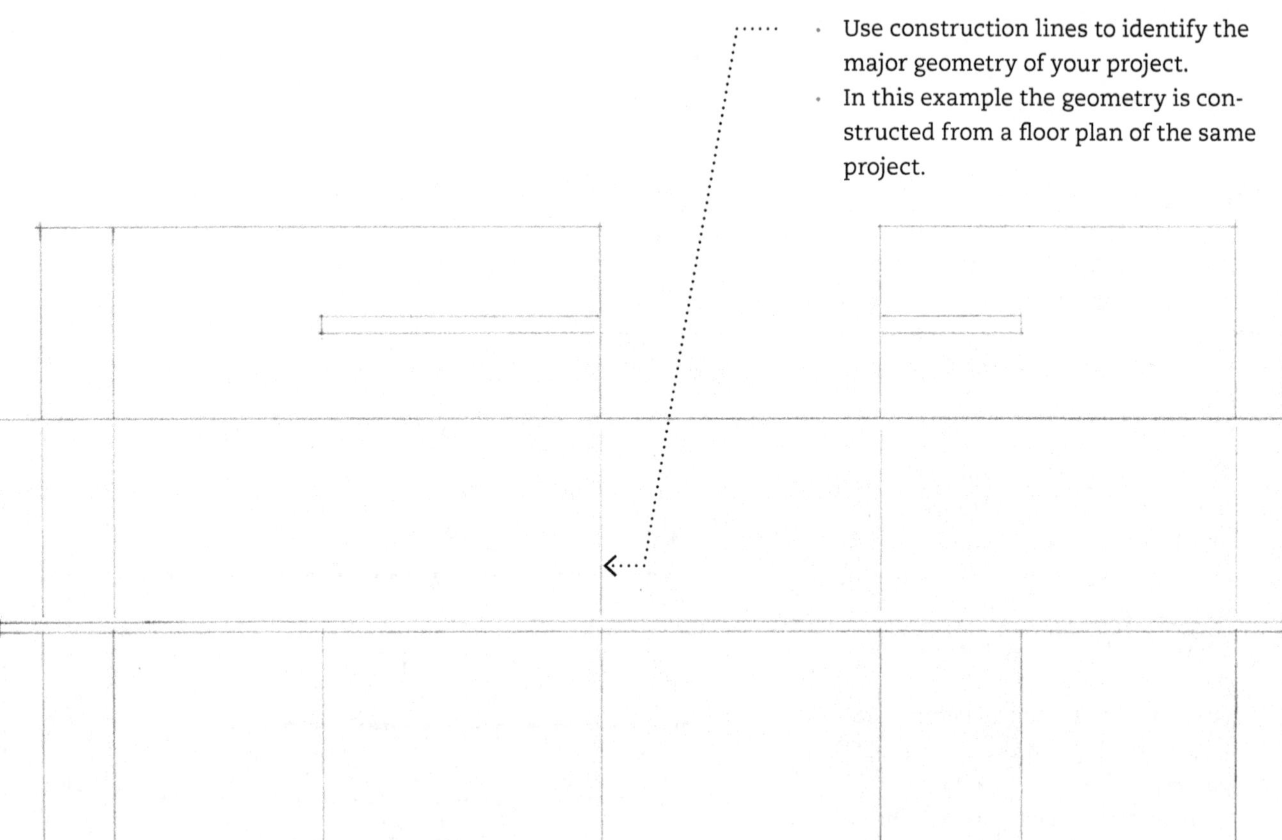

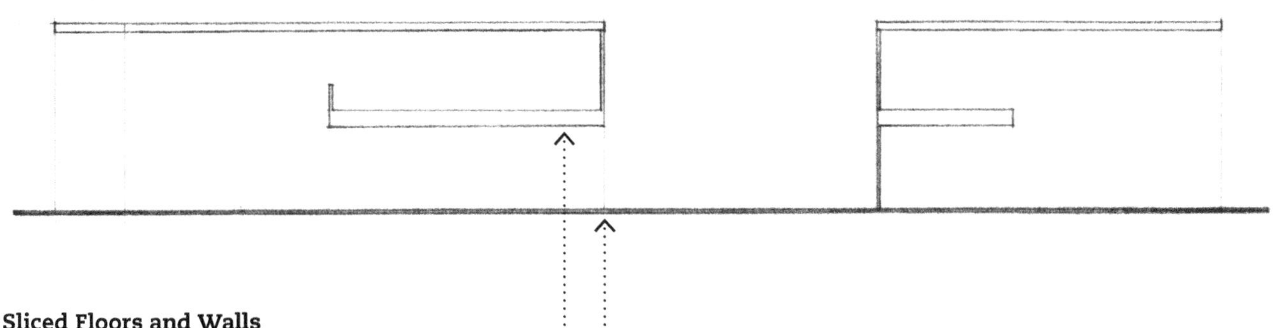

Sliced Floors and Walls
Draw the perimeter around any object that is sliced by the section cut plane.

- Use dark lines to draw all objects sliced by the cut plane, including floors and walls.
- Use a very dark line to draw the ground plane.
- It is important that building sections accurately communicate the proportional difference between wall thickness and ceiling thickness. In most buildings, wall thickness varies from 4" to 10". Floor-to-ceiling thickness varies from 10" to 24".

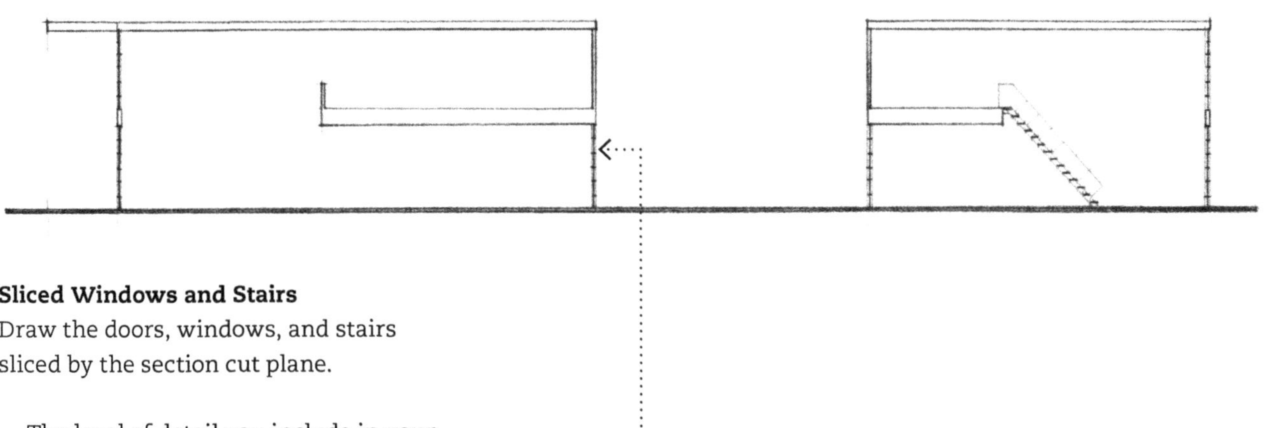

Sliced Windows and Stairs
Draw the doors, windows, and stairs sliced by the section cut plane.

- The level of detail you include in your section drawings will increase with the scale of the drawing.

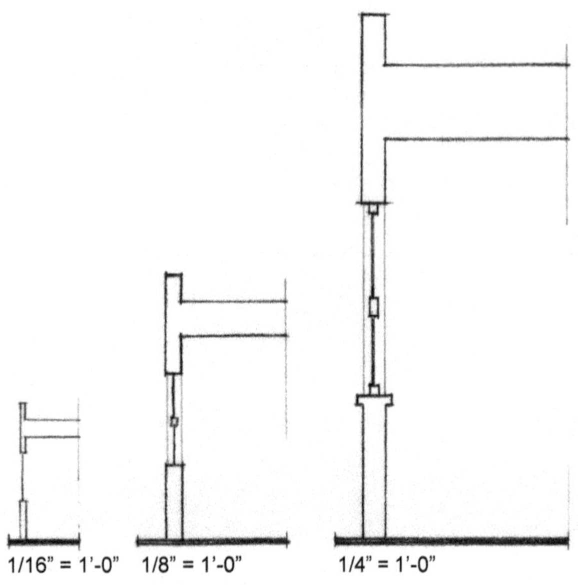

Scale and Detail
The amount of information included in a section drawing is directly related to the scale of the drawing. Larger scale drawings contain more building detail, and smaller scale drawings contain less building detail.

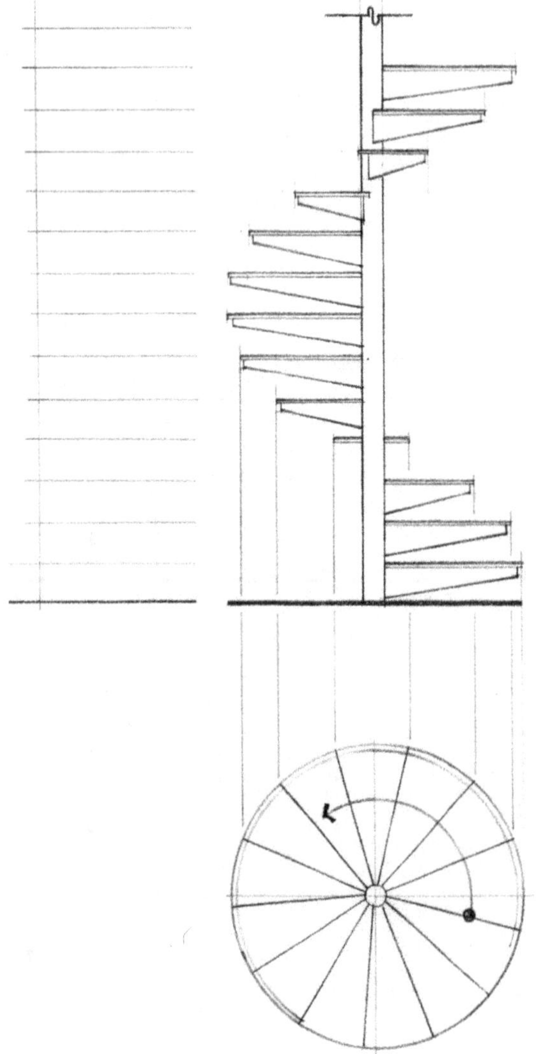

Constructing Complex Shapes
Complex shapes, like this circular stair, can be constructed from an existing plan and elevation drawing. This strategy may be used to construct any complex shape in section when you know both the shape in plan and the vertical height of the object or objects.

- The elevation drawing is used to locate the top of each stair tread and is positioned to the side of the section drawing. Vertical distances can be constructed from this drawing.
- Using medium lines, draw the central support for the circular stair.
- The floor plan is used to locate the edge of each tread in the section drawing.
- Use construction lines to connect the edge of each tread in plan with the top of the tread in elevation.

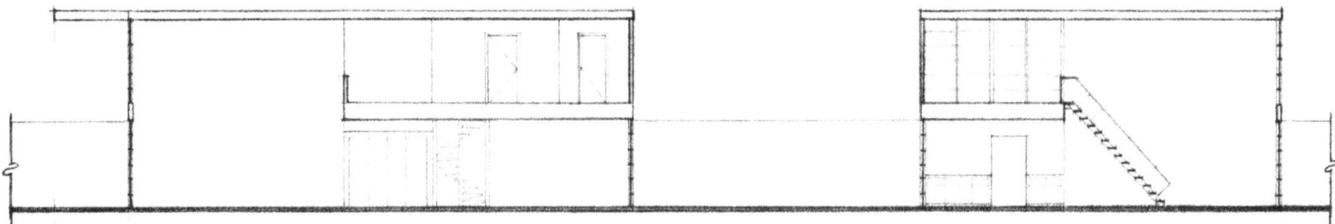

Objects in Elevations
Draw the objects, windows, and doors visible in elevation.

- Use medium lines to draw the perimeter around all objects visible in elevation.
- Use light lines to draw surface patterns and joints between materials that are visible in elevation.

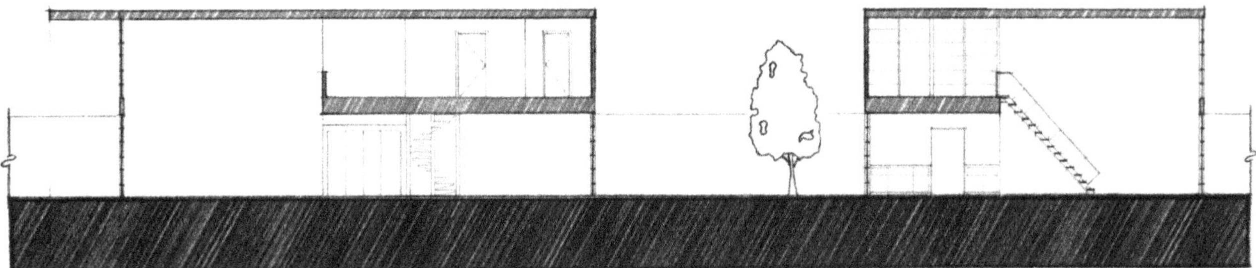

Poché
To communicate space, add tone to the sliced walls, floors, and ceilings in the drawing. This creates contrast between the mass and the void in a project.

- The solid dark tone is added with a soft lead pencil to the front or back of the sheet of paper.
- Grayscale tone is added with multiple angled lines. Depending on the density of the lines, this technique creates different grayscale values for the poché.

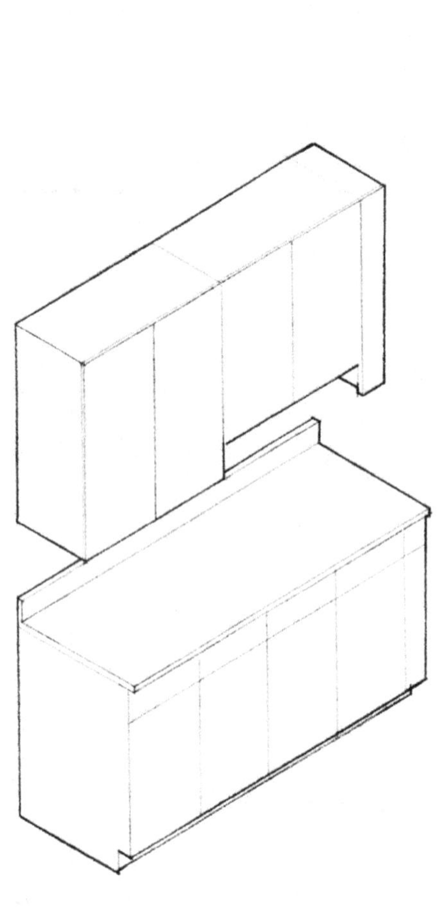

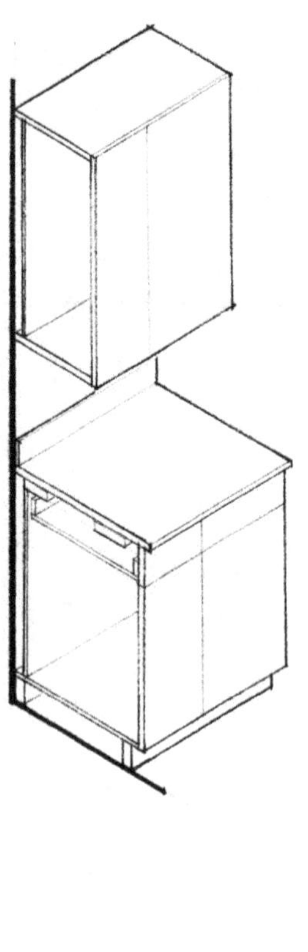

Casework Furniture Sections
Casework furniture sections are submitted to a contractor or fabricator to communicate your design intent. Using your design drawings as the starting point, a contractor or fabricator will redraw your casework elevations at a high level of detail and resubmit these detailed drawings for your approval.

- The most common casework elevations are kitchen and bathroom cabinets.
- Casework sections are also used to design and communicate any furniture attached to the building, including bookcases, entertainment centers, and custom seating.
- These details are usually drawn between ¾" = 1'-0" and 1 ½" = 1'-0". On very complex designs, portions of the furniture may be drawn at full scale.

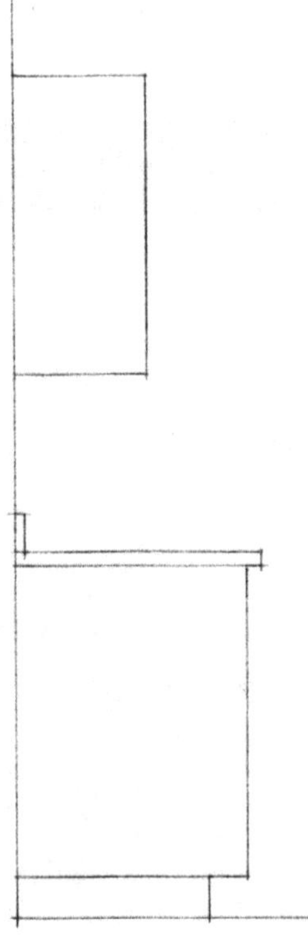

Boundaries and Geometry
When starting a new casework section, it is important to identify the boundaries of the drawing with construction lines.

- Use construction lines to identify the major geometry of your design.

Thickness of Material

- Use dark lines to draw the thickness of all the materials in your furniture detail. Most cabinets are made from plywood or medium-density fiberboard (MDF) that is laminated with wood veneer or plastic laminates. The thickness of this wood is usually ½".
- Use a very dark line to draw the ground plane. If the furniture is attached to a wall, draw the location of the wall with a single very dark line.

Material Hatches

In section details, materials are identified by standard hatch patterns. These patterns are drawn for any material that is sliced by the section plane.

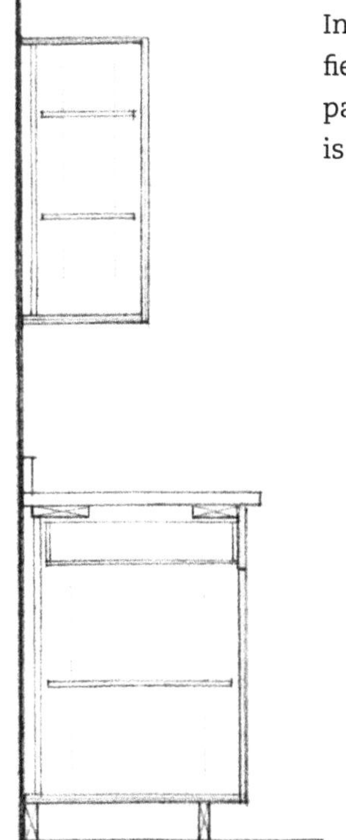

Standard Hatch Patterns

The following patterns are appropriate for objects sliced in furniture sections and construction details.

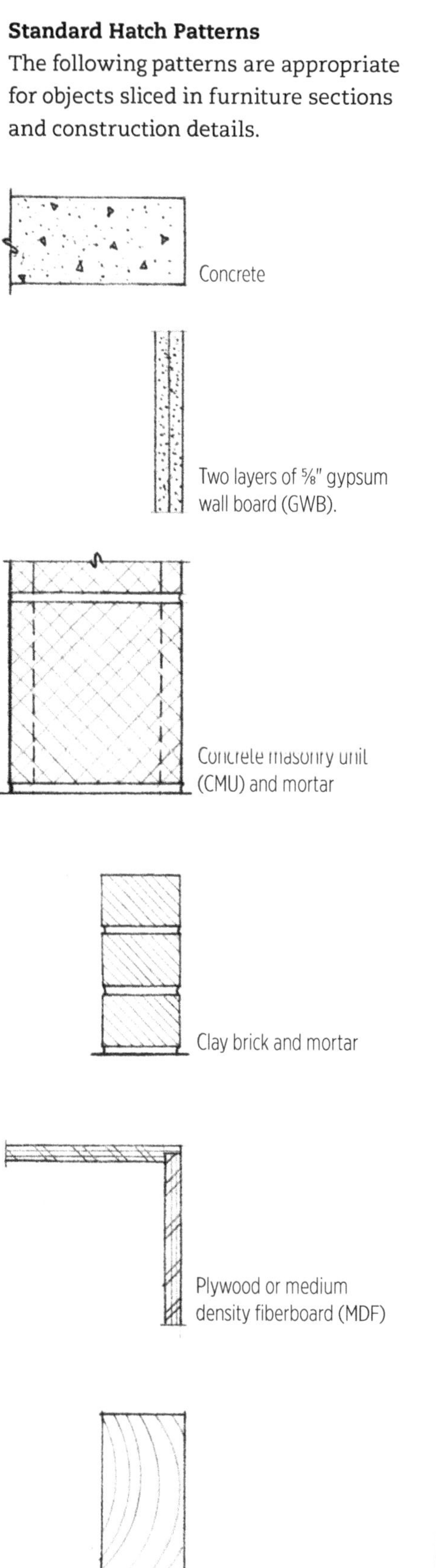

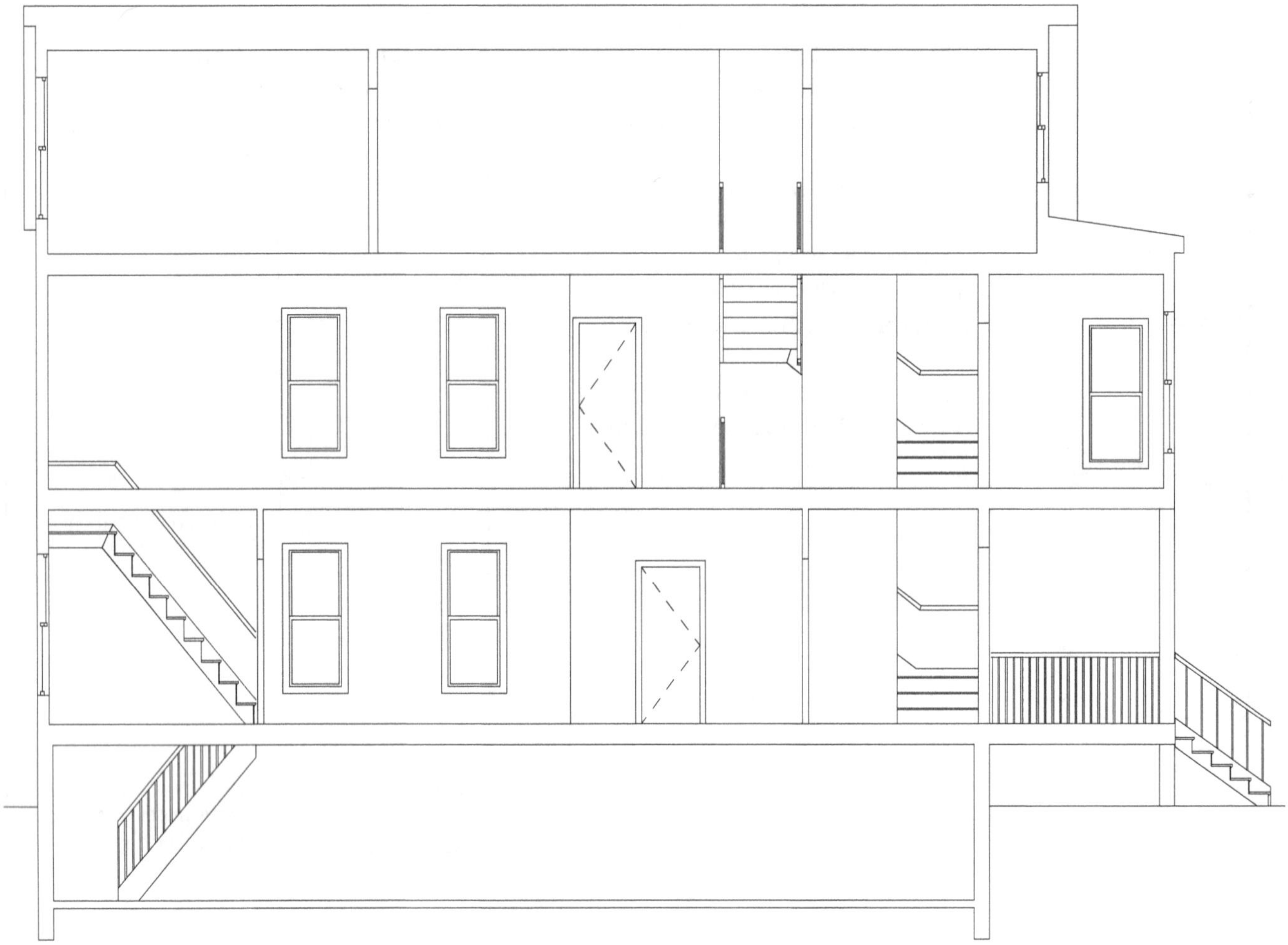

Section A
Scale: ¼" = 1'-0"

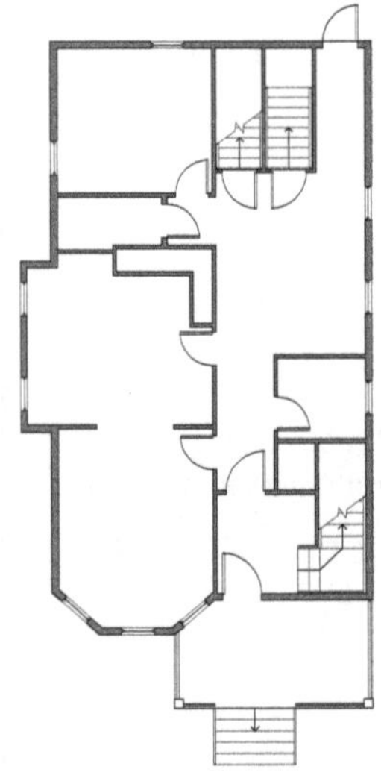

Key plan

Learning Exercise: Line Weight
This exercise is intended to help you improve your understanding of line weight in communicating the spatial properties of a building section.

- Identify the location of this section in the key plan.
- Using a dark line, carefully trace over all the sliced walls and floors in this drawing.
- Using a medium line, carefully trace over the profile lines in this drawing.
- Use poché to fill the walls and floors in this drawing.

Learning Exercise: Drawing Sections
This exercise is intended to help you improve your understanding of constructing sections.

- On the facing page, construct section B as indicated by the section line in the floor plan.
- Draw section B at ¼" = 1'-0".

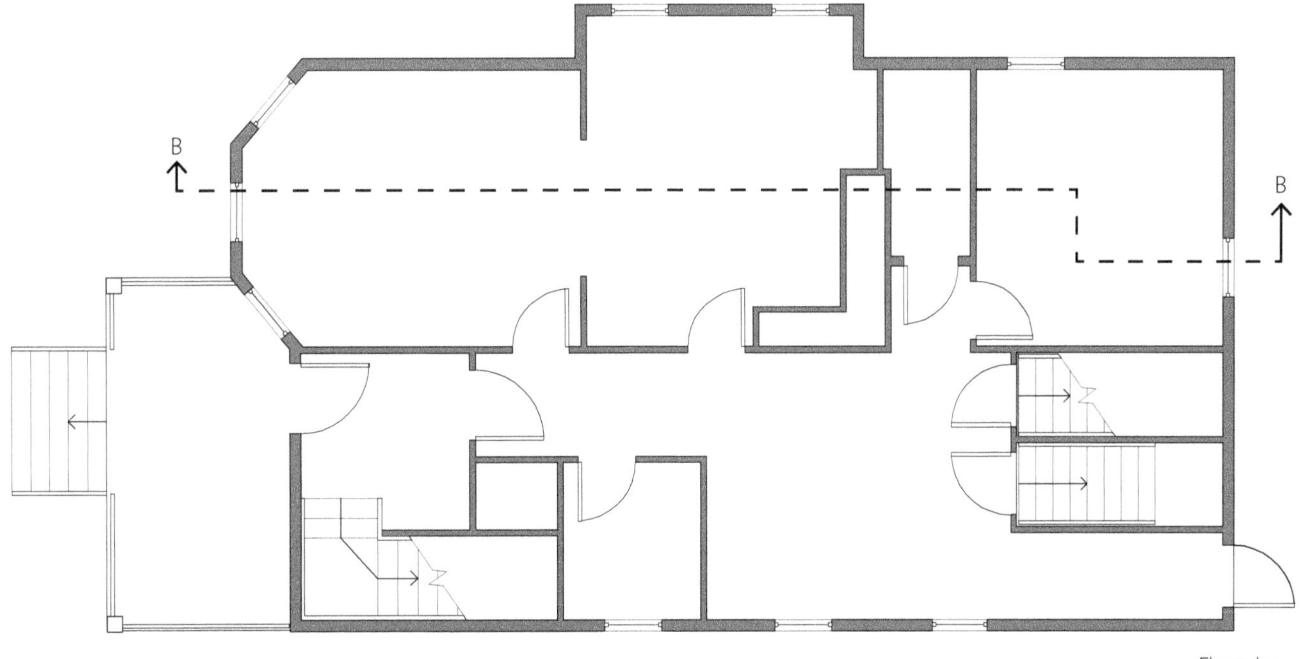

Floor plan
Scale: ¼" = 1'-0"

EXTERIOR AND INTERIOR ELEVATIONS

This chapter introduces students to both interior and exterior elevations. The instruction directly addresses what students and instructors are trying to accomplish in the design studio: the translation of three-dimensional ideas into two-dimensional presentation drawings.

Some designers use the elevation drawing as a primary tool for design. Other designers use the elevation drawing at the end of a project to communicate the proportional organization or ideas in constructed models. Regardless of when you introduce elevations in your design process, it is an important tool for refining and clarifying your design ideas and intent.

In the professional design office, elevations are used in a set of construction documents to communicate both vertical measurements and surface patterns that are not evident in the floor plan. In addition to drawing the interior and exterior surfaces of a design project, elevations are also used to communicate the design intent for cabinets, fixtures, and furniture in interior design.

Consider the following questions as you read this chapter:

- How is hand drawing used in both school and in professional practice to explore, develop, and communicate ideas?
- What are the fundamental conventions used to construct elevation drawings?
- How do elevation drawings support the design process?

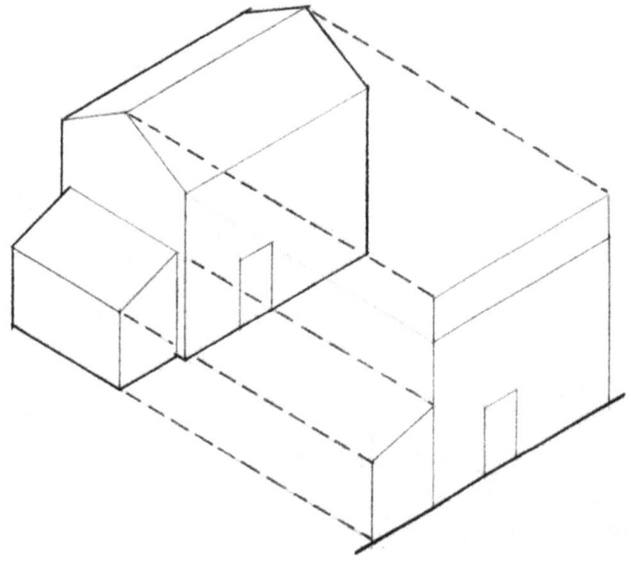

Exterior Elevations

The exterior elevation is a scaled oblique projection drawing of a building's exterior surface. Objects that parallel the building surface are drawn to scale with the same proportion they appear to have in real life. Objects that do not parallel the building surface (like a sloped roof) appear distorted in an exterior elevation.

These drawings are often drawn at 1/16" = 1'-0" or 1/8" = 1'-0" and contain enough graphic information to visually communicate the location of doors, windows, and materials on the exterior surface of a building.

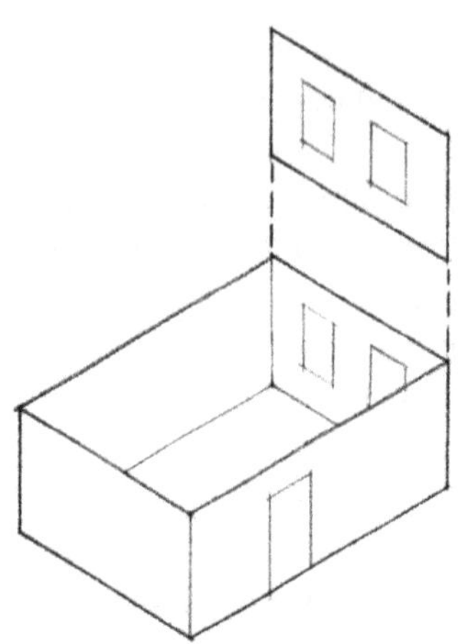

Interior Elevations

The interior elevation is also a scaled oblique projection drawing of the walls inside a room.

These drawings are often drawn at 1/8" = 1'-0" or 1/4" = 1'-0" and contain enough graphic information to visually communicate the location of doors, windows, openings, woodwork, and materials on the interior surface of a room. Interior elevations are also used in the design profession to identify the location of wall switches, electrical outlets, and bathroom fixtures.

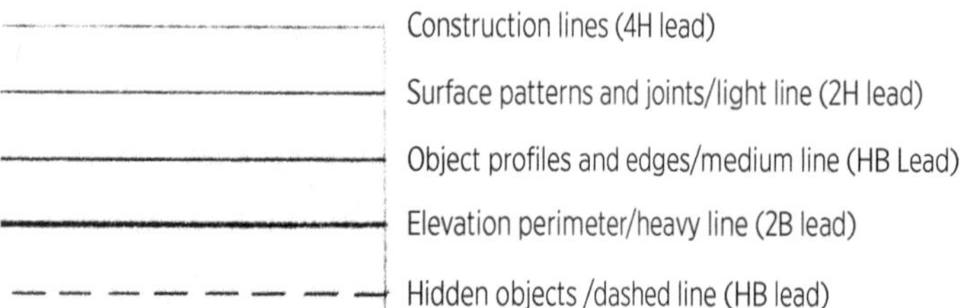

Line Weight

Designers communicate the three-dimensional space represented in elevations through clear and legible line weight.

- When drafting by hand, adjust line thickness by adjusting the type of lead in your pencil, the thickness of your pen, and the pressure applied to the paper.

Ideation through Hand Drawing

As with the other drawing conventions, elevation drawings develop from large ideas about scale and proportion. They evolve into more refined drawings that describe surface material and locate wall openings including windows and doors.

Initial elevation drawings are loosely drawn by hand. They clarify ideas of scale and proportion as they relate to site conditions and the floor plan. Through the design process, these hand drawings are refined to address the programmatic requirements for a particular elevation.

This ideation process is developed through the rapid and thoughtful execution of multiple hand drawings. These hand drawings should be proportionally accurate, drawn to an approximate architectural scale, and use line weight that is appropriate for an elevation drawing.

Hand and Digital Drafting

At some point in the design process, you will need to create a more precise drawing for a presentation, client meeting, or set of construction drawings. Using the accuracy of a drafting table or computer drafting software, you can quickly translate your hand drawings into drafted elevations that contain appropriate line weight and that conform to drawing conventions. These more precise drawings often contain additional information, such as material patterns, notes, and dimensions.

It is important to note that a strong elevation is measured both in its technical accuracy and in the strength of the design solution. Loose hand drawings remain the most effective method for exploring, refining, and strengthening a design drawing. Hand-drafted or digitally drafted drawings are the most effective methods for creating technically accurate and consistent elevation drawings.

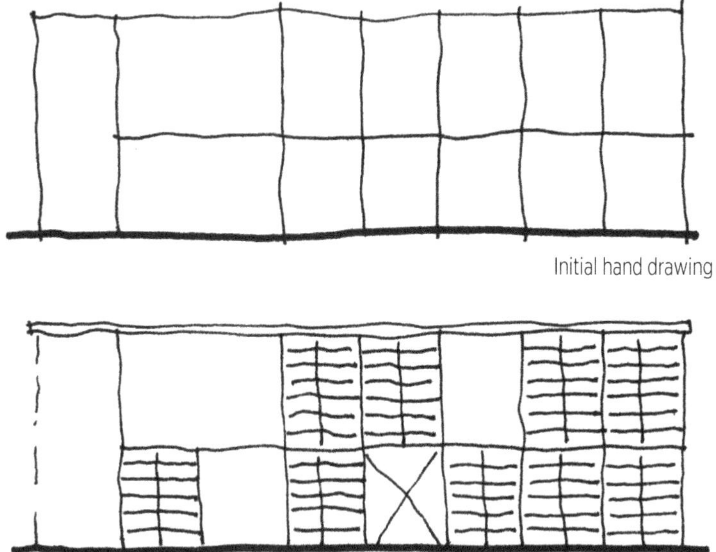

Initial hand drawing

Refined hand drawing

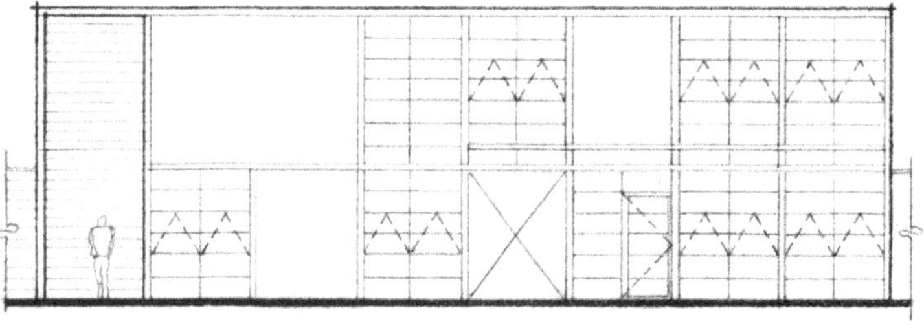

Hand-drafted elevation

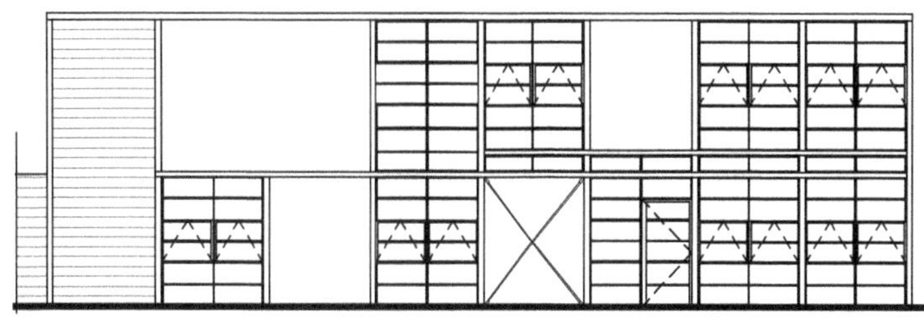

Digitally drafted elevation

CHARLES (1907–78) AND RAY (1912–88) EAMES
Eames House (1949)
Drawings by Douglas Seidler

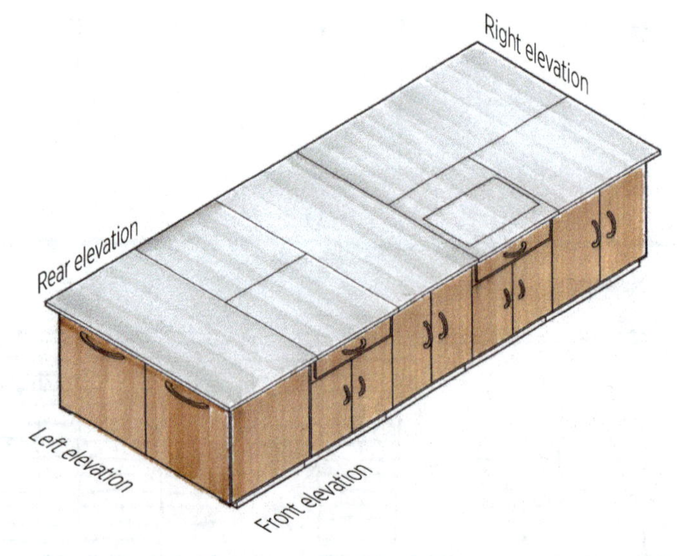

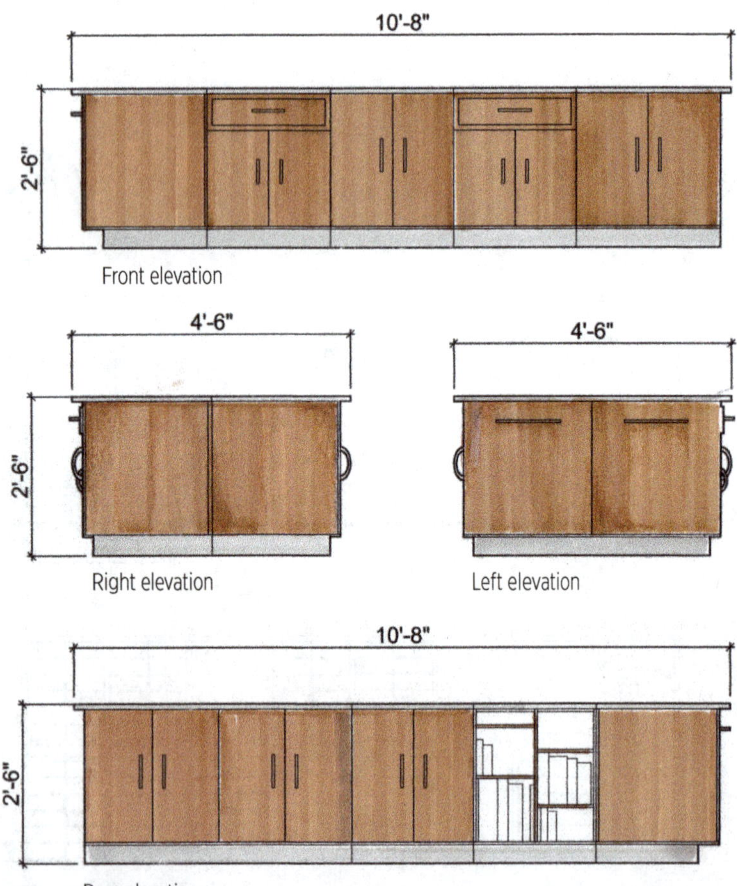

KATE MCGOLDRICK

Furniture elevations

Furniture and Detailing Studio,
The New England School of
Art & Design at Suffolk University

The concept development sketches provided a way of capturing several initial ideas that would meet the constraints of the lamp design assignment. The addition of the human figure enabled the sketches to be drawn with a sense of the intended proportions for each fixture, and that, in turn, provided a first pass at the exact sizes I would need to make each component when I constructed an actual model of the lamp.

In the modeling process, I made some changes in the lamp's proportions. The section-elevation presentation drawing was a way of communicating how I constructed the model, since after the model was built, its construction method was no longer visible.

—Tamison Rose

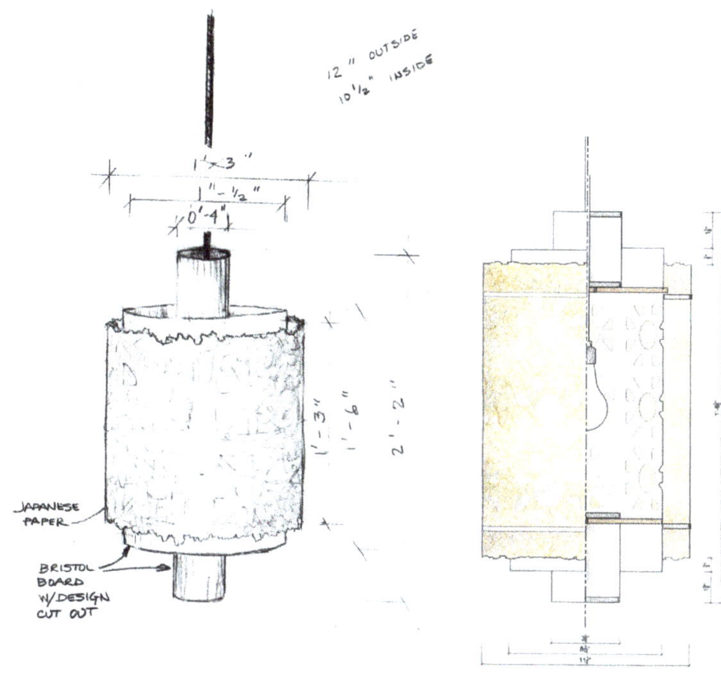

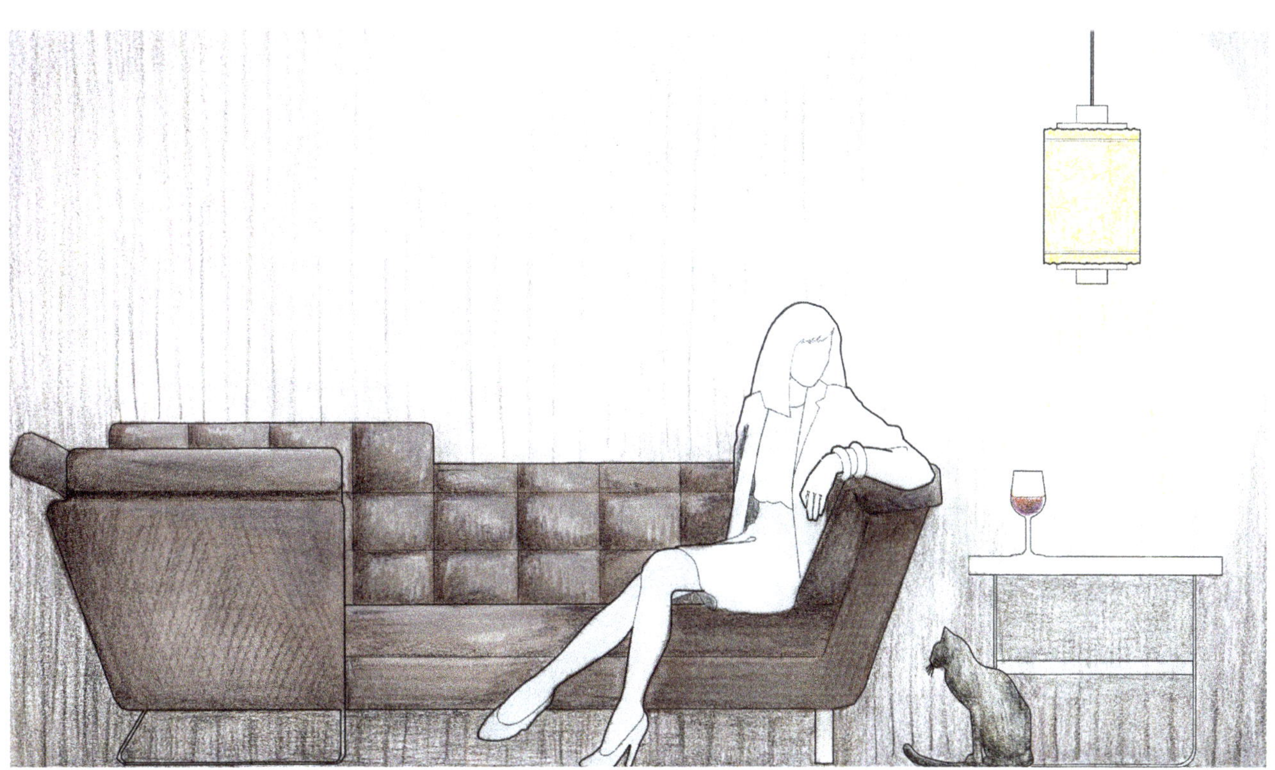

Tamison Rose

Lamp design

Furniture and Detailing Studio, The New England School of Art & Design at Suffolk University

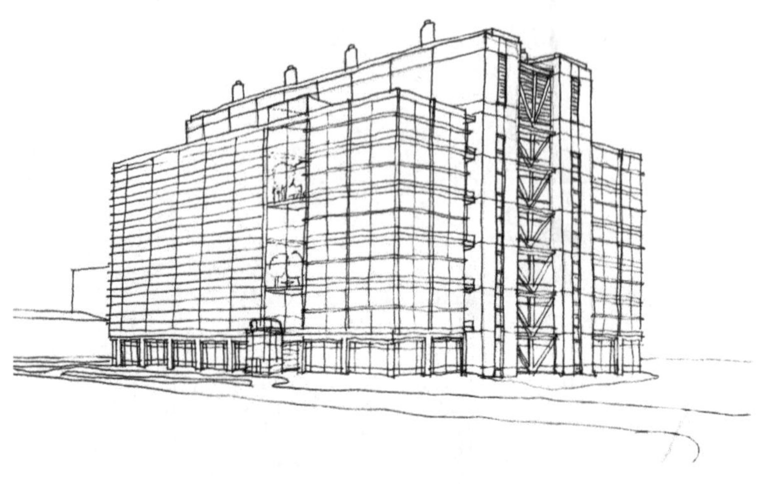

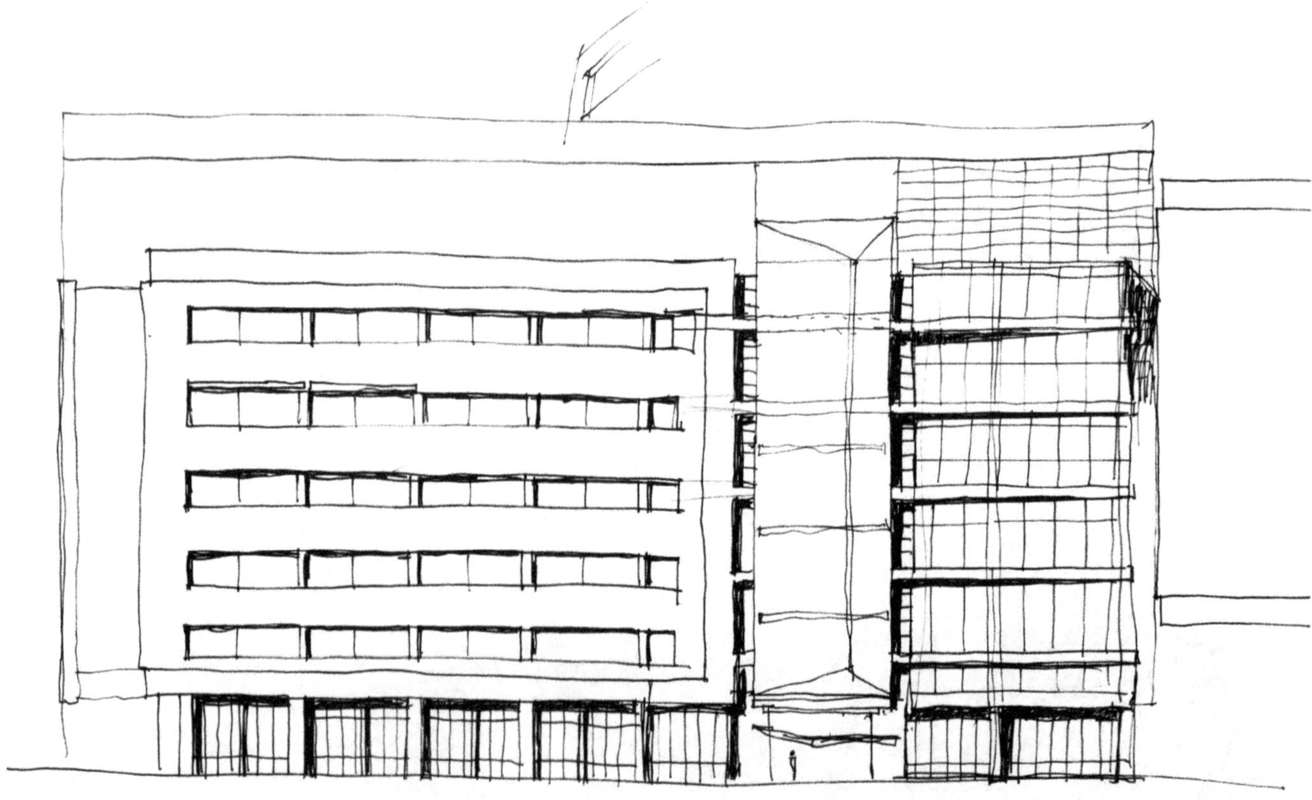

CHRISTOPHER ANGELAKIS
Elevation ideation drawings
ARC/Architectural Resources Cambridge

For me, to draw is to discover and to draw by hand allows for a stronger connection between my conceptual ideas and the actual drawing. When I am drawing with the computer, I tend to think more about the act of drawing than the actual drawing. When I draw by hand, I am free to intuitively explore larger design concepts.

When I design, I iterate a specific drawing multiple times, trying never to draw anything the same way twice. I'm not making changes to change the project as much as I use the drawings to study unique solutions to see how I may be able to use them in the future.

In these elevations, we were studying the nature of different kinds of glazing. In the drawing there are three primary glazing areas: the large curtain wall on the left of the elevation, the vertical entry, and the smaller office block on the right of the elevation.

All of these elevations are drawn by hand and presented to our client as various design options. We rendered the bottom image to begin the conversation with our client about the use of material on this project.

—CHRISTOPHER ANGELAKIS

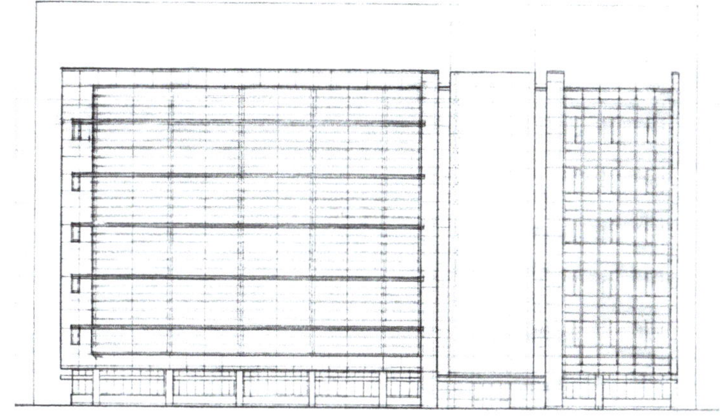

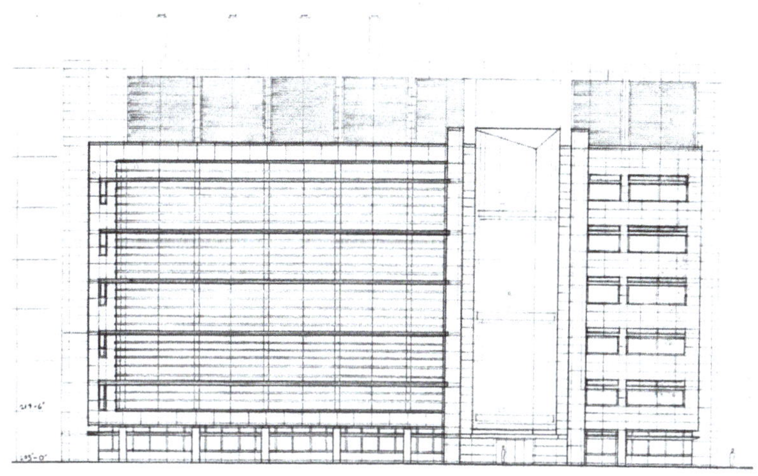

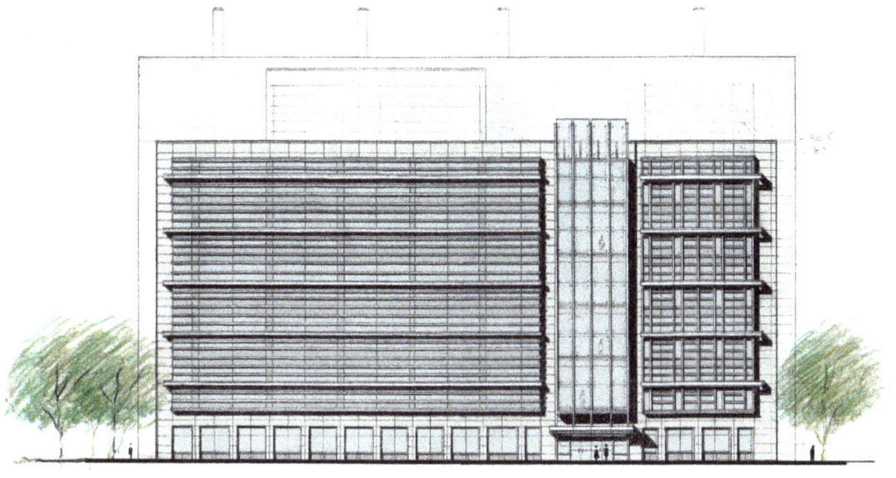

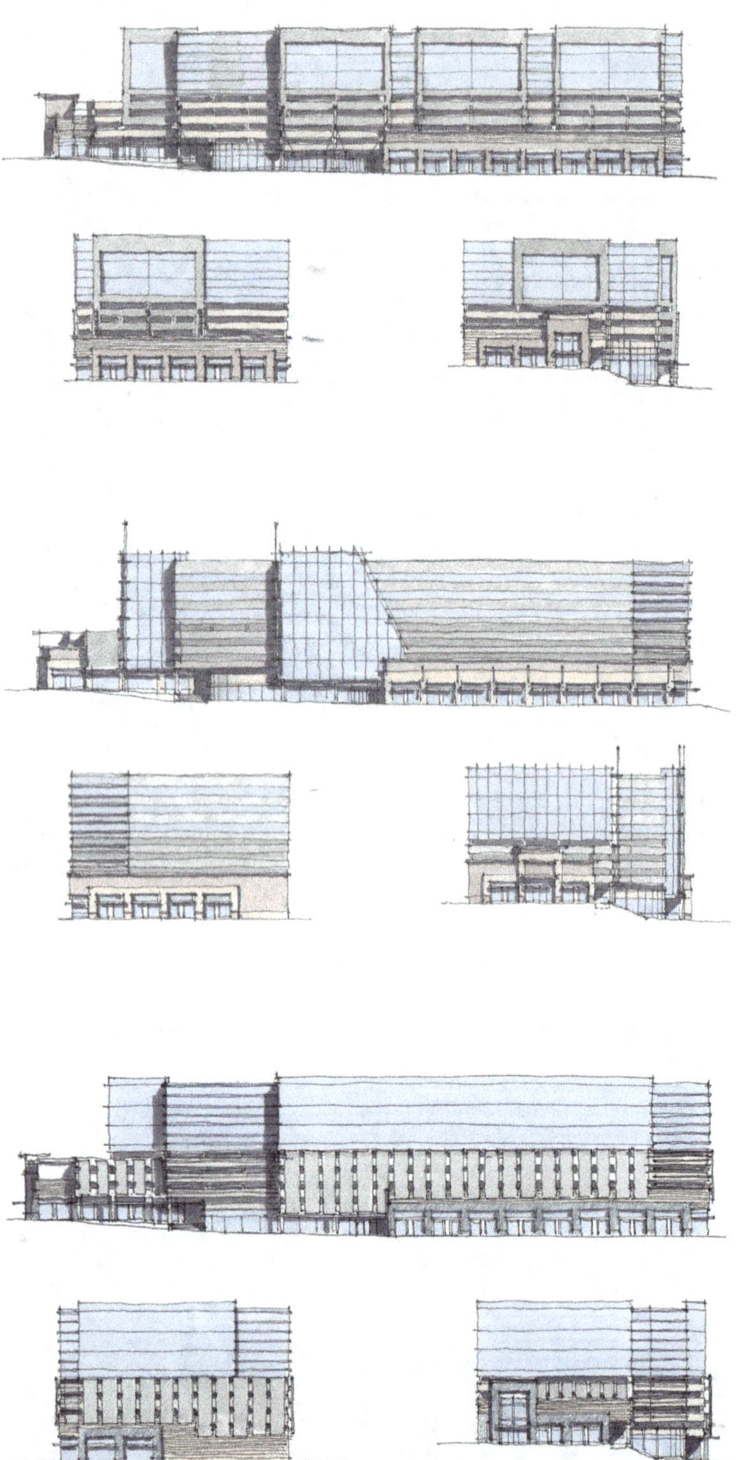

JOHN RUFO
Elevation studies for mixed-use building
Arrowstreet

Elevations have always been my favorite kind of design drawing because it is exact and rigorous while also conveying a diagrammatic essence of the building exterior. As a visual tool, it is able to both explore ideas quickly for the designer as well as convey the idea effectively to a client. On most projects I will try to explore a few distinct ideas at the same time and use elevations to convey the pros and cons to the design team and the client.

Delineation of materials is done primarily through layering colors to try to convey transparency and opacity. Cast shadows are critical to convey mass and highlights are important to express edges that will literally catch the light and help create a certain dynamic quality to the form.

On this project in particular the task of massing the office above parking, above retail in a building with a very large footprint, is really daunting. The elevation studies were an important part of identifying a strategy of exterior design that mitigates the massing issues and supports the goals of a modern building with multiple uses.

—JOHN RUFO

This project's big challenge was marrying the rigorous grid of the existing concrete building with something that had to be inherently different for construction purposes. Through the process of creating these drawings, one of the things that happened was a discovery of how the existing building was designed. The act of drawing gave me an intimate understanding of the system of the existing building so I could then pick up on that system and integrate the modules of our new addition. The new and the old fit together seamlessly.

Each of these elevations looks at a specific issue while also making slight modifications to the larger idea, allowing other ideas to influence the larger scheme. The first two elevations only have minor differences. We are looking at how we place objects on the facade and the elevations' proportional relationships. The third elevation looked more closely at the end elevation and contains a unique scheme for the base of the building.

—CHRISTOPHER ANGELAKIS

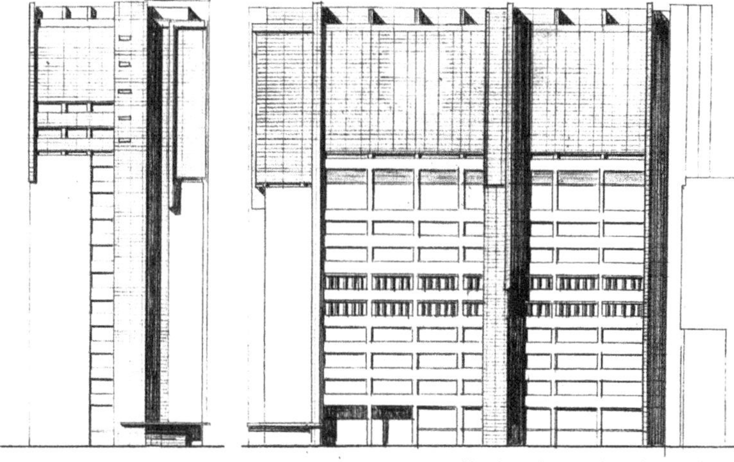

North and west elevation study 5a

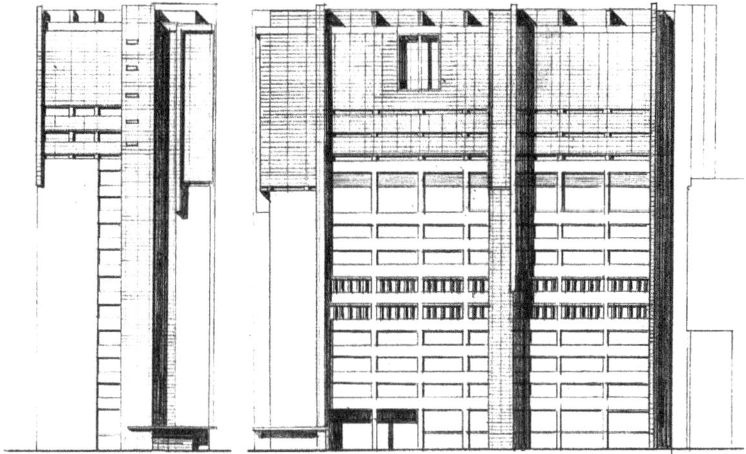

North and west elevation study 5b

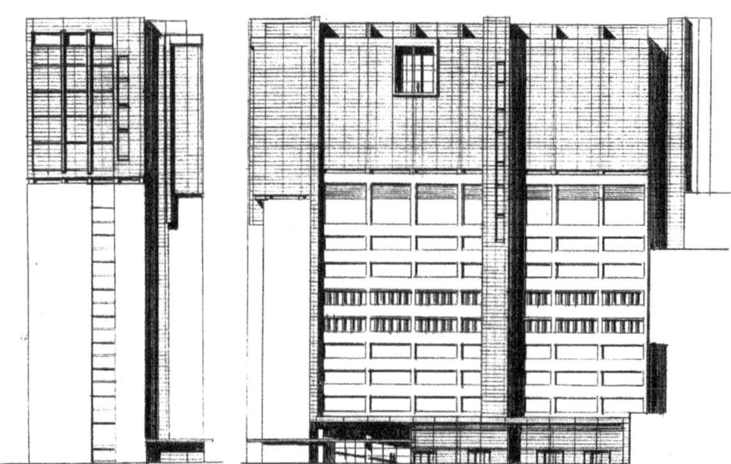

North and west elevation study 6

CHRISTOPHER ANGELAKIS
Elevation ideation drawings
ARC/Architectural Resources Cambridge

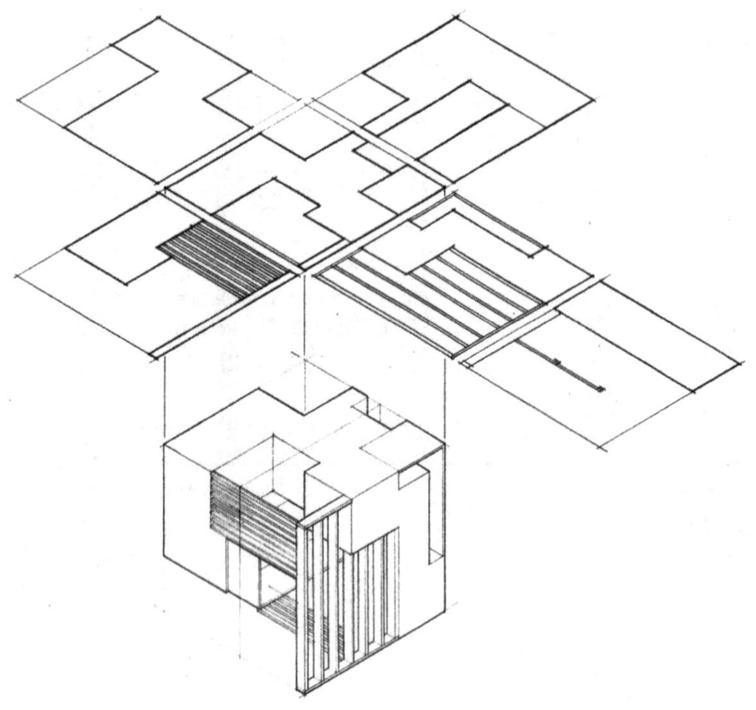

Design Elevations

In early foundation design projects, like the 9" cube model, you may begin a design exploration through a physical model and then further develop the project with elevation drawings. The elevation drawings you complete are oblique projections of your model.

The elevation drawing is an opportunity to visually communicate the spatial relationships, scale of occupation, and proportions in a project.

- The six elevations of this cube model are unfolded to illustrate the relationship between each elevation and the corresponding surface on the model.

In this and other foundation design projects, the elevation drawing is also an opportunity to refine and clarify your project, based on the new information revealed through these drawings.

- As you draw elevations, evaluate the spatial conditions and proportions visible in the drawing. Compare this evaluation with your original design intentions, which can be gleaned in built model or in written conceptual statements.
- Rotating an elevation drawing may reveal new and interesting spatial conditions already present in your project. In this series of the same elevation drawing, each is rotated 90 degrees.

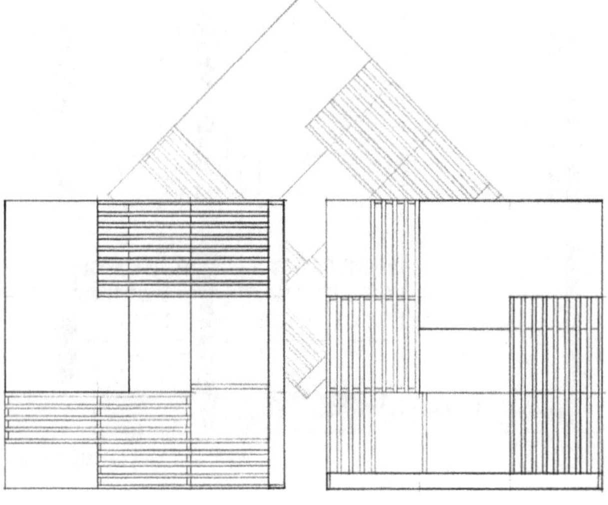

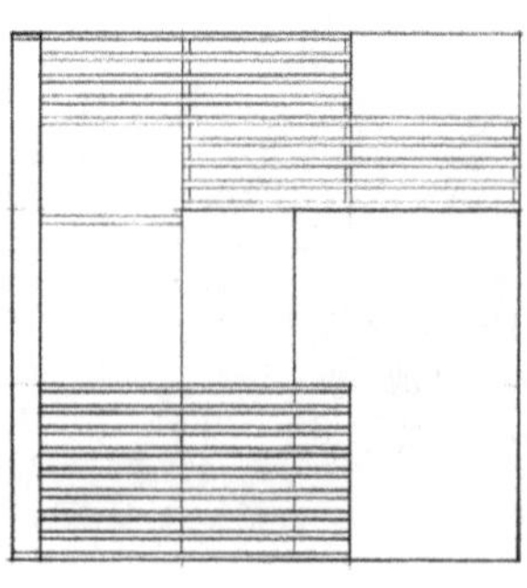

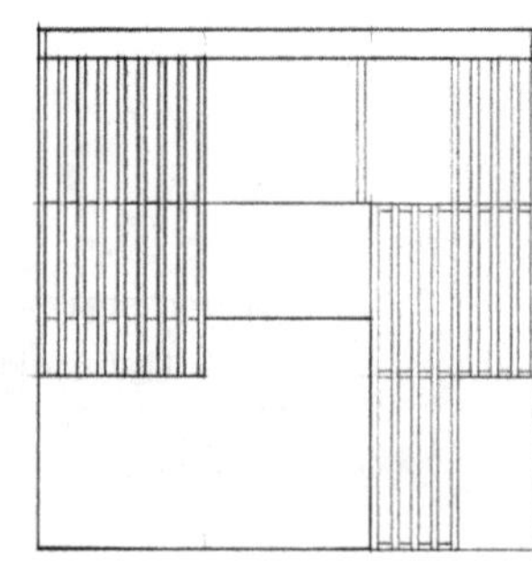

Drawing Elevations

A strong understanding of architectural graphic standards is critical for clearly communicating and developing design ideas through elevation. The remaining portion of this chapter introduces drawing techniques, terminology, and graphic standards. The goal is to increase your understanding and your ability to draw legible elevations, including interior elevations and exterior building elevations.

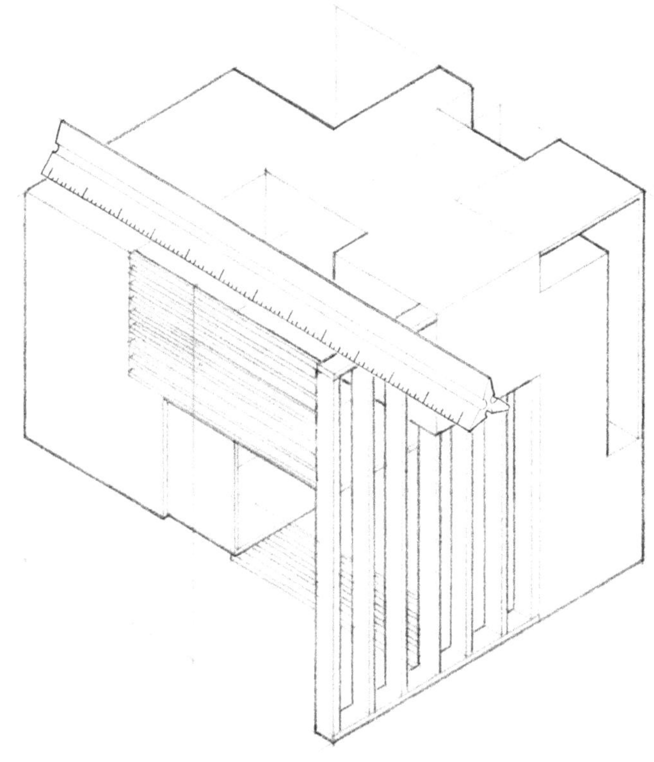

Constructing Elevations from a Design Model

In foundation design studio it is common for elevations to be drawn at the same scale as the physical model.

- Use an architectural scale or ruler to measure your model and construct your elevation drawing. Objects that are 3" wide in the model will be 3" wide in the drawing.
- In this example the cube model measures 9" wide, and the elevation is drawn 9" wide.
- Drawings are thoughtfully arranged on the sheet of paper, with an appropriate margin on all four sides of each drawing.

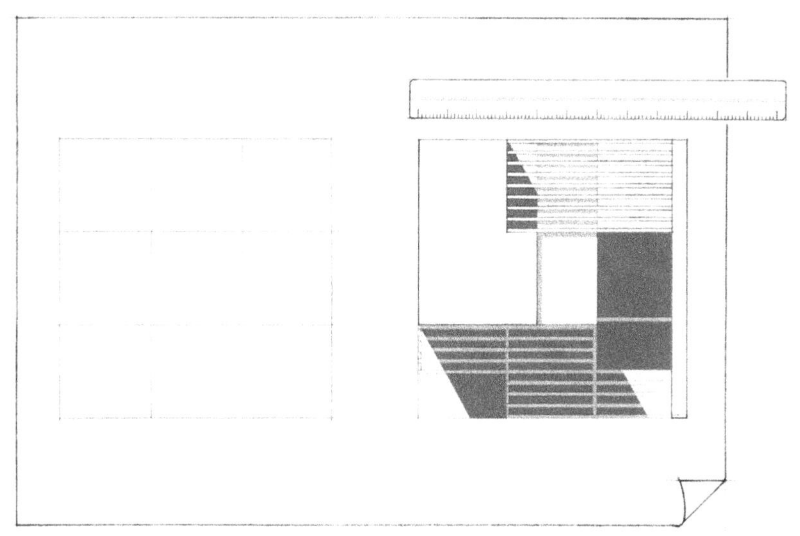

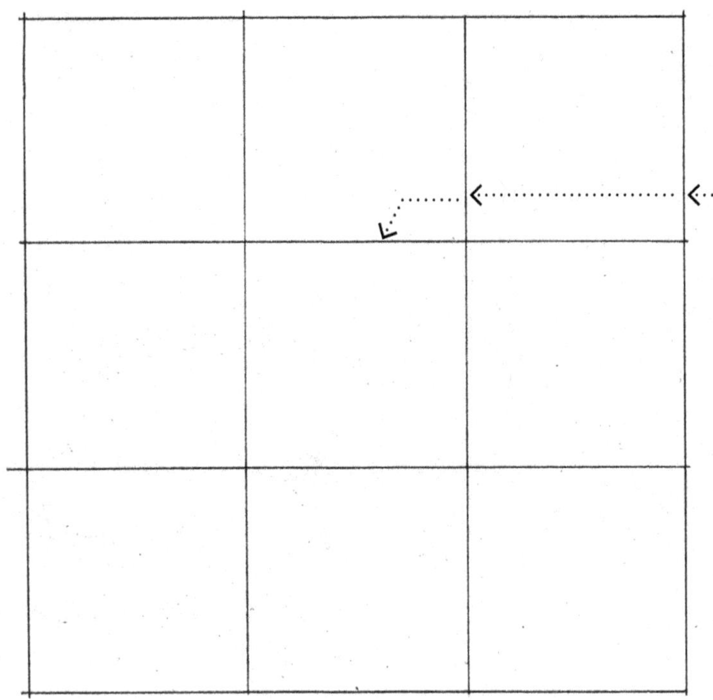

Boundaries and Geometry
When starting a new elevation, it is important to identify the boundaries of the drawing with construction lines.

- Use construction lines to identify the major geometry of your model.
- In this example the 9"× 9" square is divided into nine 3" modules.

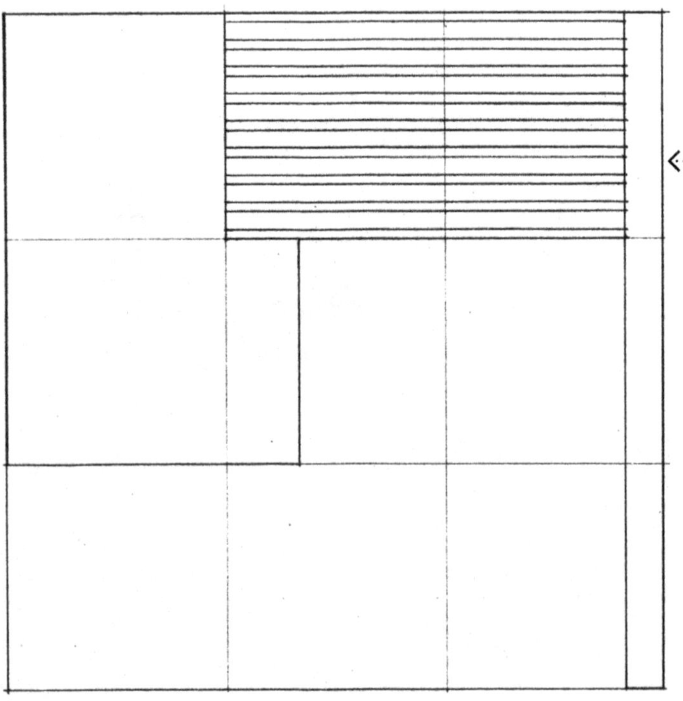

Objects on the Elevation Surface
Draw the perimeter around any object that is on the model's elevated surface.

- Use medium lines to draw all objects that are on the elevated surface. These lines identify the spatial edge of each object in elevation.

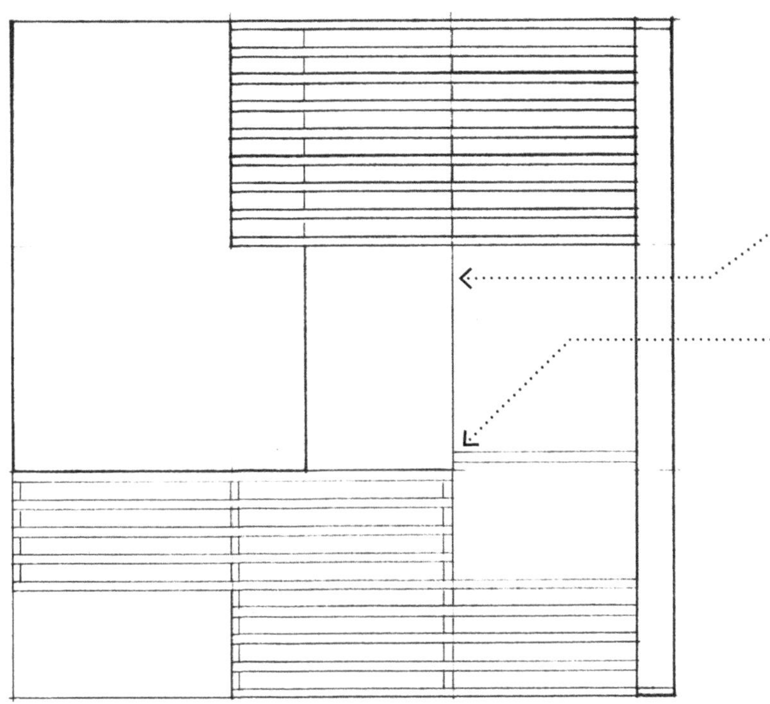

Objects beyond the Elevation Surface
Draw the perimeter around any object that is beyond the primary surface of the elevation and that is visible in elevation.

- Use light lines to draw the perimeter around all objects visible beyond the elevation surface.
- Use light lines to draw surface patterns and joints between materials that are visible in elevation.

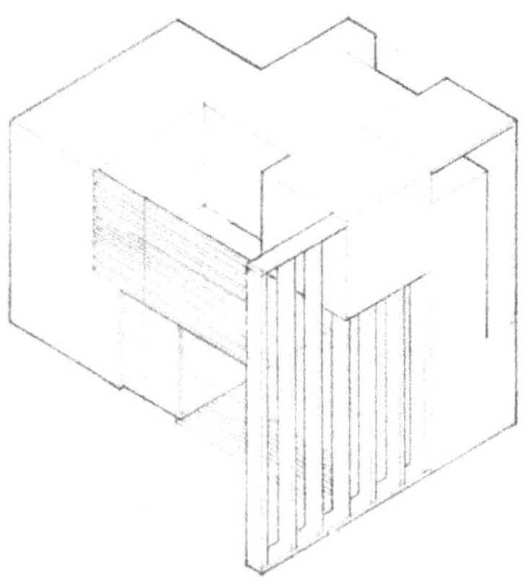

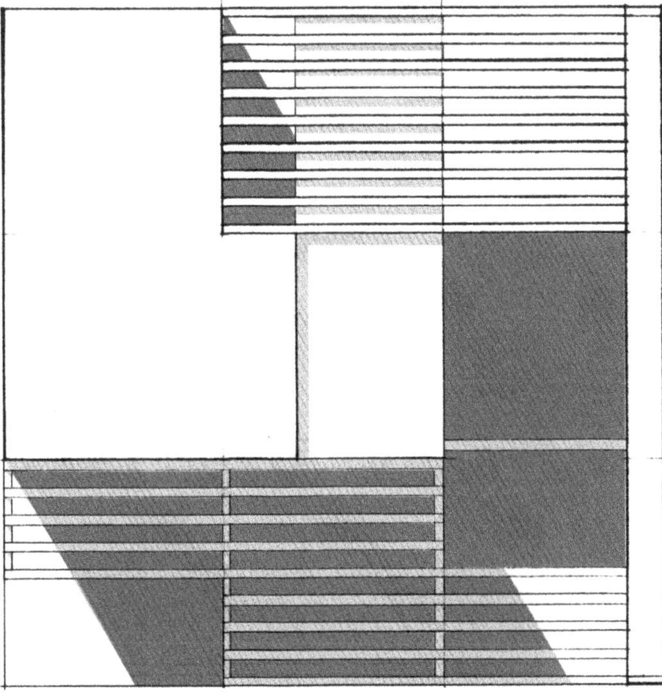

Shadows
Shadows communicate the space in an elevation by implying the depth between parallel surfaces in elevation.

- The solid dark tone is added with a soft lead pencil to the front or back of the sheet of paper.
- Grayscale tone is added with multiple angled lines. Depending on the density of the lines, this technique creates different grayscale values for the poché.

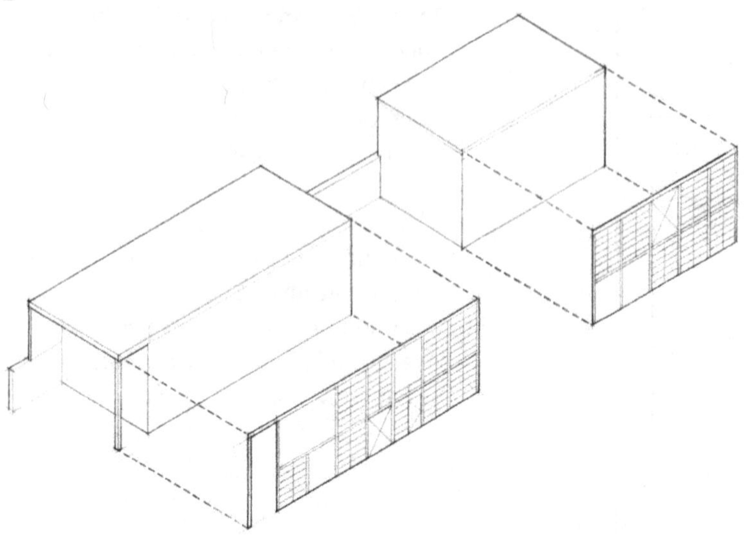

Exterior Building Elevations
The exterior building elevation is an opportunity to reveal proportions and exterior spatial relationships in a design project. Depending on the individual project and your design process, these drawings may be completed at the beginning, middle, or end of a design project.

- Exterior elevations are oblique projections of your building surface.
- Exterior elevation drawings are usually drawn parallel to a perimeter surface or wall.

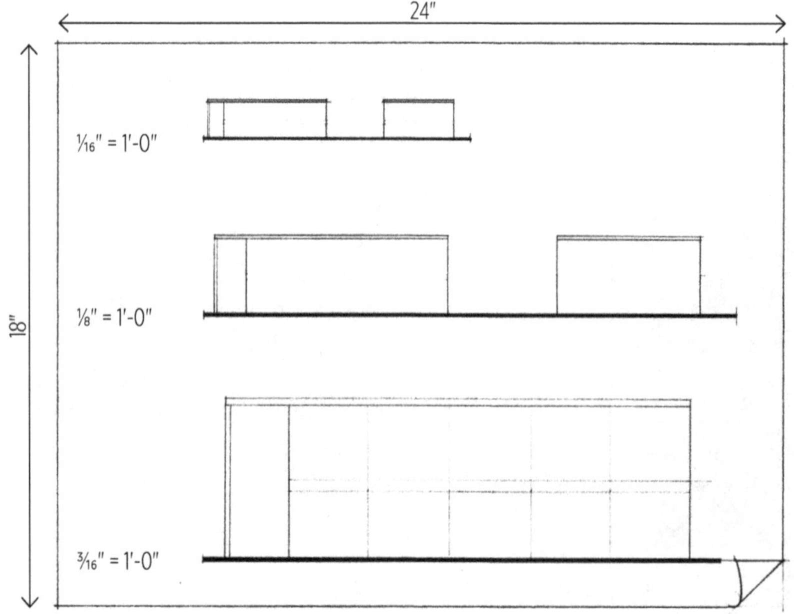

Drawing Scale

- Calculate the drawn size of your exterior elevation to determine what size sheet of paper you will need to complete your drawing.
- Exterior elevations drawn at a larger scale occupy a larger portion of the paper.
- In this example the 1/8" = 1'-0" drawing is the most appropriate size for the selected 18" × 24" sheet of paper.

Scale and Detail

The amount of information included in an elevation drawing is directly related to the scale of the drawing. Larger scale drawings contain more building detail, and smaller scale drawings contain less building detail.

- In the 1/16" = 1'-0" drawing, window mullions are drawn with a single line, and the operable windows with a dashed "swing line."
- In the 1/8" = 1'-0" drawing, window mullions are drawn with two lines, and the operable windows are clearly drawn as a separate part of the window system.
- In the 3/16" = 1'-0" drawing, the vertical steel columns accurately include the thickness of the steel W section. The window systems are accurately drawn and indicate the proper relationships between the vertical and horizontal mullions.

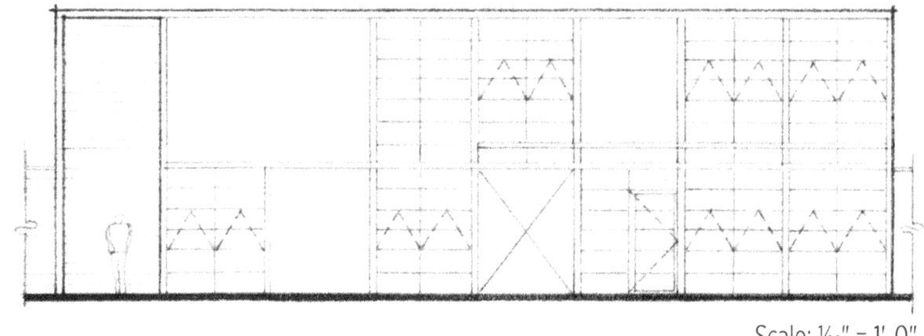

Scale: 1/16" = 1'-0"

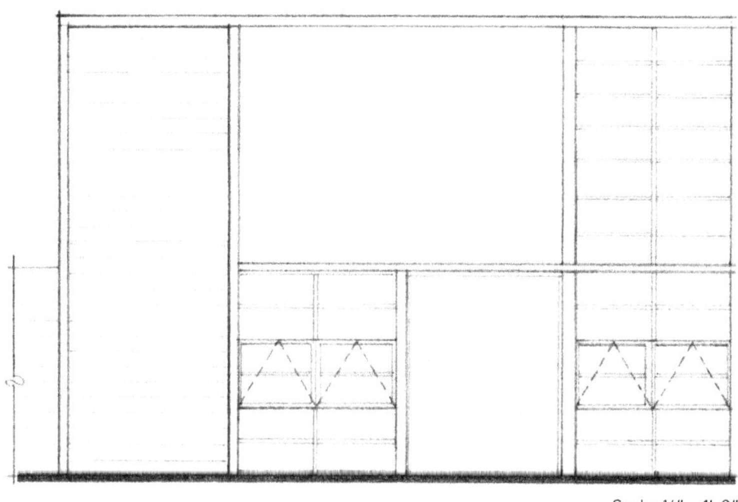

Scale: 1/8" = 1'-0"

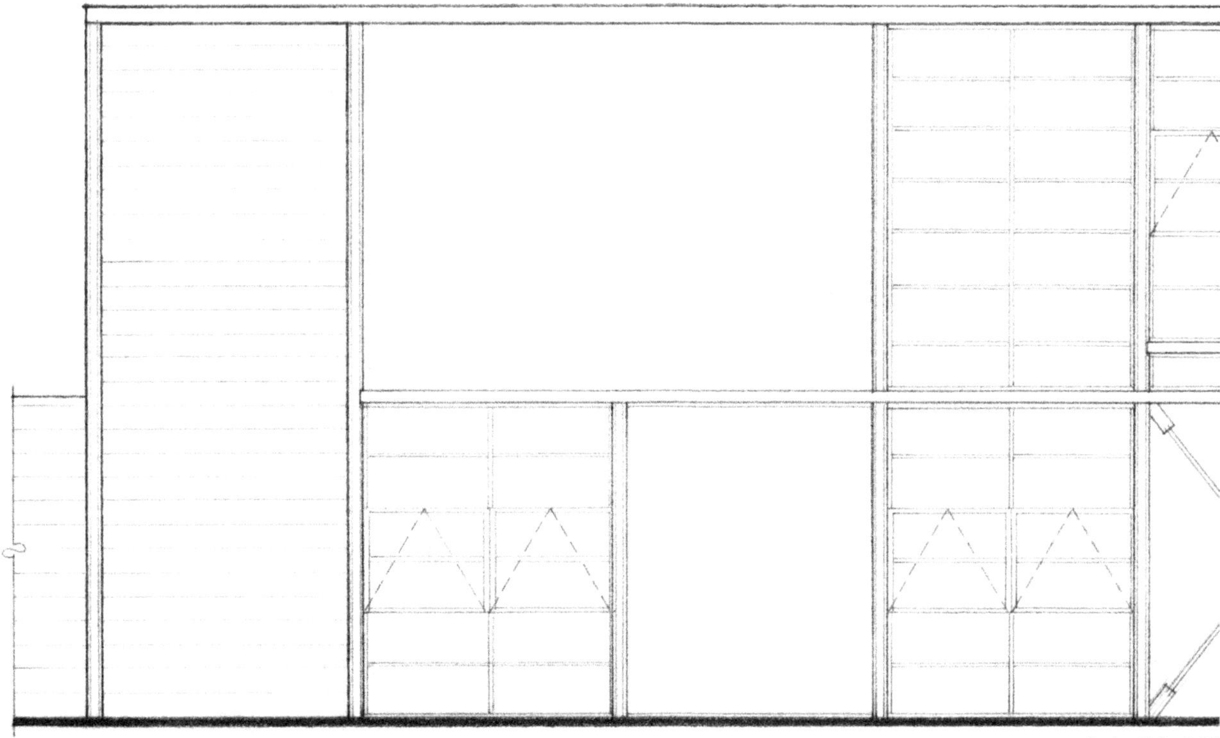

Scale: 3/16" = 1'-0"

Naming Exterior Elevations
Exterior elevations are referenced by their position on the building's surface. The exterior elevation of the north wall in a building plan is called the north elevation.

The north, east, south, and west exterior elevations reference plan north, not true north.

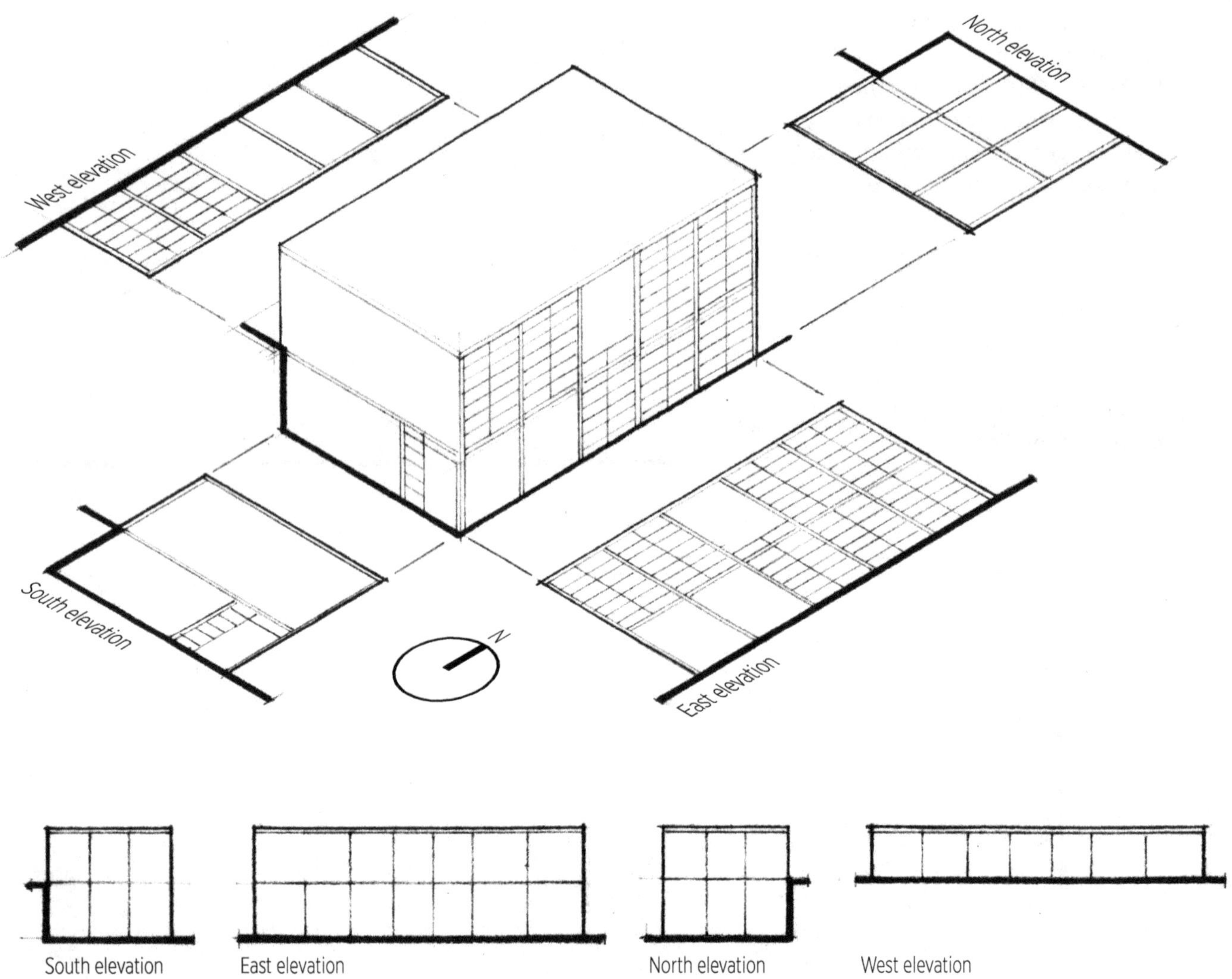

CHARLES (1907–78) AND RAY (1912–88) EAMES
Eames House Studio (1949)
Pacific Palisades, California
Drawings by Douglas Seidler

Overlay Method

Most exterior elevations are constructed from a floor plan.

- Use translucent vellum to overlay and construct new drawings from an existing floor plan. Rotate the floor plan to construct each elevation so that the bottom wall of the plan is the elevated surface.
- Insert a white sheet of paper between the two sheets of translucent vellum to review your progress and hide the existing floor plan.
- Use very light lines to construct the horizontal geometry in the elevation from the floor plan.
- Use an architectural scale to measure the vertical distances in the elevation.

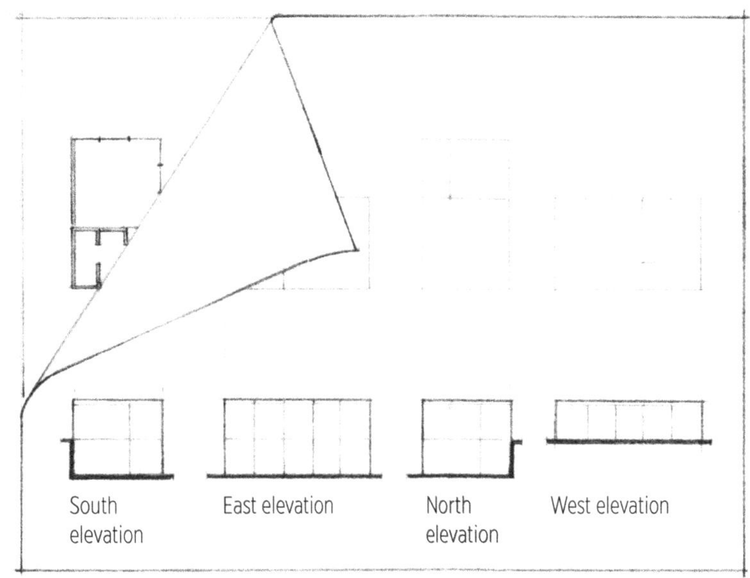

Drawing Composition

Drawing composition involves the thoughtful arrangement of a set of drawings on a sheet of paper. Before you begin a new drawing, identify the boundaries of the elevation or elevations using construction lines.

- Organize the elevations so that they wrap the exterior surface of the building. Adjacent elevations in your drawing should share a common corner in the building design.
- The ground plane should be consistent across a row of elevations. If the ground plane shifts up or down, the base of the elevations should also shift up or down.
- Leave a ¾" to 1" margin on all sides of your paper and between different drawings on the same sheet of paper.
- Center your drawings on the sheet.

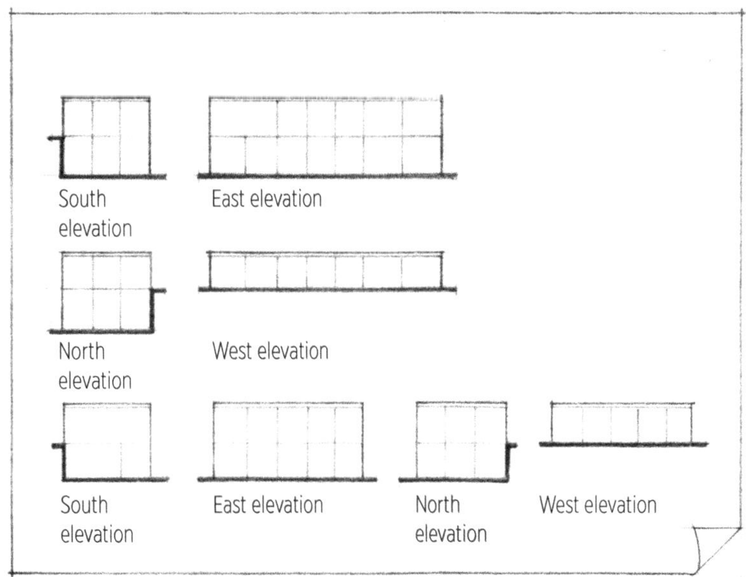

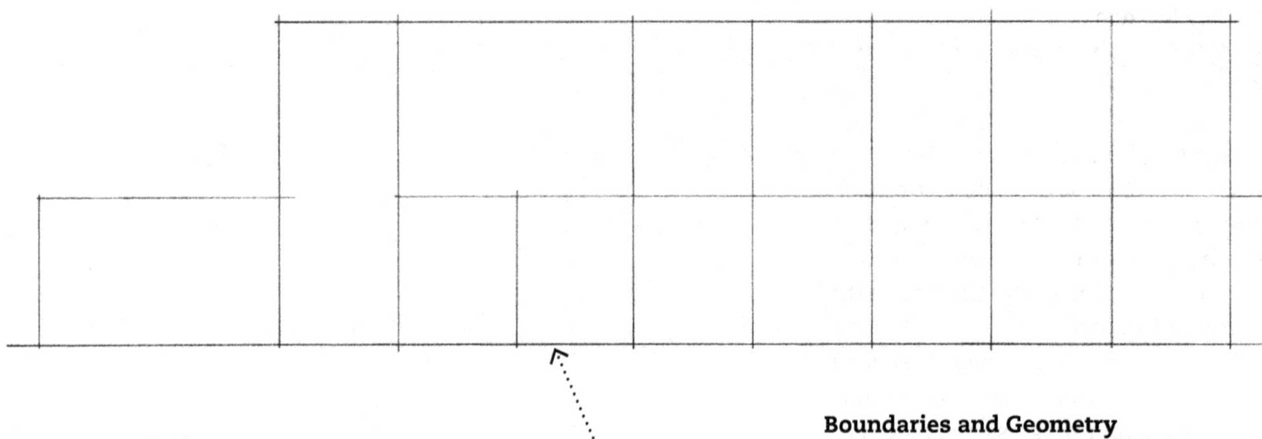

Boundaries and Geometry
When starting a new elevation, it is important to identify the boundaries of the drawing with construction lines.

- Use construction lines to identify the major geometry of your project.

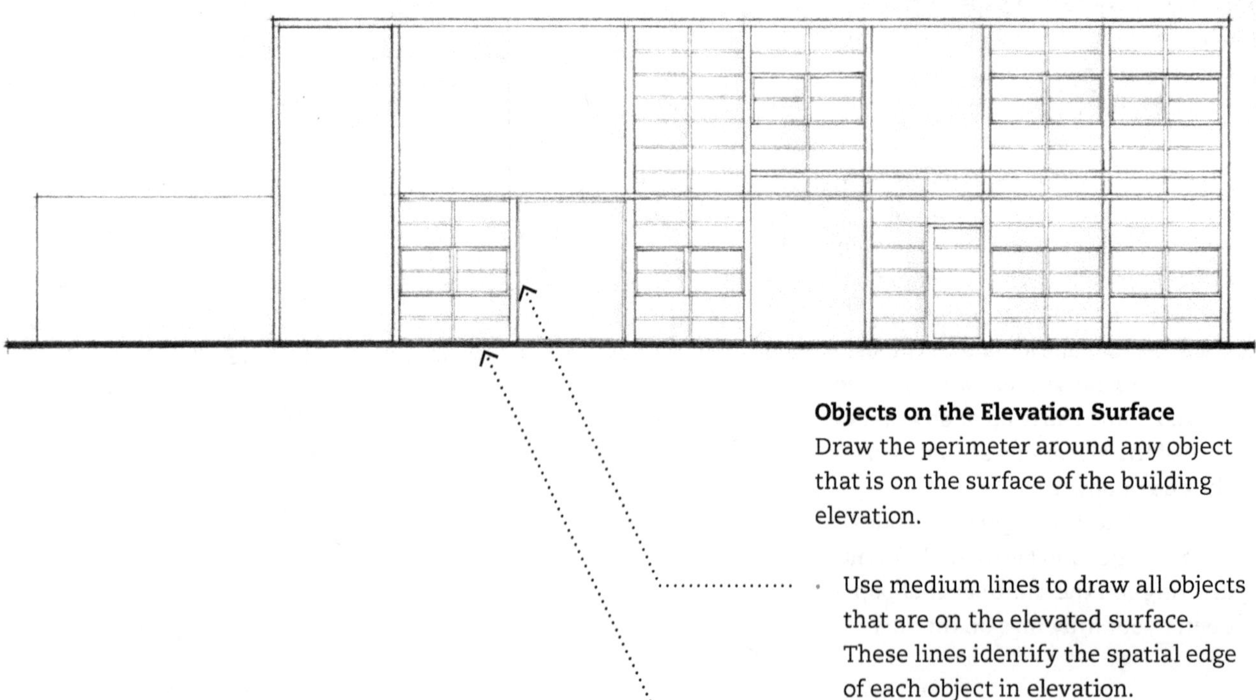

Objects on the Elevation Surface
Draw the perimeter around any object that is on the surface of the building elevation.

- Use medium lines to draw all objects that are on the elevated surface. These lines identify the spatial edge of each object in elevation.
- Use a dark line to draw the ground plane.

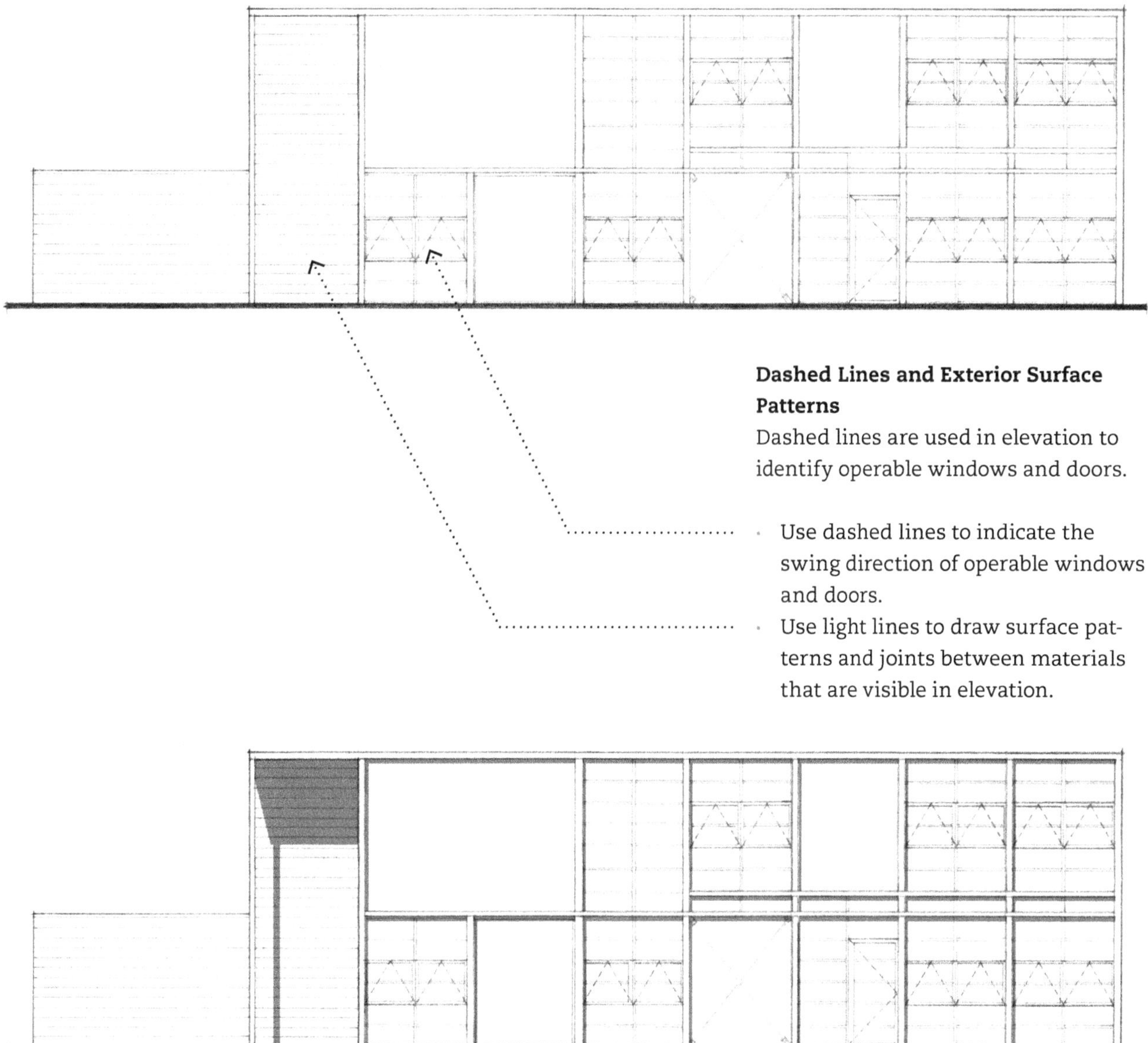

Dashed Lines and Exterior Surface Patterns
Dashed lines are used in elevation to identify operable windows and doors.

- Use dashed lines to indicate the swing direction of operable windows and doors.
- Use light lines to draw surface patterns and joints between materials that are visible in elevation.

Shadows
The final, optional step in drawing elevations involves adding tone to indicate shadows on the surfaces in the drawing. These shadows communicate space by implying the depth between parallel surfaces in elevation.

- The solid dark tone is added with a soft lead pencil to the front or back of the sheet of paper.
- Grayscale tone is added with multiple angled lines. Depending on the density of the lines, this technique creates different grayscale values for the poché.

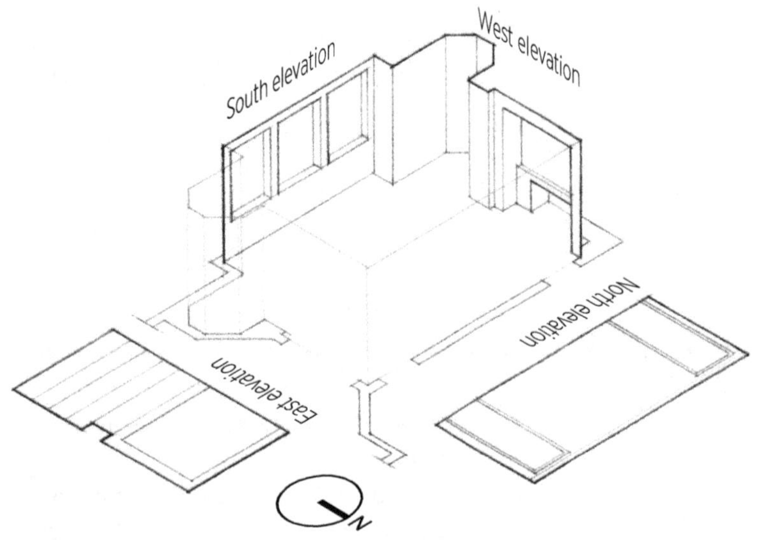

North elevation

East elevation

South elevation

West elevation

FRANK LLOYD WRIGHT (1867–1959)
George Furbeck House (1897)
Drawings by Douglas Seidler

Interior Elevations
The interior elevation is an opportunity to reveal proportions and interior spatial relationships in a design project. Depending on the individual project and your design process, these drawings may be completed at the beginning, middle, or end of a design project.

- Interior elevations are oblique projections of your interior building design.
- Interior elevation drawings are usually drawn parallel to an interior surface or wall.

Naming Interior Elevations
Interior elevations are referenced by their position within an interior room. The interior elevation of the north wall in a room is called the north room elevation.

- Like exterior elevations, the north, east, south, and west interior elevations reference plan north, not true north.

Drawing Composition
Drawing composition involves the thoughtful arrangement of a set of drawings on a sheet of paper. Before you begin a new drawing, identify the boundaries of the elevation or elevations, using construction lines.

- Organize the elevations so that they wrap the interior surface of the building. Adjacent elevations in your drawing should share a common corner in the room or interior space.
- The ground plane should be consistent across a row of elevations. If the ground plane shifts up or down, the base of the elevations should also shift up or down.
- Leave a ¾" to 1" margin on all sides of your paper and between different drawings on the same sheet of paper.
- Center your drawings on the sheet.

Overlay Method
Most interior elevations are constructed from a floor plan.

- Use translucent vellum to overlay and construct new drawings from an existing floor plan. Rotate the floor plan to construct each elevation so that the bottom wall of the plan is the elevated surface.
- Insert a white sheet of paper between the two sheets of translucent vellum to review your progress and hide the existing floor plan.
- Use very light lines to construct the horizontal geometry in the elevation from the floor plan.
- Use an architectural scale to measure the vertical distances in the elevation.

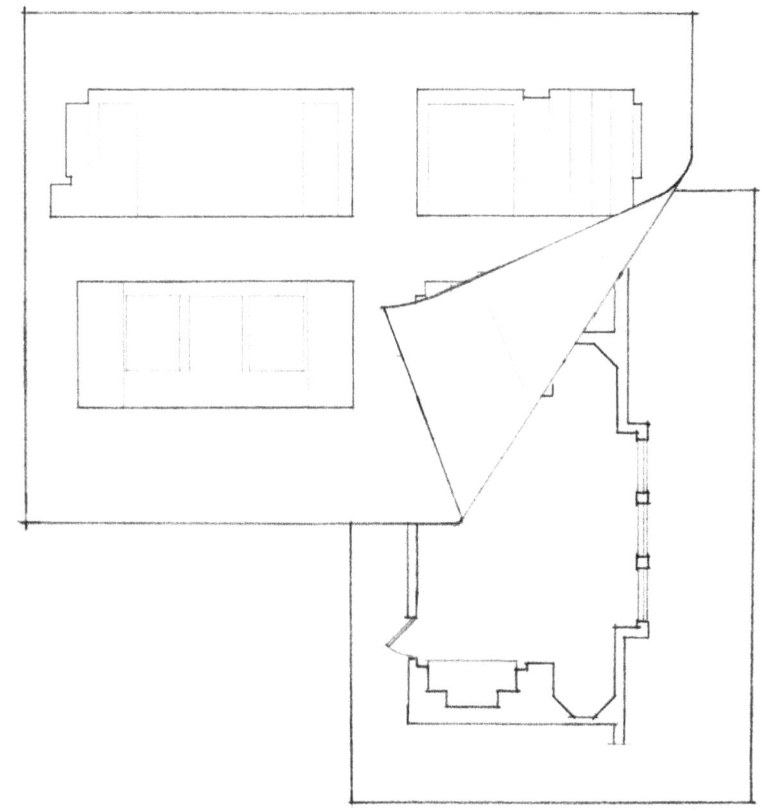

Drawing Scale
Calculate the size of your interior elevation to determine what size sheet of paper you will need. Most interior elevations are drawn at ⅛" = 1'-0" or ¼" = 1'-0".

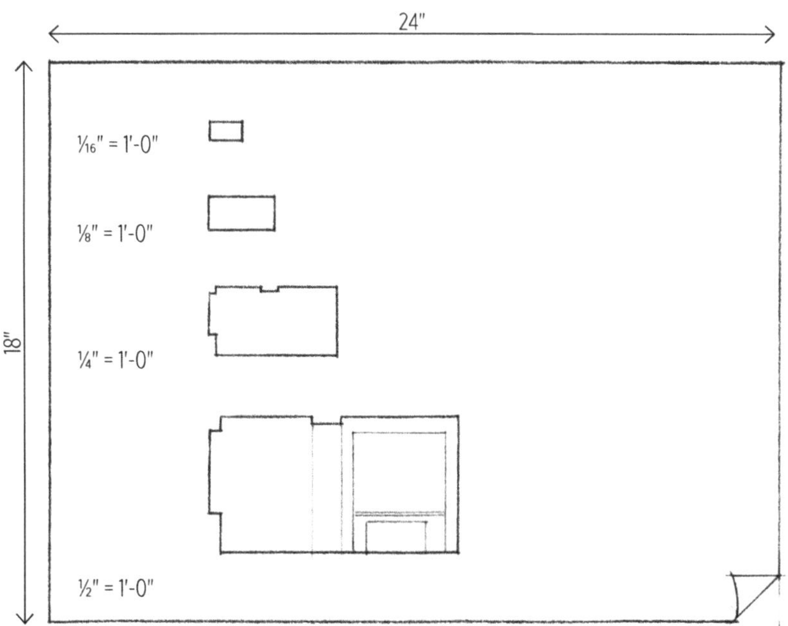

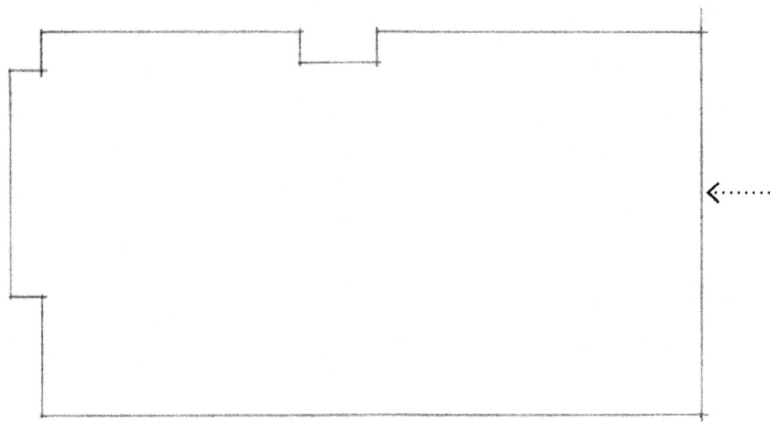

Interior Boundaries and Geometry
When starting a new elevation, it is important to identify the boundaries of the drawing with construction lines.

- Use construction lines to identify the major geometry of your project.

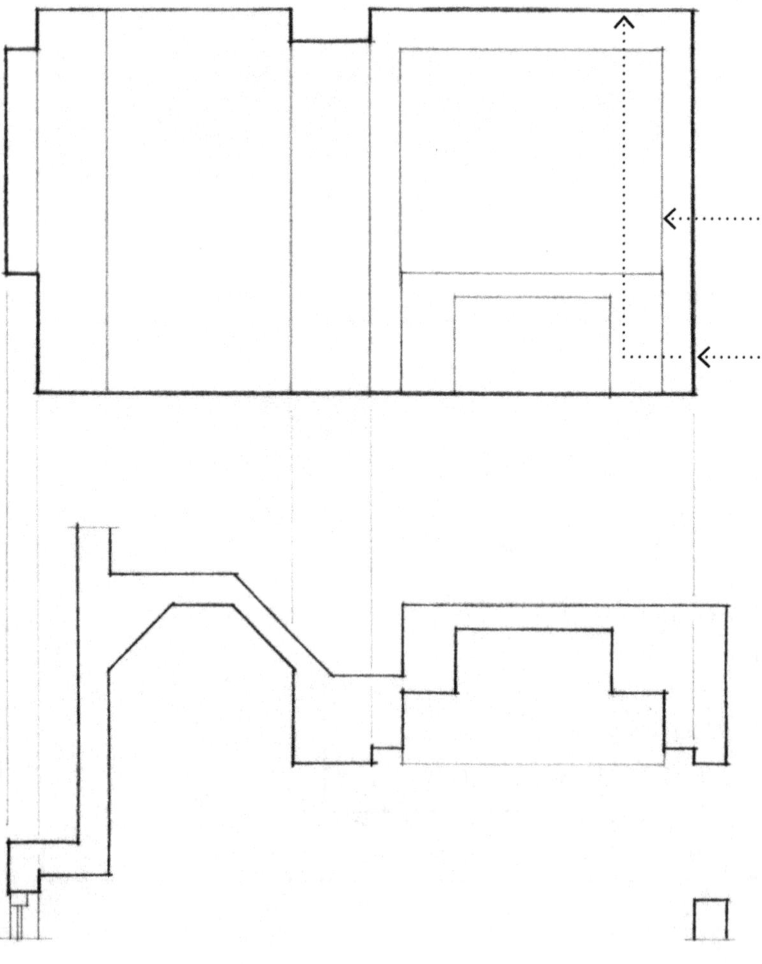

Objects on the Interior Elevation Surface
Draw the perimeter around any object that is on the surface of the interior elevation.

- Use medium lines to draw all objects that are elevated surface. These lines identify the spatial edge of each object in elevation.
- Use a dark line to draw the ground plane and the perimeter walls in the elevation.

Drawing Doors in Elevation
In elevation, interior doors are always drawn in the closed position.

- The swing direction of a hinged door is identified with a dashed line.
- The slide direction of a sliding pocket door is identified with a solid arrow.

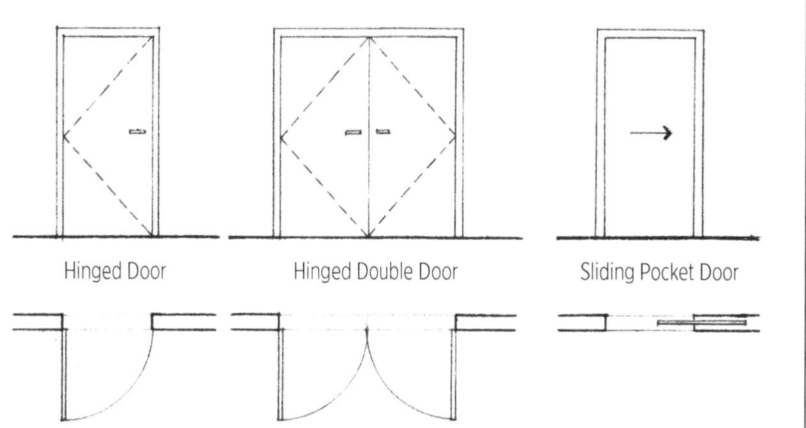

Dashed Lines and Interior Surface Patterns
Dashed lines are used in elevation to identify operable windows and doors.

- Use dashed lines to indicate the swing direction of operable windows and doors.
- Use light lines to draw surface patterns and joints between materials that are visible in elevation.

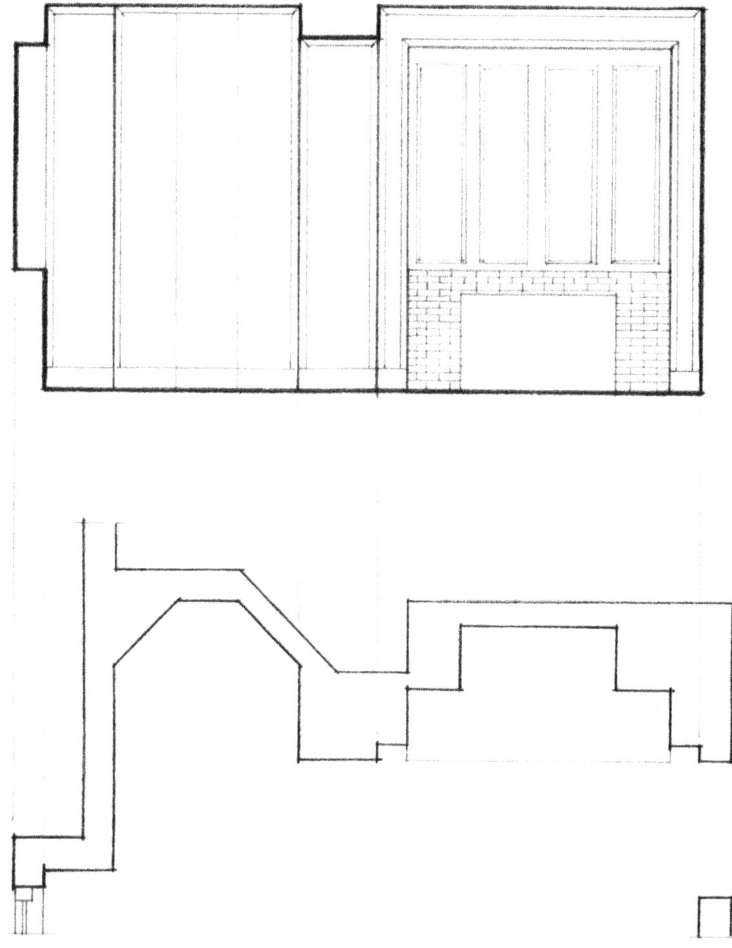

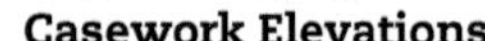

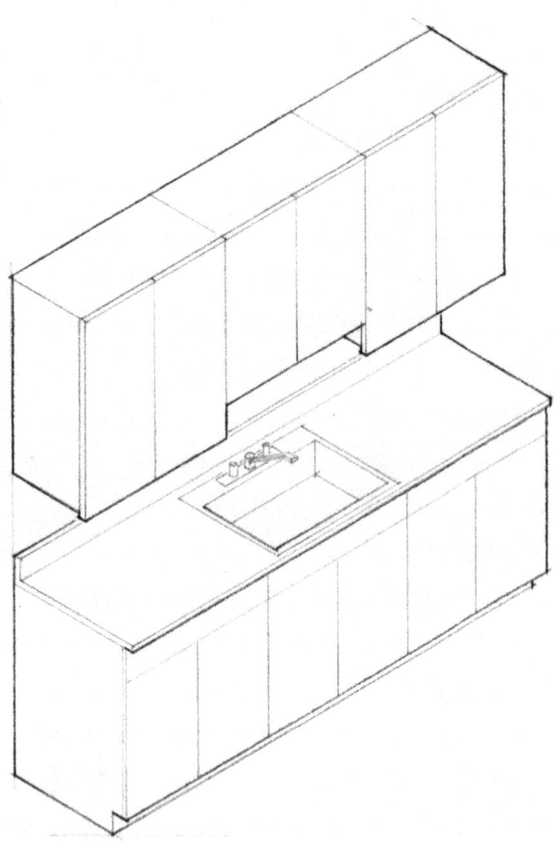

Casework Elevations

Casework elevations are often included with interior elevations but may be a separate set of drawings. These drawings communicate your design intent to an instructor or a contractor. Using your design drawings as the starting point, a contractor or subcontractor will redraw your casework elevations at a high level of detail.

- The most common casework elevations are kitchen and bathroom cabinets.
- Casework elevations are also used to design and communicate any furniture that is attached to the building, including bookcases, entertainment centers, and custom seating.
- Most casework elevations are drawn at ½" = 1'-0" or ¾" = 1'-0".

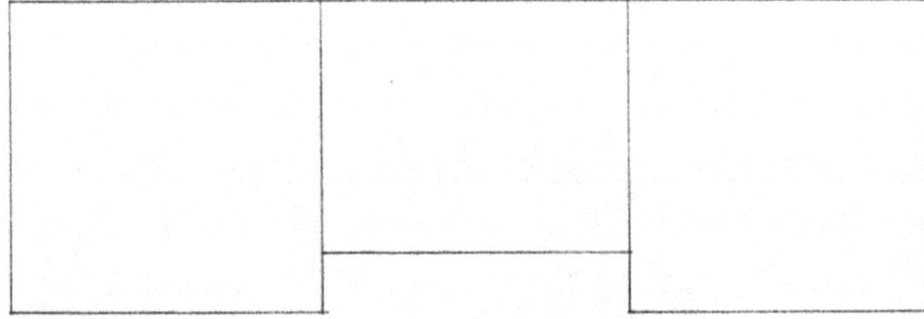

Boundaries and Geometry

When starting a new casework elevation, it is important to identify the boundaries of the drawing with construction lines.

- Use construction lines to identify the major geometry of your project.

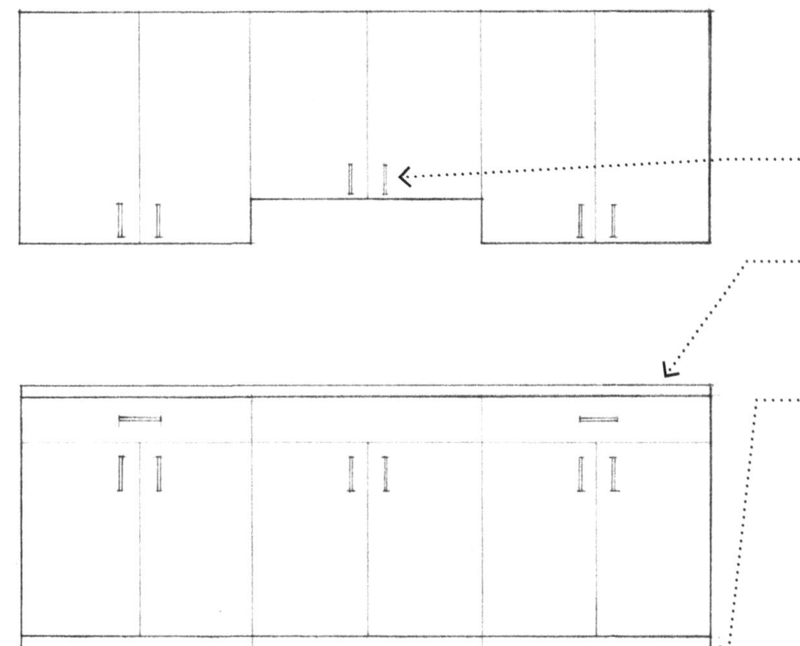

Cabinets, Drawers, and Hardware

- Use light lines to draw the individual cabinet doors, drawers, and cabinet hardware.
- Use medium lines to draw the perimeter around the casework. These lines identify the spatial edge of each object in elevation.
- Use a dark line to draw the ground plane.

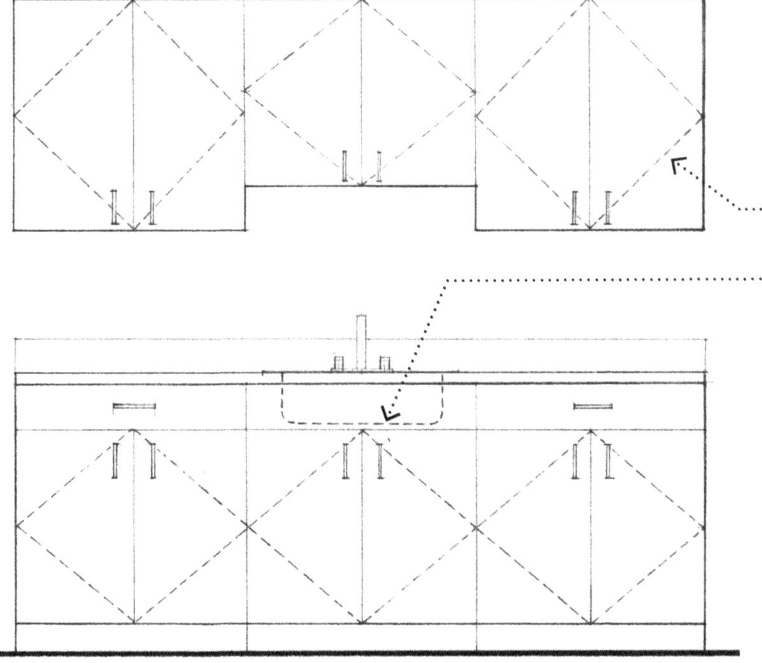

Dashed Lines and Surface Patterns
Dashed lines are used in casework elevations to identify operable doors.

- Use dashed lines to indicate the swing direction of operable doors.
- Dashed lines are also used to indicate objects that are hidden beyond the built-in, like this kitchen sink.
- Use light lines to draw surface patterns, molding patterns, and joints between materials that are visible in elevation.

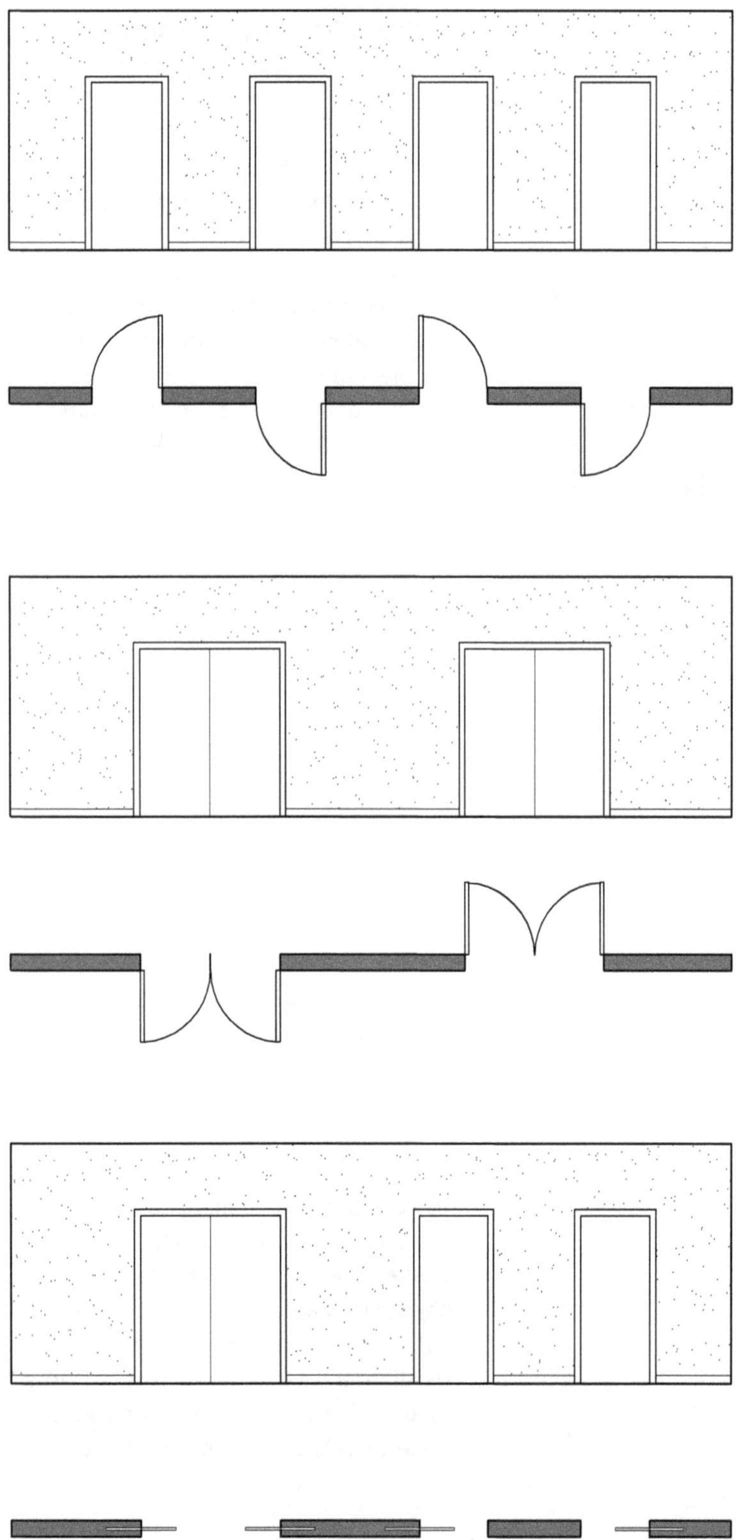

Learning Exercise: Door Swings
This exercise is intended to help you improve your understanding of annotating door swings in elevation.

- On each of these elevations, draw the appropriate annotation to indicate the door's swing direction.
- For the pocket doors, draw the appropriate annotation to indicate the door's pocket direction.

Learning Exercise: Shadows
This exercise is intended to help you improve your understanding of adding shadows to an elevation.

- Shadows are constructed on an elevation using projected lines from the floor plan.
- By understanding these primary geometries and their corresponding shadow projections, you can add shadows to elevations with complex geometries.
- Referencing these methods to construct shadows in elevation, project the appropriate shadows in this drawing.

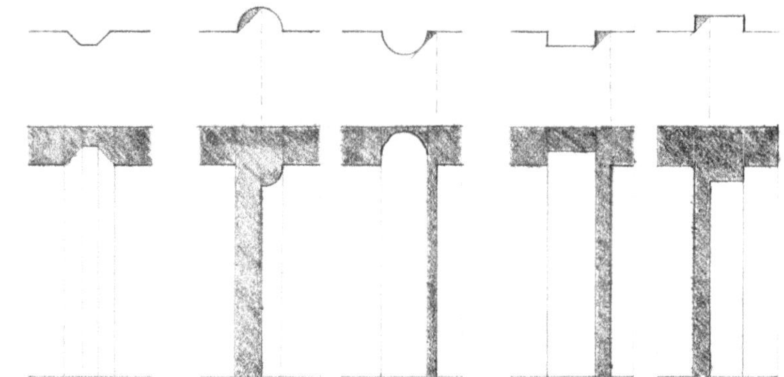

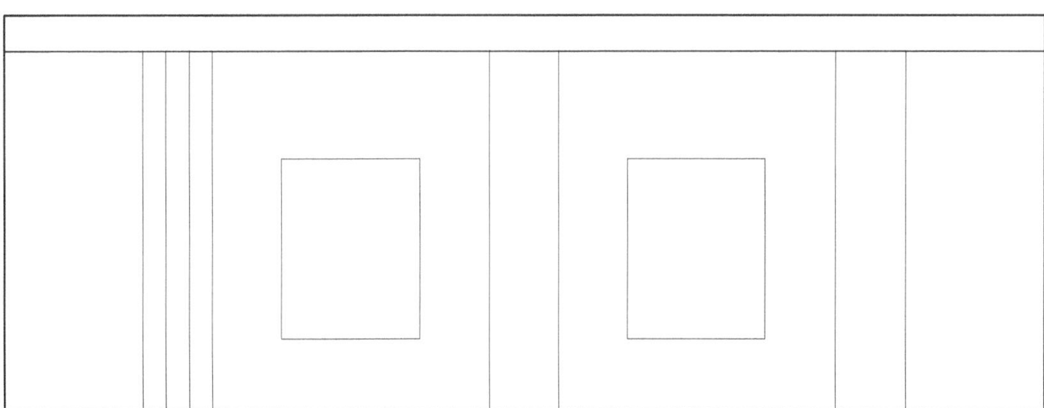

Elevation

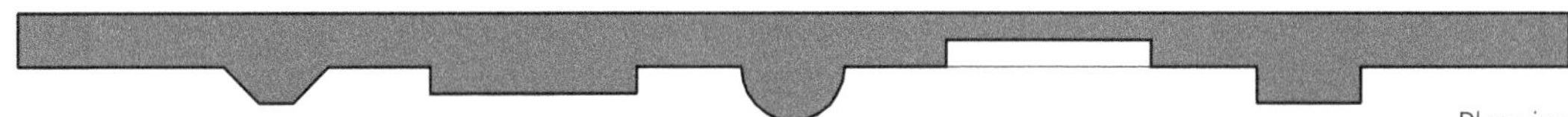

Plan view

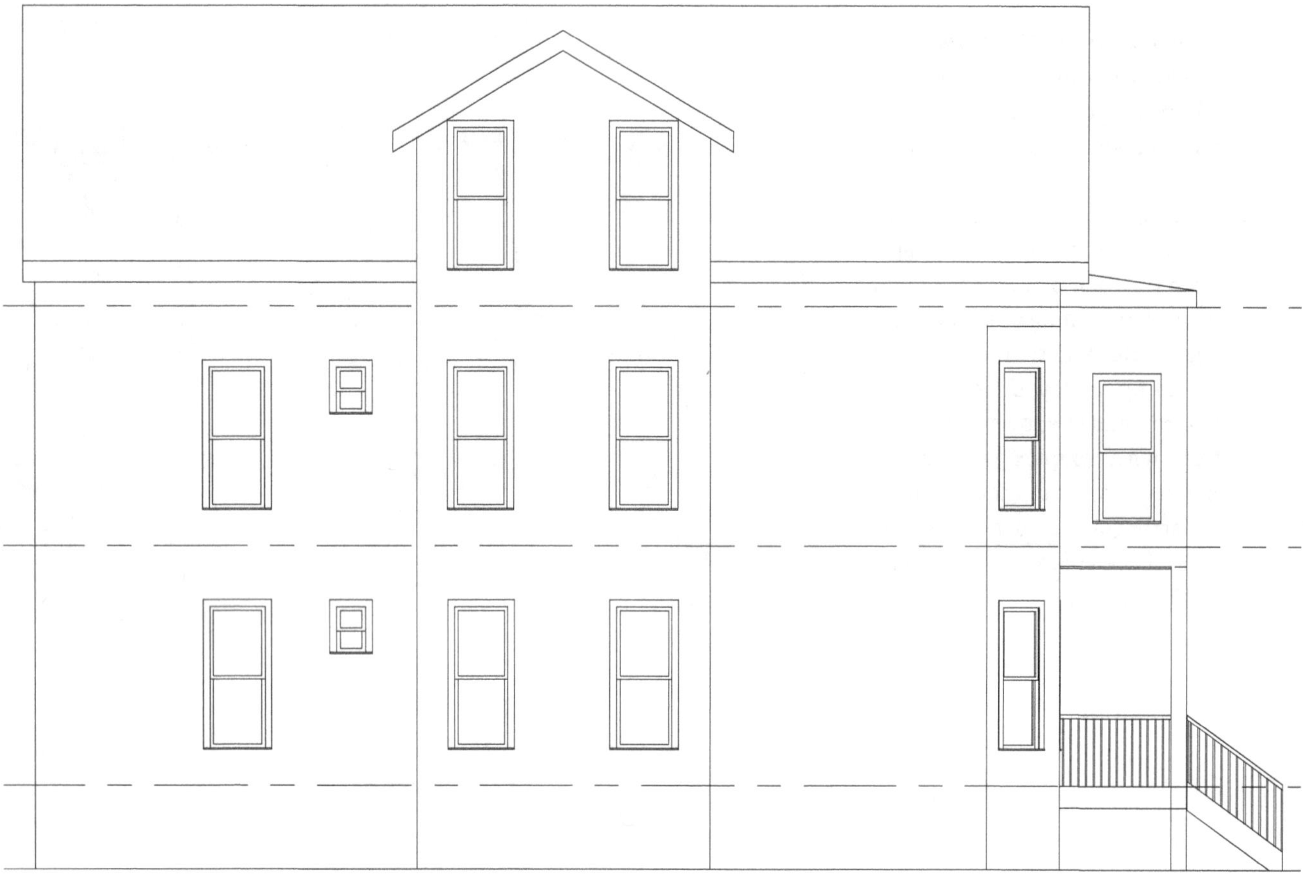

Elevation
Scale: ⅛" = 1'-0"

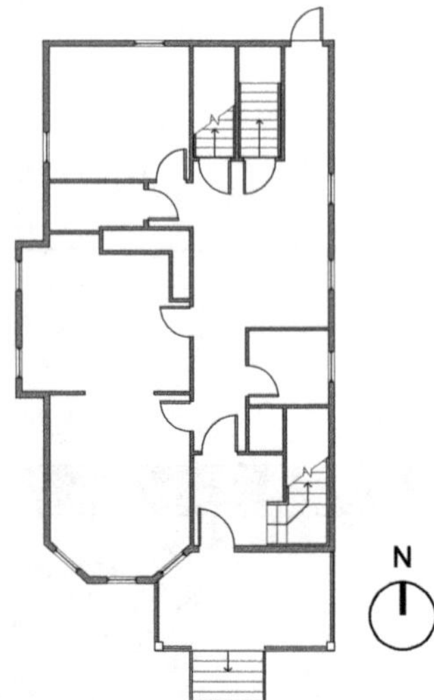

Key plan

Learning Exercise: Line Weight
This exercise is intended to help you improve your understanding of line weight in communicating the spatial properties of building elevations. Complete the following steps for the elevations on this page and the following page:

- Reference the key plan to label the elevation with the appropriate north, east, south, or west direction.
- Using a very dark line, carefully trace the ground plane line in this drawing.
- Using a dark line, carefully trace the perimeter of this drawing.
- Using a medium line, carefully trace over the profile lines in this drawing.
- Use a light line to draw 4" wood siding on this drawing.
- Project and shade the appropriate shadows in this drawing.

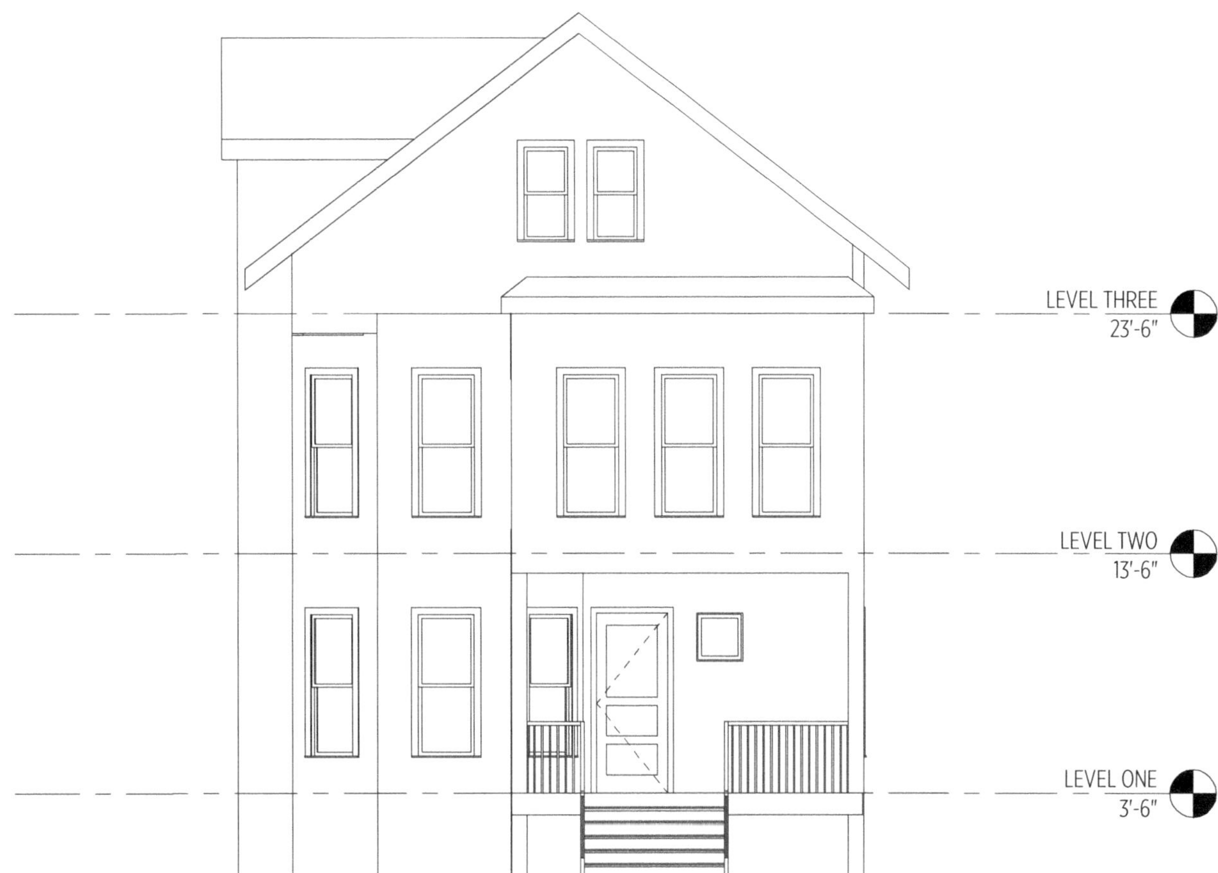

Elevation
Scale: ⅛" = 1'-0"

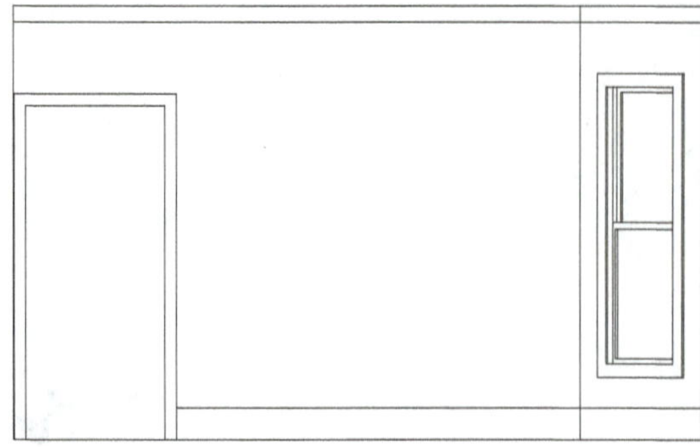

Elevation
Scale: 3/16" = 1'-0"

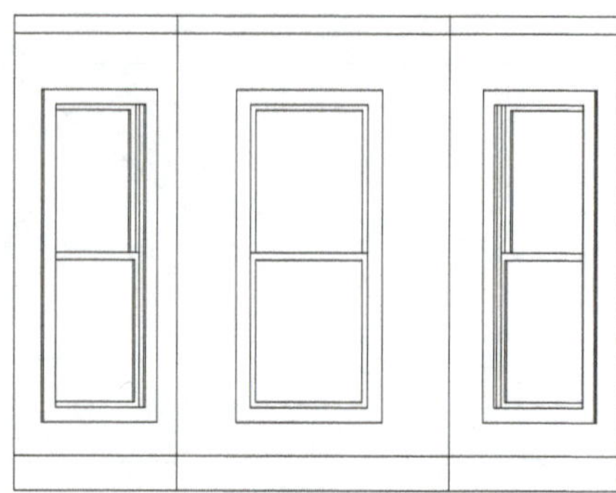

Elevation
Scale: 3/16" = 1'-0"

Elevation
Scale: 3/16" = 1'-0"

Elevation
Scale: 3/16" = 1'-0"

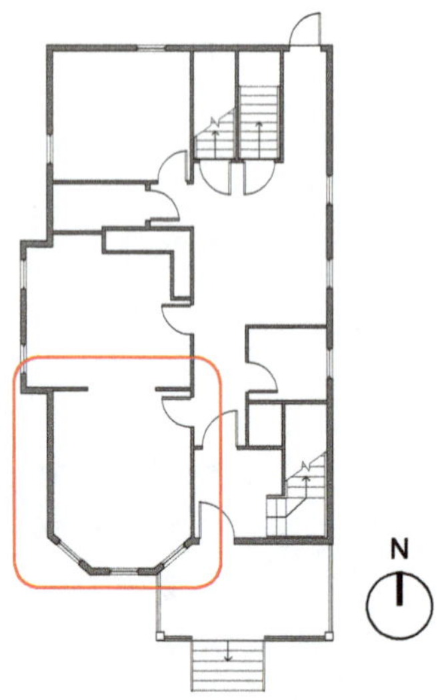

Key plan

N

Learning Exercise: Line Weight

This exercise is intended to help you improve your understanding of line weight in communicating the spatial properties of interior elevations. Complete the following steps for each elevation on this page:

- Reference the key plan to label the elevation with the appropriate north, east, south, or west direction.
- Using a dark line, carefully trace the perimeter of this drawing.
- Using a medium line, carefully trace over the profile lines and openings in this drawing.
- Use a light line to draw 4" wood siding on this drawing.
- Project and shade the appropriate shadows in this drawing.

Elevation
Scale: 3/16" = 1'-0"

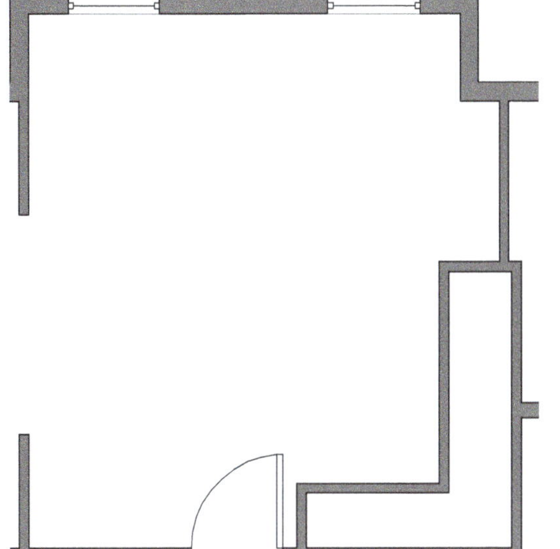

Elevation
Scale: 3/16" = 1'-0"

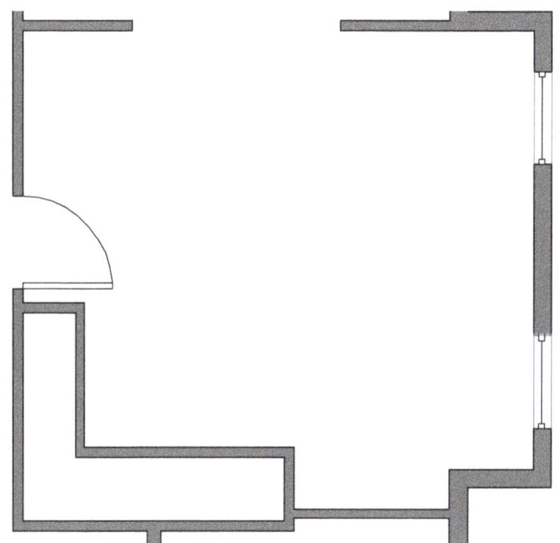

Learning Exercise: Drawing Elevations

This exercise is intended to help you improve your understanding of constructing elevations from a floor plan.

- On the facing page, construct elevation 4 as indicated by the elevation symbol in the floor plan.
- Draw elevation 4 at 3/8" = 1'-0".

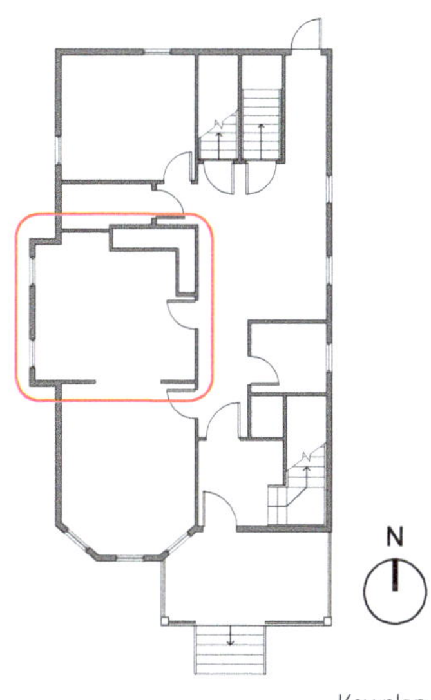

Key plan

PARALINE PROJECTIONS

Paraline drawings are a unique form of architectural representation in that they combine the measured aspect of orthogonal drawings with the three-dimensional quality of a perspective. This family of drawings is particularly useful in early project design, diagramming, and analysis because they allow a three-dimensional investigation in a single measured drawing.

For the same reasons, paraline drawings are also useful in the detailing phase of a project because they visually communicate the three-dimensional nature of complex building details, furniture details, or material connections.

Hand-drawn and hand-drafted paraline drawings have several advantages over computer-generated drawings, including:

- You have the ability to rapidly generate multiple schemes or options by overlaying a base drawing with trace paper or translucent vellum.
- You can selectively draw the information that is most important to the current design exploration, reducing drawing time and focusing the discussion or critique of the design solution in the drawing.

In this chapter, you will learn the differences between the three types of paraline drawings most used in architectural representation, including plan oblique axonometric, isometric projection, and elevation oblique.

Consider the following questions as you read this chapter:

- How is hand drawing used in both school and in practice to explore, develop, and communicate ideas?
- What are the fundamental conventions used to construct paraline drawings?
- How do paraline drawings support the design process?

About Paraline Drawings

All paraline drawings share a subset of rules used in their construction:

- Lines that are parallel in plan, elevation, or section are also parallel to each other in a paraline drawing.
- Each drawing is measured to a specific architectural scale. All lines that are parallel to a primary axis are drawn at this measured scale.

Plan Oblique Axonometric Drawing

The plan oblique, also called an axonometric drawing, is constructed by rotating a floor plan 30 degrees or 45 degrees from horizontal. The drawing is projected from the floor plan, using vertical lines drawn 90 degrees from horizontal. In addition to the general rules applied to paraline drawings:

- Lines that are perpendicular to each other in plan are also perpendicular in axonometric.
- 45/45/90 axonometric drawings are constructed with all lines in plan drawn at a 45-degree angle to horizontal.
- 30/60/90 axonometric drawings are constructed with all lines in plan drawn at either a 30-degree angle or a 60-degree angle to horizontal.

Isometric Projection

The isometric projection is unique in that it cannot be constructed directly from a floor plan, because horizontal and vertical lines in plan are drawn at a 120-degree angle in isometric. In addition to the general rules applied to paraline drawings:

- Isometric drawings are constructed with all lines in plan drawn at a 30-degree angle to horizontal.

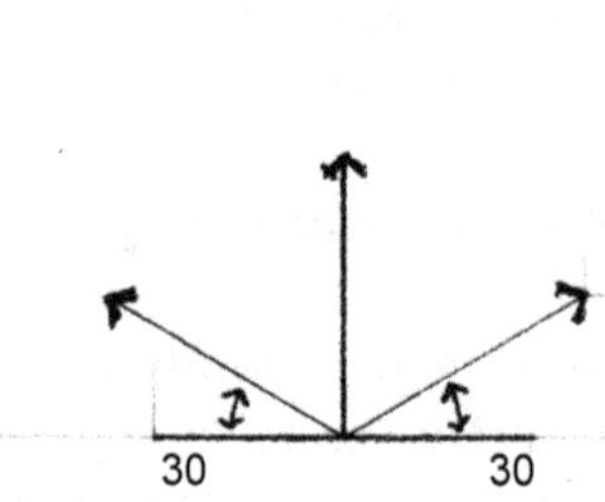

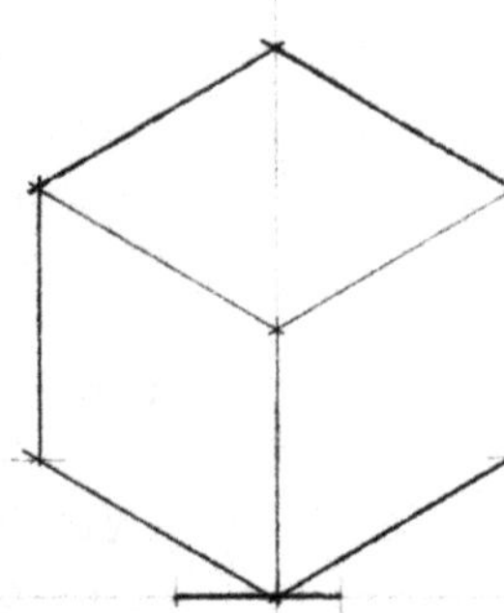

Elevation Oblique

The elevation oblique drawing is a three-dimensional drawing that is constructed from a measured elevation.

- The drawing is projected from an elevation, using lines drawn at 30 degrees, 45 degrees, or 60 degrees from horizontal.

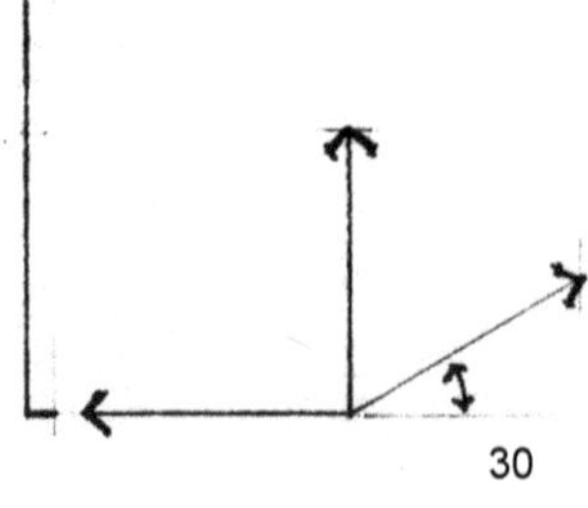

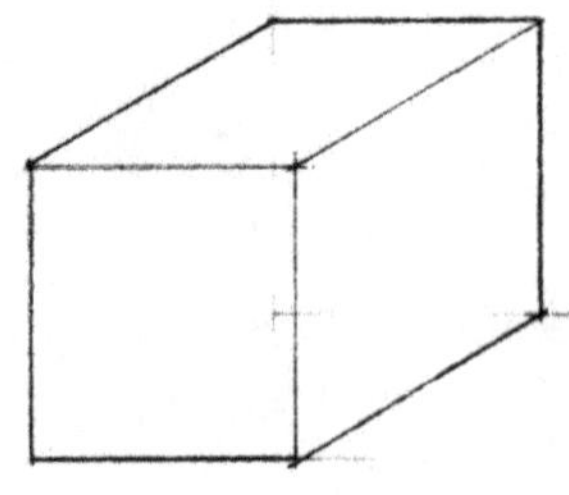

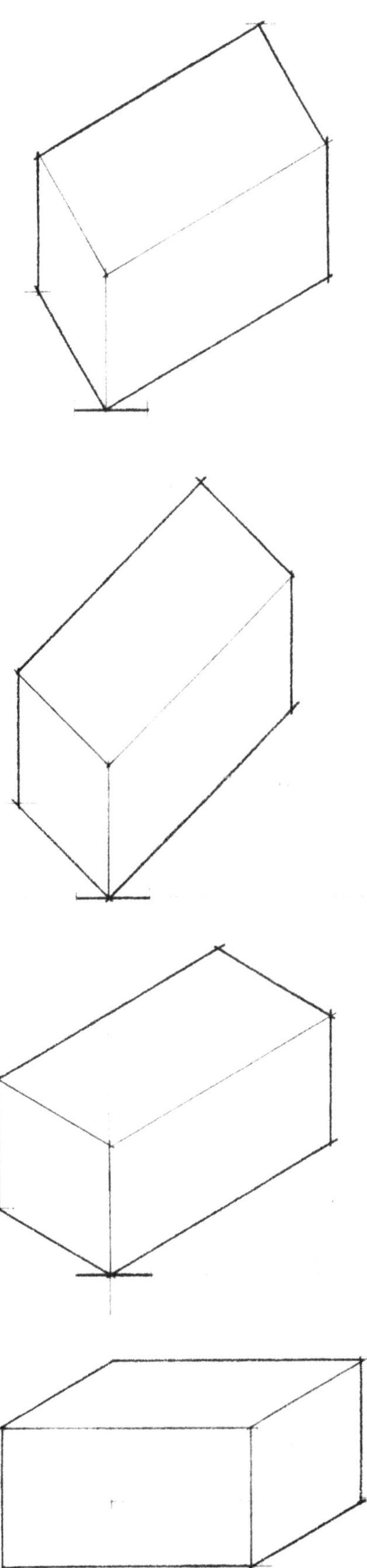

Exploded Paraline Drawing

The exploded drawing provides an opportunity to visually communicate different pieces in a design and the spatial relationship between each piece. Companies like IKEA use this type of drawing to help consumers assemble furniture.

- Construction lines or dashed lines are used to connect exploded objects back to the primary object.

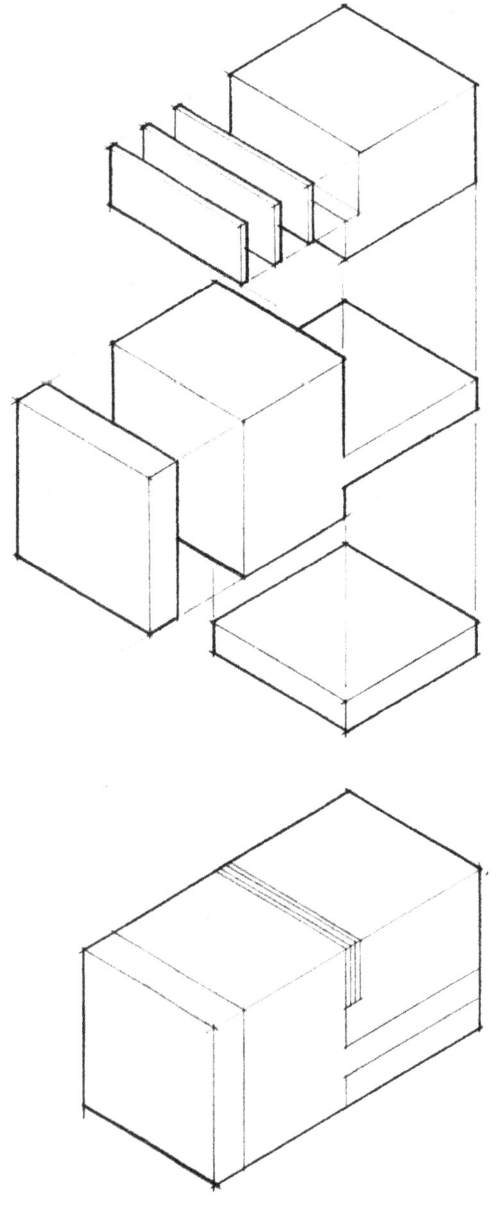

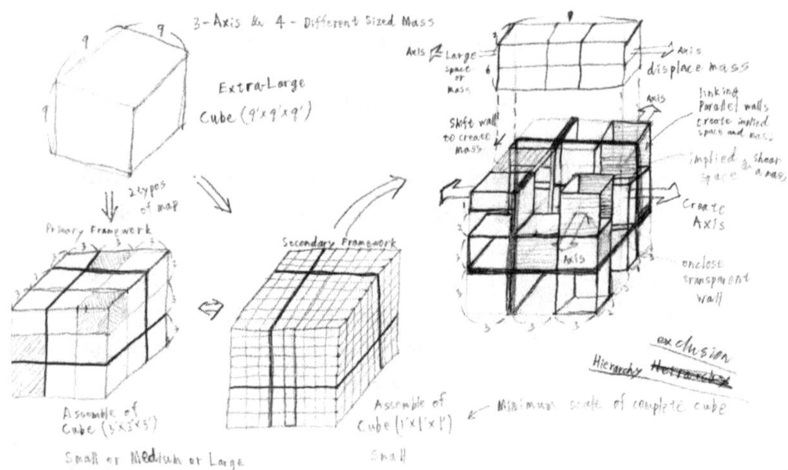

Ideation

Ideation, also referred to as conceptual design, is the process of exploring multiple design iterations and critically evaluating each as an appropriate solution to a design problem. Ideation involves the translation of a written design problem to a spatial design solution.

The written comments and notes on these drawings are an important part of the conceptual design process. They document the designer's thought process and evaluation of each solution.

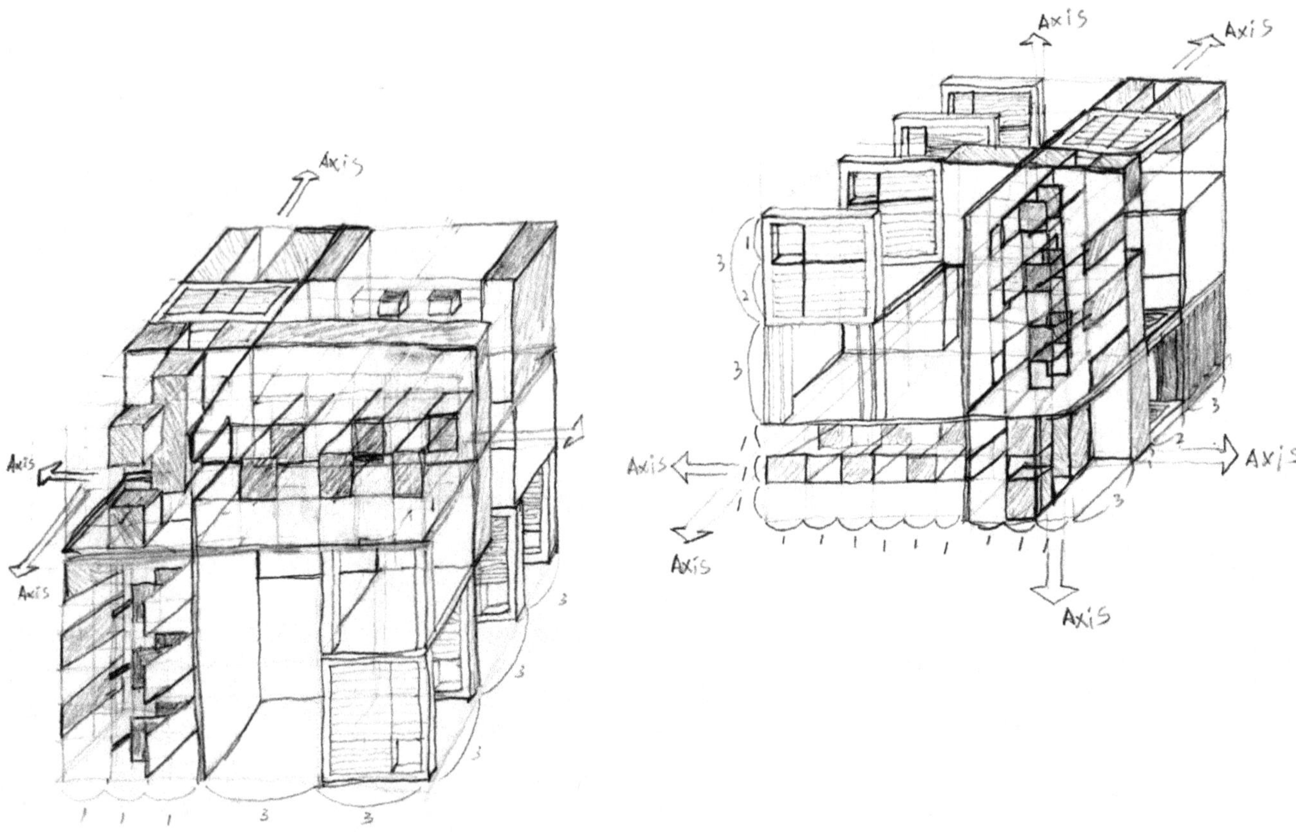

RYOTA UCHIDA
Process sketches
Masters A Design Studio,
Boston Architectural College

By sketching my ideas in three dimensions, I start to understand my ideas in very concrete ways and can use the drawings to further develop my design. Exploring my idea with sketches like these not only helps me to understand my project's core idea they also help me communicate these ideas with my colleagues and instructors.

—RYOTA UCHIDA

- Paraline drawings are a common drawing convention used in the ideation process because they allow a designer to critically investigate the spatial and formal qualities in a given project.
- Paraline drawings allow designers to explore the spatial relationships in plan, section, and elevation simultaneously during the design process.
- Because these three-dimensional sketches are drawn at a specific architectural scale, they can be used at a later design phase to create more precise plans, sections, and elevations.

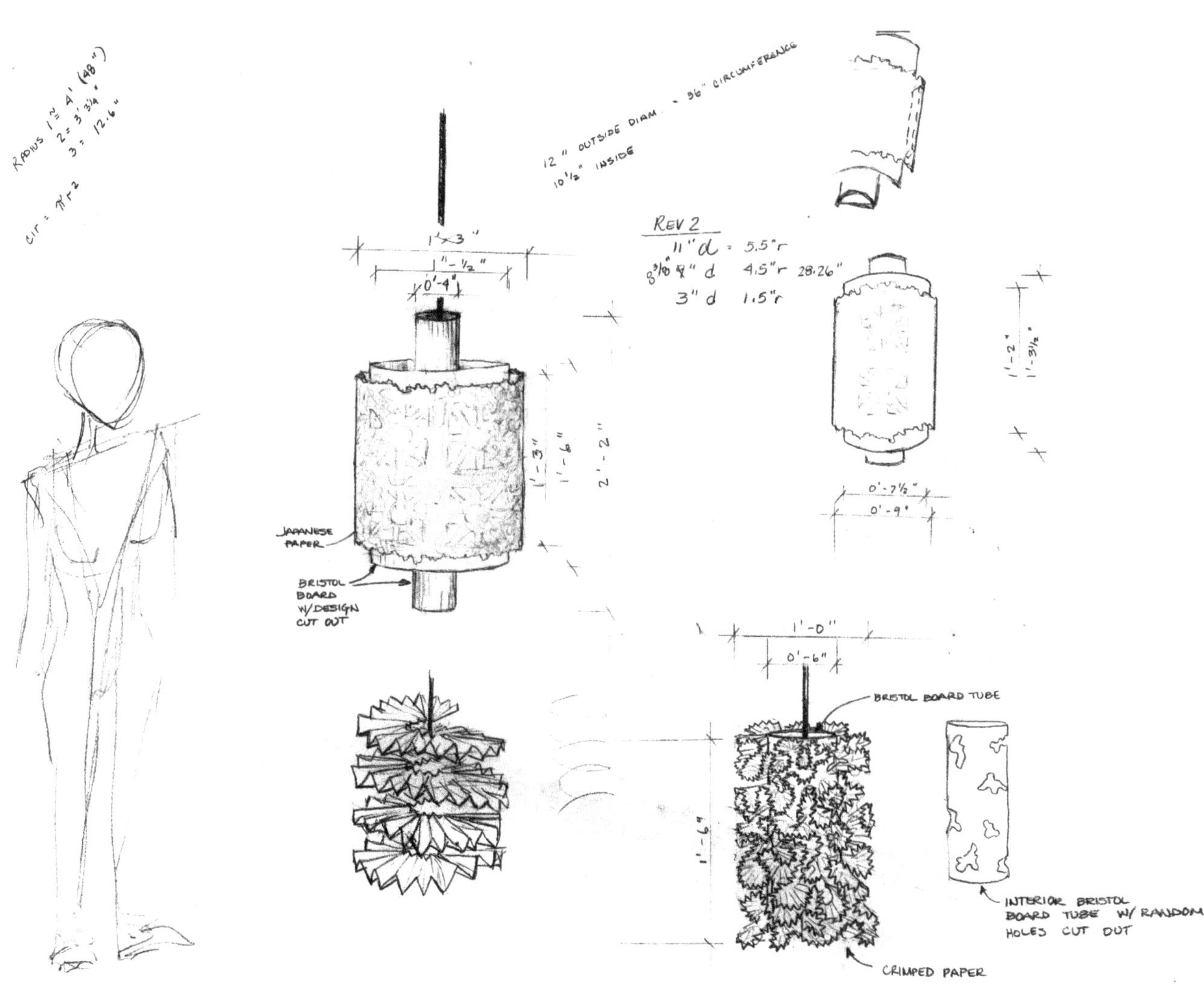

TAMISON ROSE
Process sketches
Furniture and Detailing Studio,
The New England School of
Art & Design at Suffolk University

LUDWIG MIES VAN DER ROHE
Barcelona Pavilion (1929) (Rebuilt 1988), Berlin, Germany
Drawings by Douglas Seidler

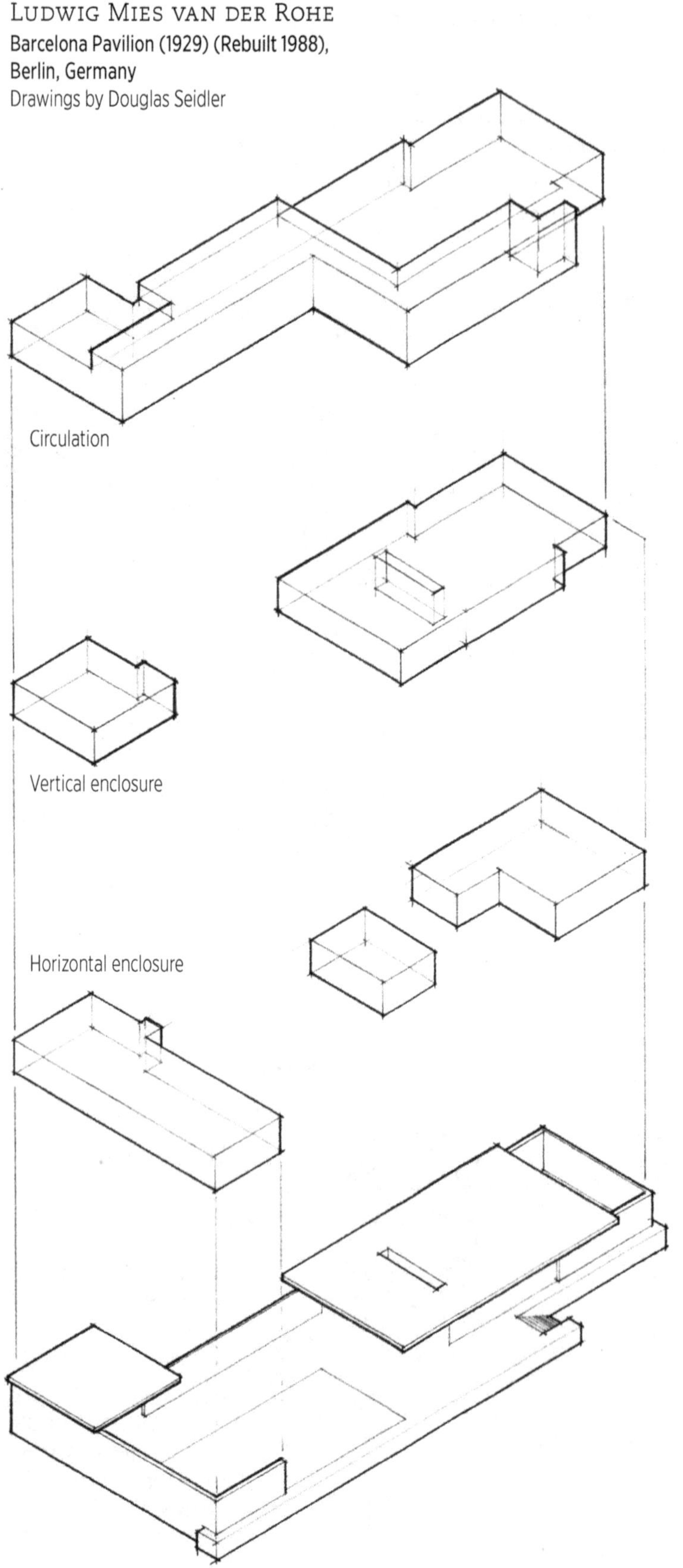

Analysis
Analysis drawings are a useful tool for investigating a project's context, precedents, and human occupation and for evaluating the strength of a current design. Good analysis drawings clearly identify the portion of the project that is under critique by editing or removing unnecessary information from the drawing. They also visually communicate the conclusions learned through the focused research or analysis.

Designers use precedent analysis drawings to investigate a piece of furniture, a building, a city, an artifact, or anything else that relates to a current design problem. Although the content of an investigatory drawing may vary in scale or scope, these drawings share the common objective of revealing new or pertinent information about a given project.

These drawings, and the information they communicate, are often used as the basis for new design decisions in a project that shares a similar set of challenges or objectives. Through this critical analysis, new designs can build on the results of previous projects without imitating style or form.

Building Analysis
This exploded isometric drawing of the Barcelona Pavilion (1929; rebuilt 1988) explores the different spatial conditions in the pavilion. Circulation, vertical enclosure, and horizontal enclosure are individually isolated in the drawing, allowing a comparative analysis of each.

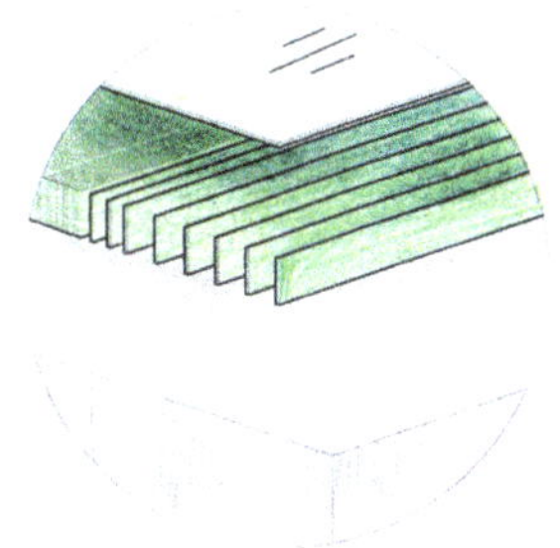

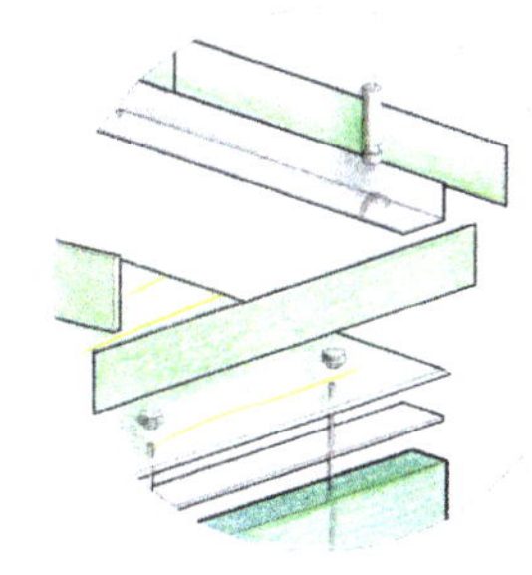

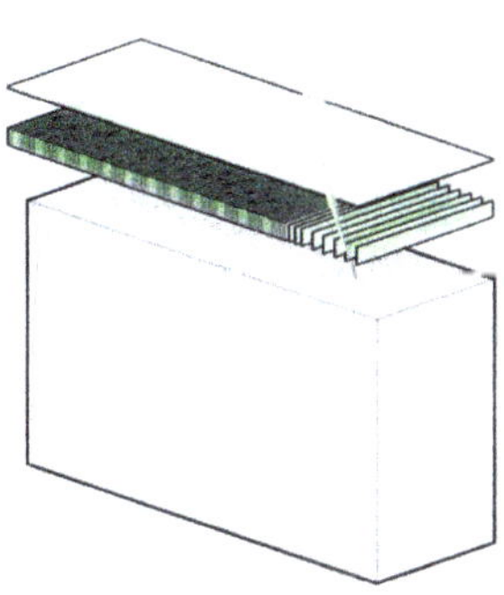

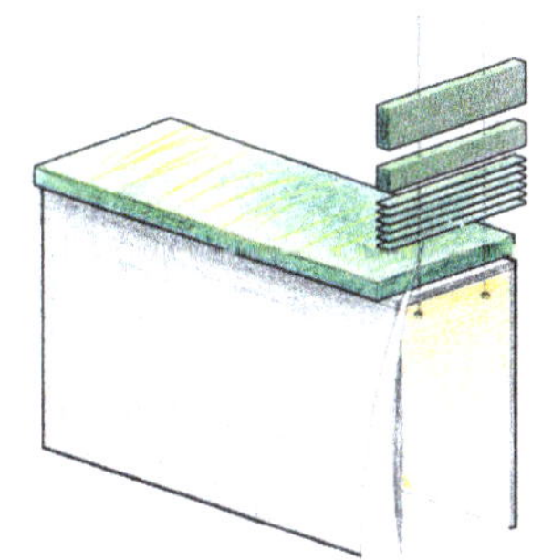

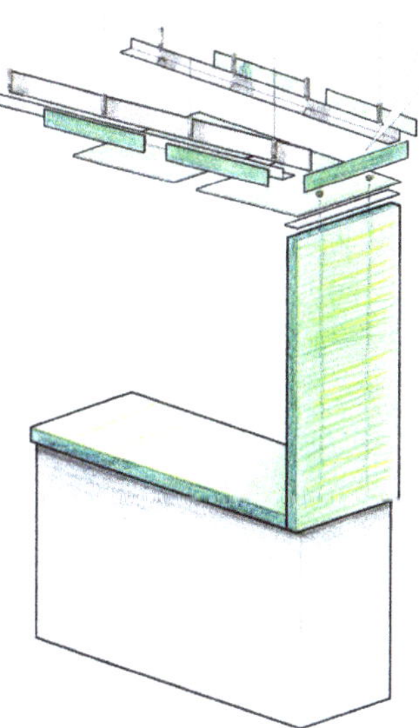

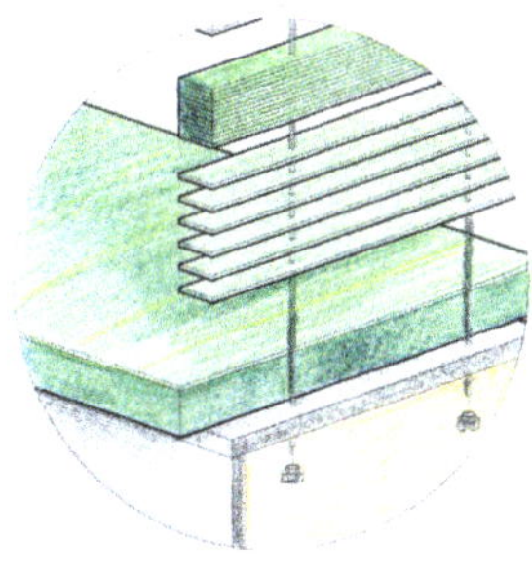

Detail Precedent Analysis
This detail analysis of the bar at Xing restaurant (2005) in New York City investigates the innovative material use and assembly.

- The isometric drawings are used to communicate the spatial relationships between the different materials used in this detail.
- Color is used to identify common materials in each of the drawings.
- Multiple scales are used in the drawings to communicate an increasingly complex level of detail.

ALISON SMITH
Isometric analysis drawing
Advanced Materials and Detailing Studio, The New England School of Art & Design at Suffolk University

Drawing has always been the primary tool I utilize for generating and developing my ideas in the conceptualization process. It is the recorded thought process of someone engaged in the visual arts and architecture.

These particular stair drawings are further developed than my initial hand drawn. After evolving the initial design direction and establishing the design intent I developed the hand-drawn sketches in a 3-D model using Sketchup. The final presentation is a combination of hand-drawn and computer-generated images to illustrate the design intent, conceptual focus, materiality, and assembly of the final stair.

—CIARA LANGLEY

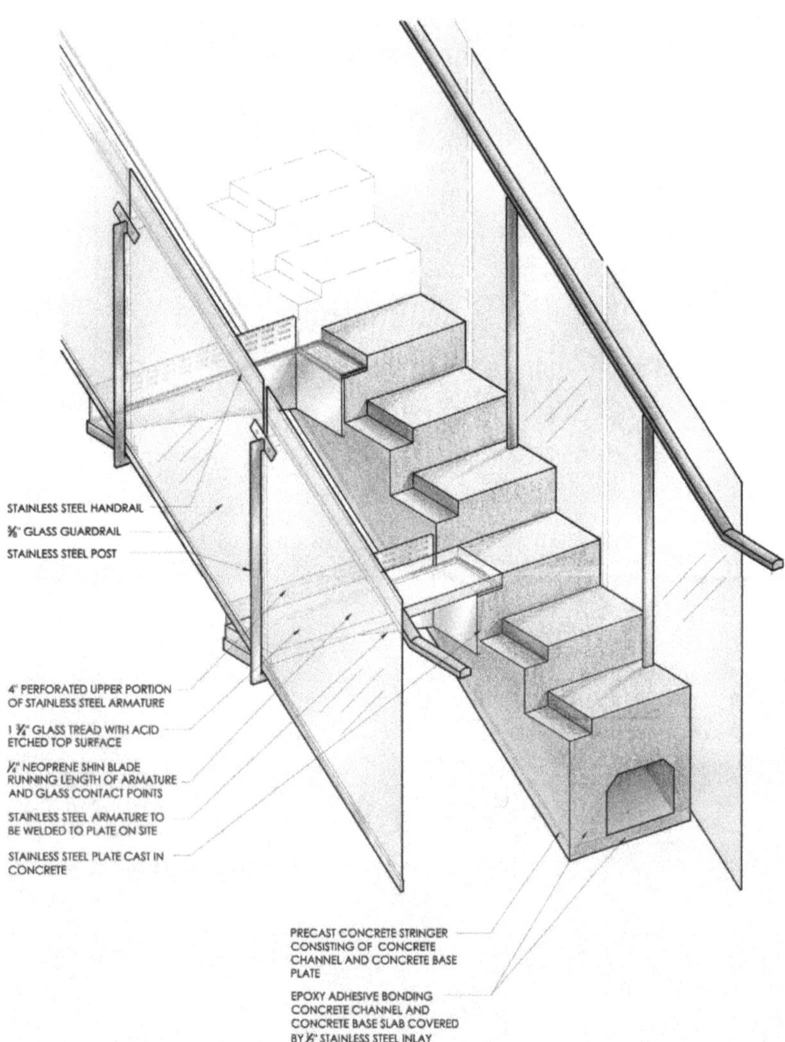

CIARA LANGLEY
Stair assembly drawing
Advanced Materials and Detailing Studio,
The New England School of
Art & Design at Suffolk University

Detail and Assembly

Detailing is one of the more complex aspects of architecture and interior design. Two-dimensional construction details layered with notes, assembly instructions, and dimensions are often overwhelming to young designers. A three-dimensional investigation of these drawings can build an understanding of the spatial information and component relationships inherent in construction details.

Exploded Detail Drawing

This detail stair drawing communicates the relationship between materials and methods of assembly in stair detail. The drawing was created for a design presentation to communicate the student's understanding of detailing, assembly, and the conceptual relationship between the detail and the project.

In creating this isometric, I was given the opportunity to explore various aspects of the design and its assembly. Constructing each component separately allowed me to pull together the design as if I were actually building it, prompting questions such as "What is this component connected to?" and "Does it look the way I originally intended?" By exploding the isometric, this drawing made it easier to communicate design intent and detail assembly to a critic, team member, or client.

—Rania Makkas

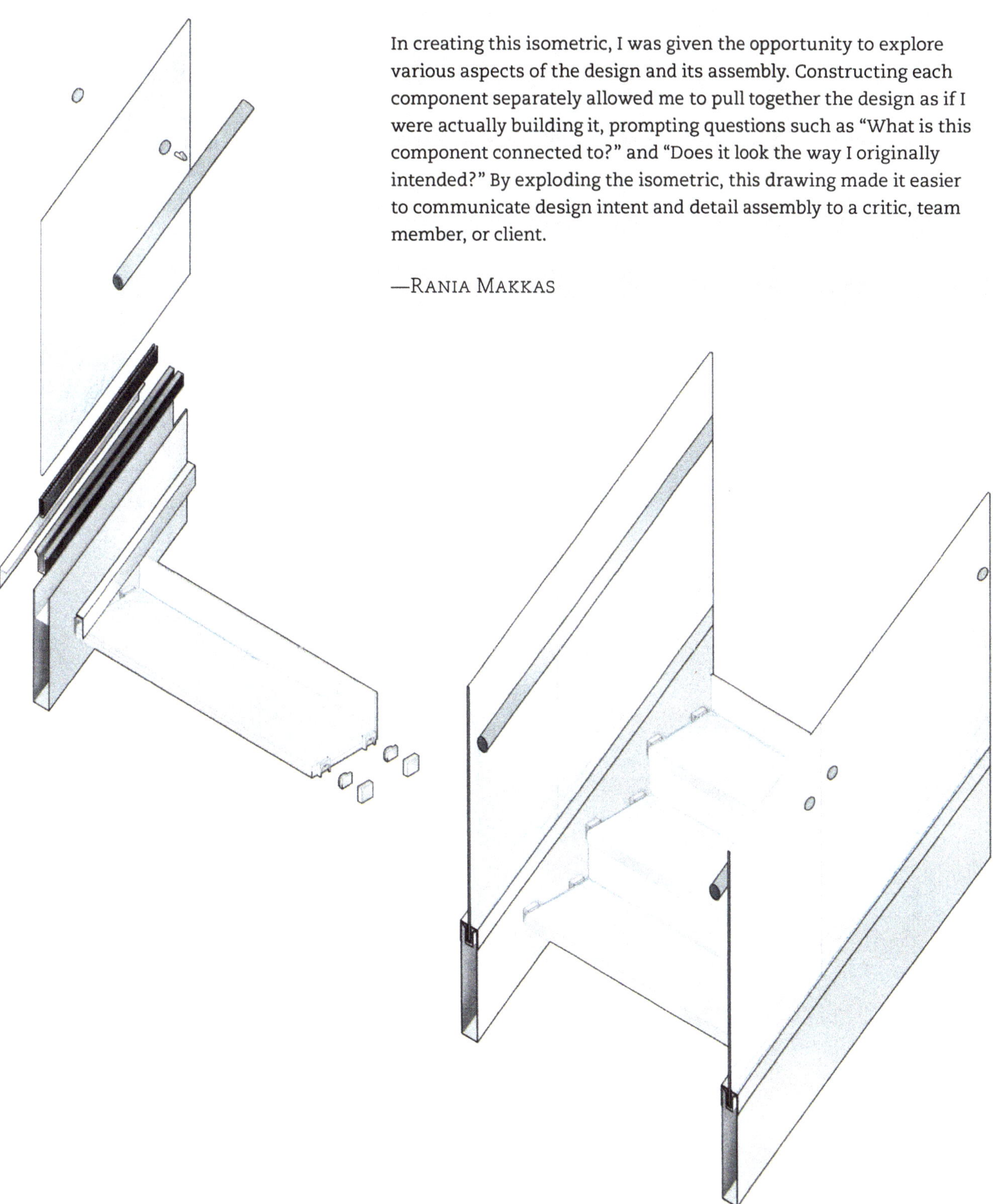

Rania Makkas
Stair assembly drawing
Advanced Material and Detailing Studio,
The New England School of
Art & Design at Suffolk University

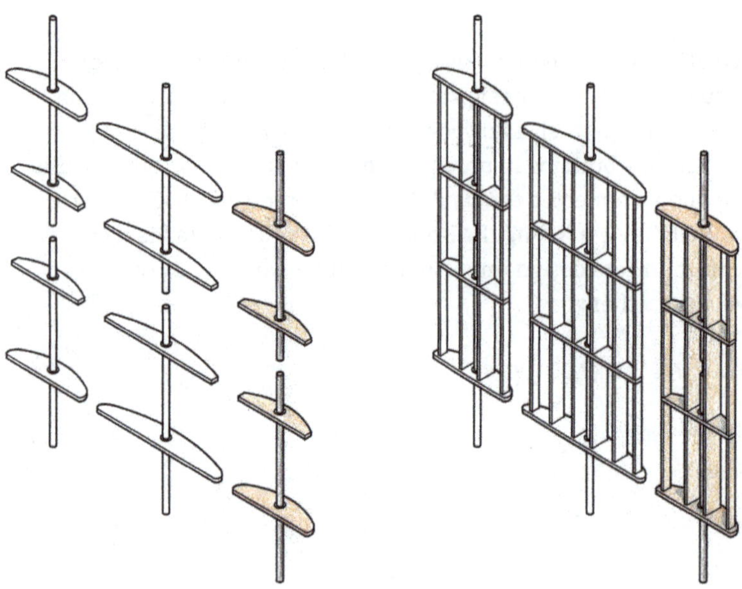

With this project, I was exploring different construction methods as a part of my design process. I started with a basic sketch or idea. By drawing the exploded isometrics, I was able to refine the design until I reached something that was both functional for the user, buildable, and aesthetically pleasing.

The step-by-step assembly drawings help communicate why I made the choices that I did during my project presentation. Since the design jury could clearly see what construction choices I made, we were able to discuss alternative solutions for achieving my design goals.

—THEADORA ELLIOTT

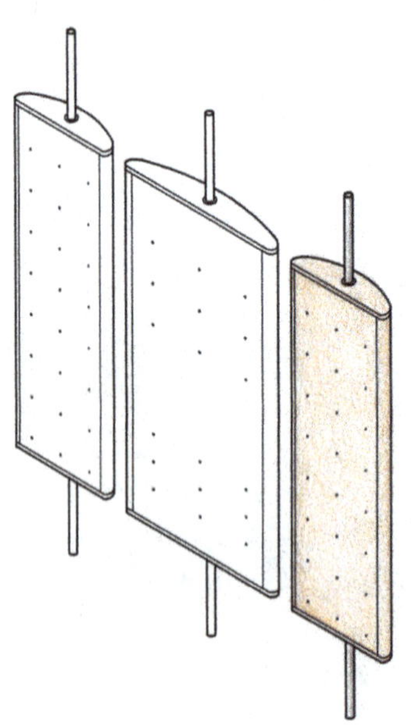

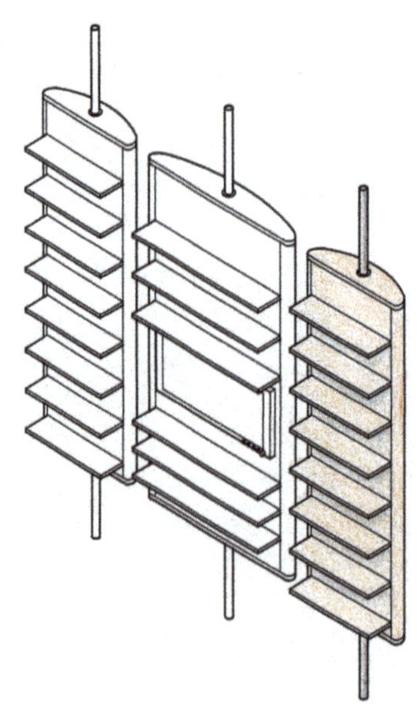

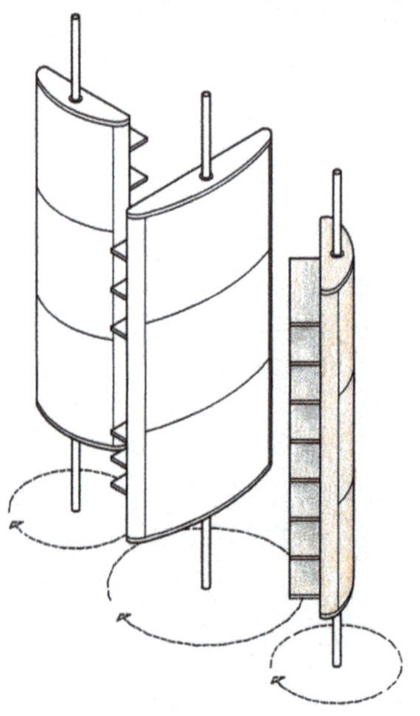

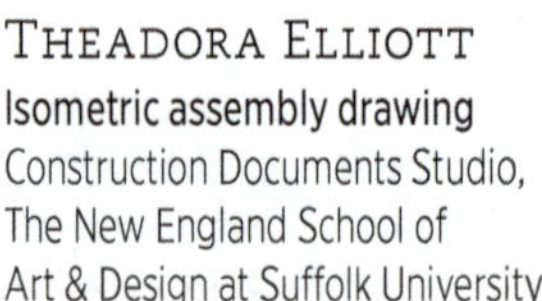

THEADORA ELLIOTT
Isometric assembly drawing
Construction Documents Studio, The New England School of Art & Design at Suffolk University

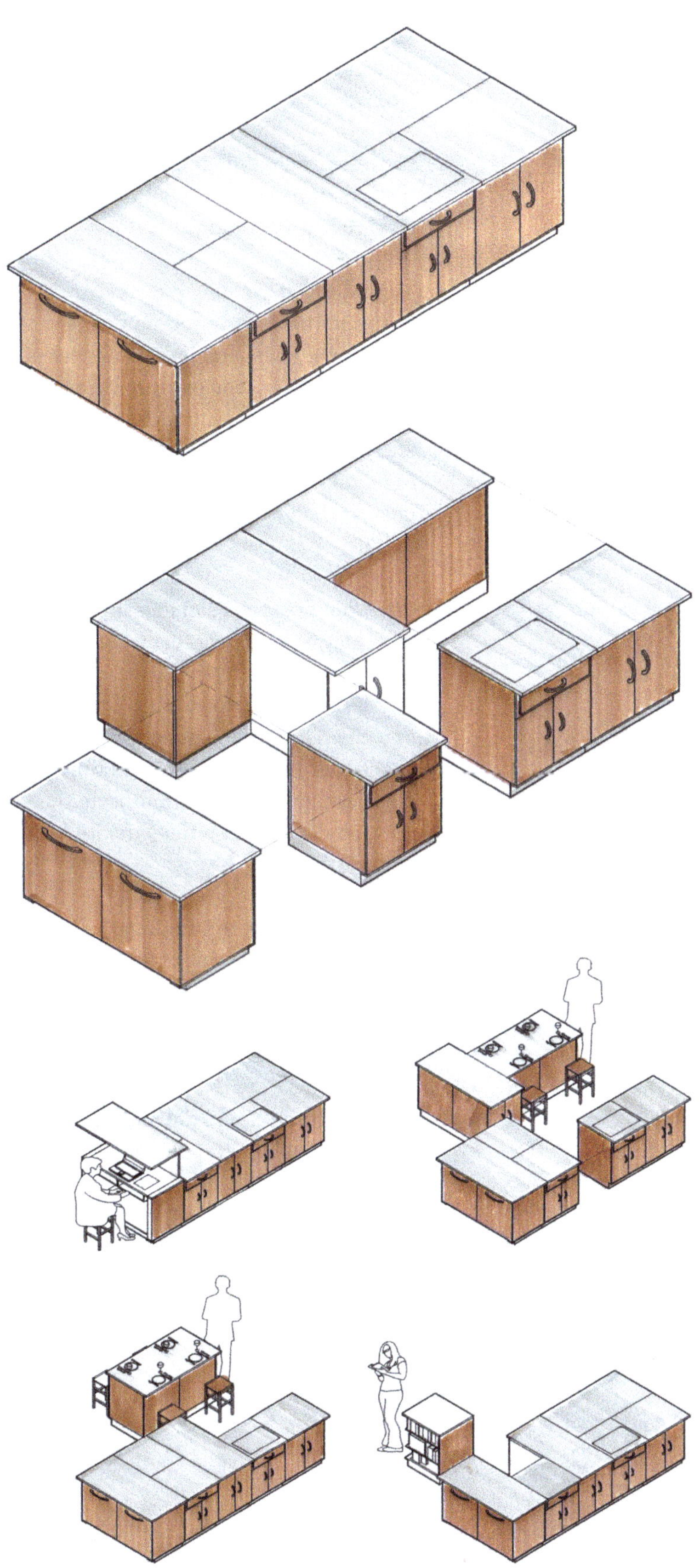

KATE MCGOLDRICK
Isometric presentation drawings
Furniture and Detailing Studio,
The New England School of
Art & Design at Suffolk University

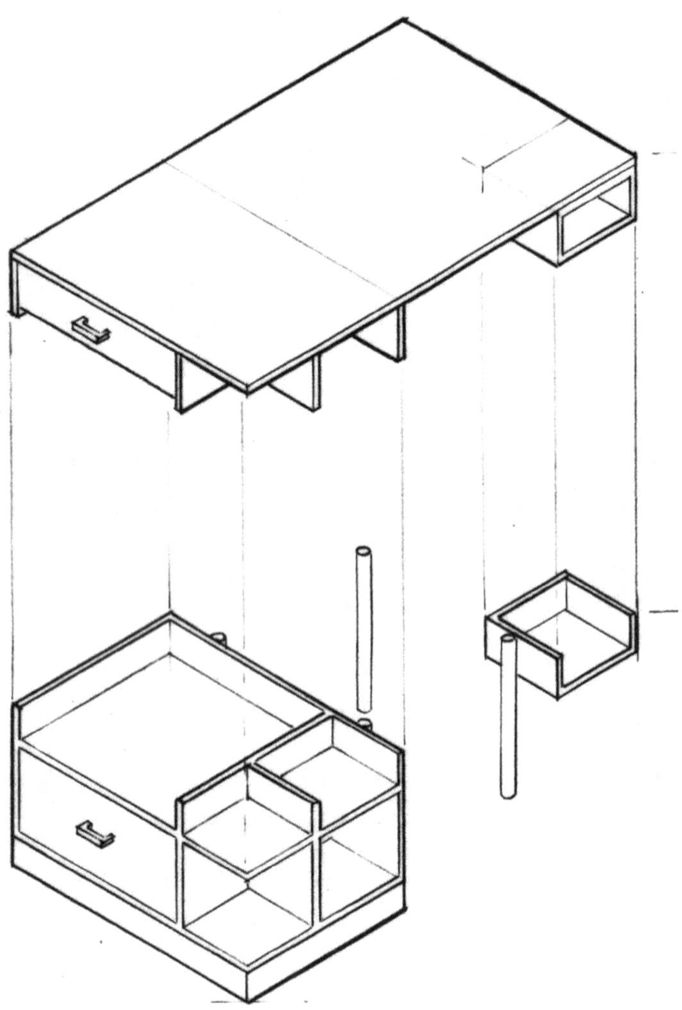

GERRIT REITVELD (1888–1964)
Bureau (1931)
Drawings by Douglas Seidler

Exploded Paraline Drawings
As a presentation drawing, the exploded isometric and axonometric drawing types communicate a project's spatial qualities and relationships by combining the information contained on plan, elevation, and section.

The exploded drawing provides an opportunity to visually communicate the relationship between individual pieces and the whole. Good exploded paraline drawings clearly identify the relationship between the larger object and the individual parts by pulling each part off of a centrally drawn building, object, or detail.

Exploded drawings can investigate the assembly of a piece of furniture, a detail, or a building. They can also explore any series of systems within a building or a city. The various scales and scopes of these drawings share a common objective: to clearly communicate the relationship between the parts and the whole.

Exploded Furniture Drawing
This exploded drawing of Reitveld's bureau (1931) reveals the difference between two types of furniture drawings: the top view and the horizontal section. This drawing was created to communicate the spatial nature of each two-dimensional drawing for an earlier chapter in this book.

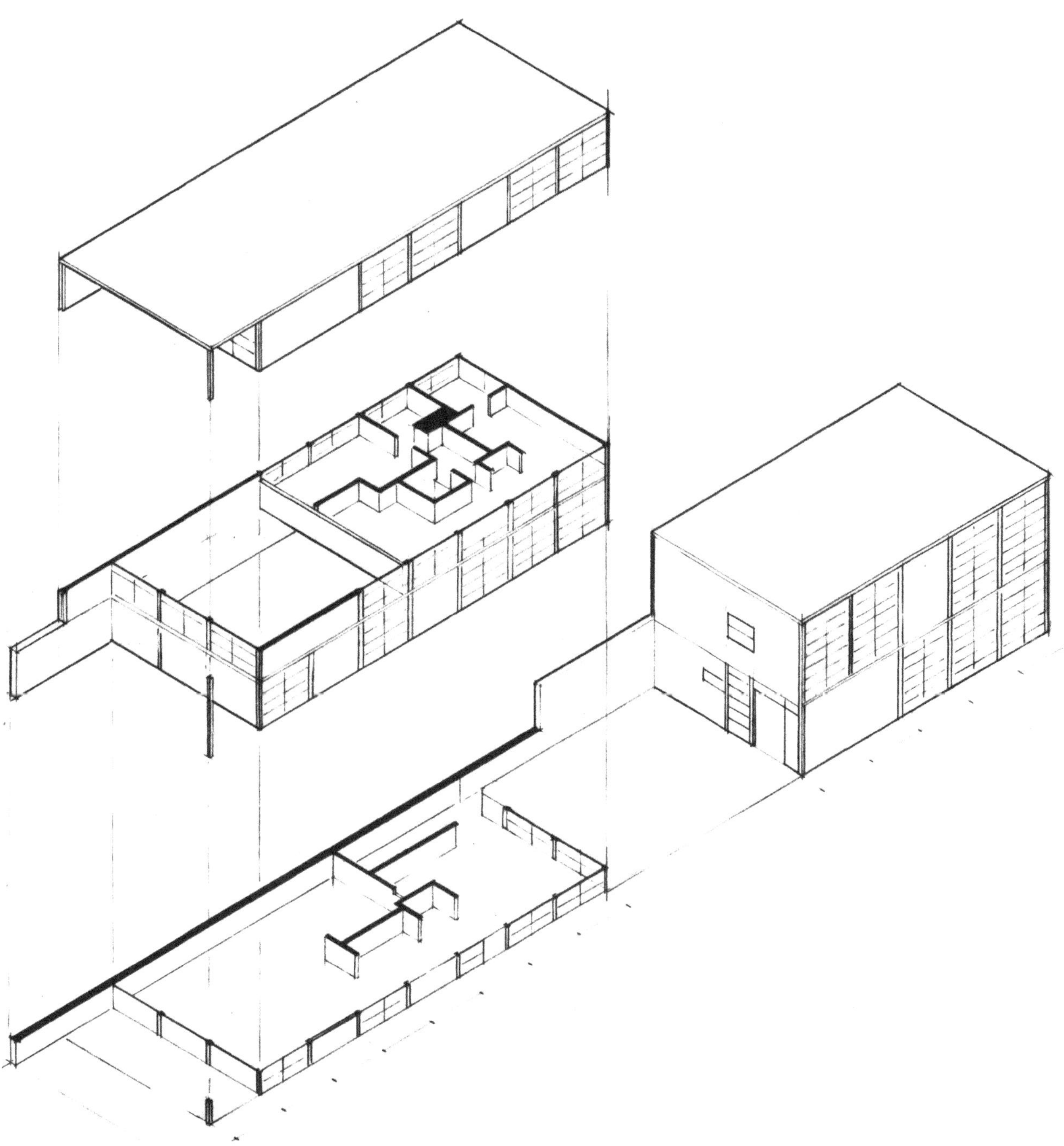

Exploded Building Drawing
This exploded isometric of the Eames House (1949) communicates the relationship between the first and second floor. The exploded nature of the drawing also accurately describes the spatial conditions of each floor without the need to hide exterior walls. For example, the drawing reveals the relationship between the bedrooms on the second floor and the adjacent double-height living room space on the first floor.

CHARLES (1907–78) AND RAY (1912–88) EAMES
Eames House (1949)
Drawings by Douglas Seidler

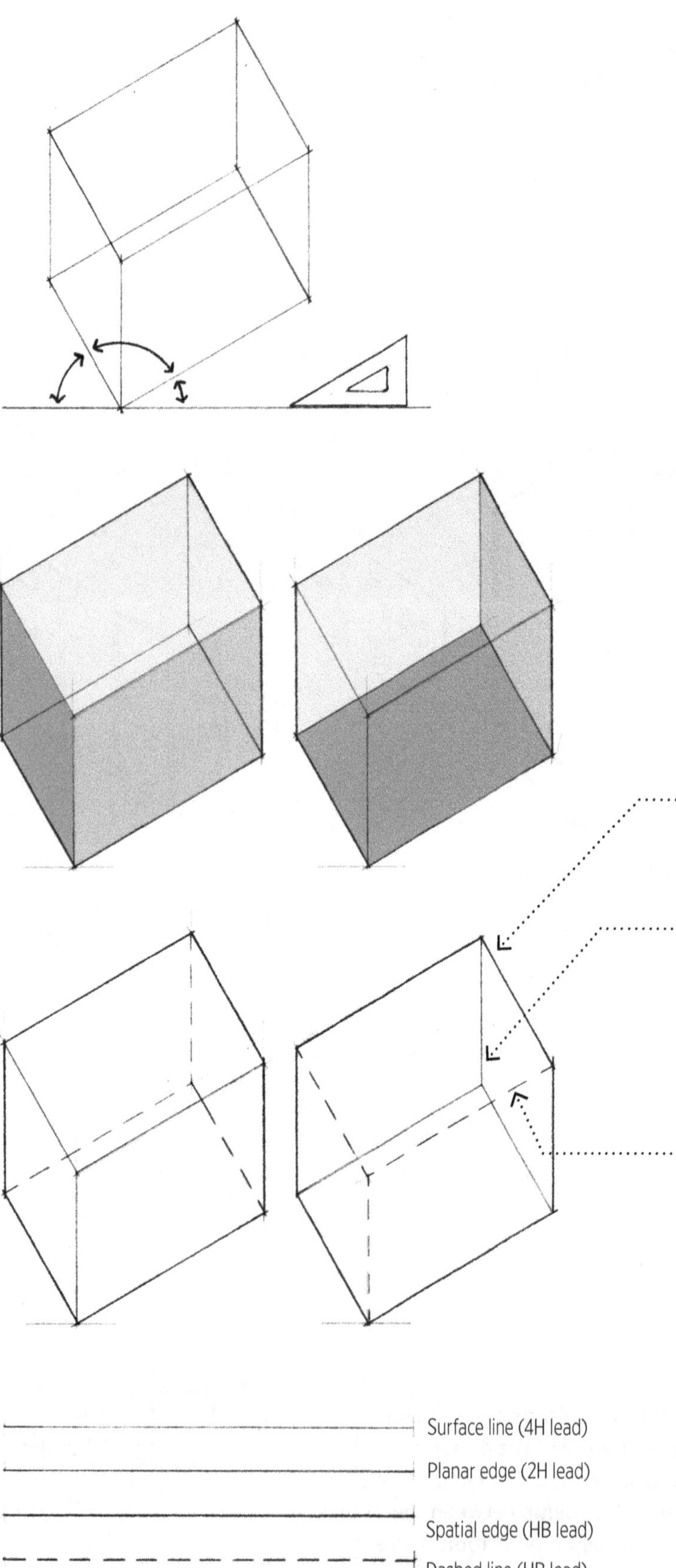

Isometric and Axonometric Drawings
A strong understanding of architectural graphic standards is critical in order to clearly communicate and develop design ideas through isometric and axonometric drawings. The remaining portion of this chapter introduces drawing techniques, terminology, and graphic standards to increase your understanding and your ability to draw legible paraline drawings.

The two drawings to the left were shaded to communicate the different visual reading and orientation of a paraline drawing that does not use a hierarchy of line weight.

In this example appropriate line weight was used to communicate the desired orientation for the object.

- **Spatial edges** are drawn with medium lines. These are edges of objects in the drawing that are separated from their background by space.
- **Planar edges** are drawn with light lines. These are edges of objects in the drawing where both adjacent planes are visible.
- **Surface lines** are very light lines that represent a change in surface material.
- **Dashed lines** are used to identify major architectural objects hidden from view or major architectural elements that have been removed from the drawing.

Line Weight
Designers communicate the three-dimensional space represented in a paraline drawing through clear and legible line weight.

- The paraline drawing has a tendency to flip on itself if it is not drawn with appropriate line weight.

Constructing Paraline Drawings
There are three primary methods used to construct paraline drawings:

- **Projection method** – Plan and elevation oblique drawings can be projected from an existing measured drawing.

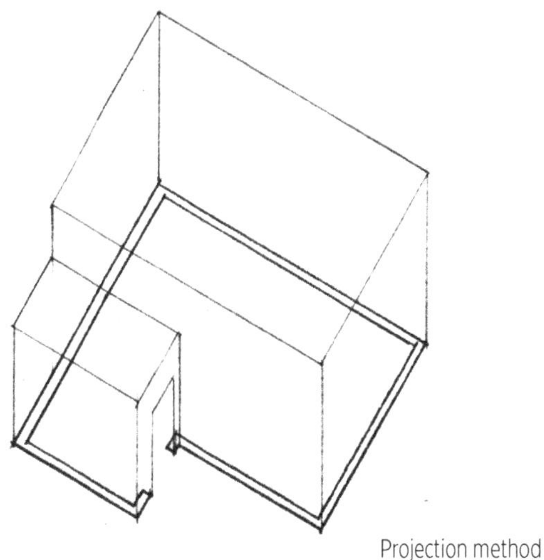
Projection method

- **Additive method** – Axonometric and isometric drawings can be constructed by combining a series of volumes to create the overall object of a building.

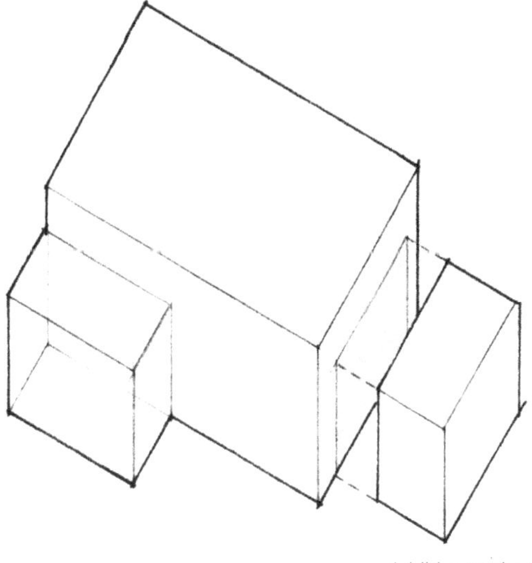
Additive method

- **Subtractive method** – Axonometric and isometric drawings can be constructed by drawing the overall volume of an object or building and then removing the portions of the rectangular solid that are not a part of the object.

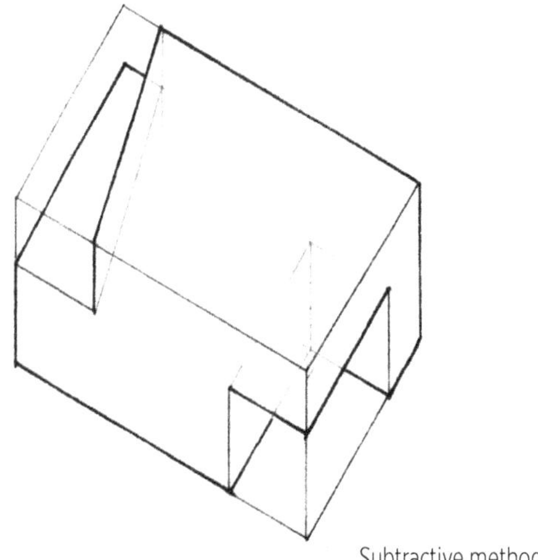
Subtractive method

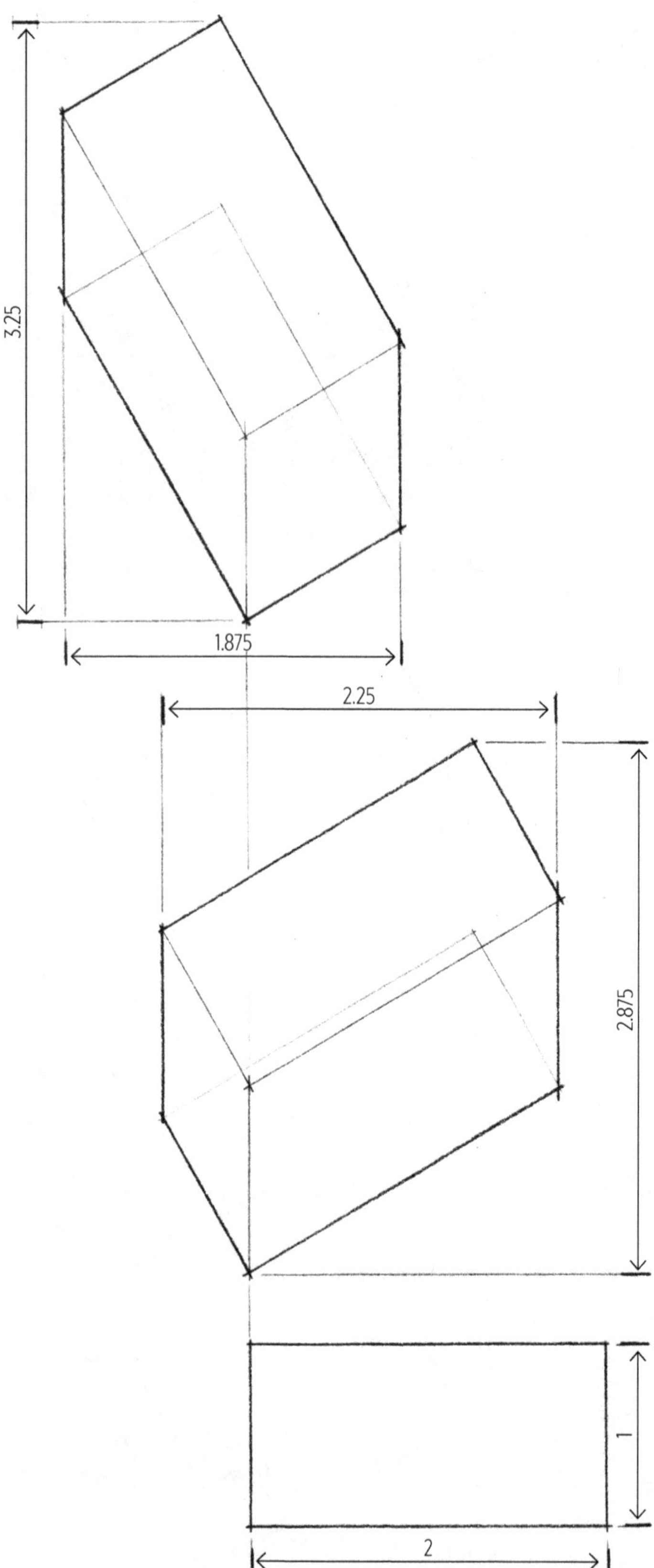

Drawing Orientation

Before you begin a paraline drawing, identify the most appropriate orientation and the overall volume of the design. Paraline drawings occupy a larger portion of a sheet of paper than orthographic drawings drawn at the same scale because they include multiple object planes instead of the single plane drawn in floor plan.

- Orient the drawing so that the most important corner is located at the front of the drawing.
- If the overall form is rectangular, orient the drawing so that the longer edge is drawn along the 30-degree axis.
- If one side of your design is more important to describe than the other, orient the prominent side along the 30-degree axis.
- If both sides of your design are equally important, using a 45-degree axis will emphasize both faces equally.

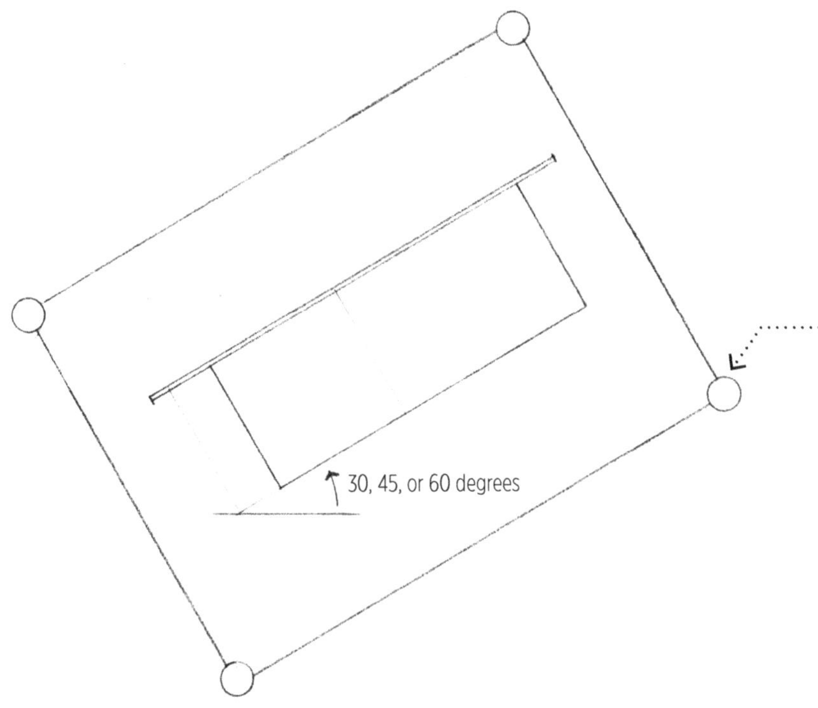

Drawing Composition
Axonometric drawings are most often constructed from floor plans.

- If you are constructing your axonometric from a floor plan, rotate the drawing 30 degrees, 45 degrees, or 60 degrees from horizontal on your drawing surface.
- Fasten the floor plan to the drafting surface with drafting dots or drafting tape.

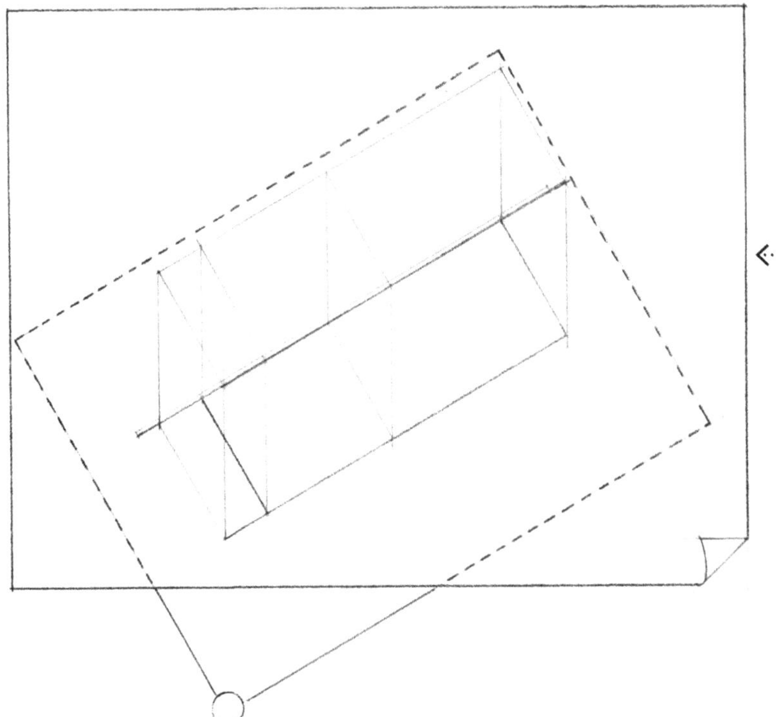

Drawing composition involves the thoughtful arrangement of the drawing on a sheet of paper. For paraline drawings, the length, width, and height of the three-dimensional drawing should be considered.

- Overlay a new sheet of paper on top of the rotated floor plan.
- Consider the overall size of the axonometric drawing as you position the new sheet of paper. To estimate how much space your drawing will take up, project lines up from the outside corners of the floor plan to construct the overall volume of the building. Then center the volume on your paper.
- Fasten the new sheet of paper to the drafting surface with drafting dots or drafting tape.

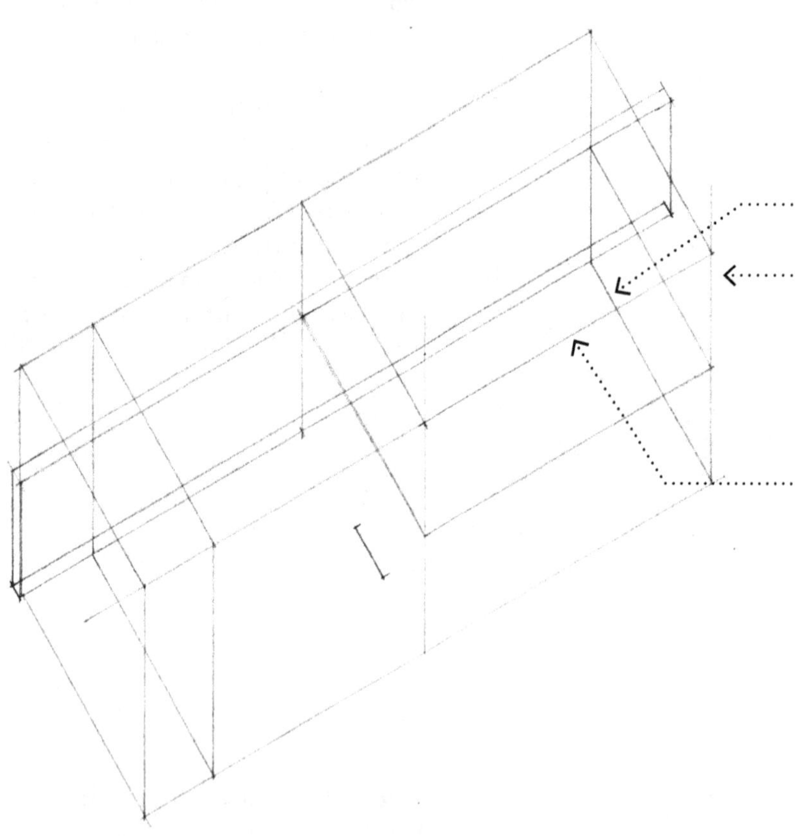

Boundaries and Geometry

- Identify the boundaries and major geometry of the axonometric with construction lines. Construction lines are very light lines that help define the overall scope of the drawing or drawings on a sheet of paper.
- Construct horizontal geometry directly from the floor plan.
- Project lines up at a 90-degree angle from the floor plan to construct vertical geometry. Transfer measurements from the elevation and section drawings to determine the length of these lines.
- Connect the top of each vertical line. This new line should be parallel to the floor plan.

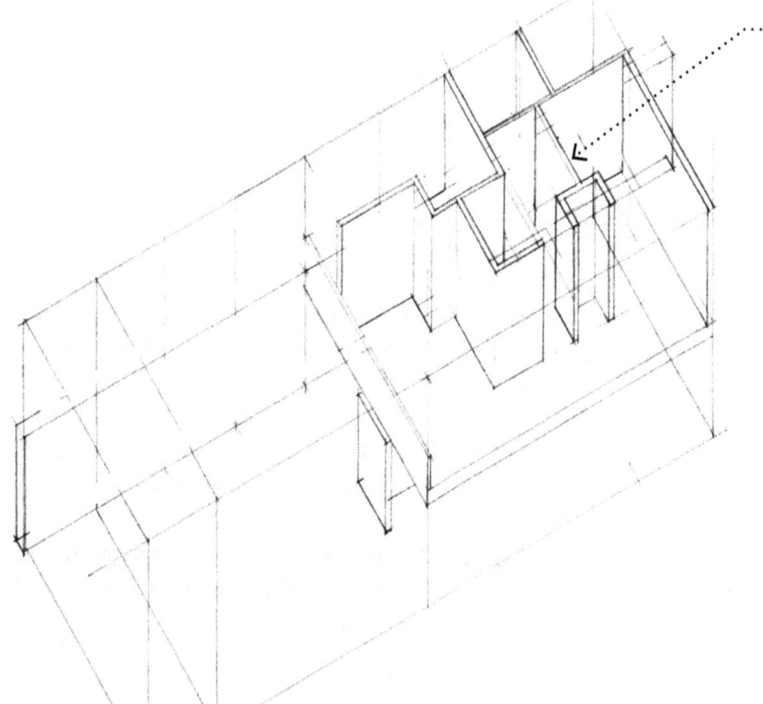

Primary Spaces

- Use light lines to locate the major spaces, walls, and surface openings in your project.
- In this example the roof, front, and left facade were intentionally not drawn to better communicate the interior space.

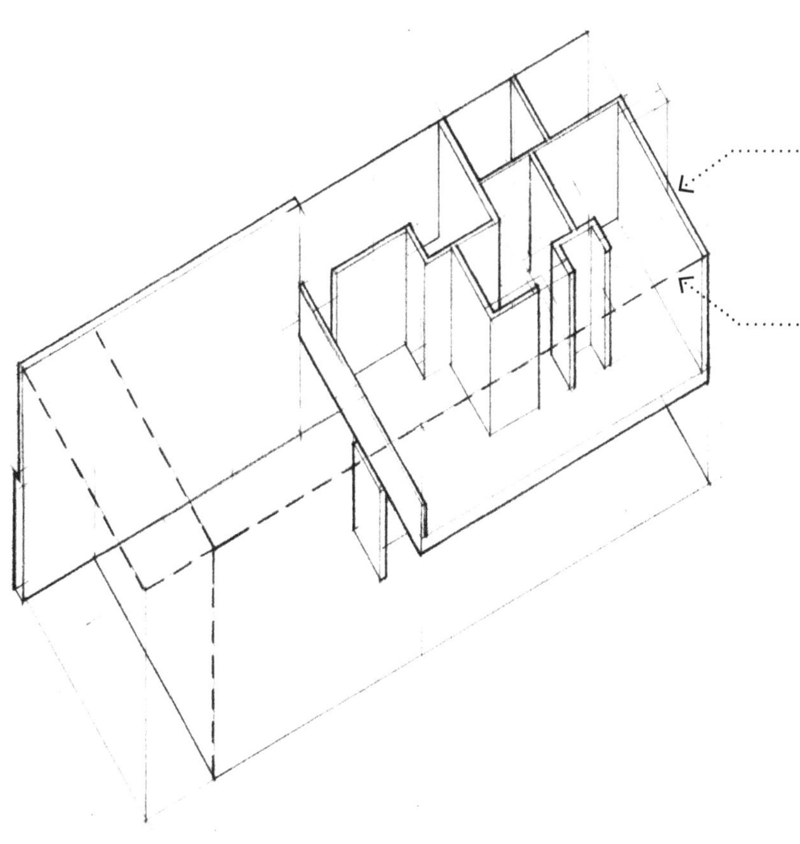

Spatial Edges and Dashed Lines
Spatial edges and dashed lines define the relationships between objects in the drawing.

- Use medium lines to identify the spatial edges for each form in the drawing.
- Use dashed lines to identify major surfaces that were removed from the drawing.

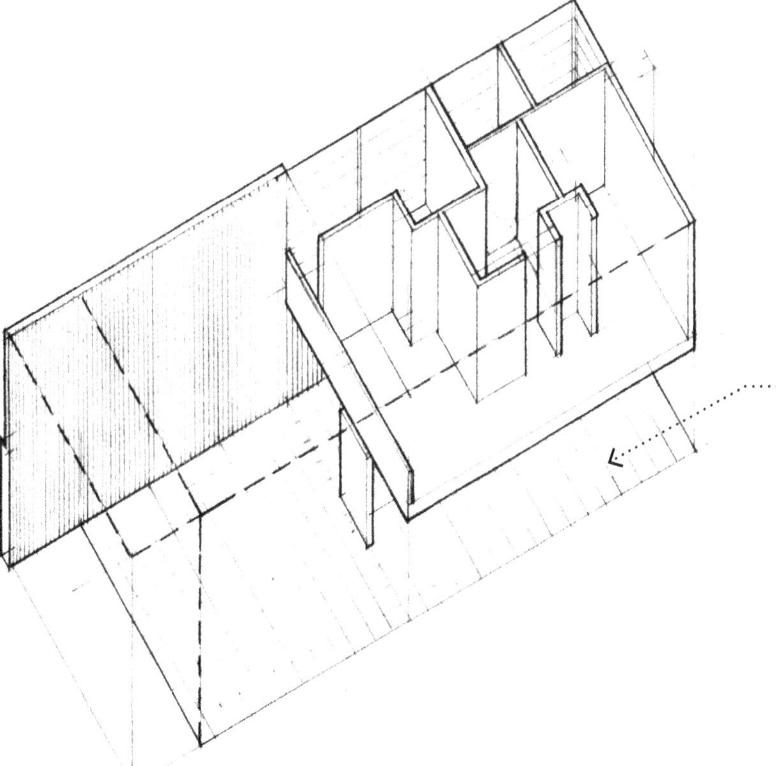

Surface Patterns
Surface patterns and material properties help visually locate each surface in the drawing.

- Use light lines to indicate surface patterns or changes in surface material.

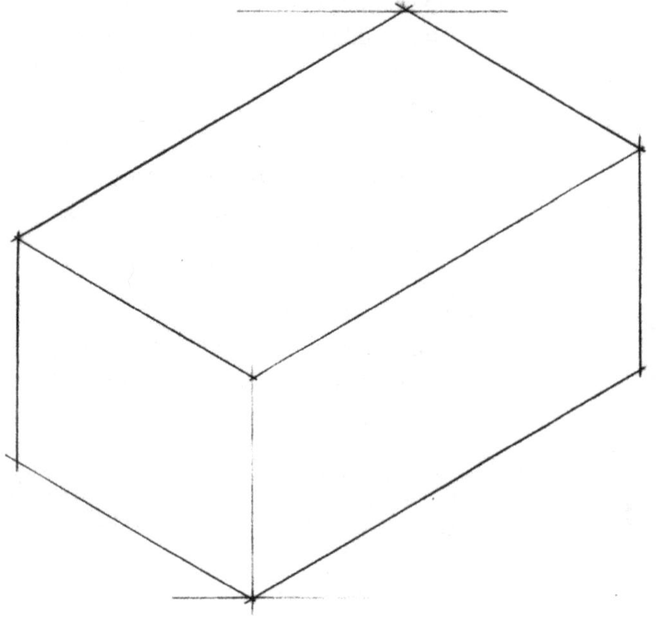

Constructing Isometric Projections
Because isometric projections cannot be constructed directly from floor plans, these drawings are most often constructed through an additive or subtractive volumetric method.

Boundaries

- Identify the boundaries of the isometric drawing with construction lines.
- Construction lines are very light lines that help define the overall scope of the drawing or drawings on a sheet of paper.
- This drawing is a 30-degree isometric projection.
- Horizontal and vertical lines in plan are drawn at 30 degrees from horizontal.
- The length of each line is drawn to scale.

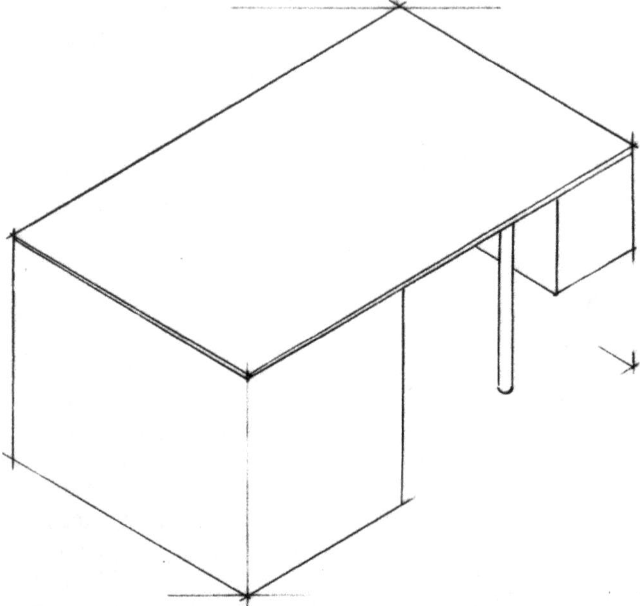

Primary Massing

- Use light lines to locate the major massing in the design.
- In this example the massing was measured from an existing furniture plan and elevations.

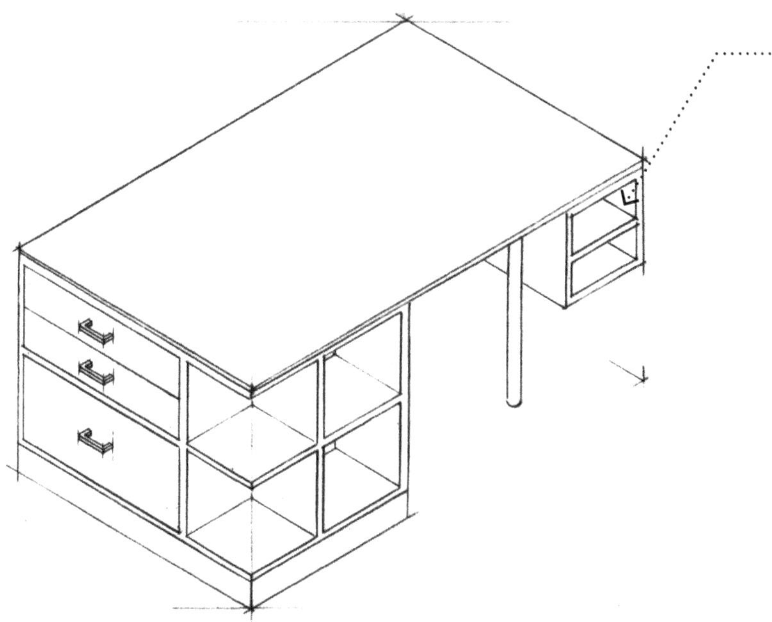

Planar Edges

- Use light lines to identify the planar edges for each form in the drawing.
- In this example the shelves and drawers were drawn, using light lines.

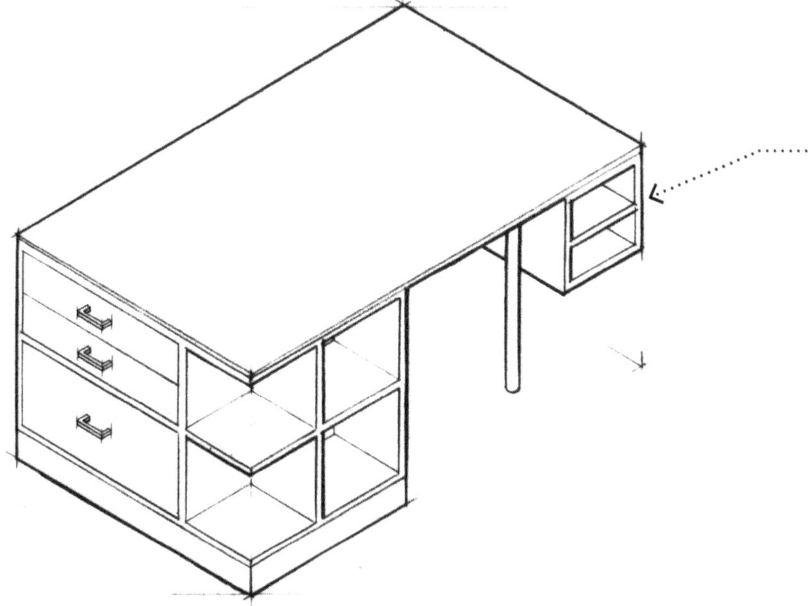

Spatial Edges

Spatial edges define the spatial relationships between objects in the drawing.

- Use medium lines to identify the spatial edges for each form in the drawing.

Constructing Isometric Projections
An isometric projection drawing can be constructed from a section through an object or a building.

- Using the section as a guide, draw the overall volume of the object.
- Draw complex angles by locating the start and end of each line on the perimeter around the volume.

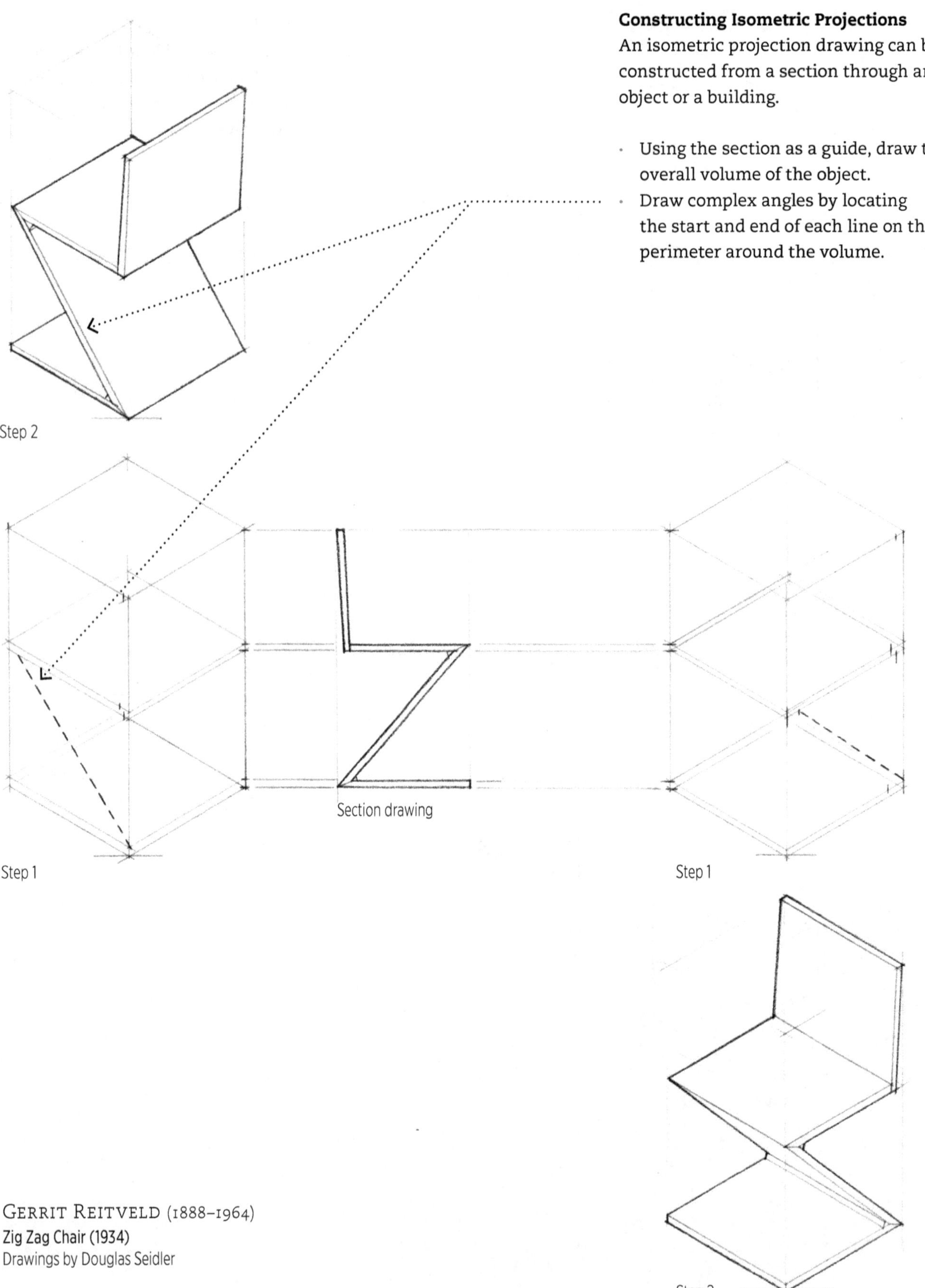

GERRIT REITVELD (1888–1964)
Zig Zag Chair (1934)
Drawings by Douglas Seidler

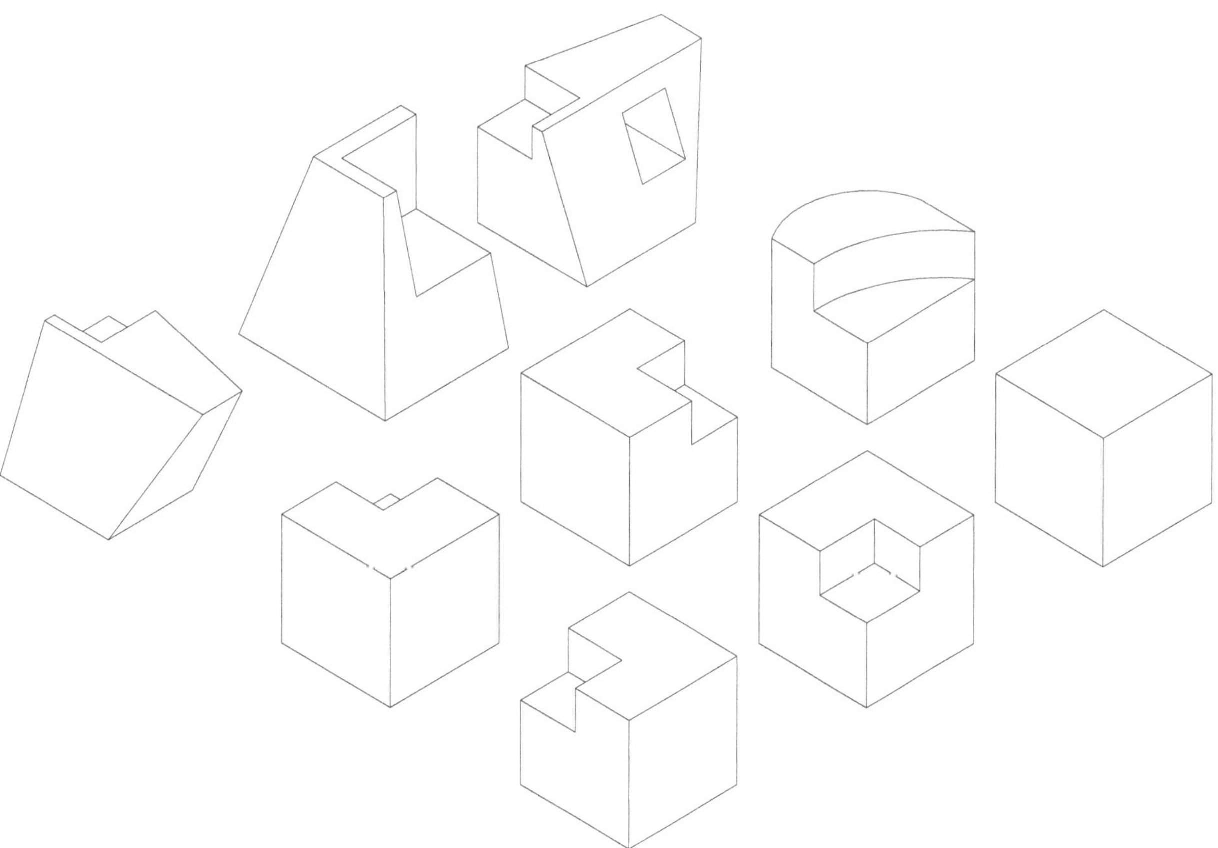

Learning Exercise: Line Weight
This exercise is intended to help you improve your understanding of line weight in communicating the spatial properties of paraline projections.

- Using a dark line, carefully trace the profile of each drawing.

Learning Exercise: Line Weight

This exercise is intended to help you improve your understanding of line weight in communicating the spatial properties of paraline projections.

- Using a dark line, carefully trace the perimeter profile of this drawing.
- Using a medium line, carefully trace over the internal profile lines and openings in this drawing.
- Use a light line to draw 4" wood siding on this drawing.

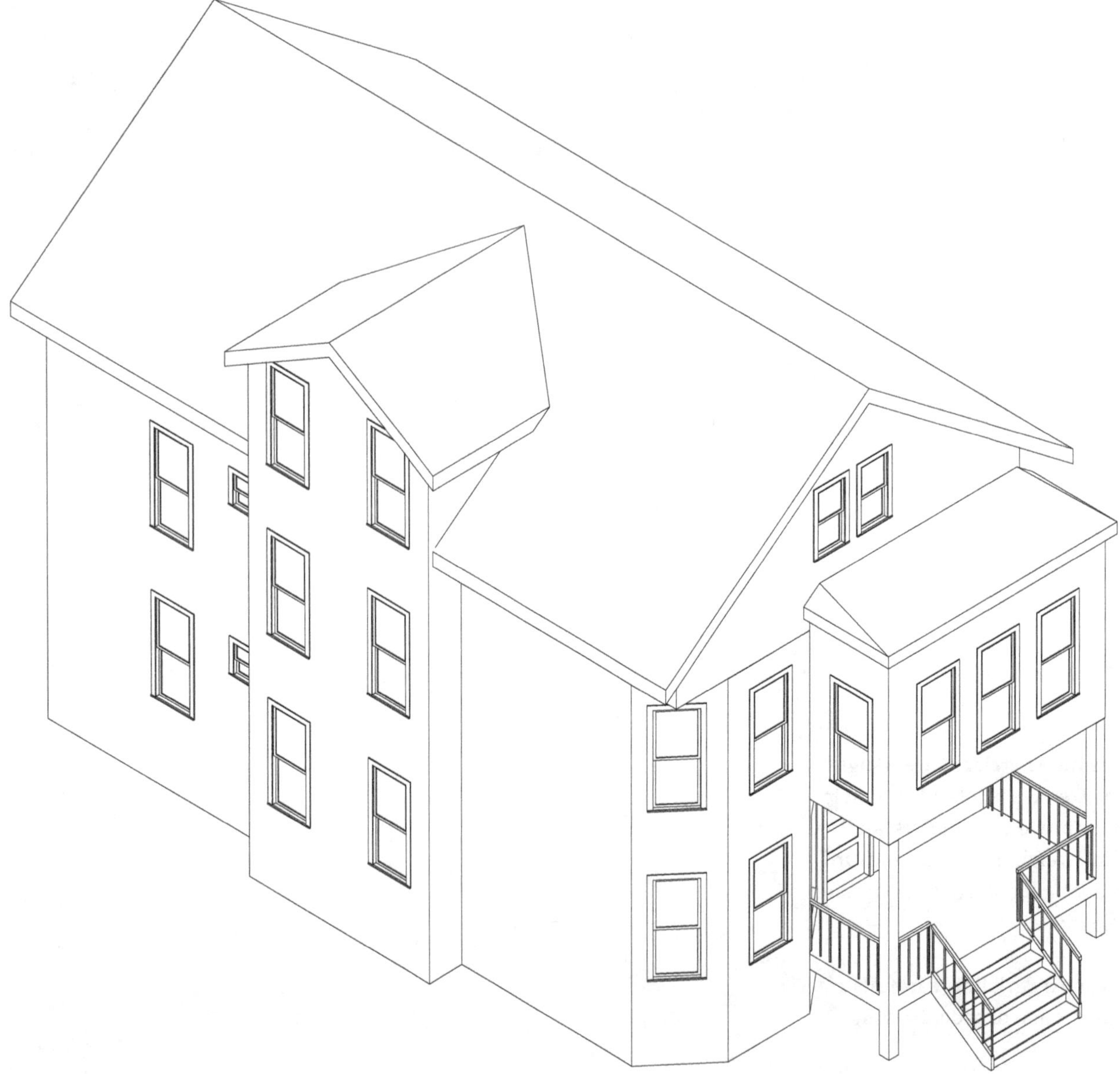

Isometric projection
Not to scale

Learning Exercise: Drawing Axonometric Projections

This exercise is intended to help you improve your understanding of constructing axonometric projections from a floor plan.

- Using the floor plan as the base of your drawing, construct an axonometric projection of this room.
- Draw the axonometric at ³⁄₈"= 1'-0".
- Door heads and openings are 7'-6" above the finish floor.
- Window heads are 7'-6" above the finish floor.
- Window sills are 2'-0" above the finish floor.

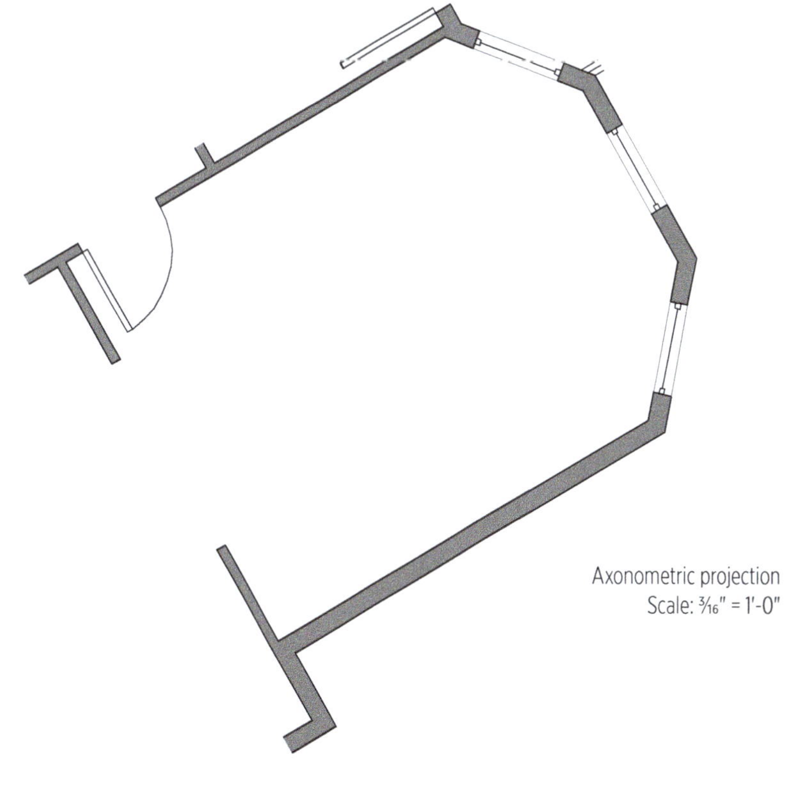

Axonometric projection
Scale: ³⁄₁₆" = 1'-0"

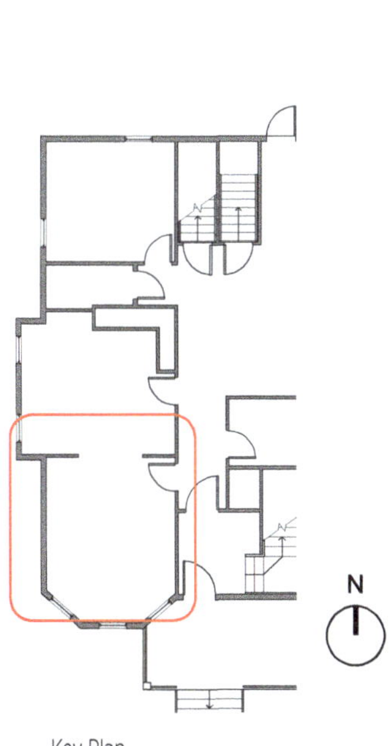

Key Plan

PERSPECTIVES

This chapter introduces students to perspective drawing. Of all the drawing conventions, perspectives convey the most experiential view of an interior room or building. When drawn during ideation, perspectives allow designers to more fully understand how their designs might be perceived and experienced.

In this chapter, you will learn how to draw freehand and drafted perspectives by applying basic perspective principles. One-point, two-point, and three-point perspectives will be introduced with an emphasis on how perspectives are used as a tool for ideation.

Consider the following questions as you read this chapter:

- How can you use perspective drawings to help generate and develop design ideas?
- How can the basic principles of perspective be applied to construct more complex objects, like furniture?
- How are perspectives used to support the design process?

Perspective drawings simulate how a space might look when seen from a single vantage point and a particular direction. Perspectives are similar to photographs, in that they capture a singular point of view or a snapshot of a space.

The use of perspectives to develop the design of a space is typically a nonlinear process. Designers, in both school and practice, move back and forth between hand-sketched perspectives, drafted perspectives, and digital models to develop and refine their ideas. Design changes that occur in perspective are projected back into plans, sections, and elevations; refined; and then reprojected back into perspective to create a final rendering of the space.

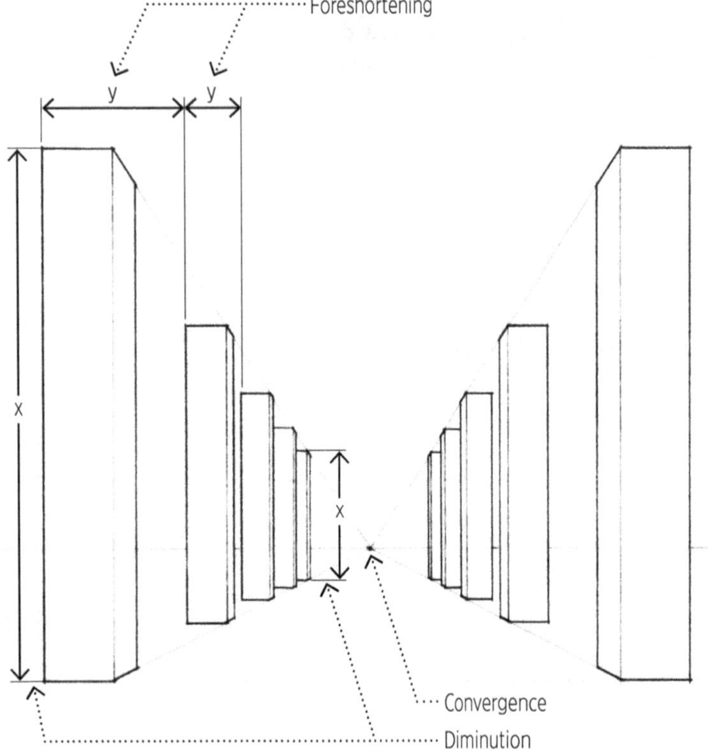

Basic Principles of Perspective

All perspective drawings are governed by three basic principles:

- Convergence – Elements that are parallel to each other, such as walls and furniture, appear to converge to a single point within the perspective drawing.
- Diminution – Equally sized elements that are farther away from the viewer are drawn smaller than elements that are closer to the viewer.
- Foreshortening – The dimension between objects appears to decrease as the distance between the object and viewer increases.

Perspective Types

There are three types of perspective drawings commonly used in architecture and interior design: one-point perspectives, two-point perspectives, and three-point perspectives. In a one-point perspective horizontal lines converge to a single point within the perspective drawing. In a two-point perspective horizontal lines converge to two main points within the drawing; in a three-point perspective horizontal and vertical lines converge to three main points within the drawing. One-, two-, and three-point perspectives are explained in more detail in the second half of this chapter.

Hand-Drawn Perspectives
Freehand perspectives are used at the beginning of ideation to quickly explore and design the spatial experience. These loosely sketched perspectives are drawn before the floor plan is finalized and are typically created by first drawing a three-dimensional cube to use as an underlay for the perspective drawing. Hand-drawn perspectives can also be created by sketching over a photograph of an interior space or physical model to develop a design.

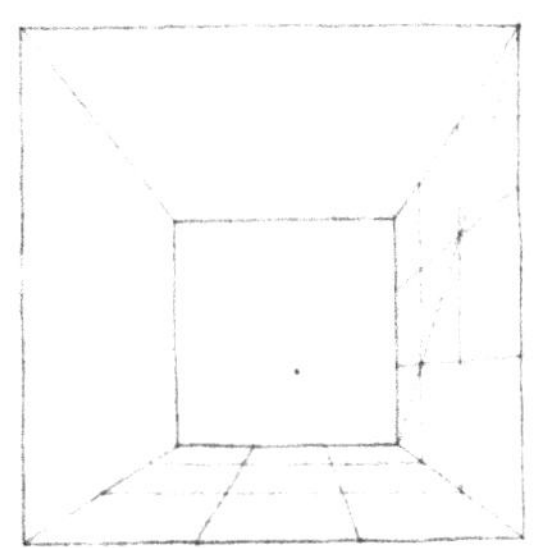

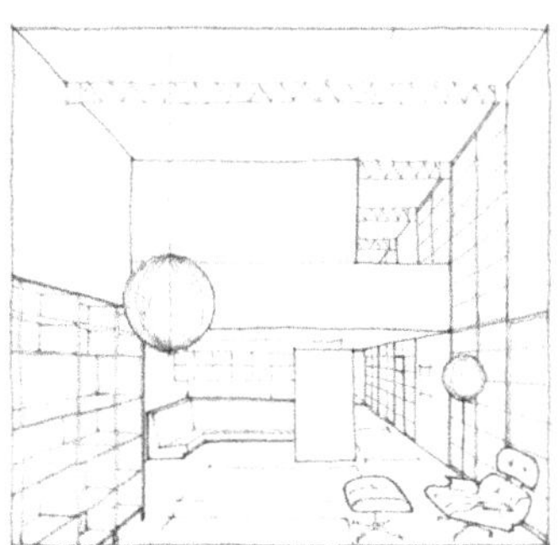

Hand-Drafted Perspectives
Hand-drafted perspectives create a more accurate representation of a space than freehand perspectives because they are constructed with measurements from a floor plan and section or elevation. Drafted perspectives are used less during ideation because they are more time consuming to draw and usually require the design to be finalized before the perspective can be constructed. Although hand-drafted perspectives are not commonly used in practice, it is critical for students to be familiar with the projection techniques used to construct one-point and two-point perspectives in order to apply these rules to their freehand perspectives.

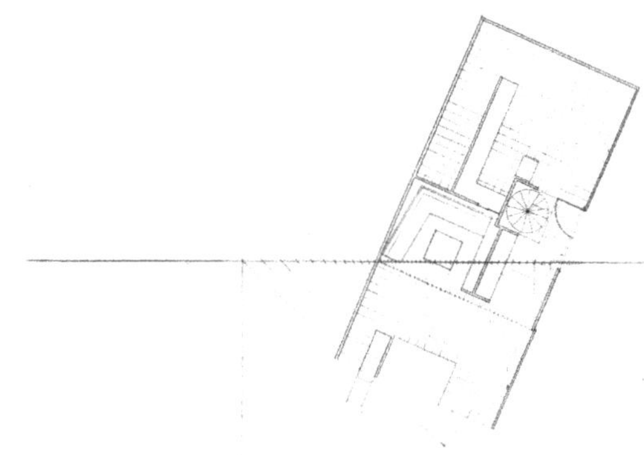

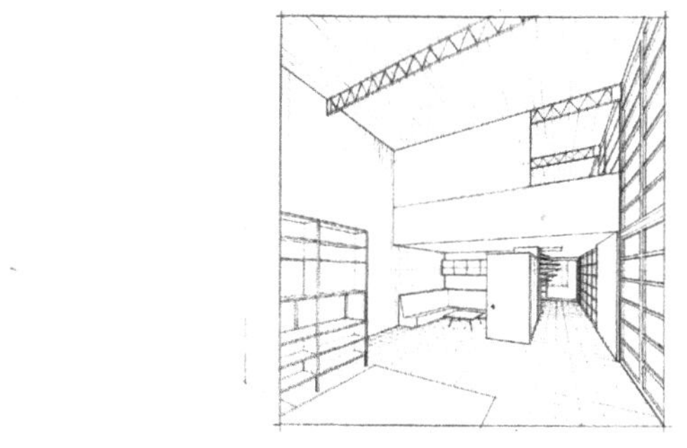

Digitally Generated Perspectives
One common way to design in perspective is to use a digital model to generate rough perspective views. Designers use the printed views as an underlay, to help them determine vanishing points and the overall perspective outline of a building mass or interior space. They then trace over the printed line work and develop their spaces through a series of freehand perspective sketches. A simple digital model, showing the overall volume of a space and critical heights, can be quicker to construct than a hand-drafted perspective, and an infinite number of views can be generated from a single model, allowing designers to study their designs from multiple points of view.

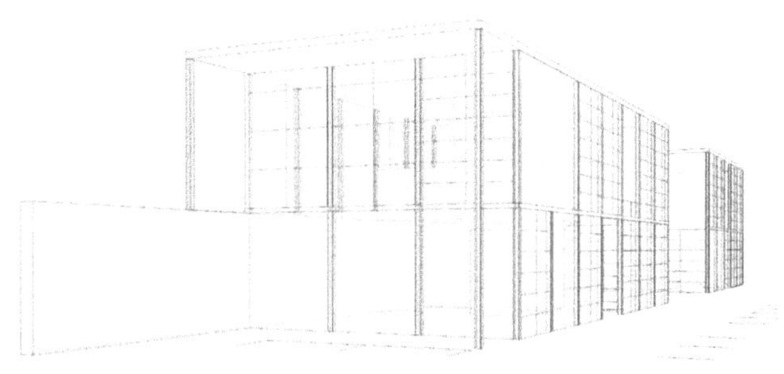

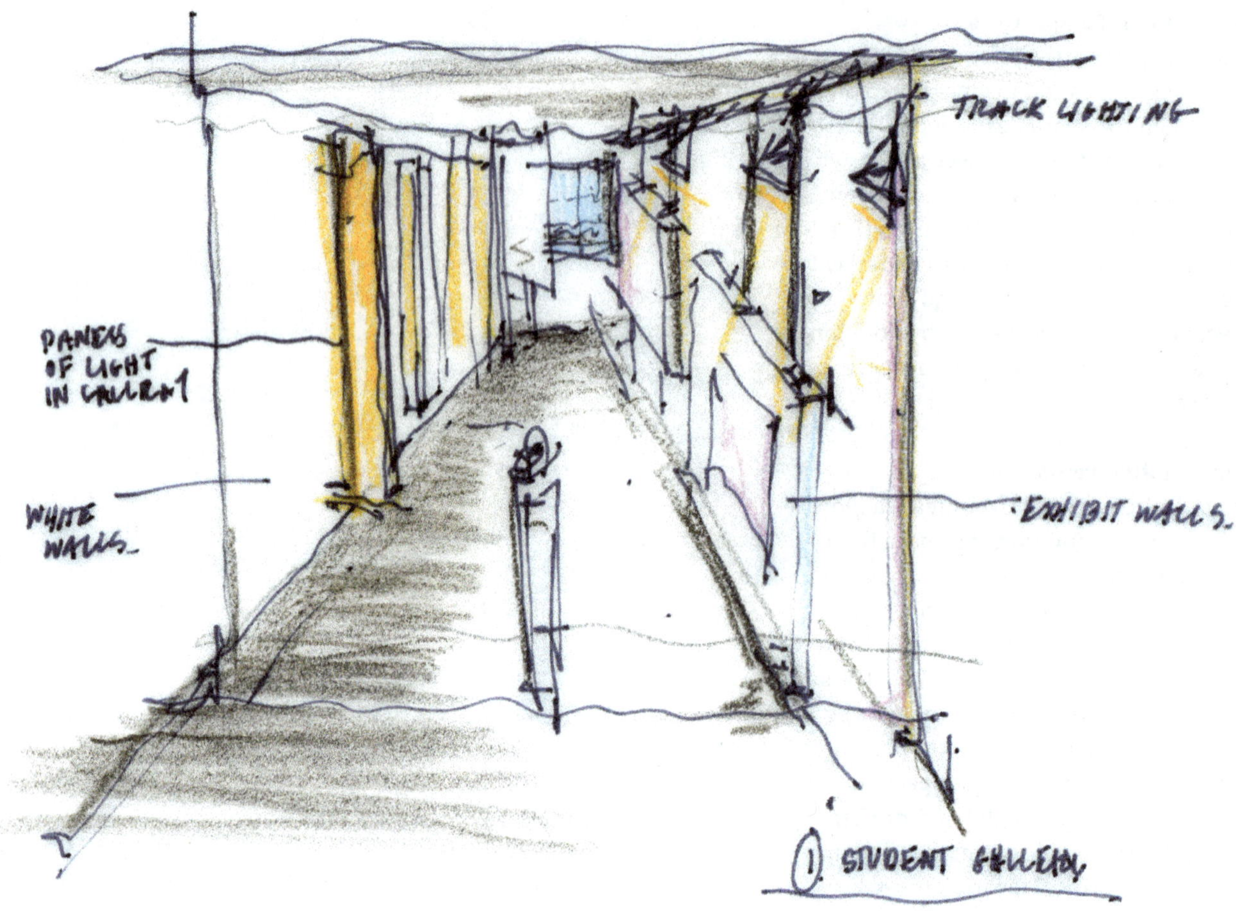

SARAH EIGEN
Perspective sketches in ink and colored pencil
Paris Studio,
Boston Architectural College

These freehand perspectives were drawn to explore a person's movement through a series of spaces. The sketches are one-point perspectives that build upon the geometry of a simple three-dimensional cube to create a wide variety of perspective views. Text and color were used to call out different materials and focal points within the views. A person is drawn within each perspective to communicate the scale of each space. Arrows also appear in many of the perspectives, noting what a person would look at or how they would move through the space.

Textual annotations are useful in early perspectives because they help designers recall their ideas at later stages of the design process. Small notations, such as text and arrows, allow designers to communicate their ideas when they are unable to present a design in person, as is often the case in practice, with sketches being e-mailed to clients and discussed during conference calls.

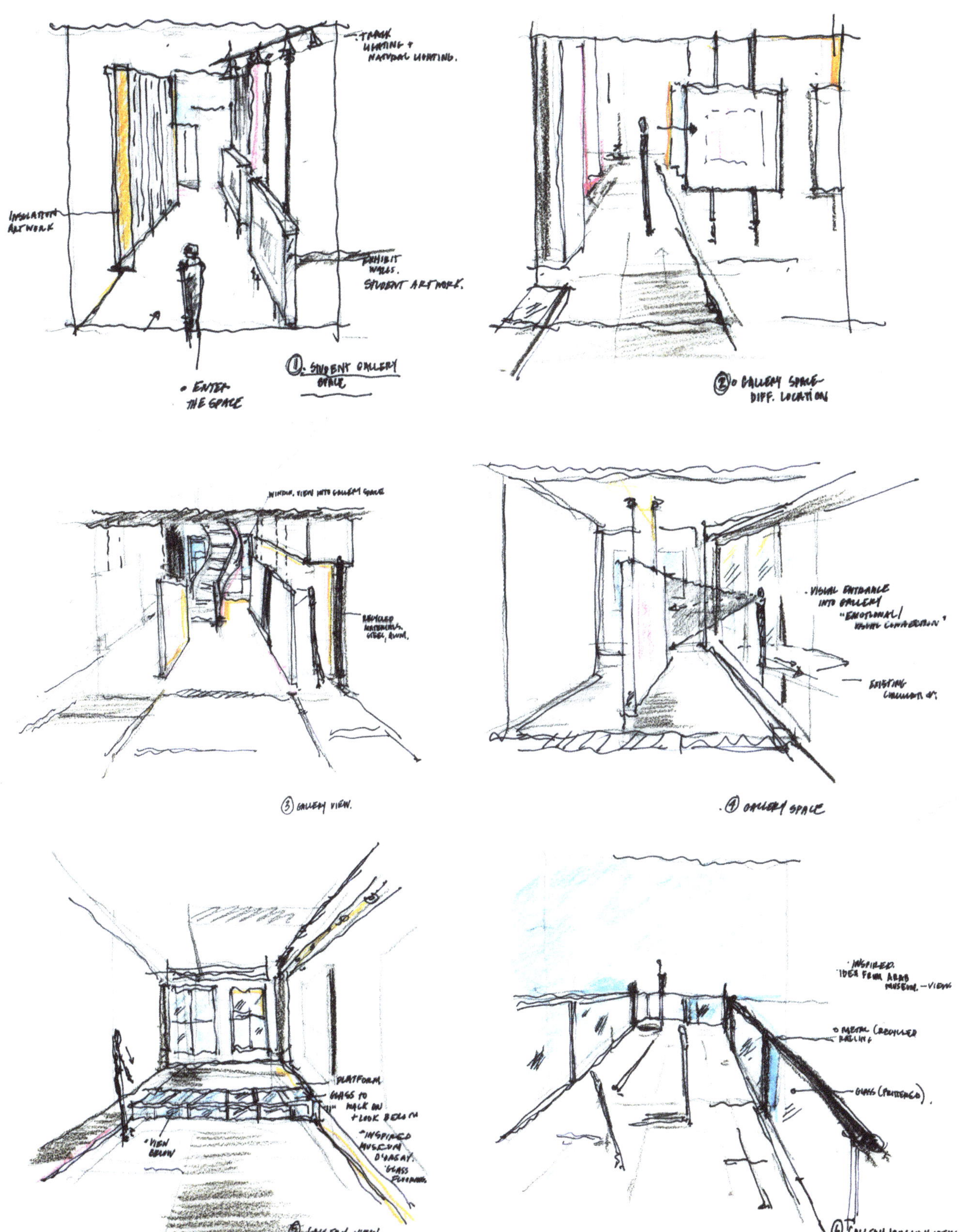
TRACK LIGHTING + NATURAL LIGHTING.
INSTALLATION ARTWORK
EXHIBIT WALLS.
STUDENT ARTWORK.
• ENTER THE SPACE
①. STUDENT GALLERY SPACE
② GALLERY SPACE - DIFF. LOCATION
WINDOW, VIEW INTO GALLERY SPACE
RECYCLED MATERIALS. STEEL, ALUM.
③ GALLERY VIEW.
VISUAL ENTRANCE INTO GALLERY
"EMOTIONAL / VISUAL CONNECTION"
EXISTING COLUMNS
④ GALLERY SPACE
PLATFORM
GLASS TO WALK ON + LOOK BENEATH
*INSPIRED MUSEUM D'ORSAY. GLASS FLOORING
• VIEW BELOW
⑤ GALLERY VIEW.
INSPIRED. IDEA FROM ARAB MUSEUM. - VIEW
METAL (RECYCLED) RAILING
GLASS (FRITTED).
⑥ GALLERY BALCONY VIEW.

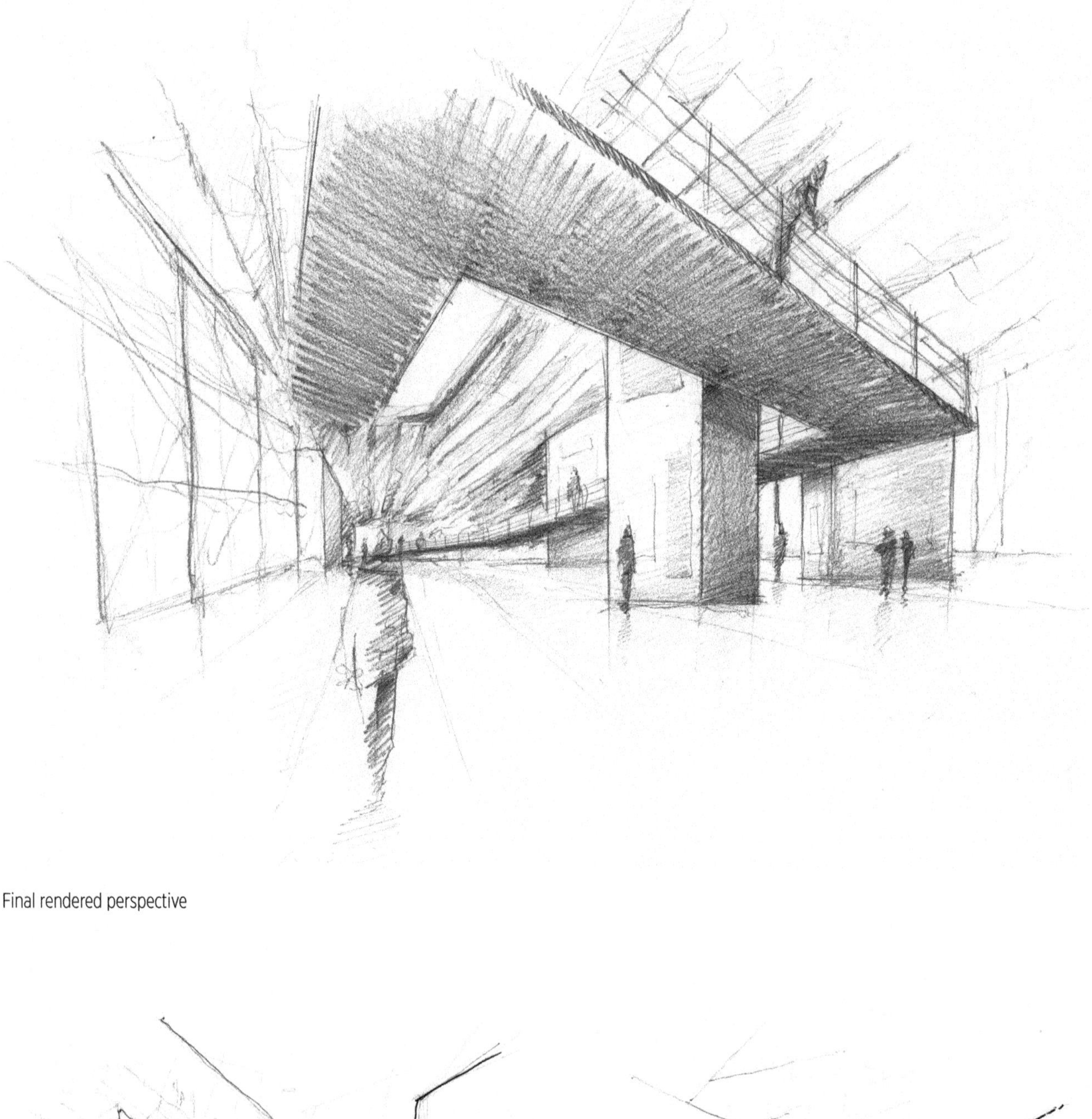

Final rendered perspective

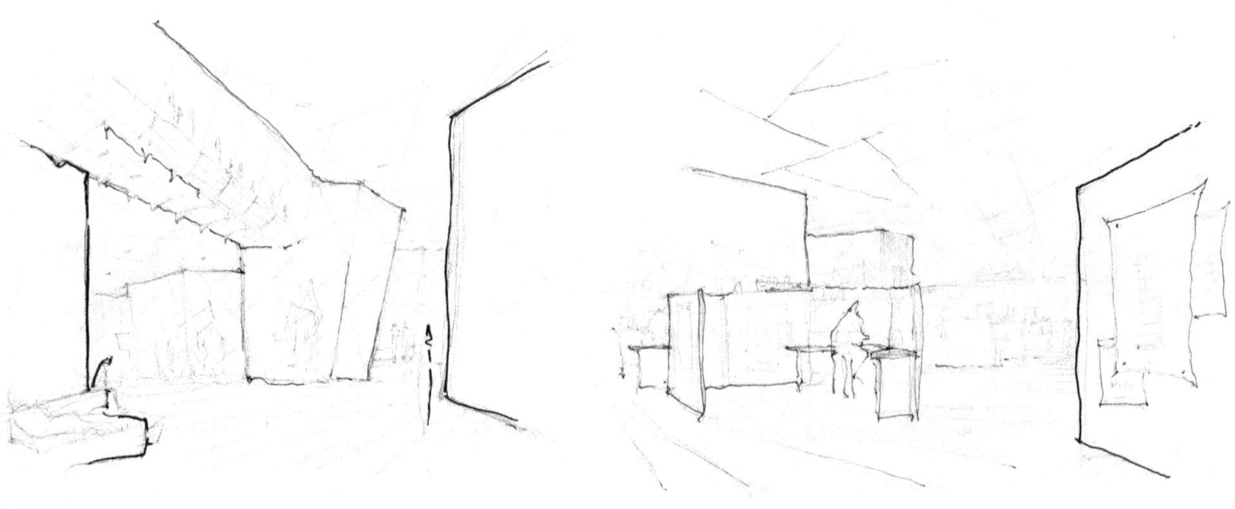

Ink sketches

Although the two-point perspectives shown on this and the facing page illustrate more complex spatial relationships than what are typically associated with freehand perspectives, they are entirely possible for a beginning student to create with a basic knowledge of perspective principles.

The views were estimated by the student and drawn without any projections from the floor plan or other drawings. The student used his understanding of perspective principles, such as convergence and diminution, in order to make the spaces look perspectively correct. The loose line quality and light lines in the background also help the perspectives look visually correct, in that they create a sense of the space while allowing a viewer to fill in the details.

The drawings were created at different times during the student's design process. The rendered perspective was created for a final presentation. The four ink sketches were drawn for an informal review, to communicate the qualities of the interior spaces.

KEVIN ASMUS
Perspective sketches in ink on trace, graphite on opaque paper
Degree Project Studio,
Boston Architectural College

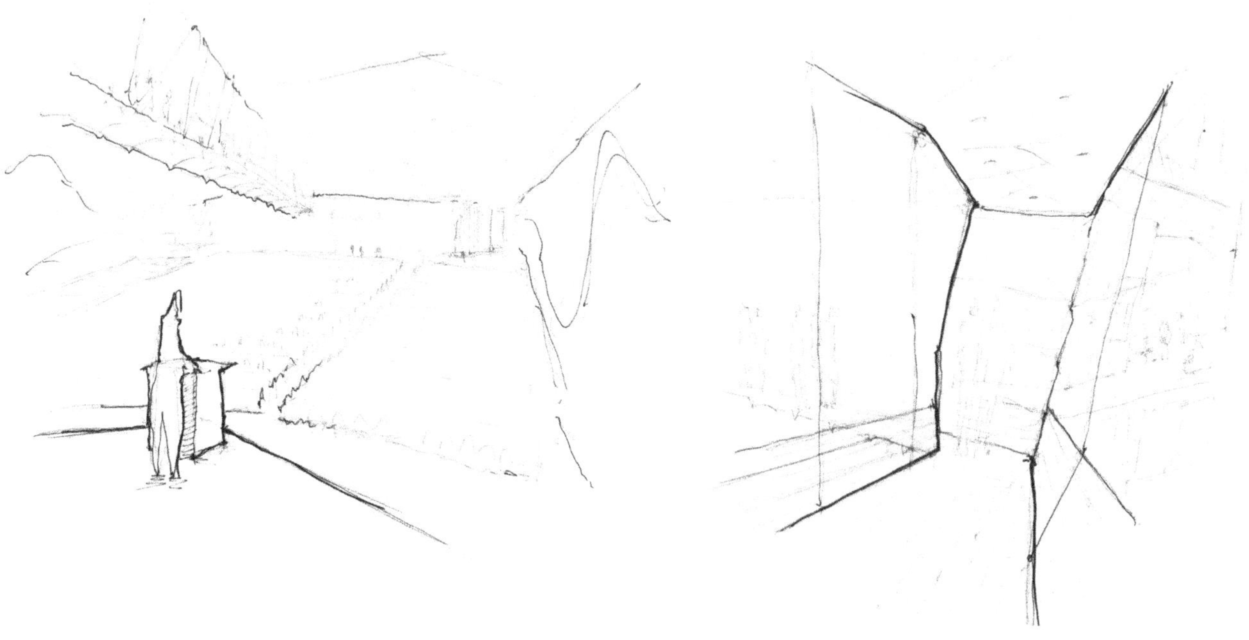

Ink sketches

The perspectives on the following pages are hand-drafted perspectives. They were constructed toward the end of the studio project in order to explore what a person would see while moving through the interior spaces.

In this type of hand-drafted perspective, the perspective view is constructed directly from a floor plan. The viewer's location (called the station point) is marked on the plan, and sightlines are drawn from the viewer to the plan and then projected down into the perspective view. When the floor plan is used to construct a perspective drawing, design revisions made within the perspective view can be projected back and refined within the plan drawing.

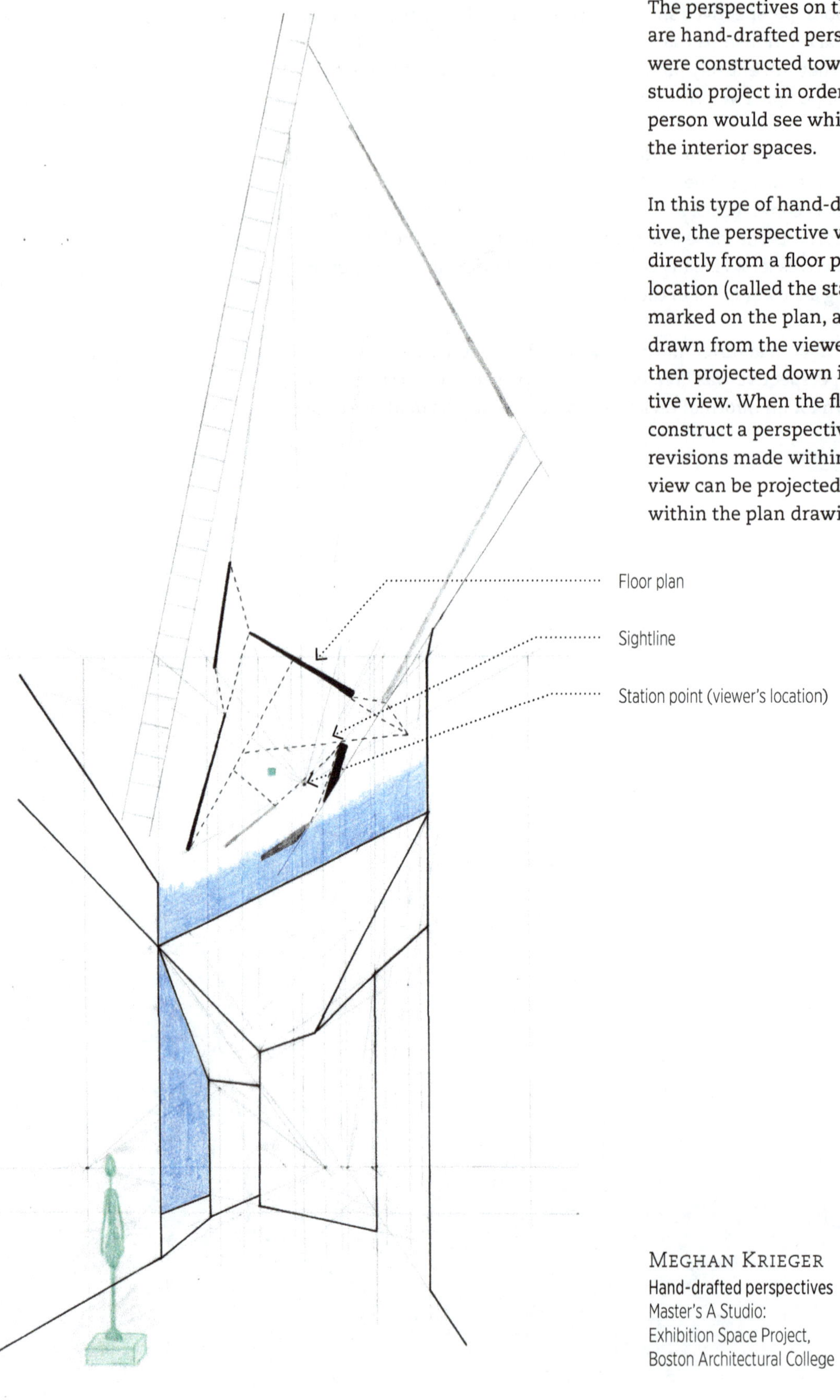

MEGHAN KRIEGER
Hand-drafted perspectives
Master's A Studio:
Exhibition Space Project,
Boston Architectural College

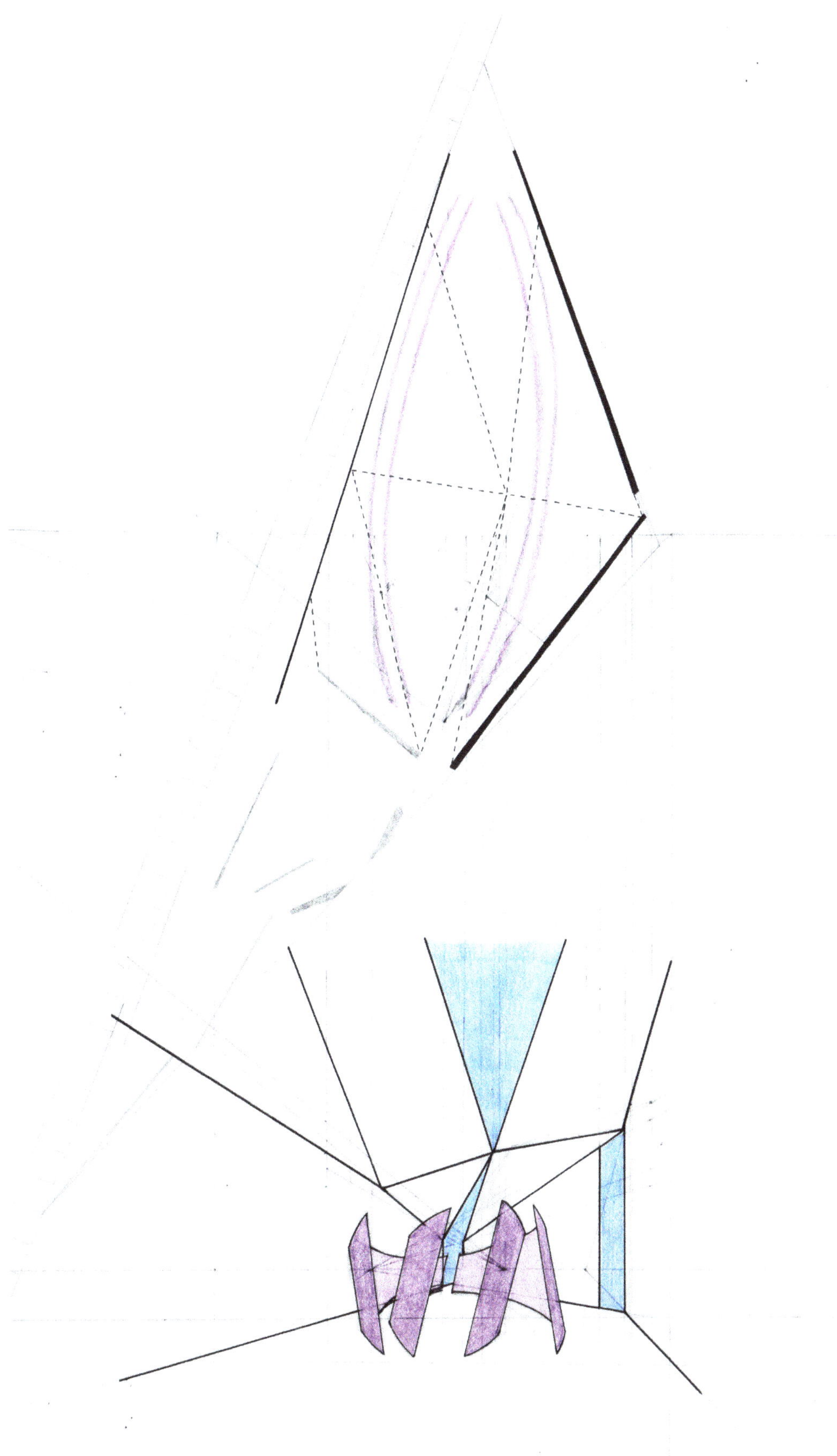

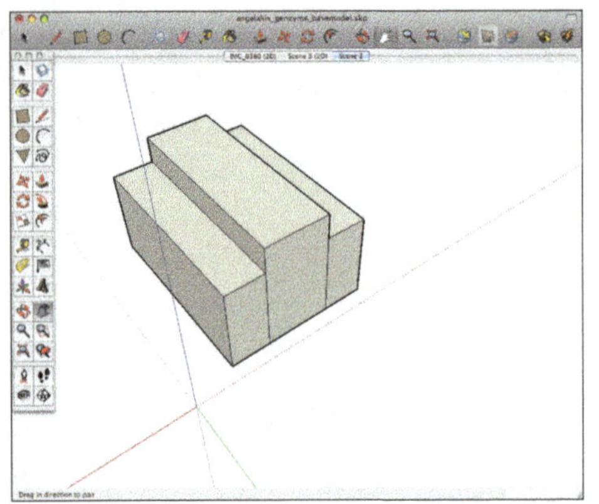
1

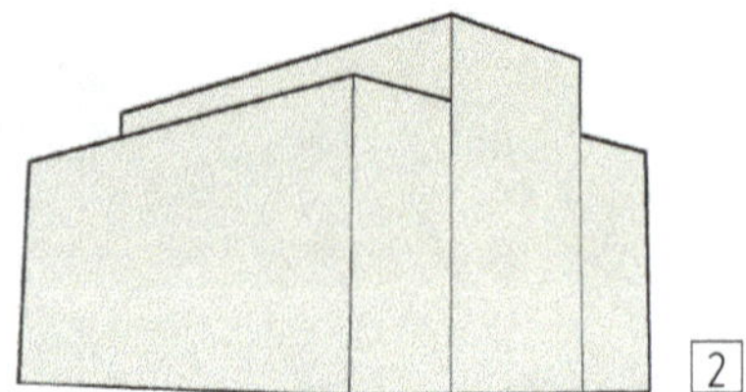
2

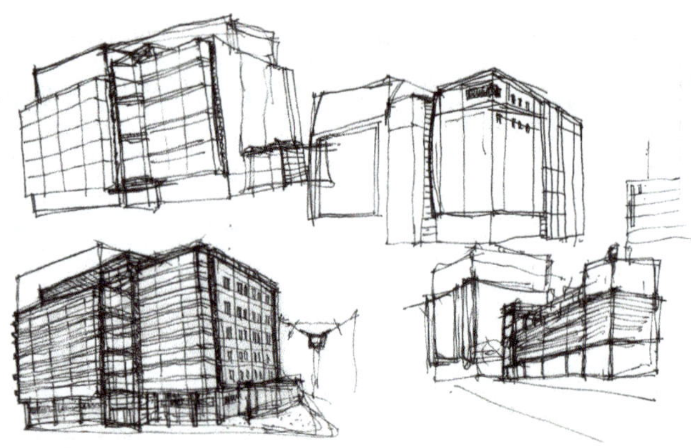

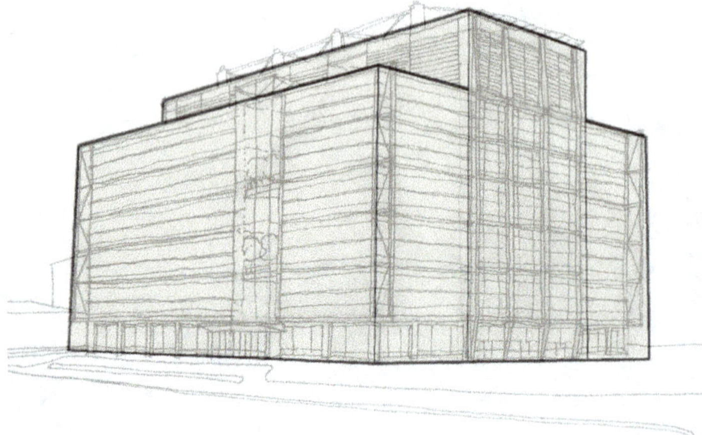
3

These sketches were generated from a digital underlay to help the designer draw a more accurate perspective of an exterior elevation design. The following steps were used to develop the perspectives:

- Step 1: A simple massing model was created in SketchUp, a digital drawing program, to simulate a view from the street.
- Step 2: The view was printed as an underlay to explore the building's elevation design.
- Step 3: The designer created a series of quick sketches by overlaying trace paper on top of the view. These initial sketches were used to study the entrance design, locations of windows, and the exterior skin of the building.
- Step 4: More refined perspectives were generated from the initial sketches to create different elevation options for the building. In developing more than one design option, a designer is able to more quickly explore his or her design ideas by comparing and evaluating the strengths and weaknesses of each design iteration.

CHRISTOPHER ANGELAKIS
Perspective sketches
ARC/Architectural Resources Cambridge

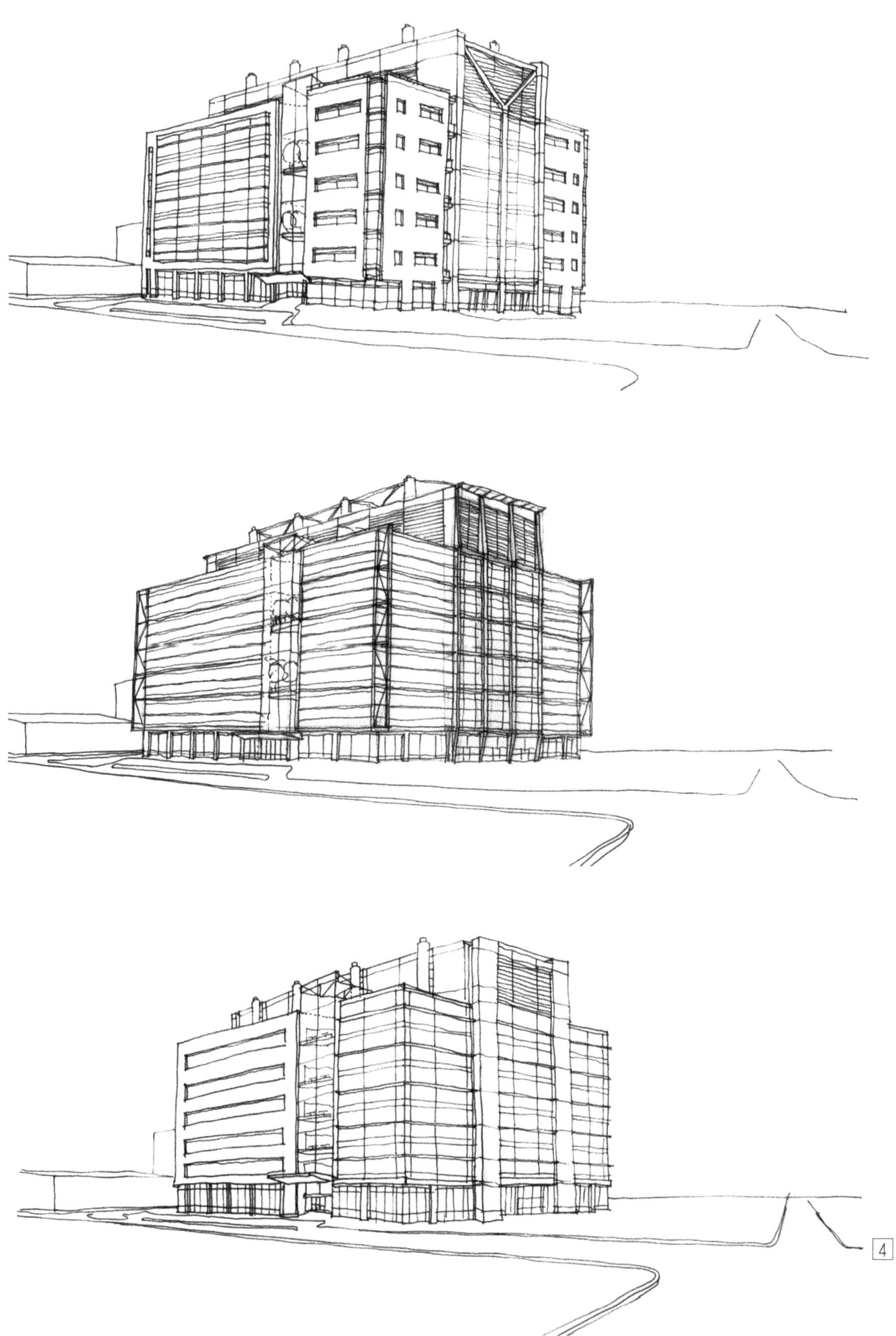
4

Perspective drawings have their own terminology unique to this drawing convention. To understand how to draw perspectives, it is important to first have a grasp of the following terms:

Picture Plane (PP)

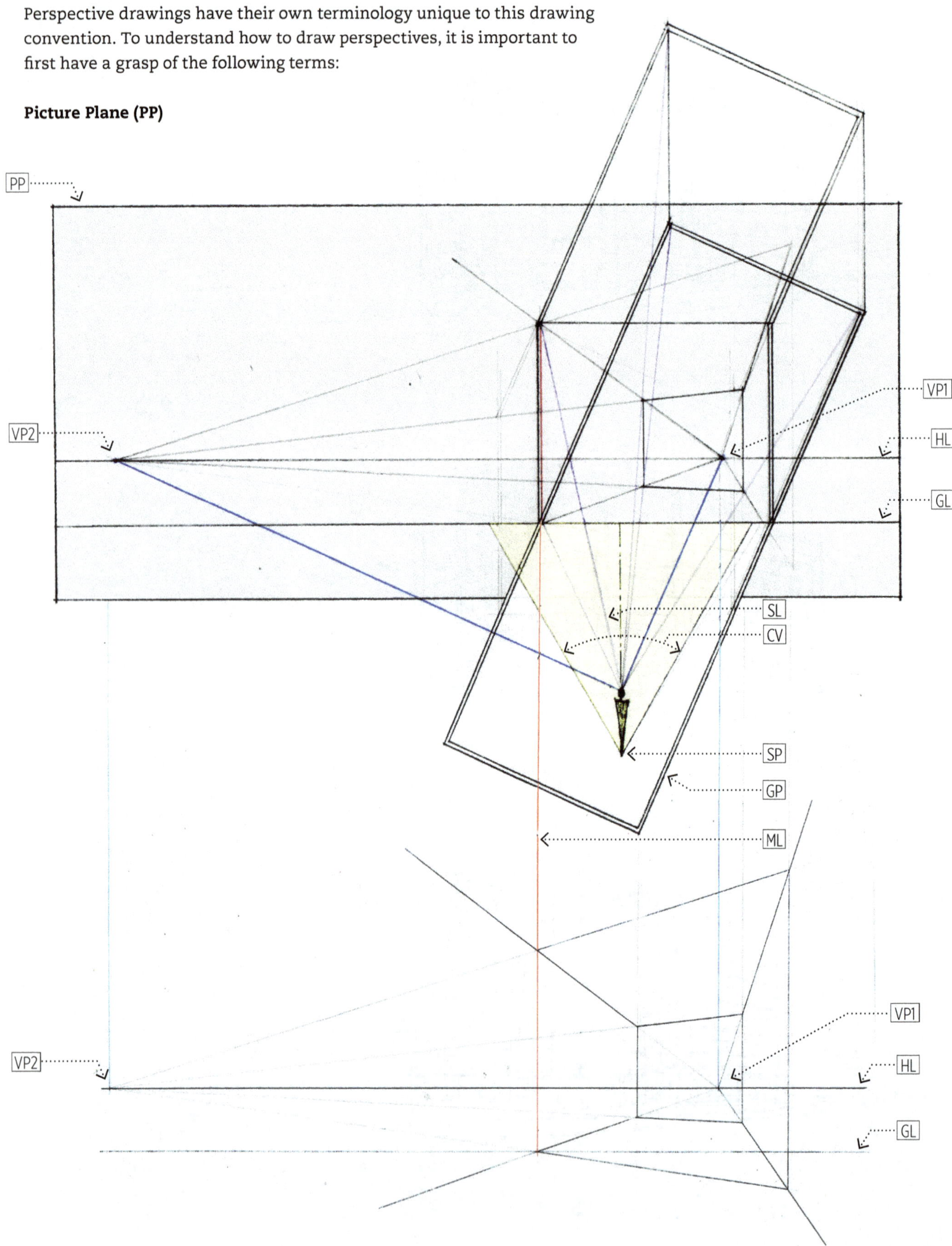

- The picture plane is a transparent surface onto which the perspective view is drawn. In most perspectives the picture plane is positioned between the station point and the object being viewed. The best way to visualize the picture plane is to look out the window at a scene beyond. If you were to trace the scene onto the glass, the window would be defined as the picture plane.
- The location of the picture plane, relative to the object and the station point, determines the scale of the perspective drawing.
- The angle of the picture plane to the central axis of vision is always 90 degrees, and the angle of the picture plane to a space or object determines if the view is a one-, two-, or three-point perspective.

Vanishing Point (VP)

Elements that are parallel to each other converge to a single vanishing point on the horizon line. One-point perspectives have one primary vanishing point. Two-point perspectives have two main vanishing points, and three-point perspectives have three vanishing points.

Horizon Line (HL)

- The horizon line represents the eye level of the viewer. If the viewer is standing, the horizon line will be 5 to 6 feet above the ground line. If the viewer is elevated, such as standing at the top of a stairway, the distance between the horizon line and ground line will equal the distance between the viewer's eye level and the ground.
- In one-, two-, and three-point perspectives, horizontal lines converge to a point located on the horizon line.

Ground Line (GL)

The intersection of the ground plane with the picture plane.

Sightlines (SL)

Sightlines are lines that are projected from the station point to the object being drawn. The intersection of a sightline and the picture plane determines the location of a point within the drawing.

Cone of Vision (CV)

- The cone of vision represents what a viewer will see within a perspective drawing. This cone is drawn on the floor plan as a 60-degree triangle and is used to guide the designer in planning the boundaries of a perspective view. Objects located outside the 60-degree cone will appear more distorted, whereas circular objects become more distorted outside a 30-degree angle.
- The central axis of vision (CAV) is drawn as the centerline of the cone of vision and defines the direction that the viewer is looking.

Station Point (SP)

The station point is the position of the viewer within the space. This point is marked on a floor plan when drafting perspectives.

Ground Plane (GP)

A plane that represents the floor or ground within the perspective view

Measuring Line (ML)

The measuring line is a horizontal or vertical line used to measure true heights or widths. In one- and two-point perspectives, this line coincides with the picture plane. The measuring line is typically located at the intersection of a major vertical wall and the picture plane in order to more easily transfer vertical measurements within the perspective view.

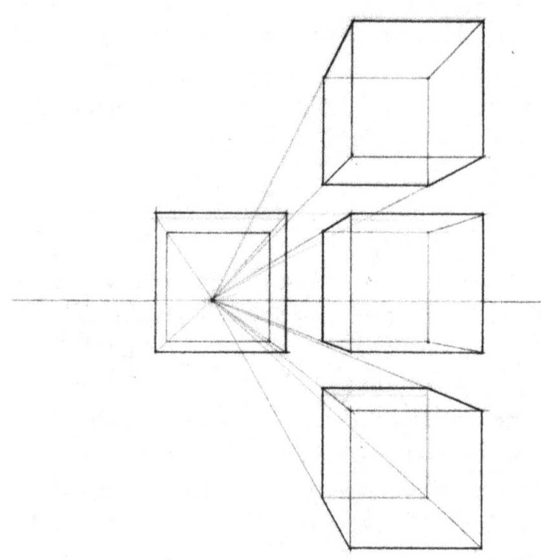

The three main types of perspective drawings are differentiated by the angle of a person's view to a space or object.

One-Point Perspectives

In one-point perspectives the front and back elevations of a space or object are parallel to the picture plane and are drawn as true elevations. There are three different types of lines in one-point perspectives: horizontal lines, vertical lines, and perspective lines. Perspective lines define the sides of the object and converge at a single vanishing point.

One-point perspectives are frequently used during ideation because they can be easily constructed from an elevation or section drawing. They create a more static view of a space than two- or three-point perspectives, owing to the frontally drawn elevations. However, this makes a one-point perspective a great drawing to use when emphasizing symmetrical or axial qualities in a space.

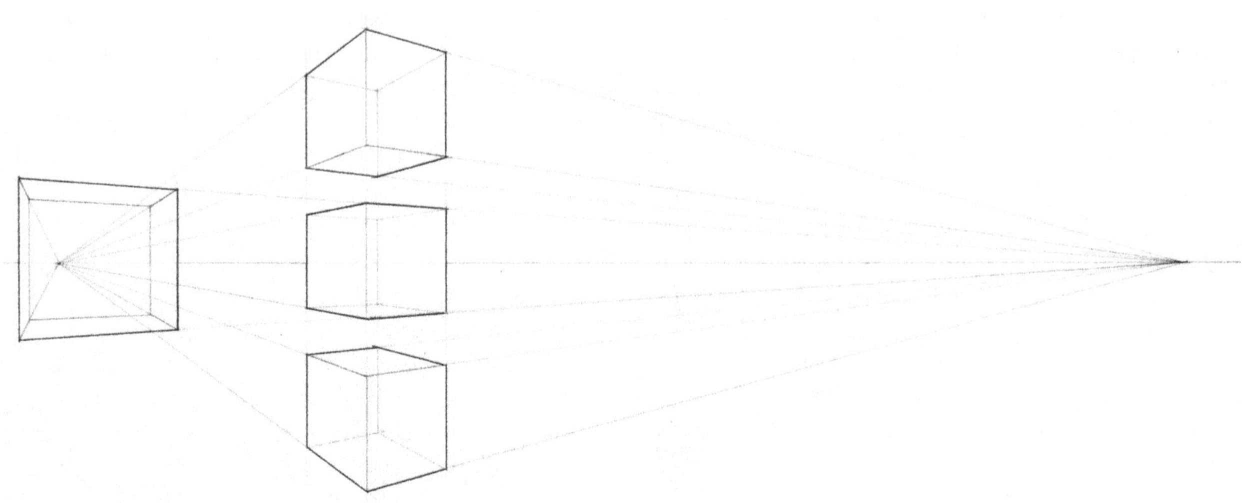

Two-Point Perspectives

In two-point perspectives the vertical edges of a room, building, or object are parallel to the picture plane. All lines in two-point perspectives are either vertical lines or perspective lines. The horizontal edges of a space converge to two main vanishing points as perspective lines; the vertical edges of a space remain vertical. Most of the spaces we see in our environment are understood as two-point perspectives, with walls oriented obliquely to our central axis of vision.

Two-point perspectives simulate a more natural view of a space and are typically less distorted than one- or three-point perspectives. Depending on the cropping of the perspective view and the location of the cone of vision relative to the object, designers can create highly dynamic views with two-point perspectives.

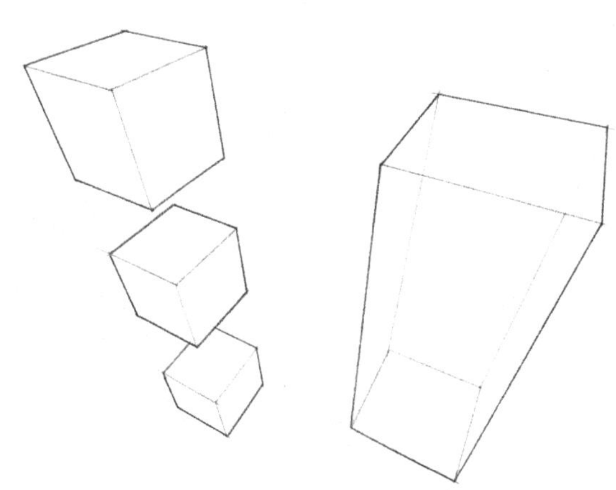

Three-Point Perspectives
In three-point perspectives all edges are oblique to the picture plane, and all lines are perspective lines. Horizontal edges converge to two main vanishing points on the horizon line, and vertical edges converge to a third vanishing point located either above or below the horizon line. Spaces are seen in three-point perspective when a viewer is looking at something from above or below.

Three-point perspectives are the most dynamic of the three types and, because of the third vanishing point, are also the most difficult to draw. Objects and spaces appear more distorted because vertical lines are angled in the view. Three-point perspectives are seldom used in interior perspectives but are used to describe aerial and worm's-eye views of buildings and cities.

Almost anything can be drawn in perspective using the basic geometry of a cube. By subdividing, extending, and manipulating the limits of a cube, more complex shapes can be created. The following techniques ultimately help designers draw perspectives faster and can be applied to all three types of perspective drawing.

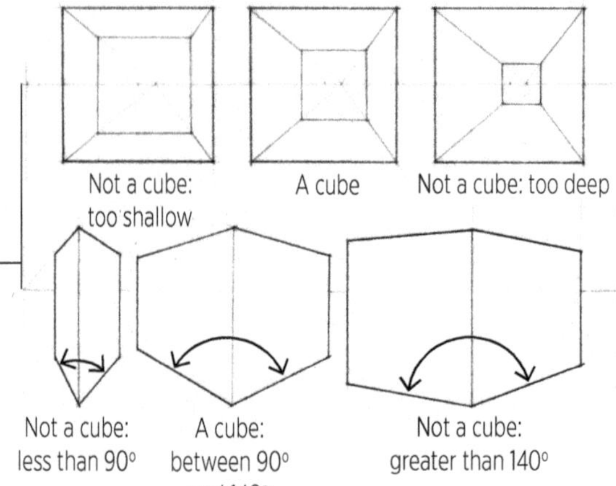

Drawing Cubes

Drawing cubes in perspective allows designers to approximate depth, width, and height measurements and to use this proportional system of measurement to develop freehand perspective drawings. Therefore, it is critical to learn how to sketch a one- and two-point cube in perspective and to be able to visually estimate when the cube looks correct.

Finding the Center of an Object

To locate the center of a rectangular plane or volume in perspective, draw two diagonal lines to connect the opposite corners. The center point and centerline are at the intersection of the two diagonal lines. This technique is frequently used to locate the center of a volume and to draw a base for a piece of furniture.

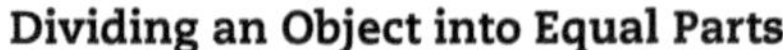

Dividing an Object into Equal Parts

A rectangular object can be divided into equal parts by first locating the center of the object and then subdividing the face of the object with additional diagonals to divide each half into two more sections.

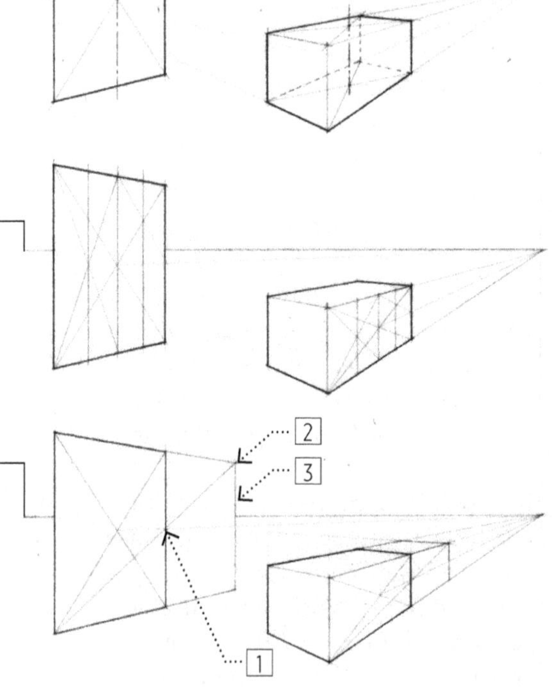

Extending an Object

An object's depth or height can be doubled through the following steps:

- Step 1: Locate the midpoint of the edge the object will be extended from.
- Step 2: Draw a diagonal line from one of the opposite corners through the midpoint, until the diagonal line intersects a line extended from the top edge of the object.
- Step 3: Complete the object's outline by extending the bottom edge and drawing a vertical line parallel to the front edge.

This technique is useful for quickly drawing window bays, columns, and other repetitive and equally spaced elements.

Dividing an Object with a Measuring Line

By using one side of the object as a vertical measuring line, an object can be divided into unequal parts, and height measurements can be transferred into depth measurements.

- Step 1: Mark off the desired depth measurements on the measuring line.
- Step 2: Draw perspective lines from each of the height marks back to VP1.
- Step 3: Draw a diagonal line connecting opposite corners of the rectangular plane.
- Step 4: At the intersection of the diagonal and the perspective lines, draw vertical lines to transfer the height measurements into depth measurements on the vertical surface.
- Step 5: To transfer the depth measurements onto the floor plane, draw perspective lines from VP2 through the intersection of the vertical lines and the floor plane.
- Step 6: Repeat steps 3–5 to subdivide the floor plane in the opposite direction.

This technique is useful for drawing floor patterns or creating a perspective grid to guide the positioning of objects within a perspective view.

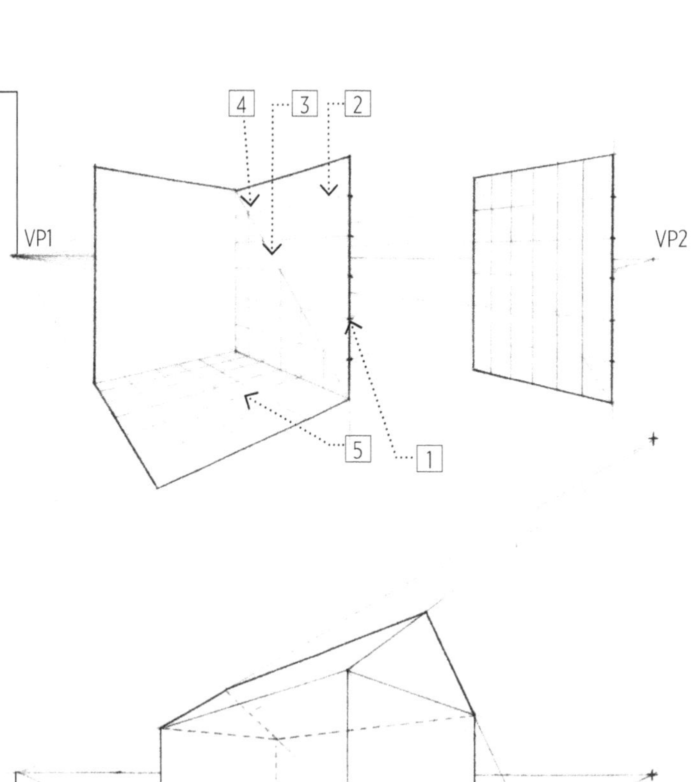

Drawing Inclined Lines

Parallel inclined lines that are oblique to the picture plane converge at a single vanishing point located directly above or below the horizon line. For symmetrical slopes, such as the roof on the left, these vanishing points are equidistant from the horizon line.

Drawing Circles

When circles are oblique to the picture plane, they are drawn as ellipses. To draw a circle, first draw a square plane and then subdivide the plane with diagonals to locate the centerline of the object. To locate the ellipse within the square, intermediate points are plotted by dividing each half of the diagonal line into thirds. The circle intersects the point that is one-third away from the corner.

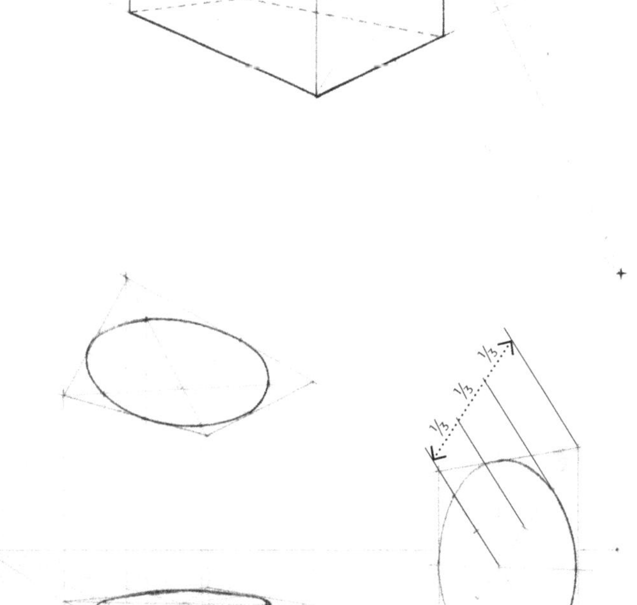

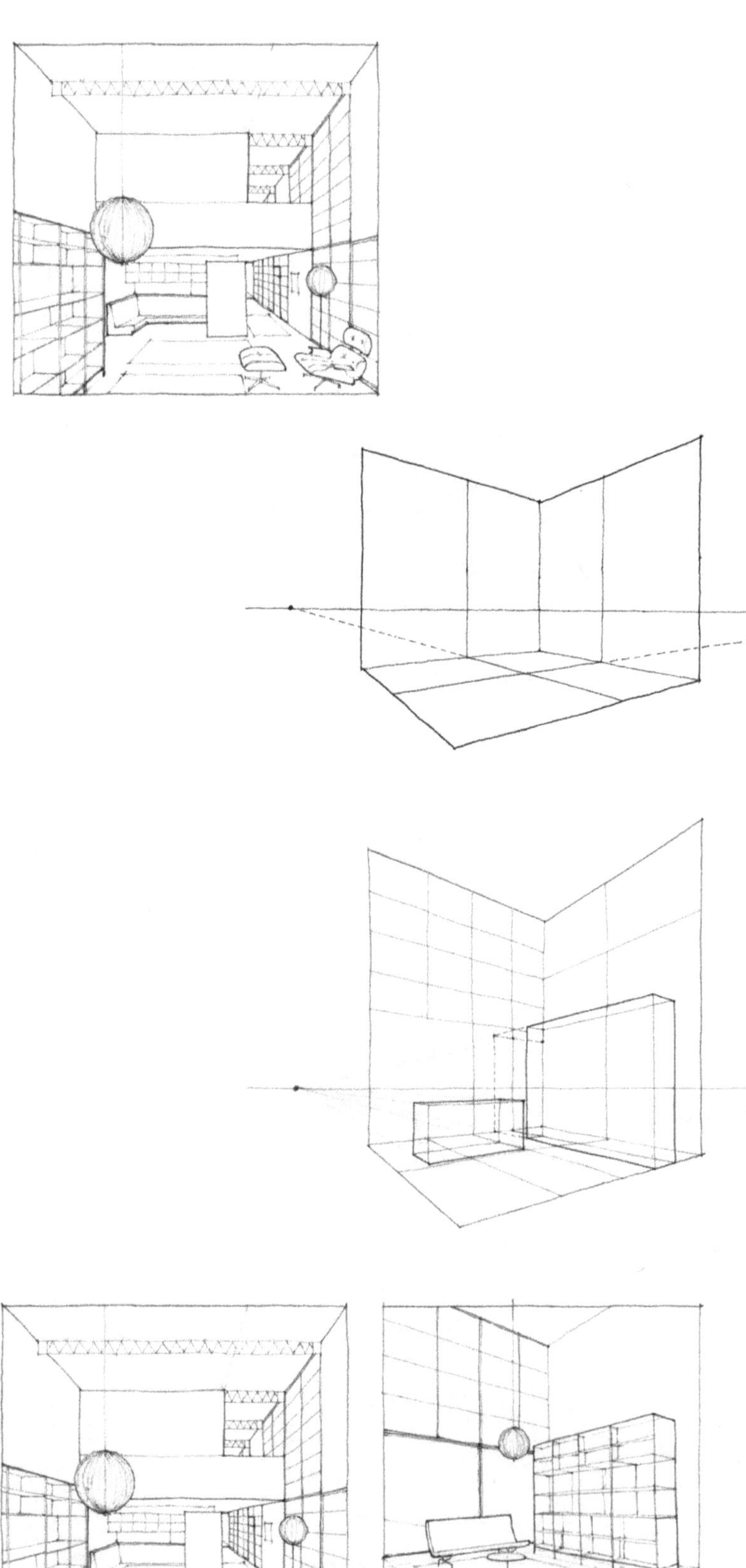

There are many different ways to construct perspective drawings. The type of method used depends on where the designer is within the design process, the amount of time he or she has to draw a perspective, and what type of precision is desired. An overview of the most popular methods of construction are described as follows, and step-by-step examples are provided for each method in the remaining pages of this chapter.

Freehand, Estimated Method

Freehand, estimated perspectives are sketched from the height and width measurements of a space. The depth of the space is estimated, based on a designer's ability to make the view look correct. This depth estimation comes with experience: the more perspectives you draw, the greater your facility to approximate the correct proportions of a space, building, or piece of furniture. The simplest way to estimate depth, and to draw a freehand perspective, is to first draw a cube in perspective and then subdivide it or expand it using diagonals, as explained in the previous section on perspective measurements.

Freehand, estimated perspectives can be constructed without floor plans, sections, or elevations, making them ideal drawings to use at the beginning of ideation. Of all the methods of constructing perspectives, these are the quickest to create and are used by designers throughout the design process to explore their ideas in three dimensions. Some freehand perspectives, such as the sketches in Ideation Case Studies 1 and 2, do not use any measurements and are instead created through a designer's understanding of proportion and scale. Step-by-step examples of how to create one-point and two-point freehand perspectives are included in this chapter.

Diagonal Point Method

The diagonal point method builds on the techniques of the freehand perspective and utilizes a point located off to the side of the drawing to measure the depth within a one-point perspective view. The following are two of the advantages of this method:

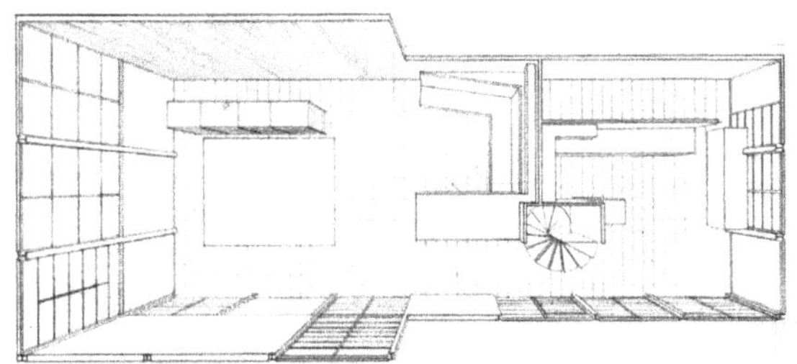

- The perspective is built up from a plan or section drawing, making it easier to visualize where objects are located within the view.
- A smaller drawing surface is able to be used, compared with the common method (discussed next), because the vanishing points are located closer to the perspective view.

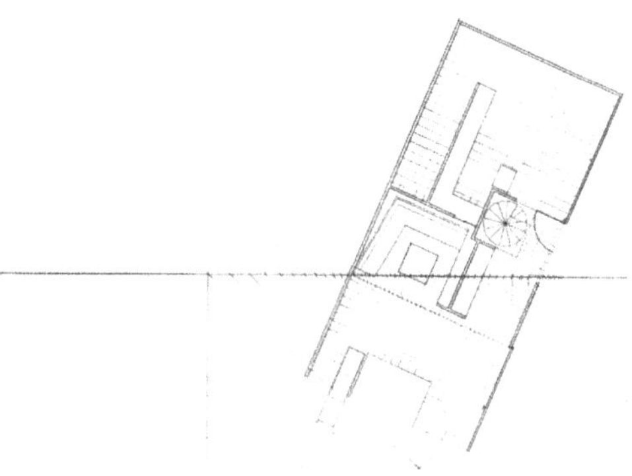

Common (or Office) Method

The common method requires a plan and either a section or elevation drawing to project vertical heights from. The floor plan is typically located at the top of the paper, and its scale determines the scale of the perspective view. The common method takes the longest to construct, but also produces the most accurate perspective view because depth measurements are projected directly from the floor plan. Because of the length of time required to draw a perspective using this method, perspectives are drawn with the common method at the end of the design process. A step-by-step example of constructing a two-point perspective using the common method is included in this chapter, along with instruction on how the steps can be adapted to draw a one-point perspective.

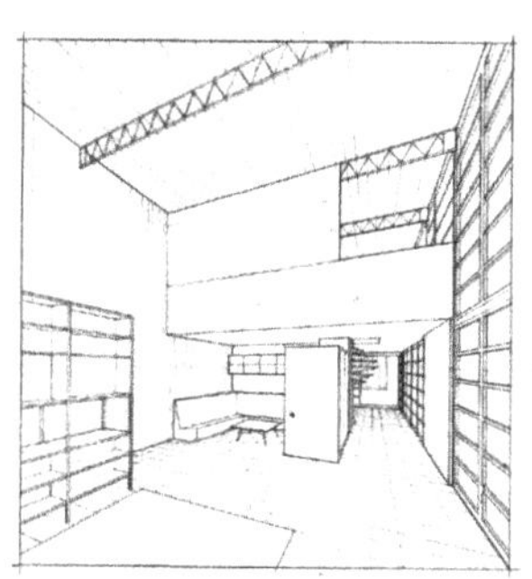

Digital Underlay Method

The digital underlay method uses the drawing techniques of freehand perspectives to develop a printed perspective view of a digital model. This method requires a basic understanding of a digital drawing program, such as SketchUp or Revit, to create a base model, along with the overall height, width, and depth measurements of the space. The model can be constructed from hand-drawn floor plans and elevations that are scanned into the model, or can be built from scratch, as shown in Ideation Case Study 4. A step-by-step example of the digital underlay method is included in Chapter 10.

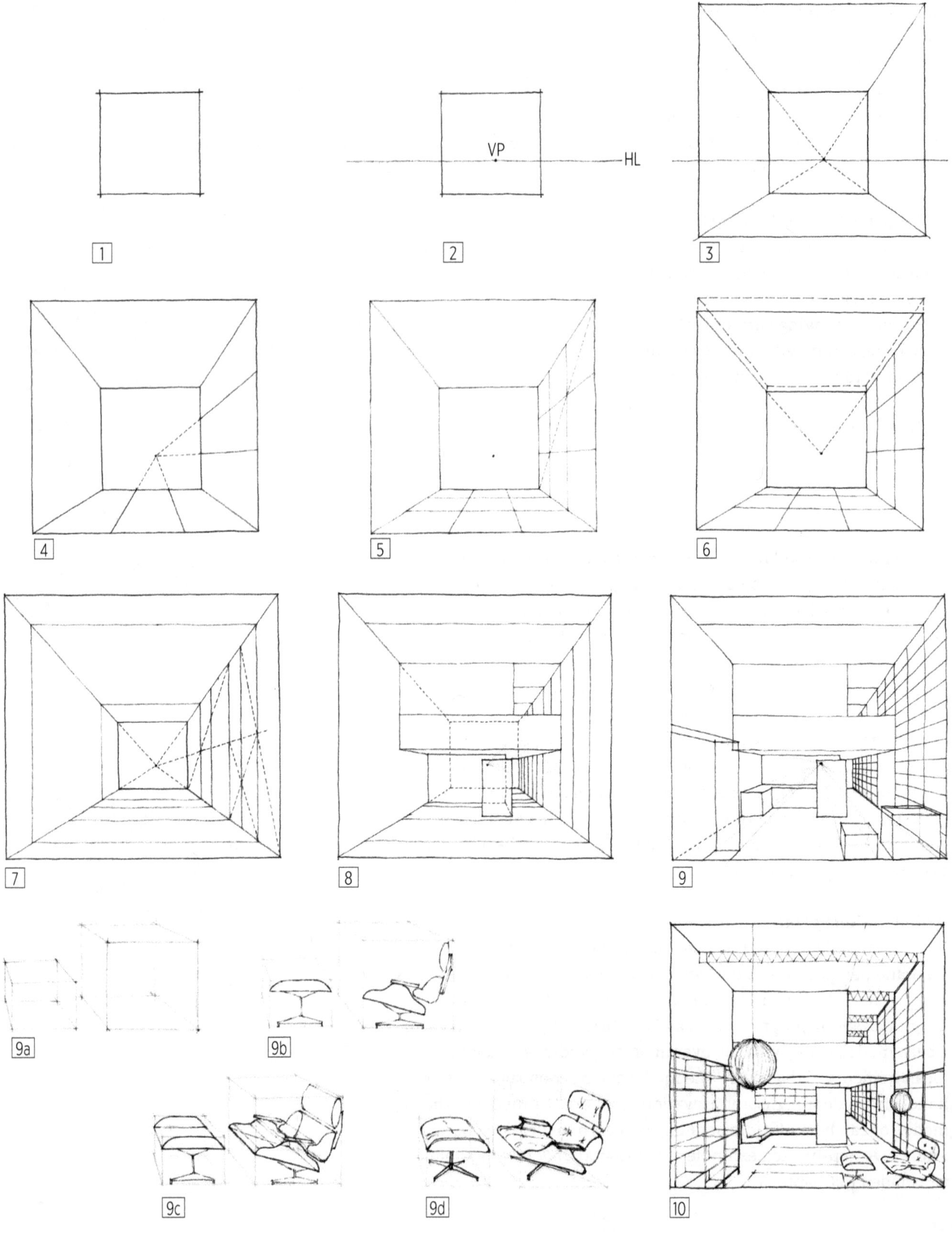
VP
HL
1
2
3
4
5
6
7
8
9
9a
9b
9c
9d
10

Step 1: Draw the Picture Plane
Draw a square with one side scaled to the width or height of the space you are drawing. In this case the width of the Eames living room is 20'-0" wide. The edges of this square will be used as measuring lines for the view.

Step 2: Horizon Line and Vanishing Point
Draw a horizontal line, approximately 5 or 6 feet above the base of the square. This line is the horizon line (HL), which represents a person's eye level within the space. Locate the vanishing point (VP) on the horizon line.

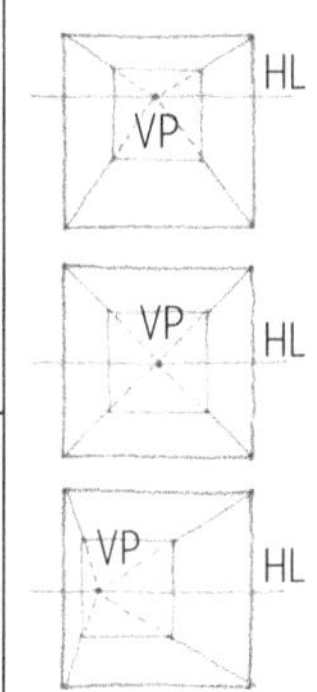

To study a higher or lower point of view, locate the horizon line toward the top or bottom of the square.

To create a more symmetrical composition, position the vanishing point close to the center of the square.

To emphasize one wall plane more than the other, locate the vanishing point toward the sides of the square.

Step 3: Draw a Cube
Draw perspective lines from the vanishing point through the corners of the square. These lines represent the edges of the floor, wall, and ceiling planes. Connect these lines with a larger square, to create a three-dimensional cube.

Step 4: Establish Width and Height Measurements
Divide the side and bottom edges of the first square into equal sections, and draw perspective lines from the vanishing point, through each tick mark, to divide the width and height of the cube into equal segments.

Step 5: Establish Depth Measurements
Draw a diagonal line connecting the corners of the wall plane. Where the diagonal intersects the height measurements, project vertical lines to divide the depth of the cube into equal bays.

Step 6: Adjust the Height and Width of the Room
Adjust the outline of the original square to match the shape of room you are drawing. Draw new perspective lines through the corners to project the shape forward. In step 6, the ceiling was lowered by 1'-0", to create a 19'-0" x 20'-0" room.

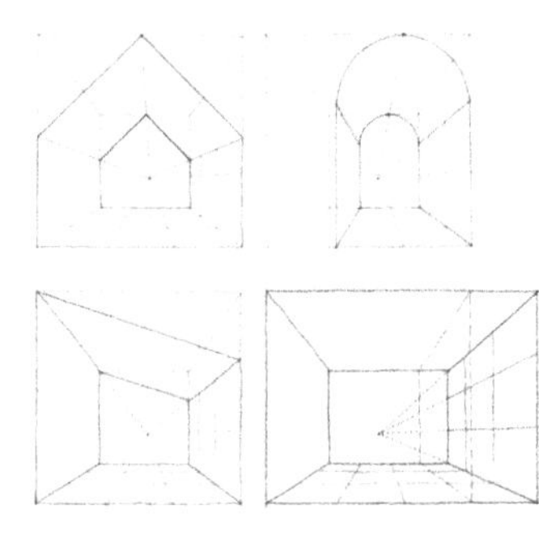

The original cube can be adjusted to create an infinite number of more complex room shapes. In the vaulted option, the curved ceiling is drawn as a true circle because it is parallel to the picture plane.

Step 7: Adjust the Depth
Extend the depth of the room by subdividing the original depth measurements with diagonals. In the example the space was extended forward by half a bay and backwards by two bays.

Step 8: Draw the Interior Walls
Using the perspective grid as a guide, draw the interior walls. Additional height and width measurements can be projected from the edges of the original square.

Step 9: Locate and Draw the Furniture
Draw the overall limits of the furniture using boxes to locate them within the floor plan. For rectilinear furniture, the boxes can be further subdivided to create a perspective. More complex furniture, like the Eames chair, can be constructed from a cube (9a), using the following steps:

- 9b: Draw the chair elevation on the front plane of the cube.
- 9c: Extend the elevation toward the vanishing point, and draw a smaller elevation where the lines intersect the rear face of the cube.
- 9d: Sketch over the extruded elevation to refine the form of the chair.

10: Draw in the Details
Continue to build up the perspective by drawing in smaller elements and surface patterns. Spherical objects are drawn as circles in perspective.

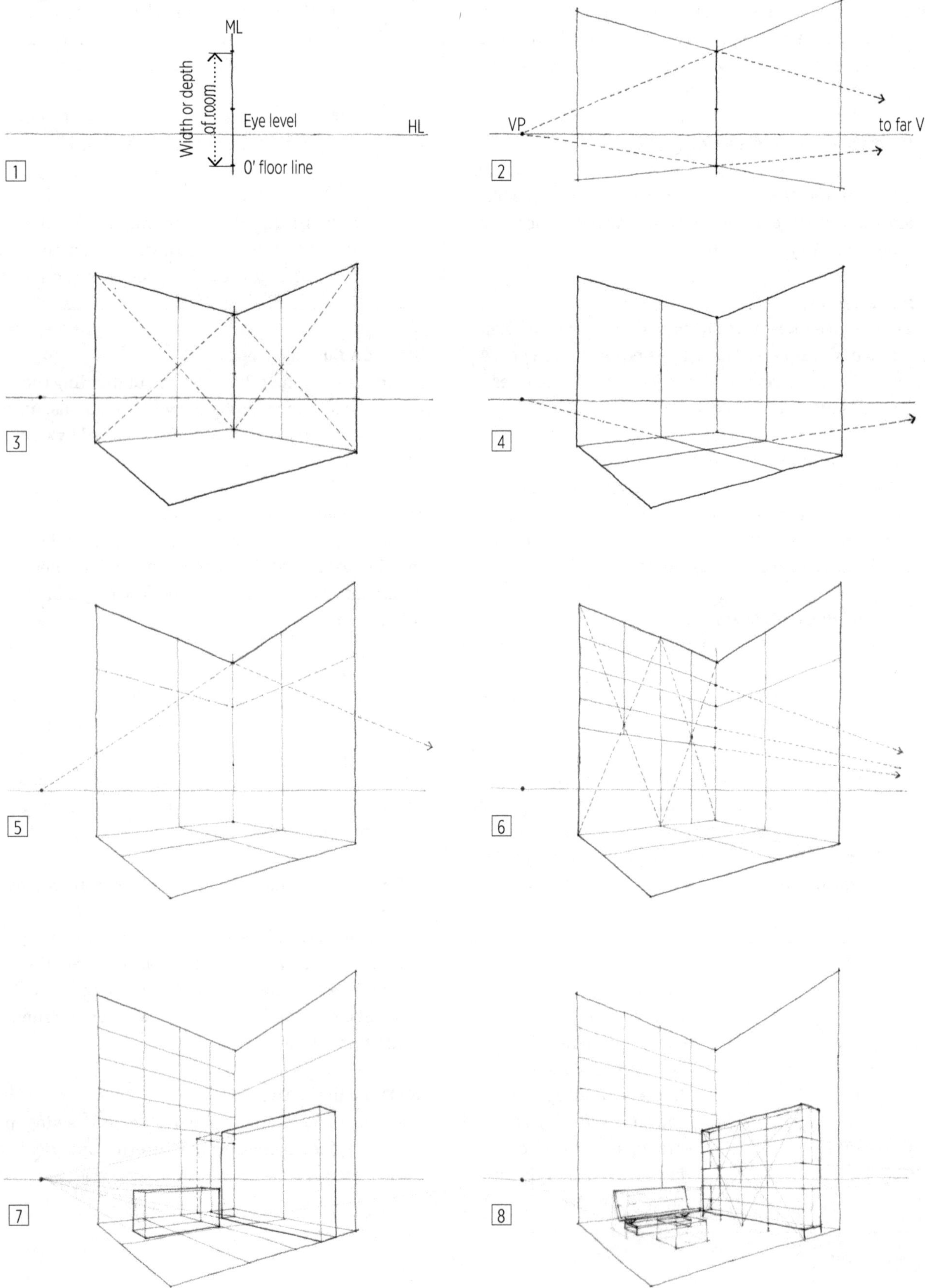
ML
Width or depth of room
Eye level
HL
0' floor line
1
VP
to far VP
2
3
4
5
6
7
8

Step 1: Perspective Setup

Draw a vertical measuring line (ML) to scale, and mark off three measurements: the floor line (0' elevation), the eye level of the viewer, and the width of the room. Draw a horizontal line through the eye level mark to represent the horizon line.

Step 2: Draw the Sides of the Room

- Locate one vanishing point near the measuring line and a second vanishing point farther away from the measuring line.
- Draw perspective lines from the vanishing points through the top and bottom marks on the measuring line.
- Draw a vertical line to define the front edge of each plane. Position the line so that each plane, or wall, looks square.

Step 3: Locate the Centerline of the Space

- Draw perspective lines from each vanishing point through the lower front corner of each wall to define the floor plane.
- Draw diagonal lines connecting the opposite corners of each wall. Project a vertical line at the intersection of each set of diagonals to find the center of the planes.

Step 4: Transfer Depth Measurements onto the Floor Plane

Draw perspective lines from each vanishing point, through the intersection of the centerline and the wall planes, to divide the floor plane into four equal squares. Depending on the complexity of the room, you may wish to subdivide the space into smaller units in order to more easily locate the interior elements.

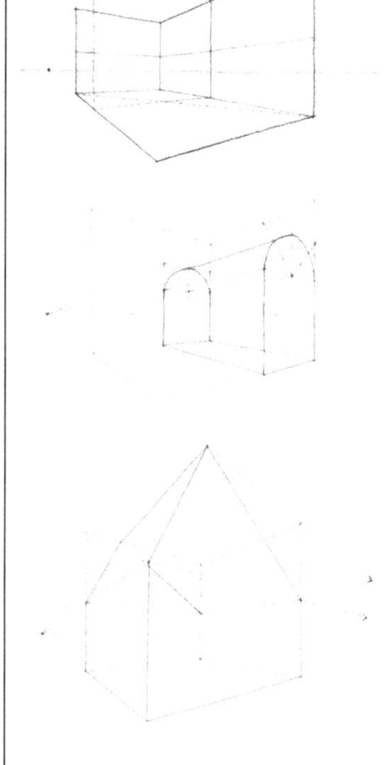

Once the overall rectangular limits are established, the room shape can be modified further into more complex forms.

Step 5: Adjust the Height and Width of the Room

Expand the limits of the room by either marking a new height on the measuring line or extending the depth through diagonals.

Step 6: Draw in Objects Located on Either Wall

Sketch in the limits of objects located on or adjacent to the walls such as windows, furniture, or doors. Drawing these objects first will help you locate objects floating within the center of the room.

Step 7: Locate the Overall Limits of Ojects within the Room

Using the depth lines from steps 4 and 6, draw rectangular volumes to represent the overall limits of interior elements within the room.

Step 8: Develop Forms of Interior Elements

Subdivide the rectangular volumes to proportionally draw the interior elements in perspective.

Step 9: Add Detail, and Crop the View

Sketch in additional details and draw a box around the perspective to crop the view. Extend the floor and wall surfaces to the edge of the box.

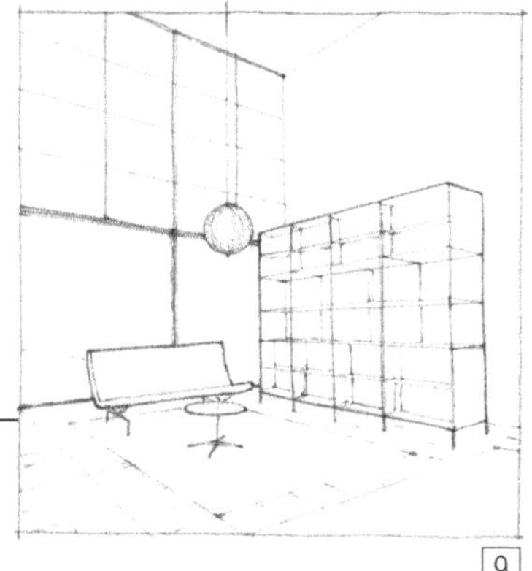

9

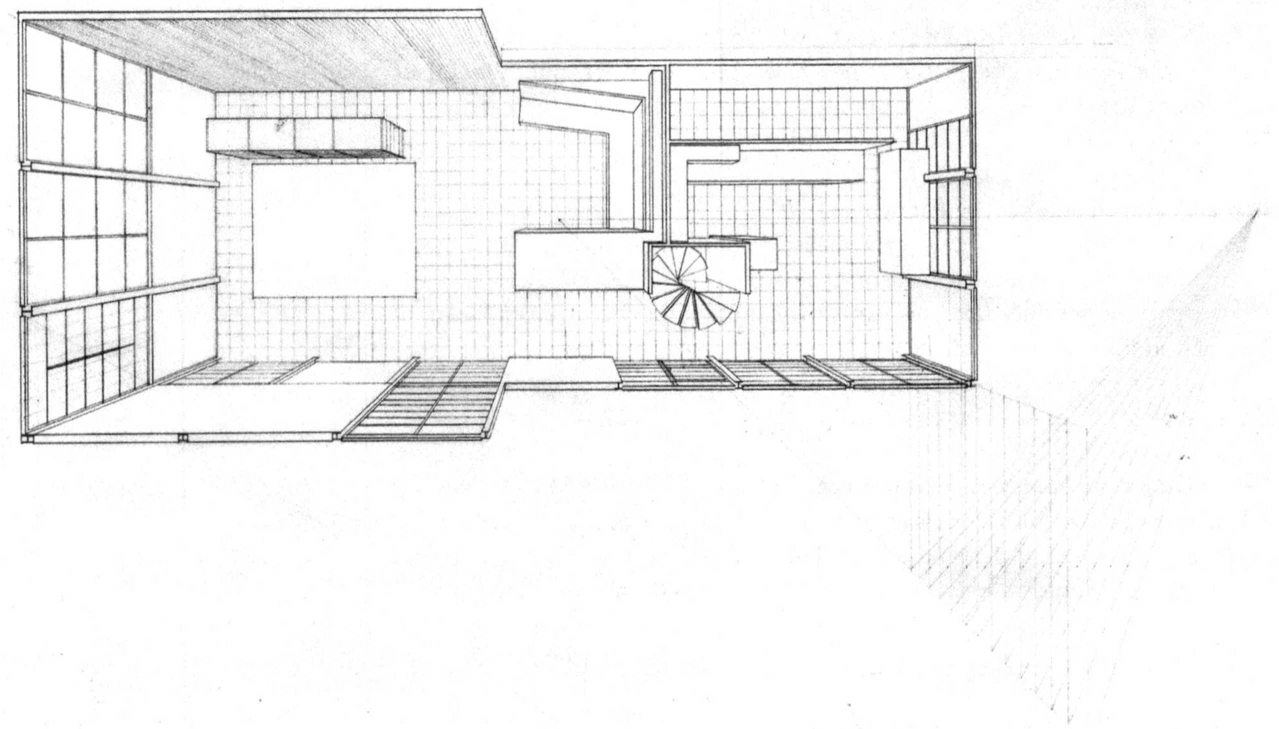

Diagonal Point Method

The following example introduces the diagonal point method, through a one-point plan perspective drawing. A plan perspective drawing combines a conventional plan drawing with a perspective to show an aerial view of a room or building. This type of drawing is useful for showing the overall layout of small interior spaces and is often used instead of a plan drawing to convey the spatial relationships between multiple rooms of a building.

Plan perspectives are constructed directly on top of a floor plan, and everything is projected back to a single vanishing point, located near the center of the drawing. Depending on the size of the space being drawn, the floor plan scale can range from 1/8" = 1'-0" for a building to ½" = 1'-0" for a small room, such as a bathroom.

The step-by-step method can also be adapted to create a section perspective drawing. To do this, use a section drawing instead of a plan, and draw the horizon line prior to locating the vanishing point at the center of the drawing. The remaining steps can be followed to create a section perspective.

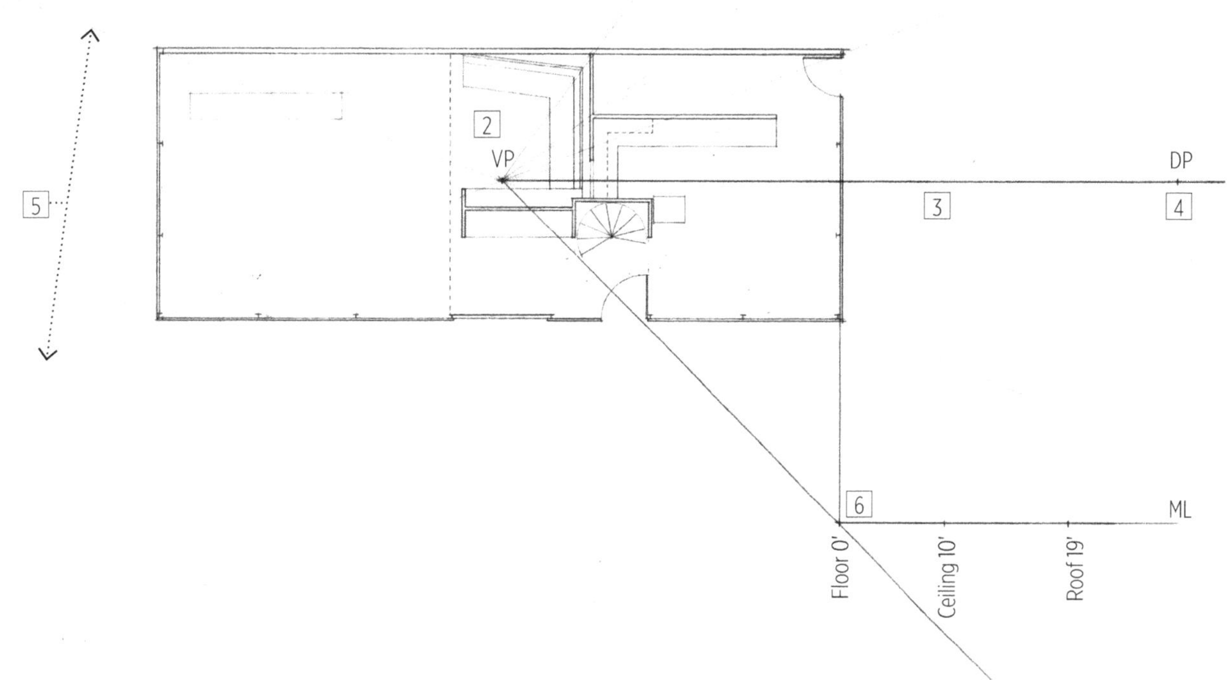

Step 1: Drawing Setup
Position the floor plan under a sheet of vellum or trace, toward the left two-thirds of the paper.

Step 2: Locate the Vanishing Point
Draw a dot near the center of the plan or within the space you wish to emphasize, to locate the vanishing point (VP). The vanishing point location will determine the focal point of the drawing.

Step 3: Draw the Horizon Line
Draw a horizontal line, to represent the horizon line, through the vanishing point, toward the right half of the drawing.

Step 4: Locate the Diagonal Point
Locate the diagonal point (DP) on the horizon line. The distance between the vanishing and diagonal points should be equal to or greater than the width of the floor plan. This distance will determine how much the walls will be foreshortened.

Step 5: Draw the Corners of the Spaces
Draw perspective lines from the vanishing point, extending through the corners of major walls.

Step 6: Locate the Measuring Line

- Locate the measuring line by drawing a vertical construction line from the bottom right corner of the plan and drawing a horizontal line at the endpoint of the construction line, extending to the right side of the page. This horizontal line is the measuring line for all vertical dimensions.
- Mark off the overall vertical dimensions on the measuring line, at the same scale as the plan.
- Draw a diagonal line from the vanishing point through the floor elevation mark (0'). This line is used to transfer perspective measurements into the plan.

Alternate Measuring Line Location
If the measuring line is drawn to the right, the plan perspective will be projected up from the plan.
If the measuring line is extended to the left, the vertical walls will be projected down from the plan, creating a smaller perspective.

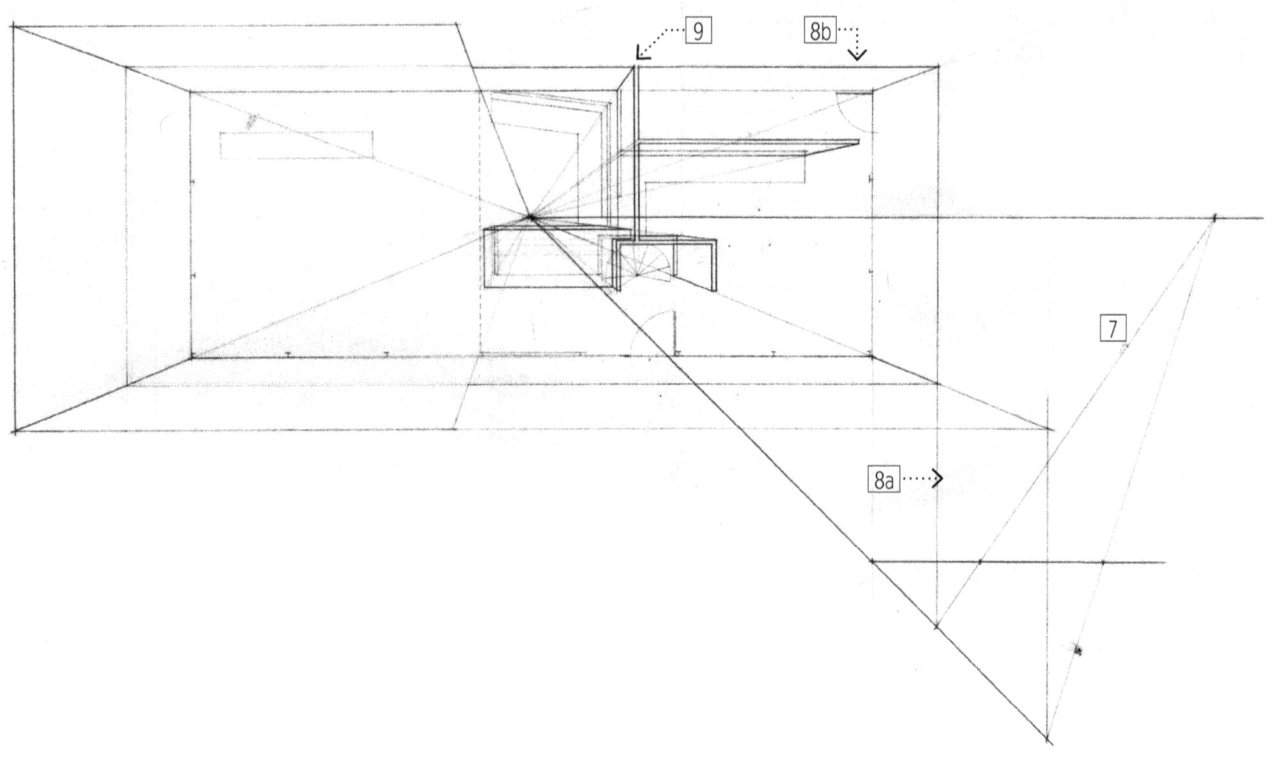

Step 7: Transfer Heights into Perspective View

- Draw a line from the diagonal point, through the height mark for the ceiling, and extend it to the diagonal measuring line.

Step 8: Draw the Exterior Walls

- 8a: At its intersection with the diagonal measuring line, draw a vertical line up to the perspective line defining one of the corners of the room. The wall plane is now drawn in perspective.
- 8b: Continue to draw the ceiling height around the room, to define the exterior walls.

Step 9: Draw the Interior Walls

- After the exterior walls are defined, draw the interior walls by first starting where the interior partitions meet the exterior wall.
- Additional lines can be projected from the vanishing point, as required, in order to define the edges of the interior partitions.

Note: The plan view represents the floor of the room; the wall outline in plan is the bottom of the wall. The floor plan also equals the picture plane, meaning that true width and depth measurements may be taken from the plan and projected up to the correct elevation by drawing perspective lines from the vanishing point through the object.

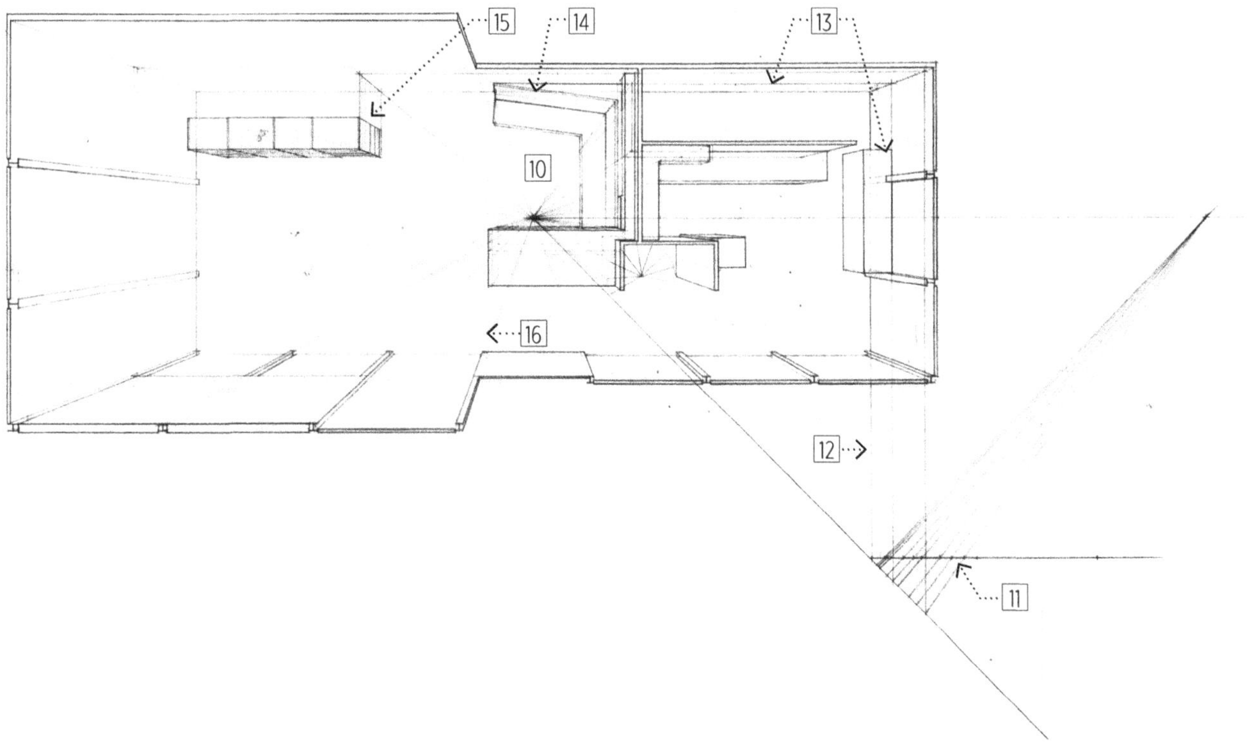

Step 10: Define the Corners of Furniture in Perspective
To add furniture to the drawing, draw perspective lines from the vanishing point through the corners of the furniture that are adjacent to the exterior walls.

Step 11: Measure Furniture Heights
Mark off the heights of the furniture on the measuring line and draw a line through these height marks from the diagonal point to the diagonal measuring lines.

Step 12: Project Height Measurements Back to Perspective
Project these heights up to one of the exterior corners of the room by drawing vertical lines up from the intersection of the height lines and the diagonal measuring line.

Step 13: Transfer Height Measurements to Object
Transfer the height measurements around the outer edges of the room, using horizontal and vertical lines, until they meet the furniture perspective lines that were drawn in step 10.

Step 14: Draw Top of Furniture
Draw the top plane of the furniture by projecting additional perspective lines through the remaining corners of each object. The lines defining the top furniture plane will always be parallel to the furniture outline in the floor plan.

Step 15: Draw Furniture Not Located on an Exterior Wall
To draw furniture that is located in the middle of an interior space, draw a horizontal or vertical construction line from the object until it intersects an exterior wall. Draw a perspective line from the vanishing point through the intersection, and repeat steps 11 through 13 to transfer the height measurements to the perspective line. Draw a horizontal or vertical line back from this perspective line to define the top edge of the object.

Step 16: Draw Exterior Fenestration
Draw the overall outline of any window, column, and door opening on the walls, after the furniture has been drawn, in order to minimize confusion with the other construction lines within the drawing. In the previous example, perspective lines were projected through the corners of the columns, up to the level of the ceiling.

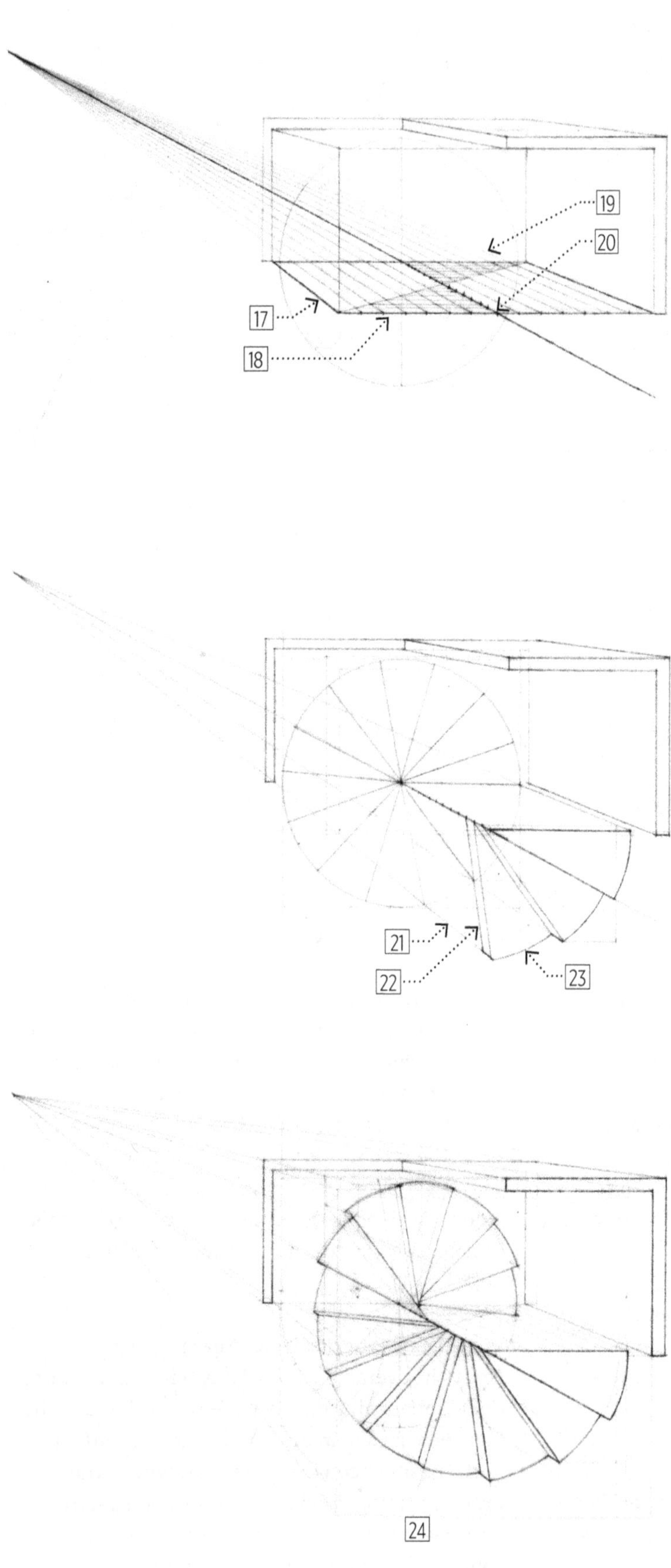

To draw more complex or smaller scale objects in the room, draw these elements at a larger scale, separate from the perspective drawing. After completion the drawing is reduced in size and then traced back into the perspective.

In this example the spiral stairs were drawn as a separate, large-scale drawing. The process for drawing the stairs utilizes the perspective measurement techniques in order to proportionally measure the heights of the stair risers. It is simpler and quicker to use these techniques because they allow the stair heights to be drawn in perspective without transferring heights from the more remotely located measuring line.

Step 17: Draw a rectangular plane, bisecting the center of the spiral stair. (Note: the left side of the stairwell wall has been omitted for clarity.)

Step 18: Subdivide the top edge of the plane into equal segments, corresponding to the number of risers on the stair.

Step 19: Draw perspective lines from the vanishing point to the measurements on the top edge.

Step 20: Draw a diagonal line connecting the opposite corners of the plane. Where the diagonal intersects the perspective lines, draw horizontal lines back to the center of the rectangle. These marks correspond to the top of each stair tread.

Step 21: Draw perspective lines from the vanishing point through the plan view of the stair for the top couple of steps.

Step 22: Draw a line parallel to the edge of each tread from the corresponding height marks to the perspective lines.

Step 23: Using a compass or circle template, draw an arc to close off the end of each stair.

Step 24: Draw the remaining stairs, repeating steps 5 through 7, until the stairway is complete.

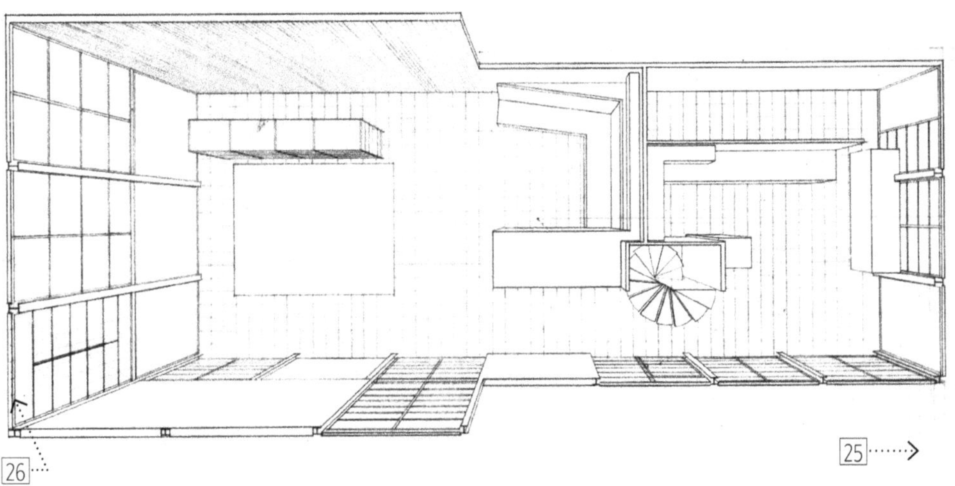

Finish the drawing by adding detail, such as floor and wall materials.

Step 25: In the example above, the location of the horizontal mullions on the lower and right walls were marked on the measuring line and then transferred to the walls.

Step 26: The mullions on the left wall were located, using the perspective measurement techniques. The upper two bays of windows were subdivided with diagonals to find the centerline. For the lower bay, the top edge of the wall was used as a measuring line and divided into seven equal sections. These measurements were transferred into height measurements by projecting perspective lines back to the vanishing point and using a diagonal to determine the location of the mullions.

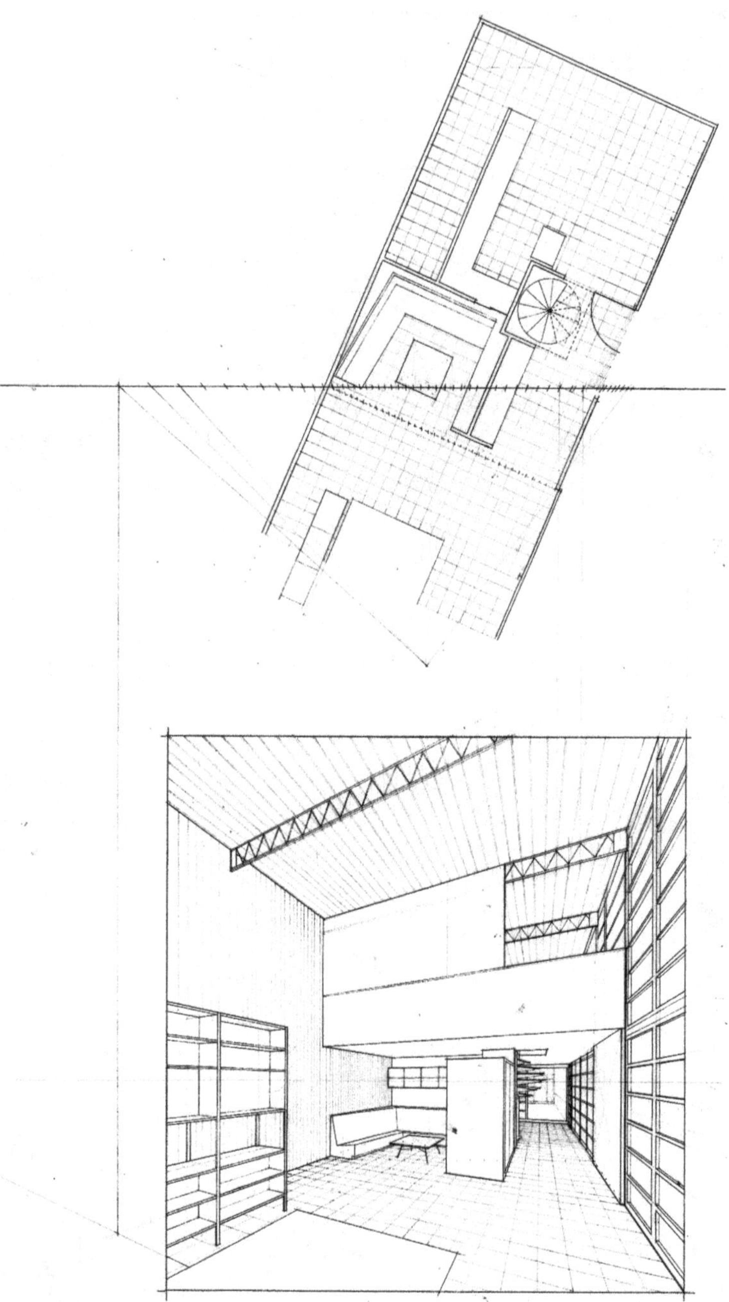

Common Method
The following example introduces the common method of constructing perspectives through a two-point interior perspective drawing. Although the example is of an interior space, these same steps can be applied to construct an exterior perspective as well as a one-point and three-point perspective.

Similar to the diagonal point method, the common method uses a scaled plan drawing and elevation heights to construct a perspective view. The station point, cone of vision, and picture plane are located on the plan in order to draw the perspective view and determine more accurate depth measurements.

Depending on the size of the space being drawn and the location of the picture plane, the floor plan can range from 3/16" = 1'-0" for a large room to ½" = 1'-0" for a small room, such as a bathroom.

Locate the Station Point and Direction of View

The first step in constructing any perspective is to decide what you want the perspective to show.

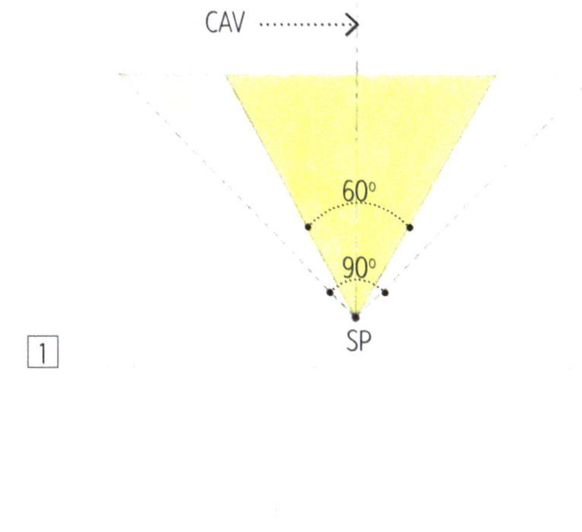

1

Step 1: Drawing the Cone of Vision and Viewer

- Draw a dot and a 60-degree triangle on a sheet of trace paper. The dot represents the station point (SP), and the 60-degree triangle is a person's normal cone of vision (CV).
- Bisect the triangle with a centerline and dash in a second triangle at 90 degrees. The centerline is the central axis of vision (CAV). The 90-degree triangle represents the limits of a person's peripheral vision. Objects located outside the 60-degree cone and within the 90-degree cone will be distorted within the perspective view.

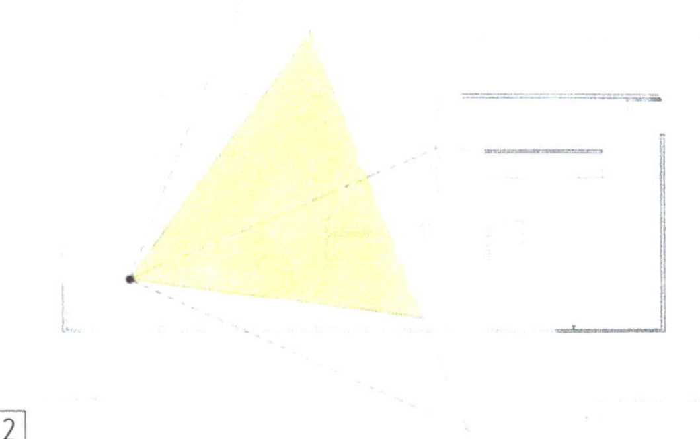

2

Step 2: Positioning the Viewer on the Plan

- Position the trace paper over a scaled floor plan and locate it so that the desired view is within the 60-degree cone of vision. Tape the trace paper onto your floor plan.
- Exterior perspectives are typically constructed with a 60-degree cone of vision. Many interior perspectives show objects within a 70- or 80-degree cone of vision in order to reveal more of the interior space. If you are drawing a perspective of a small space, it is common to position the station point outside the room and remove one of the walls so as to capture more of the space within the cone of vision.

Drawing Setup

- **Step 3:** Tape the plan onto your drafting board so the CAV is parallel to the sides of your board.
- **Step 4:** Overlay a sheet of trace or vellum paper on top of the floor plan, with the plan toward the upper portion of the page. This paper is what your perspective will be constructed on. Mark the station point on this top sheet of paper, and remove the cone of vision underlay to more clearly see the floor plan in future steps.

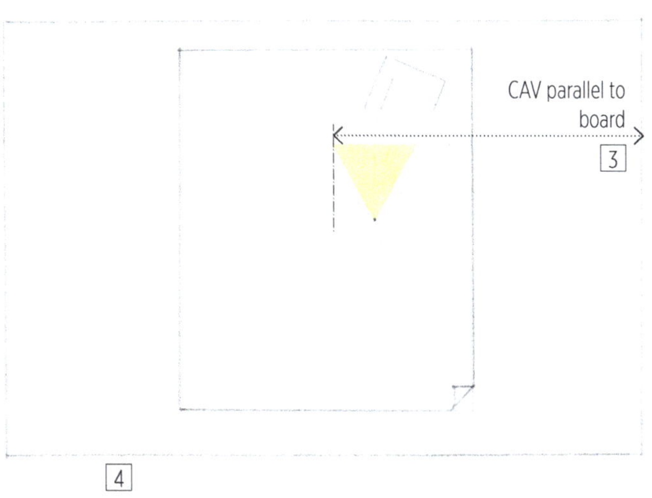

4

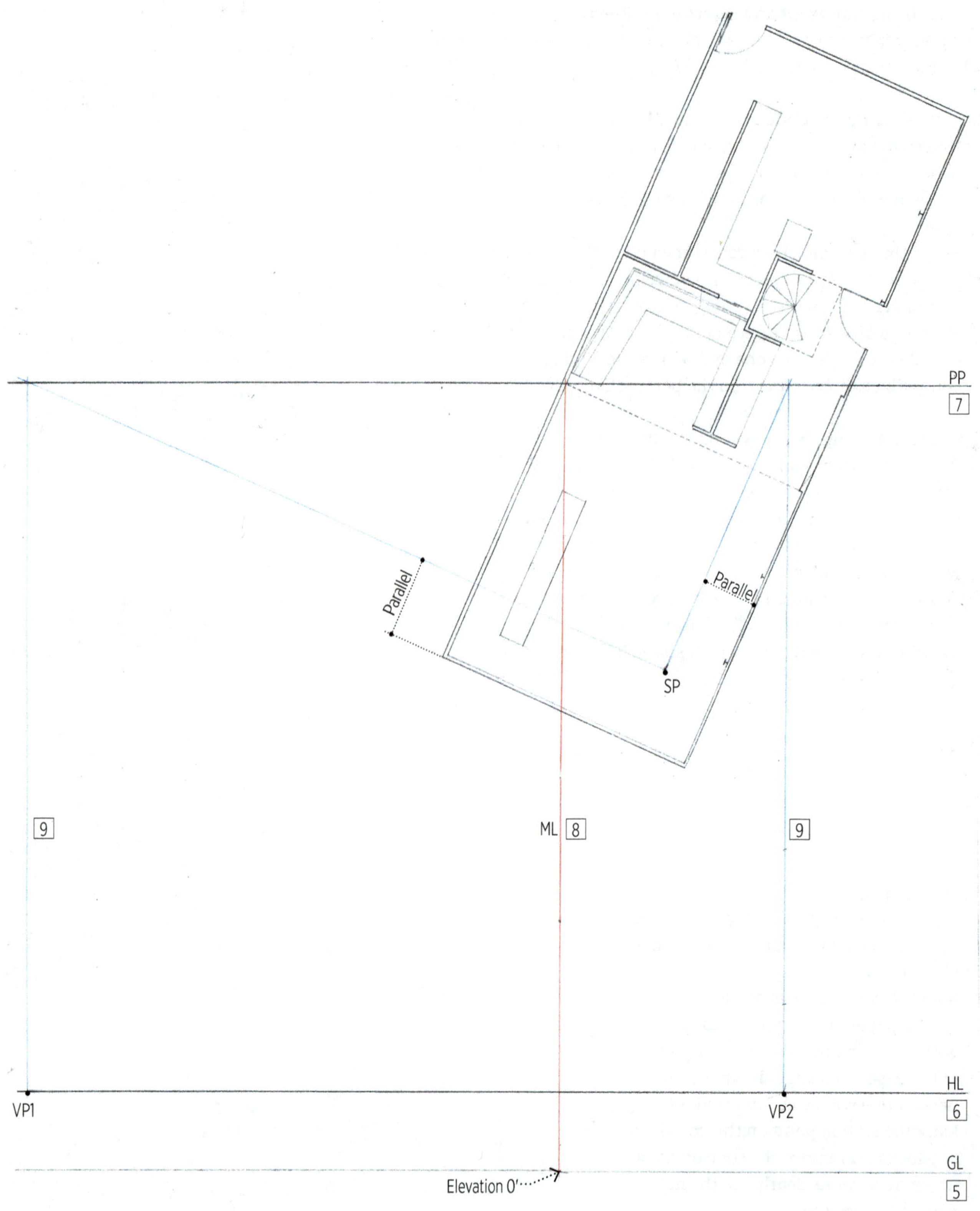
PP
7
Parallel
Parallel
SP
9
ML
8
9
HL
VP1
VP2
6
GL
Elevation 0'
5

Perspective Setup

Step 5: Ground Line

Draw a horizontal line near the bottom of the paper to create the ground line (GL).

Step 6: Horizon Line

- Draw a horizontal line above the ground plane to create the horizon line (HL). The distance between the ground line and the horizon line equals the height of the viewer's eye level above the ground plane and is drawn at the same scale as the floor plan. In the example the horizon line was located at 6'-0" to simulate a person standing within the space.

Step 7: Picture Plane

- Locate the picture plane (PP) by drawing a horizontal line through the floor plan. Because the picture plane is used to generate scaled height measurements, the line of the picture plane typically intersects an important vertical edge within the space.
- The picture plane location also controls the scale of the objects within the perspective view. All objects between the picture plane and the station point will be drawn larger than the scale of the floor plane; objects behind the picture plane will be smaller. To increase the scale of the perspective view, locate the picture plane farther away from the station point. To decrease the scale, move the picture plane closer.

Step 8: Measuring Line (ML)

In the example the picture plane intersects the point where the mezzanine meets the wall. This intersection will become the measuring line for vertical heights. To draw this measuring line, project a vertical line down to meet the ground line.

Step 9: Vanishing Points (VP)

- To locate the vanishing points for the walls of the floor plan, draw a construction line parallel to the front wall from the station point to the picture plane. Repeat this process for the side wall.
- At the point where the construction line intersects the picture plane, project a vertical line down to the horizon line. These points (VP1 and VP2) are the two main vanishing points for the perspective.

The most difficult thing for beginning students to understand is which vanishing point the perspective lines should be projected from. If you get confused, look at the plan drawing to locate the side of the object that you are drawing. If the side is parallel to the construction line for the left vanishing point, draw the perspective lines back to the left vanishing point. If the side is parallel to the right construction line, draw perspective lines back to the right vanishing point.

Drawing Objects in Perspective

In most perspectives, you want to first draw the overall limits of the room or object. There are five basic steps for drawing objects in perspective. These steps are repeated for each object in order to complete the perspective drawing.

Step 10: Mark the object's height on the ML. Mark the ceiling height on the measuring line. The distance between the floor and ceiling marks is measured at the same scale as the floor plan.

Step 11: Draw sightlines from the station point to the overall corners of the object or room.

Step 12: Where the sightlines intersect the picture plane, draw vertical construction lines down into the perspective view.

Step 13: Draw perspective lines from the appropriate vanishing point through the height lines. Draw perspective lines from VP2 and VP1 through the floor and ceiling height marks on the measuring line, to define the plane of the side and front walls.

Step 14: Stop the perspective lines at the corresponding vertical line of the object to define its edges in perspective.

Step 15: Repeat steps 4 and 5 to finish drawing all sides of the object. Draw perspective lines through the rear corners of the side walls to define the back and right side wall.

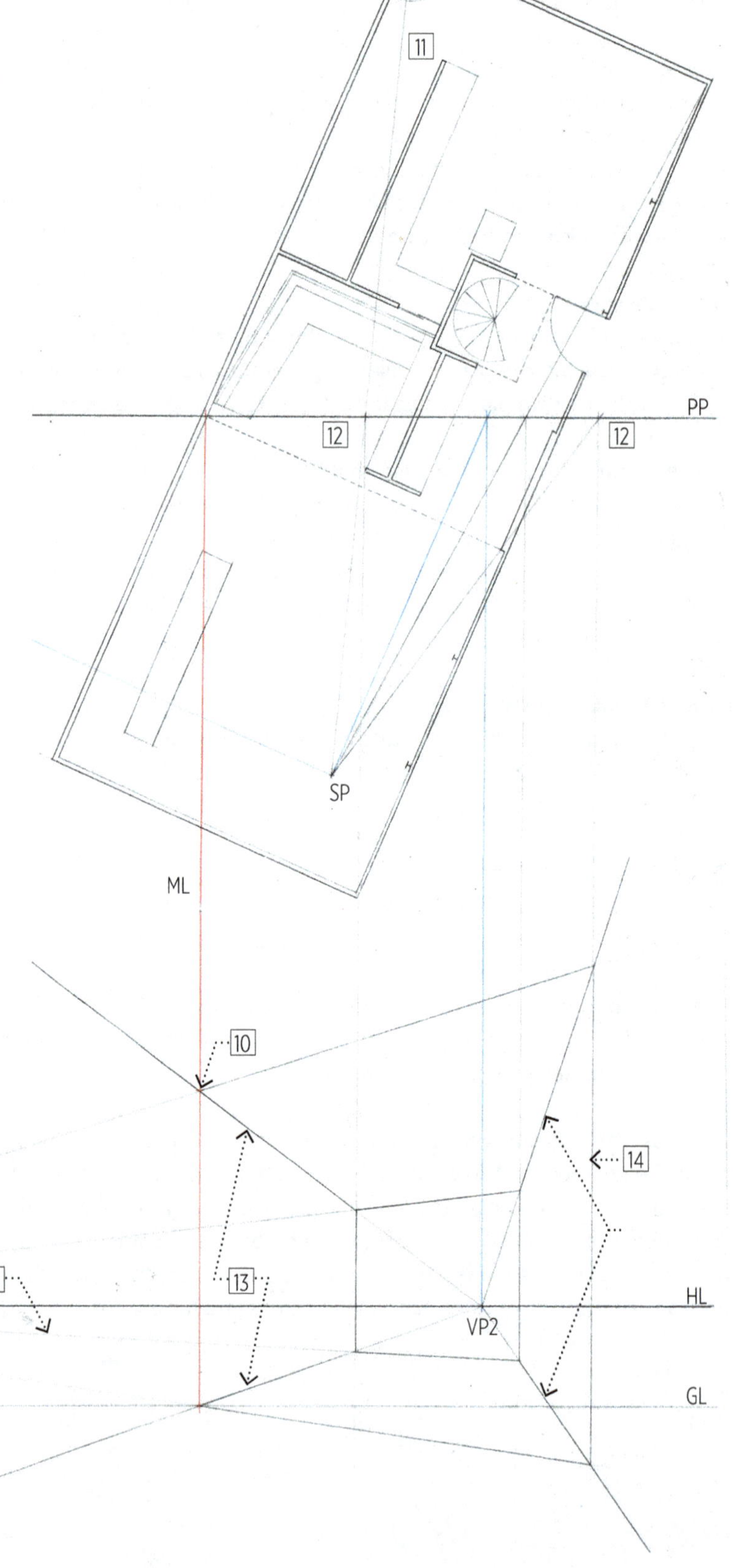

Drawing the Interior Elements

Step 16: Draw the Mezzanine

16a: Mark the mezzanine heights on the measuring line, and draw perspective lines from VP1 through the height marks, until the lines intersect the front right corner of the room.

16b: Draw perspective lines back to VP2 to define the underside of the mezzanine.

Step 17: Locate Objects in the Center of the Room

17a: Using the same technique as the plan perspective, draw an extension line from the bookcase to the exterior wall. This line should be parallel with one side of the bookcase.

17b: Draw sightlines from the station point to the picture plane through the intersection of the extension line and the wall as well as the corners of the bookcase. Project these lines down vertically into the perspective view.

17c: Mark the bookcase heights on the measuring line, and draw perspective lines from VP2 through the height marks, until the lines intersect the vertical extension line.

17d: Transfer the heights toward the center of the room by drawing perspective lines from VP1 in order to define the back plane of the bookcase.

17e: Define the side planes of the bookcase by drawing perspective lines from VP2.

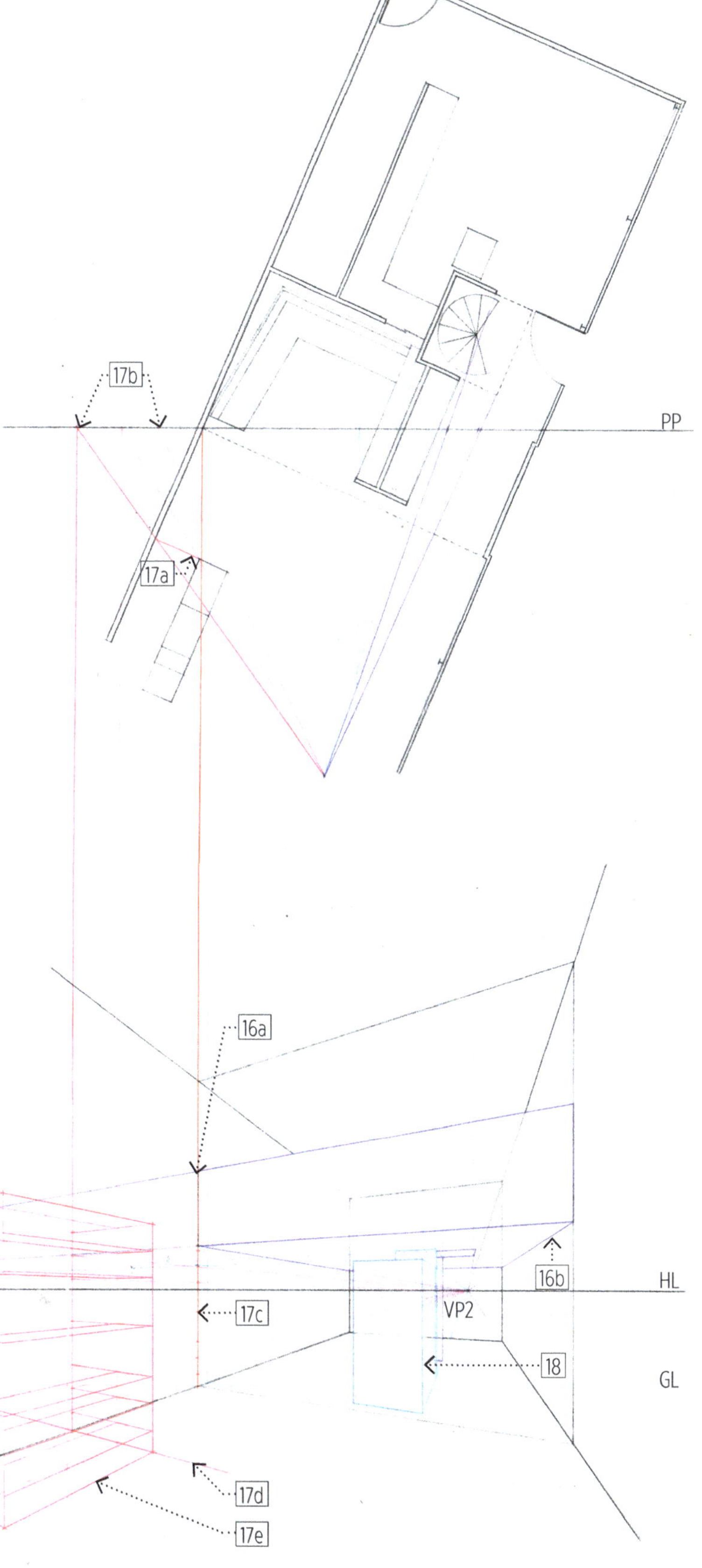

Step 18: Drawing the Interior Walls

The interior walls under the mezzanine were drawn by repeating the steps for locating the bookcase.

Drawing Furniture Set at an Angle in the Room

Objects not parallel to the main walls of a space have their own vanishing point within a drawing.

Step 19: Locate the Third Vanishing Point

- 19a: To locate the vanishing point for the angled bench, draw a line parallel to the built -n seating from the station point to the picture point.
- 19b: Draw a vertical line down to the horizon line. This is the vanishing point for the angled side of the built-in seating (VP3).

Step 20: Draw the Built-in Seating

The seat can now be drawn using the five basic steps for drawing objects in perspective.

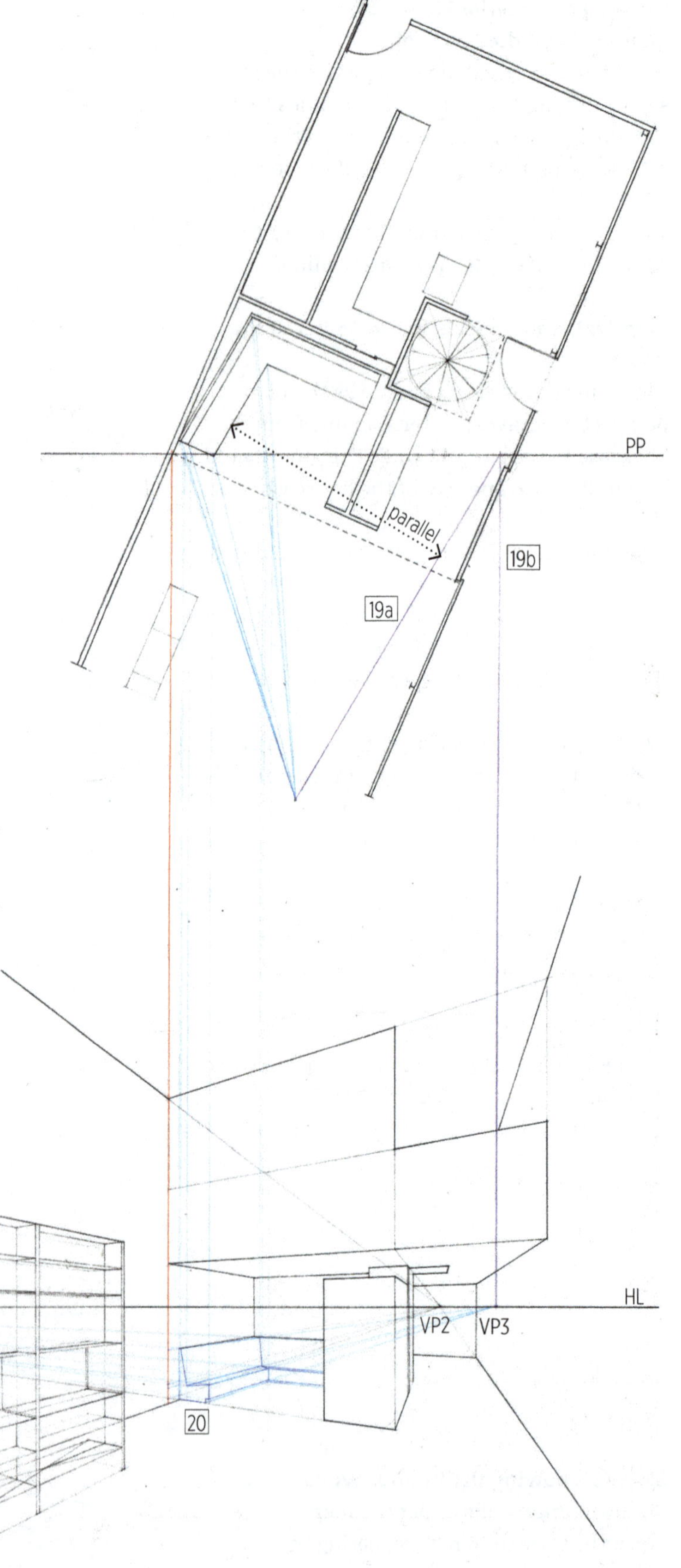

Finishing the Perspective

Complete the perspective by adding floor pattern and other details.

Step 21: Crop the Perspective

- Draw a box around the perspective to define the limits of the view.
- In the example the cone of vision is almost 90 degrees, resulting in some distortion on the sides of the walls.

Step 22: Darken the Drawing

- Line weight in perspective drawings shares the same logic as in paraline drawings.
- Spatial edges are drawn with the darkest lines and define the profile of an object.
- Planar edges are drawn with light lines. These are edges of objects or corners of a room where both adjacent planes are visible.
- Surface lines are very light lines that represent a change in material.

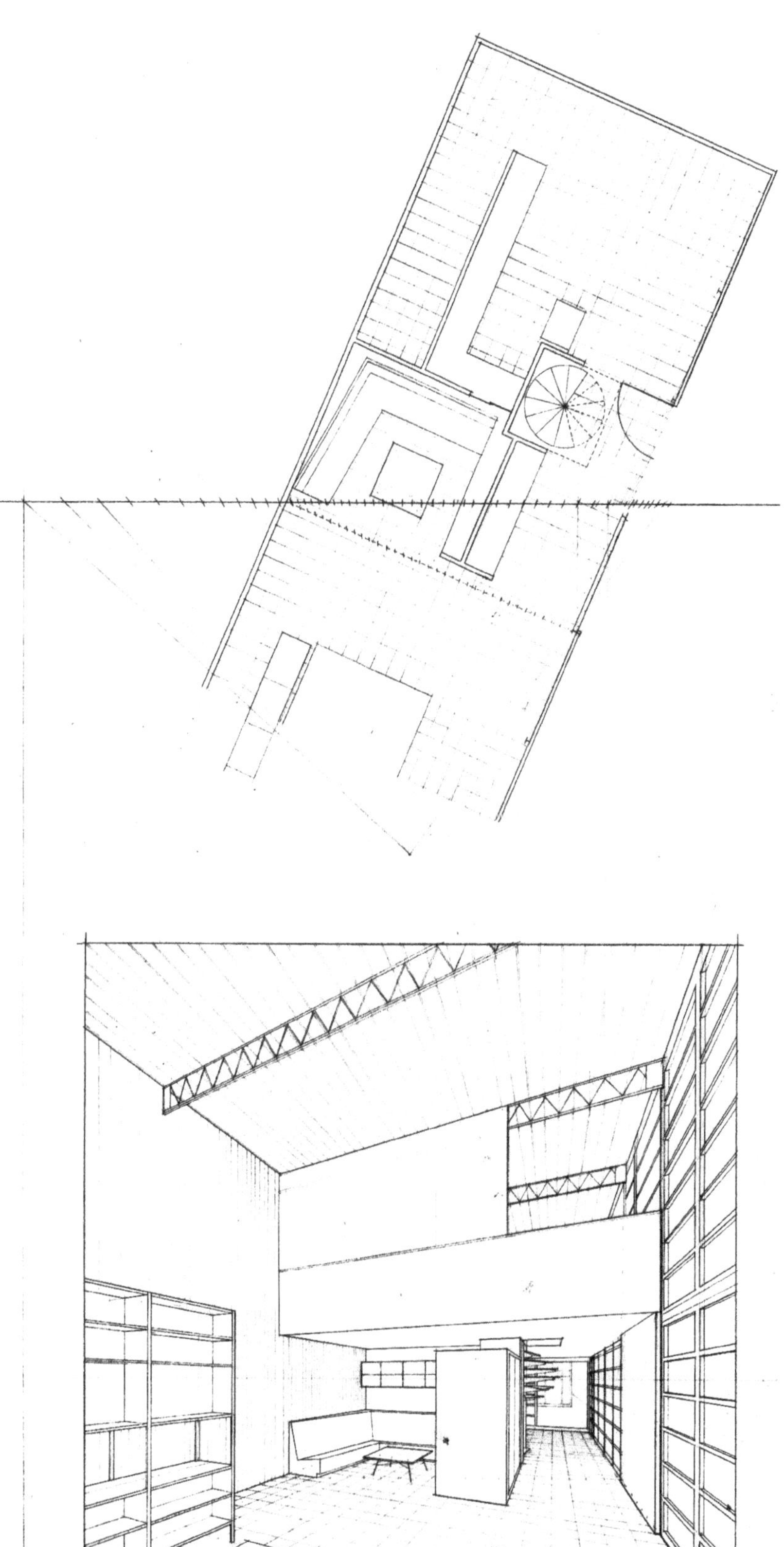

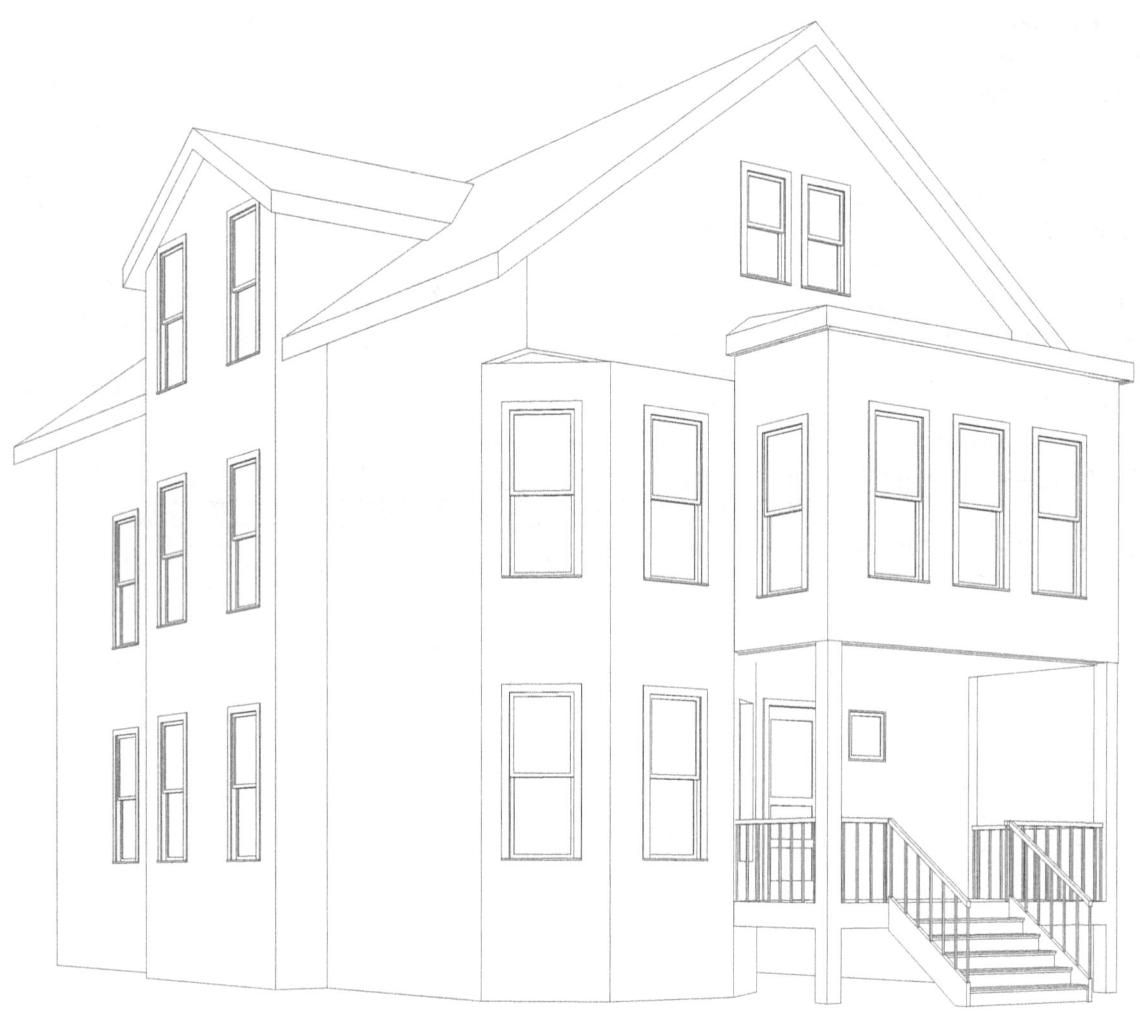

Learning Exercise: Line Weight
This exercise is intended to help you improve your understanding of line weight in communicating the spatial properties of a perspective.

- Using a dark line, carefully trace the perimeter profile of this drawing.
- Using a medium line, carefully trace over the internal profile lines and openings in this drawing.
- Using a light line, draw the exterior surface materials or items that are within the same plane as the façade, such as the window trim and frames.
- After tracing over the drawing, locate the two vanishing points and the horizon line.

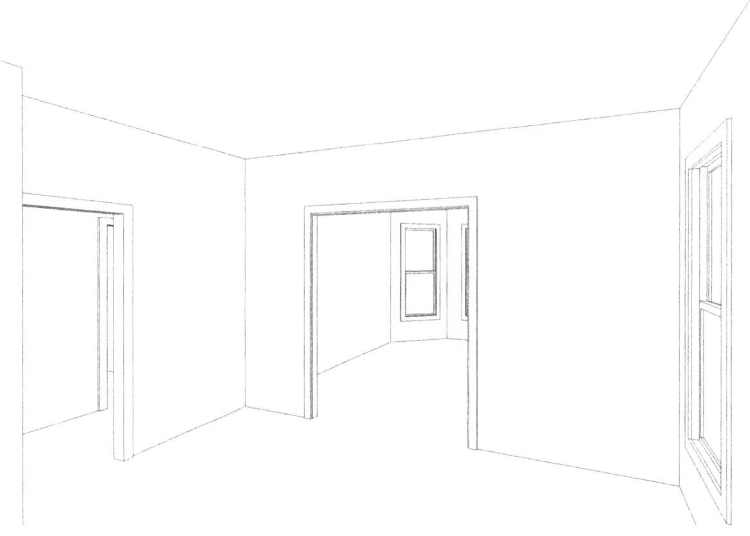

Learning Exercise: Drawing Perspectives

This exercise is intended to help you improve your understanding of perspective relationships and proportional measuring techniques.

- Locate the horizon line and vanishing points for this two-point perspective.
- Using the horizon line as a guide, proportionally determine the height of the walls.
- Proportionally increase the height of the walls to be one and a half times the current wall height. For example, if the walls are 10'-0" high, they would be drawn at a height of 15'-0". Refer to the Perspective Measurements section for how to extend an object's size.
- Draw a dining table and pendant in the front room. Use the vanishing points to help draw the furniture in two-point perspective.

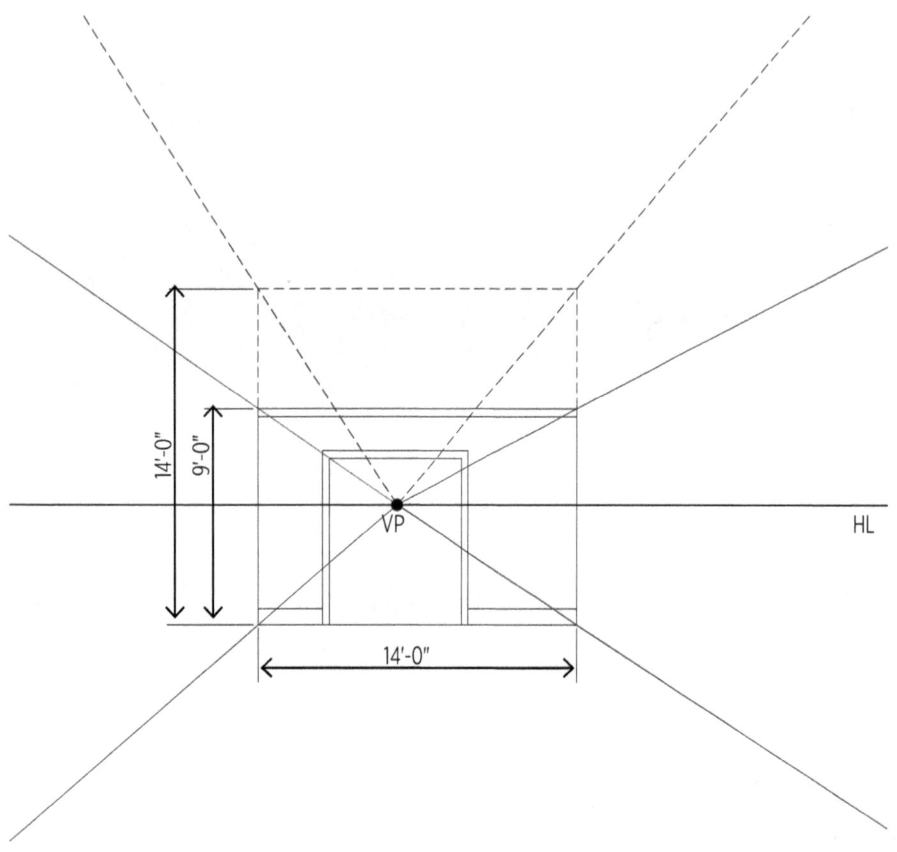
14'-0"
9'-0"
VP
HL
14'-0"

Learning Exercise: One-Point Perspective

This exercise is intended to help you improve your understanding of drawing a one-point freehand perspective.

- The plan and interior elevations on the right should be used for scale measurements to help you draw the freehand perspective. The station point, shown on the plan to the right, shows the viewer's location for the perspective. The shaded area shows a 60-degree cone of vision and the limits of this person's view. The station point is located outside of the dining area, and the wall is removed, in order to capture more of the space in the view.
- Using the drawing on the left as a base for your perspective, draw a 14'-0" × 14'-0" × 14'-0" cube to define the width and depth of the dining room. The vanishing point and a horizon line at 5'-0" have been located for your reference.
- All the elements drawn on the back wall coincide with the picture plane. This means that they can be used as measuring lines to help you draw the rest of the perspective.
- Lower the height of the cube to define the ceiling plane. Your cube should now be adjusted to 14'-0" wide x 14'-0" deep × 9'-0" high.
- Draw the limits of the living room beyond by proportionally extending the cube toward the vanishing point.
- Draw the outline of the windows and door in perspective.
- Draw a table, chairs, and suspended ceiling light in the dining room. Add materials, such as a wood floor, to complete the perspective.

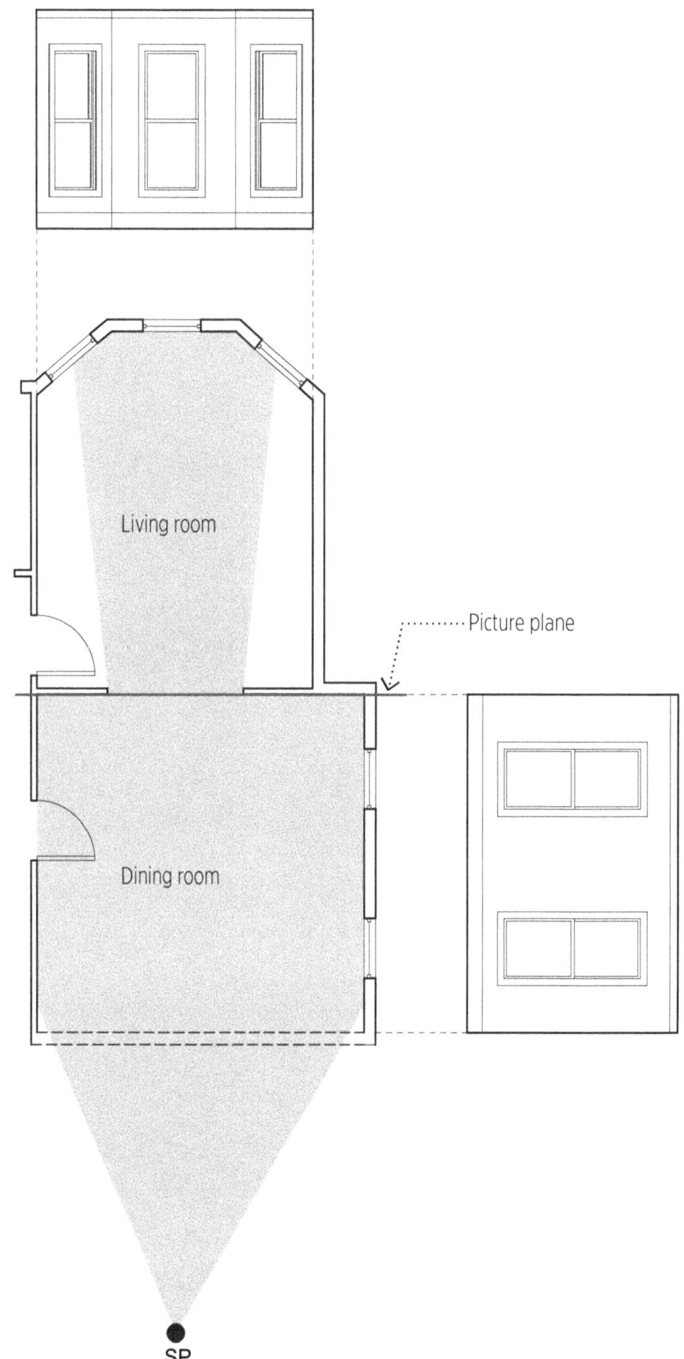

COMPLEX GEOMETRY

This chapter introduces how to represent complex geometry, such as curved and angled forms, in plan, section, elevation, perspective, and paraline drawings.

By learning how to draft complex forms by hand, you can broaden your ability to design and communicate a wide variety of complex spatial conditions through freehand sketching.

This chapter is organized into three main sections:

- Drawing oblique geometry
- Drawing curved geometry
- Using SketchUp to draw complex geometry in perspective

Consider the following questions as you read this chapter:

- How can you apply the drawing conventions that you learned in Chapters 3 through 9 to draw complex shapes?
- What drawing techniques can you use to help make your drawings read three dimensionally?
- How can you use freehand sketching, hand drafting, and digital drawing to represent complex forms in plan, section, elevation, perspective, and paraline?

Complex geometry is geometry that is nonrectilinear, such as curved, organically shaped forms or oblique forms.

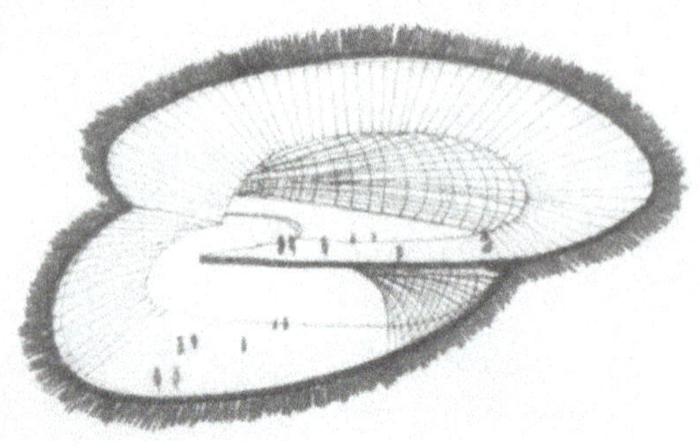

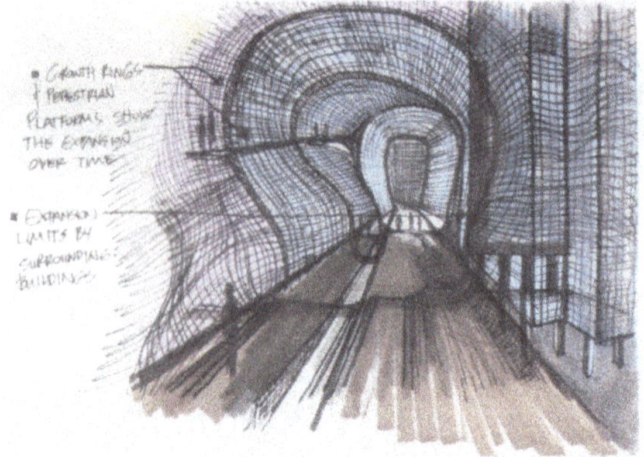

MATTHEW VARLEY
Freehand interior perspectives
Degree Project Studio,
Boston Architectural College

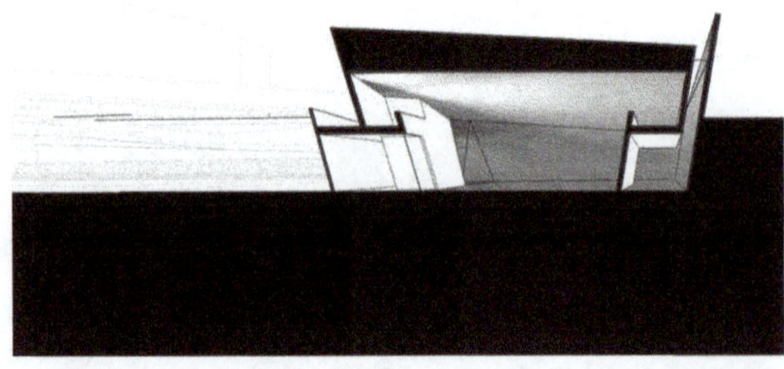

PATRICK S. LAUSELL
Section-perspective
Degree Project Studio,
Boston Architectural College

Representing Complex Geometry
Both curved and oblique geometries are drawn using the same basic projection techniques described in Chapters 3 through 9. The primary difference is that more attention is paid to drawing the elevation or plan of the spaces beyond. For example, in the top left drawing, the light lines show the elevation of the curved walls beyond. This helps convey how the space is curving in both section and plan.

Curved and angled surfaces are often rendered with shading or parallel lines to help make forms more legible.

- In the freehand sketches on the left (top and middle), a grid of lines was used to draw the curved wall surfaces. When the lines are closely spaced, the curve is read as having a tighter radius. When the lines are spaced farther apart, a larger radius is represented. Deformations within the curved surface are represented by shifting the pattern of the grid.
- The lower left drawing uses shading to communicate the depth of the space and to emphasize the angled walls.

Hybrid drawings, such as section-perspectives or plan-perspectives, are extremely effective ways to represent complex geometry because they allow the spaces to read more three dimensionally. The section-perspectives on this page (top and bottom images) merge a section cut with a one-point perspective of the interior of the space. By drawing the walls in both section and perspective, a greater understanding of the spatial qualities can be obtained.

Digital Underlays
Digital drawings are often used to help designers draw complex forms. Portions of a design are built in a digital program, such as SketchUp or DataCAD, and are used as an underlay for perspective, elevation, and paraline drawings. This process allows a designer to quickly get into the space of a project and test out different views or options before investing the time to create a presentation drawing.

Freehand Sketches
Freehand sketches are often used to refine the geometry of complex forms and develop the design of a space. When a digital model is used, a sheet of trace paper is overlaid on the printed view, and the geometry is traced and adjusted as part of the ideation process. The middle sketch on the right is an example of using a digital underlay. It was created by tracing over the digital view (top image) and adding elements such as railings, ceiling planes, and walls to develop the project.

Once you understand how to represent complex forms through orthogonal, perspective, and paraline drawing conventions, you can more easily develop your designs through freehand sketching. Loose freehand sketches often create a more convincing representation of complex geometry because they allow the viewer to interpret a wide range of spatial conditions. Case Study 2 in Chapter 9 and the freehand sketches on the facing page were created solely from the designers' imagination, without a reliance on digital underlays or other drawings.

Hand-Drafted and Presentation Drawings
These types of drawings are a more precise representation of complex geometry and are used to refine the representation of a space from a freehand sketch. The presentation drawing on the bottom right is a more refined freehand drawing developed from the middle sketch on the right.

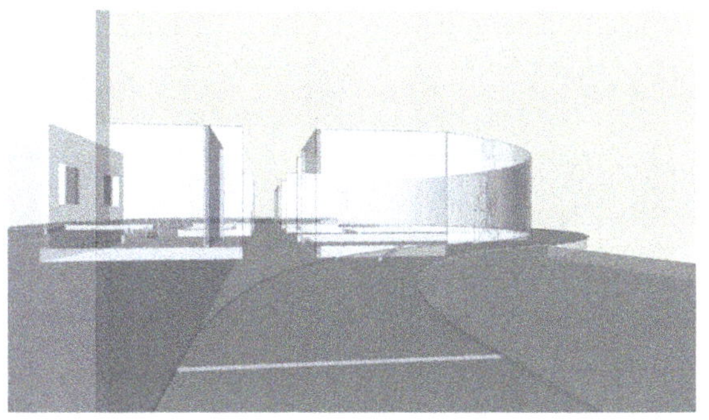

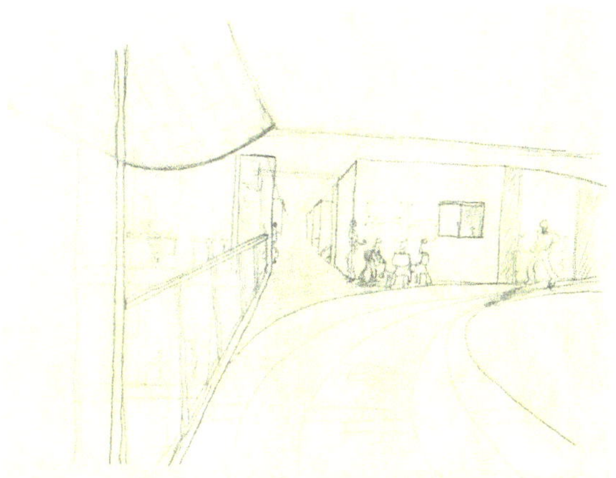

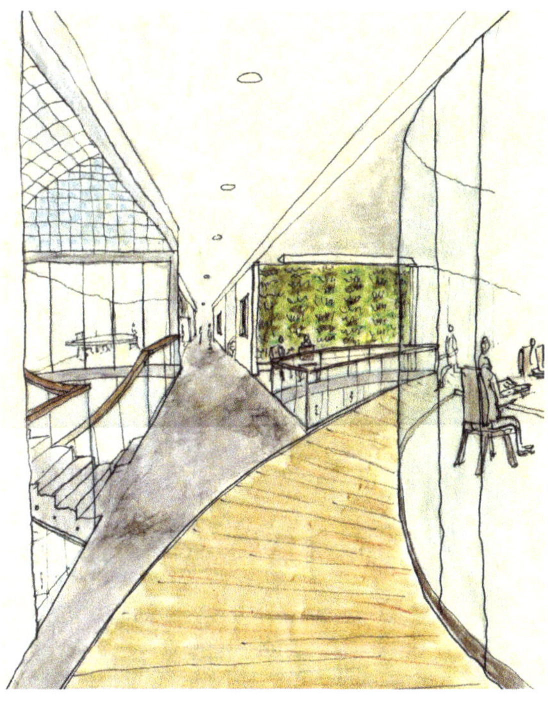

RYAN NEVIDOMSKY
Digital and freehand interior perspectives
Degree Project Studio,
Boston Architectural College

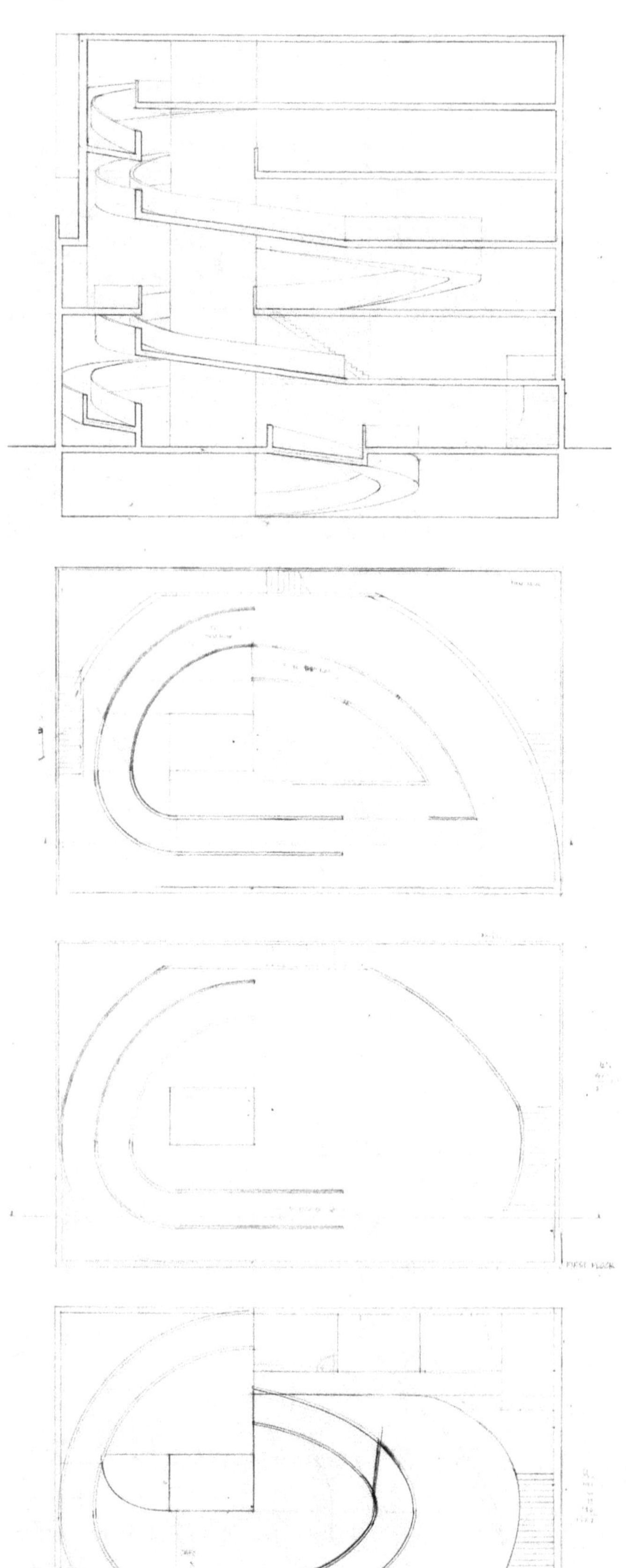

Developing Curved Forms: Hand Drafting and Freehand Sketching
This student worked back and forth between plan, section, and paraline drawings to develop his design for a curved ramp and building form. In the section drawing the elevation of the ramps beyond the section cut are drawn in order to make the curved geometry legible.

To understand the three-dimensional qualities of curved geometry, it is always necessary to draw the elevation of the surfaces beyond.

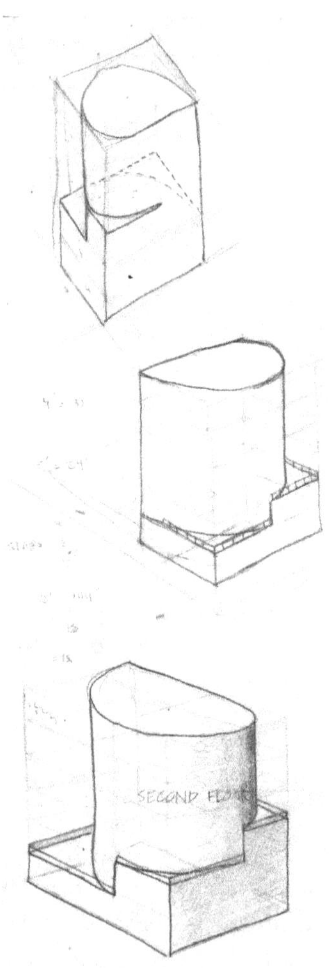

ROBERT BESON
Curved ramp and building form sketches
Architectural Studio,
Harvard Graduate School of Design
Career Discovery Program

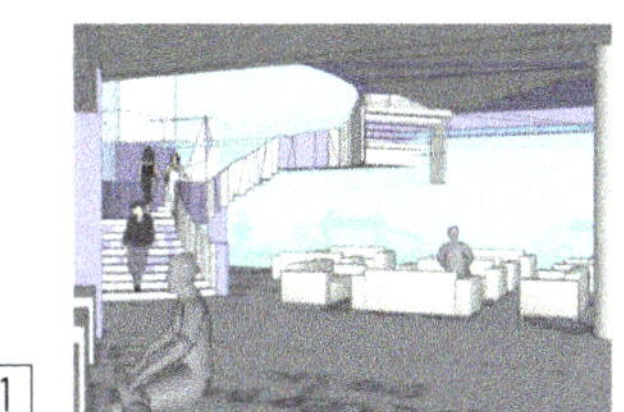
1

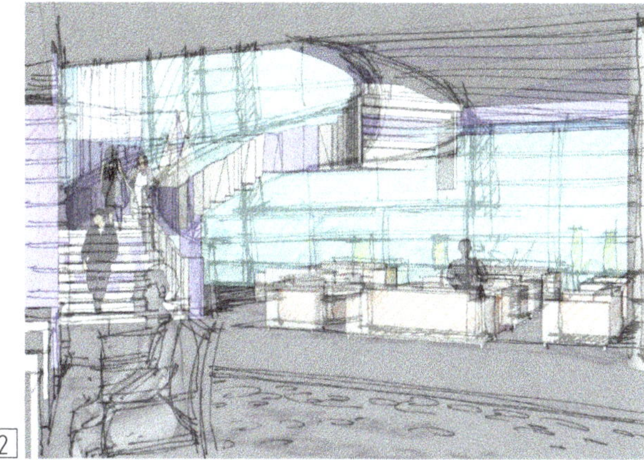
2

Developing Curved Forms: Digital Drawing and Freehand Sketching
The design of this lobby space was developed in perspective by sketching over a digital underlay.

Step 1: A rough digital model of the proposed design was built in SketchUp.

Steps 2 and 3: The designer sketched over a printed view of the digital model to refine the curved staircase and lobby design.

Step 4: The design of the stair railing and intersection of the stair and the ceiling was adjusted with a second freehand sketch iteration. Shadows were added to the sketch to help the curved stair read three dimensionally.

Step 5: A more refined presentation drawing was created, using ink and watercolor to render the curved surfaces.

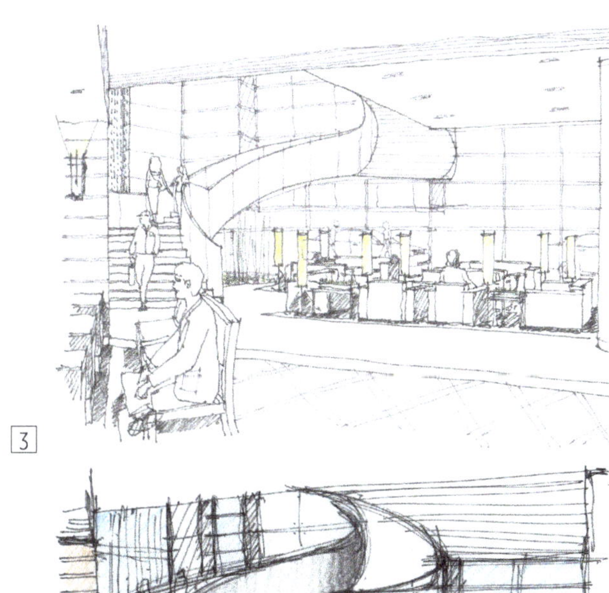
3

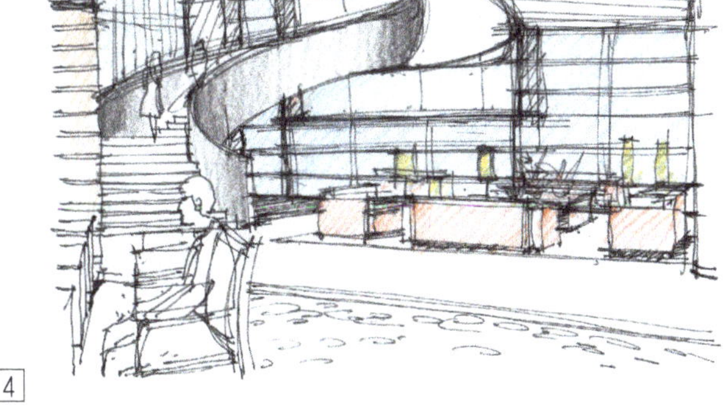
4

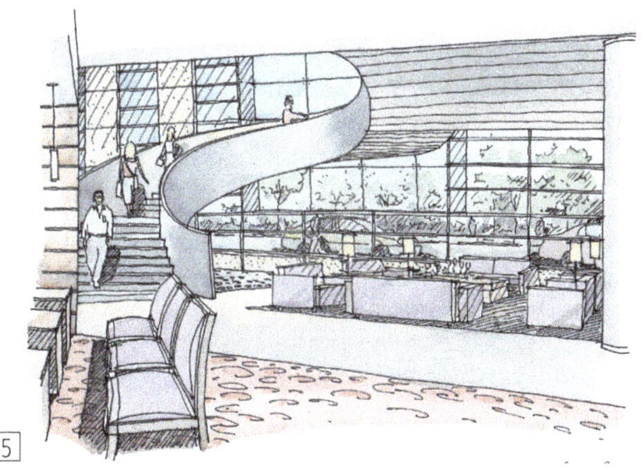
5

ARROWSTREET
Interior lobby study

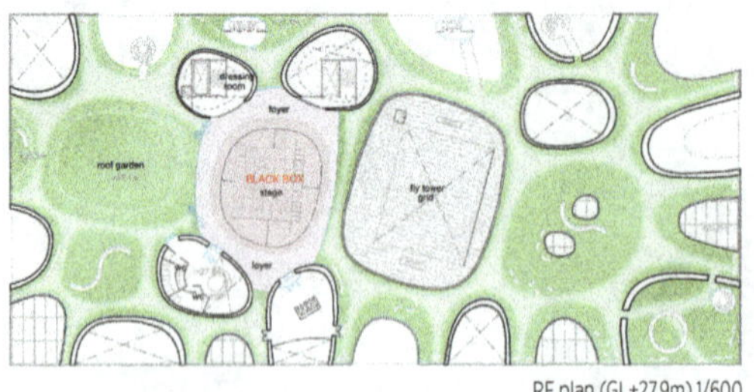
RF plan (GL+27.9m) 1/600

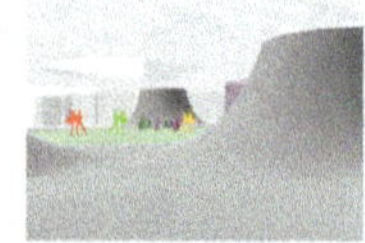
open-air arena

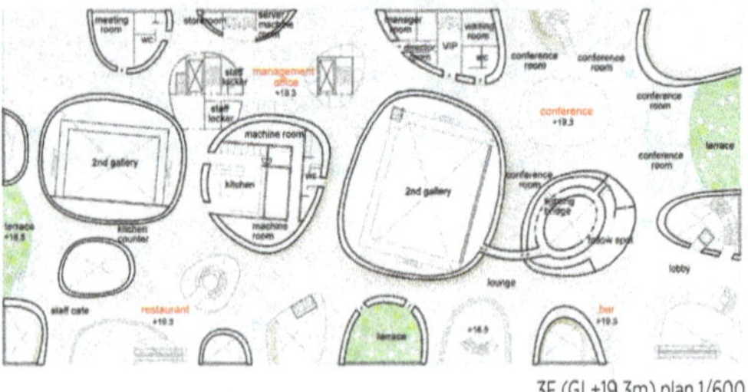
3F (GL+19.3m) plan 1/600

restaurant

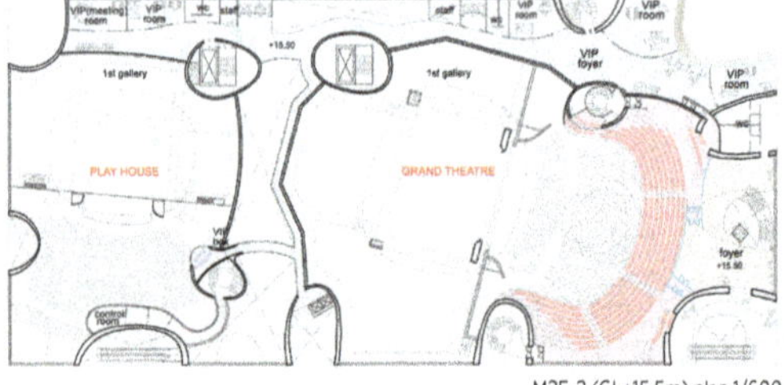
M2F-2 (GL+15.5m) plan 1/600

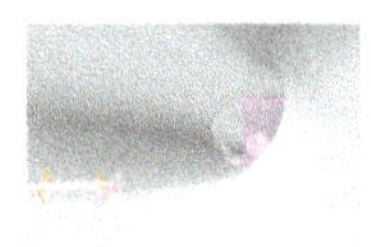
office

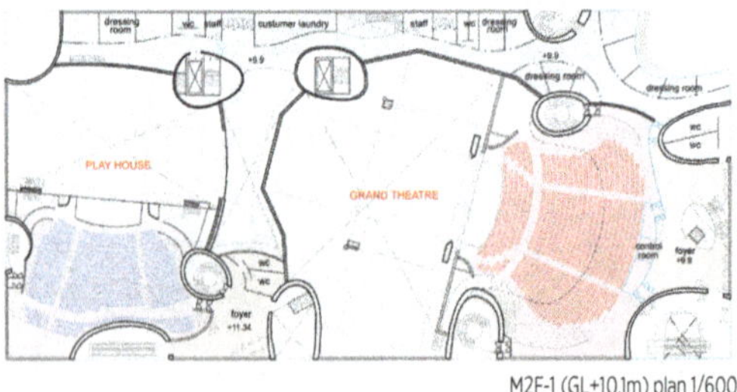
M2F-1 (GL+10.1m) plan 1/600

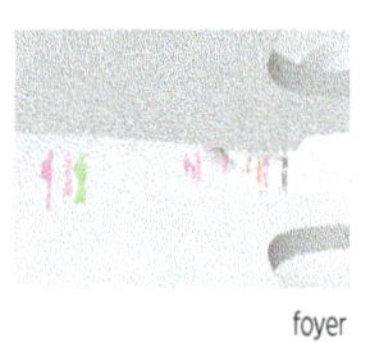
foyer

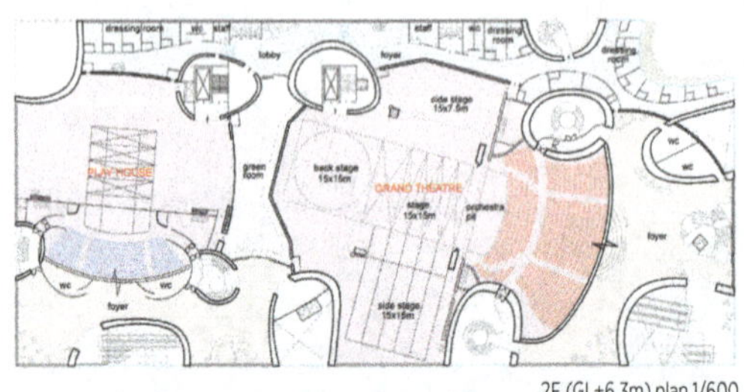
2F (GL+6.3m) plan 1/600

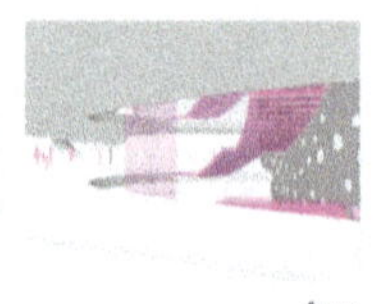
foyer

TOYO ITO & ASSOCIATES, ARCHITECTS
Competition drawings for the Taichung Metropolitan Opera House
The Taichung Metropolitan Opera House is built by the Taichung City Government, Republic of China (Taiwan)

Developing Curved Forms: Digital Drawing and Freehand Sketching
These drawings, by architect Toyo Ito, effectively convey the spatial qualities of complex curved surfaces in perspective, section, and plan.

Shading was applied to the curved surfaces in perspective to make the curves legible.

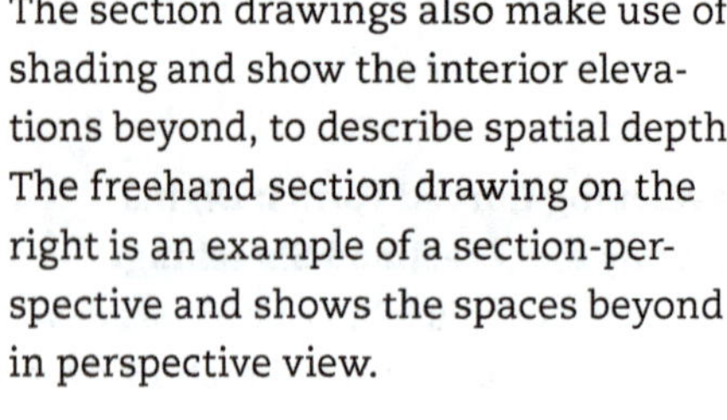

The section drawings also make use of shading and show the interior elevations beyond, to describe spatial depth. The freehand section drawing on the right is an example of a section-perspective and shows the spaces beyond in perspective view.

The floor plans are more diagrammatically drawn, with the curved walls represented through the plan cut. By aligning all the plans in a single column, Ito allows the changes between the curved forms, from one floor to the next, to be easily understood.

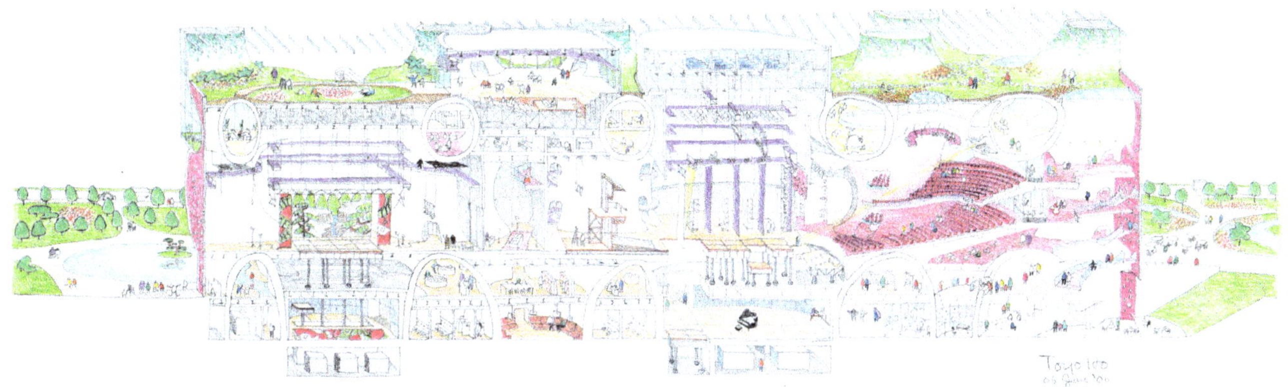

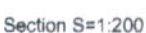

Section S=1:200

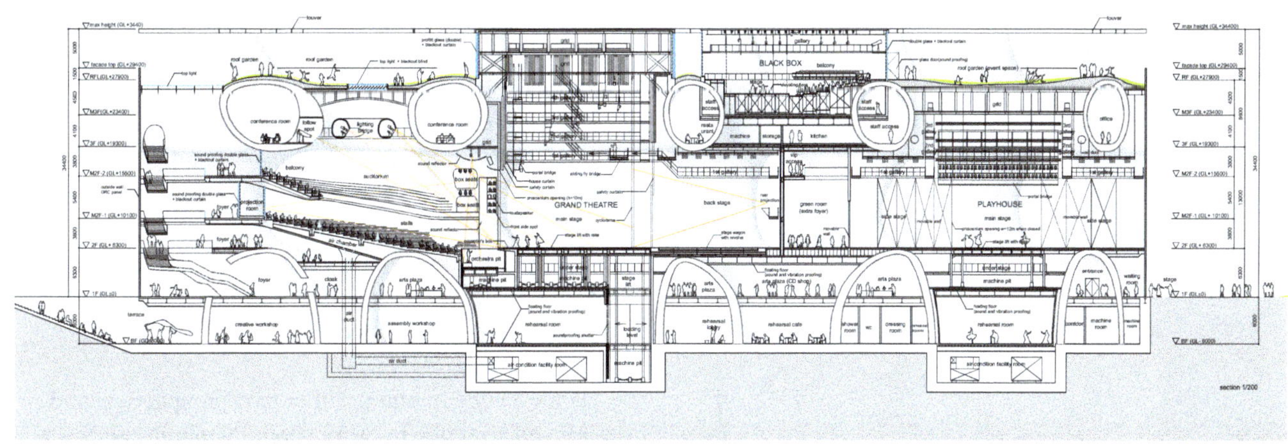

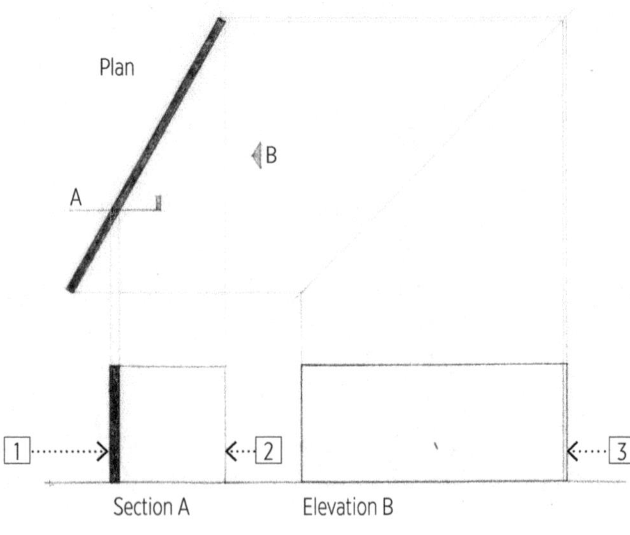

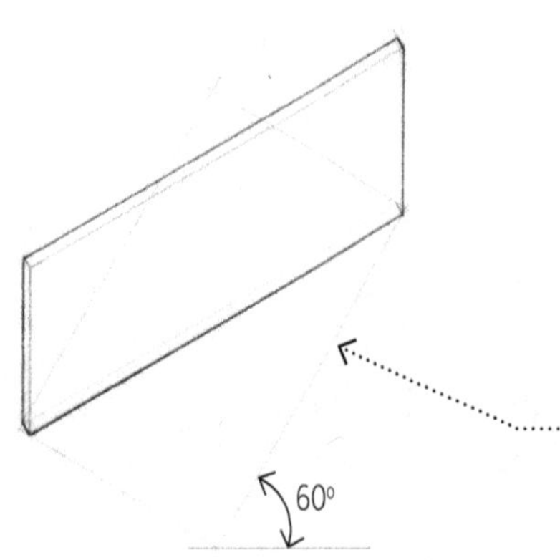

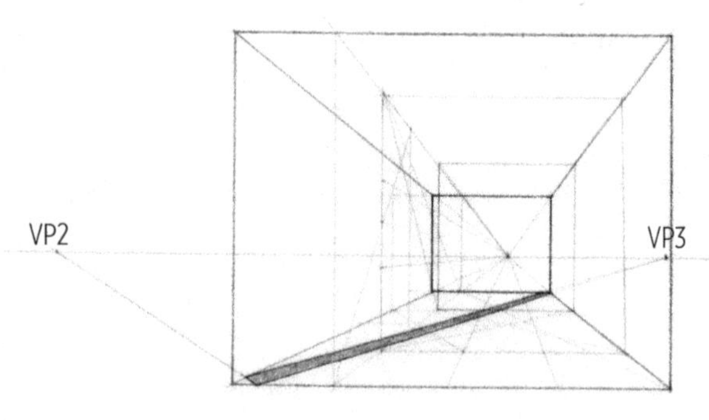

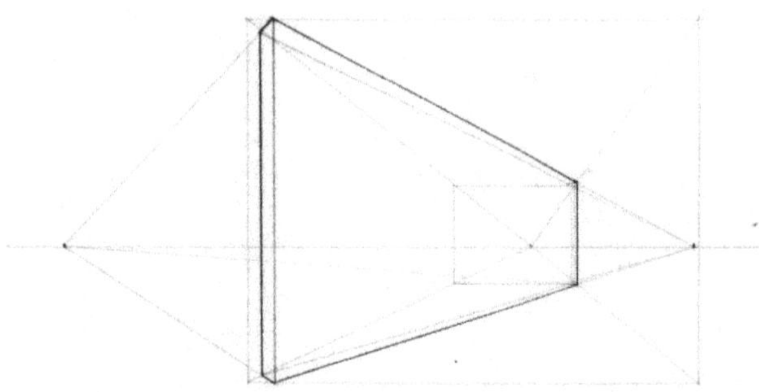

Drawing Oblique Geometry

This next section illustrates how to draw oblique forms in plan, section, elevation, paraline, and perspective drawing. When drawing nonrectilinear forms, it is useful to work back and forth between different drawing conventions in order to ensure that you are positioning the element in the correct location. The top left drawing on each page shows how construction lines were projected between plan, section, and elevation drawings to develop the geometric relationships.

Walls Angled in Plan

When a wall is angled in plan, the surface beyond is visible in the section cut, and its edges are seen in the elevation view.

Section and Elevation

- The thickness of the wall in section is greater than the wall thickness because it is cut at an angle (1).
- The elevation beyond is visible in the section drawing (2).
- The edge of the angled wall is visible in elevation (3).

Axonometric

- To draw the angled wall in axonometric and isometric, locate the wall within a rectangle.

Perspective

In all these examples the perspective steps follow the freehand one-point and two-point methods introduced in Chapter 9.

- Draw a cube in one-point or two-perspective, and extend the cube to proportionally match the height, width, and depth measurements of the rectangle used in the axonometric drawing. This cube will be a guide for locating the angled wall.
- Using the cube as a guide, draw the plan of the wall in perspective. Extend the edges of the wall back to the horizon line to locate its vanishing points (VP2 and VP3).
- Project the corners of the wall up to meet the top of the box, and draw perspective lines from the upper corners back to the vanishing points to complete the wall.

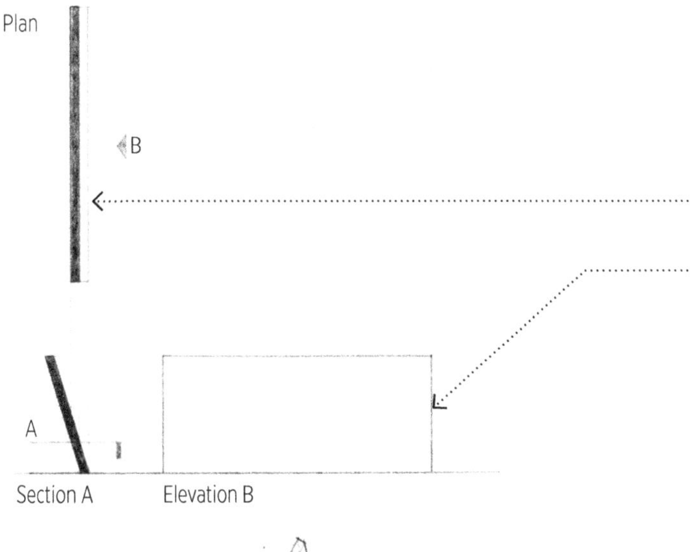

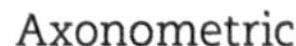

Walls Angled in Section

When a wall is angled in section, the surface beyond is visible in the plan drawing.

Plan and Elevation

- The bottom edge of the wall is visible in the plan drawing.
- The angle of the wall is not visible in the front and rear elevation drawings.

Axonometric

- Draw a box to locate the top and bottom edges of the wall.
- Connect the edges to draw the angle of the wall.

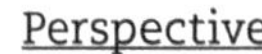

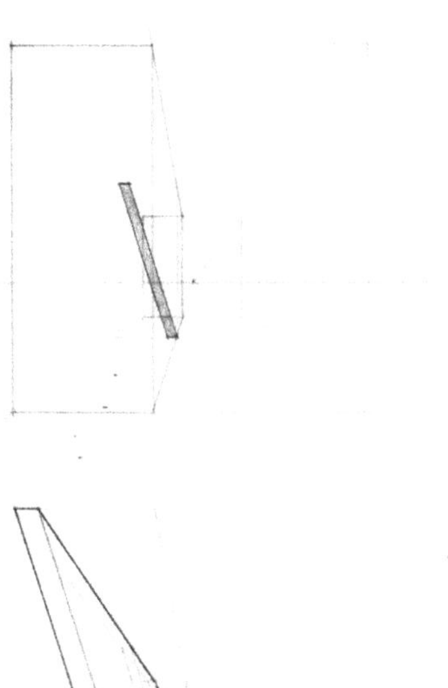

Perspective

- Draw a cube in perspective, and adjust it proportionally to match the overall limits of the angled wall.
- Draw the section of the wall on the rear face of the cube.
- Draw perspective lines from the vanishing point, through the corners of the section to the front plane of the cube.
- Connect the top and bottom edges to draw the angle of the wall.
- In this example, because the front face of the wall is parallel to the picture plane, the angled lines are also parallel to each other. This perspective is called a section perspective. It merges a true section with a one-point perspective and was projected directly from the section cut.

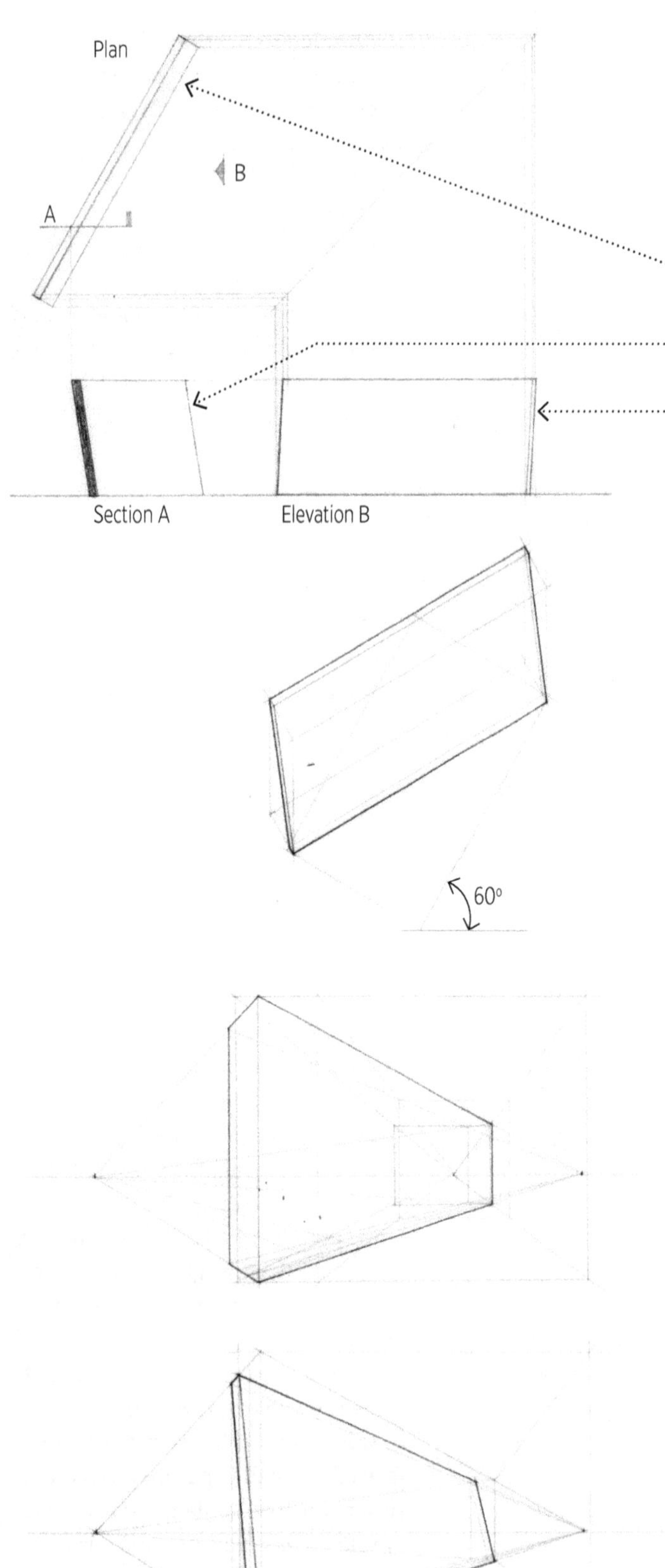

Walls Angled in Plan and Section

When a wall is angled in both plan and section, the oblique geometry is legible in the plan, section, and elevation drawings.

Plan, Section, and Elevation

- The bottom edge of the wall is visible in the plan drawing.
- The elevation beyond is visible in the section drawing.
- The angled edge of the wall is visible in all four elevations.

Axonometric

- Draw a box to locate the top and bottom edges of the wall.
- Draw the top and bottom faces of the wall on the box.
- Draw lines connecting the faces to draw the angle of the wall.

Perspective

- Draw a cube in perspective, and adjust it proportionally to match the overall limits of the angled wall.
- Draw a rectangular box in perspective to define the overall limits of the angled wall.
- Draw the top face of the wall on the box, extending perspective lines back to the vanishing points.
- Connect the top and bottom edges of the box to draw the angle of the wall. These angled lines converge at a single perspective point located above vanishing point 1.

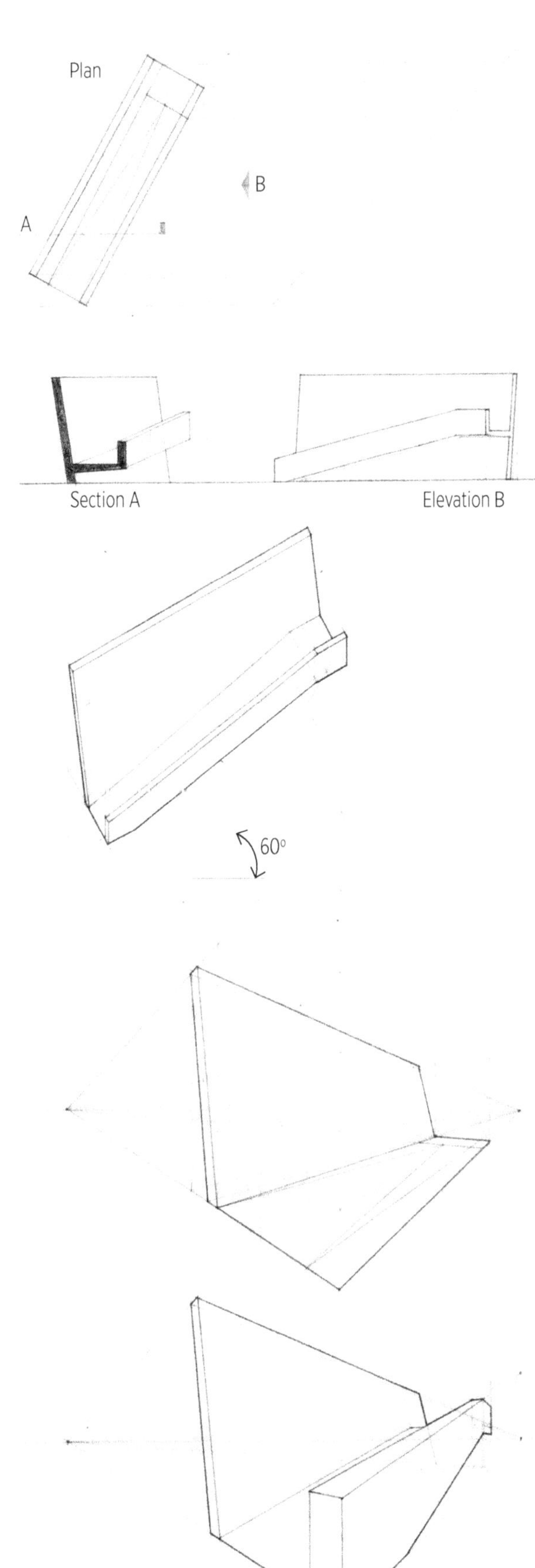

Walls and Floors Angled in Plan and Section

In this example a ramp has been added to an angled wall. As on the facing page, the oblique geometry is visible in all the drawing types. The same techniques that are used to draw a ramp can be applied to any sloping horizontal surface, such as a roof plane.

Plan, Section, and Elevation

When drawing more complex forms, it is necessary to draw the overall limits of the elements before adding more detailed forms.

- The plan, elevation, and section of the angled wall were drawn before the ramp.
- The ramp was then drawn on the plan and elevation drawings in order to establish the rise and run of the ramp.
- Next, the section cut of the ramp was drawn.
- To complete the series of drawings, the elevation of the ramp and wall beyond were drawn in section.
- When drawing ramps in plan, two angled lines are drawn on the plan view to designate the direction of the ramp slope.

Axonometric

- Repeat the steps of the axonometric example on the preceding page to draw the angled wall.
- Draw the plan of the ramp and project construction lines up from the ramp to draw the landing. Use the elevation drawing to measure the landing height.
- Connect the landings with diagonal lines to complete the ramp. The angled lines of the railing are parallel to each other.

Perspective

- Repeat the steps of the previous perspective example to draw the angled wall in perspective.
- Draw the plan of the ramp in perspective by proportionally extending the rectangle surrounding the angled wall.
- Subdivide the rear face of the rectangle to find the height of the landing. The railing heights were proportionally measured by dividing the front edge of the rectangle into six equal parts.
- Connect the height measurements to complete the two-point perspective drawing.

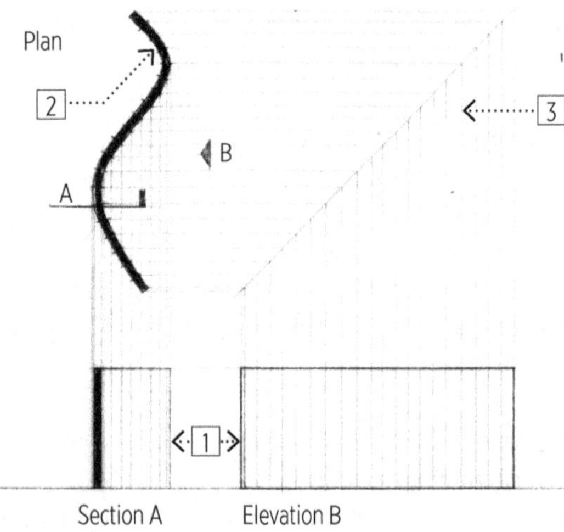

This next section illustrates how to draw curved forms. When drawing these forms, it is useful to subdivide the curved surface into equal segments. These segments are projected onto the other drawing types as either vertical or horizontal lines. The spacing between these lines conveys the radius of the curve and creates the illusion of depth.

Walls Curved in Plan

When a wall is curved in plan, the surface beyond is visible in the section cut, and its edges are seen in the elevation view.

<u>Section and Elevation</u>

- Draw the outline of the wall in elevation and section. Project the elevation and section from the plan, using construction lines. The curved wall does not curve in section or elevation, so the overall limits of the wall are drawn as a rectangle (1).
- To suggest the curved surface in section and elevation, subdivide the plan of the curved wall into equal segments (2).
- Draw construction lines from these segments to the elevation and section (3).

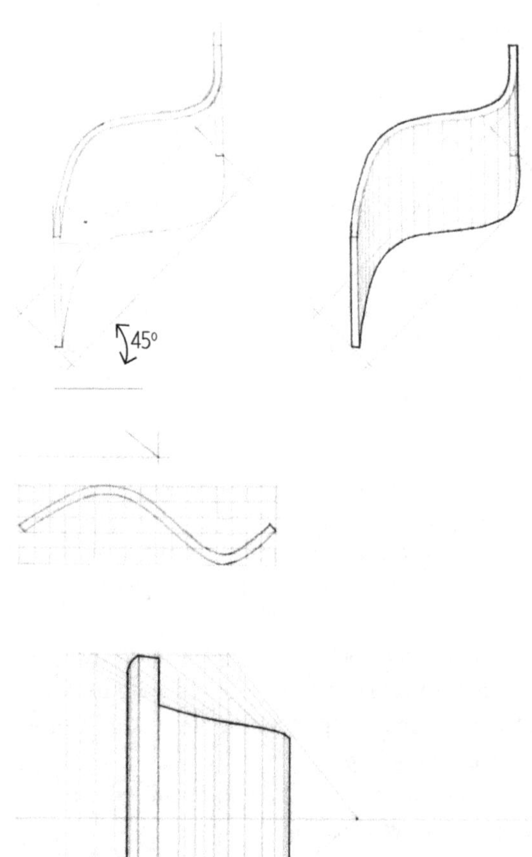

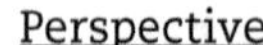

<u>Axonometric</u>

- Locate the plan of the wall within a rectangle to help you orient the axonometric.
- Draw vertical lines up from the wall to establish the outer edges of the curve. Mark off the wall height on one of the vertical edges to locate the top view of the wall. The top view is drawn at the same scale and orientation as the plan.
- Subdivide the plan into equal segments, and draw vertical lines up from segments to emphasize the curved surface.

<u>Perspective</u>

- Draw a cube in perspective, and adjust it proportionally to match the overall limits of the curved wall.
- Draw the plan of the curve in perspective. Subdivide the cube to create a perspective grid that will help you locate the curved wall.
- Transfer the vertical measurements of the curve to the top plane of the cube.
- Connect the height marks to draw the top of the curved wall.

Walls Curved in Section

When a wall is curved in section, the surface beyond is visible in plan view.

Plan and Elevation

- Draw the outline of the curved wall in section. Project the elevation and plan from the section, using construction lines. The curved wall does not curve in plan or elevation, so the overall limits of the wall are drawn as a rectangle (1).
- To suggest the curved surface in plan and elevation, subdivide the section of the curved wall into equal segments (2).
- Draw construction lines from these segments to the plan and elevation to describe the curved surface (3).
- As an alternative to the construction lines, you could also shade the plan and elevation to suggest the shadows on the curved surface (4).

Axonometric

- Locate the plan of the wall within a rectangle to help you orient the axonometric.
- Use the section drawing as a guide to transfer height measurements for the curve on one side of the rectangle.
- Connect the height measurements to draw the side elevation of the curved wall.
- Extend these measurements to the opposite side to draw the other elevation and complete the drawing.

Perspective

- Draw a cube in perspective, and adjust it proportionally to match the overall limits of the curved wall.
- Draw the section of the wall on the rear face of the cube. Draw vertical lines on the rear face to divide it into equal parts.
- Draw perspective lines from the vanishing point, through the vertical lines to front plane of the cube.
- Transfer the measurements of the curve to the front face of the cube.
- Connect the height marks to draw the front of the curved wall.

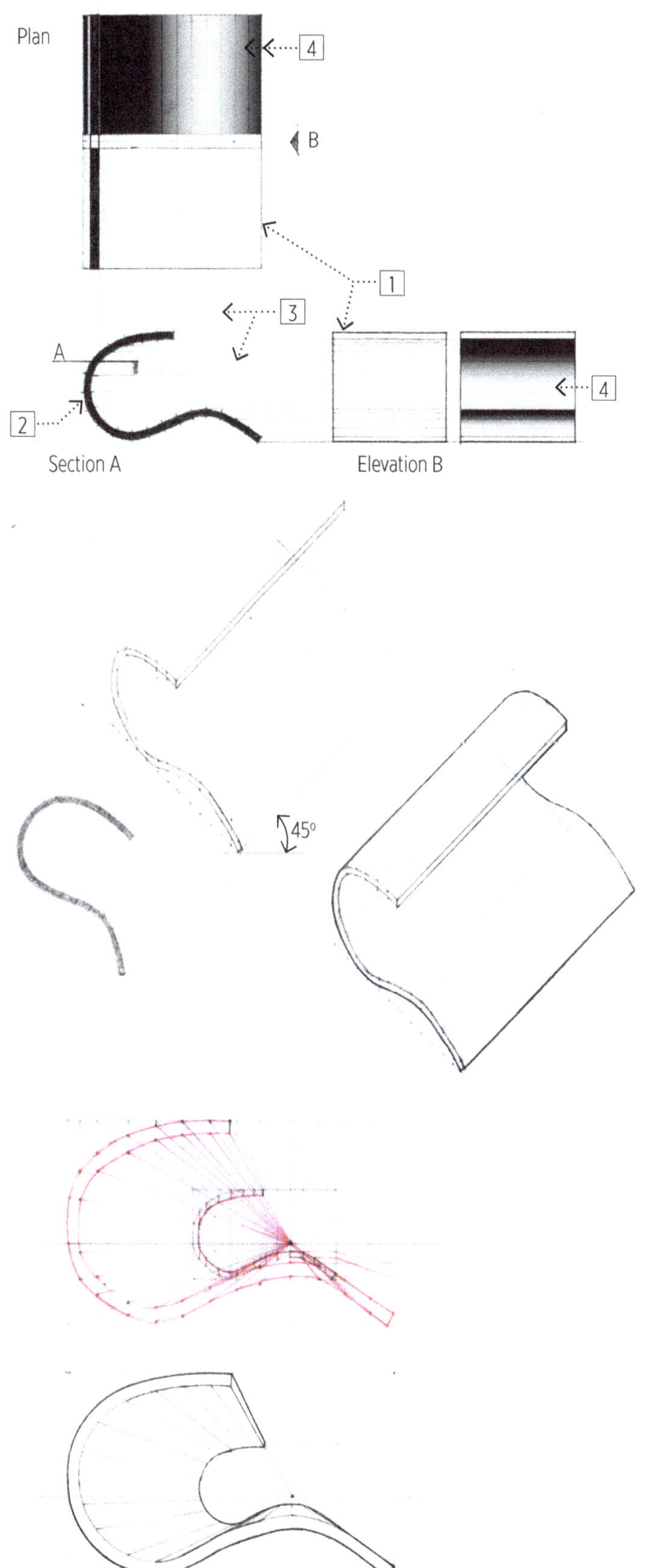

Using SketchUp to Draw Complex Geometry

Digital programs, such as Google SketchUp, are often used as an aid when drawing complex geometry. Although most students and firms construct full digital models to develop perspective views of their designs, a quicker method is to import a hand-drawn plan into SketchUp to use as a guide for the perspectives.

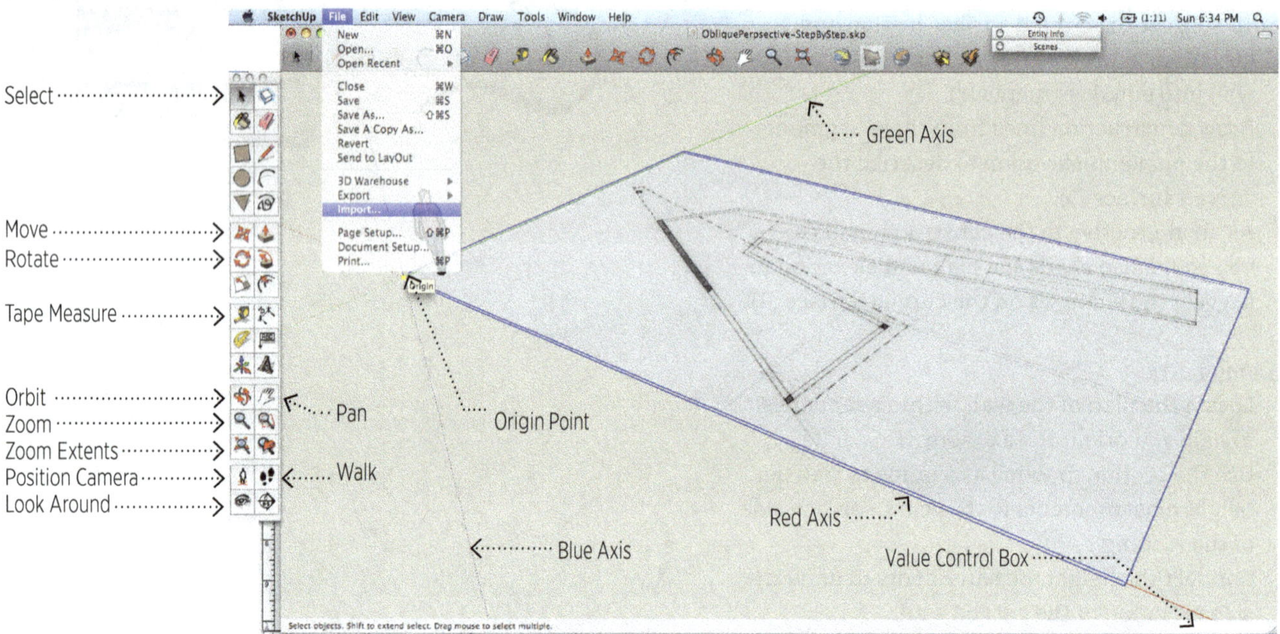

This step-by-step example introduces the basic tools needed to create a digital underlay from a scanned hand drawing. Additional SketchUp tools and commands can be easily learned from the tutorials provided with the program. This SketchUp file can be downloaded from the companion Web site for reference.

Mouse Wheel Shortcut Commands

With the mouse wheel middle button:

- CLICK + DRAG = Orbit
- SHIFT + CLICK + DRAG = Pan
- SCROLL= Zoom
- DOUBLE CLICK = Recenter the view

Step 1: Import Drawing into SketchUp

- Select FILE > IMPORT to choose the plan you wish to import. AutoCAD drawings and most image files can all be imported into SketchUp.
- To place the image, move your cursor to the origin point, located at the intersection of RED, GREEN, and BLUE AXIS lines. Click the mouse button to position the image.
- After placing the image, you will need to set its scale. Drag your mouse away from the origin point until the plan enlarges to a scale that you can see easily. Click once to set the scale. The plan will be scaled more precisely in a later step.
- Note: Elevation and section drawings can also be imported into SketchUp. To place these drawings perpendicular to the plan drawing, follow the same steps as above, and move your cursor to the BLUE AXIS when importing the image.

Step 2: Change the View

- Select CAMERA > STANDARD > TOP to change the view to a plan orientation.
- Select CAMERA > PARALLEL PROJECTION from the same menu to turn off perspctive.
- Select CAMERA > TWO-POINT PERSPECTIVE to return the SketchUp window to a two-point perspective view.
- Select CAMERA > PERSPECTIVE to return the SketchUp window to a three-point perspective view.
- Additional views, such as elevation and isometric, can be selected in the CAMERA > STANDARD menu.

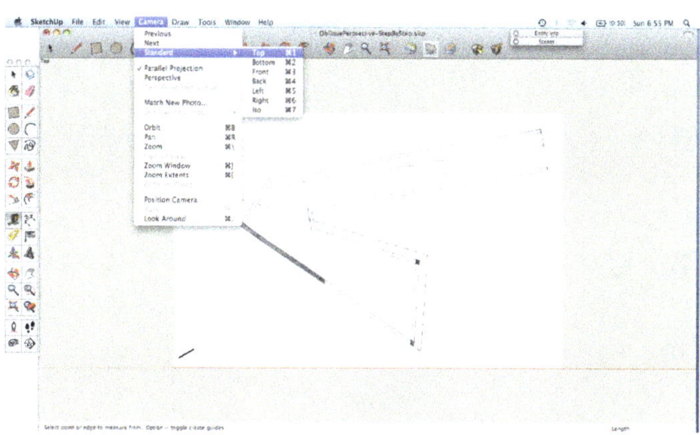

Step 3: Scale the Plan

- Select the Tape Measure tool, and click on each of two endpoints of a wall with a known dimension.
- A dimension string will appear along the wall, and the wall's measurement will appear in the Value Control Box.
- To change the scale of the wall, type the correct dimension in the Value Control Box, and press ENTER.
- A pop-up box will confirm that you want to resize the model. Click YES to proceed.

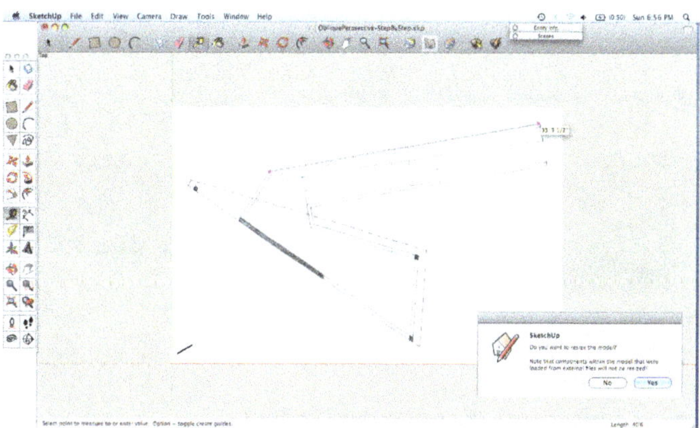

Step 4: Define the Ceiling Height

- Select CAMERA > TWO-POINT PERSPECTIVE to return to a perspective view.
- Rotate the view from plan by using the Orbit tool or by pressing down on your mouse scroll wheel.
- Use the SELECT tool to select the floor plan.
- Click the MOVE/COPY tool. Press the OPTION key (Mac) or the CTRL key (Windows) to toggle to copy mode.
- Click and drag the plan up along the blue axis any distance.
- Type in the desired ceiling height or top of your building in the Value Control Box, and press ENTER. The plan in the example was located at 10'-0" above the ground plane.

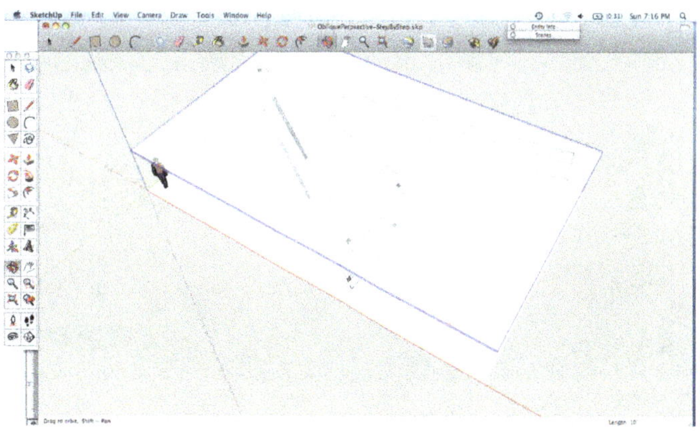

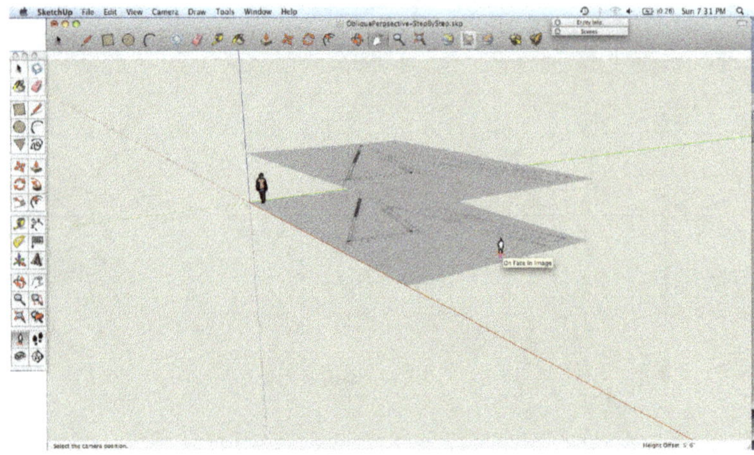

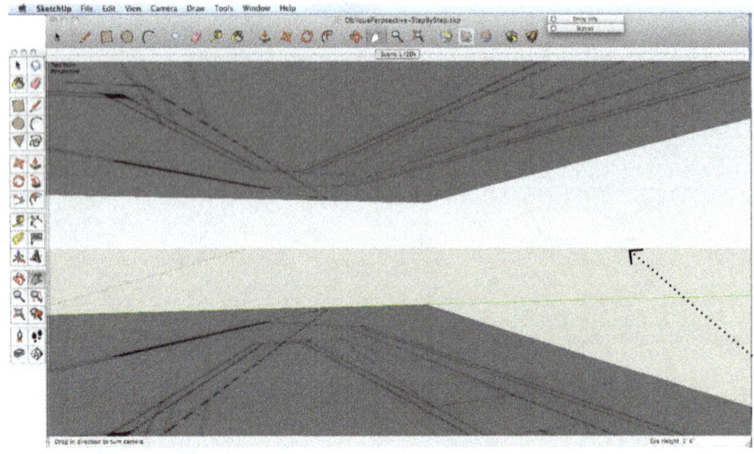

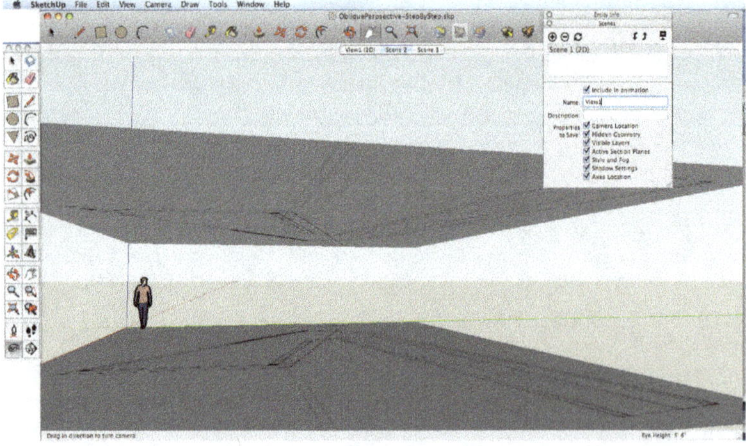

Step 5: Position Camera

- Select the POSITION CAMERA tool, and click on the face of the drawing, close to where you would like your perspective.
- SketchUp will fly down and position the initial perspective.
- The active command turns to LOOK AROUND. Use your mouse to click and drag in order to refine your perspective view.
- The camera height default is 5'-6". To change the height of the camera, type a new height in the VALUE CONTROL box.
- SketchUp perspectives default to a 50 mm field of view, which is appropriate for exterior building perspectives. Change the field of view to 28 mm for interior perspectives. Click once on the ZOOM tool. Type 28 mm, and press ENTER.

Step 6: Move around the Perspective

- Use the WALK tool to reposition the camera. Click and drag the mouse to walk; hold down the SHIFT key to move sideways or vertically.
- The horizontal line separating the ground and sky planes is the horizon line.

Step 7: Save the Perspective

- You can save perspective views as a scene.
- Open the scene window from WINDOW > SCENES.
- In the scene window, select the plus symbol to save and name the current view.
- To restore a scene, click on the SCENE tab at the top of the screen.
- Print the perspective by selecting FILE > PRINT. From the Print dialog box, set the page orientation to landscape and the print quality to high.

Step 8: Locate the Vanishing Points

- Trace over the printed SketchUp image to establish the vanishing points of the major walls.
- Locate a measuring line to help you establish the vertical heights of objects. In this example the measuring line was divided into ten equal segments, corresponding to the 10'-0" height between the planes.

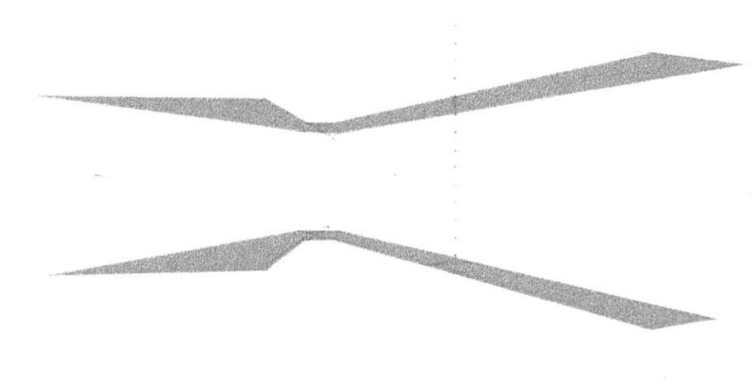

Step 9: Draw the Overall Geometry

- Draw vertical lines up from the plans to develop the outlines of the elements in perspective. The measuring line was used to determine the vertical height of objects.

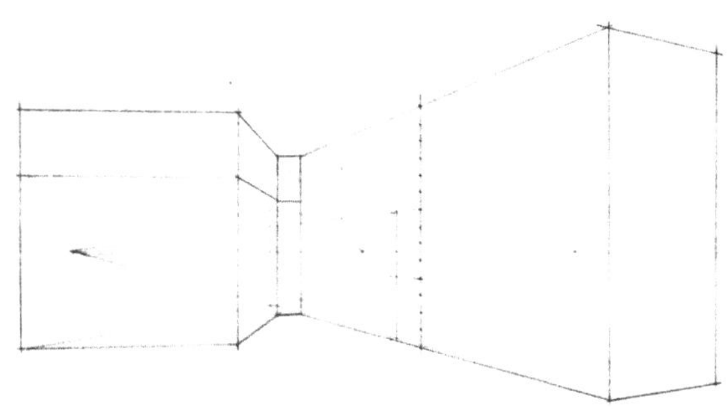

Step 10: Draw the Wall and Floor Surfaces

- Complete the perspective by drawing in each element in perspective. In the example the angled wall was drawn first, to serve as a guide for locating the ramp.

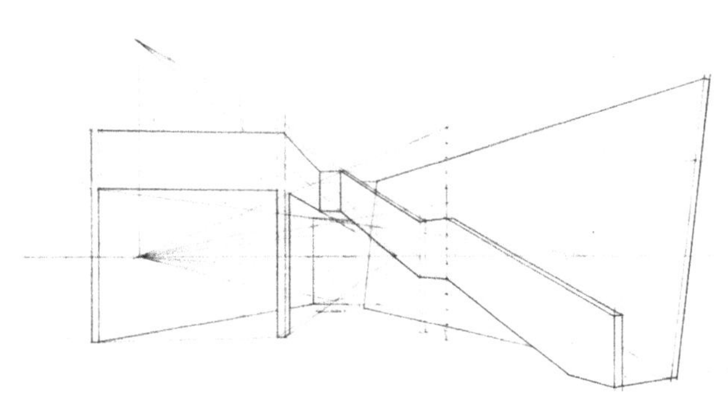

Step 11: Develop the Design through Sketching

- The design can be refined further, or different iterations can be developed by sketching over the perspective. By using the underlying drawing and vanishing points as a guide, you can design in perspective and more easily integrate perspective studies into your ideation process.

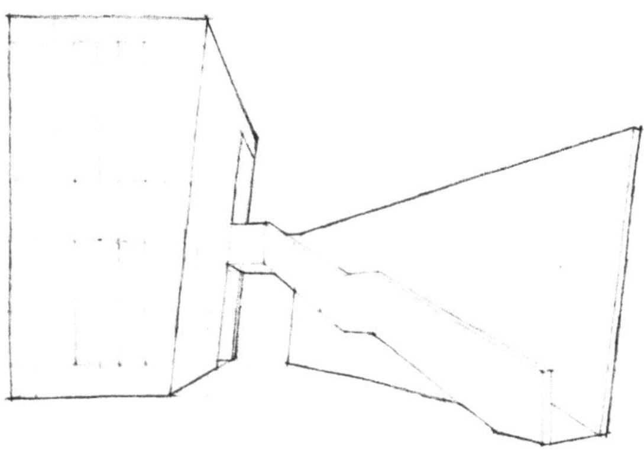

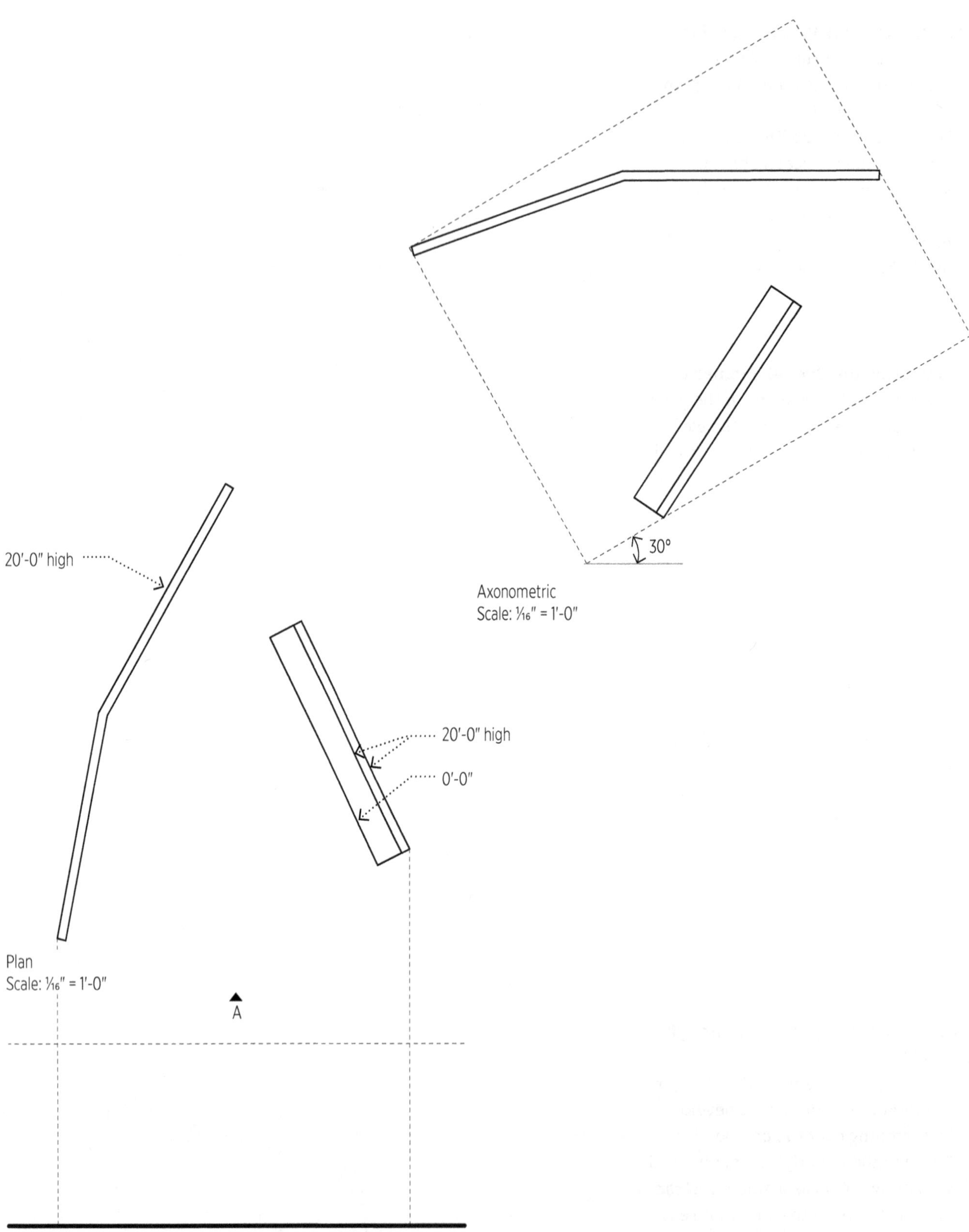

30°
Axonometric
Scale: 1/16" = 1'-0"
20'-0" high
20'-0" high
0'-0"
Plan
Scale: 1/16" = 1'-0"
A
Elevation A
Scale: 1/16" = 1'-0"

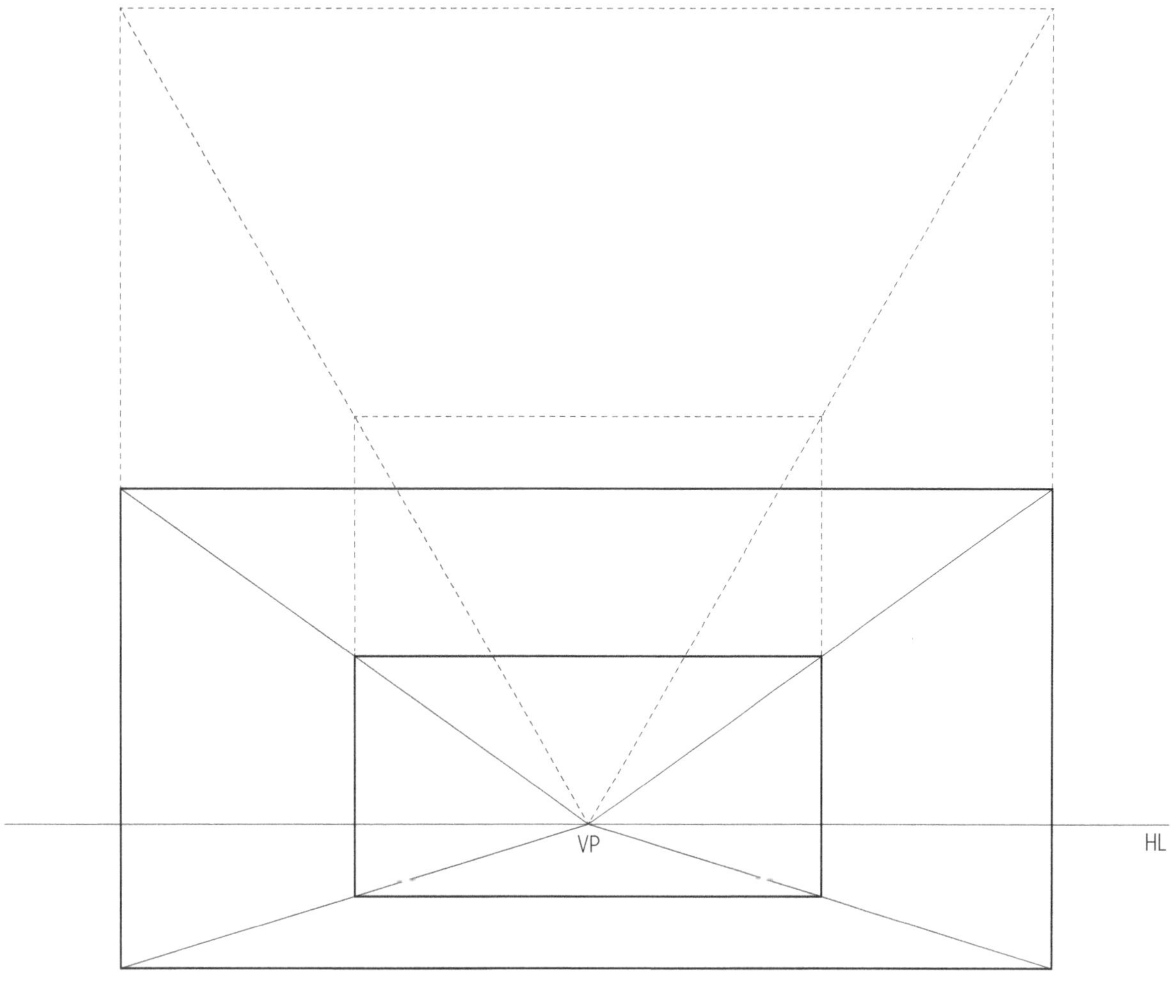

Perspective

Learning Exercise: Oblique Geometry
This exercise is intended to help you improve your understanding of drawing objects that are oblique or angled.

- Construct elevation A from the floor plan at 1/16" = 1'-0" scale.
- Using the upper right plan drawing on the facing page as a guide, construct an axonometric drawing of the angled walls.
- On this page, draw a one-point perspective of the angled walls within the given box. The reference box is drawn at 40'-0" wide × 40'-0" deep × 20'-0" high.

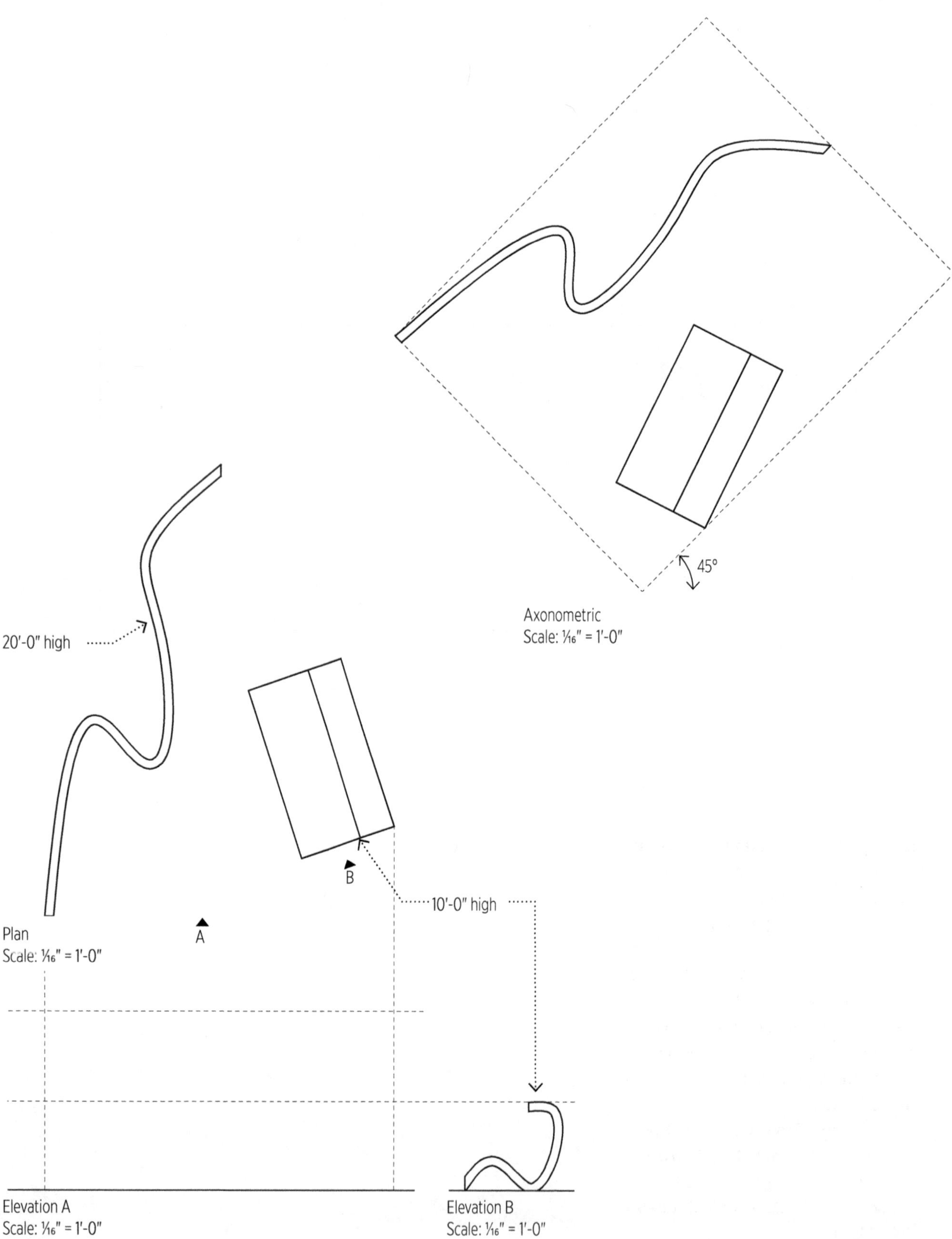

Axonometric
Scale: 1⁄16" = 1'-0"

Plan
Scale: 1⁄16" = 1'-0"

Elevation A
Scale: 1⁄16" = 1'-0"

Elevation B
Scale: 1⁄16" = 1'-0"

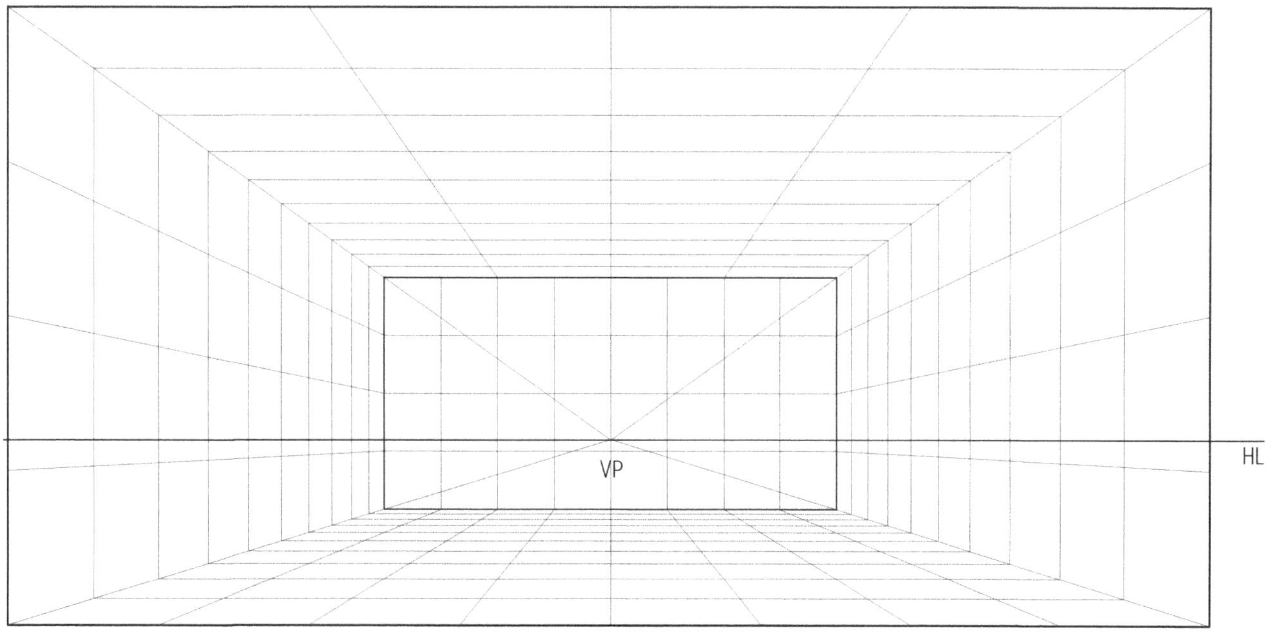

Perspective with 5'-0" × 5'-0" Grid

Learning Exercise: Curved Geometry
This exercise is intended to help you improve your understanding of drawing objects that are curved in plan and section.

- Construct elevation A from the floor plan at 1/16" = 1'-0" scale on the facing page. Elevation B shows the side profile of the wall that is curved in section.
- Construct an axonometric drawing of the curved walls, using the plan drawing on the facing page as a base.
- On this page, draw a one-point perspective of the curved walls within the given box. A 5'-0" × 5-'0" grid has been drawn in perspective and plan to serve as a guide. Use this grid to plot the location of the curved wall in perspective.

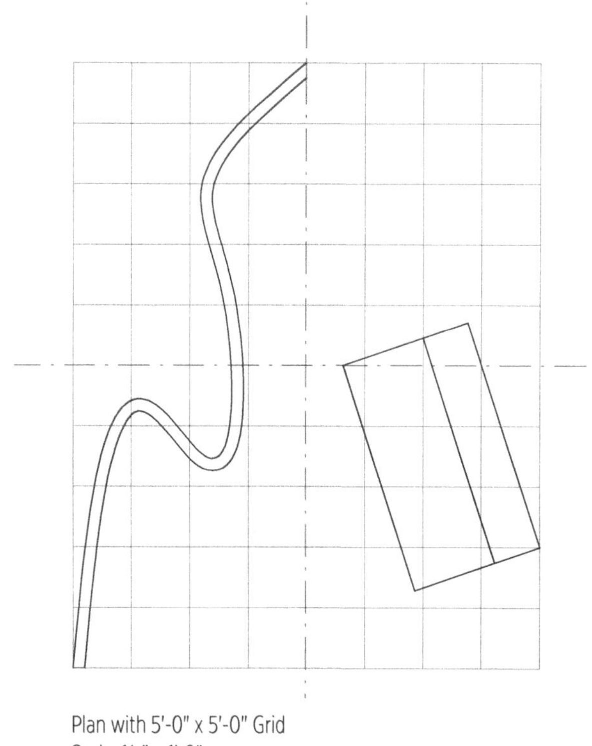

Plan with 5'-0" x 5'-0" Grid
Scale: 1/16" = 1'-0"

DIAGRAMMING AND ANALYTICAL DRAWINGS

Diagrams and analytical drawings rely on a system of notations and techniques to represent spatial systems, processes, relationships, and ideas. Both types of drawings are integral to the process of ideation, in that they help designers identify and define the important design criteria and relationships within their projects in order to make meaningful design decisions.

In this chapter, you will learn how to use and apply graphic notations, compositional techniques, and the drawing conventions of plan, section, elevation, isometric projection, and perspective to create diagrams and analytical drawings. Common diagram and analytical variables, or topics, will also be described.

Consider the following questions as you read this chapter:

- How are analytical drawings and different types of diagrams used to explore, develop, and communicate ideas?
- How do different drawing types and compositional strategies affect the meaning of diagrams and analytical drawings?
- How do diagrams and analytical drawings support the design process?

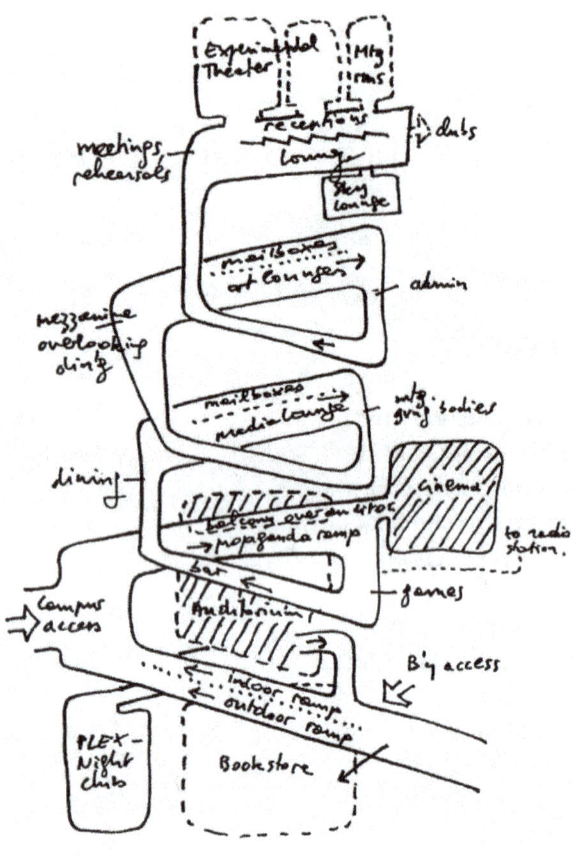

BERNARD TSCHUMI ARCHITECTS
Circulation diagram
Lerner Hall, Columbia University

A diagram is a drawing that shows the overall ideas, concepts, or relationships of a design. By reducing the amount of information shown within the drawing through a system of graphic notations, the diagram allows designers to isolate and evaluate key issues during ideation.

Diagrams are named for the topic they describe (circulation, program), their composition (bubble, block), or the type of drawing that is used to create them (plan, section). All these diagrams fall into one of two categories: freehand diagrams or presentation diagrams.

The diagram to the left, by the architect Bernard Tschumi, describes the relationship between the building circulation and program for his design of Alfred Lerner Hall, at Columbia University. The diagram focuses on how to create a central meeting space, described by Tschumi as "a vertical social space," by situating the public spaces of the program directly off a system of stacked ramps. Because Tschumi draws only the ramps and notates the main interior spaces with text or outlines, the spatial configuration and relationships within the interior of the building can be more clearly understood and explored.

Parti Diagrams

Parti diagrams convey the overall design concept or organizational ideas for a project. These diagrams use a minimal amount of graphic and textual notation to represent the essential components of a designer's project. A parti diagram can be both a freehand and a presentation diagram.

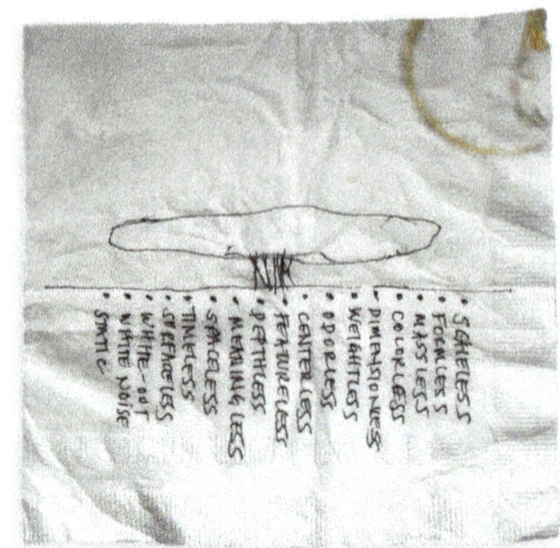

DILLER SCOFIDIO + RENFRO
Parti Diagram
Blur Building, Swiss Expo 2002

Freehand Diagrams

These quickly drawn diagrams are used extensively during ideation to generate and to clarify design ideas. Freehand diagrams are typically drawn with loose, hand-drawn strokes and at a small scale, to facilitate multiple iterations. They can also be liberally annotated with text to help capture a designer's thought process. Most freehand diagrams are used internally by design firms or by the individual designer and are rarely presented to clients.

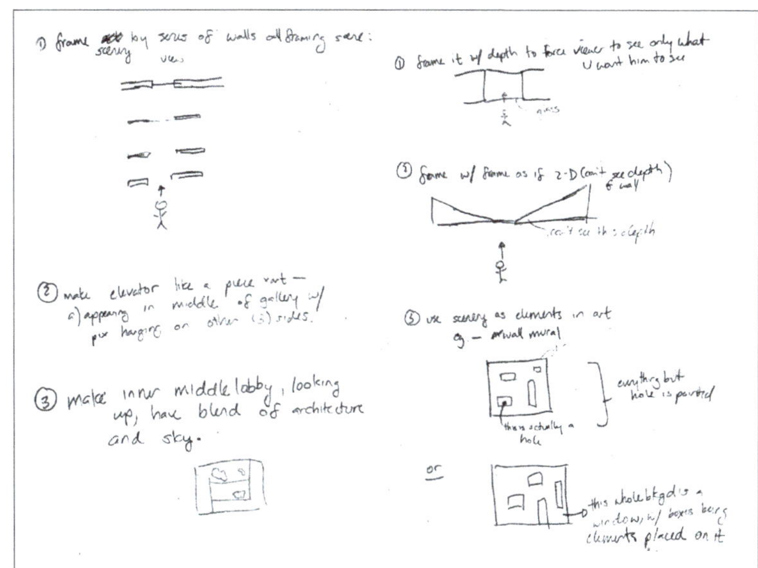

CHIENLAN HSU
Freehand diagram
Career Discovery Studio,
Harvard University, Graduate School of Design

Presentation Diagrams

Presentation diagrams are used to explain the design of a project to someone who is not familiar with it. These diagrams can describe how design decisions were made during the ideation process and the overall organization of the project as well as the important relationships within the project. Presentation diagrams are much more refined than freehand diagrams, with more precise relationships between text and image. These drawings are often created solely through the computer or from scanned hand drawings, with text and additional graphics added electronically.

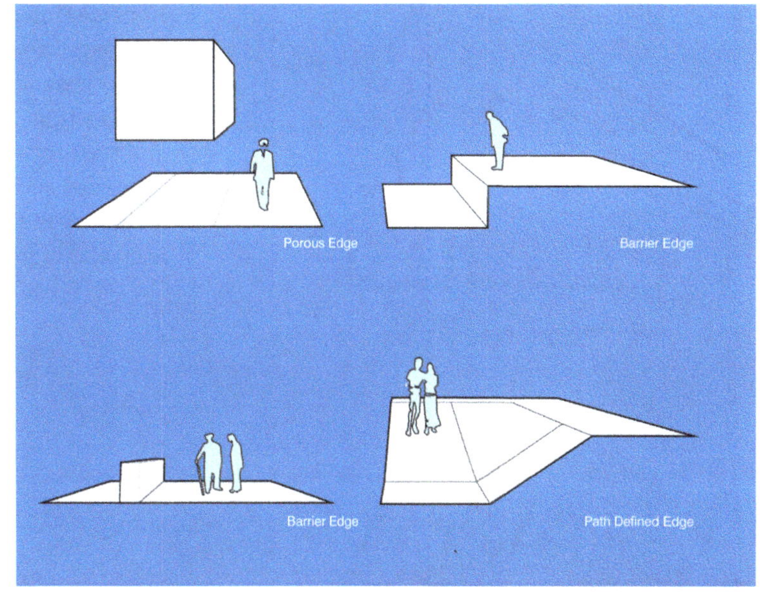

PATRICK S. LAUSELL
Presentation diagram
Degree Project Studio,
Boston Architectural College

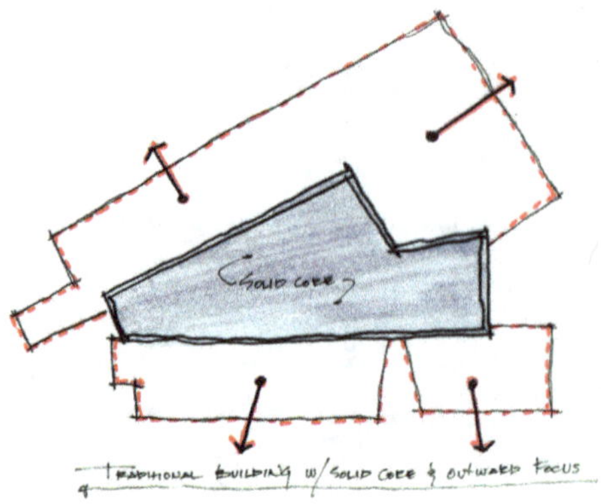

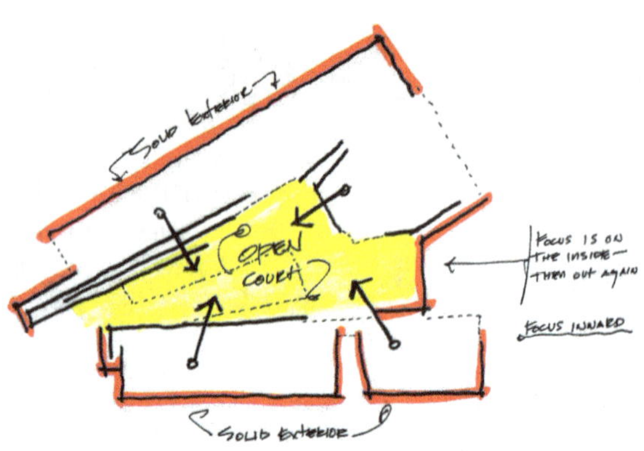

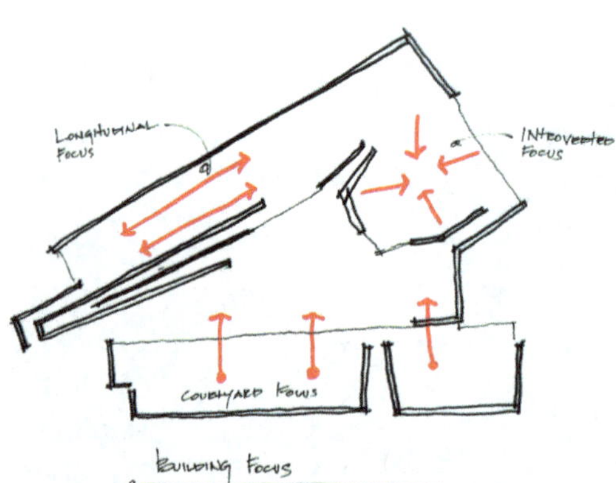

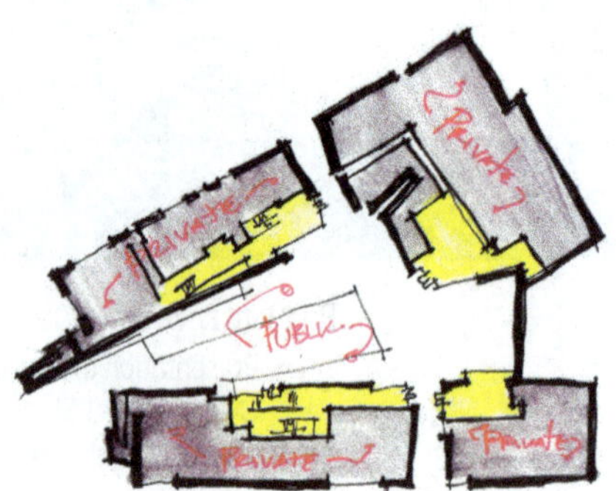

Analytical Drawings

An analytical drawing can be understood as a type of diagram that abstracts existing conditions or processes in order to make relationships legible and interpretations of the conditions possible. These drawings are used at the beginning of the design process to develop an understanding of an existing site, building, or interior space. The two most common types of analytical drawings are precedent analysis drawings and site analysis drawings.

Analytical drawings are a useful tool for investigating a project's context, precedents, and human occupation and for evaluating the strength of a current design. Good analysis drawings clearly identify the portion of the project that is under critique by editing or removing unnecessary information from the drawing. They also visually communicate the conclusions learned through the focused research or analysis.

Precedent Analysis Drawings

Precedent analysis drawings are used to investigate a building or space, a piece of furniture, or anything else that relates to a current design problem. Although the content of an investigatory drawing may vary in scale or scope, these drawings share the common objective of revealing new or pertinent information as it relates to a current project.

These analytical drawings of the Mattin Center, at The Johns Hopkins University, are examples of a precedent analysis for a building. The drawings explore how the building is organized into private and public zones that are separated by a series of transitional spaces that negotiate between the interior and the central court on the exterior. By isolating different elements, such as views, circulation, and spatial types, the student was able to compare how they influenced the experience and organization of the building.

TIM ERVIN
Degree Project Studio,
Boston Architectural College

Site Analysis Drawings

Site analysis drawings give designers the opportunity to discover, reformulate, and represent the existing context to reveal latent conditions that were not legible at the start of the design process. A site analysis drawing determines how the site, or context of a project, is understood and influences what areas are subsequently prioritized or ignored in design proposals. Therefore, the types of information that are chosen or excluded and how contextual data are assembled, scaled, and abstracted within the drawing affect future design decisions and what ultimately gets built.

The site analysis drawings on the right examine different types of activities along Detroit's waterfront. Although on first impression the site seemed to have many vacant buildings and not a lot of activity, a close reading of different newspapers and media reports revealed a different understanding.

Using photocopied text from news articles written about the site, four different drawings were created, mapping the location and density of activities relating to transportation, open space, building development, and pollution. The text is arranged to simulate the form of activity, with the text spacing relating to the frequency of activity. The drawings were created as a series of overlays that reveal a density of activities along the outer edges of the site. The design proposal for the project focused on how to build on these uses as a way to revitalize the waterfront.

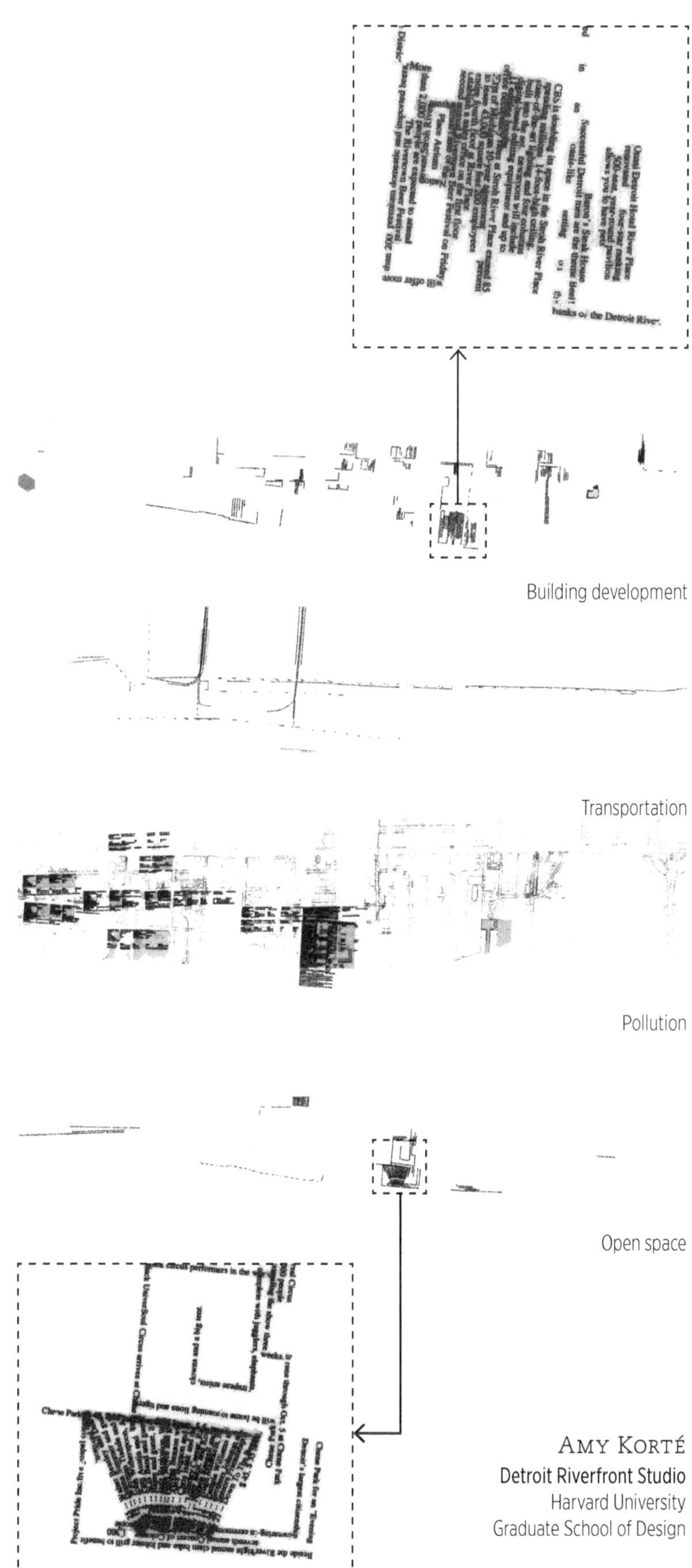

AMY KORTÉ
Detroit Riverfront Studio
Harvard University
Graduate School of Design

The variables designers choose to evaluate within diagrams and analytical drawings influence how design decisions are made during the design process while also helping construct a position on the subject(s) being studied. The following pages list some of the variables, or topics, that diagrams and analytical drawings can examine. Drawings that focus on a single topic are typically named for the topic: for example, a diagram that describes circulation is called a circulation diagram; a diagram that examines program is called a programmatic diagram.

The most compelling diagrams and analyses typically examine multiple variables in order to develop a comprehensive understanding of how these influence the built environment. By making meaningful comparisons between variables, designers can reveal latent conditions not evident at the start of the diagramming or analytical process.

pedestrian
vehicular
horizontal / vertical
entry / egress
nodes
service
CIRCULATION

values meanings
traditions
CULTURAL

focal points
physical boundaries implied
boundaries threshold
enclosure framing
sequences
SPATIAL

news
blogs
marketing
advertising
MEDIA

time
temperature
speed/sound
sun / wind
TEMPORAL

development
consumerism
costs (initial vs lifetime)
market value
tax revenue
vacancy-occupancy
ECONOMIC

qualities
types
construction
performance
MATERIALS

proportion
hierarchy
axis
pattern
scale
form
regulating lines
solid
void
interior
exterior
symmetry
rhythm
massing
FORMAL

use of space
area requirements
proximity
flexibility
adaptability
PROGRAM

historical
current
recurring
EVENTS

international relations
globalization
policy
POLITICAL

environmental control
sustainable
structural
mechanical
SYSTEMS

zoning codes
laws
design guidelines
community reviews
REGULATORY

topography
landscape
water
access
adjacent conditions
SITE | CONTEXT

past uses
landmarks
change over time
HISTORICAL

commuter
tourist
resident
USERS

networks
interactions
private-public
SOCIAL

walking
running
sitting
gathering
illicit
prescribed
ACTIVITIES

memory
views
point-of-view
sense of place
EXPERIENTIAL

Bubble, block, and network diagrams are more abstract types of diagrams, in that they do not typically appear to follow the form of the building. These types of diagrams are typically produced in the programming phase and help designers determine the organization and form of their interior spaces.

The composition of these diagrams has a tremendous impact on how a designer's ideas are perceived and interpreted. Changing the scale, placement, color, organization, and repetition of the variables affects the meaning of the relationships between elements.

Bubble diagrams compare the size and proximity of spaces through the use of loosely drawn circles or rectangles. During the design process, bubble diagrams are often refined into block diagrams, which more precisely represent the scale and configuration of spaces and their adjacency to one another.

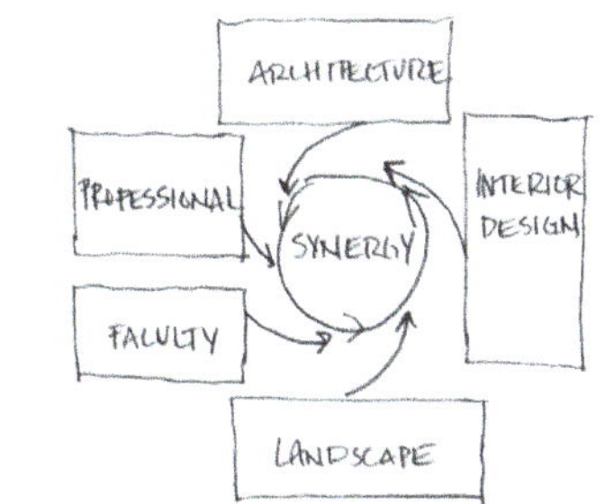

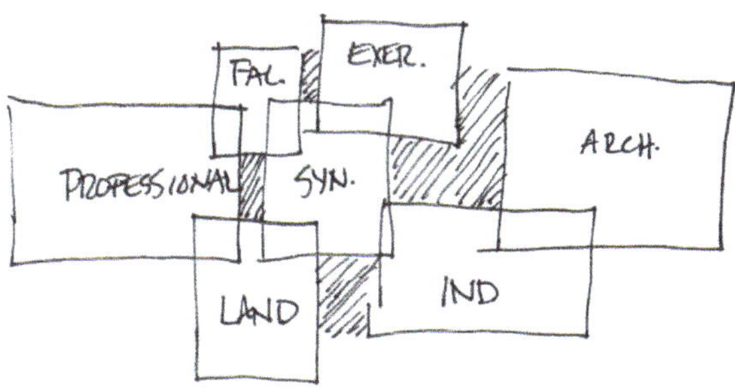

RYAN NEVIDOMSKY
Bubble diagrams
Degree Project Studio,
Boston Architectural College

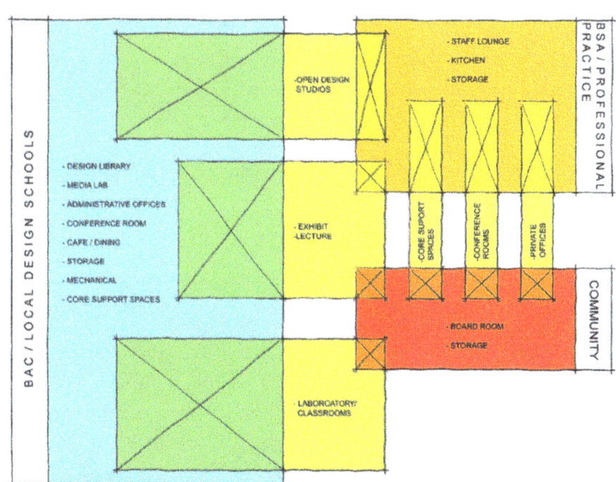

PROGRAM DIAGRAM: SPATIAL RELATIONSHIPS

TIM ERVIN
Block diagrams
Degree Project Studio,
Boston Architectural College

NODES

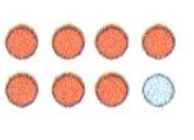
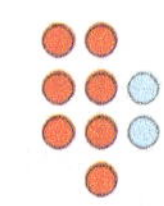

A group of nodes can define relationships between people in plan, whereas color can differentiate between different types of occupants.

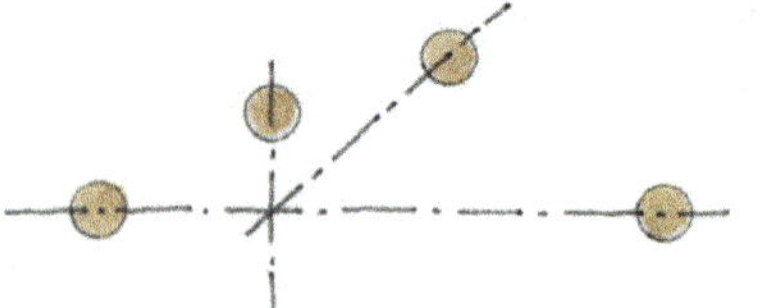

A node on an axial line defines a landmark or focal point in plan.

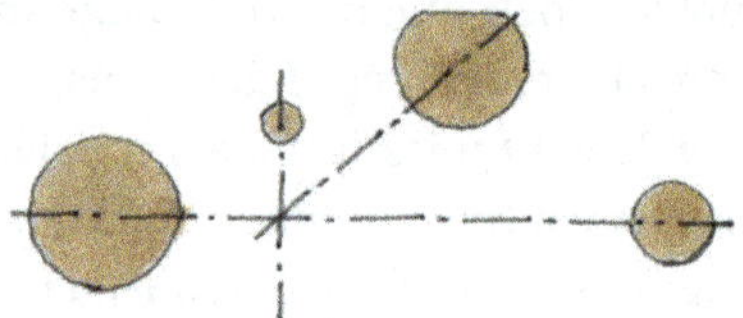

Adjusting the scale of the nodes changes the hierarchy between them.

LINKING LINES

Lines with an arrow on one end show causality, influence, or the relationship of one variable to another.

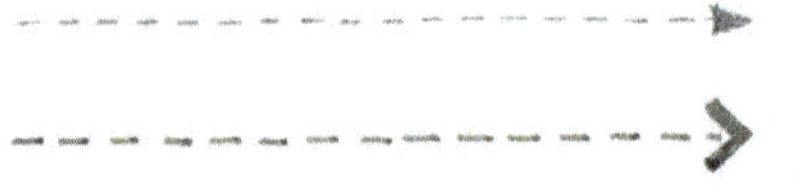

A dashed line can represent a potential connection or relationship.

A line with an arrow on both ends conveys a reciprocating relationship.

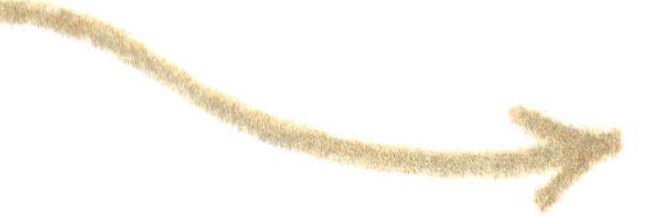

A curved line with an arrow at one end can represent a temporal force, such as wind or solar gain.

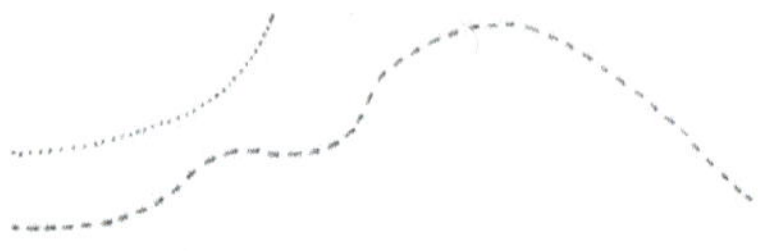

A dashed or dotted line in a curved shape can represent a path of movement.

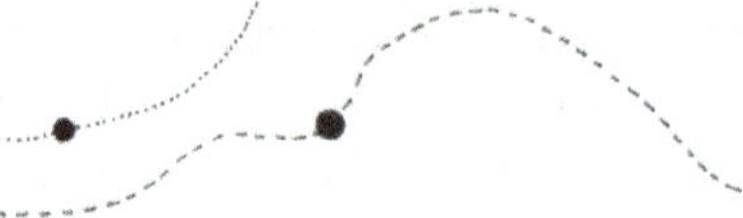

When a node is added to the same line, the node defines a position along the path.

SPATIAL ZONES

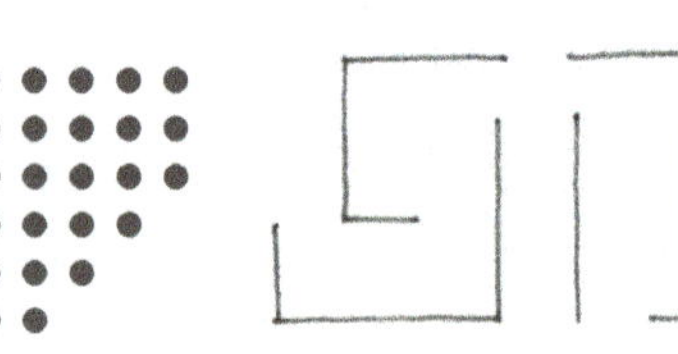

A grid of nodes or offset lines can define an implied spatial zone.

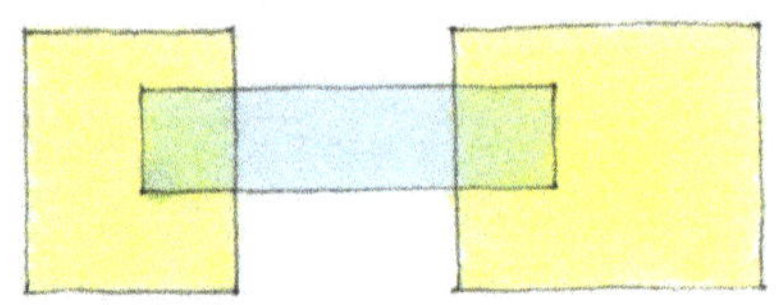

The intersection of two planes defines an overlapping spatial zone.

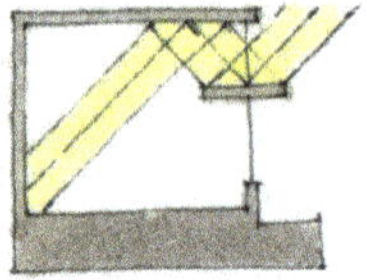

Temporal elements, such as light and water, can be created with planes.

SYMBOLS

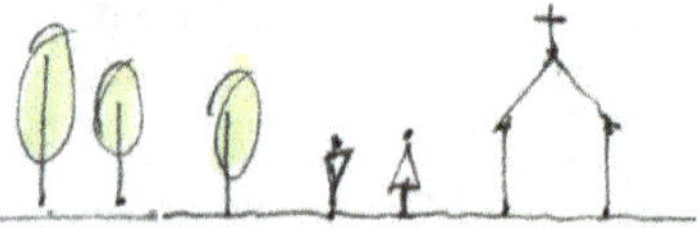

People, trees, and buildings can be drawn abstractly, with symbols.

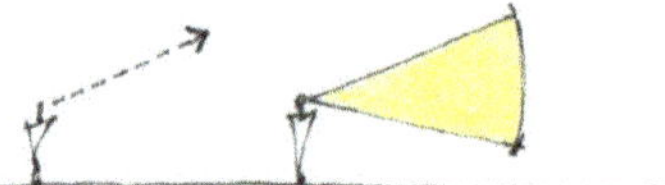

Symbols, such as a person's view, are drawn as a plane or lines.

TEXT ANNOTATIONS

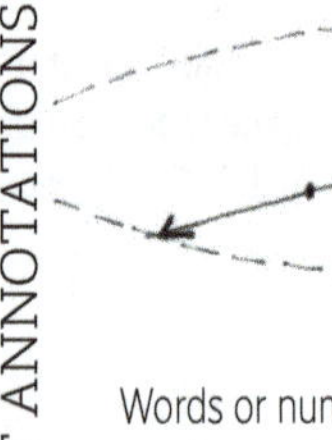

Words or numbers added to a linking line create an additional layer of meaning for the drawing.

1

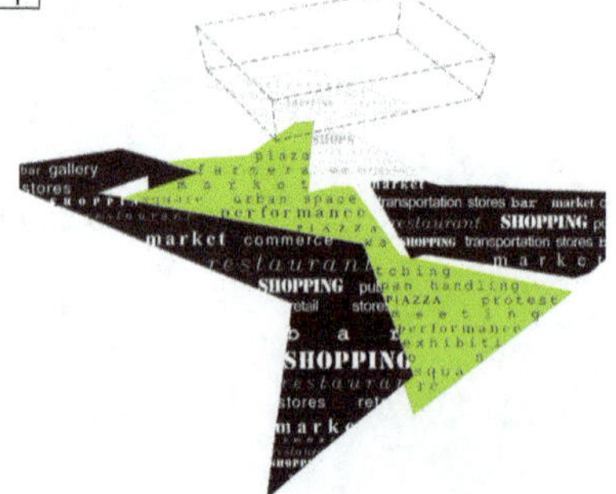

Text can be integrated into planes to describe activities that occur in each area. The dashed outline represents a building, creating a scalar and locational reference.

2

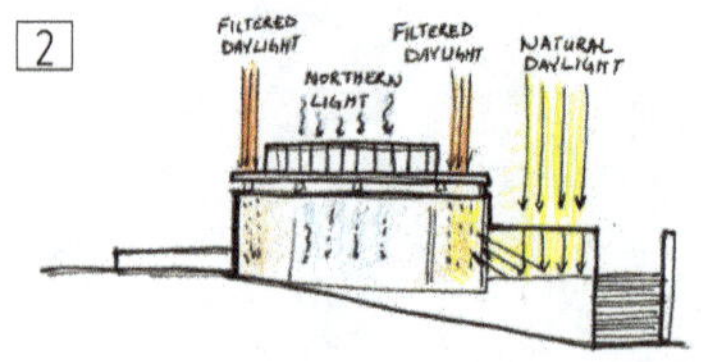

Text can be used to describe the type of light that enters a building.

Nodes
A node is a directionless point that represents position within a diagram. Nodes can define intersections, centers, points of origin, termination, and data points. In plan and axonometric diagrams, nodes can convey a person's location or landmarks within a space.

Linking Lines
A linking line represents a relationship between two or more things. Depending on the line weight, line type, scale, geometry, and demarcation at the beginning and endpoints, linking lines can define a path, direction, influence, causality, movement, or force. By increasing the scale and size of the line or arrow, a stronger force or relationship can be suggested.

Spatial Zones
A spatial zone is a plane that represents an area volume, boundary, or field within a diagram. Spatial zones can be defined through color, hatch, tone, and outline. They can also be implied by drawing closely spaced nodes or offset lines; the negative space is read as a plane. When a diagram consists primarily of planes, it is called a bubble or block diagram.

Symbols
Symbols are abstract, simplified representations of people, places, or objects. Most symbols used in the design disciplines bear some resemblance to the object, such as people and trees.

Textual Annotations
Textual annotations are words embedded into diagrams and analytical drawings to give more specific information on the relationship or variables. Textual annotations can also convey facts or research to help others understand the content of diagrams and support a designer's ideas. Typically, these words are integrated into the graphics in order to be read simultaneously with the image.

Graphic Notations
Graphic notations are a system of visual shorthand consisting of simple strokes, symbols, and brief textual annotations that give meaning to diagrams and analytical drawings. Graphic notations are based on the conventions of drawing and the fundamentals of point, line, and plane. Designers rely on these notations to help them quickly represent relationships abstractly while also developing their own notational systems to give more specific meaning to their diagrams.

Designers deploy a wide variety of media to create different notational meanings. For example, markers create a thicker notation on a page, to evoke a broader and looser relationship between variables. This type of mark complements the large scale of site diagrams and early programmatic diagrams, in which the relationships between different areas are not figured out. Pencils and pens create marks with a greater level of precision and are used to suggest more specific and smaller scale relationships between variables. Simple computer graphics can also be used as graphic notations, allowing designers to create presentation diagrams that seamlessly integrate text, color, and line.

1

PATRICK S. LAUSELL
Degree Project Studio,
Boston Architectural College

2

DONALD BARANY
Paris Studio,
Boston Architectural College

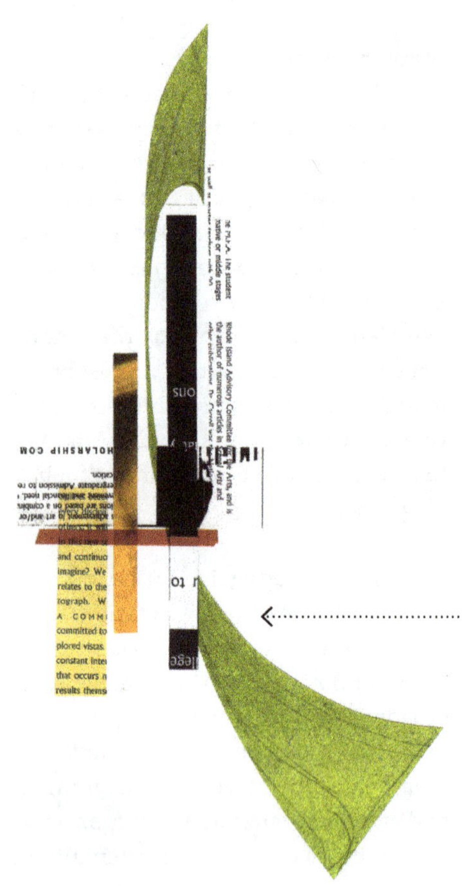

ELENA RAYA
Plan diagram
Harvard University,
Graduate School of Design

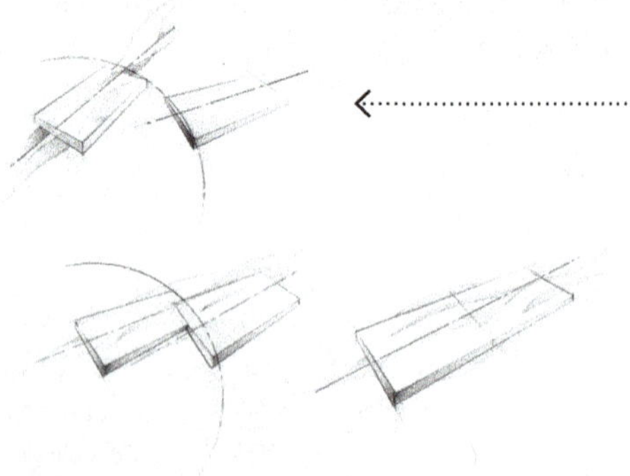

KEVIN ASMUS
Isometric diagrams
Degree Project Studio,
Boston Architectural College

Drawing Types and Meaning

Plans, sections, elevations, isometrics, and perspectives are all used to create diagrams and analytical drawings. The choice of which drawing type to use is determined by a number of factors, ranging from the variables or relationships that are being studied to the stage of the design process that the designer is in.

Plan and Section Diagrams

Plan and section diagrams share many of the same traits and are often used interchangeably. For example, it is common to draw a plan diagram and then interpret it as a section, and vice versa. These drawings convey the relationship between interior and exterior spaces, program adjacencies, formal organization of rooms, site relationships, light, and views. Section diagrams typically include symbols (such as people or trees) for scale and a ground plane to locate the building or space to its surroundings.

This plan diagram abstracts the spatial relationships between different types of uses. Uses are coded through color with green signifying landscape elements.

Elevation Diagrams and Analytical Drawings

Elevation diagrams and analytical drawings convey the compositional relationships and organizing principles of building facades, interior surfaces of rooms, and profiles of furniture. Materials and color choices are also frequently explored, using elevation drawings.

Isometric Diagrams and Analytical Drawings

Isometric diagrams describe the relationship of a system of parts to a whole. These types of diagrams are great for evaluating multiple variables, complex processes, and spatial relationships because they allow the designer to explore plan and section relationships in three dimensions.

These isometric diagrams describe three different levels of a building and were used to explain the rotation of the floor plan at each level.

Perspective Diagrams and Analytical Drawings

Perspective diagrams are frequently used to evaluate the experience of moving through space, emphasizing views, paths of movement, and focal points. By drawing perspectives in a series and showing different points of view along a path, a cinematic understanding of a design can be presented. When used in conjunction with a plan, section, or isometric drawing, the position of the observer in relation to the view can also be understood.

This section diagram of a building (at right) was used to explore vertical and horizontal program relationships.

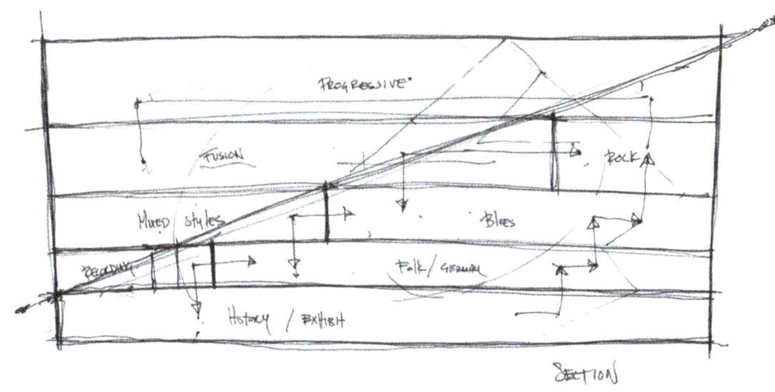

KEVIN ASMUS
Section diagram
Degree Project Studio,
Boston Architectural College

This elevation diagram of a final review presentation layout (at right) shows the drawing sizes and their relationship to each other on the wall. The student used the diagram to figure out how she would organize her drawings and present her project.

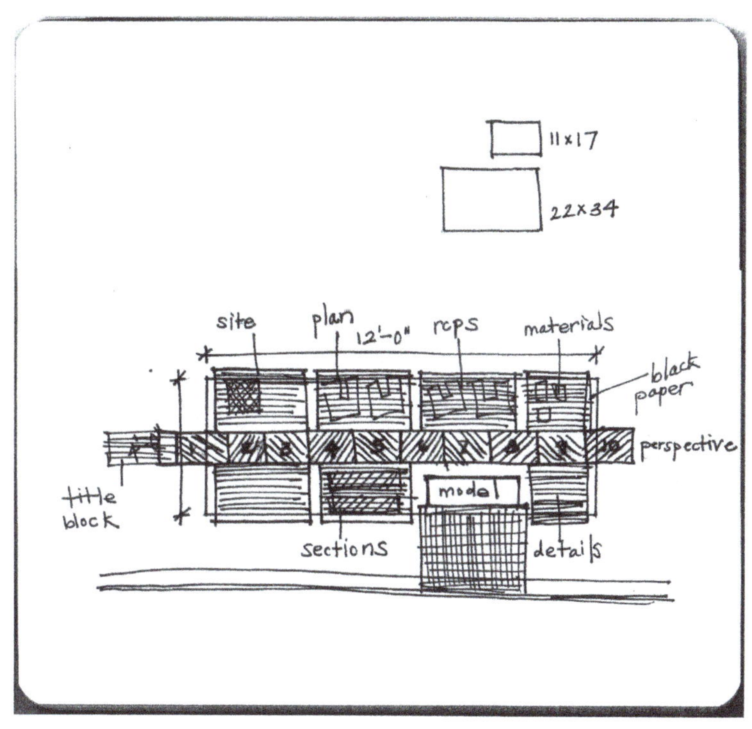

LORI ANDERSON WIER
Elevation diagram
Thesis Studio,
The New England School of
Art & Design at Suffolk University

These analytical perspectives (below) were used to map and understand the pedestrian views around Boston's City Hall Plaza.

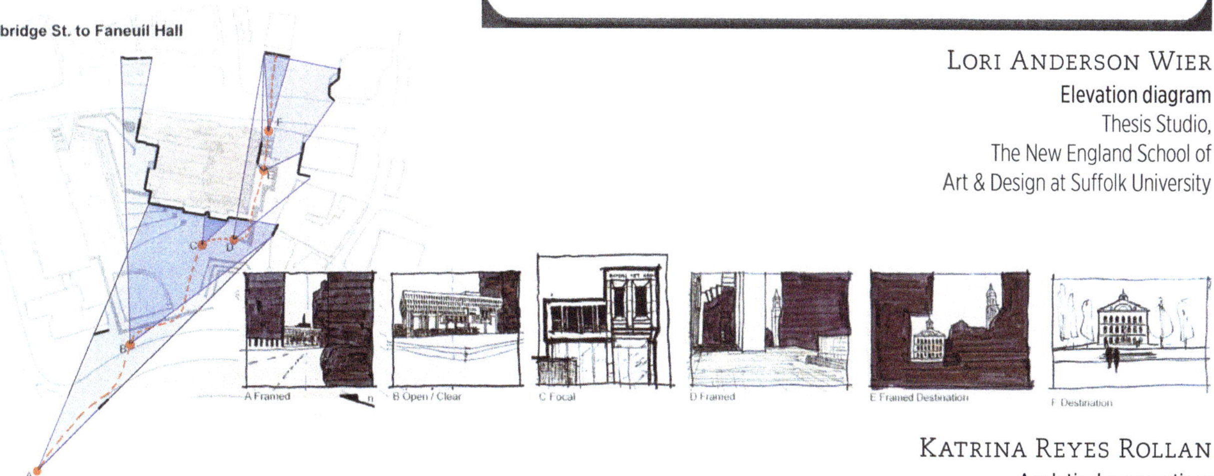

KATRINA REYES ROLLAN
Analytical perspectives
Degree Project Studio,
Boston Architectural College

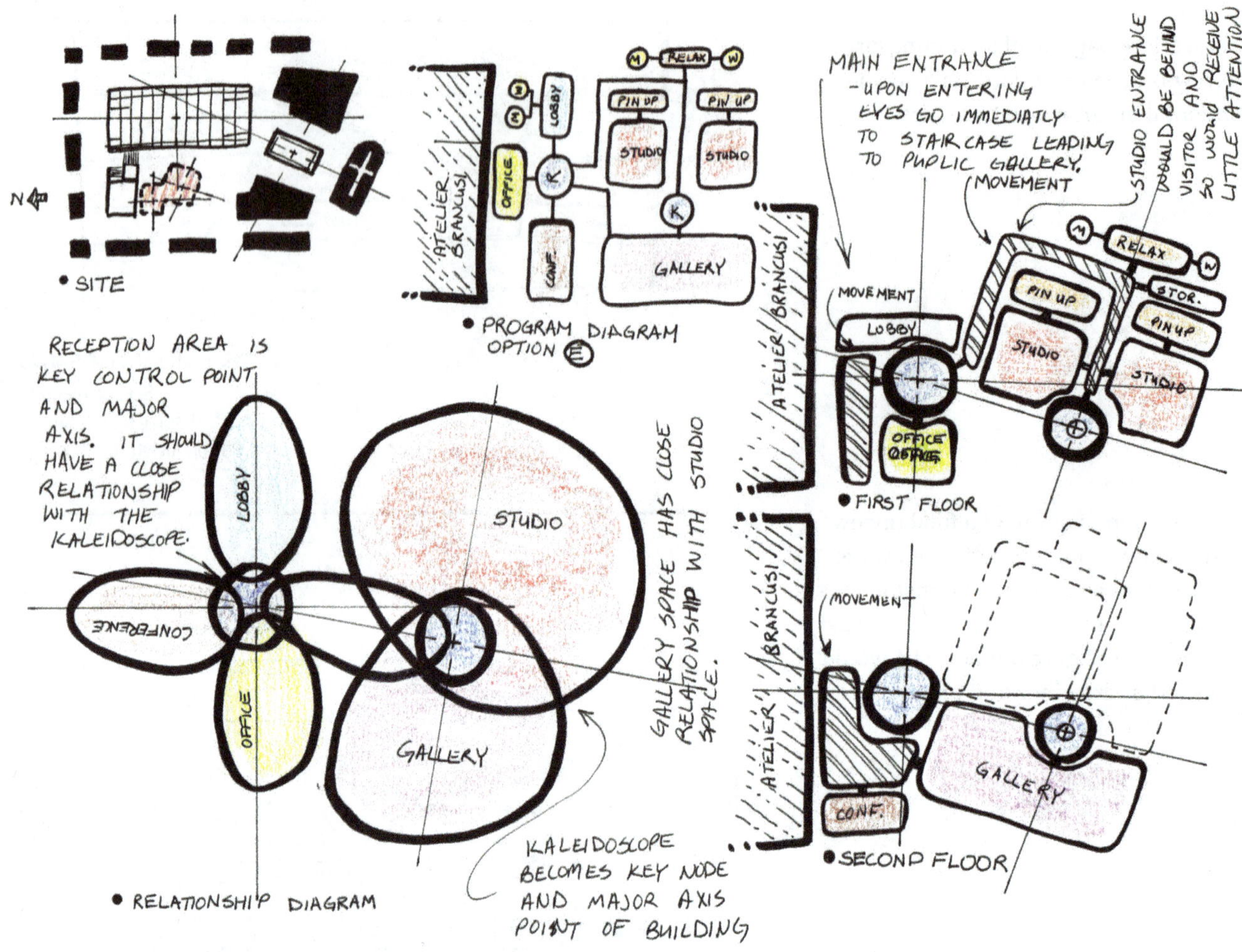

DONALD BARANY
Freehand diagram
Paris Studio,
Boston Architectural College

Freehand diagramming allowed me to quickly build up layers of information. First, the diagrams were used to analyze the site and develop an understanding of the relationships between buildings and open space. Next, the basic volume of the building was proposed and located on the site. Bubble diagrams were used to develop the basic relationship of spaces. The spaces were then developed into a program diagram. Finally, the program was developed to fit within the proposed building volume.

—DONALD BARANY

PROJECT STATEMENT

GIVEN THE PROGRAM OF A STUDY ABROAD STUDENT CENTER - MY GOAL FOR THIS PROJECT IS TO CREATE A BUILDING THAT NOT ONLY ALLOWS FOR BUT WILL ACTIVELY CREATE AN ENVIRONMENT THAT EXPOSES TRAVELLING STUDENTS TO THE URBAN CONTEXT THEY HAVE TRAVELLED SO FAR TO LEARN FROM. IN PURSUIT OF THIS THE PROJECT CANNOT INSULATE ITS OCCUPANTS FROM THEIR SURROUNDINGS OR FROM EACHOTHER - SINCE TRAVELLING ABROAD IS IN MANY WAYS A SOCIAL AND CULTURAL EXPERIENCE THAT IS AS IMPORTANT AS ITS ACADEMIC GOALS. THE COUNTER TO THIS IS THE NEED FOR PRIVATE 'REFUGE' SPACE WHERE ONE CAN ESCAPE THE BUSY AND SOMETIMES OVERSTIMULATING WORLD THAT IS STUDY ABROAD.

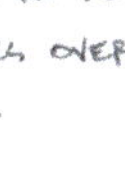

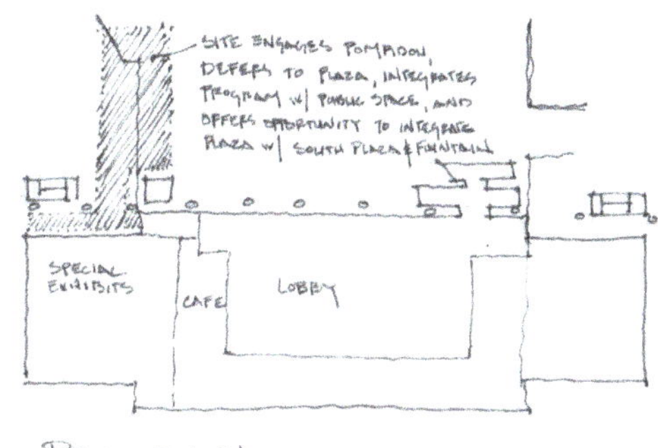

PROJECT SITING

UNIT : MODULE : SYSTEM

UNIT: "CELL" FOR INDIVIDUAL DWELLING. REDUNDANCY IN UNITS CAN BE OVERLAPPED AND SHARED.

MODULE: THE NUMBER OF UNITS THAT CAN BE SUPPORTED BY A SINGLE SHARED SPACE MAKE UP THE BASIC RESIDENTIAL MODULE

SYSTEM: A SERIES OF MODULES ORGANIZED WITH ELEMENTS NECESSARY TO THE FUNCTION OF THE WHOLE BUT COMMON TO ALL MODULES.

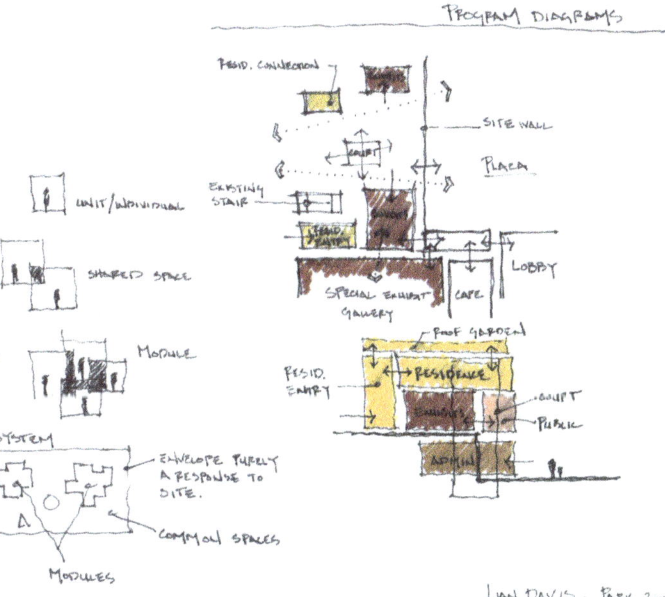

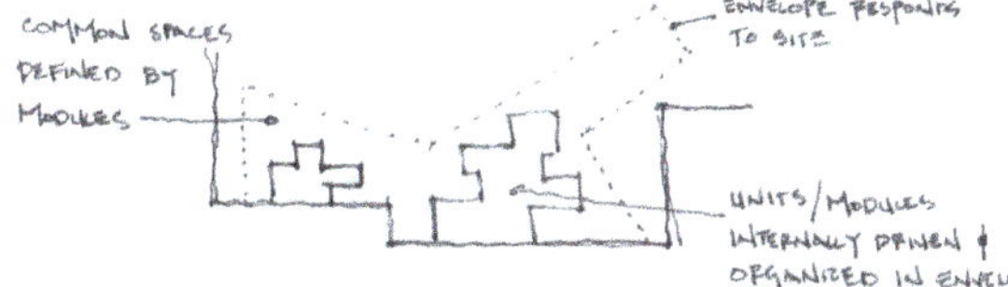

LIAN DAVIS PARIS 2008

This studio project was unique in that the entire design process was limited to sketching. Diagramming the relationships between individual program elements and the surrounding context allowed me to turn an abstract approach into meaningful spaces that engage the existing building and site. These sketches illustrate that approach, along with the first steps I took to transform my parti into a design.

—LIAN DAVIS

LIAN DAVIS
Freehand diagram
Paris Studio,
Boston Architectural College

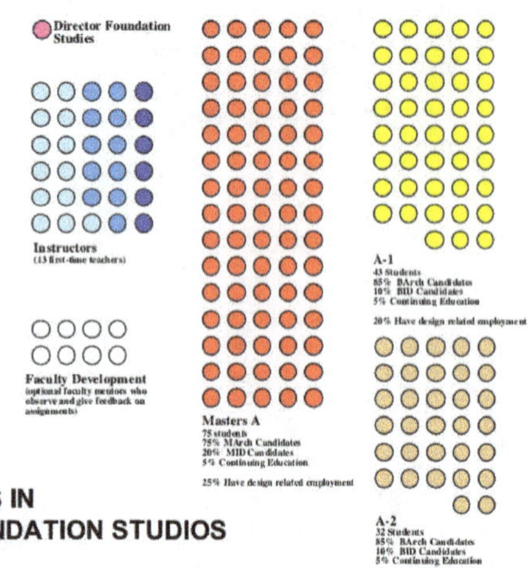

181 LEARNERS IN EVENING FOUNDATION STUDIOS Fall 2005

Slide 1

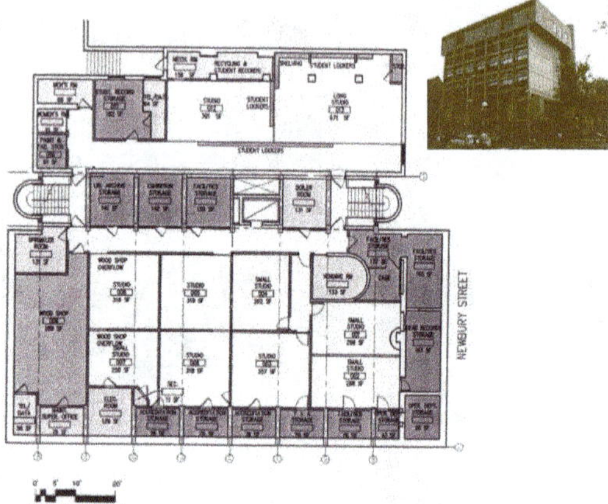

SETTING: The Basement at 320 Newbury Street, Boston

Slide 2

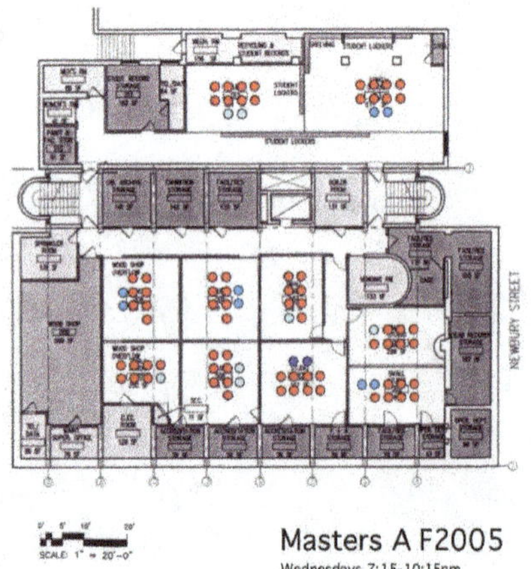

Masters A F2005
Wednesdays 7:15-10:15pm

Slide 3

This series of presentation diagrams demonstrate many of the principles of strong analytical and diagram drawings. Created by Richard Griswold for a conference slide lecture on teaching beginning design students, they explain how the first year foundation studios are organized at the Boston Architectural College. Although all these diagrams were created through the computer, the simple graphics could also easily have been created through hand drawing.

Clearly Defined Variables and Graphic Notations

In Slide 1, Griswold begins his series of diagrams with a legend, to clearly define and identify the primary graphic notations that he will use in subsequent slides. Each circle, or node, represents a person, and color defines different user groups: instructors, mentors, three different levels of students, and the foundation director.

Authenticating the Diagram with Textual Annotations

Textual annotations are integrated into the array of nodes on Slide 1 and provide additional statistical information for each category of users. This additional factual data give the audience a greater understanding of the context of teaching and learning at the BAC while also making Griswold's analysis more credible. The two different scales of text allow the larger text to be read simultaneously with the colored nodes; the smaller text is read as a secondary, supporting element.

Slides 2 and 3 introduce the studio space context within the college. These two slides can be seen as a continuation of Slide 1, in that additional contextual information is given to define the studio spaces; they also act as a transition to Slide 4, in which the image of the plan background is removed, and an understanding of the spatial arrangement of each classroom remains.

In Slides 4 through 6, Griswold focuses on the social interactions that occur within the design studios between the different user groups. By removing the plan background in Slide 4 and replacing it with a single rectangle, representing a central, unoccupied space within the plan, Griswold minimizes visual distractions and makes the relationships between the nodes the primary focal point within the composition.

Defining Multiple Relationships between Variables with Linking Lines

Slide 5 uses three types of linking lines to explain the interactions among four different users. Griswold draws dashed lines, dotted lines, and solid lines with arrows to illustrate faculty mentor connections to individual studio instructors, the management path of the foundation director overseeing the design studios, and the pairings of experienced faculty with new instructors. Each linking line is defined in a small legend at the bottom of the slide.

Slides 4 and 5 represent the primary organization of the design studios on a weekly basis: seven to eight students divided into ten classrooms with one to two instructors. Slide 6 describes a temporal relationship between the studio classes. This last slide diagrams the walk-through that occurs after the final review of each project by organizing all the nodes on a single path that curves through each studio space.

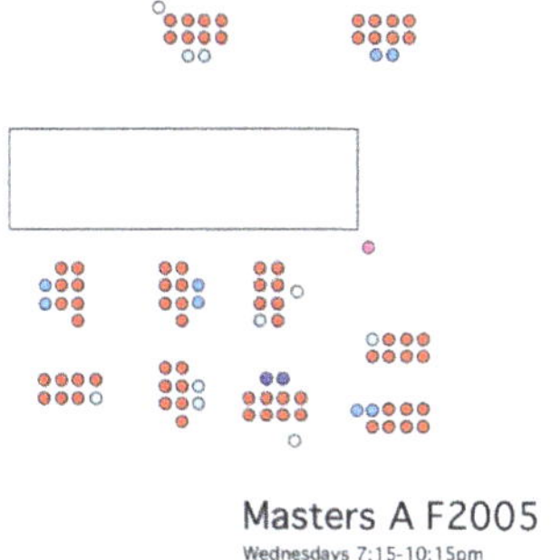

Slide 4

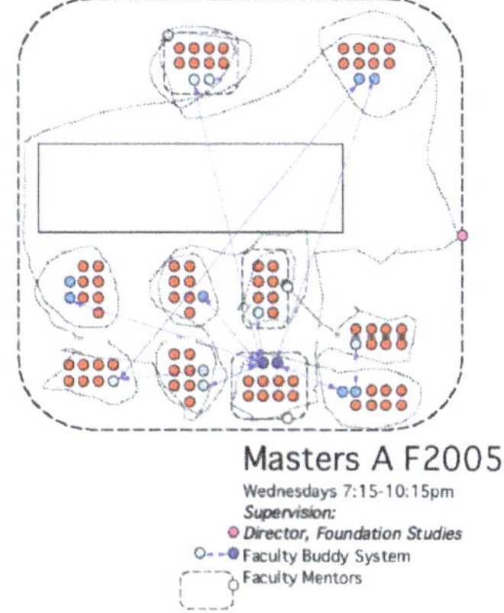

Slide 5

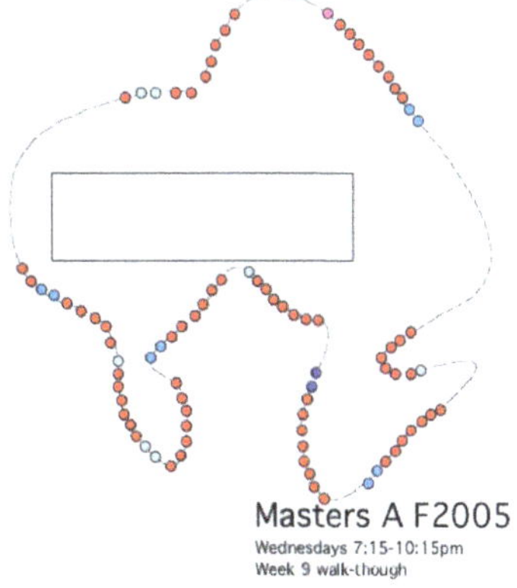

Slide 6

RICHARD GRISWOLD
Presentation Slides
Associate Provost for
Student Development,
Boston Architectural College

RENDERING TECHNIQUES

Rendering allows designers to clarify and communicate their design intentions for the scale, materiality, spatial qualities, and function of spaces.

This chapter is organized into four main sections:

- Tone and color: rendering techniques for graphite washes, colored pencils, markers, watercolors, charcoal, and pastel
- Entourage: adding scale elements, such as people, furniture, and plants to drawings
- Collage techniques: gluing papers or photographs onto a surface to create a rendered image
- Digitally supported ideation: using digital graphics programs, such as Photoshop, to render drawings and as a tool for ideation

Examples of student and professional renderings are used throughout the chapter to illustrate the wide variety of rendering techniques available to designers. As you are reading this chapter, you should also revisit the rendered ideation examples in previous chapters.

Consider the following questions as you read this chapter:

- How can you use different rendering techniques to clarify and explore your design ideas?
- How do different color combinations affect the reading of your design?
- How can you integrate digital and hand techniques to support your design process?

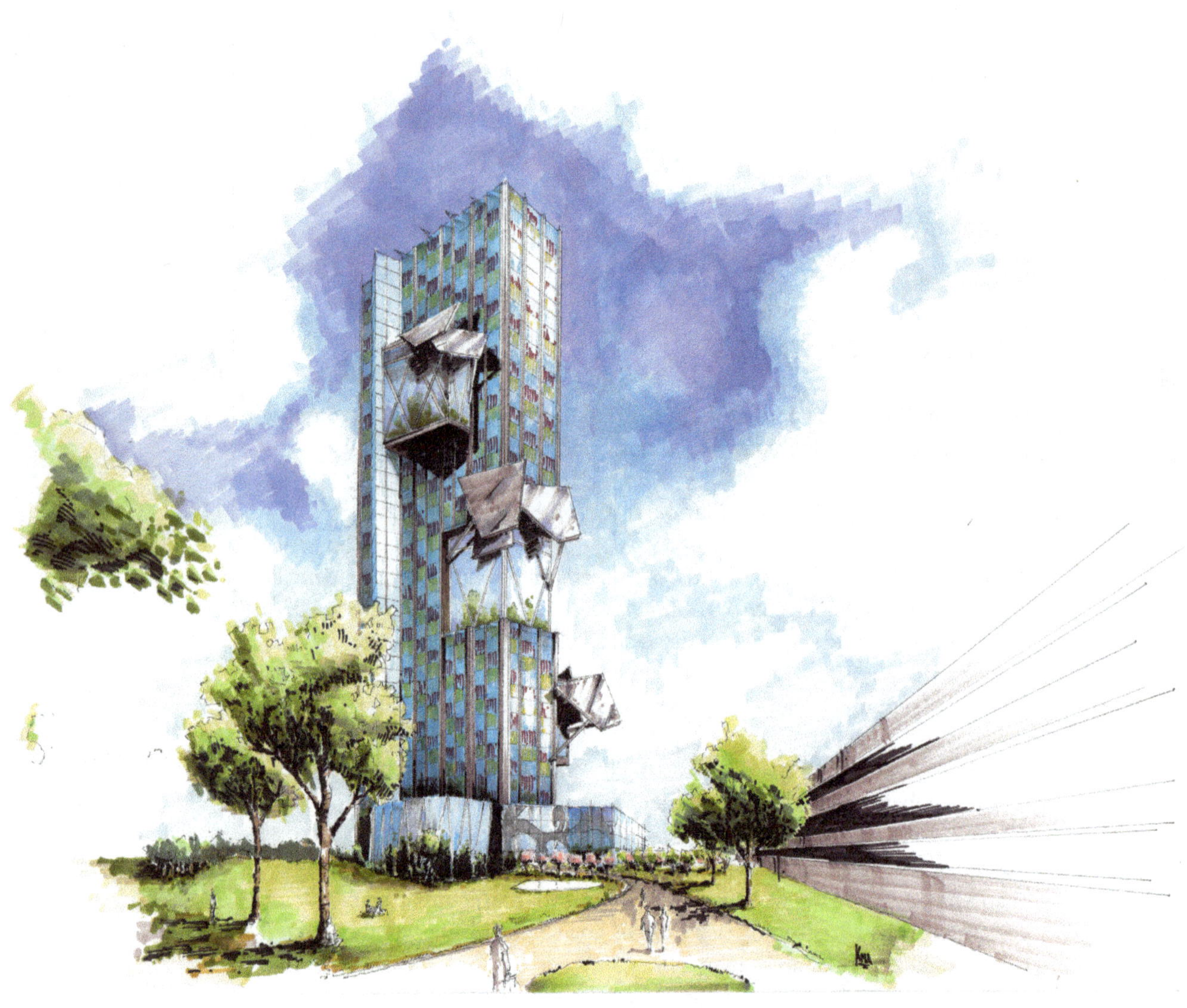

KEVIN ASMUS
Rendered perspective with markers
C-2 Studio,
Boston Architectural College

Rendering is the act of adding color, tone, and scalar elements, such as people, plants, and furniture, to drawings. Designers use rendering during ideation to test out different materials and color options; to understand the proportion, form, and scale of spaces; and to communicate how these spaces are used.

Although there is a wide range of rendering techniques available to designers, there is no one correct way to render drawings. The media and tools chosen will depend on what you are trying to represent, the amount of time you have, and your comfort level with the chosen media.

It is important to be open to testing out new techniques and media in order to develop your rendering skills. Study rendered drawings by other designers to learn from their techniques. Talk with your peers about how they are representing their designs. Look carefully at the world around you to understand how light and shadow, materials, and objects within a space affect its appearance and use.

Hand-Rendered Drawings

Rendering can occur anytime during the design process. During the early concept phases, quick, freehand strokes of color and tone are added to drawings to convey the depth of spaces or different programmatic relationships or to study different design options. People and plants are more simply drawn, with a minimal amount of strokes to suggest the scale and form.

The perspective on the top right is one example of how rendering can be used during ideation. Color, people, and furniture were added to the drawing to study the scale and spatial experience.

For presentation drawings, more careful renderings are made to create a highly realistic image of the design proposal. More detail is added in order to communicate the design intent to those unfamiliar with the project. The perspectives on the right and facing page are examples of presentation renderings.

Digitally Rendered Drawings

In a digital rendering, tone, color, and entourage are added to a drawing using a computer graphics program, such as Photoshop. Digitally rendered drawings are typically presentation drawings completed toward the end of ideation. In the rendered elevation on the lower right, material, landscape elements, and the adjacent site context were merged with a line drawing, using Photoshop.

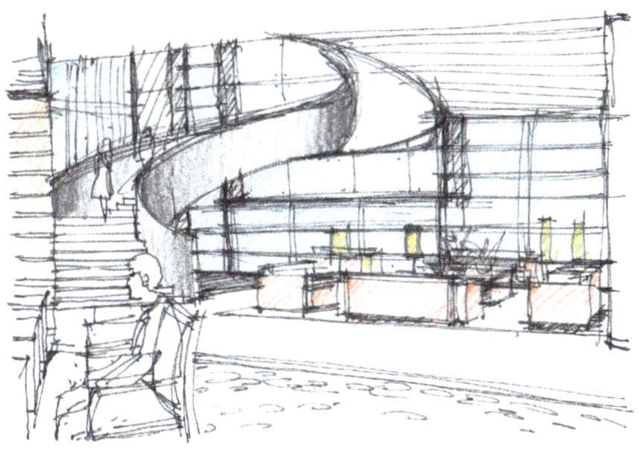

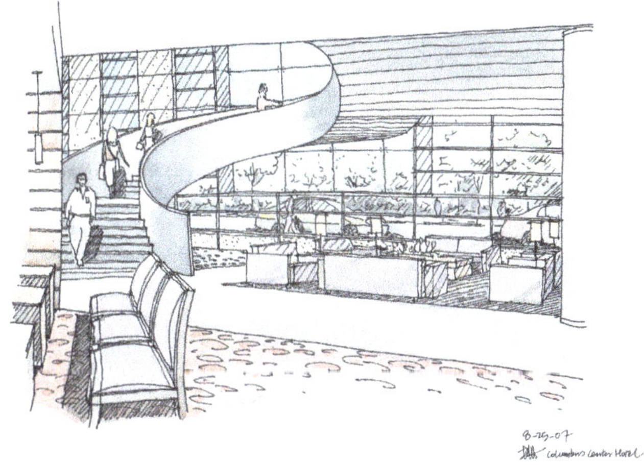

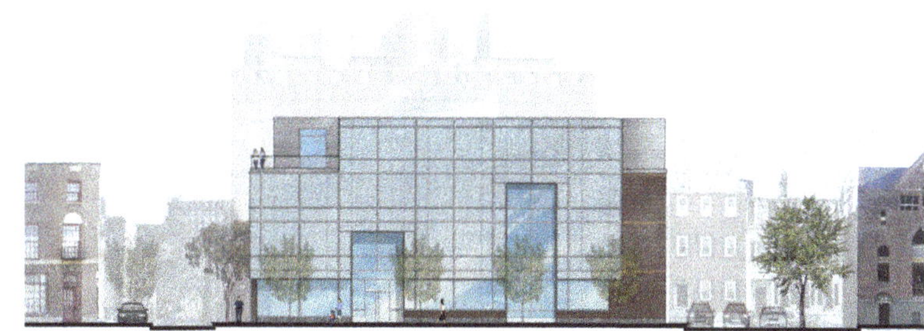

ARROWSTREET

Top and middle images:
Perspectives rendered with colored pencils, interior lobby study

Bottom image:
Rendered elevation using Photoshop

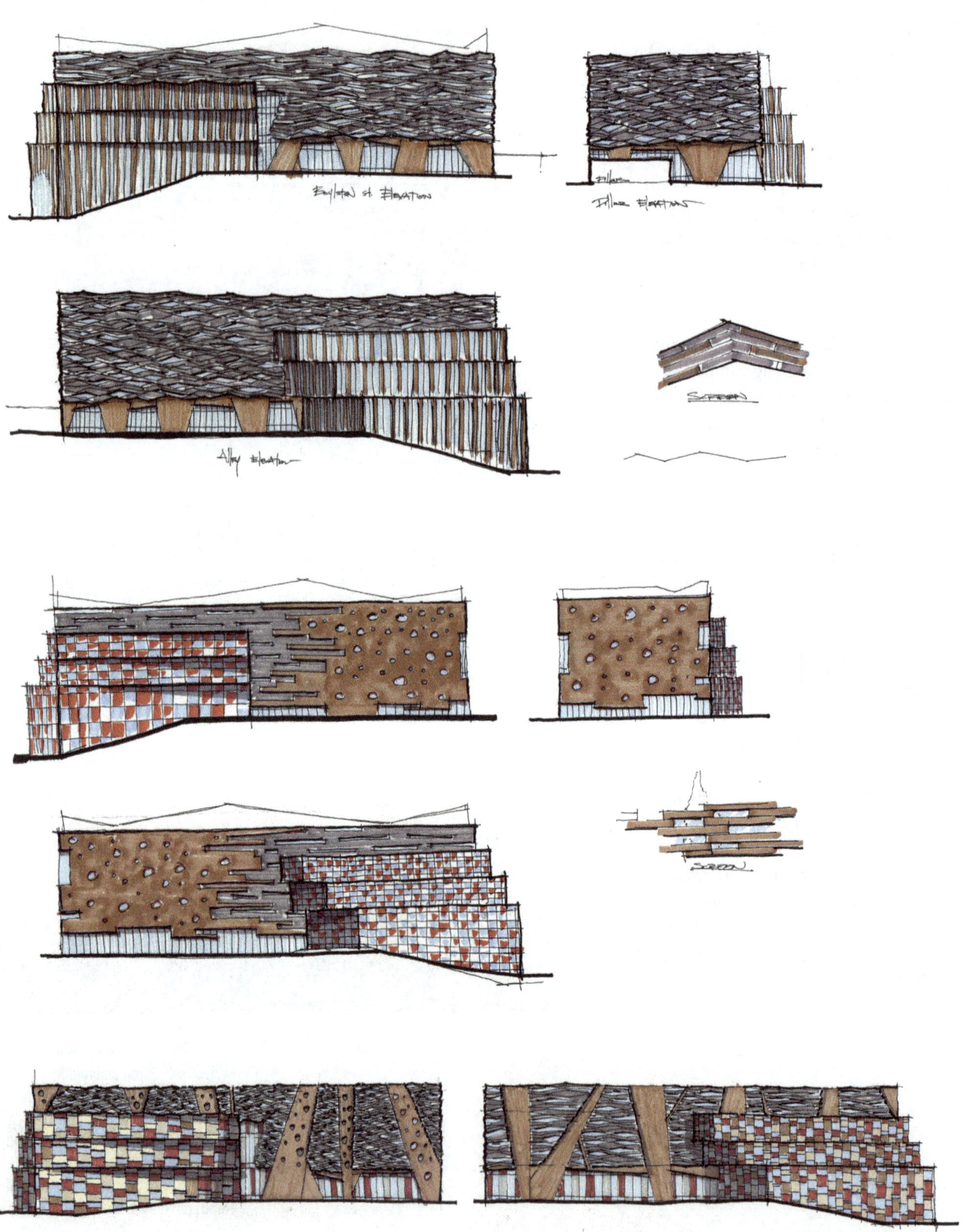
Boylston St. Elevation
Alley Elevation
Screen
Screen

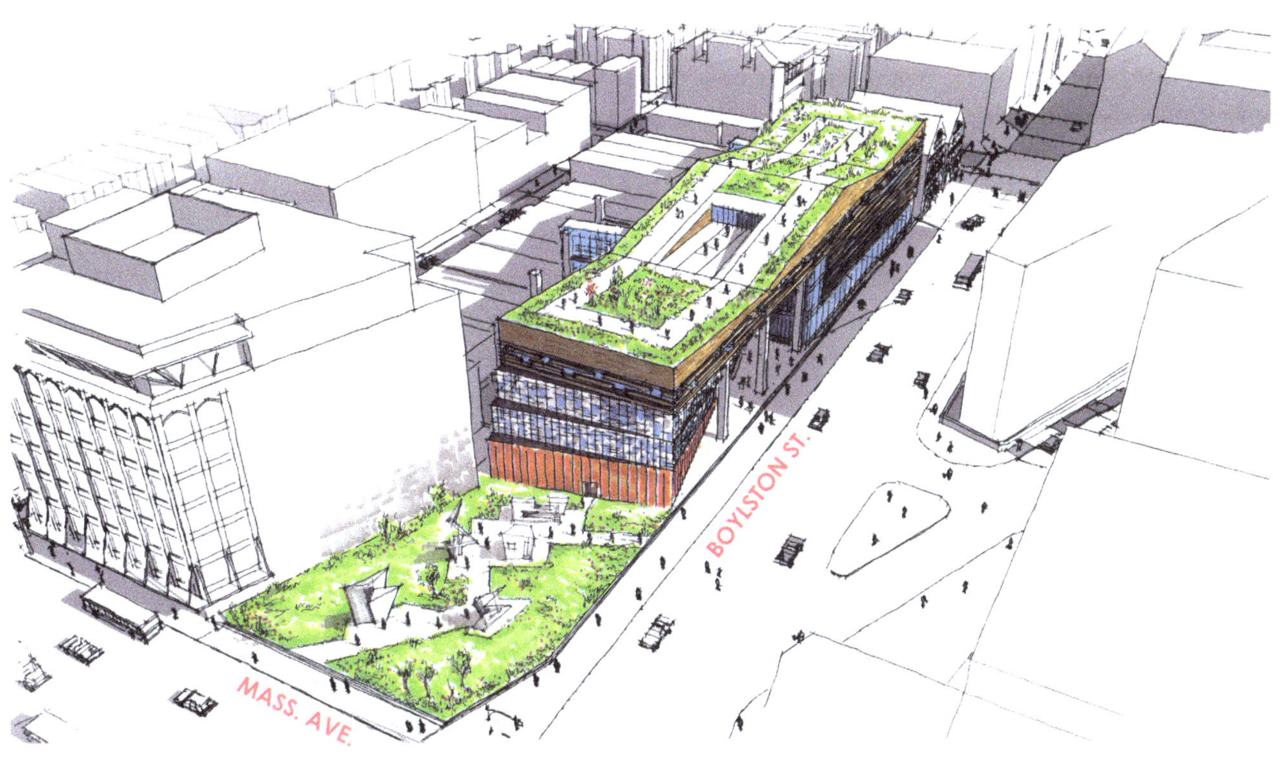

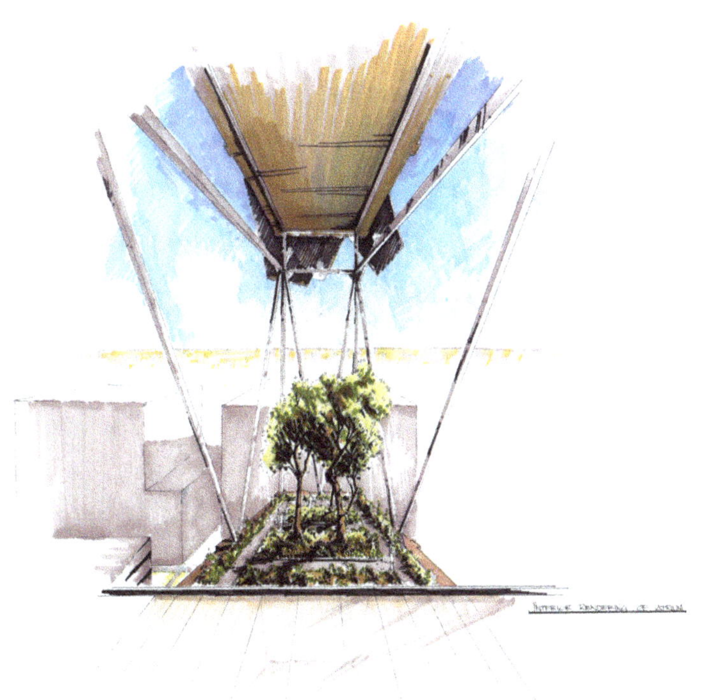

Simple colors can be quickly used to illustrate many different properties of a design. I use color to express materiality, differences in opacity, what is in the background and foreground, shade, shadow, and changes in direction. By altering shades of a color to imply changes in light value, I can achieve a sense of volume and depth that brings certain objects to the forefront, making them more readable.

—Kevin Asmus

Kevin Asmus
Rendered elevations and perspective studies, Faber-Castell markers on bristol paper
Degree Project Studio and C-2 Studio, Boston Architectural College

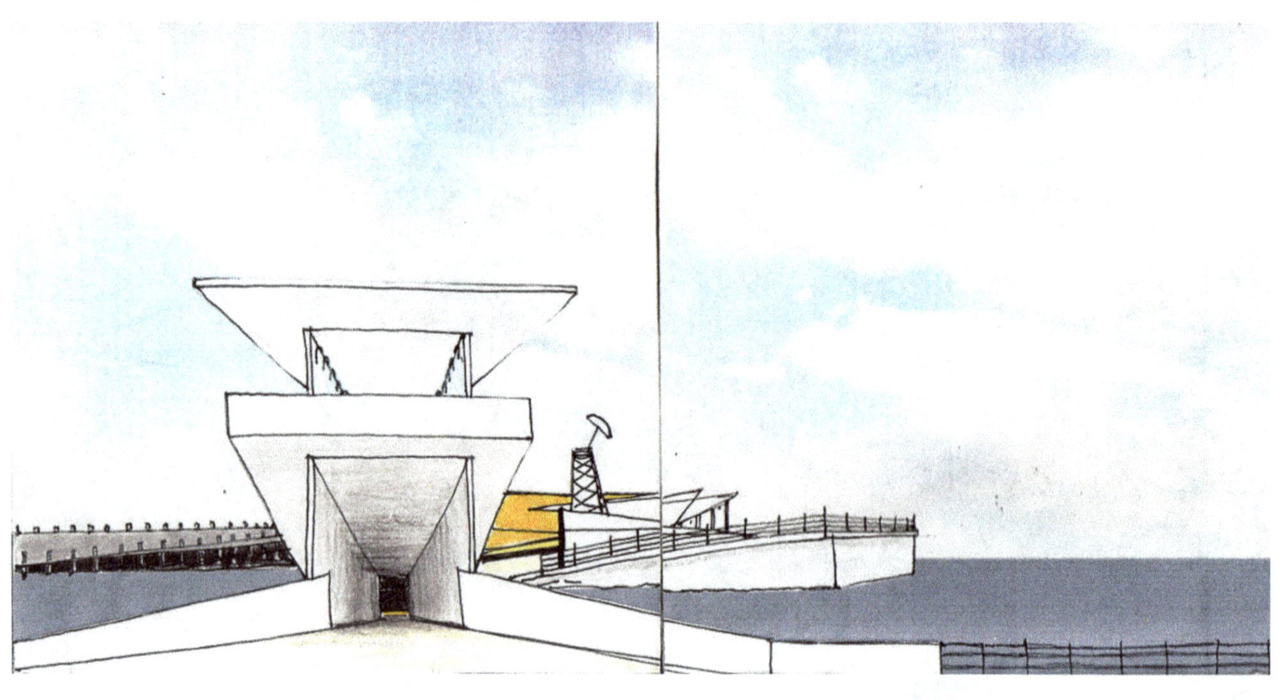

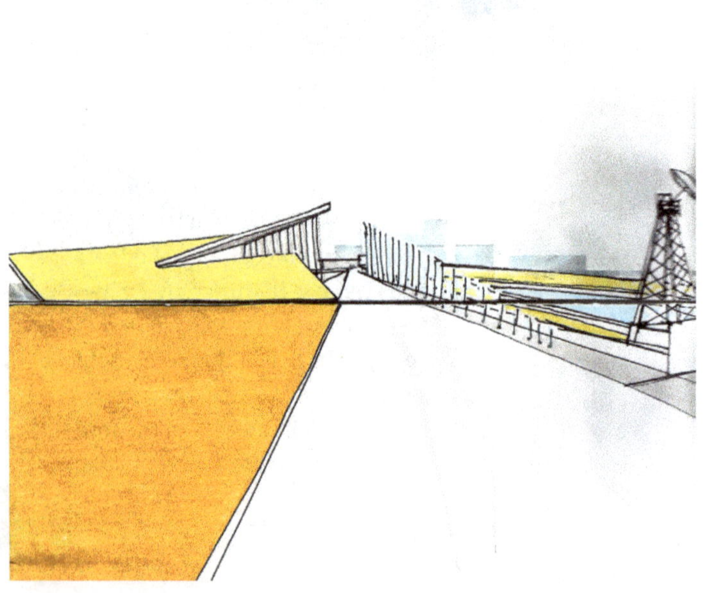

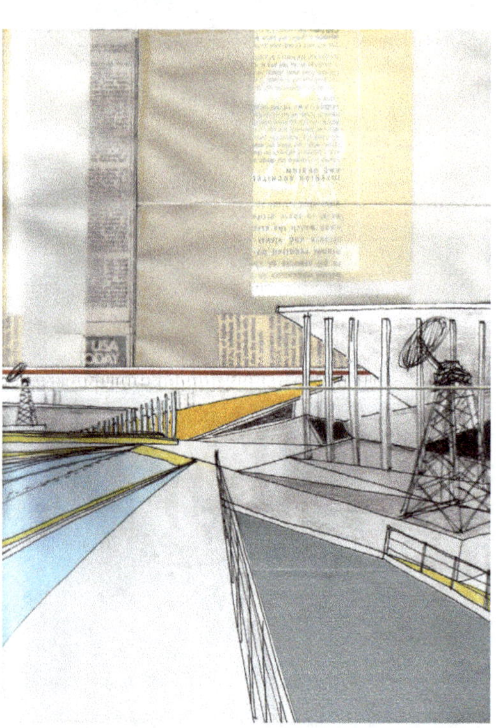

ELENA RAYA
Perspective collages,
Inked perspectives on Mylar with colored paper glued on the back
Harvard University,
Graduate School of Design

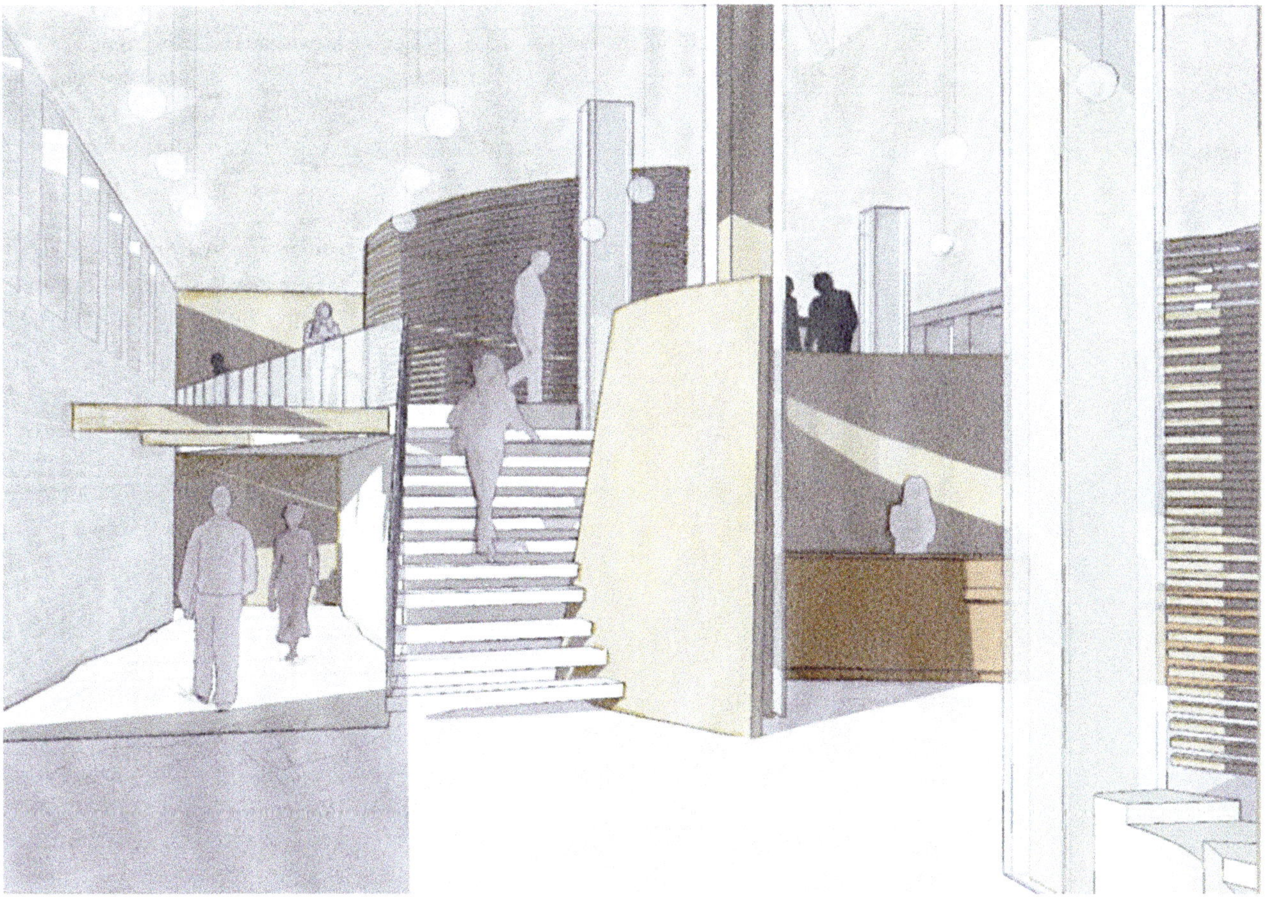

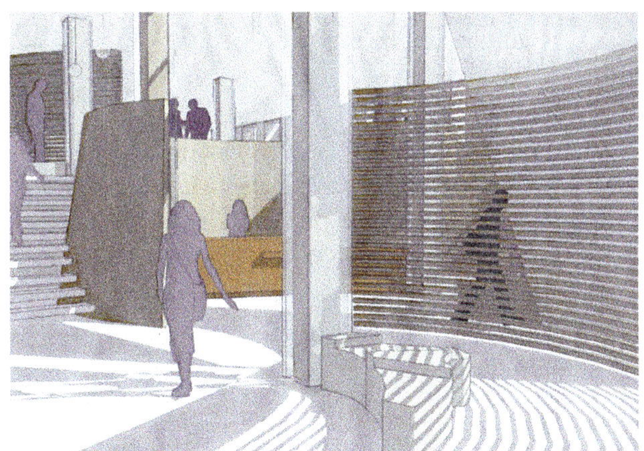

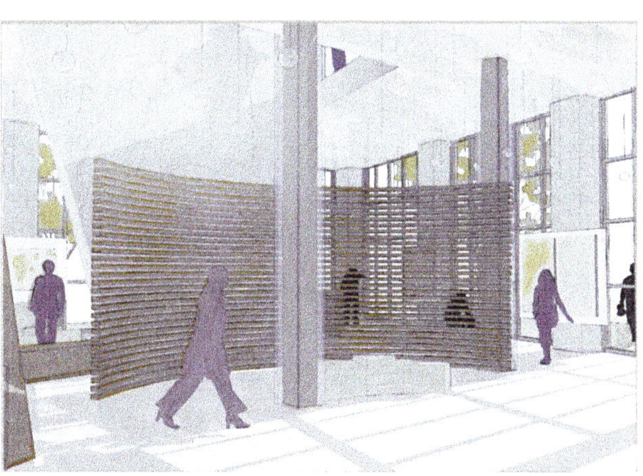

Billie Jo Baril
Digitally rendered perspectives
Thesis Studio,
The New England School of
Art & Design at Suffolk University

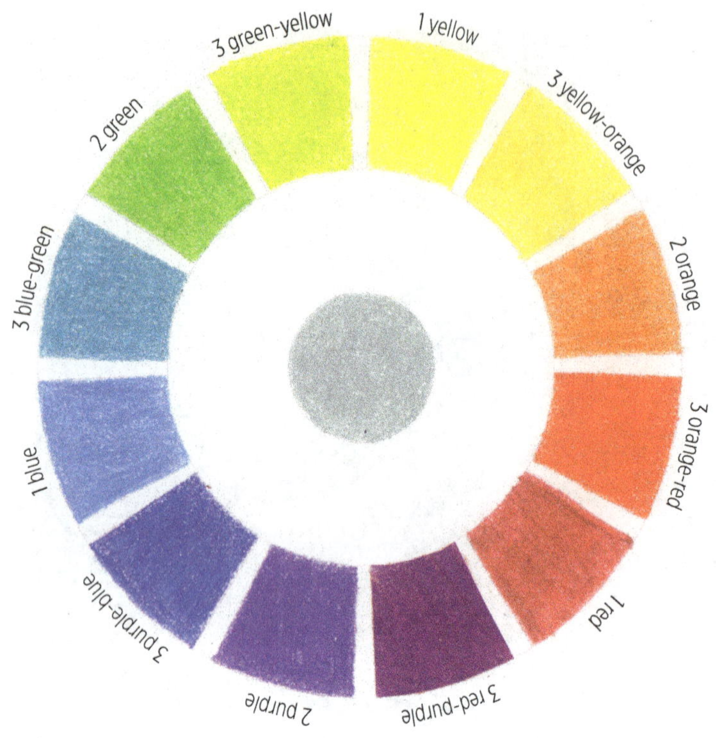

Tone and Color

Tone and color are added to drawings to make them read more three dimensionally. They define areas of light and shadow, and communicate scalar qualities by representing materials and patterns.

When rendering a drawing with gray tones or color, it helps to have an understanding of hue, value, and saturation in order to develop a more successful composition.

Hue

Hue is a measure of how we see colors, based on their wavelength. The relationship between different hues is best illustrated through a color wheel.

- The primary colors of red, blue, and yellow are the three basic hues from which all other colors can be mixed.
- Mixing the primary colors together creates secondary hues of orange, green, and purple.
- When adjacent primary and secondary colors are mixed together, they create tertiary colors, such as yellow-orange and orange-red.
- Hues that are opposite each other on the color wheel are called complementary colors and, when mixed, produce gray.

Value

Value is a measure of lightness and darkness. Values create spatial cues within a drawing, emphasizing depth and form. Successful renderings are built up from a variation of values, using light, medium, and dark shades to create a reading of spatial depth and contrast within a composition.

Saturation

Saturation is a measure of the brightness and purity of a color. The most saturated colors are those that are not mixed with their corresponding complementary color. As the amount of the complementary color increases, the saturation of a hue decreases.

Color Combinations

- In a monochromatic composition a single color with varying values and saturation is used. Choosing one shade creates a unified composition with a visual focus on the geometry and form of a space instead of the color.
- Analogous colors are adjacent to each other on the color wheel. A composition created with analogous colors also tends to create a unified composition.
- Complementary colors and triad colors (three colors equally spaced around the color wheel) create more dynamic compositions. These renderings are typically more high contrast and emphasize the colors and materials of a space.

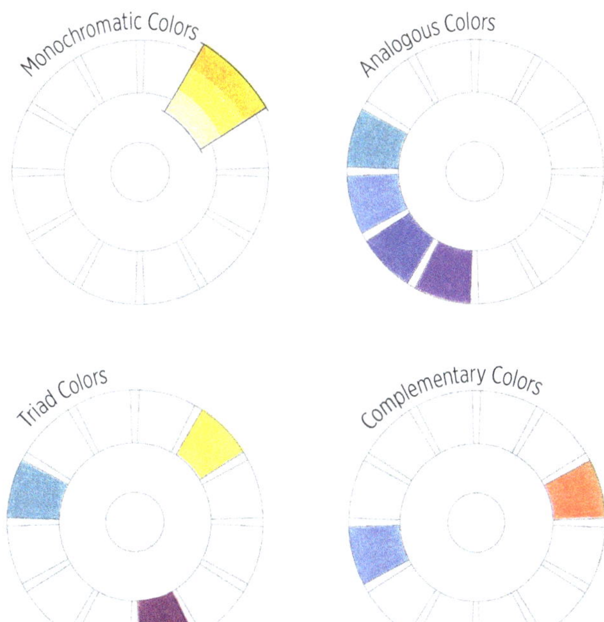

Creating Focal Points through Color

Use complementary hues to emphasize focal points within the space.

Receding and Advancing Colors

Warmer colors, such as reds, oranges, and yellows, usually appear closer; cool colors, such as blues and greens, typically recede within a composition.

Simulate Depth on a Surface

To create the illusion of light and shadow bouncing off of a surface, either render the area with analogous colors or use a single color and vary the value or saturation.

Value Study

A value study is a grayscale rendering created with either pencils or gray markers. Prior to developing a colored rendering, it is useful to first render the drawing in grayscale to develop a balance of shadows and highlights within the composition.

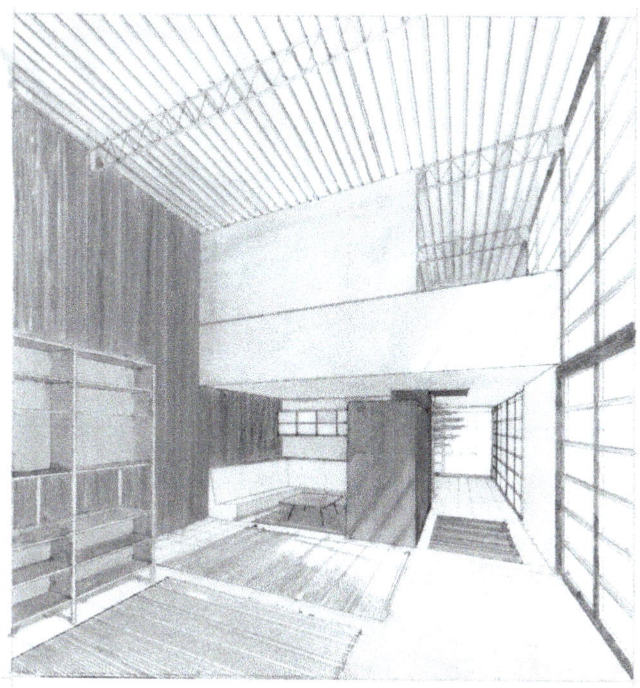

Value study

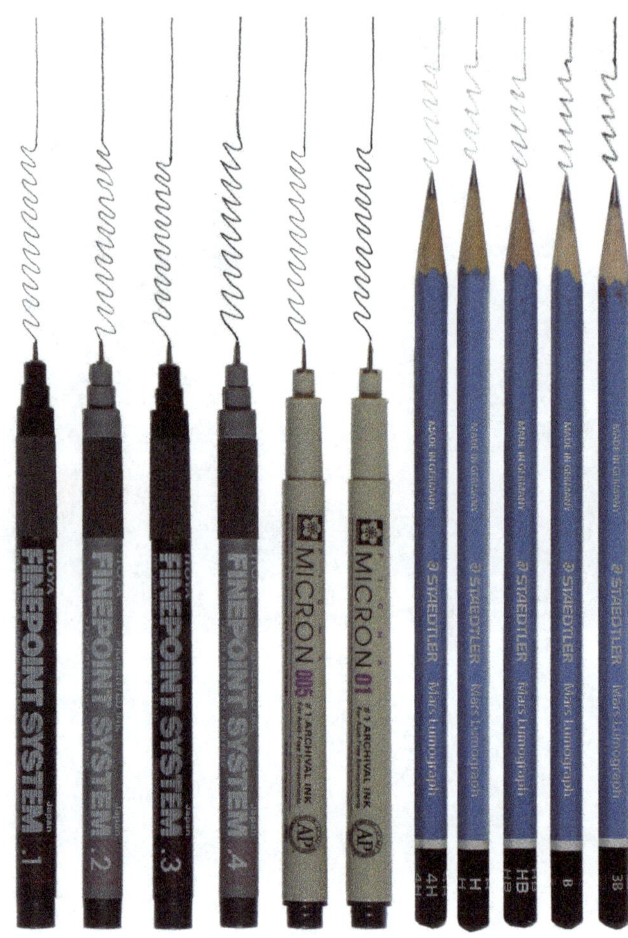

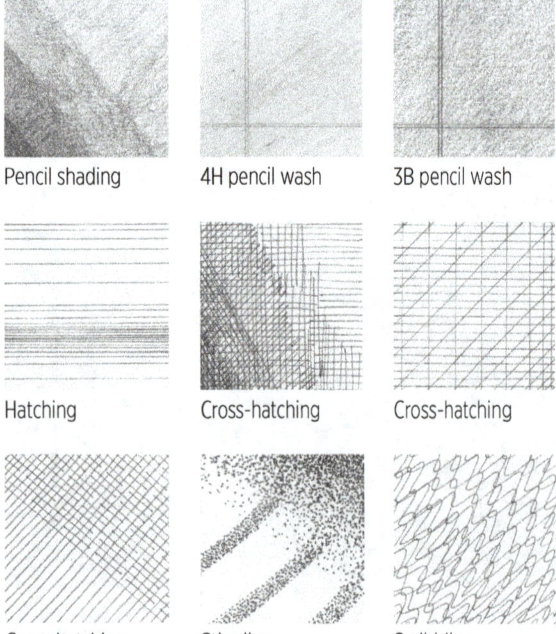

Pencil shading | 4H pencil wash | 3B pencil wash

Hatching | Cross-hatching | Cross-hatching

Cross-hatching | Stippling | Scribbling

Pencil Shading and Ink Hatching

Rendering with pencils on a drafted pencil drawing or with ink on an inked line drawing allows designers to maintain a consistency of hand while equally emphasizing both the line and tonal qualities. Ink and pencil shading work best on smooth papers, which create an even tone across the page.

Although almost any type of pen can be used to render a drawing, the artist pens, such as Micron and Itoya, are sold in varying thicknesses and are of a higher quality than the typical drugstore pen because they are acid free and dispense ink more evenly.

There are five main techniques for creating tone with pencils and ink pens:

Pencil Shading

- Diagonal pencil strokes, typically 45 degrees, are drawn on the paper to build up an even layer of graphite and tone.
- Successive layers of pencil can be applied on top of each other to minimize stroke marks and create darker tones.
- Softer pencils will create darker tones but will appear grainy when applied lightly. Harder pencils, such as 4H and 2H, will create a lighter, smoother wash.

Hatching

- Parallel lines are drawn on a page in a consistent direction to create tone.
- Closer spaced lines create darker areas; wider spaced lines create light areas.

Cross-Hatching

Perpendicular lines are drawn on a page in two or more directions to create areas of tone.

Stippling

- Dots are used to create the illusion of light and shadow.
- The density of dots creates areas of light or dark tones across the page.

Scribbling

- Repeating, curvilinear lines are used to create areas of tone.
- Scribbles typically overlap each other in order to minimize the reading of individual lines and emphasize the area as a tonal field.

Colored pencil renderings share many of the same techniques as those done in graphite and ink, such as hatching, shading, and scribbling. Colored pencils are easy to use and are one of the quickest mediums for applying color to drawings. By simply varying the pressure of the pencil on the paper, a wide range of values, from light color washes to richer, more saturated colors, can be created.

Colored pencils work well on a variety of papers, from white and yellow trace paper to bristol paper. Smoother papers typically produce a more continuous line and even tone; textured papers can sometimes create a grainy look. The artist quality brands, such as Prismacolor and Berol, are softer and of a higher quality than the commercial brands, making it easier to create tonal transitions.

Conceptual and Final Rendering Techniques

- For more conceptual drawings, color is added through diagonal strokes of a single pencil.
- For more developed drawings, color is usually built up through layered washes of similar color hues, to create the illusion of depth, light and shadow on a surface.
- To render shadows, apply a graphite pencil wash on top of the colored pencil.

Scoring the Paper to Create Patterns

Paper can be scored or etched, using an Xacto knife or bone folder to create subtle indentations. When color is applied, the pattern of score lines is revealed as lighter lines. This technique is useful for rendering joints on floor and elevation surfaces.

Combining Pencils and Markers

Colored pencils are also frequently layered over markers to add detail, highlights, and shadows to marker renderings.

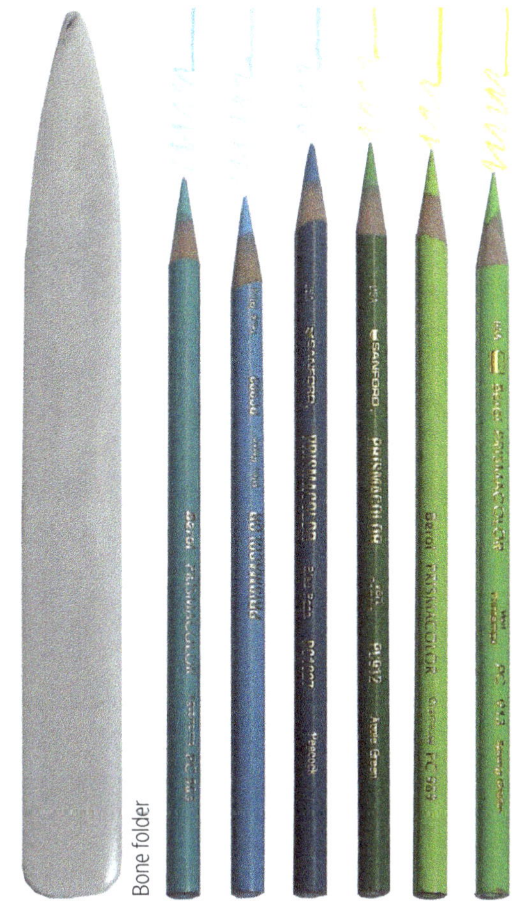

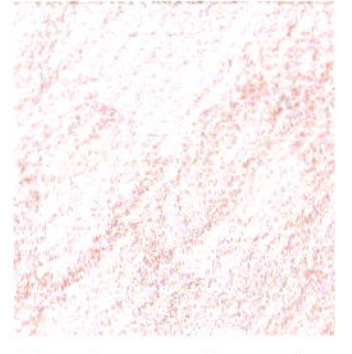
Single pencil wash

Layered pencil wash, 4 analogous colors

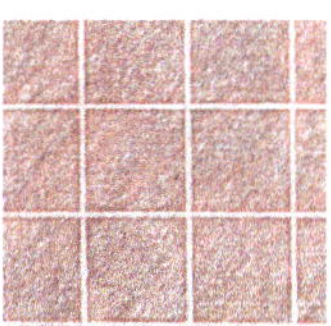
Scored paper with colored pencil wash

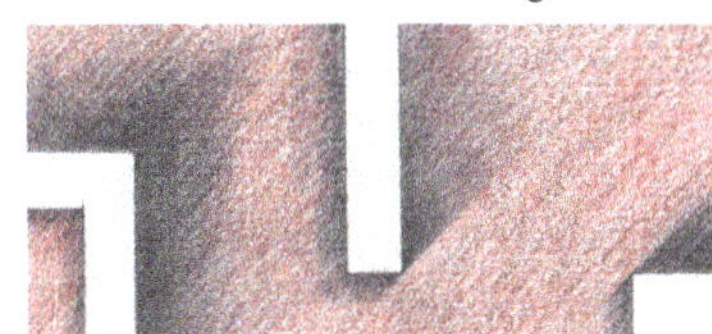
Graphite pencil wash over colored pencils

Colored pencil over marker

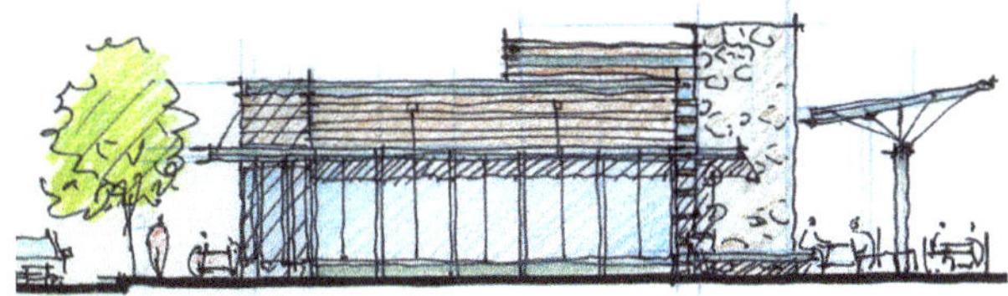
ARROWSTREET
Colored-pencil-and-ink elevation on trace

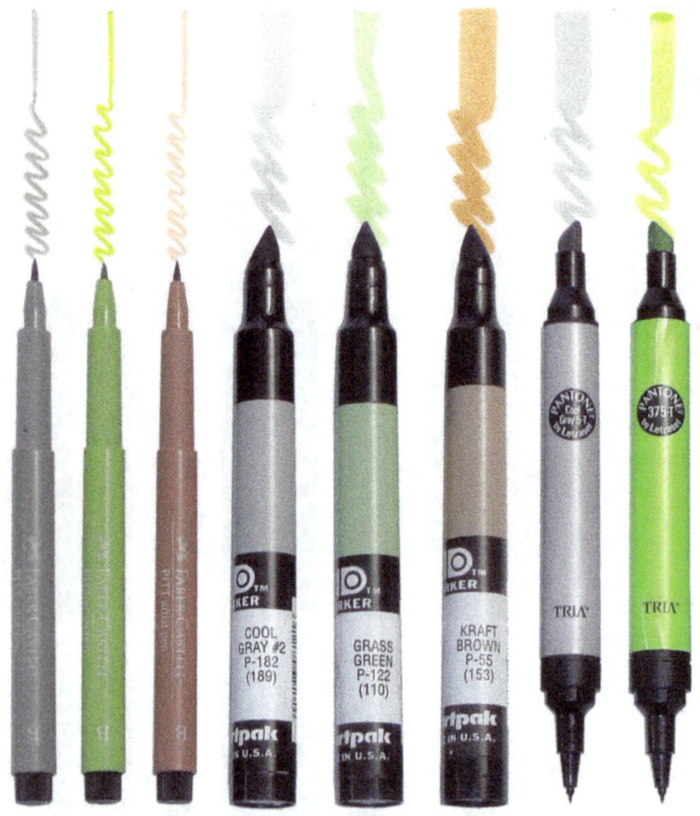

Markers are an extremely versatile medium that can be used to create quick conceptual renderings by shading in key portions of a drawing or more elaborate colored drawings. Markers dry quickly, speeding up the rendering time, and are most effective when applied over an ink line drawing. Markers come in a variety of colors and tip sizes, ranging from fine to larger, rounded shapes and chiseled shapes that can create both thin and thick lines, depending on how the marker is held in relation to the paper.

When marker is used on nonabsorbent paper, such as vellum, Mylar, and trace paper, the colors are more muted and lighter. On absorbent papers, such as bond and bristol, the colors appear richer and stronger and blend less easily.

Application Techniques

- Consistent direction of stroke is critical, especially on the absorbent papers, which tend to show strokes more prominently. Irregular strokes can create visual distractions within the drawing; a lack of visible stroke lines emphasizes the forms and shapes of objects.
- Color washes can be applied on top of each other and blended together to create a quality similar to that of watercolor renderings.
- Markers can be applied to the back of translucent papers to create a lighter tone.
- Use a straight edge and vertical strokes to simulate reflections on horizontal surfaces, such as floors and counters.
- Add details, such as highlights, shadows, and surface pattern, with colored pencils applied over a marker base.
- Because marker colors are so vibrant, many designers use a limited palette of colors in order to create more unified renderings.

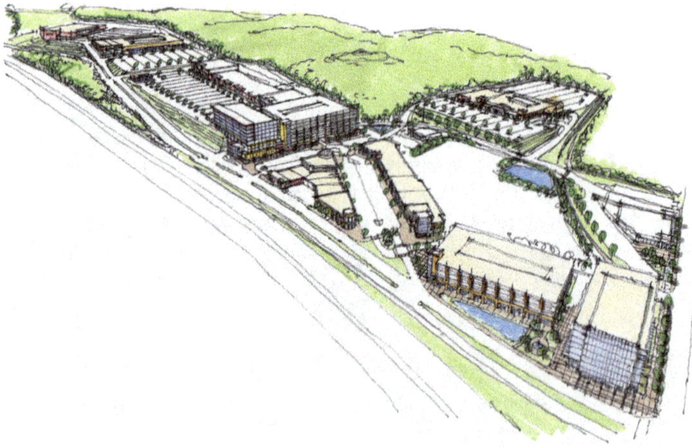

ARROWSTREET
Aerial perspective
Markers and ink on trace

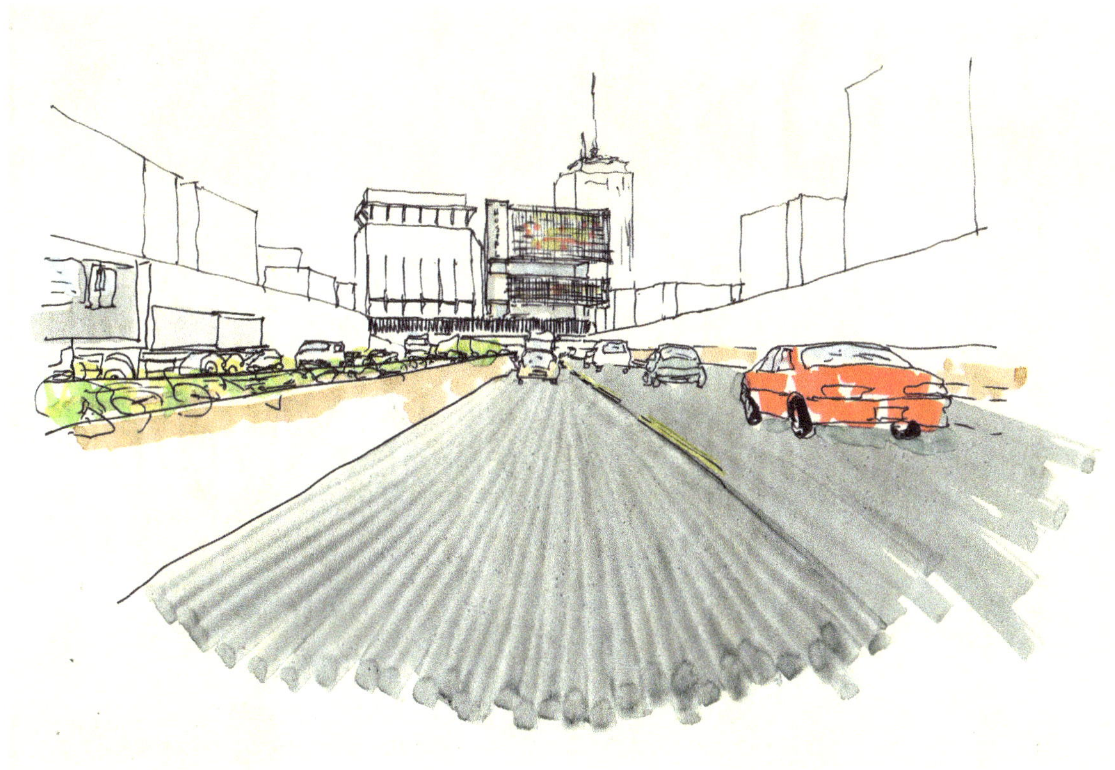

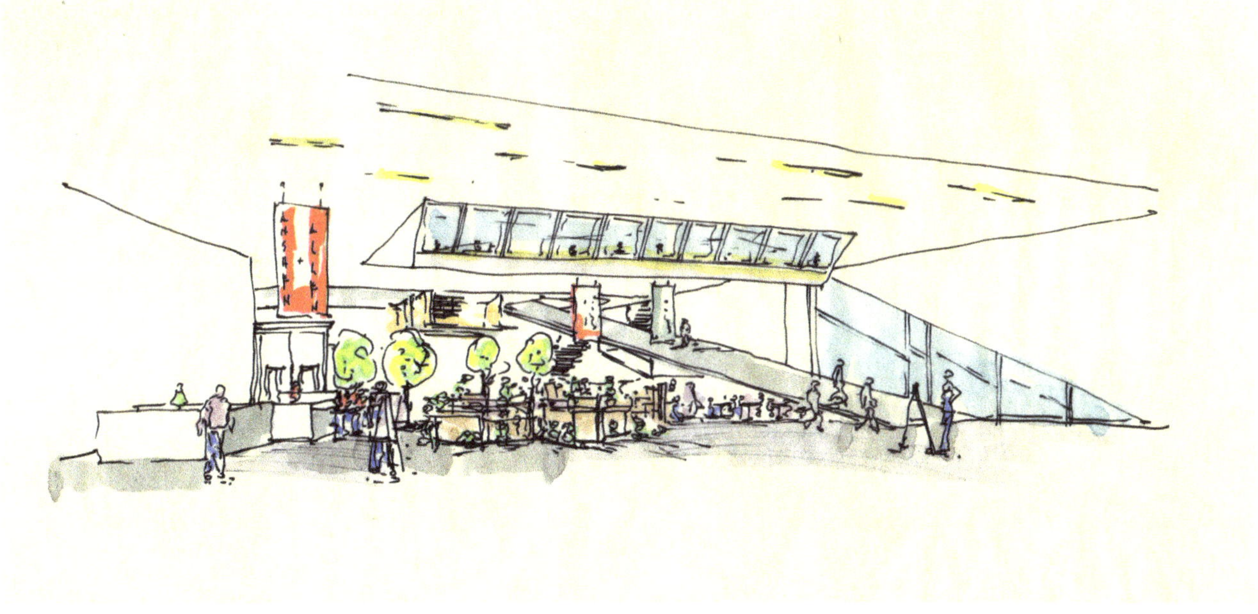

In the marker drawings above, color was added to emphasize key elements within the design and the rest of the drawing was left as an ink drawing. The road was colored with a perspectival marker stroke, which both emphasizes the movement of traffic and draws the viewer's eye to the elevation in the distance.

JONATHAN C. GARLAND
Markers and ink on yellow trace
Degree Project Studio,
Boston Architectural College

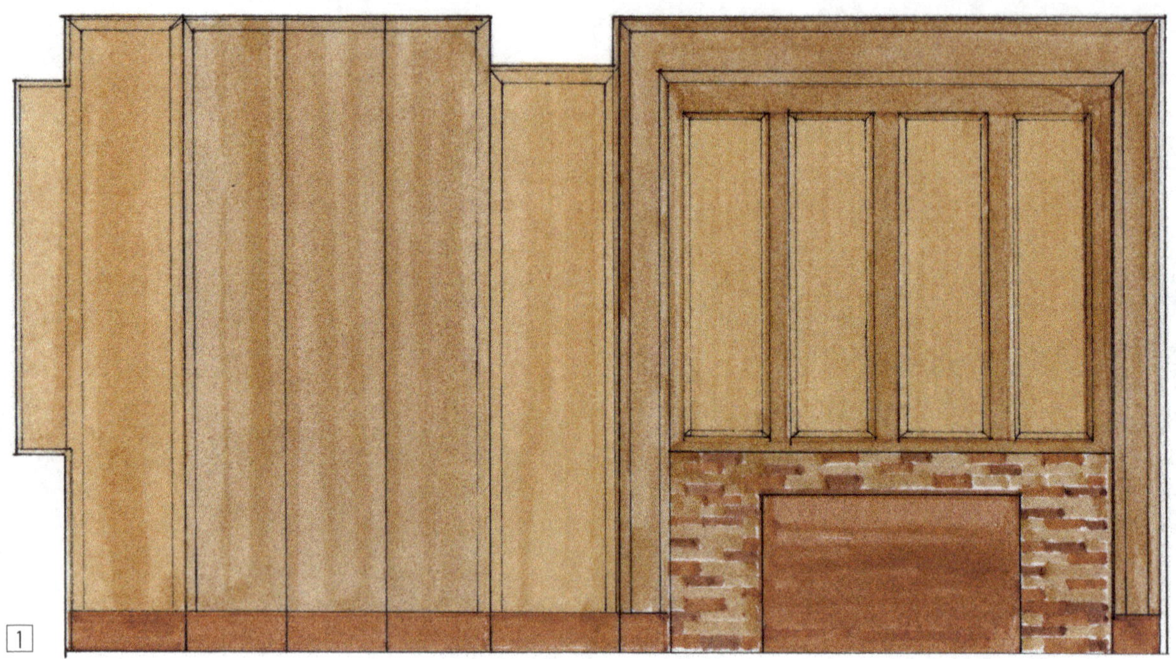

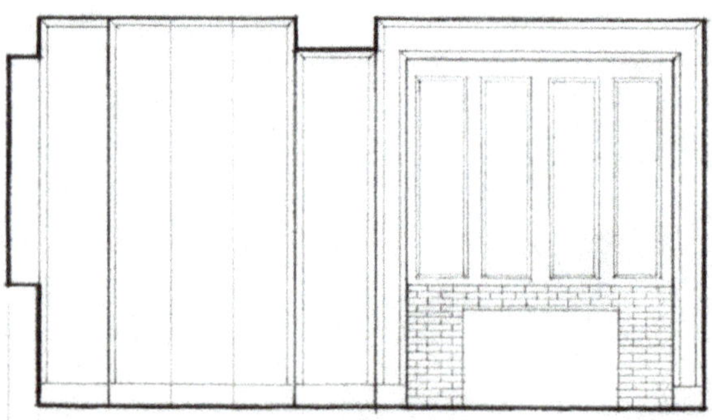

To render a drawing with markers, first print out the line work on vellum, bond, or marker paper, or ink over the drawing if it is in pencil.

Step 1: Overall Color Washes

- Apply the overall color and material hues to the elevation with consistent marker strokes.
- In the example above, the overlapping vertical strokes were used as a base for the wood grain pattern in step 3.

Step 2: Shadows

Add shadows with gray, dark blue, or black colored pencil.

Step 3: Details

- Using colored pencils, add wood grain details, as well as highlights and low lights.
- In this example, an ink pen was used to define the brick coursing on the fireplace.

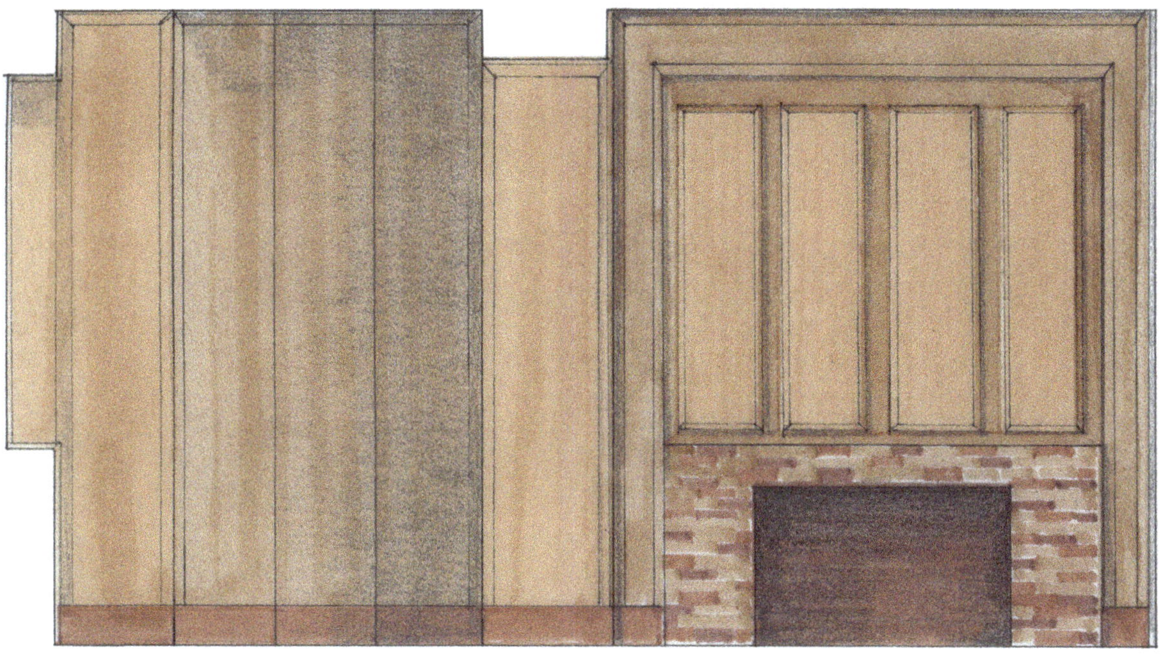

2

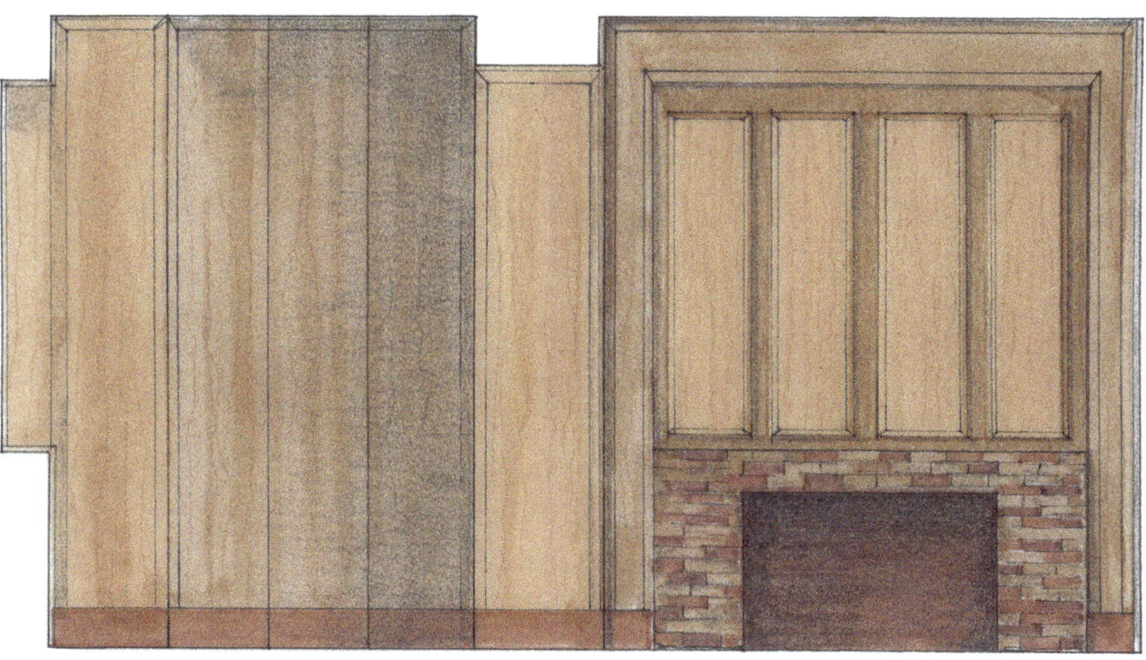

3

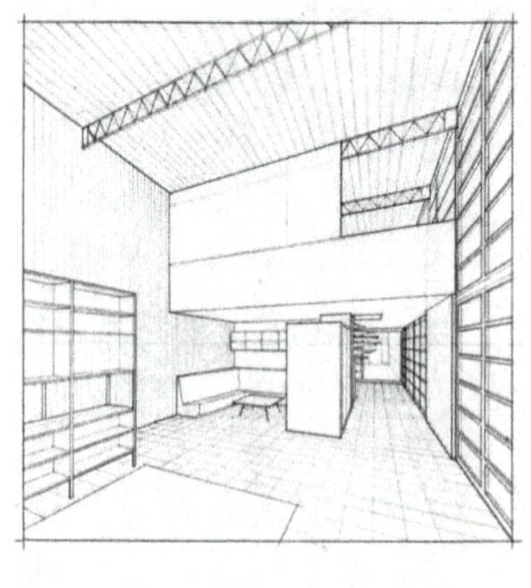

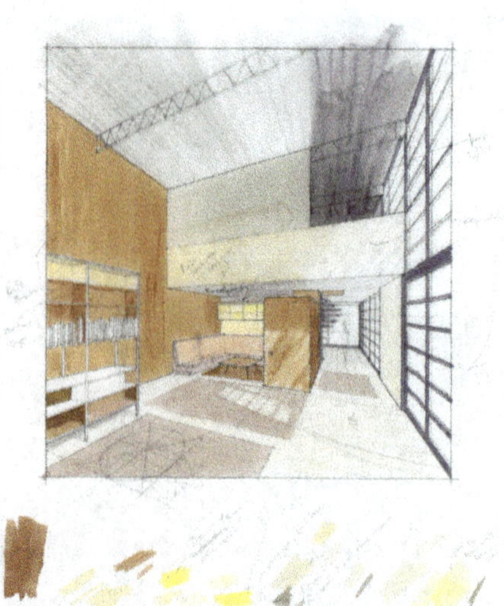

1

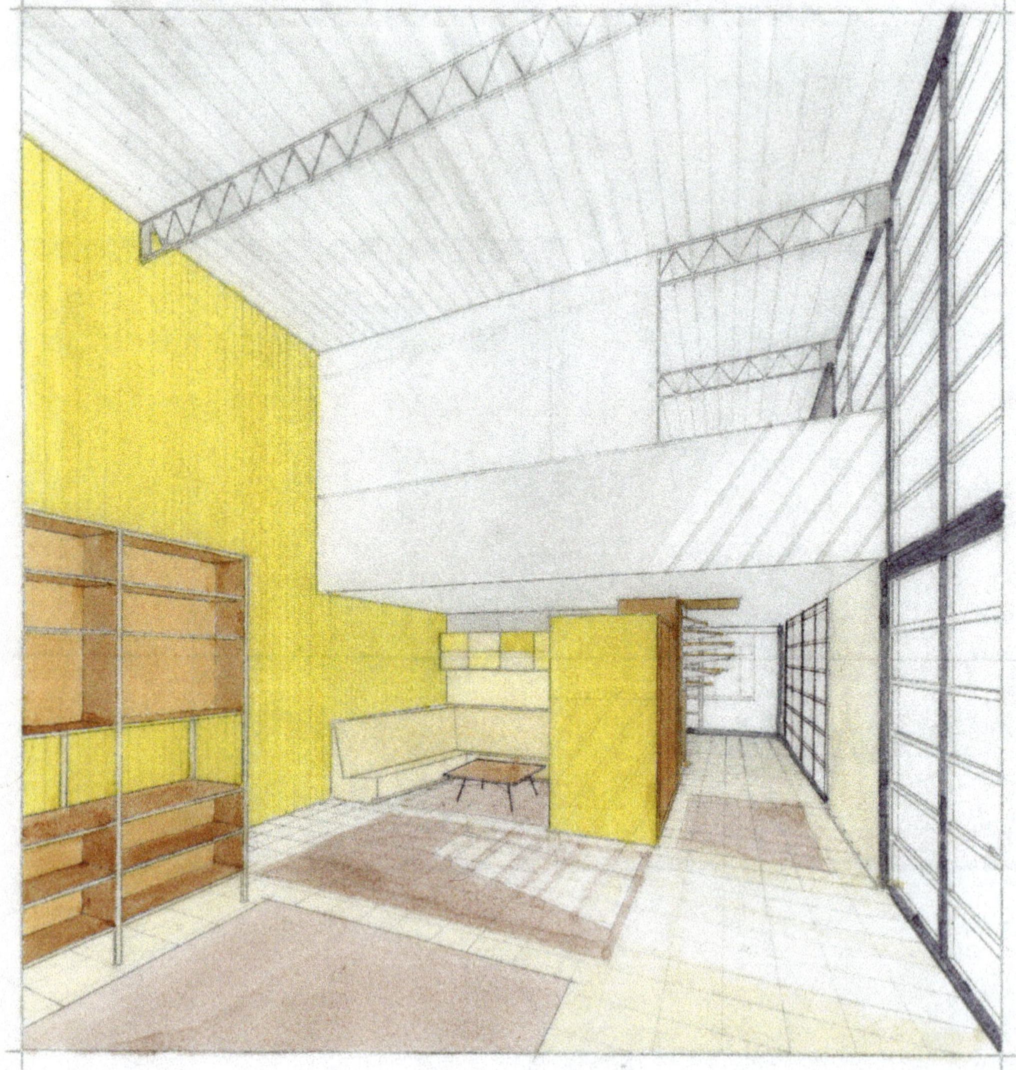

2

Step 1: Color Study

- The first step in rendering this perspective was a quick color study to determine which colors to use and the shadow locations.
- Initial color or value studies can save time when rendering more complex drawings because they allow the designer to quickly test out techniques and evaluate the overall composition.

Step 2: Overall Color Washes

- Apply the overall color and material hues to the line work with consistent marker strokes.
- In the example, the yellow was applied as a base color to give more depth to the final wood-paneled wall.

Step 3: Shadows and Details

- A second layer of marker was added to render shadows and surface details. The shadows on the ceiling plane were created with light and dark gray pen, using ruled strokes.
- To minimize the pooling of ink on the paper and to help blend colors together, you can use your finger to smear the marker ink while it is still wet. This technique was used to create a transition between areas of light and shadow on the center wood wall.
- For further development, colored pencil could have been added as a third layer to develop smaller details.

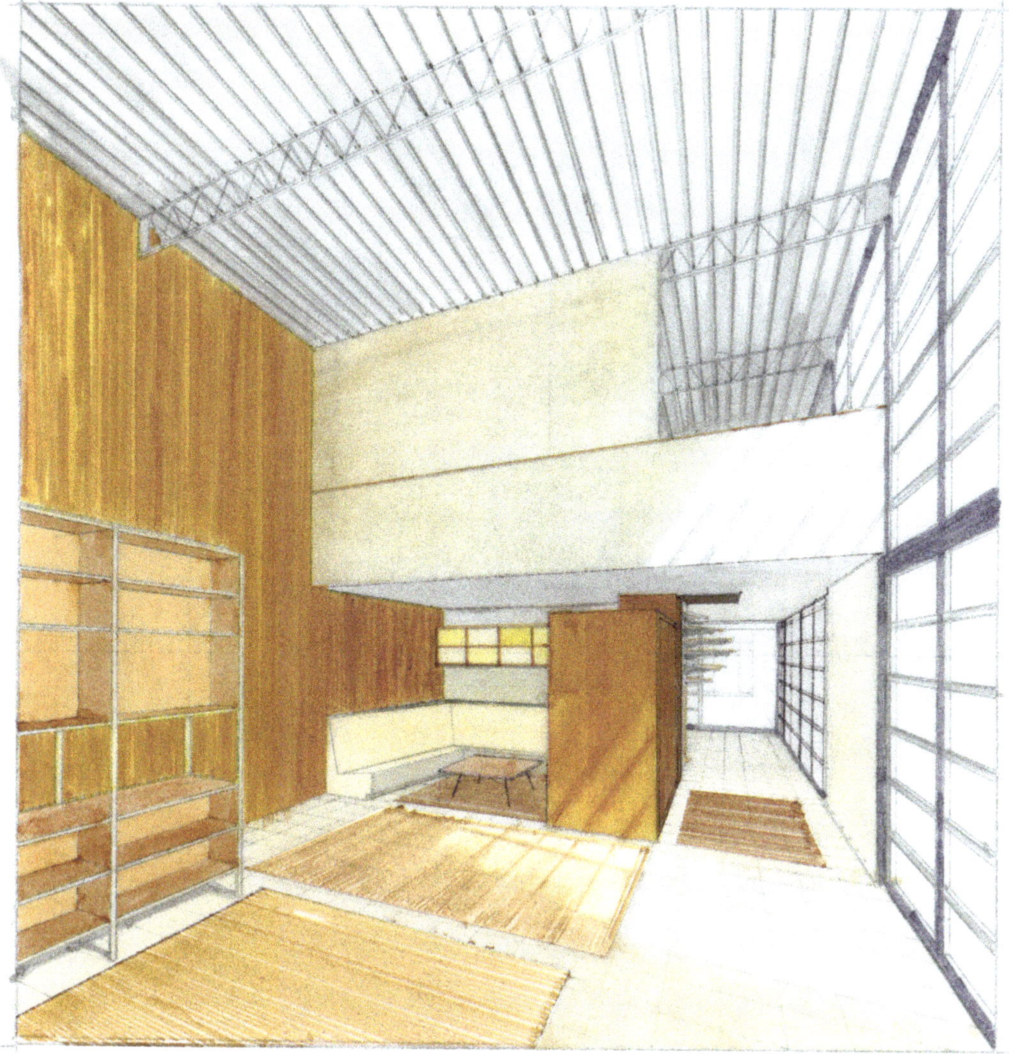

3

Watercolor is a versatile medium, characterized by seamless blends of translucent color. A wide range of values and hues can be achieved, depending on the ratio of water to pigment as well as the technique.

Watercolor is a more involved medium to work with because the paper has to be mounted onto a board before painting and can take a while to dry.

Heavier papers with a tooth, or grain, to them are an ideal base for watercolors because they absorb the color and water more readily. Line work is typically printed out on heavy paper and mounted or taped to a board, to prevent the sheet from curling or wrinkling.

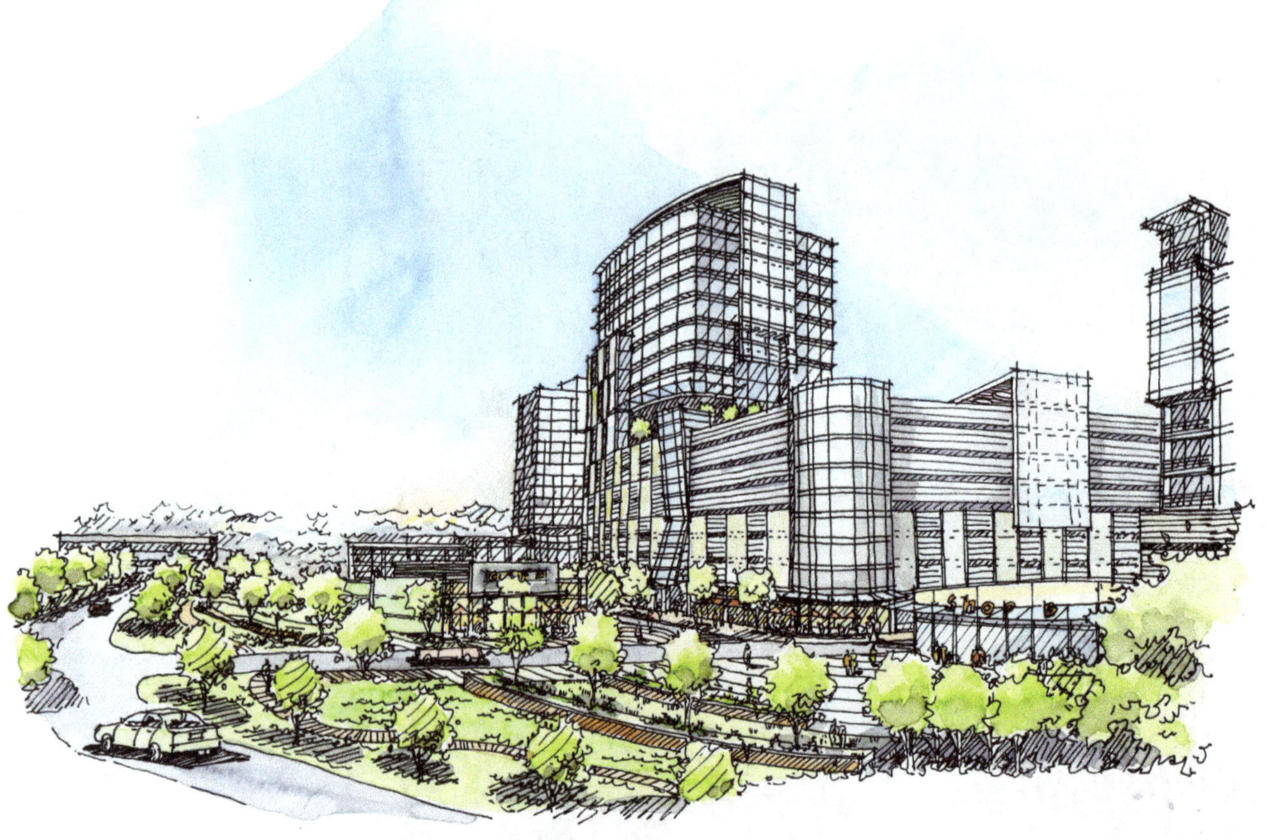

ARROWSTREET
Watercolor perspective
with ink line work
Example of the wet brush technique

Flat Wash Technique

- For a flat wash, a single color is applied to the page to create an even tone or gradation of color. The paper is first moistened with water, in the area to receive color, and then pigment is brushed on with even strokes.
- To create a gradation of color from dark to light, simply dilute the color with water for each subsequent stroke.

Wet Brush Technique

- This technique uses an ample amount of water to create dynamic blends of color across the page.
- The area to be rendered is first moistened liberally with pools of water. The brush is loaded with pigment and then lightly touched to the page, allowing the water to distribute the color. Multiple colors can be applied to the pools of water to create transitions between different colors.
- This technique works well for background elements where a softer, blurry quality is desired.

Dry Brush Technique

- A small amount of water is added to the brush before applying color to the page. More detailed drawings can be produced because the brush strokes are thinner.
- This technique works well for foreground elements for which a crisper and finer grain of detail is desired.

Glazing Technique

- A flat wash of very light color is applied over dry, existing colors. This wash subtly blends the colors together on the page and can help unify the colors of a composition.
- Colors such as yellow, blue, and rose work well for glazing and can be applied in multiple layers until the desired affect is achieved.

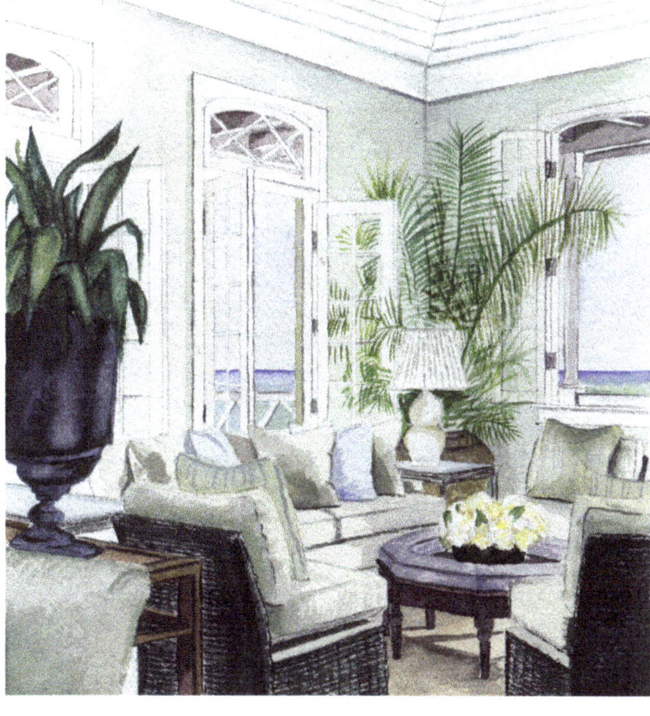

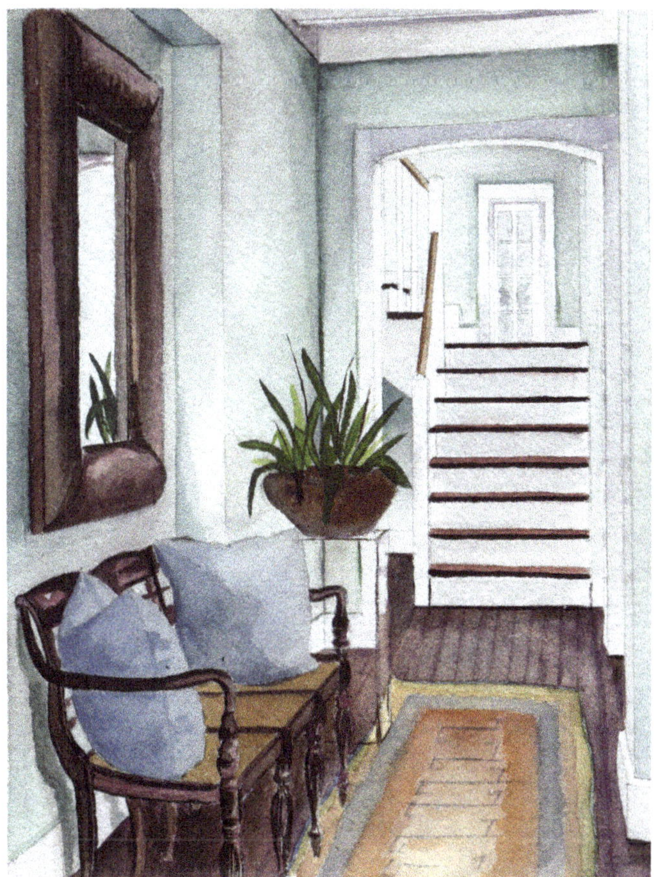

THARON ANDERSON
Interior watercolor

Creating a Pastel Dust Wash

Step 1:

- Tape off the area to receive color.
- Using an Xacto knife, scrape the edge of a pastel stick, to produce a small pile of dust.

Step 2:

- Smooth the dust across the page with a cotton ball.
- Work the pastel into the paper until the desired value is achieved.
- Remove the tape, and repeat steps 1 and 2 for the rest of the drawing.

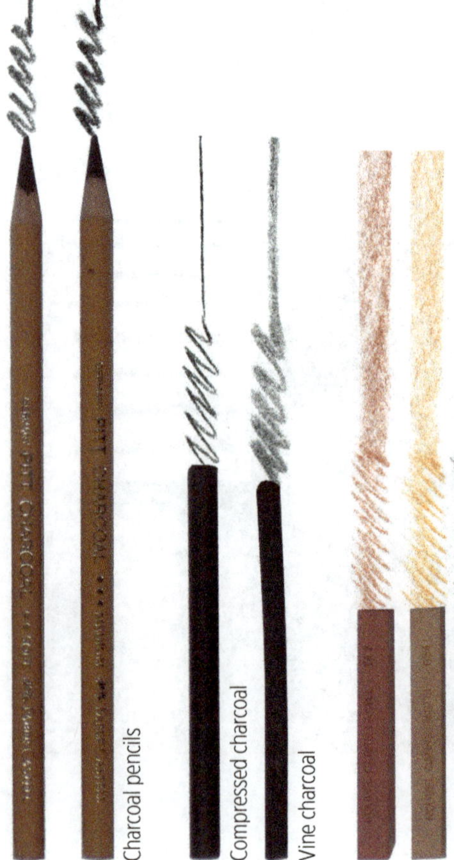

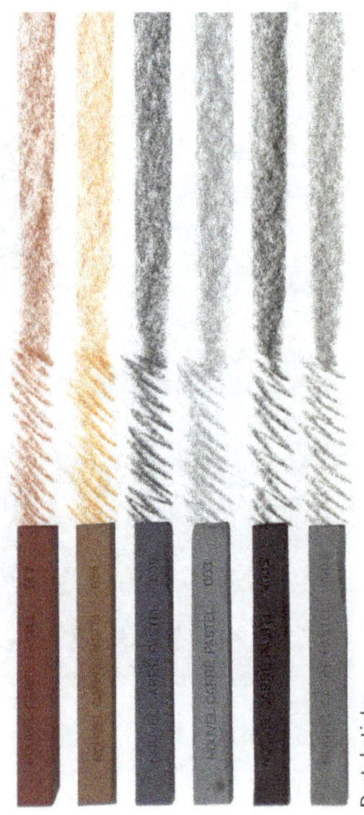

Charcoal and pastels typically create less detailed renderings than other types of media because of their wide, soft tips. Both can be used quite effectively on colored paper and blended easily using a blending stick, cotton ball, or Q-tip. Erasers or chalk sticks can be used after tone is applied to create lighter lines or highlights within the drawing.

Pastels create translucent washes of color that should be applied with a light touch so as not to look overworked. One technique for applying pastels is to use pastel dust to create solid washes of color.

Charcoal can be used to create highly evocative drawings because of the darkness of the media and the use of blending to create seamless transitions from light to dark. There are different types of charcoal, ranging from vine charcoal, which creates a soft, dark stroke, to compressed charcoal, which creates a thinner line and doesn't blend as easily. Charcoal pencils are used to create more detailed lines within a drawing and come in soft, medium, and hard varieties.

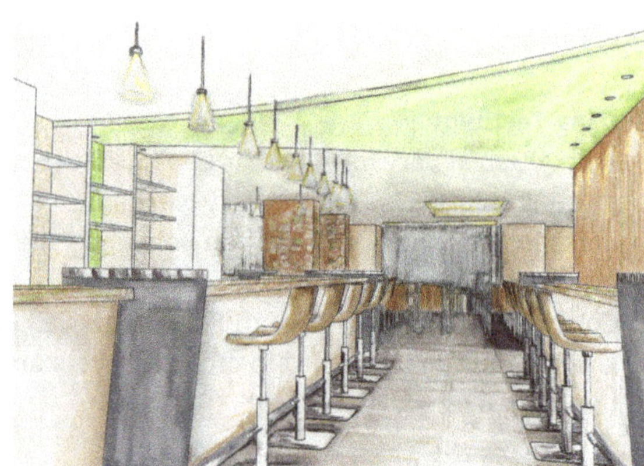

KIBWE DAISY
Interior Design concept for a restaurant
Pastel perspective with colored pencil highlights
Arrowstreet

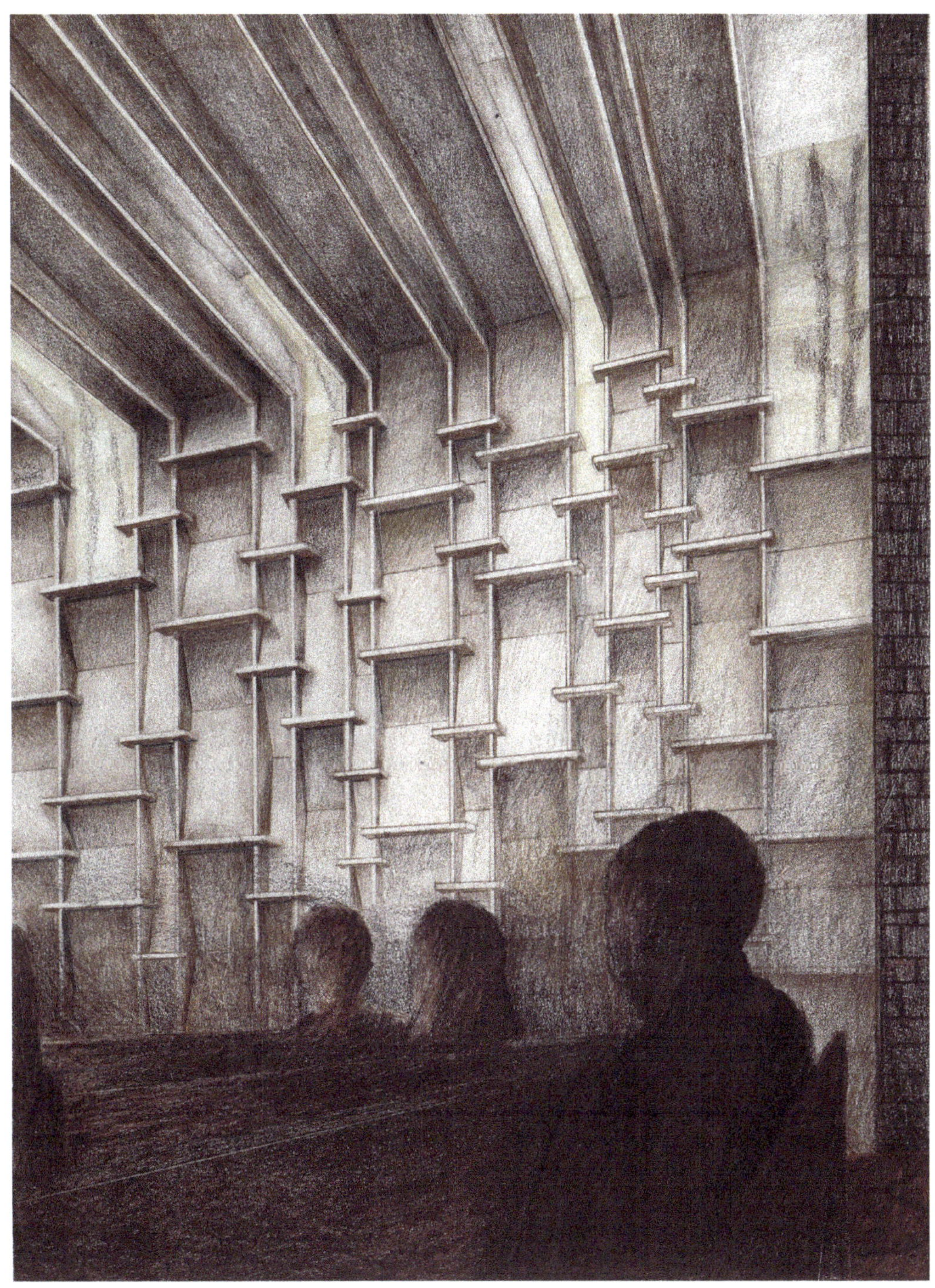

Soo Im
Colored pencil perspective
Design Studio,
Massachusetts Institute of Technology

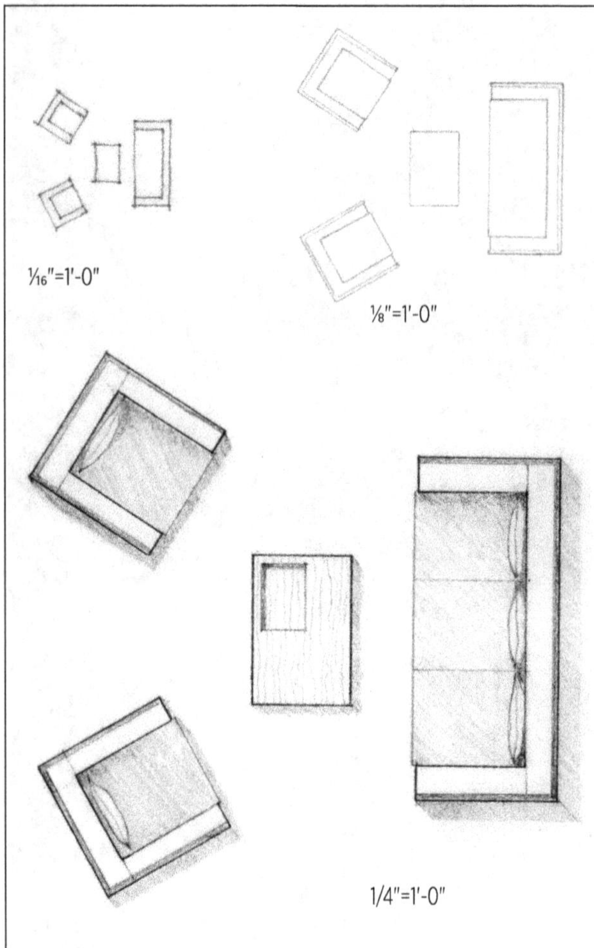

Furniture Scale and Detail
As the scale of your drawing increases, you are required to include additional information for the furniture in your drawing.

- Furniture drawn at 1/16" = 1'-0" and 1/8" = 1'-0" are drawn as outlines with furniture templates or freehand sketching.
- Furniture drawn at 1/4" = 1'-0" or larger include more detail in order to show how the design is specific to the project and include shadows.

Adding Entourage
Entourage is a term that describes scaled elements within a space, such as people, cars, furniture, and plants and other decorative objects.

Designers add entourage to a drawing to test out the proportion and scale of the spaces they are designing and to convey to others how the space is to be used.

There are many different techniques for adding entourage to a drawing. In early concept and process drawings, people and objects are usually sketched in with a pencil or pen. For more developed drawings, people are more carefully drawn, and furniture is usually drawn with templates or drafted with more detail. The level of detail is dependent on the scale of the drawing.

Relationship of Entourage to Drawing
Regardless of the method chosen to add entourage, it is important that people and objects are added to the drawing in a way that complements the line work or rendering techniques. If the entourage is added using a completely different technique, it can overpower the drawing. The drawings on the facing page illustrate a close relationship between hand-drawn entourage and the style of the rendered drawing.

1

JONATHAN C. GARLAND
Facing page, top
Marker perspective
Degree Project Studio,
Boston Architectural College

2

KEVIN ASMUS
Facing page, middle
Ink and pencil perspectives
Degree Project Studio,
Boston Architectural College

3

ARROWSTREET
Facing page, bottom
Colored pencil elevation

Marker Rendered Entourage

- The crowd of people, in the marker drawing on the right, were delineated with loose ink lines and rendered with random swatches of color.
- This technique allowed the student to quickly render the drawing and communicate the use and scale of the space.

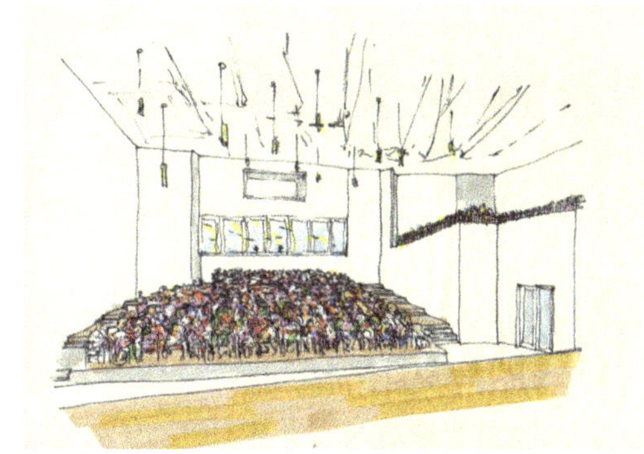

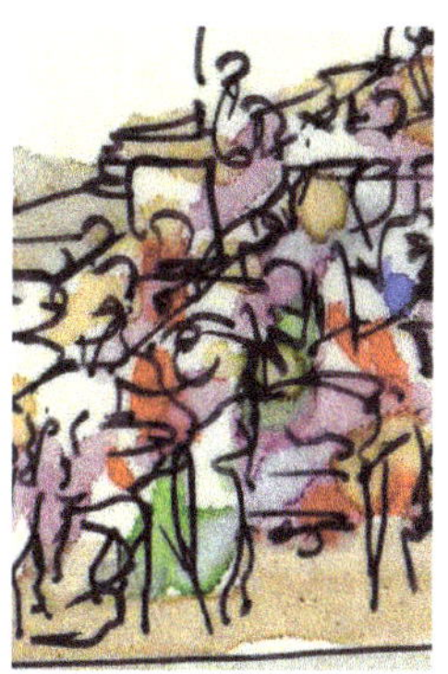

1

Ink-and-Pencil-Rendered Entourage

- In the pen-and-ink perspective on the right, figures of people were suggested with a minimal amount of lines and drawn to match the rest of the perspective.
- In the more developed pencil rendering the closest figure contains the most detail, and the figure's shadow is used to define the ground plane. The figures in the distance are suggested with looser line work.
- When inserting people in perspective, the eye level of figures standing on the ground plane should always align with the horizon line, no matter how far away they are from the viewer.

2

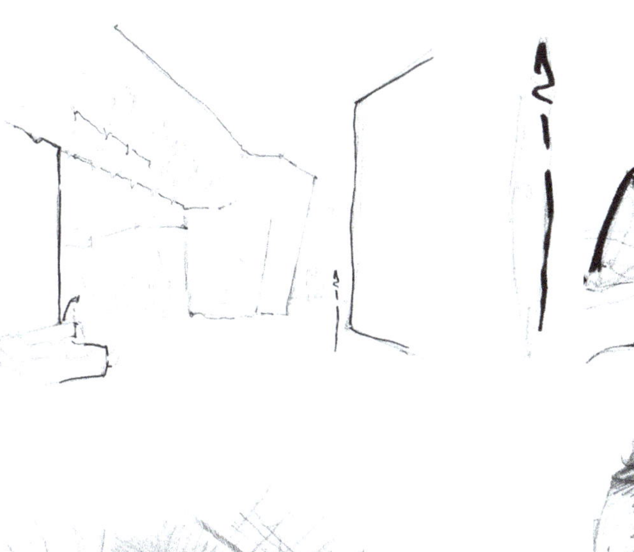

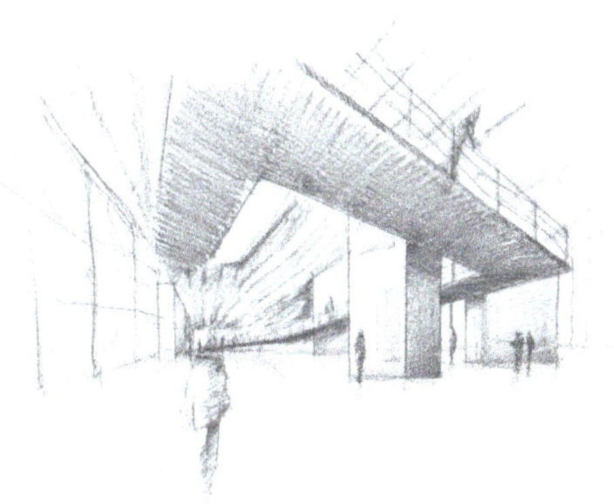

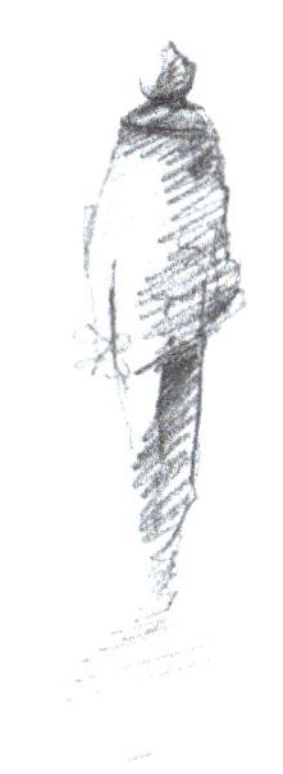

Colored Pencil–Rendered Entourage

The people, trees, cars, and furniture in the colored-pencil-and-ink rendering below all share the same line and tone quality as the building.

3

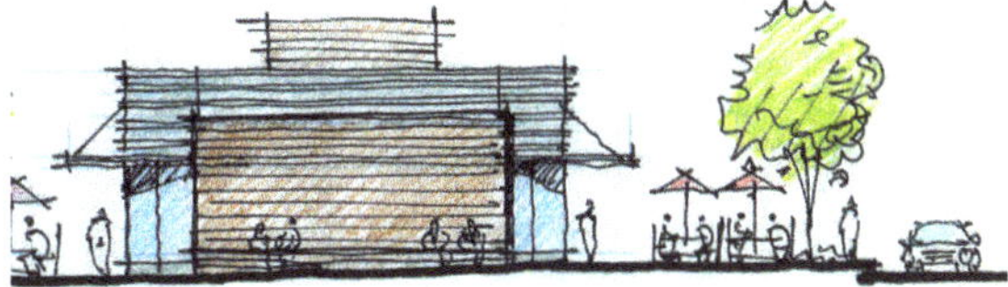

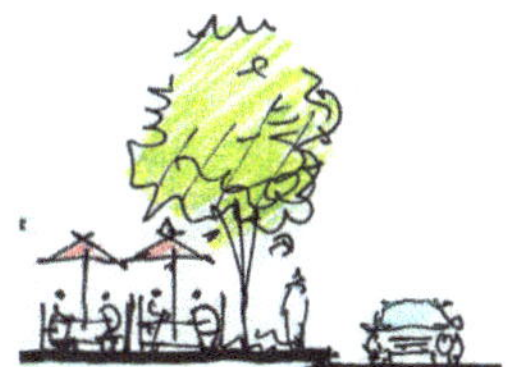

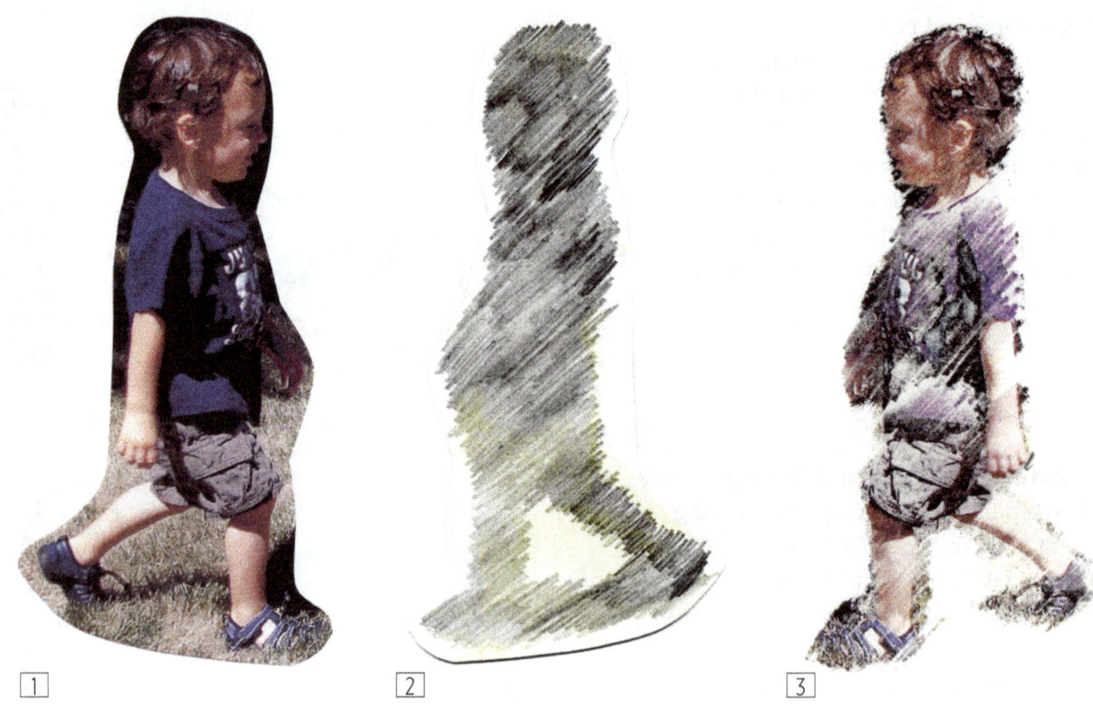

1 2 3

Acetone Transfer Technique

Acetone, or nail polish remover, is highly effective for transferring people and objects onto drawings from existing photographs. The technique has a hand-drawn quality that complements pencil, ink, and colored pencil renderings.

Step 1: Select Image

Choose a magazine image (on matte paper), or print out a photograph, and cut out the profile of the object that you wish to transfer.

Step 2: Transfer Image

- Place the image facedown on your drawing, and apply a liberal amount of acetone to the back, using a cotton ball or paintbrush.
- With a pencil, or other hard-tipped object, rub the entire back side of the image to transfer the photo to your drawing. You will need to apply a fair amount of pressure in order for the ink to transfer. Keep the direction of your pencil strokes consistent because these will be visible in the final image. If the acetone starts to evaporate before you have finished rubbing, simply apply more acetone to the back of the image.

Step 3: Reveal Image

- Before lifting the image off of the drawing, peel away a corner of the image to make sure it has fully transferred.
- After confirming, peel away the image to reveal the transferred photo.
- This technique can also be used to transfer printed text onto paper, such as vellum or Mylar, and onto model building materials, such as chipboard and basswood.

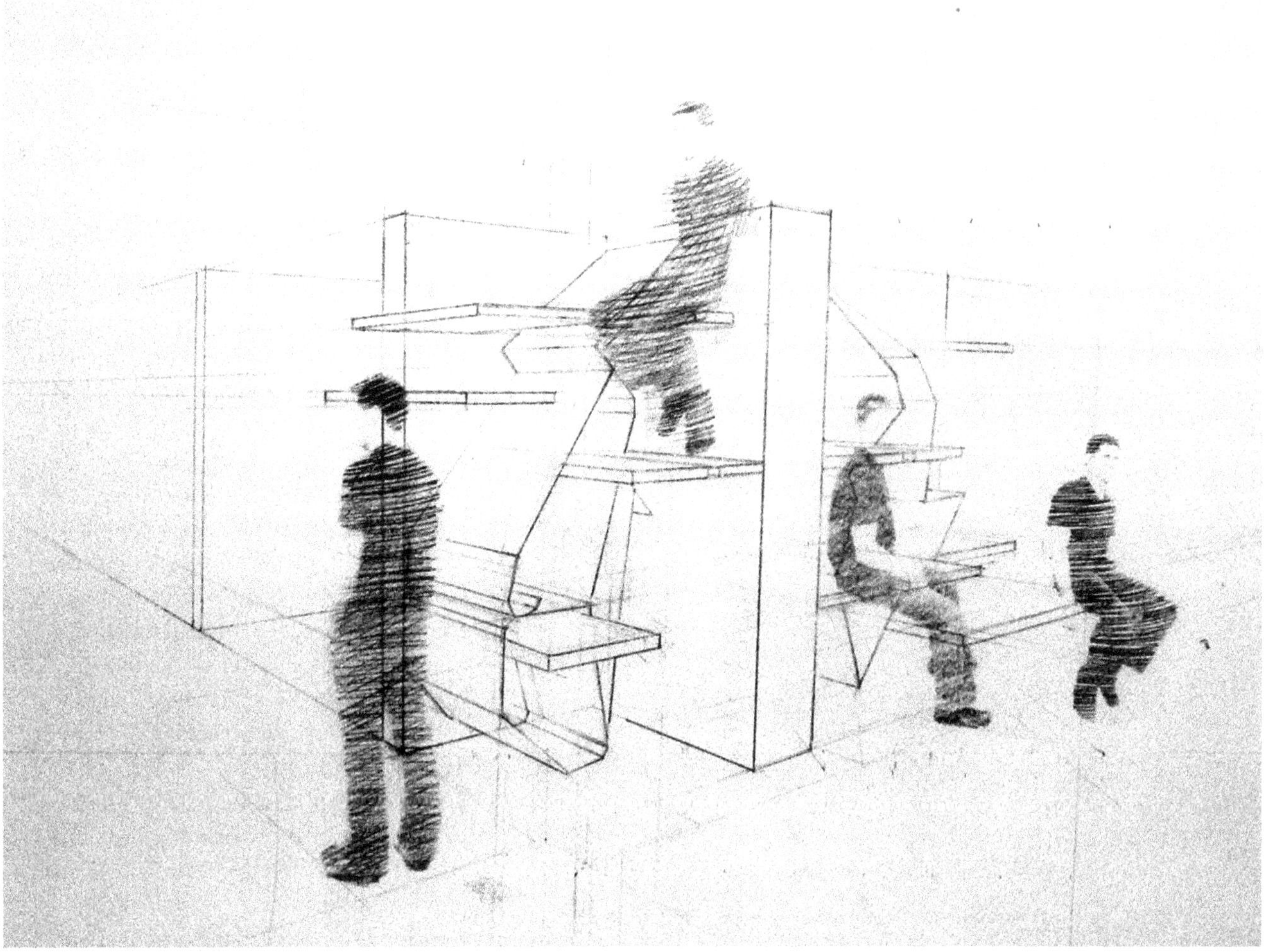

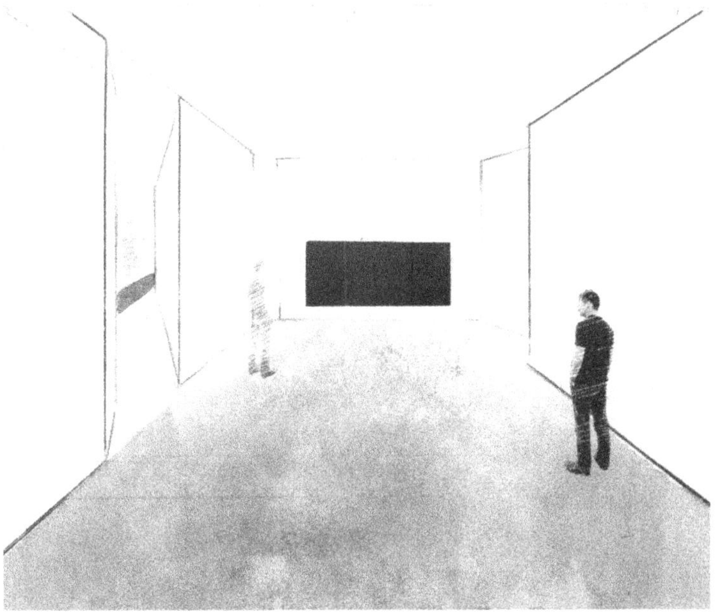

BRIAN KERR
Pencil drawings with acetone transfer people
Master's A Studio,
Boston Architectural College

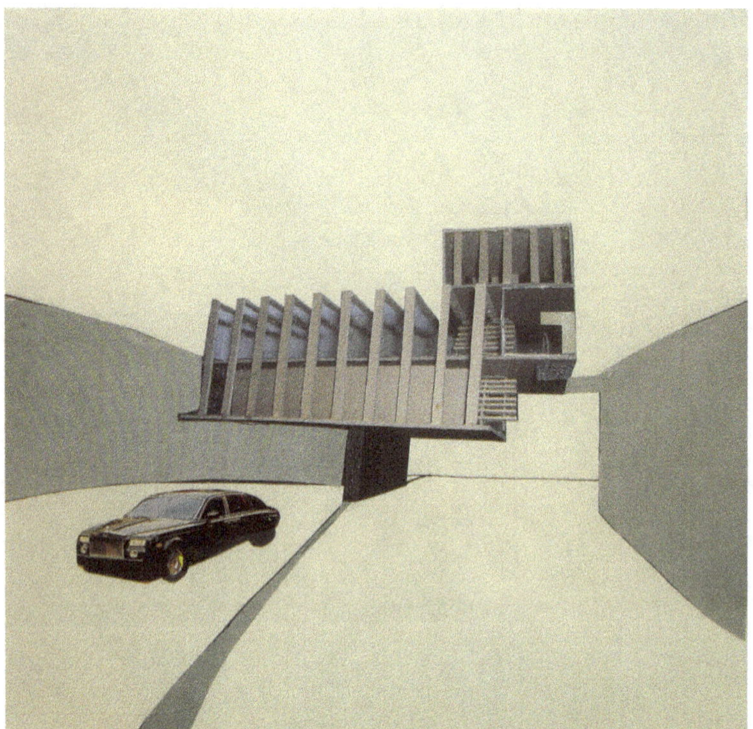

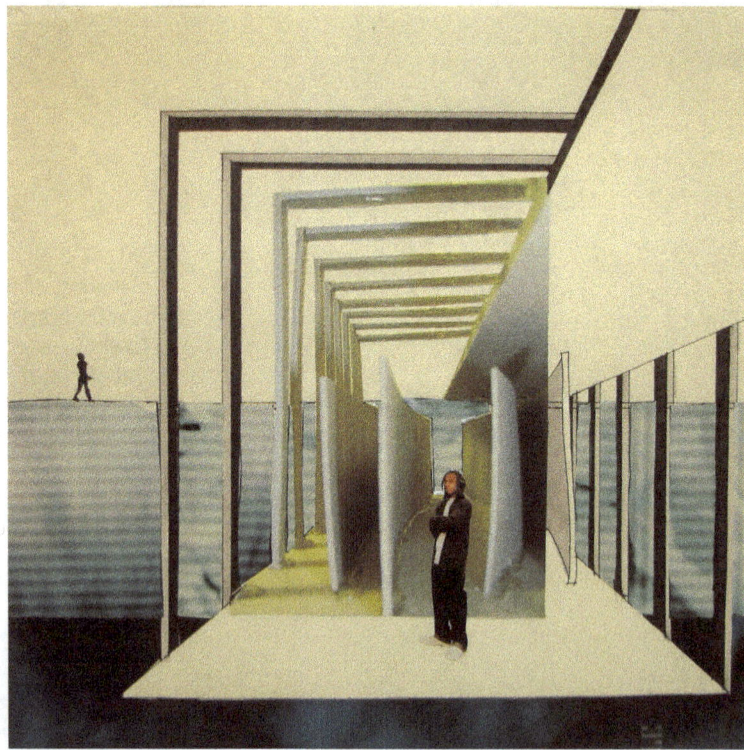

KIRSTEN A. LAWSON
Model photos, colored paper, and magazine photos
Master's A Studio,
Boston Architectural College

Collage adds tone, color, and entourage to drawings by gluing papers onto a two-dimensional surface. Collage typically creates a more abstract image than the photo-realistic rendering techniques outlined earlier in the chapter, making it a great medium to use during ideation.

Collage Techniques

- The most basic technique is to cut papers with solid colors or abstract patterns into shapes and use them to fill in wall and floor surfaces within a pencil or ink line drawing.
- More successful collages add color, tone, and surface pattern by using papers without recognizable imagery on them. For example, choosing papers with solid colors or abstract patterns instead of a magazine image with a photo of a window or door allows the designer to create a collage that is more specific to his or her design intentions.
- Photographs of the site context can be combined with hand drawings to illustrate the relationships between the design and its context.
- Another effective collage technique is to merge photographs of a physical model with images of scale figures and site photos to simulate perspective views of the project. This is a quick technique to use when you do not have time to draw a perspective.
- The decision on how to splice different collage elements together also influences the reading of the collage. In general, you want to locate the seam at a corner or edge of an object.
- To create a more uniform surface quality, a final collage can be scanned in or photocopied. This eliminates the reflective surface typically found on collages created with magazine papers and can reduce the emphasis on the splices between the various papers.

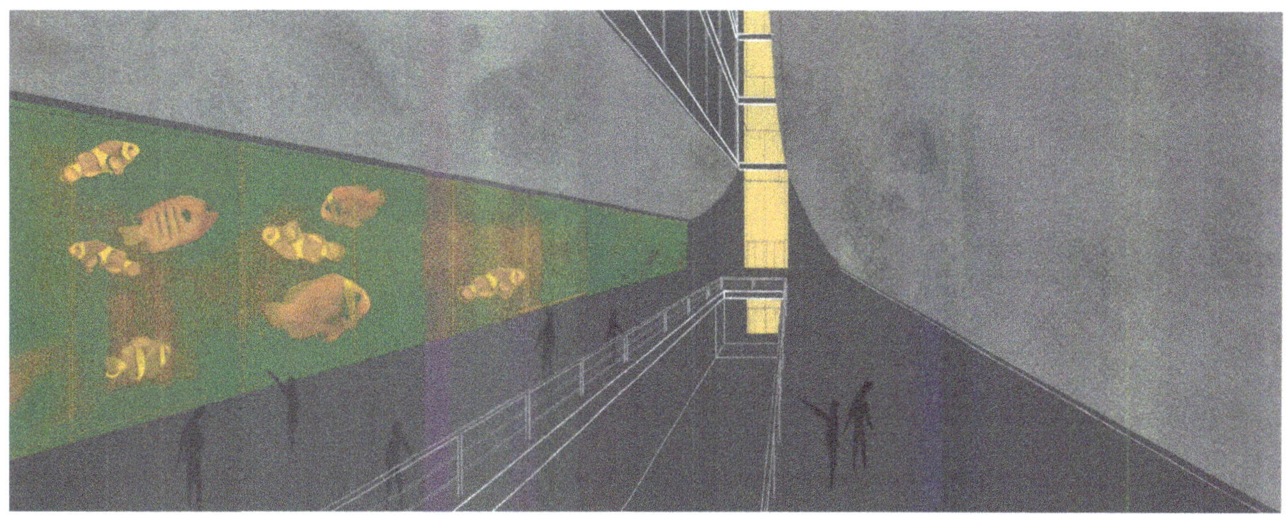

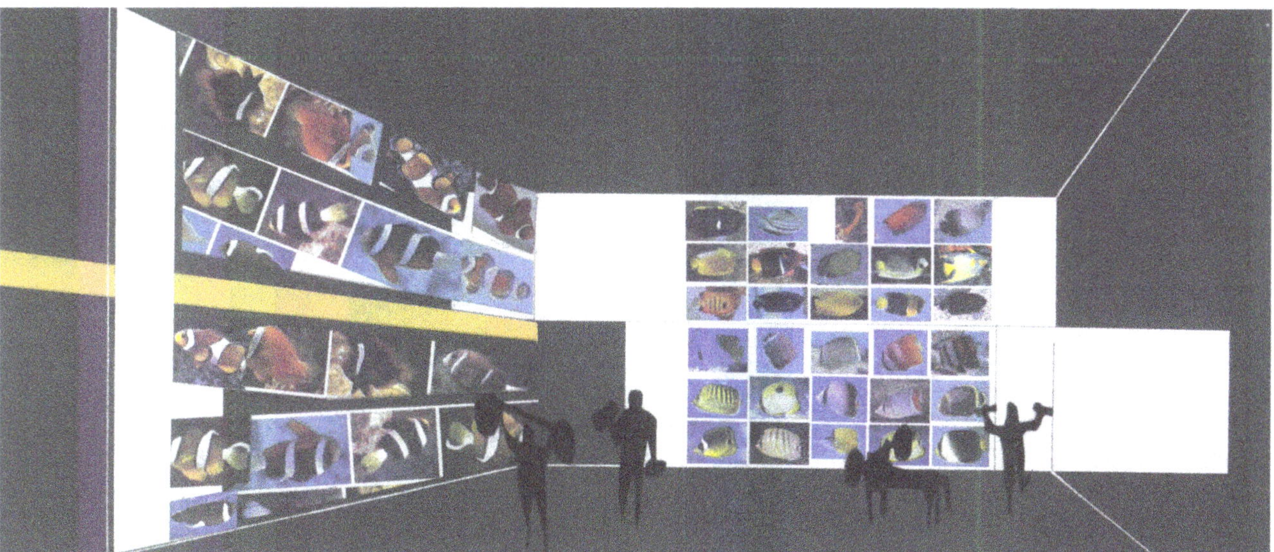

ELENA RAYA
Perspective collages
Design Studio,
Harvard Graduate School of Design

Photoshop Overview

With a mastery of just a few basic tools, beginning students can use Photoshop to digitally render and add entourage to hand drawings. This section introduces common Photoshop tools and commands.

Options Palette

When you select a tool icon, additional options for the tool will appear in a row below the menu.

History Palette

Shows all past actions. You can undo previous actions by dragging an action into the trash.

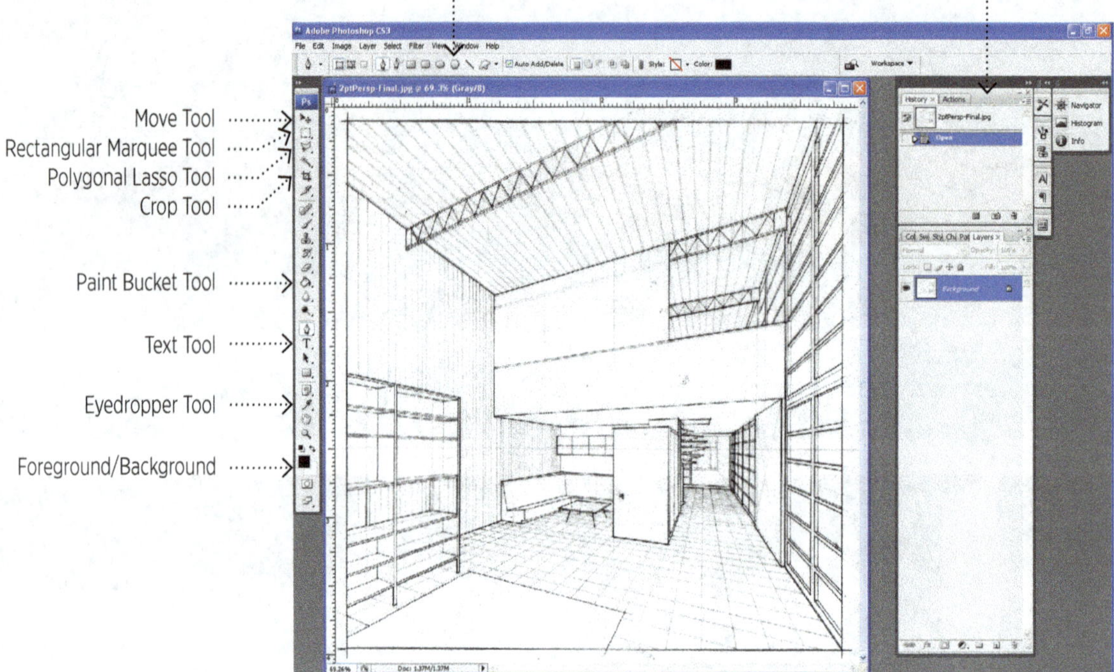

Tools Palette

- The TOOLS palette is located on the left side of Photoshop. Icons with an arrow in the lower right corner can be expanded to reveal additional tools.

Common Tools in the Tools Palette:

- **Move:** selects and moves layers within a drawing. To make a layer current, **RIGHT CLICK** on the layer when this tool is active.
- **Rectangular Marquee:** selects rectilinear shaped areas.
- **Polygonal Lasso:** selects irregular areas.
- **Crop:** crops a drawing.
- **Paint Bucket:** applies color to an area.
- **Text:** adds text to a drawing.
- **Eyedropper:** used to match colors from an existing drawing.
- **Foreground/Background Colors:** shows what colors are currently selected.

Layers Palette

Manages the layers within your drawing and allows you to set the opacity of each layer.

Keyboard Commands

Keyboard shortcuts are used to perform an action more quickly or when another tool is in use. Common shortcuts are listed below. (These may differ slightly for Macintosh users.)

- Zoom in: CTRL +
- Zoom out: CTRL -
- Select all: CTRL A
- Copy: CTRL C
- Paste: CTRL V
- Pan: press SPACEBAR

Rendering Step by Step

The step-by-step example on the following pages illustrates how to digitally render a perspective drawing. These same steps can be applied to render an elevation, plan, or section drawing. The first step in rendering any drawing in Photoshop is to apply fields of color to all the surfaces within the drawing.

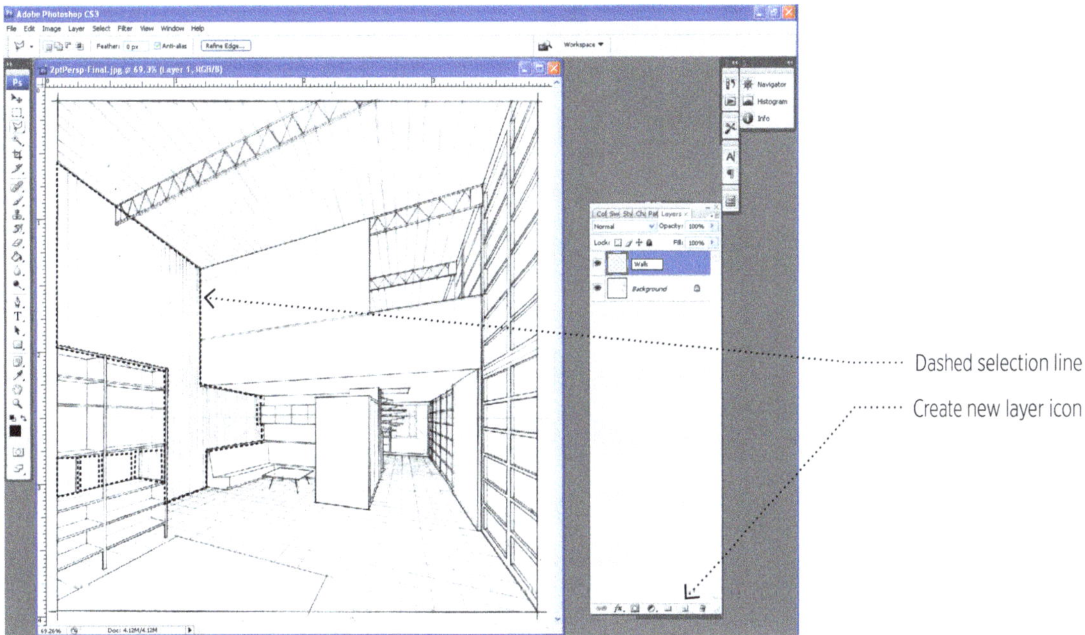

Step 1: Open Drawing

- Open your freehand drawing in Photoshop by choosing FILE > OPEN.
- Go to IMAGE > IMAGE SIZE to make your drawing smaller or larger and to change the resolution.

Step 2: Select a Surface to Be Colored

- Select the POLYGONAL LASSO tool in the TOOLS palette.
- Using the Lasso, CLICK ONCE on the corners of the area you wish to color, drawing a dashed selection line around the entire surface.
- To draw a horizontal or vertical line with the Lasso, hold down the SHIFT key.
- To close the outline, DOUBLE CLICK, or hold the mouse over the start point until a small circle appears under the Lasso icon.
- After closing the outline, you can add areas to the selection by holding down the SHIFT key or delete areas by holding down the ALT key and clicking on the corners of the area to add or subtract.

Step 3: Create a New Layer for the Color

- Create a new layer by clicking the CREATE NEW LAYER icon under the LAYERS palette. Re-name the layer by DOUBLE CLICKING the LAYER NAME. To make a layer current, click the LAYER NAME within the LAYERS palette so that it is highlighted in blue.
- This new layer will be used on which to place the wall material. You will want to create a new layer for each color in your drawing in order to more readily adjust the colors as your rendering develops.

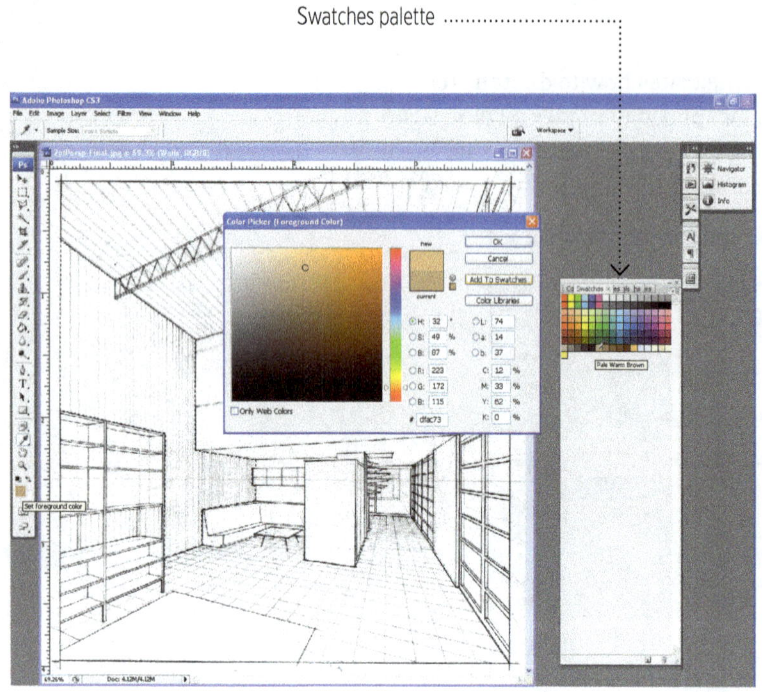

Step 4: Select a Color

- To choose a color for the wall, select the SWATCHES palette, and click on one of the standard colors. The color should appear in the FOREGROUND/ BACKGROUND square in the TOOLS palette.
- To adjust the color, DOUBLE-CLICK on the foreground or background color in the TOOLS palette to bring up the COLOR PICKER box. In this box you can type in the RGB or CMYK value or adjust the color by picking a new hue and value.

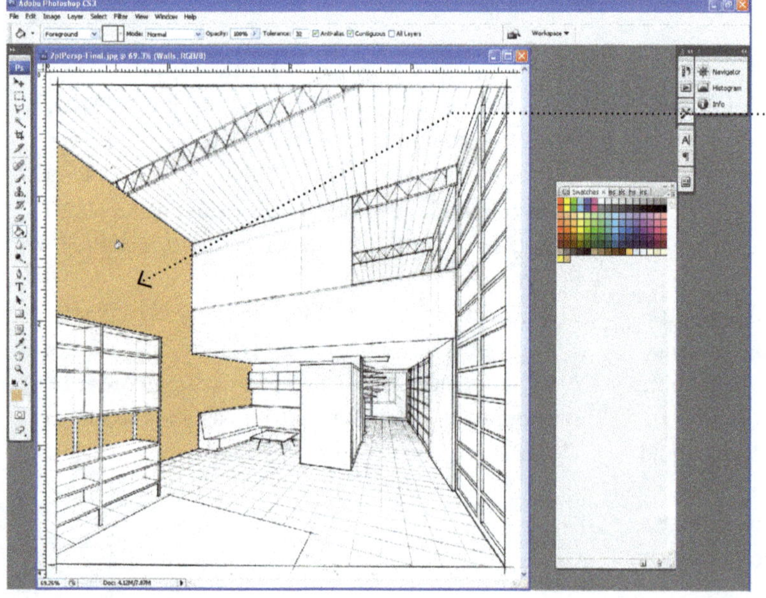

Step 5: Paint the Selected Area

- Select the PAINT BUCKET tool from the TOOLS palette.
- CLICK anywhere within the selection outline to fill the area with color.

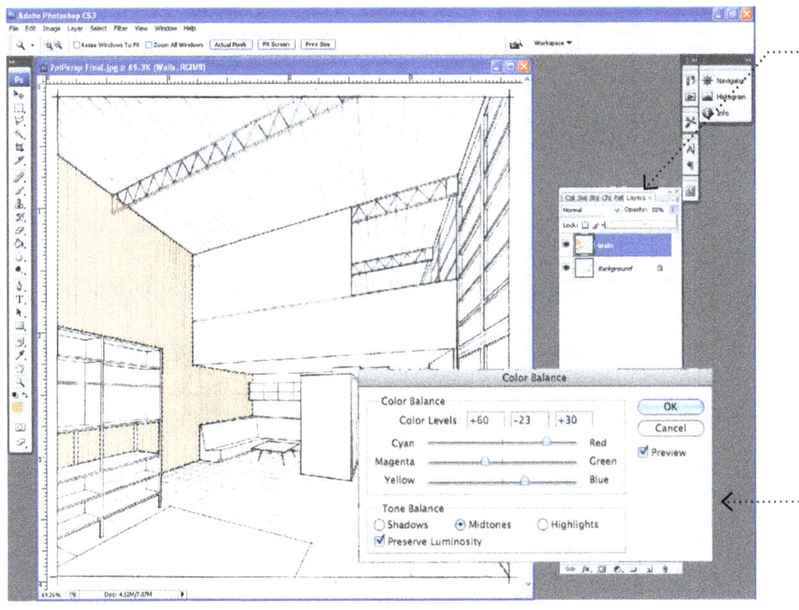

Step 6: Adjust the Opacity of the Color

- To view the line work underneath the newly painted wall, select the LAYERS palette, and adjust the opacity of the layer by either dragging the opacity bar or typing in a new percentage.
- You may also change the blending mode, located to the left of the opacity percentage, from NORMAL to MULTIPLY or OVERLAY.
- To remove a portion of the color, use the POLYGONAL LASSO tool to select the area, and press DELETE on the keyboard.
- To adjust colors once they have been applied, go to IMAGE > ADJUSTMENTS > COLOR BALANCE to pull up the COLOR BALANCE box.

Step 7: Add Color to the Rest of the Drawing

- Repeat steps 2 through 6 to color in the remaining areas of the drawing.
- Remember to create a new layer for each new color that you add.
- A gradation of color can be created with the GRADIENT tool.
- To use the GRADIENT tool, first DOUBLE-CLICK on FOREGROUND COLOR and BACKGROUND COLOR to select light and dark color values for your gradient.
- Choose the GRADIENT tool from the TOOLS palette, and DRAG YOUR MOUSE within the selected area to apply the gradient.
- The gradient will be applied in the direction of your mouse stroke.
- In this example the ceiling plane was rendered with the GRADIENT tool.

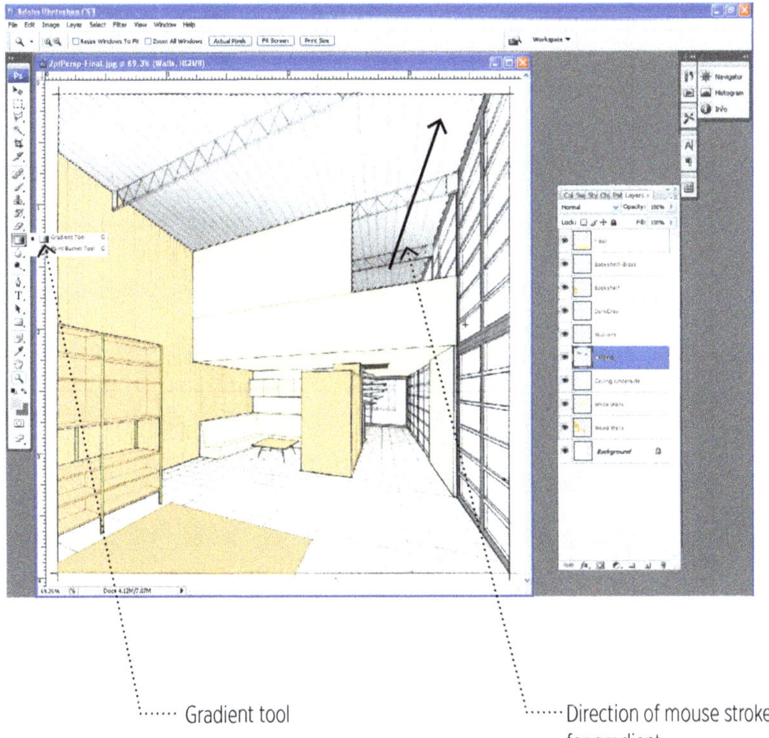

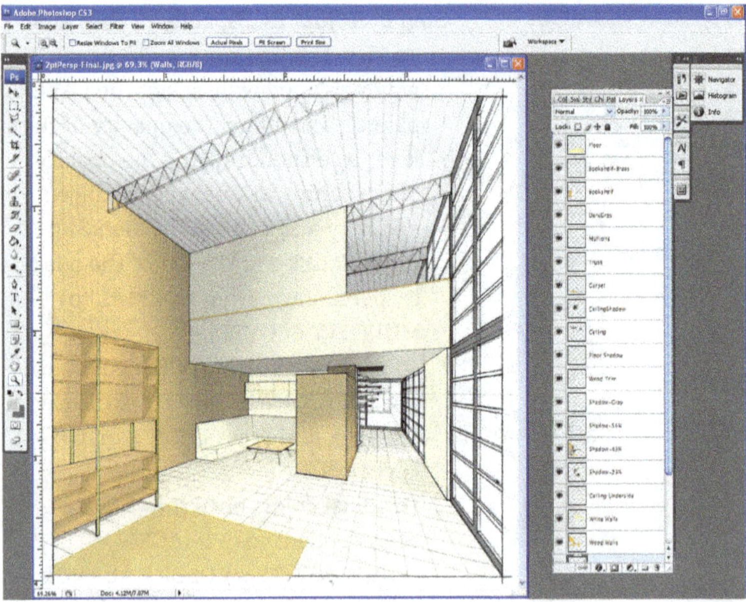

Step 8: Add Shadows and Detail

- Select the area to receive the shadow with the POLYGONAL LASSO tool.
- Create a new layer to put the shadow on.
- In the example the shadows were grouped onto five different layers so that the opacity could be adjusted for different areas of the drawing.
- Choose the light and dark color values for the gradient by DOUBLE-CLICKING FOREGROUND/ BACKGROUND COLORS under the TOOLS palette.
- Select the GRADIENT tool from the TOOLS palette.
- Click and drag the mouse within the selected area to apply the gradient.
- Adjust the OPACITY of the shadow layer to achieve the desired shadow value.
- You may also change the BLEND MODE of your shadow layer to DARKEN or MULTIPLY.
- This image shows the areas of shadows that were applied to the drawing.

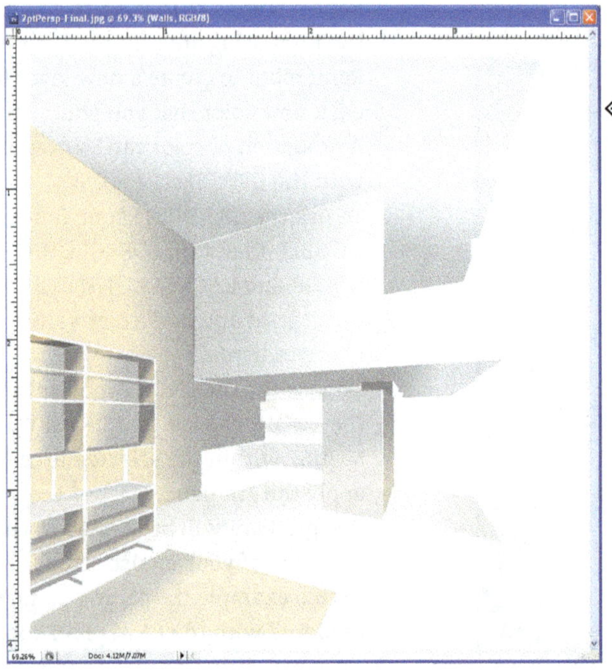

Step 9: Add Background Photo
The landscape outside the building was added, using a photograph of trees as a base.

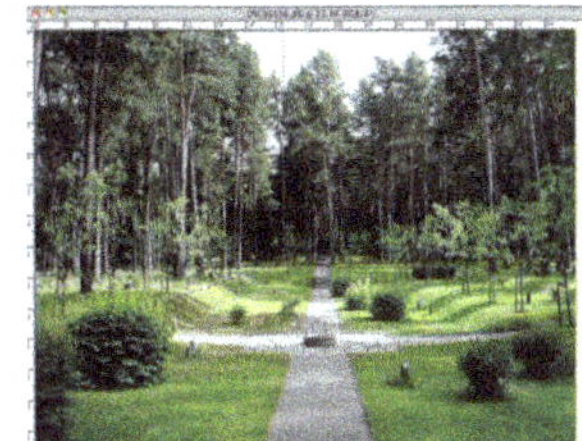
9A

Step 9A:
- Select the area of the photo to use with the POLYGONAL LASSO tool.

Step 9B:
- The area was copied into Photoshop and mirrored to align with the perspective in the drawing.
- To mirror an object, go to EDIT > TRANSFORM > FLIP HORIZONTAL.
- Using the DISTORT tool, the photograph was stretched to align with the windows.
- To distort an object, go to EDIT > TRANSFORM > DISTORT, and drag the grips to adjust the image.

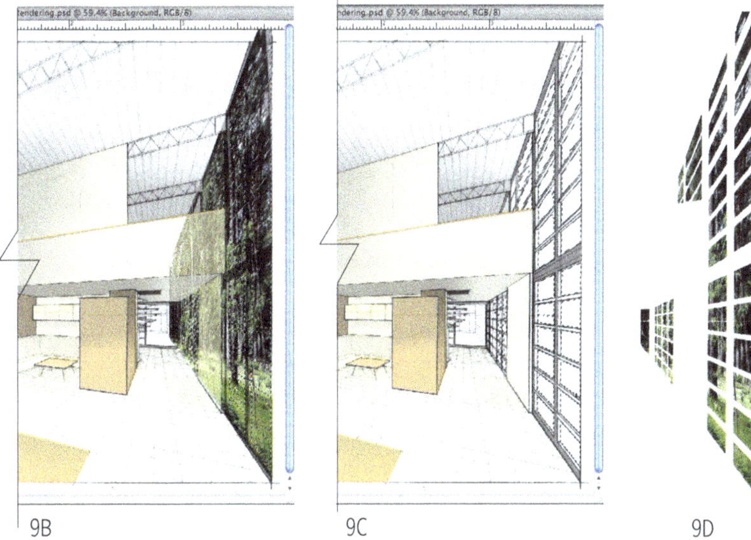
9B 9C 9D

Step 9C:
- After turning off the background photo layer, the window outlines were selected on the background drawing layer, using the MAGIC WAND tool, from the TOOLS palette.
- To use the MAGIC WAND tool, click in the center of the area you wish to select. You can adjust the tolerance in the options bar.

Step 9D:
- The background photo layer was turned on and made current. CTRL + C was used to copy the areas of the photo within the window outlines.

Step 9E:
- The opacity of the background photo layer was set at 40% to help blend the photo with the rest of the rendering.

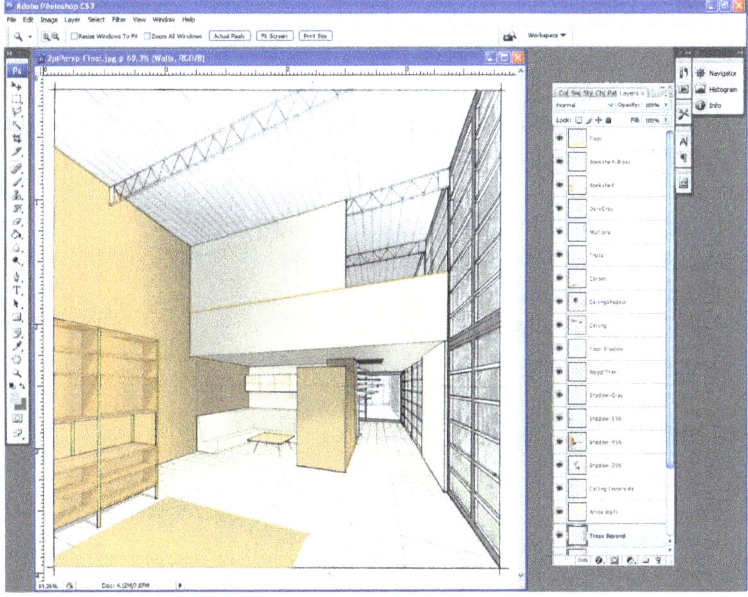
9E

Adding Entourage with Photoshop

Most designers and design firms build their own entourage libraries, using photographs of people, objects, and vehicles that have been downloaded from the Internet or photographed by the designer. Many students start building their own libraries during school, taking photos of people and objects in plan, elevation, and perspective and using these images to populate their drawings. In general, it is better to photograph your own entourage in order to maintain a higher resolution and more control over the angle of view.

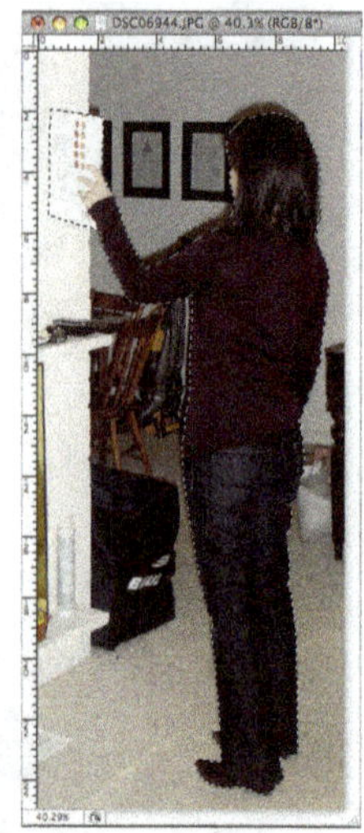

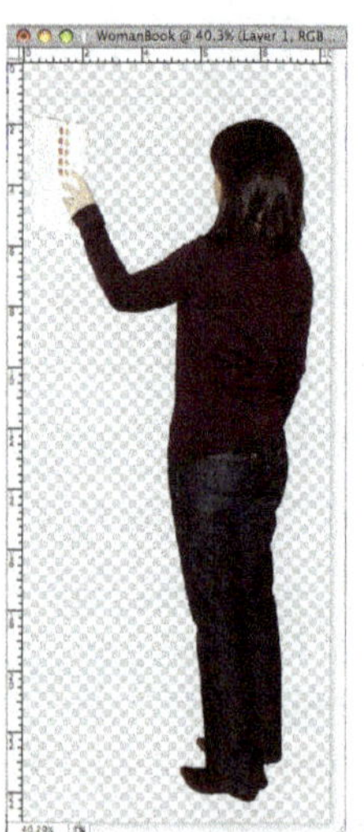

10A

Step 10A: Add Entourage

- OPEN the photograph in Photoshop.
- Select the POLYGONAL LASSO tool, and draw an outline around the person or object.
- To save the image into your library, copy and paste the selection into a new window, using CTRL + C, CTRL + N, and CTRL + V.
- SAVE the image as an EPS file to maintain the object without a background.

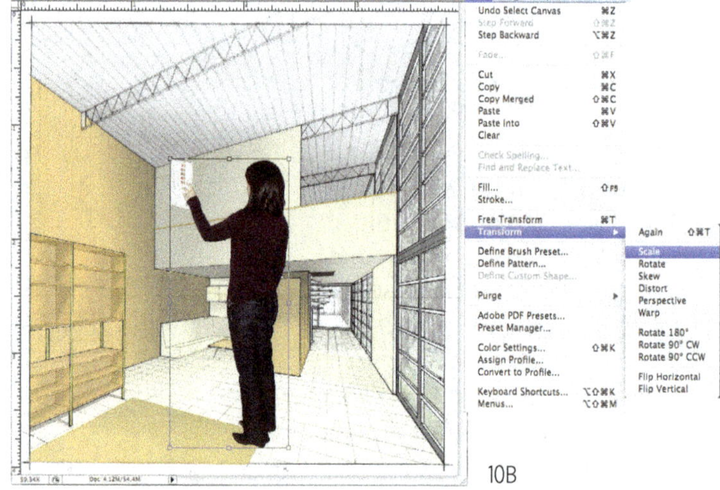

10B

Step 10B:

- COPY the selection into your main drawing. The image will be put on a new layer and will most likely be at a larger or smaller scale than your drawing.
- To SCALE the person or object, go to EDIT > TRANSFORM > SCALE to activate the scale command.
- Hold down the SHIFT key to scale the image proportionally, and drag your mouse from the corner grips of the image to the center of the image to decrease the scale. Drag your mouse the opposite way to increase the scale.

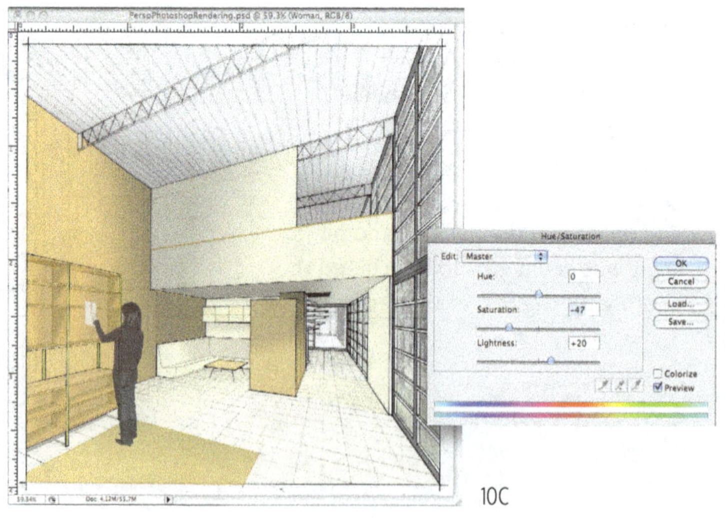

10C

Step 10C:

- MOVE the image to the desired location on the drawing.
- To help blend the photograph with the hand drawing, it is common to change the OPACITY of the image to 75%, making it semitransparent.
- Another way to integrate the image with the drawing is to decrease the saturation and increase the lightness, by selecting the HUE/SATURATION box from IMAGE > ADJUSTMENTS > HUE/SATURATION.

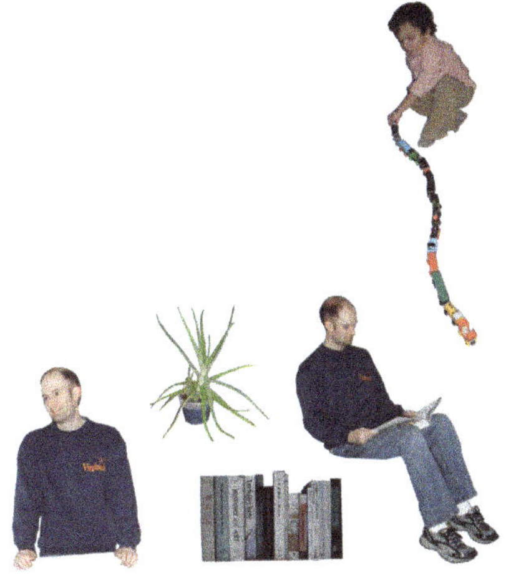

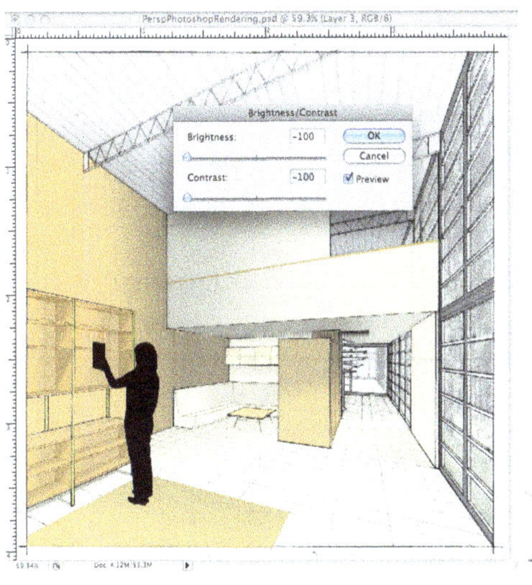

11A

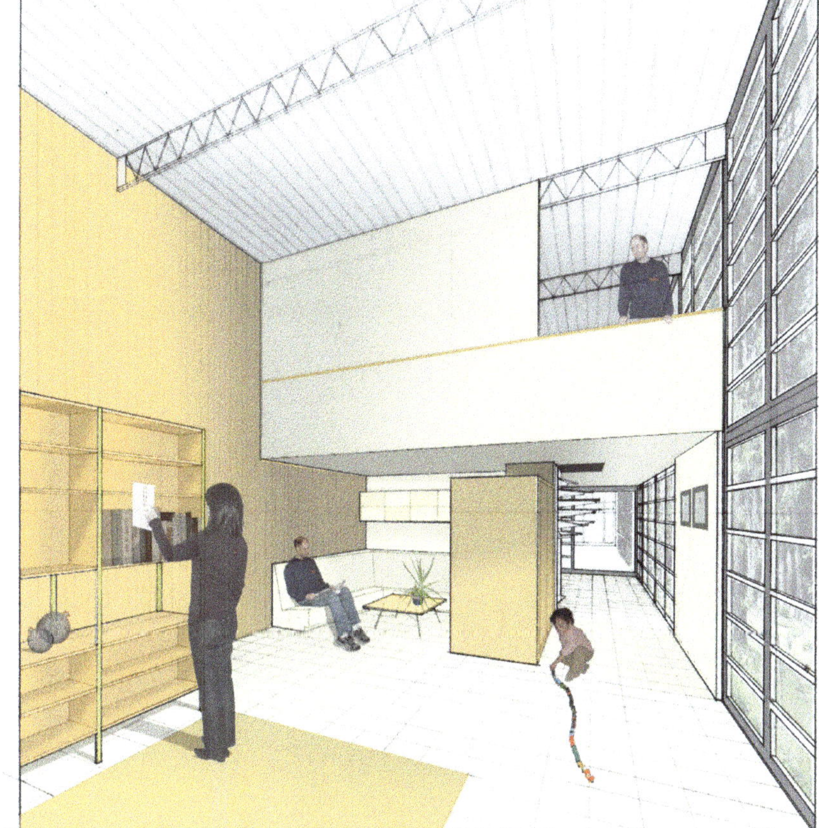

11C

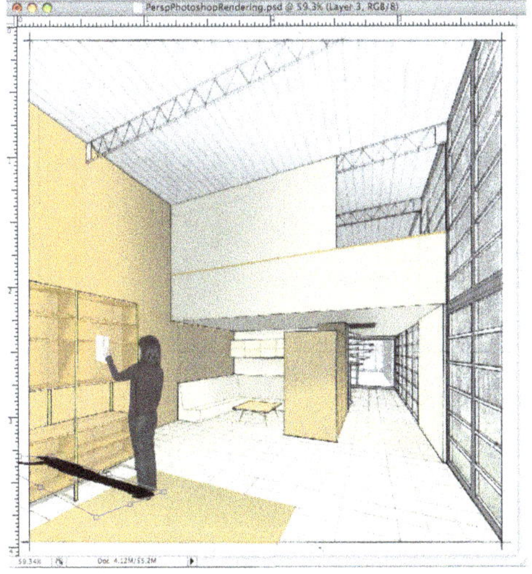

11B

Step 11A: Create Shadows

- To create a shadow, make a copy of the person, and change the brightness and contrast to -100, under IMAGE > ADJUSTMENTS > BRIGHTNESS/ CONTRAST.

Step 11B:

- Move the shadow layer below the person layer, in the LAYERS palette. Select EDIT > TRANSFORM > DISTORT, and drag the corner grips to make the shadow appear as if it is projected on the floor.

Step 11C:

- Change the OPACITY of the shadow to SEMI-TRANSPARENT, matching the other shadows within the rendering.
- Complete the rendering by repeating these steps to populate the drawing with additional objects and people.

Rendering Exterior Elevations in Photoshop

In this example the same tools and techniques were used to render the elevation as for the perspective Photoshop rendering. The main difference between the two is the use of photographs to depict the materials on the exterior facade and to create a more realistic rendering.

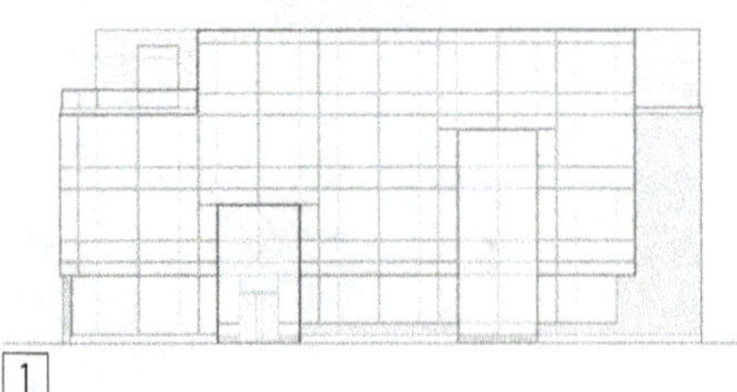

1

Step 1: Open Line Drawing into Photoshop

- The elevation was exported from AutoCAD as an **EPS** file and opened in Photoshop. An **EPS** file export preserves the line work and does not contain a background. This allows the line work to be layered on top of the photos in Photoshop.
- A hand-drawn elevation could also be used as a base for the digital rendering.

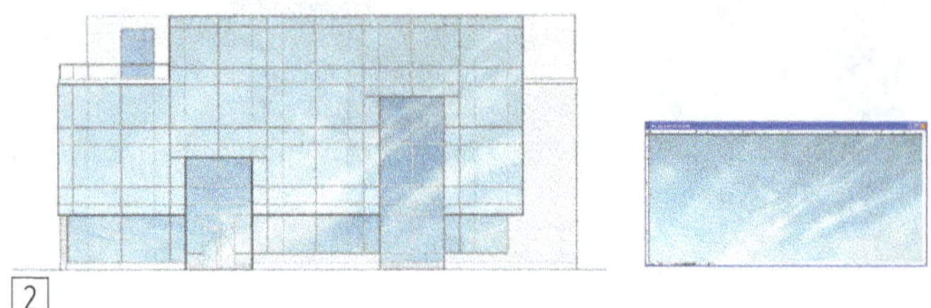

2

Step 2: Adding Materials (glazing)

- A photo of the sky was opened in Photoshop and copied into the elevation, to represent the window reflections.
- The POLYGONAL LASSO tool was used to trim the sky so that it aligned with the glazing.

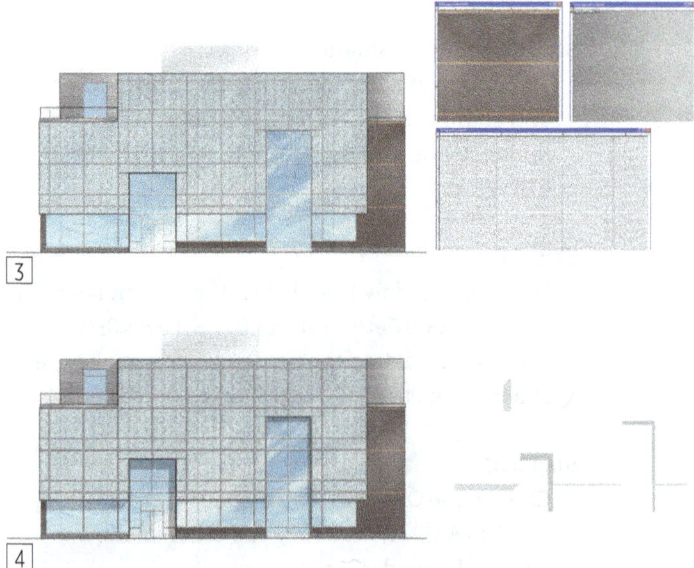

3

4

Step 3: Adding Materials

- Additional images, for the brick, metal, and screen pattern, were opened and copied into the elevation rendering.
- These images were also trimmed with the LASSO tool to align with the elevation.

Step 4: Adding Shadows

- All the shadows were created on a single layer with the opacity set at 30 percent.
- The LASSO tool was used to select the areas for shadows, and the PAINT BUCKET tool was used to fill in the areas with a gray tone.

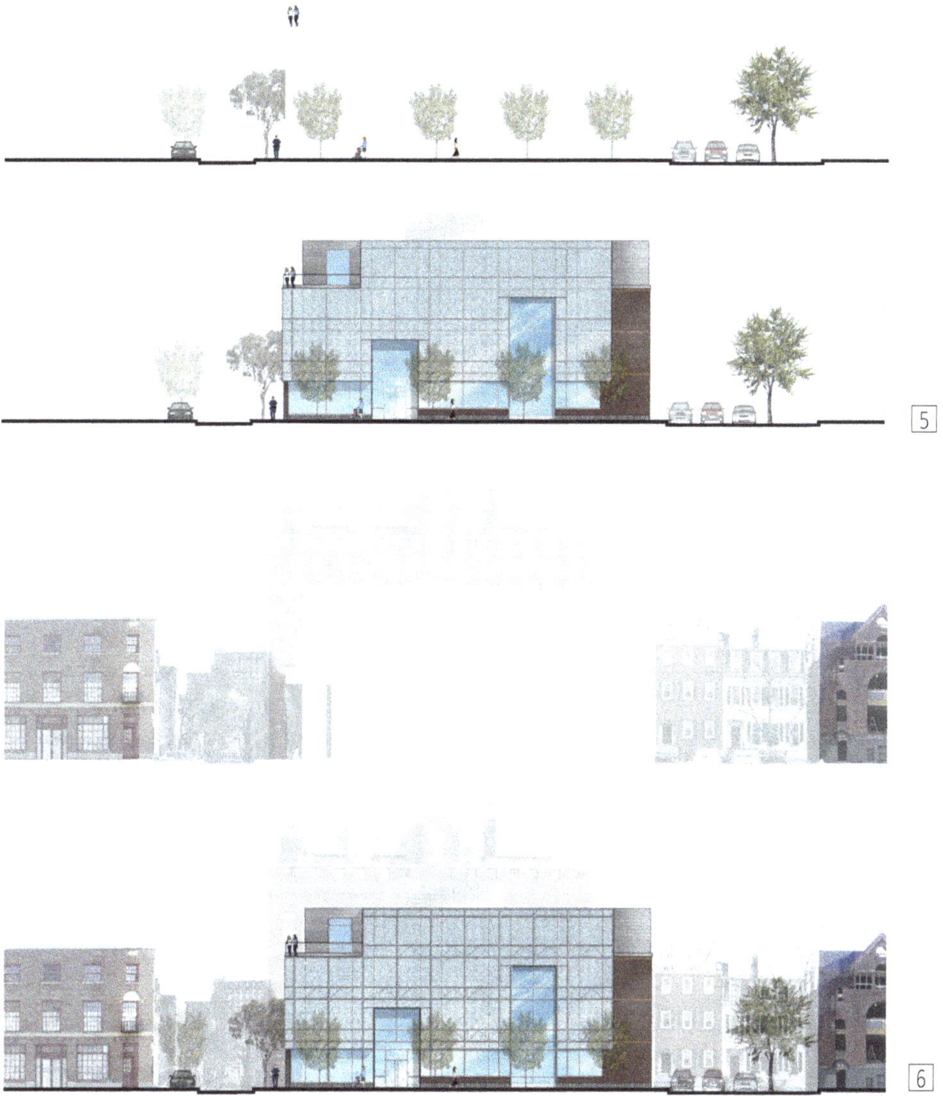

Step 5: Adding Entourage

- Trees, people, and vehicles were added to the rendering, using the same techniques outlined in the perspective step-by-step.

Step 6: Adding Site Context

- Adjacent buildings were added by copying in photos of their elevations and scaling them to the appropriate size.
- The opacity was set at 50 percent for the foreground buildings and 20 percent for the buildings beyond in order not to overpower the proposed elevation.

ARROWSTREET
Elevation study

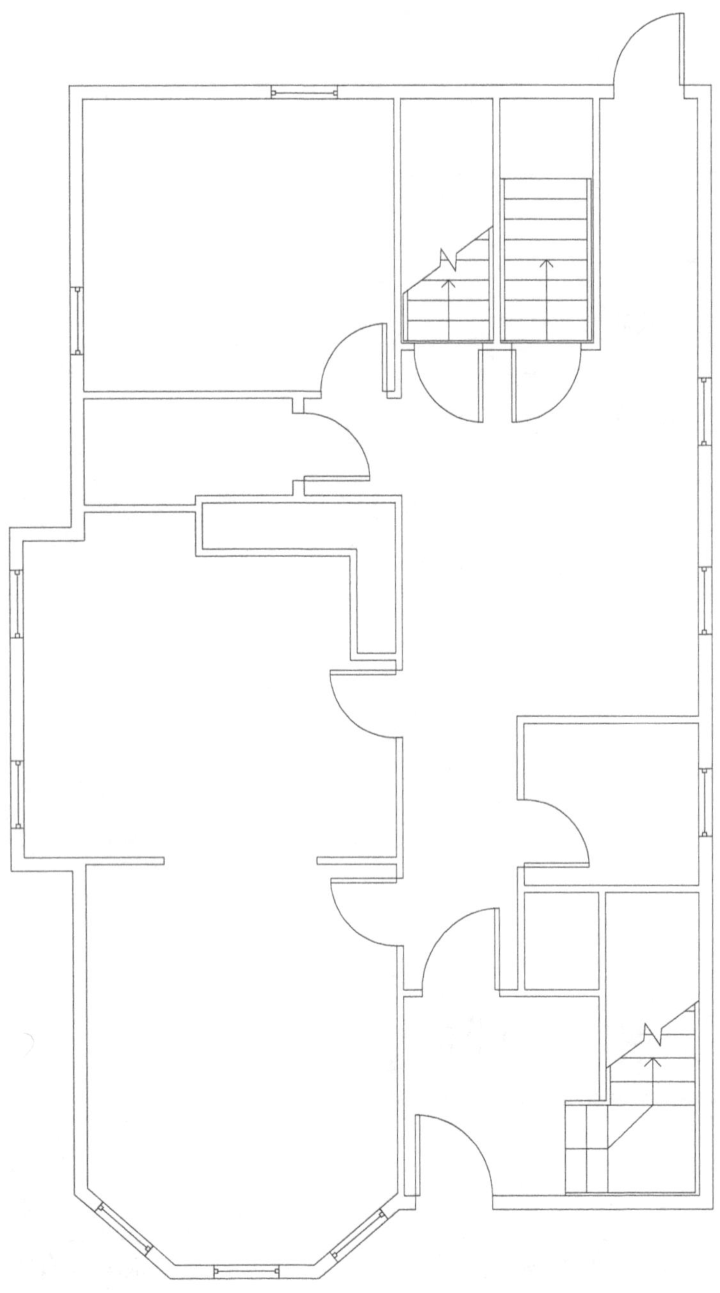

Floor plan
Scale: ⅛" = 1'-0"

Learning Exercise: Adding Entourage

This exercise is intended to help you improve your understanding of adding entourage at different scales to a plan drawing.

- Using the room names as a guide, add furniture, plants, and floor coverings to the ⅛" = 1'0" plan on this page, using your furniture templates.
- Draw in furniture on the ¼" = 1'-0" partial plan of the living and dining room on the facing page. This furniture should be drawn with more detail.
- The furniture for both plans should be located within the rooms to allow adequate clearance between items. For example, 3'-6" clearance should be maintained between a dining table and wall.

Learning Exercise: Rendering Plans

This exercise is intended to help you improve your understanding of rendering a floor plan to show materials. For this exercise, you will need four to six colors of marker or colored pencil.

- Apply an initial wash of color to all the areas of the drawing with controlled and consistent marker or colored pencil strokes.
- Add a second wash of color to areas that are in shadow, using marker or colored pencil.
- Render the surface details, to suggest materials, textures, and highlights, with colored pencil.
- Trace over the lines of the plan with a pencil or pen to convey the correct line weights. You may wish to poché the walls of the plan, to emphasize the plan cut.

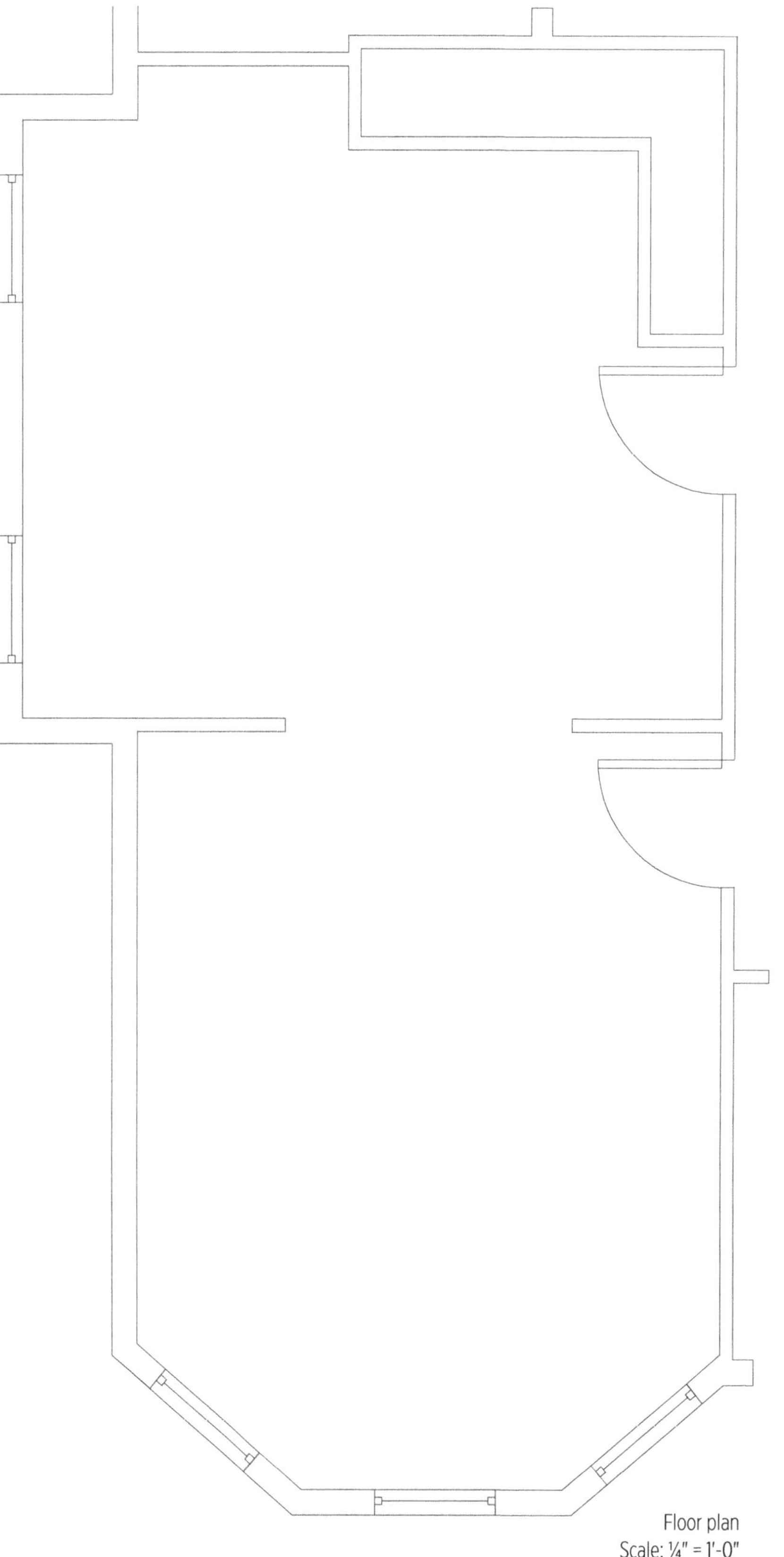

Floor plan
Scale: ¼" = 1'-0"

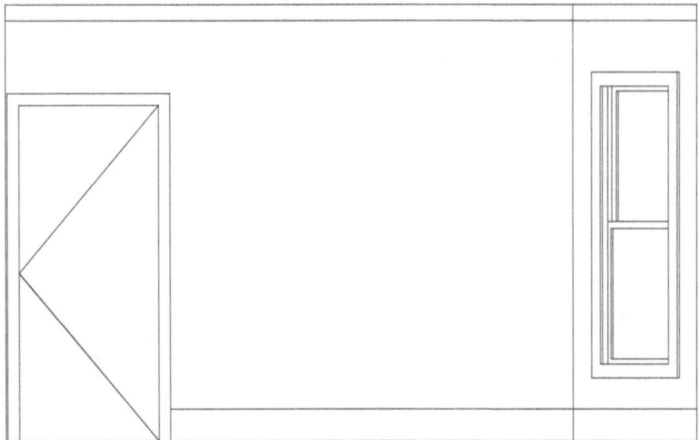

Interior elevation A
Scale: ¼" = 1'-0"

Interior elevation B
Scale: ¼" = 1'-0"

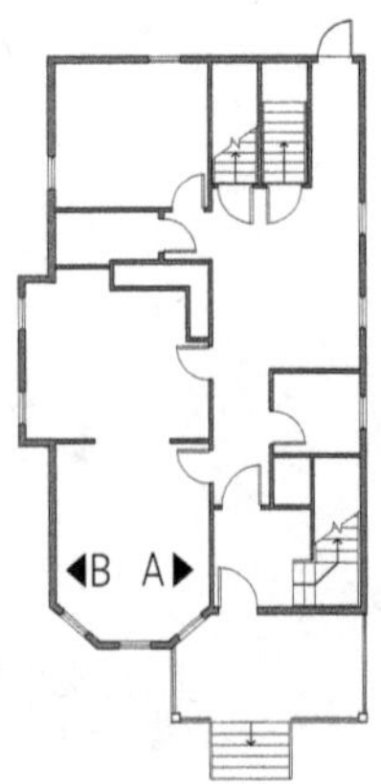

Key plan

Learning Exercise: Rendering Elevations

This exercise is intended to help you improve your understanding of rendering an elevation to show furniture and materials. For this exercise, you will need four to six colors of marker or colored pencil.

- These elevations are showing the side walls of the living room. Reference the key plan for details.
- Using your furniture plans on the preceding pages as a guide, draw the furniture in elevation.
- To render the elevation with color, apply an initial wash of color to all the areas of the drawing with controlled and consistent marker or colored pencil strokes.
- Add a second wash of color to areas that are in shadow, using marker or colored pencil.
- Render the surface details, to suggest materials, textures, and highlights, with colored pencil.
- Trace over the lines of the plan with a pencil or pen to convey the correct line weights. Refer to Chapter 7 for information on line weights in elevation.
- Add a person to one of the elevations. This person should be drawn in the same style that you used to render the colors and materials.

Learning Exercise: Value Studies

This exercise is intended to help you improve your understanding of using a variation of values to create spatial depth in a rendered drawing. To help you understand how shadows are cast on exterior surfaces, you may wish to do some quick value sketches from observing buildings in your neighborhood.

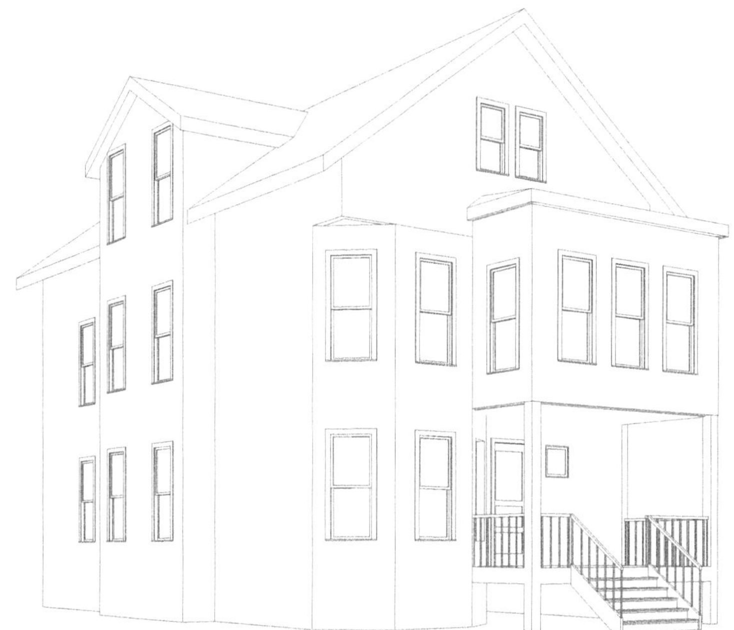

For this exercise, you will need at least three different gray markers or colored pencils, ranging from light to dark. As an alternative, you can also use pencils or pens to develop light, medium, and dark hatched areas within the rendering.

- Decide on the direction and location of the sun. For example, if you want the sun to shine on the front of the house, the front planes would be colored lighter than the side facade of the house.
- Using a light gray marker, fill in the areas of the facade that are facing the direction of the sun.
- Using a medium gray marker, fill in the areas that are not getting direct sunlight. The gray marker can also be used to color in elements that are darker in value, such as the window trim.
- Using a dark gray marker, fill in the areas that are in shadow. For example, the ceiling of the front porch would be rendered darker than the facade above. The roof overhang will also cast a shadow onto the adjacent wall. This dark gray marker can also be used to color in elements that are dark in value.
- Sketch in a ground plane, using a mix of all three shades.
- After creating two different value studies, evaluate how they are working. Do you have a balance of shadows and highlights? Do the values emphasize focal points and create a reading of depth within the rendering?

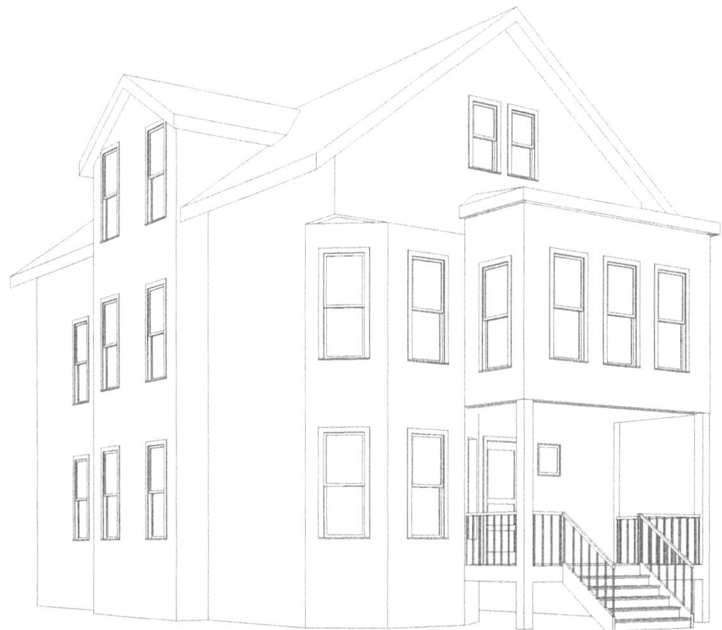

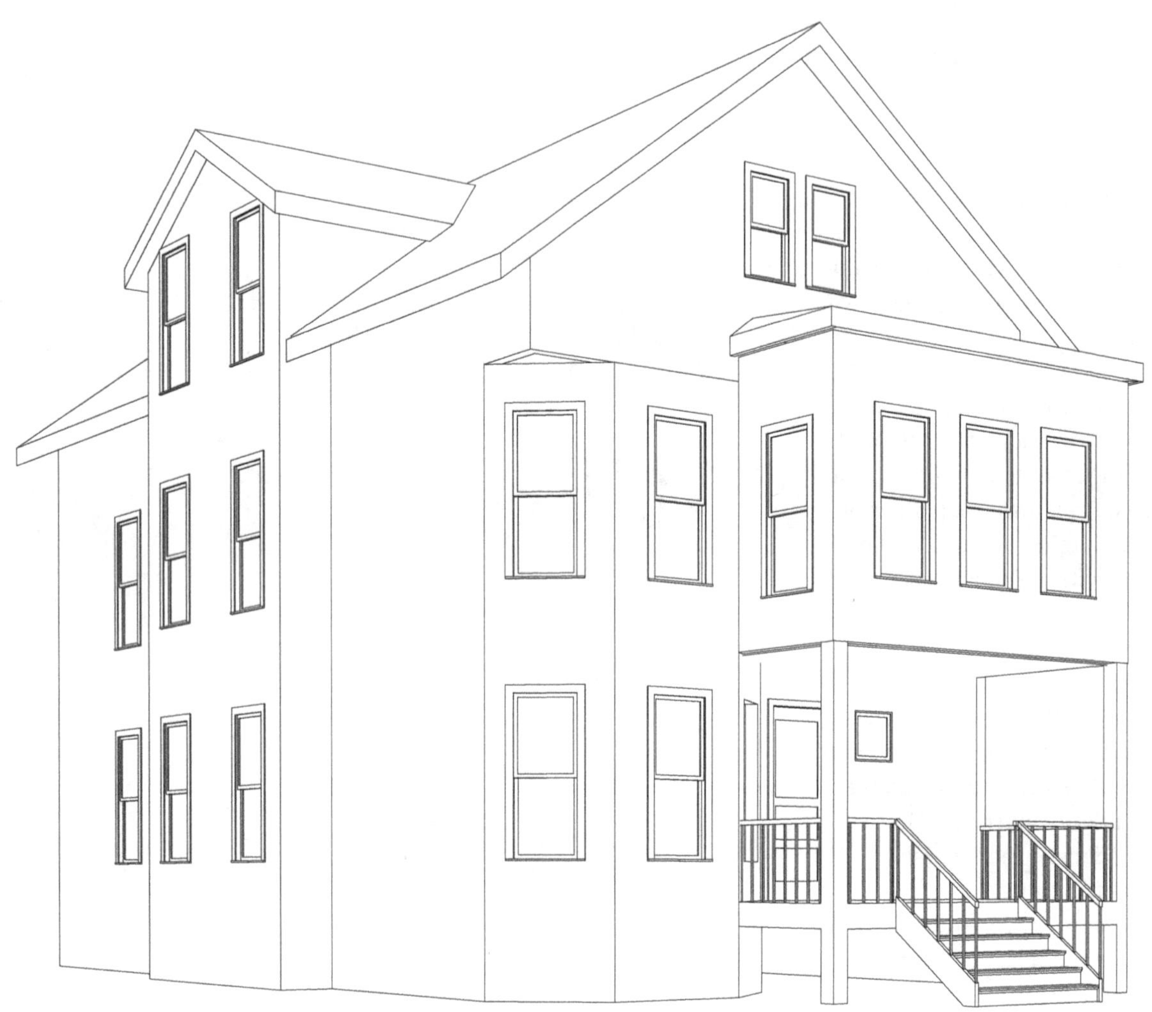

Learning Exercise: Color Study

This exercise is intended to help you improve your understanding of using color to render a drawing. A color study is a quick, preliminary rendering that is done to test out composition and techniques prior to the final rendering. For this exercise, you will need four to six different colored markers or colored pencils.

- Using your value studies as a guide, apply an initial wash of color to all the areas of the drawing with controlled and consistent marker strokes.
- Add a second layer of color to those areas that are in shadow, using marker or colored pencil.
- Render the surface details, to suggest materials, textures, and highlights, with colored pencil.
- Evaluate your composition. Are you using a complementary, analogous, triad, or monochromatic color scheme? What does your placement and choice of colors emphasize within the drawing? What techniques did you use to apply the color?

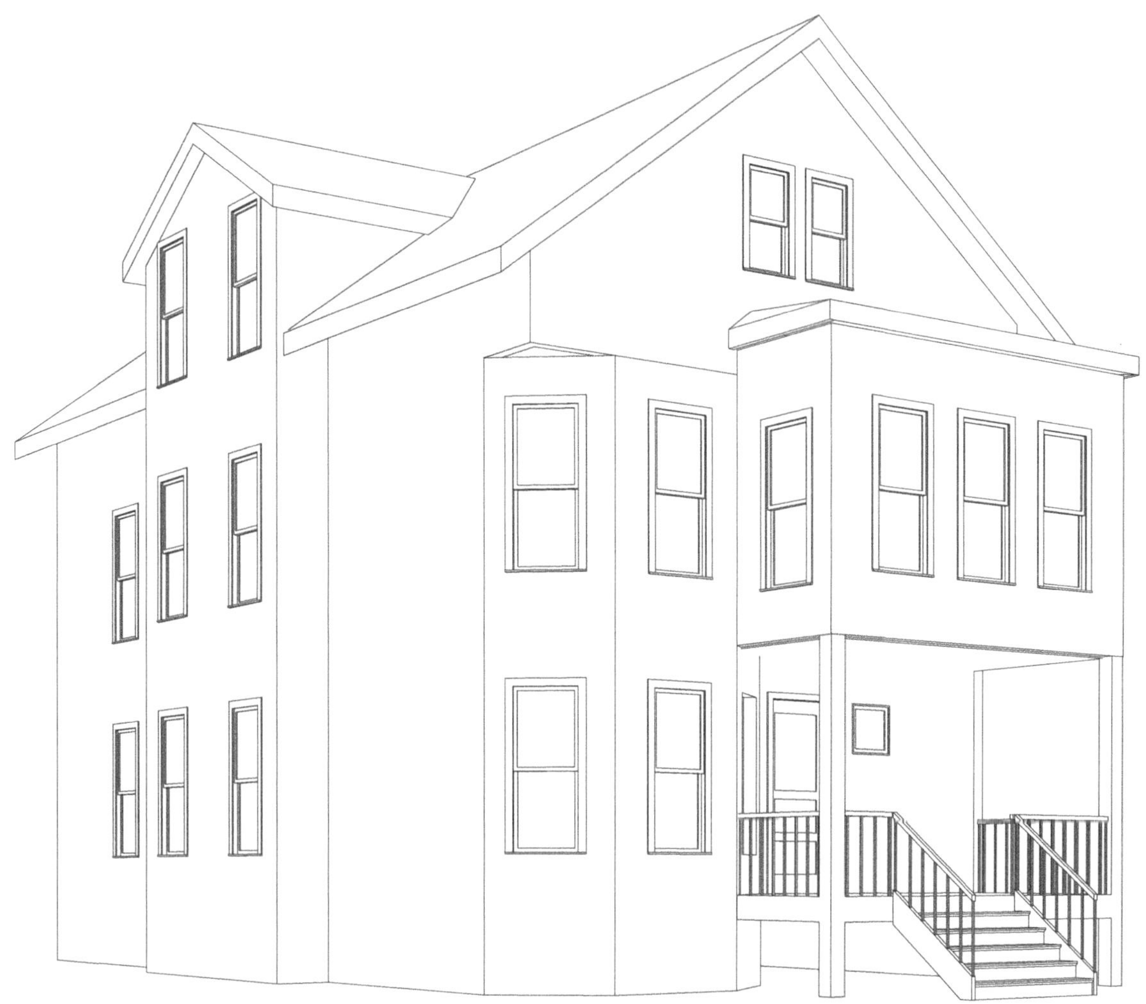

Learning Exercise: Color Rendering

This exercise is intended to help you improve your understanding of using color to render a drawing. Prior to doing this exercise, you should complete the value and color studies on the previous pages. For this exercise, you will need four to six different colored markers or colored pencils.

- Using your value and color studies as a guide, apply an initial wash of color to all the areas of the drawing with controlled and consistent marker strokes.
- Add a second layer of color to those areas that are in shadow, using marker or colored pencils.
- Render the surface details, to suggest materials, textures, and highlights, with colored pencils.
- Draw a person standing on the porch, and add a second person, walking by the side of the house. The people should be drawn in a style consistent with the rest of your rendering.

Printed in the USA
CPSIA information can be obtained
at www.ICGtesting.com
LVHW020223260824
789260LV00010B/513

9 781563 677809